'Network management is not necessarily about keeping the network optimized, but about knowing who or what to blame when things go wrong!'

The Network Manager's Dream

'I had a dream...
I had a dream that all users were identical and equal,
I had a dream that all the workstations were using the same hardware, and no matter what their colour or position, they all had equal access to the network resources.
I had a dream that all users were running the same applications and treated on an equal basis across the network.
I had a dream.'

But life is just not like that!

Managing NetWare®

Data Communications and Networks Series

Consulting Editor: Dr C. Smythe, University of Sheffield

Selected titles

NetWare Lite
  S. Broadhead

PC-Host Communications: Strategies for Implementation
  H.-G. Göhring and E. Jasper

Token Ring: Principles, Perspectives and Strategies
  H.-G. Göhring and F.-J. Kauffels

Ethernet LANs
  H.G. Hegering

Local Area Networks: Making the Right Choices
  P. Hunter

Network Management: Problems, Standards and Strategies
  F.-J. Kauffels

Distributed Systems Management
  A. Langsford and J.D. Moffett

X400 Message Handling: Standards, Interworking, Applications
  B. Plattner, C. Lanz, H. Lubich, M. Müller and T. Walter

Systems Network Architecture
  W.Schäfer and H. an de Meulen

Frame Relay: Principles and Applications
  P. Smith

TCP/IP: Running a Successful Network
  K. Washburn and J.T. Evans

Managing NetWare®

Farshad Nowshadi

ADDISON-WESLEY PUBLISHING COMPANY

WOKINGHAM, ENGLAND • READING, MASSACHUSETTS • MENLO PARK, CALIFORNIA • NEW YORK
DON MILLS, ONTARIO • AMSTERDAM • BONN • SYDNEY • SINGAPORE
TOKYO • MADRID • SAN JUAN • MILAN • PARIS • MEXICO CITY • SEOUL • TAIPEI

Cover designed by Designers & Partners, Oxford
Text and illustrations from files prepared by the author
Printed and bound in the United States of America.

First printed 1993. Reprinted 1994.

ISBN 0–201–63194–6

British Library Cataloguing-in-Publication Data
A catalogue record for this book is available from the British Library.

Library of Congress Cataloging-in-Publication Data is available

Preface

The aim of this book is to fill the gaps left by the standard manuals. It will provide you with guidelines and practical suggestions on managing and configuring your networks. One of the main themes is to point out the things to avoid and the things that are worth looking out for.

I hope to convey the basic concepts in network management, and suggest some of the issues that you need to consider when devising a coherent strategy. I also hope to avoid unnecessary complications.

I shall also explain the underlying concepts, and highlight the current trends in PC local area networks. In looking at networks from a Novell perspective, I hope to pinpoint a whole series of practical points and tricks of the trade.

Reading technical manuals is not the most exciting pastime; they often assume (wrongly) that the reader is familiar with the underlying theory of the topic at hand. This book contains numerous sections explaining the theory of topics of which the modern network manager should be aware.

Throughout the book I make references to the powerful new NetWare 4.x system. These references are indicated by the icon shown here. One chapter is devoted to the most significant new concepts introduced with NetWare 4.0, concentrating on the NDS (NetWare directory services), and on how to upgrade to NetWare 4.0 from NetWare 3.11.

This book does not dwell unnecessarily on discussions of syntax. Some books seem to be filled with reams of information regarding every possible syntactical command. I believe that if you understand what can be accomplished then it is easy to locate the appropriate command in the technical manuals. Furthermore, this approach is far more flexible in accommodating the development of new versions of software. Having said that, there are times when it is essential to discuss individual commands.

Throughout many years of network consultancy work, and of hands-on teaching of Novell networks for Learning Tree International, I have encountered multitudes of different types of network. What I continue to find surprising is how similar the problems are as you go from one company to another. Each company believes that their problem is unique, but in fact new problems are very rare. Somebody out there has probably already solved your problem and moved on long since; the trick is to find the person or source that can give you the solution that you need.

The big issue of the 1980s – whether or not we should network our PCs – is no longer relevant. The current issue is how to manage the multitudes of growing networks, and how to ensure that they can interoperate and work at optimum performance.

The areas that seem to be of greatest concern to most Novell network users are applications and their management, with an emphasis on Microsoft's Windows environment. I devote a large proportion of this book to how you can manage, install and configure applications on the file server, and in particular the Microsoft Windows graphical environment and all its related applications. Although on the surface this seems to be quite straightforward, it is actually a vast area. There are many different approaches and techniques available for managing your Windows environment efficiently. They are mostly neglected in the standard manuals from Novell or Microsoft, but they come in handy when you are managing a range of users utilising different Windows applications across a Novell network.

The other main area that we shall be examining is the integration of Novell networks. I shall be exploring the strategies involved in bringing the multitude of different Novell networks together. Novell provides us with some of the underlying concepts of internetworking, and in particular the connection of multiple of local area networks using routers. I shall look in some detail at the following:

- configuring and using NetWare Routers
- Novell RIP and SAP packets
- managing NetWare asynchronous communications
- TCP/IP and IPX routers

I shall be discussing these issues further, giving you some guidelines on what to look out for and the current trends.

The third major area of concentration, and this is a vast area, is network management in connection with users, user groups, network hardware and file server performance. I shall discuss some of the tools used to help you monitor the network. I shall look in particular at SNMP (simple network management protocol). I shall also cover other miscellaneous areas such as:

- virus and UPS protection
- backup systems
- how to create bootless workstations and the strategies to consider
- network printing and its management

This is a practical book, and I sincerely hope that you find it both enjoyable and informative. It is not intended to be a heavy technical manual. I would like to inspire you, trigger off your imagination and help you to realize that Novell NetWare is not necessarily a science but an art, and a beautiful art at that!

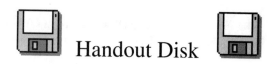

Handout Disk

Overview

In the disk accompanying this book there are a number of very useful tools, to help you manage your network. Most of them are available through bulletin boards, some are public domain and others are Shareware. Each tool is PKZIPed and when you un-zip them please read their accompanied documentation for licence agreements and instructions on their usage. A program that I wish to draw your attention to is MSET.NLM: this is a fantastic program to use on the NetWare 3.11 server. I have also enclosed the Novell PERFORM3 tool, a great tool for performance-testing your network. On this disk you will also find the version of PKZIP which recognizes the NetWare network and makes to it direct calls, thus bypassing DOS and saving you time.

Network benchmarking tools

☞	PERFORM3	Novell's excellent standard Network performance testing tool
☞	PCMAG	PC Mag's network performance testing program

Network information tools

☞	BINDIN	Lists bindery objects (DOS text based)
☞	BINDER	Lists bindery objects (Windows programs)
☞	CHKSRV	Checks users servers connection (very useful DOS batch files)
☞	CHKUSR	Displays users' disk utilization
☞	MONITOR	Monitors NetWare 3.x server information from any workstation
☞	NETUTILs	Selection of tools, including finding the Novell LOGIN drive
☞	NWHAT4	Returns information about user network environment (excellent)
☞	NWLDET	Detects the presence of NetWare Lite (useful in batch files)
☞	SST	Display FCONSOLE type information from workstation
☞	ULSORT	Displays users on network in alphabetical order

Windows management

☞ WIN_TAKE   Takes a snapshot of your Windows configuration

☞ WIN_REST   Restores a Windows configuration

A NetWare aware ZIP program

☞ PK204g   The very latest network aware set of ZIP programs

PC hardware information tools

☞ DRVTBL   Displays the PC hard disk drive tables

☞ MAPMEM   Displays a map of the PC memory

☞ VIDEO_ID   Displays the PC video configuration

Network management tools

MSET.NLM   A very useful NLM tool. This is a menu program which can change the NetWare 3.11 SET parameters

KILL   Kills the network users' connection (useful for forced log off)

COPY_CFG   Allows the copying of print job configuration, login scripts or other configuration files from one user to another

KEYLOCK   Password protects your keyboard while you are away

MOVE   Moves network files

SLEEP   Suspends operation in a DOS batch file for a specified time

TASK   Asks questions from DOS batch files ('yes' and 'no' responses)

Network printing management tools

☞ NETPRINT   Copies print job configuration from one user to another

☞ POPCAPT   A pop up version of the CAPTURE program (excellent)

☞ QSTAT   Displays the status of print queues

☞ QSWITCH   Another pop-up version of CAPTURE

☞ QUTIL   Command line print queue control program

The structure of this book

The structure of this book can be thought of as similar to a DOS directory structure. Most books are organized sequentially page by page. I would like you to consider this book as pages of information organized in a hierarchical basis, enabling you to skip over or delve deeper into sections as you wish. Each section as far as possible has been designed on a modular basis, so that they can be read on a stand-alone basis.

I shall try to organize each subject on the basis of three subsections, as follows.

Conceptual background

This section lays down the foundation for the subject. Where necessary, more detailed technical information is provided for users who require a more in-depth understanding of the subject. This is boxed within the main text.

An example of this is the large section on Ethernet. If you are already familiar with the subject, you can skip over this part. If you are uncertain of what Ethernet actually is then you will look at this section first.

Implementation issues

This section will explore implementation issues and, if necessary, show how the topic is implemented within the NetWare operating system. Some topics are so theoretical that they do not raise specific implementation issues, and consequently do not have an implementation section.

Management strategy

The last section is represented by the 'thinking man' icon shown here. It contains a discussion on management strategies regarding the topic in hand, and covers:

- how to approach the problem
- important considerations

- which approach best achieves your goal

In summary: if you understand the conceptual background of a subject, just miss the relevant section out. If you are sure of what you can do from a Novell viewpoint but would like to explore the management approach then skip over the first two parts and move to the third part: the management section.

This book includes information about the NetWare 4.0 operating system. Where appropriate, any information that is specifically relevant to NetWare 4.x is highlighted by the NetWare 4.x icon shown here.

Throughout the book there are literally hundreds of practical points. They are shown as follows:

This is a practical point regarding the subject under discussion.

They contain information not normally given anywhere in the manuals but which has come through my own experiences, sometimes good and sometimes bitter to the point of near suicide!

Contents

Preface   **vii**

The structure of this book   **xi**

Conceptual background
Implementation issues   xi
Management strategy   xi
                                                                         xi

1   Novell and its key products
                                                                         1

2   Network cable management
                                                                         19

3   Network standards
                                                                         39

Networking and topology basics
IEEE 802 standards   39
Ethernet connectivity   43
Token ring   54
ARCnet   63
                                                                         72

4   Managing and selecting optimum file server hardware
                                                                         77

Overview
NetWare server memory   77
File server hard disk platform   78
SCSI technology   88
RAID technology   93
How much hard disk storage?   100
CPU chip selection   104
                                                                        112

5   NetWare disk, volume and file management system
                                                                        117

NetWare filing system
NetWare and volume management   117
                                                                        124

**6   Managing your PC's configuration, memory and network
     adaptor cards**
                                                                        131

Analysing your PC hardware configuration
Managing network interface cards   131
Managing the DOS workstation memory   136
                                                                        142

7   Managing the NetWare workstation environment   160

Novell shell start-up   160
The ODI IPX versus dedicated IPX   162
Novell IPX.COM native drivers   162
Novell ODI drivers   168
Comparing IPX ODI and dedicated IPX   174
Installing ODI drivers   176
NDIS drivers   186
ODI versus NDIS   188
ODINSUP.COM: the ODI to NDIS converter   190
Novell Shell for DOS workstations   195
Managing shell updates   214
Burst mode and IPX technology   217
VLM redirector (introduced with NetWare 4.0)   224
NetWare workstation drivers management strategy   231

8   Managing network drives, directories and applications   233

Evaluate new applications   233
Types of network application   234
The anatomy of an application   235
Mapping Novell drives   237
Organizing file server directory structure   242
A simple framework for installing applications   259
Archiving using PKZIP   263

9   Windows and NetWare: a happy marriage?   265

The Microsoft Windows product range   265
Microsoft Windows 3.1   266
Windows for Workgroups   267
Windows NT (new technology)   270
NetWare 4.x and Windows NT   272
Comparing Microsoft Windows products   273
Windows basics   273
Windows .INI files   276
Installing Windows over the network   282
Running Windows over NetWare   292
NetWare drivers for Windows   293
Managing TSRs and Windows   299
EMM386.EXE and Windows   300
TBM12 program   301
Some Windows secrets   305

10   Managing Windows application over NetWare   311

Managing installation of Windows applications   311
Top tips for networking Windows   319
NetWare standard tools for Windows   320
Creating a corporate-wide Windows menu   323
Restricting the Program Manager for network users   326

Word for Windows: installation case study 328
Saber Windows Menu System 336
Windows Workstation 342

11 Managing IPX numbers and network interconnections 345

Managing NetWare IPX network numbers 345
Internetworking NetWare 358

12 Managing Novell routers 371

Overview 371
Warning: Novell bridge name confusion! 372
Understanding NetWare routers 372
RIP (Routing Information Protocol) 376
SAP (Service Advertising Protocol) 377
NetWare external router 380
NetWare MultiProtocol Router Extension disk 384
NetWare internal router 387
Tracking RIP packets 395
Quick external router installation guide 396
NetWare gateways 397

13 Asynchronous NetWare communication 399

Overview 399
NetWare Asynchronous Remote Router (external) 400
Asynchronous remote workstations 407
Asynchronous management issues 411
NetWare Access Server (NAS) 414
The NetWare Asynchronous Communication Server (NACS) 415

14 TCP/IP and NetWare 419

TCP/IP overview 419
TCP/IP NetWare applications 421
TCP/IP on NetWare servers 423
NetWare TCP/IP files and directories 424
Configuring TCP/IP on a NetWare server 425

15 Managing users and groups 437

Basic overview 437
Managing users' accounts 440
Managing group assignments 443
Managing workgroup managers 445
How to create large numbers of users quickly 445
Management issues 449
Management administration tools 449

**16 Cracking the NetWare 3.x supervisor password, NetWare security 455
and the virus threat**

Cracking the NetWare 3.x Supervisor password 456

What are the Novell bindery files?   457
NetWare security   464
Managing NetWare users   468
Secure your workstation from unauthorized access   472
Virus overview   473
Network and virus fundamentals   474
Viruses: how they work   474
Viruses and NetWare   475
File server-based virus protection (SiteLock)   476
Management virus summary   479
Virus summary   479

17   Network management tools   **481**

Overview   481
SNMP network management   483
The OSI view of network management   488
NetWare management tools   489
NetWare Management System   494
SNMP and NetWare   509

18   NetWare 4.0   **513**

Overview   513
NetWare 4.0 objectives   514
NetWare 3.11 versus NetWare 4.0 performance   515
NetWare 4.0 Directory Services   516
X.500 Directory Services   535
Installing and upgrading to NetWare 4.0   537
Improved file server memory management   544
Internationalizing NetWare 4.01   546
Demonstrating multi-language support of NetWare 4.01   548
Improved disk storage arrangement   549
File compression system   550
Media manager   553
CD-ROM support   554
Security auditing NetWare   556
Improved on-line help documentation   557
NetWare 4.0 utilities   560

19   Managing NetWare printing   **565**

NetWare printing basics   565
Print servers and queue directories   570
NetWare Queue Management Services   571
Print server management strategy   572
NetWare 4.0 printing enhancements   574
Optimizing network printing   576

20   Managing diskless workstations   **585**

Overview   585

How it works   586
How to create boot image files   586
Supporting multiple different remote boot disk images   589
Management issues   590

21   Managing backups and Uninterruptible Power Supplies (UPSs)   593

Overview   593
NetWare backup programs   594
SBACKUP.NLM   594
NetWare 4.x   595
Backup technology   595
Dedicated tape backup servers   597
Permanent archiving   597
Backup management strategy   598
Power protection overview   601
UPS management issues   604
The PowerChute UPS package   604

22   Network performance issues   607

Components affecting network performance   607
How to performance test the file server   609
Strategy for improving network performance   613
The NetWare 386 SPEED test   615

23   Documenting and auditing network hardware and procedures   619

Auditing the network   619
Why document?   619
LAN Automatic Inventory   620
The 'Don't Panic' book   624
A final word of advice   626

Appendix A   627

Sample network number register form   627

Appendix B   629

Quick installation guides   629
NetWare 386 (Version 3.11)   630

Appendix C   643

Novell worldwide addresses   643

Appendix D   645

Networking abbreviations   645

Index   647

1

Novell and its key products

Novell the company

Novell nowadays is synonymous with PC local area networks; this is predominantly because it dominates the world markets. According to recent estimates, 60–70% of all the connected PCs worldwide run under the Novell NetWare operating system.

    The company has come a long way from its inception in the late 1970s. The original founders of Novell had a vision of the future. They envisaged using interconnecting personal computers (PCs), and the creation of an efficient network operating system that would provide a sharing of common resources.

An interesting fact regarding the original founders of Novell is that they were all Mormons. The top management of Novell remain faithful to this set of beliefs, which perhaps explains why you may hear the Novell system being described as such a beautiful system that it must be the work of God!

In their endeavour to achieve PC networking, they assembled a group of keen undergraduate students studying computer-related courses. Their brief was to create a network operating system that would utilize network interface cards plugged into PCs. It was to provide a means by which users could share resources from a dedicated PC, to be called a file server.

This group is now referred to as the legendary 'Super Set' group. They laid the foundation for the NetWare operating system. The legend lives on to this day. Novell's current Chief Scientist is Drew Major, an original member of the Super Set. Because the group was working to such a tight schedule, so the rumours go, they used an operating system that they were familiar with, and that was UNIX, thus explaining the large number of similarities between the Novell NetWare and UNIX operating systems. Examples of these similarities are seen in the procedures for mounting volumes and for logging-in in Novell and UNIX.

The Super Set originally developed NetWare to run on Motorola MC68000 microprocessors. The Novell S-Net program, as it was then called, was at the time an extremely minor player in the PC networking market. Novell made its first major step in 1983 when it announced NetWare for the newly announced IBM XT PC, which was to run under the new PC DOS version 2. These products set a completely new standard: the IBM XT was the first PC from IBM that actually included hard disk drives without any patches intrinsic to its operating system.

One could argue that Novell's good fortune was in backing the right horse at the right time; it saw the IBM XT and DOS as the main forum for future development, and history has proved it to have been an extremely shrewd move.

The product at that time was called NetWare 86, since it was designed for the 8086 processor. In 1985 IBM introduced the IBM 286 (referred to as the IBM AT). Novell decided to use the 80286 CPU in the IBM AT as its hardware platform for the production of the NetWare 286 (advanced) operating system. This brought NetWare to the serious local area network market. NetWare 286 fully utilized the power of the new 80286 CPU, giving companies a choice for the first time between either purchasing a mini- or mainframe computer, or utilizing the new IBM AT with, for example, a 40 Mbyte hard disk, running NetWare 286 over Ethernet. NetWare 286 had put Novell on the world map.

In 1989 Novell continued its tremendous growth and success in selling NetWare, while moving upwards to another generation by utilizing the new Intel 80386 and announcing NetWare 386, the first operating system to take full advantage of the new 386 processor. The 80386 was specifically designed to make possible a full multi-user environment.

NetWare 386 was at the top of Novell's product range: the Rolls-Royce of PC local area networks. It was a product compatible in its specification and breadth of coverage with the average mainframe specifications of that time. The product entered the large corporate markets, and it has now reached the stage where it is extremely rare for large organizations to install new mainframes. Most of the time they are considering downsizing their mainframe operations to a networked file-server-based environment, probably a Novell NetWare 386 environment, running on a 486 or Pentium microprocessor.

Things could hardly be better for Novell. Sales of its core product, NetWare, are at an all-time high. In the last five years Novell has almost trebled its revenue, which topped $200 million for the first quarter of fiscal year 1992/93, 52% up on the same period last year. Profits have been soaring over the last few years, having now risen 72% on the previous year.

To a large extent this is thanks to the co-founder and current president of Novell, Ray Noorda, who has directed Novell into its pivotal position of today. Over the last few years he has slowly manoeuvred the company from dominating the small PC workgroup market (usually quoted at around 70%) to its current position as provider of one of the premium network operating systems used worldwide for interconnecting PCs at all levels. This includes governmental, corporate and small workgroup environments.

As Novell concentrated more and more on the corporate market, it dropped the hardware products that it formerly marketed, such as the network adaptor cards, disk subsystems and complete PC systems. By dumping these low-margin hardware products Novell's earning potential has now grown exponentially, resulting in a substantial cash injection that has led in turn to Novell's engaging in a whole series of acquisitions.

The first and most significant merger came with Excelan in the summer of 1989: a move that meant that UNIX, Macintosh and TCP/IP network expertise could be incorporated into the Novell NetWare series of products. In 1989 Novell continued its investment plan by taking a minority stake in Gupta Technology, a leading developer of DOS-based and Windows-based SQL products. Novell has continued a whole series of ventures with companies such as Toshiba and Canon, and even came close to agreeing a merger with Lotus Development in 1990, but this was called off because of a disagreement on how the board was to be organized.

The biggest coup and collaboration was made in 1991, when an agreement was made with IBM for it to support and distribute NetWare. This took the PC LAN market by storm, as IBM until that time had a very strong affiliation with Microsoft. NetWare from Novell is seen as being in direct competition to Microsoft's LAN Manager network operating system, now called Windows NT Advanced Server. Under the new Novell–IBM agreement the two companies agreed to work towards interoperability between their respective network environments: Novell's NetWare and IBM's SNA (System Network Architecture). Most importantly of all, IBM agreed to sell Novell NetWare through its own distribution lines, ensuring Novell a guaranteed increase in NetWare sales.

Last year Digital Research, developers of the DR-DOS operating system, merged with Novell, with the intention of incorporating the technology developed by Digital Research into the next releases of the Novell shell into one harmonized workstation environment. MS DOS would no longer be required to run the Novell shell from workstations. The fruits of this collaboration can be seen in the new NetWare 4.0. It is supplied automatically with DR-DOS, enabling the server to boot up without having to use Microsoft DOS.

Novell currently seem to be going through a phase where everybody wants to be its friend. For example, Compaq has renewed close ties with Novell with the hope of reinstating interest in the System Pro; Oracle (the makers of the popular SQL products) is busy promoting the use of its products in the form of NetWare loadable modules (NLMs); and Lotus Development has recently announced that it will develop its workgroup product to work with NetWare.

In 1992 Novell announced a major joint venture, code-named Univell. This is a collaboration with AT&T System Laboratories (the developers of UNIX system 5), with Novell owning 55% and AT&T owning 45%. The purpose of this collaboration is to produce a UNIX environment at the workstation level totally integrated with Novell NetWare. This 'easy to use' UNIX would be positioned in direct competition with Microsoft's Windows NT. While Microsoft has been promoting Windows NT, Novell has been quietly working on the new Univell project.

Novell is now in the happy position of having penetrated practically every technological arena of strategic importance. There are several questions that have to be asked, however. Can Novell sustain the attack from Microsoft with LAN Manager and, more significantly, the up-and-coming Windows NT technology, claimed by Microsoft to be a NetWare killer? Can Novell continue its tremendous profit growth rate? In answer one should look at Novell's track record over the last decade, and its ability to continue to meet the demands of its increasingly sophisticated existing user base. Novell as a whole is an extremely successful company run by a shrewd competent management, with a sharp eye on current trends developing in the market, but will this continue?

Novell product overview

There follows a list of the most important software packages provided by Novell. The most important of all these is the new NetWare 4.x. This is Novell's flagship product. Its success, or lack of it, will significantly determine Novell's profits margins for the near future.

NetWare 4.0

The new NetWare 4.x builds upon the success of NetWare 386 3.11, by incorporating a number of major improvements over the old version. This release lays the foundation for some extremely exciting developments that are to be included in the next major release, NetWare 5.x.

For a more detailed look at 'NetWare 4.x' see Chapter 18.

There follows a list of the most important new functions included in the NetWare 4.x package.

Directory services

The most significant new feature of NetWare 4.x is the Directory Services. This introduces the superb concept of identifying all resources on a network not from a file server's perspective, but from a worldwide internetwork perspective. The idea is to move away from file-server-based user accounts, and to introduce the idea of universal domains. In this environment you log into the network once, and will automatically log into a whole community of synchronized file servers.

Novell has also introduced a hierarchical naming space. Every object that can be shared across the network is given a universal address. This addressing system is based upon the X500 naming convention: part of the International Organization for Standardization's seven-layer model. NetWare 4.0 treats every item on the network as a universal object; these can be users, printers or directories, which are made sharable from given file servers.

Each object can be qualified by asking from which worldwide organization, in which country, at which site, within which department and, finally, from which file server, the object has been made available. Therefore, for example, if we have a user at Reuters in Geneva called Hans he might be given a universal address such as:

    HANS.TRAINING.GENEVA.REUTERS.

This means that Hans is from the training department of Reuters in Geneva. NetWare 4.0 achieves this by implementing the 'GLOB' or global database. This is a single hierarchy database which stores all the objects on a worldwide basis as a hierarchical tree structure. At the top level will be a description of the international company. At each regional centre, information regarding the departments' resources is stored. In each department, information regarding the users and printers, file and communication servers is stored.

Novell NetWare 4.0 allows tremendous flexibility in defining the structure of this tree. A number of useful tools are provided to manipulate the tree and to browse through the hierarchy, in order to examine each object in turn. Once an object is defined at a given level, it will be immediately recognized network-wide. This is a form of distributed database system. When a user makes a request to access a resource on the other side of the world, the appropriate request is transmitted along the hierarchical directory services and is authenticated at the other side.

Novell has attempted to make this new service backward-compatible, but it is not fully compatible with the old NNS (NetWare naming services). A lot of users when upgrading might be better off using the new system from scratch, learning from their old method, and reorganizing their account under the new Novell global directory services. All the services on the network will be given a universal address.

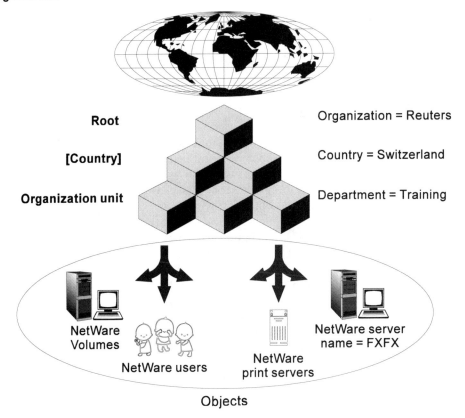

Figure 1.1 NetWare 4.x directory services.

Novell has produced an electronic yellow pages tool, which will publicize the global services available to users.

Internationalizing NetWare

For a long time, the Novell manual and operating system have only been available in English. Different language versions will now be available; most major languages will be supported.

File server memory structure

NetWare 4.0 has defined a completely new memory structure, that will allow selected NLMs to run under protected memory mode. The new memory management uses a whole new set of algorithms. Not only can it run NLM under protected mode, it also significantly improves the overall server memory performance compared with the old NetWare 3.x servers.

Auditing of files

You can now audit files for read and writes. It is possible to open up an audit trail showing which user opened any given file for reading or writing, and when.

New media manager

It is now possible to have a removable hard disk on the file server, and to incorporate CD-ROM drives as standard on the Novell file server. There is also the very clever concept of automatically putting files onto another medium off the main file server hard disk, depending on the last time the file was accessed. For example, if a file is not used for six months you can put it onto a backup device. This sort of tool has been available from third-party software manufacturers for some time, but it now comes as standard with NetWare 4.x.

Novell Windows-based tools

Novell has incorporated all the old DOS-based tools into a few Windows-based tools. The most widely used of these is the NWADMIN program.

 For more information see Chapter 18 on 'NetWare 4.x'.

Multiple processor support

Using an asymmetric multiple processor, it is possible to break down the functions of NetWare 4.0 and run multiple NLMs simultaneously. This means that, for example, SYBASE or Btrieve can be running on their own CPU, while all the functions of the NetWare operating system are running on the other CPU.

NetWare 3.12

Overview

NetWare 3.12 updates the successful NetWare 3.11 operating system. It incorporates all the latest fixes and patches that were distributed as addons to the standard package. NetWare 3.12 will retain the popularity of NetWare 3.11 as the industry standard for networking PCs. It also incorporates extra functionality that was first introduced with the NetWare 4.0 operating system. NetWare 3.12 reflects Novell continued commitment to the NetWare 3.x operating system line. However, it should be noted that the additional enhancements incorporated in NetWare 3.12 enable upgrading to NetWare 4.0 operating system far easier than the old NetWare 3.11 operating system. The NetWare 3.X operating systems is perceived as an open standard, which means it allows for other functions to be glued into it in a complete open environment, therefore DOS, Apple Mac and UNIX workstations can all be supported from the Novell 3.x file server. These are all achieved by NetWare Loadable Modules (NLMs), a series of software modules which can be added to the base of the NetWare operating system, thus enhancing the functions of the Novell

NetWare environment. NetWare 3.12 supports the same application programming interface (API) as the NetWare 3.11 environment.

What new in NetWare 3.12

Patches and fixes

NetWare 3.12 fixes a number of known problems and updates a series of NetWare utilities and drivers. These updates reflect all the new technology that has been developed around the standard NetWare 3.11 package, since it's introduction. Examples of such improvements are a significantly improved (bug fixed) print server PSERVER and RPRINTER.EXE, the latest ODI drivers, and enhanced NLM disk drivers such as support for IDE disk driver controllers. With the purchase of NetWare 3.12 you are assured that as of October 1993, all relevant patches and fixes for NetWare 3.11 that were available through Novells electronic bulletin board NetWire are now incorporated into one unified product. In NetWare 3.12 over 50 new third-party device drivers are supported.

New CD-ROM support

With NetWare 3.12, users can now share a server's CD-ROM device using the CDROM.NLM program. It will support ISO 9660, High Sierra and the HFS CD-ROM file systems. This means that most of the CD-ROMs available can be supported. Each CD-ROM can be mounted and dismounted from the server console, just as if it were a disk volume. Once a CD-ROM is mounted it is given a volume name. Users can now access CD-ROM volumes in the same way that they access disk volumes. The difference is that CD-ROM volumes are read-only, whereas disk volumes are read- and write-able. This function is very similar to the CD-ROM support as introduced in NetWare 4.0 operating system.

See the 'CD-ROM support' section in Chapter 18, 'NetWare 4.0' for more details.

CD-ROM installation

It is now possible to install NetWare 3.12 from a CD-ROM just like NetWare 4.0. All the files required for installation of the NetWare 3.12 server are contained on a single CD-ROM. It is still possible to install from floppies (Figure 1.2).

Basic Message Handling Service (MHS) support

NetWare 3.12 provides a single network version of the MHS. This is a NLM server based service, which provides e-mail and FAX based applications with the services of an MHS engine. It can deliver and receive MHS messages around the network. You get a basic but powerful e-mail package called FirstMail free with NetWare 3.12. It can be used by DOS and Macintosh users to send e-mail to each other across the network. For those users who need global MHS support, Novell are also providing NetWare Global MHS. This product has to be purchased separately.

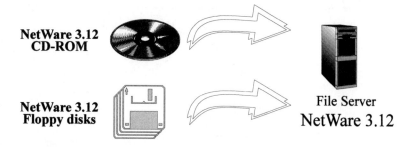

Figure 1.2 Different installation methods for NetWare 3.12.

Macintosh support

With NetWare 3.12 you get NetWare for Macintosh. This is a 5-user version. Macintosh users can now log into the NetWare 3.12 server, and use it as though it were a Macintosh file server. A new series of improved Macintosh utilities are also included in this release.

New client VLM architecture

With the release of NetWare 4.0 and NetWare 3.12 radical changes have occurred with the old NetWare shell concepts. The NETX or BNETX programs can now be replaced by the more flexible concept of the VLM (Virtual Loadable Modules). They provide greater flexibility in configuring NetWare drivers under DOS and Windows environments. Although the new VLM architecture is the standard for the future, the old NetWare shell NETX is still being supported for the time being.

    For more information on VLMs see 'VLM redirector' in Chapter 7, Managing the NetWare Workstation Environment

Improved disk performance

With NetWare 3.12 the disk system will anticipate the user's future disk read requests. It will read ahead of time anticipated read requests, and cache them into the server's memory. This cache-read function should improve the performance of disk access. It should even improve reading performance from CD-ROM drivers on the server.

Enhanced version of Btrieve

Novell uses the Btrieve API as its standard record-oriented database management system. With NetWare 3.12 you get the latest Btrieve 6.1. It offers enhanced performance over the previous version. It also includes new functions such as on-line backing up of its data files, and it can now support concurrent applications submitting simultaneous requests to a common data file.

Improved manuals and on-line help

The manuals in NetWare 3.12 have been significantly improved over those supplied with NetWare 3.11. With the CD-ROM set of NetWare 3.12 you get almost all the manuals in electronic format. A Windows-based program called ElectroText is used to display and sort through the electronic NetWare 3.12 manuals. This is equivalent to Folio, a hypertext search engine used in the NetWare 3.11 electronic manuals. ElectroText is now being shipped with the NetWare 4.0 operating system as well as NetWare 3.12. The only difference is the content of the accompanying electronic manuals, otherwise installation and usage is exactly the same.

For more information and some screen shots of the product see the section 'Improved On-line help documentation' in Chapter 18, NetWare 4.0.

Improved network performance

Novell has included its Burst Mode technology into NetWare 3.12 by default. It optimizes large file read requests across the network. This technology has been available for NetWare 3.11 as a special patch, and is now incorporated into the new system.

Novell has improved the performance of IPX packets that need to go across a series of inter-linked networks by using LIPX (Large Internet Packet Exchange) technology. It offers significant improvement to IPX packet transmission. The LIPX standard allows for the largest possible size packet to be transmitted across the network. Before the introduction of LIPX, NetWare would identify the smallest possible IPX packet size.

To find out more about Burst Mode Technology see Burst mode and IPX technology in Chapter 7, 'Managing the NetWare Workstation Environment'

Improved Novell Menu program

A new improved menu system is now shipped with NetWare 3.12. It is, in fact, Saber's Menu system. However, only the DOS system is shipped. The Saber Menu system also includes a Window-based menu management system. The new Novell Menu program is a significant improvement over the old limited MENU program that came with NetWare 3.11 and NetWare 2.2. It offers a significant reduction of memory overheads while menu option are selected. It is also now possible to disable users from being able to exit the menu system. Menu text files are now compiled and then issued to users as an object file.

To find out more about the Saber Menu system see Saber Windows menu system in Chapter 10, 'Managing Windows Applications over NetWare'

Improved Security Services

Novell has implemented a new NCP (NetWare Core Protocol) Signature security enhancement. In the old version of NetWare it was possible for a hacker to intercept the data packets as they flowed across the network and then generate data packets, fooling the server into thinking the hacker was someone else. The NCP Signature facility stop this happening. It uses a constantly changing encryption key to encrypt and decrypt data as it flows between a client PC and the server. The price for this extra data security is reduced performance. You can select to disable NCP Signature support.

NetWare Operating System architecture

The fundamentals of the NetWare 3.x servers can be broken down into a number of components: the NetWare server loader, the NetWare kernel, the NLM support bus, and NLM programs.

NetWare loader

This is the most basic component of the operating system. It starts up the NetWare operating systems on the server. From the DOS prompt line the program SERVER.EXE loads the system into machine memory. On start-up it saves the DOS environment, switching the CPU into the protected mode. It then proceeds to activate the NetWare kernel.

NetWare NLM support BUS

This provides one of the most important functions offered by the NetWare operating system (Figure 1.3). It basically acts as a run-time linker. It can add extra functionality to the NetWare operating system from the console prompt line. Such additional support modules are called NLMs.

Some of the important functions of the NLM loader are that it can:

- dynamically load and link new NLMs into the NetWare kernel
- make available to NLM programs a common set of NLM supporting routines
- dynamically unload and release any resources used by NLM programs

NLMs provide a very powerful tool, because they can be loaded and unloaded dynamically while all the other NLM programs continue to function as normal (in theory, at least). They can be used for a variety of purposes, such as hard disk drivers, for protocol support or as network adapter drivers.

NetWare kernel

The NetWare kernel lies at the core of the operating system. It provides a set of fundamental functions that the NetWare operating system is built upon. The kernel is a library of executable code, which NLM programs can use.

The functions of the kernel can be broken down into the categories shown in Table 1.1.

NLM programs

NLM programs are dynamically linked into the NetWare operating system. Broadly speaking, they can be categorized into two basic types, supporting either NLMs or server application NLMs. Some NLM applications will automatically load up other supporting NLMs before they can provide a service. There are a number of supporting NLM programs that are loaded normally by default. On their own they cannot function, but they provide important functions to application NLM. Examples of such NLMs are listed in Table 1.2.

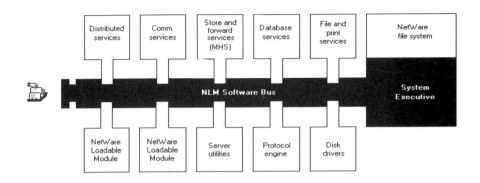

Figure 1.3 The NetWare 3.11 NLM software bus (courtesy of Novell)

Multi-workstation operating support

Although this book deals with the DOS workstation environment, the NetWare file services can be utilized on several different workstations. For many years Novell has concentrated on the DOS workstation as the premier workstation environment for NetWare interconnectivity, with support of other operating systems seeming to have been of secondary concern. However, today most of the functionality available to DOS NetWare users can also be made available to OS/2, Apple Macintosh and UNIX users. The main difference between each implementation is its NetWare shell. This acts as a translator between the standard NetWare core calls and the local workstation operating system.

OS/2 workstation support
The OS/2 NetWare requester comes as standard with NetWare 2.2, 3.x and 4.x. It allows for OS/2 v1.3 or v2.0 workstations to operate on a NetWare LAN.

OS/2 NetWare workstation environment
The OS/2 NetWare redirector acts more like the DOS VLM (virtual loadable module), as introduced with NetWare 4.x, than the NetWare DOS shell, as provided by the NETx program.

Table 1.1 Functions of the NetWare kernel.

Function	Function	Function
Memory management	Function scheduler	NetWare core protocol
Routing management	File system support	File and record locking
Transaction tracking	Device driver interface	Protocol stack support

Table 1.2 Examples of NLMs.

NLM name	Description
CLIB	This is the main programmer's interface into the NetWare operating system. Many NLM programs need this program to function correctly.
STREAMS	Defines a standard for moving data between NLMs and NetWare devices. It uses a standard data exchange protocol that is universal regardless of the protocol being used.
SPX	SPX (sequenced packet exchange) support. This NLM uses the IPX support provided by the NetWare kernel to provide guaranteed data exchange between nodes. Some NLM programs prefer to use SPX instead of calling the IPX functions.

The OS/2 NetWare requester is a standard device driver that is part of the redirection table of the OS/2 operating system. This is very different from the DOS shell concept, which garbs the DOS standard interrupt (INT 21h) and processes any DOS calls. If they are network-related it deals with them, otherwise control is passed to DOS as normal.

Macintosh workstation support

Support for Macintosh workstations is supplied as an extra module to the normal NetWare operating system. It consists of a special set of NLM programs and a set of Apple Macintosh programs for the workstations. This package will then support a native Apple protocol called LocalTalk over NetWare networks. Although the Apple Macintosh users is thereby making a LocalTalk request to the NetWare server, it is possible for the Macintosh user to see and use the NetWare server, in Apple Macintosh terms, as if it were an Apple Macintosh network server.

> There are a number of problems with the NetWare Macintosh support. First, there is no direct relationship between LocalTalk and IPX calls. Translation between the two standards can result in one function call resulting in many calls in the other. When errors occur across the network, the Macintosh workstations may not necessarily be presented with the correct error message. Another source of potential problems is the differences in the Apple Macintosh and DOS file-naming conventions. These might have to be converted from one format to the other if users on one operating system try to access files created by the other operating system across the network. This can lead to user confusion.

NetWare 2.2

This used to be considered Novell's entry-level product, ideal for small businesses. Up until 1991, life was a little confusing for the potential NetWare 286 user, who had a bewildering choice of NetWare SFT (system fault tolerance), Advanced NetWare, ELS I, and ELS II (ELS standing for entry-level system). Novell decided to trim their product range by combining the SFT functions as standard with the Advanced NetWare in the single product called NetWare 2.2. This was targeted at the small business and workgroup market. Its larger and more expensive sibling, NetWare 3.1, was described as 'the corporate solution' and positioned at the top end of the networking market, whereas NetWare 2.2 was the small business solution.

This was also reflected in the pricing structure of the two products. NetWare 2.2 was available with licences covering from 5 to 100 users, whereas the NetWare 386 product was available for users from 20 to 250. However, NetWare then proceeded to bring out NetWare 386 for the five-user market as well. Making this high-end corporate product available for just five users is directly attacking the NetWare 286 market.

The price difference between the five-user versions of NetWare 2.2 and NetWare 386 is £150 – 200: a very small price to pay for the extra sophistication and ease of use of NetWare 386. This raises the question, why bother to buy NetWare 286? For very little extra you can purchase NetWare 386: a much better option, especially when you consider the price difference of the user licence between the two products, and also bear in mind that the actual price paid for the network operating system is only a small part of the total cost of getting a network up and running. There are a whole series of other hidden costs, including installation costs, training, future flexibility, upgradability and adding third-party tools. In all these respects NetWare 386 is a far more flexible and open product, so that for that initial small extra outlay, in the long term you are making far greater savings. Table 1.3 lists the functions that are provided in NetWare 2.2 and NetWare 3.1, and outlines their comparisons.

UnixWare and Novell

Novell has acquired the UNIX System Laboratories (USL) from AT&T, at a rumoured price of around $300 million. The resulting product is called UnixWare and is sold by Novell as a desktop version of UNIX for corporate PC users. The product is basically UNIX System V release 4.2 with a seamless integration into Novell networks. It has been modified to work across SPX/IPX as well as the normal TCP/IP.

UnixWare comes in a number of different versions, as listed in Table 1.4.

If you plan to install UnixWare, bear in mind that it only comes on a CD-ROM or QIC tape cartridge. The CD-ROM should normally be on a SCSI interface.

A tremendous amount of research has gone into ensuring that NetWare will not be left behind in a rapidly expanding UNIX market. NetWare NFS has been introduced to allow workstations installed with an NFS service to share files with other NetWare clients (Figure 1.3). It is distributed and sold by both SUN and Novell.

Table 1.3 Comparison of Novell NetWare 2.2 and 3.11.

Feature	NetWare 2.2	NetWare 3.12
Maximum users per server	100	250
Minimum server processor	80286	80386
Realistic minimum RAM (server)	2.5 Mbyte	8 Mbyte
Maximum RAM (server)	12 Mbyte	4 Gbyte
Maximum disk (server)	255 Mbyte	32 000 Gbyte
Disk duplexing	Yes	Yes
Disk mirroring	Yes	Yes
Transaction tracking	Yes	Yes
Server applications base	VAP	NLM
Backup	DOS-based	NLM server
Monitor	DOS-based	NLM
NetView Interface	No	Yes
TCP/IP option	No	Yes
Macintosh support	Free	Cost option
NetWare SQL	No	NLM option
NetWare FTAM	No	NLM Option
OS/2 support	Yes	Yes
Minimum price (per server)*	£630	£770
Maximum price (per server)*	£4,230	£8,820
Best price per user	£42.30	£35.28

* Prices as of December 1992.

Table 1.4 Versions of UnixWare.

Product name	Product description
Personal Edition	Basic single-user UNIX system, with X-Windows, Mofit and Open Look window managers
Application Server Editio	Personal Edition + Multi-user UNIX system

The UNIX operating system is an extremely flexible, efficient, portable operating system with an intrinsic networking facility. The power comes from the inclusion of literally hundreds of cryptically named utilities, such as YACC, TAR and UUCP. The Univell project replaces these utilities by providing an X-Windows-based user-friendly interface based on the Open Look and Mofit desktop managers. Intrinsic protocol support for IPX/SIP and NCP comes as standard. This means that the UNIX-based PC can connect seamlessly to Novell file servers. The standard networking functions associated with UNIX are also supported, including NFS

NetWare
file server

UnixWare
Application Server
Edition running
under UNIX

UnixWare workstation
running under UNIX

Figure 1.4 UnixWare products.

(network file system) as associated with Sun microcomputers, and of course TCP/IP. The UnixWare machine can run most off-the-shelf UNIX applications. This includes, at extra cost, a special development kit to include an ANSI C compiler, a device driver development kit, and Mofit. This last is a special development GUI kit to produce user-friendly programs within the X-Windows environment.

Novell, having set up its Univell project, intends to produce a desktop version of UNIX Version 5.4 to rival Sun's Solaris Version 2. This will run on a stand-alone PC platform and will also be very much in direct competition to the Windows NT environment. Its advantages and disadvantages are as follows:

✓ runs standard UNIX applications seamless integration with Novell file servers
✓ seamless integration with Novell file servers
✓ simplified installation
✓ excellent development tools
✓ supports NFS and TCP/IP
✗ needs to build up credibility
✗ cannot run NLMs
✗ not all UNIX programs can run, but a good 99% will

NetWare Lite

NetWare Lite is designed for extremely low-volume users: for example, small businesses that do not require the sophistication that even the lower NetWare product – the 286 version 2.2 – can provide. It provides a peer-to-peer network running under DOS. NetWare Lite supports, and is compatible with, the NetWare 286 and 386 file servers. Its main drawback is that, in being DOS-based, it has very limited security control. Since it is peer-to-peer, this means that everyone can share everyone else's resources, such as floppy disks, hard disks and printers. Novell are now bundling NetWare Lite with DR-DOS as a challenge to the Microsoft DOS and Windows for Workgroup package.

The market is pretty well served by other products, such as LANtastic and Microsoft Windows for Workgroups. I have my doubts about the future of NetWare Lite. However, it should find a good following amongst the small network community looking for cheap solutions:

- ✓ cheap
- ✓ everyone can share each other's resources
- ✓ uses IPX
- ✗ works on DOS as a TSR
- ✗ not very secure
- ✗ limited number of users supported (five or ten maximum)

Novell DOS 7

Functionality overview

Novell has announced a multitasking version of DOS called Novell DOS 7. This is the next-generation product after DR-DOS 6.x. Scheduled to be available in the summer of 1993, it will contain the following enhancements:

- pre-emptive multitasking DOS operating system
- integrated NetWare client support, as part of the operating system
- peer-to-peer networking based on NetWare Lite technology
- standard support for network management agents
- enhanced memory management
- disk compression (based on Stacker technology)

This release of Novell DOS 7 is Novell's first major DOS upgrade, from Novell's Desktop System Group. This product is designed to integrate very tightly into the NetWare redirector, and provides flexible support for the range of workstations from palmtops to desktop PCs. It represents a major challenge to Microsoft's DOS 6.x.

NetWare service manager

Service management is the area in which Novell has made the greatest strides over the last few months. The majority of hardware vendors are producing network management systems. Novell, in recognizing that network management tools are essential for growing and expanding networks of today, has announced the NetWare service manager modules. These are SNMP modules which provide a series of information on managing the networks of today.

For more detailed information, see Chapter 17 on NetWare management systems.

Novell has taken a modular approach to network management. Its product supporting Windows and OS/2 is at the front end of displaying the information to the network manager. Like most similar systems, it first displays a map showing the network on a wide geographical area, and then maps it onto a series of logical interconnected computers and monitors their performances.

A series of critical triggering points are monitored. These trigger off an alarm, which the window user sees displayed on the screen represented by an icon (traditionally a red alarm clock). The mouse can then be used to investigate which aspect of the network is causing the problem.

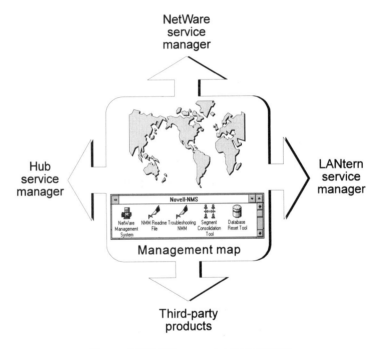

Figure 1.5 NetWare management system.

2

Network cable management

Cable overview

It was once pointed out that there is more copper running through the cables in the buildings of New York than there is available to be mined worldwide.

In this chapter we are going to look at the choices of cables that are available, and how to manage the ever-growing number of cables that are involved in today's networks.

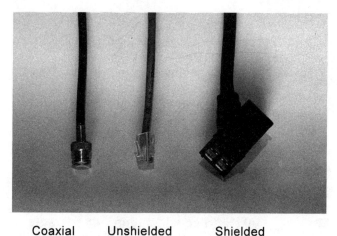

Coaxial   Unshielded   Shielded
cable   Twisted   Twisted
                 Pair cable   Pair cable

Figure 2.1 Typical cable types.

There are five major types of cable to choose from when you are constructing your network:

- Thin Ethernet coaxial cable with bayonet connection (BNC) connectors
- Thick Ethernet coaxial cable with access unit interface (AUI) connectors
- Fibre optic cable
- Shielded twisted pair (STP), normally associated with IBM Token Ring
- Unshielded twisted pair (UTP), normally associated with 10Base-T
- Cableless, known as LAWN (local area wireless networks)

We shall discuss each of these individually before moving on to structured wiring.

There is much talk about the merits of each type of cable; each has a number of positive points in its favour. I am always surprised by the way that advocates of a particular type of cable become almost evangelical in promoting it over others.

The perfect cable would:

- be very reliable
- be easy to install
- take up very little space
- be able to cope with very high transmission speeds (100–1000 Mbit/s)
- be noise-free
- be cheap and cheerful
- be very secure
- be physically robust and flexible

Chasing rainbows

The search for this kind of perfect cable is like chasing rainbows. No cable has yet been invented to meet these specifications. In the real world we have to work out which of the above requirements are our top priority, and then be prepared to compromise on the others.

However, there are a number of obvious trends worth noting. The first is that, within the PC LAN environment, there is a movement towards UTP and away from coaxial cables. This can be seen in Figure 2.2. There are several reasons for this, including their relative cheapness, the increased popularity of the star topology, and the trend towards structured wiring.

If you are going to have an Ethernet network of over 20 stations, then consider using UTP rather than coaxial cables. You should take into consideration other factors, such as building structure, interconnectivity and ease of installation and maintenance.

The second trend is that the price of fibre cables is coming down and the number of installations is beginning to rise. Fibre is the cable of the future. Its main

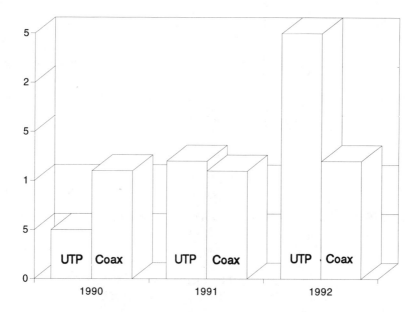

Figure 2.2 US shipments of Ethernet by media type.

disadvantage is that it is still expensive, and relatively new to the PC LAN market. This will change. It is likely that the main cable being used in ten years' time will be fibre.

Network cable types

What the cable has to carry

Copper-based cables carry digital signals in the form of electrical voltage levels. Typically a rise of voltage to 15 V denotes a binary 0, whereas a drop to –15 V means a binary 1 (Figure 2.3). When the cable is at 0 V it is in no man's land. Fibre cables carry signals using photons of light generated by miniature laser diodes.

Signal transmission problems

The signal travelling across the cable can be subjected to four types of problem.

Signal deterioration
As the signal travels along the cable it slowly decays, losing its square characteristic. This limits the length of cable that can be used. The problem can be overcome by installing signal boosters, called repeaters.

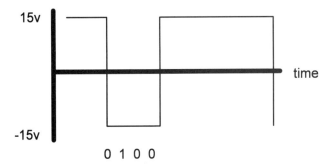

Figure 2.3 Typical voltages across a wire.

Radiation given off by the cable

Because the cable is carrying a very rapidly oscillating voltage, it starts to emit radio-frequency noise. So LAN cables can interfere with other equipment or domestic appliances.

The US Government has defined two sets of standards to tackle the problem, called Class A and Class B. The Class B standard is more stringent than Class A.

Electrical interference from outside

LAN cables must in some way protect the signals they carry, as they can easily be disrupted by outside electrical interference. Electric signals from fluorescent lights, heavy motors, radio and TV can all affect your cable.

Be aware of interference problems, particularly when using an unshielded twisted pair. For example, don't run UTP close to power lines, and never have the cable too close to fluorescent lights.

Unauthorized monitoring of the signal

Special equipment can be used to detect the signal being carried on some types of cable, without the user being aware of it. Such equipment can even be used from long distances, analysing the signal, and identifying the data being carried. This is of great concern to security-conscious establishments such as certain government departments. It is rumoured that most of the world's government information-gathering departments, such as the CIA in the USA and GCHQ in the UK, have standard equipment that can intercept, from a distance, security information data flowing through UTP or coaxial cables.

I have seen monitoring equipment in use that can pick up the radiation emanating from a coaxial cable and analyse the data. At the time of this demonstration I was logging into a Novell file server. The equipment was switched on and, from a distance of 5 m, started to monitor the radiation flow from the thin Ethernet cable that I was using. Without making any physical contact with my network it recorded my dialogue across the network, analysing the Ethernet packets. It then started to analyse the Novell protocols being used and from them deciphered the data that was being carried. At the end of this session, it printed out my user ID, the encrypted password that I had used, and all the data sent to and received from the file server.

Coaxial cable

Coaxial cable has at its centre a copper wire surrounded by an inner insulation. This is in turn surrounded by a screening cable, normally made of aluminium, copper or neutral braid. This type of cable has long been associated with Ethernet, but there is no reason why it cannot be used on Token Ring networks.

The two most widely used types of coaxial cabling in the PC LAN environment are Thin and Thick Ethernet cables.

Be careful of non-fire-retarding cable covers. Ask your cable supplier whether the cable coating confirms to any of the fire code standards.

Thick Ethernet

Thick Ethernet is the grandfather of coaxial cables. The IEEE calls it 10Base-5 cable. It is commonly found in older establishments or installations with large mini/mainframe computers. Thick Ethernet cable is mainly used either as a backbone in joining up a number of smaller LANs, or in networks where long distances (relative to Thin Ethernet) are required. It is not easy to use. Another, and I think appropriate, name for this type of cable is the 'frozen yellow garden hose', which sums up succinctly how manageable it is.

The Thick Ethernet standard states that the cable can be up to 500 m in length. Network stations are attached to the cable via a box called the transceiver. A transceiver then connects to the network station, which can be up to 50 m away, via a shielded twisted pair cable and an AUI port on the network adaptor (Figure 2.4).

Twisted pair cable

Twisted pair cables, as the name implies, are pairs of wires spiralled around each other (Figure 2.5). Variable factors are:

- the gauge (size) of the base wire
- the number of twists per turn
- whether the twisted pair is shielded or unshielded

Twisted pair normally tends to be unshielded, and as a result the cable is light, easily movable, economical and easily installed.

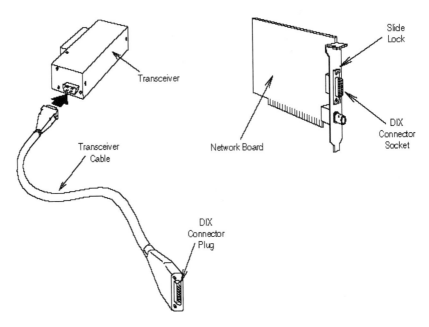

Figure 2.4 Transceiver and connecting cable.

Unshielded twisted pair (UTP)

This is most commonly associated with the telephone cabling found in offices and homes. It used to be considered a poor man's low-specification cable in the field of PC LANs, but attitudes are now changing and the UTP bandwagon has started to roll. UTP is now eclipsing coaxial cable as the cable of choice for new PC LANs. In particular, within the Ethernet market where previously the natural choice would have been Thin Ethernet coaxial cables, now the preference seems to be for UTP cables. Although UTP cables have a certain degree of resistance against electromagnetic interference because of their twist, they are best suited to small distances. Generally speaking, try to keep a single run of UTP to less than 50 m or so.

If you wire your own installation, you can expect that, on average, about 2–5% of the wired pairs will be faulty. So do check each connection thoroughly as you go along.

Most UTP wiring uses RJ-45 as connecting plugs, as found in all American-style telephones. One of the few telephone companies to use different plugs is British Telecom.

Figure 2.5 Twisted-pair cable.

Fibre optic cables

Fibre optic cables are a relative newcomer to the PC LAN scene. Basically, instead of sending electrical voltages down a cable, with fibre cables light is used to transfer the signal from one end to the other.

Digital signals are transferred to light using lasers; sensors at the end detect the laser light and either convert it back to digital signals or just pass it on to the next laser. Since the data is transferred at the speed of light, this technique allows us, in theory, to attain the ultimate data transfer rate, unless of course Einstein and his theory of relativity are proved wrong!

Because lasers are used, fibre cables can be very long; single runs of fibre cable of 100 km are not unusual.

Security

Because of the structure of the glass fibre, the light beams are trapped within the cable, and do not leak out. Hence it is extremely difficult to monitor the signals from outside as they flow through the fibre cable.

Traditionally, the main users of fibre cables in networks have been highly secure establishments, in the area of defence, for example. I was told of one application within a defence establishment, which comprised an isolated network of four users and one file server. Although the network was only used for word processing, the regulations stated that it must use fibre cables and standard Ethernet. Each PC had to have a $2,000 network card. The cost of the cable alone came to $800. This was in 1991. If Thin Ethernet had been used, the cost would have been approximately $200 per card and around $100 for the cable.

Fibre networks are no longer the extremely expensive alternative, they are just expensive! If you require a very secure, reliable and fast network, then fibre is the obvious solution, but quality has its price.

Cable key points summary

Fibre optics

- ✓ Very high data throughput: 100 Mbit/s–1 Gbit/s
- ✓ Very secure against outside monitoring
- ✓ Will in the future be able to carry voice, video and graphics
- ✓ Very long-distance runs
- ✗ Expensive
- ✗ Not many third-party vendors to choose from yet

Copper coaxial cable

- ✓ Large user base
- ✓ Easy to install

✓ Relatively high data throughput

✓ Relatively long distances: up to 500 m Thick Ethernet

✗ Not very secure

✗ Hard to locate cable failure without specialized equipment

UTP

✓ Very cheap: 30 cents per metre

✓ Lends itself well to structured wiring (see the section on Structured cable management).

✓ Easy to identify errors

✓ Very flexible and movable

✓ Failure does not cause the network to go down

✗ Susceptible to electrical noise

✗ Prone to failure, especially during installation

✗ Need greater quantities of cable compared with the bus topology of coaxial

✗ Not very secure

Cable scanners

Overview

Cable scanners (Figure 2.6) are invaluable for installers of networks and for the everyday management of a network. They are extremely powerful tools, which can be used to identify any faults on cables.

They are sometimes referred to as time domain reflectometry (TDR) equipment, because they basically work by sending out a signal and then listening for the echo to be reflected back: rather in the way that sonar works. They are intelligent pieces of equipment; for example they know that the Thin Ethernet standard is 185 m from end to end, so that when they send out a signal they expect a certain characteristic to be returned.

Cable scanners are effective in identifying problems on an assortment of different types of cable: Thin, Thick, ARCnet, shielded or unshielded twisted pair. A cable scanner can identify a breakage on the cable and tell you if the breakage is due to an open circuit or a short circuit. It will also tell you if it is on the left- or right-hand side of the cable scanner. Most scanners can also tell you the distance of the breakage from the scanner. For example, if a Thin Ethernet cable is faulty, a TDR could be used to pinpoint the error, which might for example be due to a breakage on the left-hand side of the TDR, 3 m along the cable.

Figure 2.6 TDR equipment.

Cable scanners can significantly help to eliminate all those annoying problems that often plague the network administrator, and thus can significantly reduce the network downtime. For example, if a network is running slowly, the scanners can be used to establish whether this is due to a faulty cable or whether the fault lies at some higher level.

Most TDRs cannot be used on live networks. You must log everyone off the network before you use the TDR to make sure that you get true readings.

Most cable scanners that retail at around $1,500 come with an optional tracing facility: a small extension used in conjunction with the cable scanner to trace cables in walls.

Management strategy

If you are managing a network that has more than, say, 20 PCs, you are strongly recommended to purchase this type of cable scanner, at least for the basic purpose of troubleshooting and at best for maintaining your sanity!

Structured cable management

Who needs cable management?

As networks grow, which inevitably they all do, they get proportionally harder to manage. In order to minimize this effect a management strategy is required. This is particularly true when it comes to cabling, as anybody who has installed and maintained networks will be aware.

As the network expands, there is a general need to install more and more cables around the office. New stations may extend the network cables beyond the maximum allowed length; adding a number of devices, such as network interconnection devices like routers and bridges, could require a whole assortment of different cables. These then all have to be interlinked. It is common to see networks with a whole series of redundant interconnections, to provide fault tolerance.

Before you know it you can easily find yourself amongst a massive series of spaghetti-like cables all around the office. The cumulative effect of unmanaged and undocumented cables is a potential nightmare when you need to upgrade or expand your network facility.

In general, I would strongly recommend that today's network manager should have a coherent cable management plan. However, if you are in the happy position of only managing a few stations (less than 20, say) within close proximity of each other, and you have no plans for expansion, then you can possibly avoid the overheads that a cable management strategy would involve.

What is structured cable management?

Structured cabling systems were originally conceived to ease the growing complexity of cables around offices. 'Structured cabling' has now become one of the buzz phrases in the PC network market. It is important to remember that a structured cabling system is not just a single product that can be bought off the shelf; it is a systematic approach to cabling around which you can structure your office. The aim at all times is to manage your cables easily when problems arise or when you are planning further expansion.

The EIA 568 structured wiring standard

A new worldwide standard for structured wiring has emerged over the last few years. This is the EIA 508 from the Electronic Industry Association, a US based organization which has international recognition. This standard defines how wires running along commerical buildings should be wired. It defines a recommended topology for wiring up office floors, risers and service entrances. The standard allows for Data, Voice and Video cabling. It also includes a wealth of advice on wiring your closets and administrating your cable database.

Get hold of the EIA 568 structured cable standard if you are interested in structured wiring, even if you do not intend to adhere to its recommendations; it is full of very sensible advice.

The five golden rules of structured cabling

1 Label the cables

As cables are installed they should be marked using a universal standard. The label should state which two devices the cable connects up, and where the cable starts and ends. To achieve this, rule 2 is required.

2 A planned layout

A universal addressing scheme is required to uniquely identify all devices and their location within your organization. This information can then be used to document the unique cables connecting up devices and their location.

3 Adopt a single wiring scheme

Use a minimum number of media types around your organization. The current trend is towards using UTP and fibre optic cables.

4 Document the cable layout

Record and maintain a layout plan of your cable organization. This should illustrate which cables connect which devices together. There are a number of cable management software packages available for this purpose.

5 The addressing scheme

When using structured cabling there is a need to be able to address each device individually. From this address or code any person should be able to walk round the building and point to the unique device, assuming they know the addressing scheme being operated. This addressing scheme can also be used to identify where the cable starts and terminates within your organization.

In short, the addressing scheme has to define the physical location of any item within the organization.

A suggested addressing scheme

To identify a specific location the most commonly used technique is outlined below. The addressing scheme involves three parameters. In order, these are:

(1) name of building

(2) floor or department number with in the building

(3) zone within the floor or department.

Building and floor name

The choice of building name and floor number is straightforward (Figure 2.7). However, this does mean that you must have a corporate-wide policy as to what each building will be universally known as.

You must also bear in mind that on occasions cables will travel from one building to another.

Zone address

The scheme superimposes some form of grid to identify each area.

For example, in Figure 2.8 a simple grid of A–Z for the x axis and 1–10 for the y axis is used to identify each area. In this example PC1 is in grid C1, HUB1 is in grid B1 and cable C1 goes from C1 to B1.

The only complex part of this scheme is how fine to make the grid reference floor plan. The unit area should normally be large enough to accommodate an average-size PC (normally 1 m × 1 m). This can be a major problem when working in large open-plan offices. I once visited a research centre that had an open office spanning 100 m × 200 m.

Labelling the cable

Cables should always be labelled on each end, identifying the type of cable and which two points it connects (Figure 2.9).

The cable type ID could be given:
T: **Thin Ethernet**
K: **Thick Ethernet**
F: **Fibre**
U: **Unshielded twisted pair**
S: **Shielded twisted pair**
followed by a unique reference number for that cable.

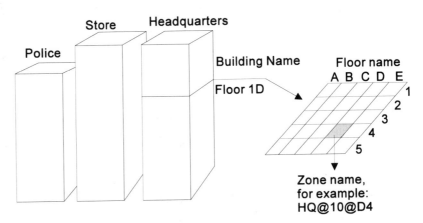

Figure 2.7 Suggested addressing scheme.

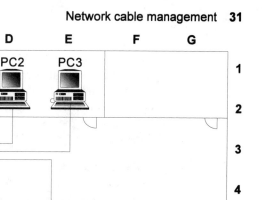

Figure 2.8 Cable labelling.

Extending the addressing scheme

There are a number of different approaches that improve the flexibility of the addressing scheme. The following suggested extension to the usual standard could be used to extend the address scheme, first country-wide and then worldwide. In practice, the addressing has to be much more complex.

Extending the scheme country-wide
There now follows the most frequently used approach to an addressing scheme, to which I have added a few suggestions of my own.

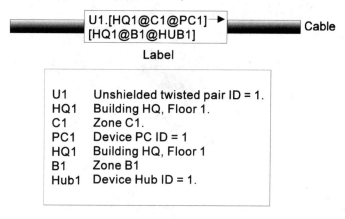

Figure 2.9 Cabel labelling

I have known organizations with a country-wide cabling system to utilize the post or zip code to identify a small part of the country. Most countries implement a postcoding system that can be used to identify small areas within that country. For example, the UK postcode can be used to pinpoint a unique area containing approximately ten buildings (Figure 2.10).

This can be used to qualify the building address, floor address and zone address.

Extending the scheme worldwide

The postal address can be further qualified by the name of the country in order to extend the concept to a worldwide basis.

 For cables that span international borders the addressing scheme can be further enhanced by using the international telephone code for that country. Cables spanning countries using different postcoding schemes, such as the UK and the USA, can result in interesting problems (Figure 2.11).

If the cable is running within a country the country ID can be omitted. Similarly, if the cable is running within the postcode area that can also be omitted, and the current default postcode will be assumed, as with the default country.

Novell and hub management architecture

Hub overview

In the classic structured wiring scheme, each machine is connected to each other via a wiring concentrator called a hub (Figure 2.12). The most common cabling used in this configuration is twisted-pair wiring running on Ethernet: 10BaseT.

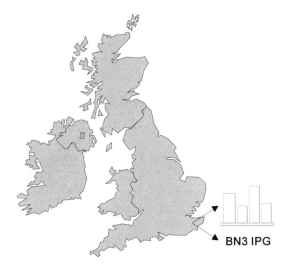

Figure 2.10 Postcoding system.

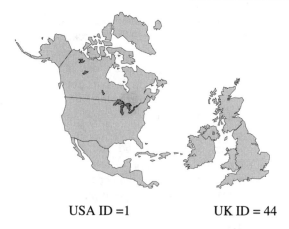

USA ID =1   UK ID = 44

Figure 2.11 Typical national cable addresses.

Since each station has a direct connection to the hub, if one cable fails the others still operate, unlike the situation with Thin Ethernet. Hubs can also provide management information, normally by using LEDs that tell the user which cables are active and are carrying information at any given time. Many hubs provide additional management data, such as how much data has been transferred on any cable, or which is the most congested cable; these are very useful statistics in managing the network. Most of the 'clever' manageable hubs communicate using SNMP (see later), a standard network management protocol. There is a small price to pay; however, although intelligent hubs represent a significant advantage to the network manager, they are not cheap.

Another problem is that since this trend towards managed cable is relatively new, there are a multitude of different approaches to the solutions. Each manufacture has developed their own approach. However, Novell has now introduced the hub management interface (HMI).

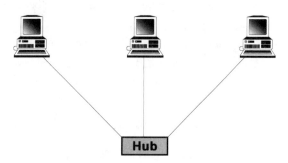

Figure 2.12 PCs on a hub.

HMI: the Novell hub management standard

Novell has been working hard to standardize hub interfaces and to encourage third parties to develop hardware that can be incorporated into the Novell networks of the future.

Novell has now moved the hub from being an external device (Figure 2.13) to be a integrated device internal to the file server (Figure 2.14). To access this type of hub, Novell has come up with the HMI standard.

These special hub cards will typically have 12 to 16 ports on them. You can have up to four network hub adaptor cards on each file server. This means that you can in theory have 4 × 16 ports coming out of each server as standard. Hub cards are already manufactured by a number of major third-party hardware vendors, such as SMC, 3-COM and Intel Corporation. The HMI solution comes with a complete management software package. A supervisor can, from any workstation, see how each HUB is performing and turn each port at the HUB on or off. These new HUBs will be manageable using SNMP protocols. I see this as a major trend. The Novell HMI standard is here to stay.

Cable management software tools

Overview

Perhaps one of the biggest growths in cable technology is that of cable management software. Network mangers need to be able to manage cable configurations and at the same time reduce the tedium associated with documentation. By using the latest cable management software, the life of the network manger can be made much easier, although if you select the wrong package it can be an administrative disaster!

Strategy decisions

When it comes to deciding which package to buy, look for answers to the following questions:

- Will it keep an inventory of all cables around your organization?
- Will it automatically print labels for the cables?
- Will it show graphically the connections between cables and devices?
- Does it have a CAD facility?
- Can you define a physical layout of your organization?
- Can it superimpose cables on the physical layout of your offices?
- Can it be used to simulate cable 'what if' scenarios?
- Does it produce a good selection of reports?

A good example of such a package is Crimp+ from Cableship.

Crimp+ cable management software

This package (Figure 2.15) is one of the leading cable management software packages in an increasingly competitive market. It shows what can be expected from

Figure 2.13 External hub.

a good cable management package. One of its unusual features is its ability to integrate with an in-house PABX system.

The package has an excellent graphics module. It can import drawings from CAD packages such as AutoCAD. On each one of these drawings you can superimpose both the devices and the cables that are used to join them up (Figure 2.16).

This product is extremely useful when structured wiring is being used. It can easily display schematic diagrams of the cable layout (Figure 2.17).

The package can produce some very interesting reports, such as what is the optimum route between any given two nodes. It will analyse your system and suggest the quickest route (Figure 2.17).

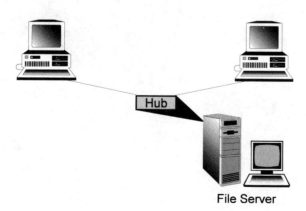

Figure 2.14 Internal hub, using Novell HMI standard.

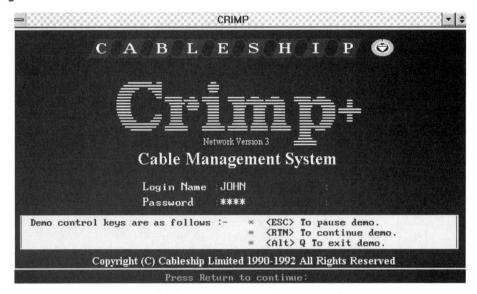

Figure 2.15 Crimp and Cable Management System.

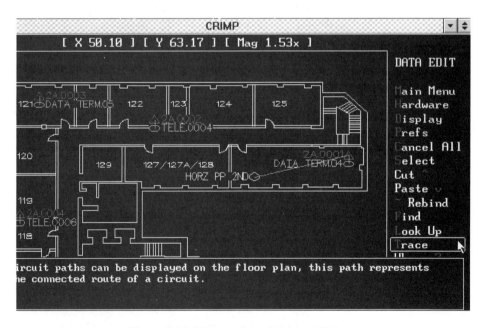

Figure 2.16 Crimp and graphics capabilities.

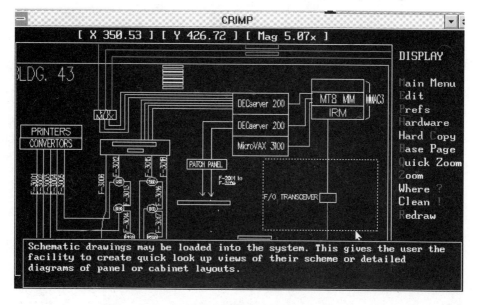

Figure 2.17 Crimp and schematic diagram cable layout.

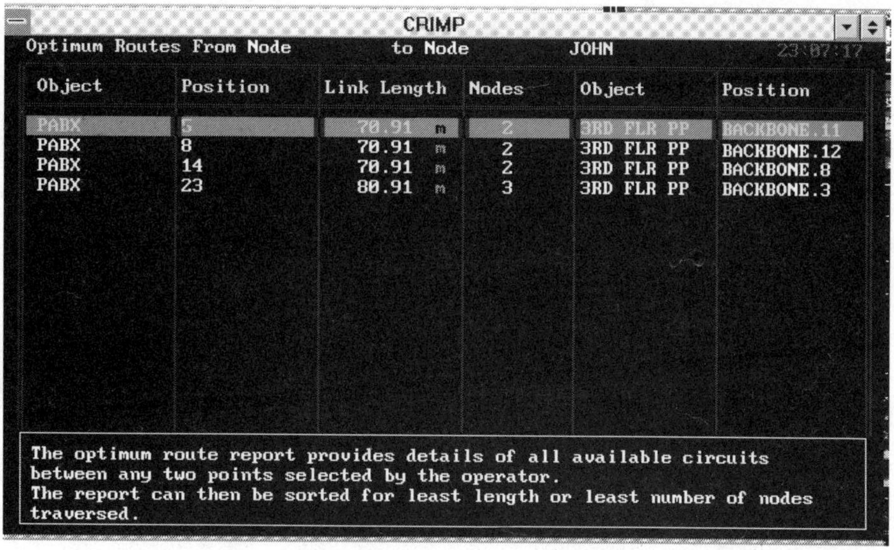

Figure 2.18 Crimp and system wiring report.

A multitude of different types of reports can be produced. These could be sorted by location or by device or by cables.

3

Network standards

Networking and topology basics

This chapter covers the fundamental concepts of networking and topology in general terms. I have assumed that most readers of this book have already used networks, and are familiar with networking concepts. I shall therefore not spend too much time on this topic, but move on quickly to the more advanced (and interesting) sections within this chapter, starting with the IEEE 802 standards. The chapter is designed around a series of key points.

If you are a seasoned network user, you can easily skip over this whole chapter.

Local area networks: basics

This section covers some of the basic concepts relating to PC networks. It covers some standard ground, which will be built upon in subsequent chapters.

There are two basic types of local area network (LAN): server-based and peer-to-peer. In the server-based type, the workstation is the client, and a special workstation is turned into a dedicated server. This stores and delivers shared files to clients. It also allows clients to share peripherals, such as printers and faxes. In a peer-to-peer network, each workstation is a client and, if the user chooses, can also become a server by sharing its local resources with other clients.

Why use LANs?
Here are some of the main reasons why many organizations decide to use a LAN:

- It utilizes equipment efficiently

- It reduces the workstation specification by increasing the specification of the server
- It reduces cost by minimizing duplicated hardware
- It increases users' access to resources
- It enables sharing of information
- It enables local staff communications

Resource sharing

The LAN, in essence, provides the means by which resources can be shared amongst users (Figure 3.1).

Basic LAN functions

- Share hard disk storage
- Share programs and data
- Share printing

Enhanced LAN functions

- Use shared communication lines, such as gateways to other computer systems
- Share database server
- Share mail and fax server

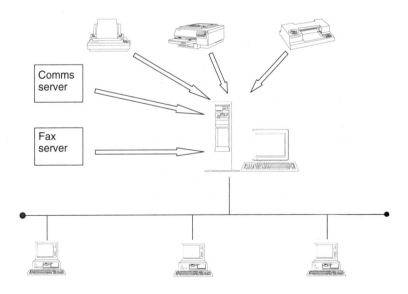

Figure 3.1 Basic server-based network functions.

- Share CD-ROM server
- Share backup hardware
- Share processing: execute programs on the server rather than on your own workstation

Communication protocols

Networks use protocols as formal rules for exchanging information between networked computers. Protocols define the exact format in which data and system messages are to be sent. They also define the network addressing system and control network traffic flow by its priority and routing. Protocols do not work in isolation; before communication can take place both parties must adhere to a common set of protocols:

- Communication is based on a common standard
- Protocols are layered
- Workstation and servers need to have compatible protocols

Topology

Topology defines the way in which nodes on the network are connected up together. There are two types of connection: point-to-point and multipoint.

Point-to-point connection (Figure 3.2) joins two machines, and only two, directly together. Information passes between the two machines without going through any intermediate workstation.

Multipoint connection (Figure 3.3) comprises a single common point shared by two or more workstations that send information to each other via the common point.

Basic topologies

These two forms of connection (Figure 3.4) lead to three basic types of topology: bus, star and ring.

Bus networks are multipoint connections, in which all workstations are connected by a common cable. In a star configuration, workstations are also connected on the multipoint basis but all connect up to a single point in a star pattern, meeting at the central point. In a ring topology, workstations only connect to their

Figure 3.2 Point-to-point connection.

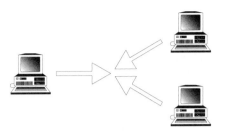

Figure 3.3 Multipoint connection.

neighbours in a ring fashion. If one workstation wishes to talk to another workstation it may have to talk to a number of intermediate neighbours, feeding the information through one workstation to another until it eventually reaches the destination workstation.

Logical versus physical topology

There are some interesting points to make regarding topology. First, there is a major difference between the logical and physical topology of a network. Very peculiar situations can arise when a network is logically connected up on a bus system but is physically connected as a ring. However, it is common to see networks that are logically connected up as a ring, but physically cabled in a star fashion. There are various practical examples of this. Ethernet, which is a logical bus network, is commonly implemented using unshielded twisted pair in a star configuration. IBM's Token Ring system, although logically connected as a ring, has traditionally always been implemented in a star configuration using MAUs (media access units).

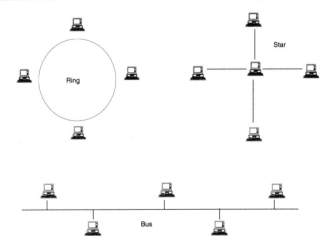

Figure 3.4 Basic topologies.

Evaluating different topologies

There is usually no choice as to the logical topology you use on your network, as this depends on the type of network that you adopt. For example, an Ethernet network will always be a logical bus, and a Token Ring network will always be logically configured as a ring. However, each type of network can be physically configured either as a bus or a star. It is quite rare to connect a network physically as a ring, so the main choice is between a physical bus or star configuration.

The advantage of a network cabled as a bus is that it requires a minimal amount of cabling, and is therefore normally an excellent choice for small networks. A major problem is that it is vulnerable to breakdowns. If any part of the bus cabling becomes faulty then the whole network fails. It is very difficult to trace where the fault has developed in the cable without using special hardware.

There is at present a definite trend towards implementing medium-sized to large size networks using physical topology; this is particularly true for structured wiring systems. One of the great things about star topology is that the whole network will not go down if the cabling in one segment fails. It is also very easy to identify the faulty cable in a star configuration because LEDs on either side will tell you which section of the cable is no longer functioning. However, it requires more cable than the bus layout and it can become far more complicated.

However, if I had to make a general recommendation for a small network (between 2 and 20 workstations), then a physical bus topology might be more appropriate. For a larger network, however, because of the complexity of the wiring and the need for managing potential future troubleshooting of the network, under most circumstances a physical star topology is more appropriate.

IEEE 802 standards

Why have standards?

Standards play a vital role in the field of communications. In order to succeed in the fast-growing field of computing and information technology, the manufacturing industry must produce equipment that is compatible with other equipment in both national and international markets. This calls for an internationally agreed computer communications standard allowing for the interconnection of different equipment. This will enable users to make selections based upon cost and performance rather than compatibility.

It could be argued that, of the many disciplines, the field of communication is the one that benefits most from common standards. By definition, a communication service is the bringing together of information from a number of information systems. The adoption of standards also helps to widen a user's choice. Paradoxically, although a given standard in the field of communication aims to limit the approach and interpretation to a single method, this actually has the effect of giving a potential user greater choice. Manufacturers starting from different standpoints are given a common ground on which to compete, which should result in the user being offered a wider choice of products.

In summary, communication standards provide:

- a common approach to information interchange
- a wider choice for users
- a guide for manufacturers of communication systems as to the exact nature of the products that are required

The first attempt to format a common standard for telecommunications was made by the International Telecommunication Union (ITU) in 1865. Since then many other bodies have joined in laying down standards. There are now organizations spanning the international sphere, such as ISO, CCITT, ANSI and the ITU, and national organizations such as BSI in the UK. Organizations have also sprung up to cater for special-interest groups: for example, ECMA is responsible for coordinating manufacturing policy across Europe.

Table 3.1 lists the most important organizations active in the field of communication standards.

IEEE 802 project

This is one of the most important bodies as far as networks are concerned. The IEEE set up the 802 project at the request of IBM, Xerox, Boeing and the world's largest company at that time, General Motors. The aim was to define a standard for LANs. The outcome was the definition of the OSI model's lowest three layers, designed predominately for LANs.

This project is best known for its formal definition of Ethernet (IEEE 802.3) and Token Ring (IEEE 802.5) Most of the IEEE 802 standards have now been fully adopted by ISO through their fast-track route. The ISO just adds an 8 in front of the IEEE standards: for example, IEEE 802.3 is defined by the ISO as 8802.3.

Incidentally, the reason why the project was called IEEE 802 is because it was set up in February 1980: hence the 80 for 1980 and the 2 for the second month, February.

There were four major objectives for the IEEE 802 committee:

(1) to define the physical, data link and network layers;

(2) to standardize the service to be provided by each layer to the higher layer;

(3) to define peer-to-peer protocols;

(4) to define selected LAN technologies, such as Ethernet and Token Ring.

Table 3.1 Standards organizations.

Abbreviation	Name	Purpose
ISO	International Organization for Standardization	Develops standards for data communication and data processing
CCITT	Comité consultatif international télégraphique et téléphonique	Prepares recommendations for communications standards including data communications (part of ITU)
ITU	International Telecommunication Union	Facilitates international communication and promotes trade by setting standards
ANSI	American National Standards Institute	Sets communications standards; coordinates with ISO and the ITU
BSI	British Standards Institution	National body for the laying down of standards within the UK (equivalent to ANSI in the USA)
ECMA	European Computer Manufacturers' Association	Association of European companies; develops and manufactures common data processing machines. ECMA is a member of ISO and CCITT
EIA	Electronic Industries Association	Association of US-based manufacturing organizations that recommends a standard approach to develop and manufacture a common data processing machine
IEEE	Institute of Electrical and Electronics Engineers	Sets standards to enhance data processing and data communications. Famous for its LAN 802 standards

The IEEE 802 reference model

The IEEE model defines the bottom three layers of the OSI seven-layer model. The relationship between each committee is shown in Figure 3.5, and the individual committees are listed below.

802.1

This committee is split into two subcommittees. Committee 802.1(a) is concerned with defining an overview and the underlying architecture for other committees to use. The second subcommittee is concerned with defining addressing, with internetworking and, most importantly, with the management issues.

802.2

This is the highest committee. It is concerned with the logical link control layer, which universally defines compulsory services from any given network, regardless of the actual network being used. So this committee sets the function that will be

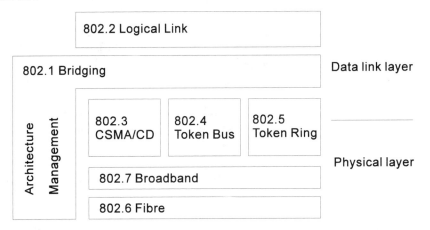

Figure 3.5 Structure of the IEEE 802 project.

required, whether you are implementing an Ethernet, Token Ring or FDDI network. Once the IEEE 802.2 committee had defined the requirements, subcommittees were set up to implement the 802.2 requirement in different ways.

802.3
This committee, working to the IEEE 802.2 committee specification, defined how it could be implemented using the CSMA/CD (Ethernet) approach. The committee was then further subdivided to explore the different types of hardware that could be used to implement CSMA/CD, which in turn is an implementation of the 802.2 requirements.

802.4
This committee, working to the IEEE 802.2 committee specification, defined how it could be implemented using the token-passing bus approach.

802.5
This committee, working to the IEEE 802.2 committee specification, defined how it could be implemented using the Token Ring bus approach.

Logical link controller IEEE 802.2

The LLC (logical link control) layer defines a method for exchanging data between SAPs (service access points), which are multiplexed over a single physical LAN. The LLC defines both connection-oriented and datagram-oriented (connectionless) services. Interestingly, these functions are very similar to the HDLC standard. The service definition resembles the definition for a WAN (wide area network), with the constraint that the two connecting devices are considered to reside on the same network.

Ethernet

Overview

Ethernet networks are currently the most popular type of network in the PC LAN environment. At the last count, the ratio of Ethernet installations to those of its closest rival, Token Ring, was 3:1.

The original Ethernet system was installed on an experimental basis at the Palo Alto Research Center of the Xerox Corporation in California in 1980. This was followed with a public paper, the DIX 1.0 standard, in September 1981. This was the joint standard from DEC, Intel and Xerox. Xerox, Digital Equipment and Intel subsequently agreed a specification for Ethernet called version 2, which is the system most commonly used today. This standard was later recognized at international level thanks to the IEEE adopting version 2 almost unaltered as the now-famous IEEE 802.3 worldwide Ethernet standard. There is now yet another standard for the Ethernet packet that is slightly different from IEEE 802.3, called Ethernet II (see later for comparison). The two standards are very similar, but unfortunately the slight difference is significant enough to make them incompatible. The chances are that if you are not sure which version you are running, you are probably running the IEEE 802.3 standard.

While a student at Sussex University in the 1970s, I witnessed one of the earliest installations of Ethernet in the UK. I could not believe how impressively fast Ethernet was, with its speed of 10 Mbit/s. It was reliable, fast and comparatively inexpensive, and at that time represented an incredible achievement. The original design objective was to allow office workstations and other computing resources to connect up and share resources.

How Ethernet works

The word 'Ethernet' itself helps to explain much of how it actually works. 'Ether' is a word derived from Greek Latin, meaning an element that fills all space: in other words, a substance that surrounds everything, so that everything is in common touch with the ether. There is really nothing new about the basic concept of Ethernet. A useful analogy is to compare it with human verbal communication.

We are all equipped with mouths and ears that we use to communicate. Since we are all tuned to use the same common frequency range, in a group situation we are able to hear any one individual who is talking. Each Ethernet card is similarly equipped with a transmitter (its mouth) and a receiver (its ears). Electronically, Ethernet is based on joining each node to a signal cable, so that through the common cable all nodes can 'talk' and can 'hear' each other's conversation. The ether in everyday conversation is ·air, which carries our conversation as a series of air pressure disturbances. In Ethernet it is an electrical voltage flowing through the common cable, which all nodes can detect. The cable works at a rate of 10 Mbit/s (megabits per second): roughly 1 million characters per second, which compares well with the average throughput that you would expect from a normal disk drive.

We can extend the analogy further. The further away you are from an individual, the harder it becomes to talk to them. Ethernet nodes suffer from the same problem; hence there is always a limit on the maximum distance between any two nodes. However, just as in everyday conversation you can boost the distance over which you can talk by using a loudspeaker or a megaphone, the flagging Ethernet signals can also be boosted by means of repeaters.

Ethernet is sometimes referred to by the abbreviation CSMA/CD. This stands for Carrier Sense Multiple Access/Collision Detection, which describes well (albeit in technical jargon) how Ethernet basically works. Before transmitting, a node must first ascertain that no one else is sending data across the cable (carrier sense); once this has been established, any node with data to send can begin to transmit (multiple access). If by chance two or more nodes were to attempt to send data across the network then the data would be corrupted. Each node is able to detect this situation since it is listening to the signal over the cable, constantly comparing it with what it is sending out. If it detects the signal differing from what it would expect as the only node sending data on the cable, it assumes that a collision of data has occurred: it then has detected a collision (collision detection). The station will now refrain from sending out its data, and the node will wait for a short time before trying to re-send the data.

In order to prevent constant collisions it is essential that each Ethernet card has a unique 'backing-off' time. How Ethernet ensures that each card has a slightly different backing-off time is very ingenious. Each Ethernet card is given a universal unique address. This is used as a seed in a random number generator, which will produce a different waiting time for each card. The Ethernet standard specifies that messages must have a maximum length of 1500 characters in order to give others the chance to have their say.

Limitations of Ethernet

Ethernet is an ideal and extremely efficient method of communication when only a small number of people wish to talk with each other. However, if everybody chose to talk at the same time it would result in massive amounts of collisions and a minimum amount of messages actually being received (Figure 3.6). One of the main problems with Ethernet is that it is a non-deterministic network: you cannot guarantee that a user will be able to communicate with another user within a set time period.

In my experience, it is extremely rare to come across a massively congested Ethernet network. It is very difficult to congest a pure Ethernet network because there are normally so many other bottlenecks in the way: for example, slowness of network cards, workstation applications being unable to keep up with the network, the file server hard disk being too slow, or the file server process being unable to keep up with the demands of the network.

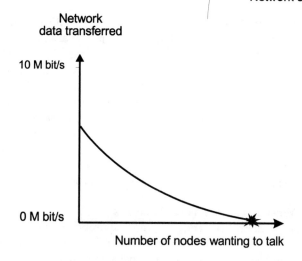

Figure 3.6 Performance deterioration on Ethernet networks.

Ethernet II and IEEE 802.3 and 802.2 frames (different standards)

These different standards often lead to confusion. There are three versions of Ethernet packets commonly being used on Novell LANs. By default, Novell used to support IEEE 802.3 packets, but when NetWare 4.0 was introduced, the Novell default packet was changed to the more flexible IEEE 802.2 frame. In fact, as of 15 April 1993, all new drivers shipped out with NetWare 3.11/3.2 and NetWare 4.x default to the IEEE 802.2 frame type.

Ethernet IEEE 802.3 packets
This used to be the Novell default setting. The IEEE 802.3 packet has a two-byte length field, set by the higher protocol layer. In most cases it is the IPX (inter packet exchange) protocol that sets up the length field.

Destination	Source	Length	Data unit
6 bytes	6 bytes	2 bytes	46–1500 bytes

Ethernet II packets
The Ethernet II packets contain a unique protocol number that is not contained in the IEEE 802.3 frames: a two-byte field called 'type', which indicates the type of data being carried:

Destination	Source	Type	Data unit
6 bytes	6 bytes	2 bytes	46–1500 bytes

Ethernet IEEE 802.2 frame format: Novell's new default

Novell decided with the introduction of NetWare 4.0 to accommodate a number of desirable features into its default Ethernet frame format. This meant doing away with the limitations of the IEEE 802.3 raw format and moving towards the far more flexible IEEE 802.2 format, which has a number of extra fields as compared with the old IEEE 802.3 frame. The IEEE 802.2 frame is shown in Figure 3.7.

With this new frame format it is now possible to support packet checksums, which is very useful over wide area networks. Extra data frame security can also be implemented. But perhaps the most important reasons for the change is that the new default frame format is far more protocol-independent. For example, IEEE 802.2 frames can easily support IPX and TCP/IP protocols.

When to use Ethernet II packets

The Ethernet II standard is more appropriate than IEEE 802.3, if multi protocols are going to be used across your network. In environments where there might be more than just Novell nodes it is advisable to use Ethernet II. It has been designed to be used in a multi protocol environment and has superior flexibility. For example, if the network is to service Novell, DEC and TCP/IP clients it is advisable to modify the Novell Ethernet packets to use the Ethernet II packets. DEC uses Ethernet II packets as standard for its DECpathworks networks.

If you will only be carrying Novell packets across your network, then you can save yourself a lot of time by installing the Novell default Ethernet frames. To do this you just follow the Novell standard installation guidelines. However, to install Ethernet II packets you need to carry out a number of extra steps at the workstation and at the file server.

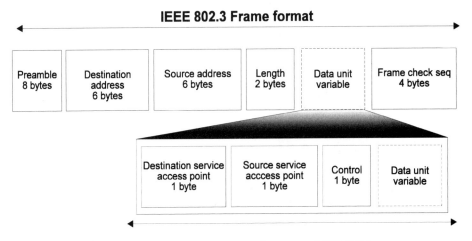

Figure 3.7 Novell's new default frame type IEEE 802.2.

It is important to note that from the Novell user's viewpoint it makes no real difference what type of Ethernet packet is being used. Testing has indicated that performance differences are negligible. So my recommendation to Novell-only organizations is: don't change anything. However, if you intend to carry any other types of protocol, such as TCP/IP traffic, then it is worth spending the time and converting to Ethernet II packets.

Detailed differences

The Ethernet IEEE 802.3 packets, which represent the Novell default setting, look like this:

Destination	Source	Length	Data unit
6 bytes	6 bytes	2 bytes	46–1500 bytes

while the Ethernet II packets look like this:

Destination	Source	Type	Data unit
6 bytes	6 bytes	2 bytes	46–1500 bytes

The type field is very important in the Ethernet II frame format. These type numbers are now well defined. There follows a list of the main service type numbers. The most important as far as this book is concerned is the number allocated to Novell (8137 hex).

Network type number (hex)	Service using the number
8137	NetWare data
0800	Internet packets (TCP/IP)
0600	XNS packets

These type descriptors are now assigned universally by IEEE. They indicate the type of user making use of a particular service. It is interesting to note that these numbers given to potential type users are always greater then 1518, or roughly 1.5 kbytes, which happens to be the maximum data size that can be sent on Ethernet packets.

Now by cleverly organizing the type field like this, it possible to distinguish between an Ethernet II and an IEEE 802.3 packet. This is how is done:

- Look at the type field
- If it is greater then 1518, then it is an Ethernet II packet
- If not, it is an IEEE 802.3 packet

Establishing which type of Ethernet packet you are using under NetWare

It is very easy to find out the type of protocol currently being supported on your Novell network.

(1) Go to the NetWare file server

(2) You can now type at the file server console two different commands: CONFIG or PROTOCOLS (Figure 3.8).

CONFIG shows the current configuration of the file server, including the type of packets being supported on each NIC card. It also shows other interesting information about the file server, such as its name and internal network number. Look for a description of each network interface card and against this will be a description of the type of data packet that has been bound to it.

You can use the PROTOCOL command to get the same information. This shows which network cards are currently active, and what protocols are currently being supported. There is another interesting frame type called VIRTUAL_LAN. This is used by the NetWare 3.x and 4.x file servers as a sort of universal internal network that brings all the real networks together.

Using Ethernet II packets on Novell

There are a number of basic steps that have to carried out:

- Specify Ethernet II packets on the file server when you load the Ethernet LAN driver during installation
- Run PROTOCOL on the file server console
- To specify a protocol other than Novell's IPX on the server
- Run ECONFIG.EXE on workstation IPX
- On the appropriate workstation (modifies IPX.COM) and router software

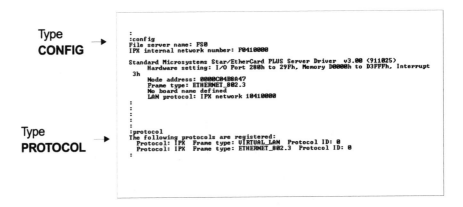

Figure 3.8 Monitoring server configuration.

Try not to mix Ethernet II and Ethernet 802.3 packets on the same cabled network, since it could lead to a lot of confusion!

Different Ethernet frame formats

Ethernet 802.3
This is the Ethernet standard frame format as defined by the IEEE committee. It is referred to as the IEEE 802.3 packet format. It is also the Novell standard default Ethernet packet format.

Preamble 8 bytes	Destination address 6 bytes	Source address 6 bytes	Length 2 bytes	Data unit variable	Frame check seq 4 bytes

Ethernet II
The other major Ethernet frame is Ethernet II, which is the default format type for such networks as TCP/IP and DEC's LAT. It uses a type field instead of a length field. When TCP/IP is used across Novell networks, in most cases this type of frame must be used. TCP/IP needs this type of frame because the ARP (address resolution protocol) can be recognized by examining the type field.

Preamble 8 bytes	Destination address 6 bytes	Source address 6 bytes	Type 2 bytes	Data unit variable	Frame check seq 4 bytes

Ethernet 802.2
This is a more comprehensive frame format since it contains, within the header, the logical link control (LLC) IEEE 802.2 information on top of the IEEE 802.3 frame (Figure 3.9). The LLC layer defines a universal service access point (SAP) which can be used to communicate over Token Ring, Ethernet or FDDI networks.

Ethernet SNAP
This format is used predominantly on networks which need to use TCP/IP over networks which do not use the standard Ethernet II packet format (Figure 3.10). It was devised to allow the IP address and ARP to be transmitted across a wide variety of local area networks.

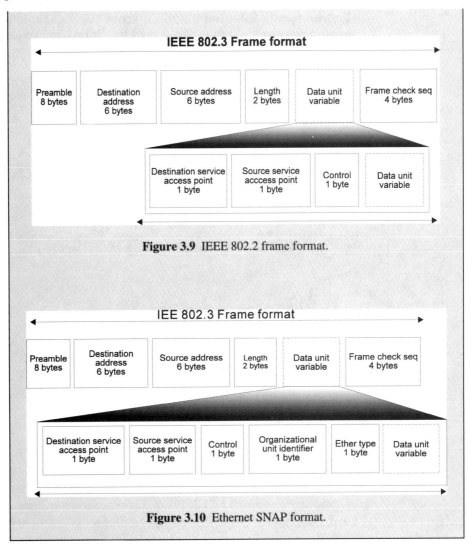

Figure 3.9 IEEE 802.2 frame format.

Figure 3.10 Ethernet SNAP format.

Ethernet connectivity

Ethernet, by its very nature, is based round a bus topology. However, it can be connected up physically in a number of ways. There is of course the bus cable topology when using thick or thin coaxial cables, but you can also use unshielded twisted pair physically connected in a star (Figure 3.11).

Thin Ethernet is the most commonly used means of connecting an Ethernet network, although 10Base-T is slowly taking over from thin Ethernet.

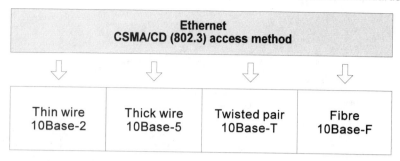

Figure 3.11 Ethernet's different cabling systems.

Thin Ethernet

Thin Ethernet uses coaxial cables. It is relatively inexpensive and the quickest to install of all the different types of cable. As an alternative to thick Ethernet, thin Ethernet coaxial cable is preferred because of its manoeuvrability and low cost. However, there are significant limitations on its distance capability and the number of devices that can be attached. Thin Ethernet, the most popular medium for Ethernet networks, uses 50 Ω BNC plugs. The plug used to connect up a thin Ethernet cable to an Ethernet card is a T-BNC plug. (See Figure 3.12.)

Not all BNC plugs are of the same quality. Whenever possible select BNC plugs with gold pins, not silver. If money is no object, insist on the higher military specification UG-274.

One of the main problems with thin Ethernet is that if at any point you disconnect the cable from either side of the T junction the whole network goes down, killing all live sessions.

Consider using no-break BNC plugs on thin Ethernet networks that are installed in a hostile environment.

There are some interesting BNC plugs on the market that are 'no-break', thus eliminating the above problem.

Sometimes thin Ethernet cabling is referred to as 'cheapernet' cable!

When buying cables from manufacturers, don't just say, 'I want some cables for thin Ethernet'. Ask for the cable that conforms to IEEE 802.3 specifications: 10Base-2 for thin Ethernet and 10Base-5 for thick Ethernet. The market is flooded with very cheap cables that barely match the standards required but claim to be thin Ethernet cable. Always remember to ground one end of thin or thick Ethernet, as defined by the standards.

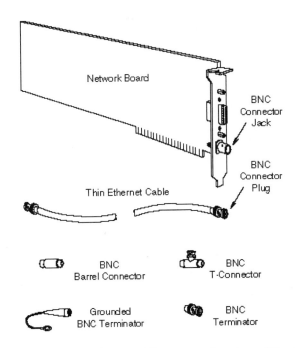

Figure 3.12 Thin Ethernet cabling system (courtesy of Novell).

According to the IEEE 802.3 rules, a thin coaxial segment may support 30 attachments up to a distance of 185 m. Devices are usually attached directly to the cable segment with BNC-T connectors.

Thick Ethernet

Thick Ethernet was the original medium for Ethernet networks. It was primarily used for connecting PCs to mainframes and microcomputers. The current trend seems to be moving away from this type of cable in favour of fibre cables. For thick coaxial cable, distance is limited to 500 m and the maximum number of attachments to 100. Each PC is attached to the thick coaxial cable by a transceiver and an attachment user interface (AUI) drop. These can be up to 50 m in length.

Always remember to ground one (and only one) end of thick Ethernet, as defined by the standards.

10Base-2, 10Base-5 and 10Base-T Ethernet cable characteristics

These are listed in Table 3.2.

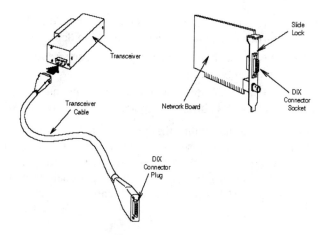

Figure 3.13 Thick Ethernet cabling system.

Table 3.2 Ethernet cable characteristics.

	Thin 10Base-2	Thick 10Base-5	Twisted pair 10Base-T
Maximum cable segment length	185 m	500 m	100 m to hub
Maximum segment	5	3 + 2 repeaters	4 + (hub-based)
Maximum span with repeaters	925 m	2500 m	Depends on hub
Minimum node spacing	0.5 m	2.5 m	N/A
Total nodes in network	1024	1024	Depends on hub
Maximum number of nodes per trunk segment	30	100	Depends on hub

The future of Ethernet

The Ethernet standard has been around for a long time; it standardizes at 10 Mbit/s. It is the most popular network standard, with nearly 4,000,000 nodes installed, in contrast with 2,500,000 Token Ring network nodes. However, people are now looking to Ethernet for greater performance. Ethernet's current proposal to the IEEE committee is a new 100 Mbit/s version of Ethernet, based around 10Base-G cabling. This proposal was initially pioneered by 3Com, who are seen as the grandfather of adaptor cards, and it is now being backed by Synoptics and Sun Microcomputers. A new consortium bandwagon has started to roll. The new standard is to have the following characteristics:

- It is to use the same access method as the old 10 Mbit/s standard; it uses carrier sense multiple access/collision detection (CSMA/CD).
- It is to use the same cable types that are associated with unshielded and shielded twisted pair.
- As far as possible it will adopt the same interfaces in terms of cabling plugs and sockets currently implemented under the 10 Mbit/s version.

I can foresee that within the next two to five years the 100 Mbit/s standard based around unshielded twisted pair technology will become as common as thin Ethernet on 10 Mbit/s today. A recently announced standard 100Base-VG (voice grade) has been proposed to the IEEE for international acceptance. This new standard, proposed by HP, allows 10Base-T cables to operate at 100 Mbit/s using special HUBs.

How Ethernet works

There now follows a technical overview of the components of the Ethernet card and how they inter-operate.

The building blocks of an Ethernet card
The basic components for an Ethernet cards are shown in Figure 3.14.

The tap makes a non-intrusive physical connection to the coaxial cable. It is sometimes known as a vampire tap as it sucks signals from the cable. The transceiver then processes the signal. It can send and receive data to the cable,

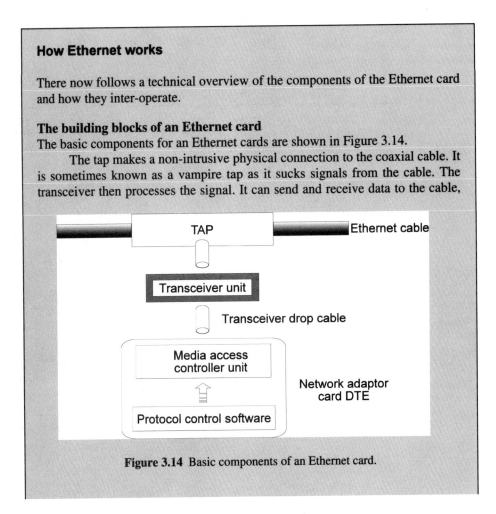

Figure 3.14 Basic components of an Ethernet card.

and also provides the mechanism to detect collisions, thus conforming to the Ethernet protocol on board the Network Interface Card (NIC).

The other important function is that the transceiver will, if functioning correctly, protect the coaxial cable from a malfunctioning NIC by detaching the NIC from the cable. This is called 'jabber' control (Figure 3.15). It is part of the transceiver function, and ensures that signals produced from the NIC destined for the cable are within acceptable voltage levels, and thus do not exceed the defined maximum length.

The aim is to ensure that the NIC is compact. The transceiver unit, when using thick Ethernet cable, is external to the NIC, whereas in thin Ethernet it is on board the NIC.

The transceiver is connected to the MAC (medium access control) unit, which always sits on the network card. Its main functions are to encapsulate and de-encapsulate data into Ethernet frames. It will then pass the incoming data onwards to the controlling microprocessor on the network that is running the Ethernet higher-level control protocols.

How Ethernet frames are constructed

Each Ethernet card address is given a unique universal 48-bit identifier by an international organization: his is known as the Ethernet address of the card.

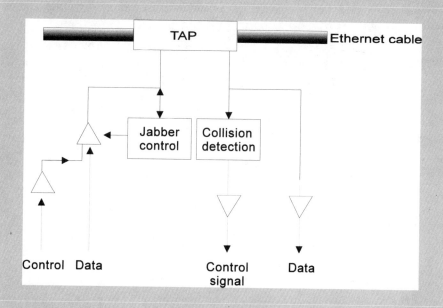

Figure 3.15 Jabber control.

Each frame when transmitted on the cable has eight distinct fields (Figure 3.16):

(1) the preamble

(2) the start of frame delimiter (SFD)

(3) the unique destination address

(4) a source network identifier (this being the unique Ethernet address)

(5) a length indicator

(6) the data field

(7) an optional padding field

(8) a frame check sequence (FCS)

All the fields are of fixed length, except for the data field and the associated padding field.

The first field, the preamble field, is at the head of the frame. Its basic function is to allow the receiving electronics via the MAC unit to synchronize before the actual frame is received. The preamble is a series of seven bytes, each having the pattern 10101010.

The next field, the start of frame delimiter (SFD), is a simple single byte having the pattern 10101011. This informs the Ethernet card that the start of the Ethernet frame is to follow.

The next two fields are the source and the destination fields. The source field simply contains the unique Ethernet address of the sending card. However,

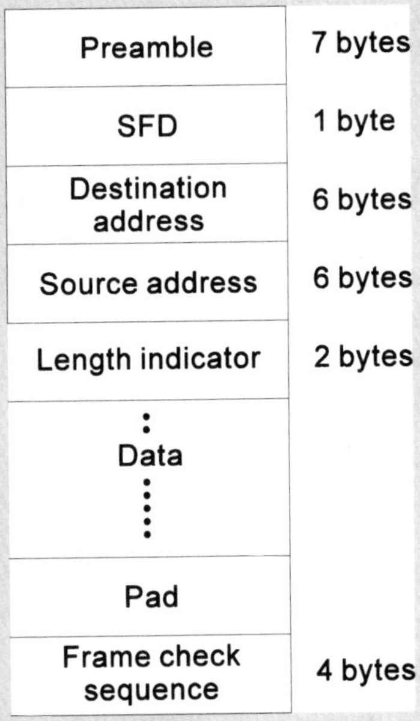

Field	Size
Preamble	7 bytes
SFD	1 byte
Destination address	6 bytes
Source address	6 bytes
Length indicator	2 bytes
Data	
Pad	
Frame check sequence	4 bytes

Figure 3.16 Ethernet frame format.

the destination field is more interesting. If the first bit of the address is set to 1 this means that it is referring to a group address, or is a general broadcast. A broadcast address is shown by all bits being set to 1 for all the 48 bits in the address. However, if the first bit is 0 then the destination address is a unique Ethernet card on the network.

The length indicator is the next field. It is two bytes long. They record the length of the user data carried by the frame. If the data field is less than the minimum frame size, then the padding field is used to bring the field to the minimum frame size. The minimum frame is 64 bytes long.

Finally, the frame check sequence (FCS) is used to trap any error that may have occurred in the frame. It is four bytes long, and uses cyclic redundancy check calculation.

Ethernet frames transmission

In order to prepare data to be sent across the Ethernet network, an Ethernet frame is initially constructed around the user data to be transmitted. Before attempting to send the frame, the Ethernet card monitors the activity on the cable, thanks to the MAC unit, by monitoring the voltage of the cable. If it finds that the cable is being used it will wait until the carrier becomes available. This is where it becomes clever; it does not attempt to send its frame immediately, but waits for a short time, called the interframe gap. This is a fixed time that is the maximum time for the Ethernet frames to go from one end of the network to the other. It must allow for this time so that the data is given time to get to its destination before the new data is sent out onto the cable.

When the cable is ready for the transmission, a series of bitstream data leaves the Ethernet card onto the cable. While this is going the transceiver will electronically monitor the cable for any collisions that may be occurring.

Detecting a collision

Ethernet does this by monitoring voltages; if they go beyond predefined levels a collision is detected. If, for example, two cards produce a signal of 5 V on the cable, the resulting voltage on the cable will be 5 V + 5 V = 10 V. The transceiver will then monitor the cable for collisions by looking for 10 V (Figure 3.17).

Managing an Ethernet collision

When a collision has been detected, the Ethernet card will go through a set recovery procedure, designed to ensure that the data can be sent as quickly as possible back onto the common cable, avoiding future collisions with cards also waiting to send their data.

On detection of a collision, the Ethernet card goes into what is called the jam sequence of operation. This ensures that all other Ethernet cards on the network are made aware of the collision. The transmission of the outgoing frame is suspended and the data already sent out is assumed lost. The card will

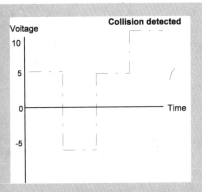

Figure 3.17 Collision detection.

then attempt to schedule a retransmission when the carrier once again becomes available. The retransmission of a frame is attempted up to a predefined number of times, known as the attempt limit, before the card gives up. The attempt limit is set by controlling software. It is one of the few interesting parameters that the user can set.

The MAC unit will now attempt to re-send, and adjusts itself to the load on the cable. It progressively increases the time delay between failed attempts at retransmission. This scheduling is known as truncated binary exponential back-off. The method of operation is shown schematically in Figure 3.18.

To ensure that every Ethernet card on the network does not attempt to retransmit simultaneously, a random number generator equation is used to ensure that the back-off times for each card will be slightly different. This should avoid multiple cards synchronizing and constantly colliding with each other. This is done by utilizing the universal Ethernet address in each card as the random number seed. This way, each card is assured of behaving slightly differently from each other. The NIC now waits a random integral number of

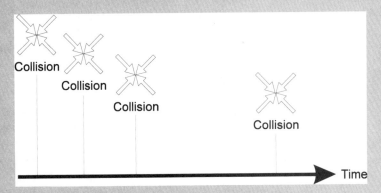

Figure 3.18 Truncated binary exponential back-off.

slot times before attempting to retransmit. The slot time is worked out as the worst-case time delay for which the NIC must wait before it can reliably know that a collision has occurred.

The formula used is:

slot time = 2 × (transmission path delay) + safety margin

The transmission path delay is the worst-case signal propagation delay going from any Ethernet card to any other on the cable. The slot time is then doubled to allow for the signal to return to the source, plus a safety margin.

Frame reception

When a transceiver detects incoming data, it informs the Ethernet MAC controller and inhibits any sending of data from the card. The preamble is used to synchronize the packet start sequence. The destination address is processed to see if a frame is destined for this particular Network card; if not, the rest is disregarded. Assuming it is meant for this Ethernet card, the source address and data fields are then loaded up into buffers for further processing.

The frame check sum is then calculated and compared with the FCS field. If it is correct, the information is then passed on to the next protocol layer. If the check sum fails, the frame is ignored and an error is reported to the protocol.

Token ring

Overview

Historically, Token Ring has been associated with IBM. It was, after all, IBM who campaigned for a worldwide standard in Token Ring; now called the IEEE 802.5 standard. The original principles of Token Ring were laid down by a Swedish engineer, Von Willemjin, in early 1972 (he later went on to make a successful claim for royalties against IBM). Token Ring is now one of the two most popular protocols being used to carry data across LANs, the other being Ethernet.

The basic idea is that nodes are connected together in a ring (Figure 3.19). Each node can only communicate with its neighbours on either side; this leads to a logical ring. However, in most cases Token Rings are physically cabled up in star topology. In my experience of network installations, most sites that implement Token Ring tend to be IBM houses. These organizations usually have a historical involvement with IBM, by using their mainframes or mainframe technology. When they decide to connect up their PCs to the existing IBM equipment, the natural IBM solution has been to use Token Ring.

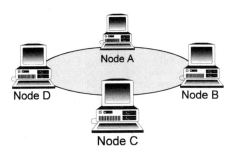

Figure 3.19 Basic Token Ring structure.

How Token Ring works (basics)

The token is a small series of bits sent round the ring from PC to PC. It is used to arbitrate who has access to the ring at any given time. When any workstation wants to communicate, it must grab an empty token. It can now send data to any other PC on the network.

An interesting analogy can be made between Token Ring and the story of William Golding's book *Lord of the Flies*. The book is basically about a group of schoolchildren marooned on a desert island. They decide to organize themselves around the 'conch', a special seashell that they find on the beach. Whoever holds the conch has power over the others: a bit like a PC workstation taking over an empty token, and using it to take control of the ring. The analogy breaks down when you realize that in Token Ring a station is only allowed to send out one message at a time; it must then relinquish control and pass it on to the next user.

Assume that we have a small Token Ring network with four nodes, and that node A suddenly decides that it need to send a message to node C. Let us follow the basic sequence of operation that would normally occur (Figure 3.20).

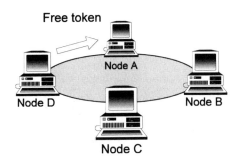

Figure 3.20 Node D forwards a free token to Node A.

Node A waits for an empty data packet to arrive, and grabs it by setting a field in the token as it flows through. It then enters the address of the destination node, in this case node C, onto the ring followed by the length of the message and then finally by the message itself. The now extended token train flows throughout the ring. As it goes through node B the token is analysed to ascertain whether it is a free token. In this case the token is already being used. Node B will investigate whether the message is destined for itself; since in this case it is not, node B would just allow the token and all the associated data to flow through without interference. There is a small one-bit delay in attempting to analyse the token (Figure 3.21).

When the token arrives at the destination node C, the data from the token is read and a flag bit on the token is set, indicating that the destination node has read the data with no problems (Figure 3.22).

The token and the message continue their journey all the way around the ring, back to the original sender, node A. The data is then stripped away from the ring and compared with the original data sent. If they match up, and the destination node has confirmed it has read the data, then node A has achieved its objective of sending data to node C (Figure 3.23).

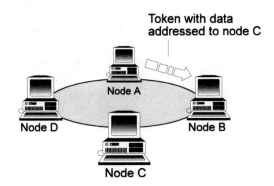

Figure 3.21 Node A sending data to Node C via Node B.

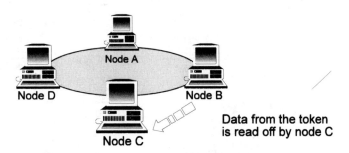

Figure 3.22 Node C receives Node A's data.

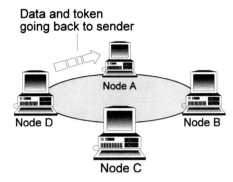

Figure 3.23 Data arrives back to sender.

The token is stripped of any data and released back onto the ring as a free token. In this case node B is the next node in line to have the opportunity to send data to any other nodes (Figure 3.24).

Although the above explanation of the operation of the token appears simple, it is in fact anything but simple. Compared with Ethernet protocol, Token Ring protocol is far more complicated. A more detailed technical explanation of Token Ring, covering important aspects of monitoring and beaconing, is given below.

However, unless you happen to be a systems engineer with a protocol analyser at hand, you really do not need to know the technical details of the Token Ring protocols. In most cases you can think of them as essential black boxes that you put into your PC to provide network connections.

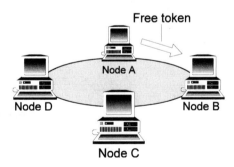

Figure 3.24 Free token is passed on to next node.

How Token Ring works

The interface to the ring

Token ring uses a wire centre (hub) that houses electromechanical relays to make the physical star into a logical ring (Figure 3.25).

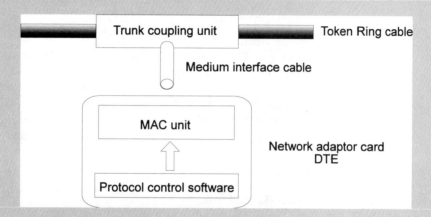

Figure 3.25 Token Ring card basic components.

The trunk coupling unit forms the physical interface with the cable. It contains a set of relays, arranged in such a way that if the power from the NIC is lost it would pass the transmission through the cable.

The MAC unit, as with Ethernet, is responsible for frame encapsulation and de-encapsulation. Also, when the network card is defined as a ring monitor it ensures that the ring has a minimum latency time; this is the time for a signal to propagate once round the ring.

Token Ring management

At all times in a Token Ring, a token is being transmitted round the network, even though it might not contain any data. At any given time one of the stations is the monitor station, and all others are on a stand-by monitor mode.

Token Ring maintenance is concerned with three basic types of problem that could cause failure: what happens if a token is lost; a physical break in the network; and the failure of the monitor station. Any station can become a monitor station, but only one at a time.

The active monitor station has a number of responsibilities. It is responsible for ensuring that a token is constantly going round the ring. It will also monitor whether a token goes missing and, if so, will initiate a new token to go around again.

When a workstation is turned on and wants to join the ring, it first has to ensure that no other Token Ring card has the same address, and then inform its neighbours that it has now joined in the ring.

The new station first sends a duplicate address test frame to check whether anyone has the same address. If no error has occurred, the new station sends a frame that informs its neighbours of its new address. Each station in the ring records the address of its neighbour upstream and uses this for fault detection.

Stand-by monitor

When a station joins in a ring it goes into stand-by monitor mode, assuming that somewhere on the ring there is already an active monitor. It then waits for an active monitor present (AMP) frame to come along within a set period of time. This tells all the other stations that there is already an active monitor on the ring.

If the stand-by monitors do not constantly see AMP frames, they assume that the active monitor is active no more, and attempt to take control of the network. This becomes a 'free for all', with the first station to grab the title becoming the new active monitor.

Beaconing (breaks in the network)

When the ring becomes damaged, which could be due either to a node failure or to a physical cable problem, the station immediately 'downstream' from the point of failure goes into beaconing mode.

All normal data packets will be suspended.

Station A, on realizing that no more packets are coming from its neighbour, would go into 'public mourning' and send out a beaconing frame telling all the other stations that (for example) station D has died and should now be bypassed. The active monitor is also informed about station D's failure. Using the mechanical relays, station D is bypassed and a new token is then placed into the ring.

Connecting Token Ring

In most cases Token Ring networks are physically connected together in a star configuration. Each station connects up to a central hub: an IBM 8228 MAU (multistation access unit).

Figure 3.26 shows a typical Token Ring community of five workstations and one file server connected up using two MAUs. Each MAU is connected to each other to produce a ring. Each MAU can normally take eight workstations, although this is largely dependent on the manufacturer of the MAU; I have an MAU that provides for up to 16 workstation connections. There are a number of classic rules when it comes to Token Ring and MAUs.

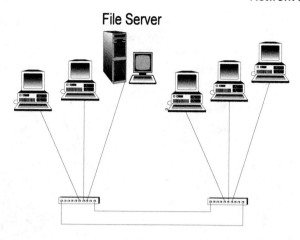

Figure 3.26 A typical way to connect Token Ring networks.

IBM MAUs are notorious for being prone to electromagnetic interference. Keep them well away from fluorescent lights. Don't forget; if the MAU does not seem to work, ask whether it has been activated by the little activator key that should have been provided.

The general limits for Token Ring when using shielded cable are:

Total length of a ring	336 m
Maximum distance of node from MAU	100 m

The cable used is normally shielded cable but UTP (unshielded twisted pair) is becoming very popular. This is partly because shielded twisted pair cable is much more expensive than UTP, especially if you buy IBM-conformant cables.

Token Ring used to work at 4 Mbit/s, but now we have a more powerful version, the 16 Mbit/s Token Ring. Equipment running at 16 Mbit/s is now becoming standard across industry. The new faster cards are compatible with the old 4 Mbit/s cards, but the price you pay is that they will flip down to the lower 4 Mbit/s speed.

Token Ring cables

IBM has identified a series of cable types that should be used be used for Token Ring. Although IBM has set the standard, you can easily buy compatible cables from other manufacturers, and they are likely to be cheaper.

The ICS (IBM cabling system) has been around for a long time. It is mainly used to connect IBM mainframes and Token Ring PCs together.

These cables are given type numbers. A new series of IBM data cables has been introduced to replace all previous incompatible cable types.

Traditionally, IBM uses copper twisted pair with double screening cables (Figure 3.27). There are seven different IBM data cable types to choose from. The first three are used mainly by today's IBM Token Ring cards.

There are basically two different types of cabling system:

- small movable cable system: can support up to 96 nodes and up to 12 MAUs; typically uses cable types 3 or 6
- large unmovable cabling system: can support up to 260 nodes and up to 33 MAUs; typically uses cable type 1

The small movable cabling is more popular then the large unmovable system. This means that most Token Ring networks use cable types 3 or 6 or both (Table 3.3). The other cable types are listed in Table 3.4.

Cabling Token Ring, using type 6

Table 3.5 shows the cabling rules for Token Ring type 6 cable.

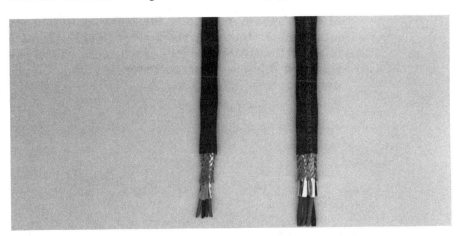

Figure 3.27 IBM copper twisted cables.

Table 3.3 IBM data cable types.

Parameters	Type 1	Type 2	Type 3	Type 6
Maximum distance between MAU and workstation	375 m	100 m	100 m	45 m
Tested data rate	16 Mbit/s	4 Mbit/s	4 Mbit/s	4 Mbit/s
MAU to MAU	200 m	120 m	120 m	45 m
Maximum devices per ring	260	72	96	96

Table 3.4 Remaining cable types.

Cable type	What it is used for
Type 5	Comprises two fibre optic cables (multimode); used for cabling between distributor rooms
Type 6	Flexible type of cable 3, used to connect terminals to Token Ring sockets; commonly called patch cables
Type 8	Flat cable used for laying under carpets
Type 9	Simple implementation of IBM type 1 cable

Table 3.5 Cabling rules for type 6 cable.

Maximum number of nodes in ring	96
Maximum number of interlinked MAUs	12
Maximum patch cable between an MAU and a node	150 ft (45 m)
Maximum patch distance between two MAUs	150 ft (45 m)
Maximum patch distance connecting all MAUs	400 ft (120 m)

Key points

- IBM backed the development of Token Ring
- Known as the IEEE 802.5 standard
- Standard 4 Mbit/s
- The new 16 Mbit/s
- Uses the token-passing access scheme
- Multiple access units (MAUs) used to connect workstations
- Novell always supported IBM Token Ring cards as standard
- Less efficient than Ethernet in low traffic
- More efficient than Ethernet when large number of multiple conversations are required simultaneously

Token Ring management issues

Using IBM Token Ring

If you are using IBM Token Ring cards, then generally speaking use IBM cable type 6 to connect workstations to the MAU. The good thing with IBM cables is that they have 'unisex' plugs, which means that they can all interconnect together. You do not need to worry about male and female connections. If you plan to run the cable across any ducts then it is better to use IBM type 9, since it is fire- and smoke-resistant.

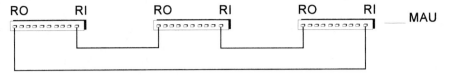

Figure 3.28 Connecting MAUs.

Where you have a number of MAUs, be careful how you connect them up together. The best way is to connect the RO (ring out) of the MAU to the RI (ring in) of the other. You do this for all the MAUs (Figure 3.28)

If you are considering installing Token Ring in a large building, such as a high-rise office block, use fibre optic cable. For a small installation, IBM type 1 cable will probably be sufficient. If you want to cable up a number of buildings together, opt for implementing 16 Mbit/s Token Ring using fibre optics.

When you buy MAUs nowadays, you do not need to go automatically to IBM. There are a number of alternative Token Ring manufacturers to choose from, such as Madge, Intel, SMC and Proteon. When you buy the cards and the relevant MAUs, ask the vendor what sort of management is provided. Also, ask whether the MAU is SNMP compliant. Check that good diagnostic tools are provided, and ensure that the appropriate driver for your current version of Novell NetWare is provided by default.

Do not confuse IBM's name for the Token Ring wiring hub – the multistation access unit, or MAU – with the MAU (medium attachment unit) used on thick Ethernet transceivers. Do not try to connect workstations to the MAU through the RO (ring out) or the RI (ring in) ports.

ARCnet

Overview

ARCnet is the third major network that is popularly used in PC LANs. Although its popularity seems to be slowly eroding away to Ethernet and Token Ring networks, It still remains a major worldwide player. ARCnet stands for Attached Resource Computer Network. It was devised by the Datapoint Corporation in 1976, uses coaxial cable and works at 2.5 Mbit/s, although there is now a new version that works at 20 Mbit/s. A number of manufacturers have now implemented ARCnet using UTP cables. Traditionally, ARCnet networks are considered to be very robust. The original ARCnet specification was largely dictated by the US Defense Department. This means that it has a large tolerance toward errors and was designed to work in hostile environments.

ARCnet technology predates Ethernet. I continue to find it fascinating that ARCnet is quite common in the USA but relatively rarely found in Europe. I put this down to the fact that the USA was originally two to three years ahead of Europe in the implementation of PC LANs. By the time European organizations came to implement PC LANs an alternative was available in the form of the 10 Mbit/s Ethernet.

SMC are one of the largest companies producing ARCnet cards. They also produce an SMC ARCnet chip set. In 1991 SMC decided to buy out Western Digital Network Card's LAN division, who at that time were a major player in the Ethernet card manufacturing market. SMC were apparently diversifying out of ARCnet and joining the bandwagon of Ethernet and Token Ring cards.

ARCnet configuration

Like Token Ring, ARCnet uses logical token passing, but implemented in a bus topology, which is why it is sometimes called a token-passing bus. However, the hubs it uses to connect the nodes are distributed round the network in a star-like configuration, as seen in Figure 3.29.

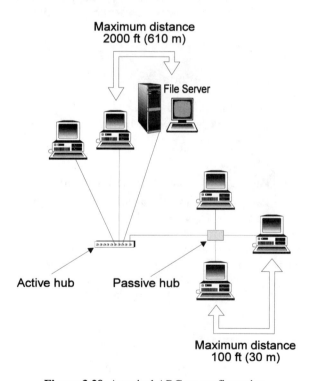

Figure 3.29 A typical ARCnet configuration.

When coaxial cables are used in ARCnet they employ the BNC plugs commonly associated with thin Ethernet cabling. The greatest distance between two nodes in the network cannot exceed 20,000 ft (6100 m). ARCnet uses two different kinds of hub to bring workstations and file servers together: active and passive.

Active hubs

These are powered via the mains and can have nodes connecting from as far as 2,000 ft (600 m). You can connect a number of nodes to an active hub; a typical number is eight.

Passive hubs

These are not powered. They can have nodes connected to them from as far as 100 ft (30 m), and are limited as to the number of nodes they can bring together (typically four).

One of the problems with ARCnet is that the users have to give each ARCnet a unique address from 1 to 255. This is often a problem, since you need to keep a list of which numbers have been assigned and which are free. Station number 0 is reserved for broadcasts.

When using ARCnet to simplify the addressing scheme, consider using the following approach: number file servers from 1 to 9 and workstations from 10 to 255.

ARCnet specifications

ARCnet cabling rules

ARCnet cabling uses the following cabling rules:

- Any unused node of a passive hub must be terminated with a 93 Ω terminator; unused active hubs do not need to be terminated.
- Passive hubs cannot connect directly to each other.
- Passive hubs cannot connect up two active hubs; they can only connect network nodes to active hubs.

Cabling specification

Tables 3.6 and 3.7 outline the ARCnet specifications. There are many different ways of configuring ARCnet, but there are two basic specifications, depending on whether you are using twisted pair or coaxial cables.

ARCnet strategy

Frankly, if you are starting your LAN from scratch, then generally speaking ARCnet would not be the first network that I would consider. The future of ARCnet is open to debate because of its diminishing popularity. However, there are a number of good things to be said about ARCnet: it is extremely reliable, and could be very appropriate if you are installing a PC LAN in a hostile environment There are also some excellent deals available on ARCnet cards.

Table 3.6 ARCnet twisted-pair specification.

	Limitations
Cable type	Twisted pair
Cable topology	Star-bus
Maximum number of nodes	254
Maximum number of active nodes	10
Maximum distance between active hub and a node	400 ft (120 m)
Data transmission	2.5 Mbit/s

Table 3.7 ARCnet coaxial cable specification.

	Limitations
Cable type	RG-62
Cable topology	Star-bus
Maximum number of nodes	254
Maximum number of active nodes	10
Maximum number of passive nodes	One per active node
Maximum distance between active hub and a node	2000 ft (610 m)
Maximum distance between active and passive hub	100 ft (30 m)
Maximum distance between passive hub and a node	100 ft (30 m)
Data transmission	2.5 Mbit/s

4

Managing and selecting optimum file server hardware

Overview

There is a general understanding that, normally, every two to three years some or all of the hardware within the file server needs to be updated. This is because technology is moving is so fast that anything older than three years should be suspected of being a technological bottleneck. This is a good rule of thumb, but obviously to be taken only as a general guideline. For example, your six-year-old AT-type keyboard should not be suspected of affecting your file server's performance.

The file server should not be seen as a single entity, but rather as a series of modules that all have to work together effectively. The performance of the file server is determined by the slowest module. It is therefore very important to ensure that all the modules are appropriately matched, and that any obvious bottlenecks are avoided.

The basic modules in a file server are:

- CPU type
- CPU clock speed
- amount of memory installed
- hard disk controller type
- hard disk performance
- the network operating system

When upgrading your file server it is not always easy to identify which module is the bottleneck. You need, if possible, to carry out a number of tests, exercising each component of the file server. From these results, you should have a better idea of which module needs updating. This approach, although potentially very time-consuming, will yield the best value for money in overall performance improvement.

An alternative approach is to purchase a complete file server from a reputable manufacturer, relying upon them to have constructed a file server with well-matched modules. If you are in the fortunate position of deciding to buy a new file server, or you are just considering upgrading your existing file server, then this is the chapter for you.

The big question

Although it is very easy to say, 'Let's run some benchmarks to assess the performance of the file server', this is in fact extremely hard to do. Normally the parameters are so numerous, affecting not only the hardware but also the software (such as the drivers used), that running a pure hardware benchmark across the network is more of an art than a science. When running benchmarks, you should always try to reduce the number of parameters in your benchmark tests, and in particular ensure that the software drivers do not change during the tests. The constant question to ask yourself is: 'Am I sure that the results just attained from some networking benchmark tool are really telling me something about the performance of the item under investigation, or could they, as is more likely, be monitoring some other bottleneck?'

What this chapter covers

This chapter will examine some of the key issues involved in deciding whether you do indeed need to update your file server and, if so, how to choose from the range of products available. Each area is discussed, with recommendations and general rules of the trade that you can use in deciding how much of your hardware needs upgrading.

What you will learn in this chapter:

- understanding NetWare 3.x and 4.x server memory structure
- how to decide on file server memory requirements
- how to decide on file server processor type
- how to decide on hard disk drive type
- how SCSI hard disk controller cards work
- whether you need to use RAID technology

NetWare server memory

Overview

NetWare 3.x and 4.x have a highly sophisticated memory management system. The NetWare kernel constantly monitors the demand on its resources and reallocates its memory: this enables it to maintain the file server performance at a maximum level.

The old NetWare 286 used a static memory-allocation model. Once the memory was allocated to a process it was then fixed for the duration of the file server. This is one of the main differences between the NetWare 286 and the NetWare 386 operating systems. NetWare 386 can load and unload memory blocks dynamically, even though all the other functions of the file servers are maintained and continue to function unaffected. This means that the NetWare 386 memory is a complicated one, and it is difficult to know what is happening at any given time. However, it is partly thanks to this function that NetWare 386 is considered to be one of the best operating systems for maintaining a good performance level as demand loads on it increase. The general rule is that the more memory available to the NetWare 386 the better the performance (up to a point).

See the test carried out in the section on file server memory and performance in Chapter 22.

File server memory structure

NetWare sees the file server as a flat memory model. In theory, it can address 4 Gbytes of main memory (Figure 4.1).

NetWare 3.x maintains five different type of memory pool (Figure 4.2):

- permanent memory pool
- allocation memory pool
- cache buffers
- cache movable memory
- cache non-movable memory

Novell 386 and memory protection

The Novell 386 file server has always been controversial in the way that it uses the 386 memory (Figure 4.3). Before discussing why this is, we need first to understand what the 386 chip provides. It can address a maximum of 4 Gbytes of system memory. However, when the 386 chip was designed it was considered an ideal chip to use for a multitasking operating system. In this kind of environment you have the concept of virtual memory. The chip can in theory support 48 Tbytes (48,000 Gbytes) of virtual memory for each process that runs on it. OS/2 uses this concept of virtual memory.

The 80386 memory chip defines four layers of security: these are called rings (Figure 4.4). At the highest level is ring 0. At this level, any program can access every byte of system memory. It is at this level that the operating system runs. The operating system will then start running programs at other ring levels. If a program is started at ring 2 then it cannot interfere with any other program at layer 1 or 0; however, it can access program memory running at ring 3. This leads to an effective protection system, so that if a program blows up or goes out of control it cannot

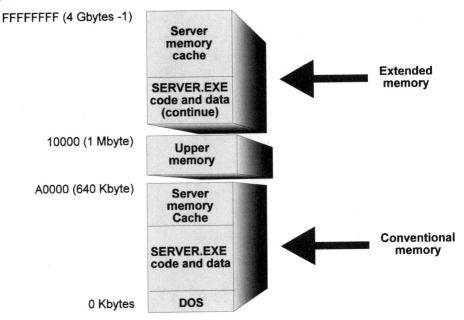

Figure 4.1 NetWare 3.x logical memory structure.

interfere with any program running at higher priority levels. However, there is a small price to pay for this kind of system: the memory management of the chip takes up processing power from the execution of programs.

Novell have decided not to use the memory ring management system of the 386 chip; they run all programs, NetWare loadable modules (NLMs) and the operating system at ring 0, assuming a flat memory model of 4 Gbytes. They argue

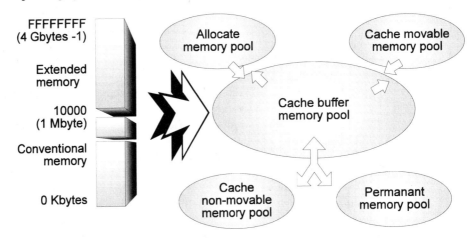

Figure 4.2 NetWare 3.x memory pools.

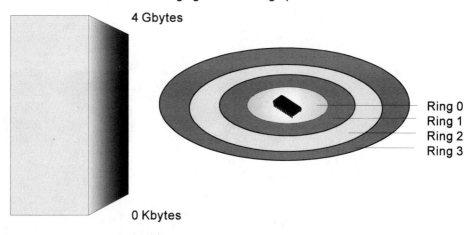

Figure 4.3 NetWare 3.x server and memory protection.

that although this could be very dangerous if you get rogue programs, the potential improvement in performance is well worth it, especially since before approving any program Novell carry out extensive tests on its NLMs and third-party NLMs. However, if they had used the ring management of the 386 CPU it would be much easier to write NLMs: I think the jury are still out on this! I would not be surprised if in the near future Novell decided to utilize the ring management from the 486 or the new P5 chip. We shall have to wait and see.

NetWare 4.0 file server memory structure

NetWare 4.0 has defined a completely new memory structure that will allow selected NLMs to run under protected memory mode (Figure 4.5). This is a radical departure from the old NetWare 3.x system, which used to run the 386 chip with no form of memory protection, at security ring 0. This meant that all the NLMs ran at the

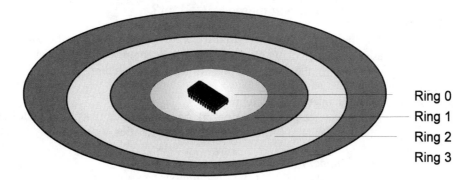

Figure 4.4 80386 memory protection structure.

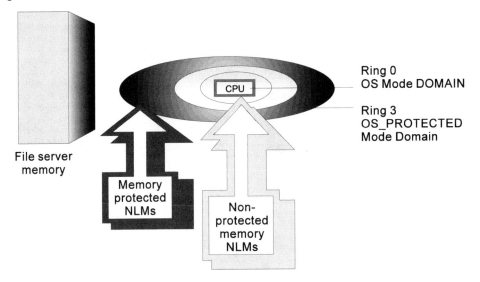

Figure 4.5 NetWare 4.0 memory protection structure.

highest level of memory security, so that in theory they could corrupt each other's memory. The new memory protection system is provided at the cost of slight performance deterioration. However, both options will be supported under the new system, which means that old NLMs can run efficiently under non-protected mode, and new NLMs can run under protected mode.

NetWare 4.0 runs its memory-protected NLMs in a domain called OS_PROTECTED. This is at privilege ring level 3. Unprotected NLMs are run in a domain called OS, at ring level 0.

The new memory management uses a whole new set of algorithms. Not only can it run NLMs under protected mode, it also significantly improves the overall server memory performance over the old NetWare 3.x servers.

What is the server memory used for?

The file server memory is used for a host of different activities; the most important uses are listed below. Note that increased memory does not always mean improved performance; there comes a point of diminishing return.

Network operating system
The executable part of the network operating system has to be kept in the memory: this lays down the kernel for all the other activities.

Active bindery objects
The active data parts of the operating system are called bindery objects. These are all kept in the available memory. They could be, for example, information on who is

currently logged in, and what their current rights are.

Data packet buffers

Area in the file server memory is set aside as buffers for incoming and outgoing packets. These are used when data is flowing into the file server quicker than it can be dealt with at that moment; the file server will then buffer the packets up until it has time to analyse the data.

File allocation table (FATs)

FATs are kept in the file server memory. All files are stored by splitting them into a number of data blocks. The average block size in a Novell file server is 4 kbytes so that, for example, a 20 kbyte file is kept in five blocks of 4 kbytes each. For each file name there is a related list of the blocks in which the data is stored, and this information is stored in the file allocation tables. The Novell operating system reads the FATs from the hard disk, and stores them in memory as far as possible.

Directory entries

All the directories currently in use are kept in memory. The file names within each directory are 'hashed' for quick access. Hashing is a clever mathematical technique for identifying a given name extremely quickly amongst a very large number of potential names. It takes the given name and applies a formula that returns a result indicating whether the name exists in the list or not.

NetWare loadable modules

NLMs are the means by which extra functionality can be added to the basic Novell 386 file server. They are in fact the only programs that can run on a Novell file server. They must use the file server memory to execute. Interestingly, NLM programs are given complete access rights to all of the file server memory.

Caching

Any memory left is given over to file caching, to improve hard disk reads and writes. Disk caching can dramatically improve the apparent hard disk performance. The disk-caching program uses part of the system's memory as a holding area. It is activated when a user makes a request to read a block of data; it then predicts what the user is going to want next time. Most of the time this is to read the next block of the file that is currently being worked on. The caching program satisfies the current request, and also grabs the next blocks and stores this information in the system memory. Assuming that the caching has done its job correctly, then when the user makes his or her next request it can satisfy the demand directly from memory. I always find it remarkable that the caching techniques used by Novell can have a success rate of 95 to 98%.

The general rule is that the more cache memory there is at the disposal of the caching program, the more effectively it can work. However, as the caching memory increases, and assuming all else remains constant, diminishing returns start to creep in, so that the performance does not continue to improve.

See the chart of benchmarks for file server versus installed memory.

You can increase the amount of system memory on a Novell 3.x file server, simply by removing DOS from the NetWare 3.x main memory pool. Just type:

REMOVE DOS

What you have done is remove all the original DOS parameters and variables that were kept in the system memory and given over to the Novell 3.x free memory pool. This will mean that you cannot return to the DOS prompt line after you have downed the file server.

One nice trick is that you can reboot the Novell 3.x file server remotely, when using the RCONSOL.EXE program:

1. REMOVE DOS

2. DOWN

3. EXIT

This can be very useful if you want to re-run the SERVER.EXE program, although it is important to make sure that your AUTOEXEC.BAT automatically loads up the SERVER.EXE program, and that you put in the command to load up the remote console support in your AUTOEXEC.NCF, such as:

: LOAD REMOTE

: LOAD RSPX

Monitoring the file server memory pools

At any given time you can see what is going on in overall terms within the file server memory by using the MONITOR.NLM program on the file server.

First start up the MONITOR program (which is probably already running on the file server) (Figure 4.6).

Permanent memory pool
This memory is used by processes that require memory blocks permanently set aside for their exclusive use, regardless of any other process. NetWare 386 tries to make as little use of this pool as possible. This area is mainly used by the NetWare operating system. It is here that the operating system sets aside memory for such things as caching directories or the buffers used to receive packets from the network interface cards.

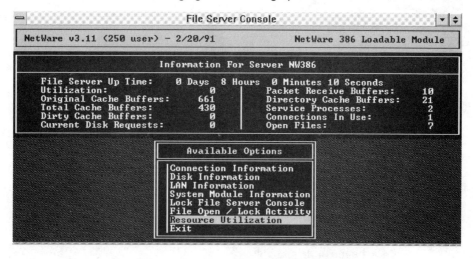

Figure 4.6 MONITOR NLM program.

To see your permanent memory pool usage on the file server:

(1) Load MONITOR.NLM

(2) Select Resource Utilization

(3) Select Permanent Memory (Bytes)

This should show you what is going on in your permanent memory pool (Figure 4.7).

Allocation memory pool
This area is used for short-term storage. Generally, applications make a request to

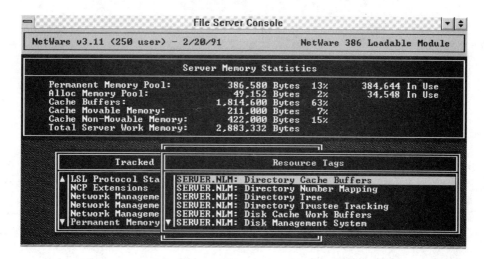

Figure 4.7 Permanent memory pool usage.

use memory on a temporary basis. Novell likes to see most NLMs making requests to use this memory pool in preference to any other. It should be easy to monitor whether this is the case; next time you are loading an NLM, check the allocation memory pool to see if it really is being used, by noting its size before and after loading.

Cache buffers

This should be the largest block of all the other memory pools. It stores the file-caching data. If it is not the largest block then there is potentially something abnormal.

Look at the cache buffers. If they are not the largest pool, then one of your memory pools may have reached its full limit. This requires further investigation.

Cache movable memory

Memory is allocated from the cache buffers to the cache movable memory. Normally, when a request is made for this type of memory, it tends to be for small areas. As the name suggests, once these blocks have been allocated, they can be moved around, so that the file server can optimize its memory. This is implemented as a background process, which searches through the file server memory, collects all the cache movable memory blocks and reorders them for efficient access. This is a bit like garbage collection, or defragmenting all the blocks on a DOS-based hard disk.

Cache non-movable memory

As the name suggests, this is exactly the same as cache movable memory, except that it cannot be relocated. Normally, when this type of memory is requested, it tends to be for large blocks of data.

Estimating the best file server memory size

When installing a new file server, you need to decide how much memory to place on the motherboard. This is a simple decision, compared with all the other more complicated decisions that you will have to make before your file server becomes active. Increasing the size of the memory you install is one of the most cost-effective ways to improve the performance of your file server, but you soon begin to suffer from diminishing returns.

There is a school of thought that says that since memory chips are so cheap nowadays, we might as well fill up the file server memory as far as we can. Memory used to cost $400 for a 1 Mbyte SIMM (single in-line memory module) in 1989, but now the price has fallen dramatically. It should be possible to pick up a 1 Mbyte SIMM for $40 and a 4 Mbyte SIMM for $200. There are already new 256 Mbyte SIMMs on the market that represents a very big quantum jump. Keep an eye on their prices; when they have come down sufficiently, consider using them. However, note that most modern 486-based motherboards are not designed to cope with 256 Mbyte SIMMs; they normally only go up to 64 Mbytes on board.

NetWare 386 needs a minimum of 4 Mbytes, but the typical memory configuration of an average Novell file server has 16 Mbytes.

Strategy in deciding on memory size

First, if your motherboard will support it, try to use the 4 Mbyte SIMM and not the 1 Mbyte. Usually, when you buy a 'ready to go' file server with memory installed by the manufacturer, you will be told that the machine can support, say, 32 Mbytes on the motherboard, and that they have already put 8 Mbytes on board. What they neglect to tell you is that the motherboard has eight SIMM slots and can take either 1 Mbyte SIMMs or 4 Mbyte SIMMs. In order to save money, they have filled all your slots with the cheap 1 Mbyte SIMMs. If you wish to go to 16 Mbytes or 32 Mbytes you must throw away all your 1 Mbyte SIMMs and start again with 4 Mbyte SIMMs. In most cases, if your motherboard will support it, it is far better to insist that they install 4 Mbyte SIMMs.

Use 4 Mbyte SIMMs instead of the 1 Mbyte SIMMs where possible.

A useful rule of thumb is as follows:

- Start with a minimum of 4 Mbytes for NetWare 386

- Add 1 Mbyte for each 100 Mbyte of shared hard disk, up to the maximum allowed by the file server

- This rule gives a good, simple (on the generous side) approximation to memory size requirements

Novell's method of working out memory requirements

(1) Calculate the memory requirements for each volume. For each DOS volume:
$M = 0.023 \times$ volume size (in Mbytes) $\div$ block size (default = 4)
For each volume with added name space:
$M = 0.032 \times$ volume size (in Mbytes) $\div$ block size (default = 4)

(2) Add the memory requirements for all volumes:
total volume memory
$= M(\text{sys:}) + M(\text{vol1:}) + M(\text{vol2:})...$

(3) Add 2 Mbytes for the operating system, and round up to the next Mbyte. If after steps 1–3 you have only arrived at 3 Mbytes, assume a minimum memory requirement of 4 Mbytes.

For the equivalent NetWare 4.0 calculation see the section on NetWare 4.0.

How to tell if you are getting low on file server memory

If memory gets very low because of the demands on the file server, a file server console error is automatically generated, warning you of the low memory. However, since prevention is better than cure, it is important to be able to judge when the file server is suffering from low memory. By using the MONITOR program from the server console you can monitor how the file server memory is being utilized.

File server hard disk platform

Using hard disks on the server

Fast file server hard disk access is very important to the overall performance of your network. The hard disk should be of the highest quality; it will be one of the most used piece of hardware on your network. Before a hard disk can be installed in your system you must select the right combination of hard disk and controller card (see Figure 4.8).

This means that you must use a hard disk controller card that can slot into your motherboard extension slots. These can be ISA, EISA, MCA or local bus slots. Next you need to select an appropriate type of hard disk controller. This can be ST-506, IDE, ESDI, or SCSI. Then you need to attach an appropriate disk driver. These can be RLL, MFM, IDE, ESDI or SCSI type. Each one of these options is now discussed.

Table 4.1 lists some typical combinations.

Since most file servers nowadays use a SCSI BUS, we shall be concentrating on SCSI. There is also a new technology called RAID (redundant array of inexpensive disks) that appears to be increasing in popularity.

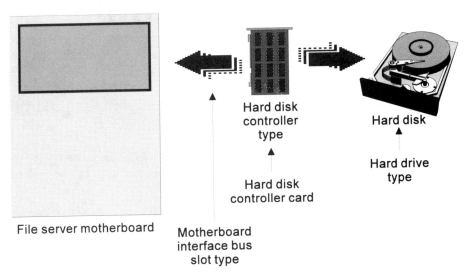

File server motherboard

Motherboard
interface bus
slot type

Hard disk
controller card

Hard disk
controller
type

Hard disk

Hard drive
type

Figure 4.8 Hard disk interface.

Table 4.1 Typical hard disk configurations.

Motherboard interface slot	Hard disk controller	Hard disk
ISA	ST-506	MFM
ISA	SCSI	SCSI
ISA	IDE	IDE
EISA	SCSI	SCSI

Hard disk drive types

There are a number of different types of disk drive available on the market: MFM, RLL, IDE, ESDI and SCSI. MFM and RLL are encoding schemes, which are normally used with ST-506 hard disk controllers, whereas IDE, ESDI and SCSI disks can only be used with their own specific disk controllers.

MFM

The MFM (modified frequency modulation) disk drive uses a coding scheme in which every bit of data is represented by two and a half bits on the disk. It is a relatively inefficient coding method, and is now considered to be out of date. Typically, MFM drivers can handle 20–80 Mbytes, and connect to the PC via ST-506 controller cards.

RLL

The RLL (run length limited) disk drive can typically store twice as much as the MFM drive: up to 100 Mbytes. Most new RLL disks are used with the newer version of ST-506, which supports RLL drives.

ESDI

These are disk drives that are compatible with the ESDI interface. They use a special version of the RLL encoding method. They are referred to as RLL 2,7 or RLL 3,9.

IDE

These drives have to be used with IDE hard disk controller cards. They are normally low-level formatted at the factory.

SCSI

These drives have to be used with SCSI controller cards.

Motherboard bus slot types

There are a number of different motherboard interface buses. The most common are ISA, EISA, MCA and local bus. On a given motherboard it is possible to have a combination of different interface slots: for example, it is common to see three ISA, two EISA and two local bus interface slots on one motherboard.

Standard ISA system bus

This is the standard ISA (industry standard architecture), first used in the IBM PC. It was originally an 8 bit interface standard, but with the introduction of the IBM AT it was extended to 16 bits. This standard has been around for a long time. It is well proven, but suffers from being too slow for most of today's input/output-intensive interface cards, such as hard disk controllers. In practice, the maximum data transfer rate through an ISA bus is around 1–3 Mbit/s. This can quickly become a bottleneck on large network systems. On the positive side, ISA interface cards tend to be very cheap. If you are very cost-conscious about hardware, an ISA interface standard would be ideal for a small or medium-sized network. The bus typically runs at 8MHz.

EISA bus

The EISA bus was designed to overcome the inadequacies of the ISA bus. It can provide direct memory access to yield a transfer rate of 10–24 Mbit/s. It is downwardly compatible with ISA drivers. The EISA BUS is a full 32 bit card, which means that it requires more pins than the standard ISA bus. A two-stage slot design is used: the first half is fully compatible with the old ISA slots, while the second half makes use of the new EISA extensions. Traditionally, Compaq was one of the major companies pushing this standard. It is a much better bus to use in the file server than ISA, and a flood of EISA machines is pouring onto the market. Since most machines have both ISA and EISA slots, it is important to set aside one of the EISA slots to take the hard disk adaptor card for the file server.

MCA bus

This is the Micro Channel Architecture from IBM, first incorporated in IBM PS/2 machines; it has not really taken off as IBM intended. The MCA bus is a signal bus design that handles memory and I/O transfer through multiplexing. This means that several processes can share the bus simultaneously. It is not ISA or EISA compatible.

Local bus

The local bus technique allows network adaptors, hard disk controllers and other interface cards to bypass the normal I/O bottlenecks and address the 32 bit CPU bus directly. This means that it can run at the same speed as the CPU clock cycle. The performance gain with a local bus can be staggering: it can, for example, improve the data transfer rate performance by 2–15 times that of the equivalent ISA interface

The problem with local bus technology is that it has been proprietary: each manufacturer, such as DEC, Northgate or Hewlett-Packard, has offered their own local bus solutions, some better then others. There is now a solution to get round this problem: the VESA (Video Electronics Standards Association) standard. This is a universal local bus standard for motherboard and adaptor card manufacturers. The resulting devices will be called VL-bus compatible. There are other attempts to define a local bus standard, but VL-bus is by far the most popular.

Intel have an alternative standard called PCI (peripheral component interconnect), which is now backed by Compaq, DEC and IBM. It will be widely available by the end of 1993, and only time will tell whether PCI can overcome the VL-bus momentum.

Comparing different interface bus systems

Table 4.2 shows the relative differences in performance that you would normally expect for the different types of interface.

Hard disk controller types

NetWare can support a variety of different hard disk controller cards. The most important types are ST-506, IDE, ESDI, SCSI and RAID controller adaptors. I shall concentrate on IDE and SCSI, since these are the most widely used types on file servers today. I shall also cover RAID technology, which is becoming more popular for large file servers.

Management tips

- Before you buy, ensure that your drive will work with NetWare 3.x or 4.x.
- Ensure that the disk controller and disk drive have all been approved by Novell.
- Ensure that the latest NetWare disk driver is available for you to use.
- Select only disk drives that are fully compatible with your hard disk controller.

ST-506 interface cards

The ST-506 is the classic standard for IBM PC hard disks. It was developed by Seagate. It can transfer data at a rate of 5 Mbit/s, which is not very much nowadays. It is now considered to be old-fashioned. It can cope with a maximum of two hard drives per controller. The new IDE cards have now taken over from ST-506 as the most popular hard disk controller. The old type of card is as standard in a number of cheap 386 and 486 machines. For reasons of performance, they are considered inadequate to drive file server hard disks on large networks. Typically, an ST-506 controller records information on hard disk using the MFM coding technique, but the latest version of ST-506 can also support RLL coding. The standard NetWare 3.x and 4.x disk driver for this type of controller card is the ISADISK.DSK module.

Table 4.2 Performance of interface bus systems.

Type	Bus size	Typical data transfer rate	Typical clock rate
ISA	16 bits	3 Mbit/s	8 MHz
EISA	32 bits	33 Mbit/s	8 MHz
MCA	32 bits	40 Mbit/s	10 MHz
Local bus	32 bits	132 Mbit/s	33 MHz

ESDI (enhanced small device interface)

This standard was originally developed by Maxtor in 1983. Typically, ESDI-compatible disks range from 40 Mbytes to 700 Mbytes. ESDI controllers were associated with high-end machines, but now SCSI cards have become much more popular. Compared with ESDI, SCSI drivers are just as powerful, more flexible, and nowadays much cheaper. The typical data transfer rate of EDSI drivers is between 10 and 24 Mbit/s. IBM used the ESDI controller in the PS/2 machines (Model 60 and above). Novell provides the PS2ESDI.DSK driver for these types of controller.

IDE controllers

Overview

The IDE drive standard was introduced to overcome the limitations of the old ISA-based ST-506 controller. In 1987 the power of hard disks was seriously beginning to outstrip the limitations imposed by the ST-506, originally developed by Seagate. There was a pressing need for a new standard for disk driver controllers. It had to be compatible with the existing BIOS in order to fool the PC into thinking it was simply another ST-506 controller. This led to the development of the IDE standard. In comparison with the old standard it is far more powerful in performance and intelligence, but as far as the PC is concerned it is using a standard ST-506, ISA disk driver controller.

The IDE standard achieves its improved speed by the digital nature of the operation of its interface, compared with the analogue approach of the ST-506. It works in a similar way to SCSI: it passes standardized requests to IDE drives, which in turn process the commands independently of any CPU intervention from the motherboard. The great advantage of the IDE standard is that it is fully compatible with ST-506, and therefore most existing software does not need altering to operate under IDE. This means that you can use the standard ST-506 NetWare 3.x and 4.x disk driver for this type of controller card. This is the ISADISK.DSK module.

These types of hard disk require low-level formatting, which is normally completed at factory level.

Note that IDE disk drives are incompatible with the ST-506 disk drives: the ST-506 type is analogue driven, while IDE-based drives are intelligent command driven.

> Many IDE drives are not compatible with each other.

IDE management and practical considerations

The cabling required is simpler than for the old ST-506, which required two different cables to connect each disk drive. IDE drives are daisychained off one ribbon cable as with SCSI 1 cables (SCSI 2 requires two cables). IDE cables do not need to be terminated, just like SCSI.

When using two IDE disks off one IDE controller (the maximum allowable), you must set the dipswitches on the first disk so that it is the primary, and inform it that a second hard disk is residing on the cable. The second IDE disk must have its jumpers set to identify it as the second disk.

An IDE controller can fool the BIOS on a PC into believing that it is using one type of drive whereas in reality the physical layout of the IDE is very different. You no longer need to hunt through all the possible options displayed by the particular BIOS used on your PC. This used to involve looking for a type number that defined the precise combination of number of heads, sectors per track and cylinders before you could use your hard disk. With IDE, you can select from the existing options a type that matches the size of the hard disk, and the IDE controller will do the rest of translating the actual physical parameters to logical parameters.

Here is an important rule that you can use when you are selecting a physical drive type on a PC to work with an IDE controller card:

You can select any combination of disk drive heads, number of cylinders and sectors per track as long as the total number of logical sectors is equal to or less than the total number of physical sectors on the IDE hard disk.

The total number of sectors on a hard disk is calculated from the following formula:

$$\text{Total sectors on hard disk} = \text{Head} \times \text{Cylinders} \times \text{Sectors per track}$$

Provided that you get this right, you should have no problems.

Since most operating systems see the hard disk as a contiguous block of sectors, if you define a hard disk to have a bigger logical size than is physically available, you could be in serious trouble. When the IDE controller attempts to translate to a non-existent sector, it will roll back to the start of the hard disk and potentially start over-writing existing data.

> Do take the above rule very seriously. If ever you are in doubt, you should always define the logical number of sectors be less than or the same as the actual number available.

There are some state-of-the-art IDE controllers that need no drive type definition at all, since they ask the IDE hard disk for the actual physical topology during the power-up sequence dynamically. These types of IDE controller tend to have large amounts of on-board cache memory, typically 4 Mbytes.

SCSI technology

Overview

SCSI, which is pronounced 'scuzzy', stands for Small Computer System Interface. Originally designed by Adaptec, it is rapidly becoming the most popular type of hard disk interface for file servers. The standard SCSI bus has a data transfer rate of 7.5 Mbit/s. Up to seven devices can be daisychained onto one SCSI controller. The original Apple Mac, and some minicomputers, have been using the SCSI bus for many years. Examples of SCSI cards are the Adaptec SCSI card (the industry standard) and the Western Digital WD7000 fast SCSI card

In this section we shall examine the SCSI bus in detail, including its basic theory of operation, implementation issues and the special software drivers that it requires.

The Adaptec card is supported as standard by Novell.

SCSI history

The standard SCSI specification became a recognized international standard in 1986, thanks to an ANSI committee. It was based on the IBM peripheral bus called the IPI (intelligent peripheral prototype), which was defined in 1980. This standard is rarely talked about nowadays. It in turn was based on an earlier bus called the IEEE 488 external bus standard. This was developed by Hewlett-Packard to connect up its range of minicomputers. The Commodore Pet used to utilize the IEEE 488 bus standard to connect the floppy and hard disk to its motherboard.

The ANSI SCSI committee have now moved on to define the SCSI 2 standard. This is a superior SCSI bus standard. It is far faster than the original SCSI; in theory, it is also compatible with all the devices that used to sit on the old SCSI 1 bus.

The basic SCSI operation

The SCSI bus is a multi-device interface. It can be used as a universal bus to daisychain an assortment of different devices together. These can be anything from a hard disk or CD-ROM, to DAT backup or even a network interface card. The great advantage of this approach is that you can easily add each device in-line on the SCSI bus, without your needing to buy another interface card to place in your PC motherboard (Figure 4.9).

SCSI software drivers

The SCSI adaptor introduces its devices to the PC by loading up special drivers, and this is where all sorts of problems seem to raise their ugly heads. It is very difficult to produce a driver for SCSI devices, as they can differ greatly in nature. Usually, in the SCSI world, you need to load a different device driver for each of the SCSI devices being used (Figure 4.10).

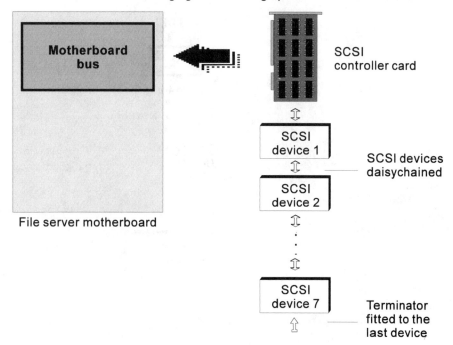

Figure 4.9 SCSI bus structure.

Although most manufacturers of SCSI adaptors and devices have agreed upon the hardware specification as defined by the ANSI standards, there is no international standard on how the software drivers for SCSI devices should be written. This has led to a number of major headaches for the users. For example, a SCSI adaptor from Vendor A would not necessarily work with a SCSI device from Vendor B. This has resulted in a large number of users being forced to buy the adaptor and device from the same vendor to ensure compatibility.

The people at Adaptec realized that there was a serious need for a universally agreed SCSI software standard, which they therefore developed and placed in the public domain. Now, when users buy an Adaptec SCSI card, they can buy a SCSI device from any vendor as long as it conforms to the Adaptec ASPI standard. This has become so popular that, despite its origins as a proprietary standard, it has now become an industry standard.

What is Adaptec ASPI?

ASPI stand for Advanced SCSI Programming Interface. It is a programming standard that allows for multiple SCSI devices to share the same SCSI host adaptor. It is a two-layered standard, similar to the ODI drivers from Novell. It defines a universal layer that describes a hypothetical SCSI adaptor card, which will then respond to

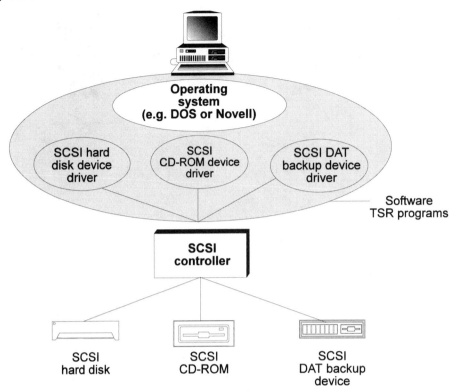

Figure 4.10 SCSI software interface.

standard ASPI requests. On top of this layer a second layer is defined, at which specific device modules are written for each device, which are then bound to layer 1. This allows for multiple types of SCSI device, such as DAT and hard disk drives, to be daisychained off one SCSI host adaptor (Figure 4.11).

If you are loading up a typical hard disk on an Adaptec adaptor you need to load at least two drivers. The first is layer 1, which defines the universal ASPI SCSI adaptor card. Then you need to bind to it a special ASPI device driver for the specific SCSI hard disk in use.

Example with NetWare operating system and ASPI

Assuming you have a SCSI hard disk connected up to an Adaptec AHA-1640 (an industry standard), then a special NLM needs to be loaded from the server console.

This normally takes place in the STARTUP.NCF:

```
:Load aha1640
    Auto-Loading Module ASPITRAN.DSK
AHA-154x/1640 ASPI Manager & SCSI Disk Module For
```

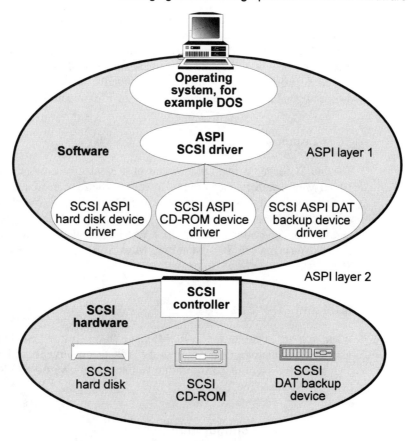

Figure 4.11 SCSI ASPI drivers.

```
NetWare 386 v3.11
Version 2.0
Copyright 1990 Adaptec, Inc.
```

In the above case the NLM AHA1640 defines ASPI layer 1.

ASPITRAN.DSK, which is automatically loaded in this case, defines the ASPI layer 2.

Laddr and Cam: SCSI software standards

The problem with standards is that there are so many to choose from. ASPI is one of a number of competing standards that define universal SCSI software drivers. NCR and Future Domain are pushing for the ANSI committee to make Cam (common access method) an international standard. Microsoft has also defined its own competing standard called Laddr (layered device driver architecture), which it was pushing to go with its OS/2 operating system. However, none of these standards has the mass credibility that ASPI from Adaptec has attained. The Cam and Laddr standards do not seem to be making a very big impact on the market; I wonder if they are going the same way as CP/M! IBM has asked Adaptec to write ASPI drivers for the new OS/2, and this is yet another reinforcement for the ASPI drivers. Novell supports the ASPI drivers as standard. If I was buying SCSI adaptors or devices I would make sure that they were ASPI-compatible.

SCSI 2 standard

The old SCSI had a maximum speed of 4 Mbit/s, whereas the new SCSI 2 has a 10–40 Mbit/s performance rating. However, when you realize that the average high-performance hard disk can only work at 5 Mbit/s, there is clearly a lot of waste. The new standard can work with any SCSI device. SCSI 2 has much-improved multitasking operations among its daisychained devices, and overall it is more efficient then the old SCSI standard. Most SCSI manufactures are now producing SCSI disks that are SCSI 2-compatible.

SCSI and CD-ROMs

When you are installing a CD-ROM, make sure that its SCSI ID address is not 0 or 1: some SCSI adaptor cards, such as the Adaptec, reserve these ID numbers for their own exclusive use. I recommend that you normally give the CD-ROM device a high SCSI ID, such as 6 or 7.

SCSI hardware configuration

Termination
When SCSI devices are daisychained at both ends of the bus, it must be properly terminated. This means that resistors have to be fitted to each wire to 'pull it up' to a defined voltage. This is similar to the terminators at the end of thin Ethernet cables. The first and last device in the daisychain must be terminated. All other devices in between must have their terminators removed (Figure 4.12).

SCSI ID numbers
Each SCSI device in the chain is given an ID number. This is normally set up using the jumpers or dipswitches found on each SCSI device. You must make sure that each device is set up with a different ID. The SCSI ID number goes from 0 to 6. Normally SCSI ID 0 is automatically used by the SCSI adaptor card itself, leaving 1–6 available for use.

There is an implied priority: devices with lower ID numbers have higher priority over the bus. This is traditionally why hard disks are set up with low SCSI ID numbers whereas relatively slow devices, such as CD-ROMs or DAT backups, are giver higher SCSI ID numbers such as 5 or 6.

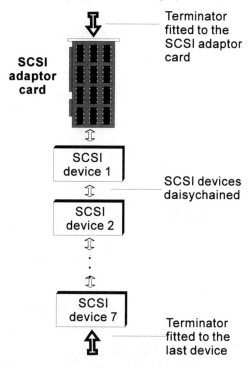

Figure 4.12 SCSI bus structure.

SCSI LUN and IDs

When a device is given a SCSI ID, when activated it will in turn report to the SCSI card the number of LUNs (logical unit numbers) that it is supporting. LUNs are normally given a number starting from 0 and working upwards. They represent the number of logical units that are being provided by that SCSI device. For a SCSI hard disk, these could be partitions or volumes (Figure 4.13).

SCSI management strategy

A number of points should be considered before installing a SCSI adaptor card.

Using SCSI only for hard disks

If you only plan to use your SCSI bus controller in conjunction with the hard disk, and have no plans to use any other types of device on the SCSI bus, then look for the ATA (AT bus attachment) standard, which is a SCSI standard that defines the way the controller should emulate the original WD-1002 AT disk controller. This means that your SCSI adaptor will be fully compatible with the IBM AT ISA hard disk controller, and you don't need to load any extra device drivers to recognize the hard disk or disks, although only two can be supported.

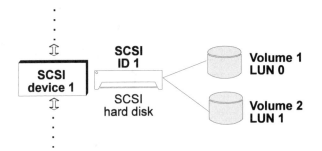

Figure 4.13 SCSI LUN and IDs.

Ensure BIOS compatibility
Many SCSI adaptor cards have to modify the PC BIOS before they can function properly. Make sure that the version of the BIOS used in your PC is compatible with the proposed SCSI card that you are about to purchase.

Go for SCSI 2 (where possible)
Nowadays the SCSI 2 adaptor is becoming very popular. Its increased performance is well worth the extra cost.

Managing SCSI ID numbers
Because the SCSI device IDs have an associated implied priority, I recommend the following use of SCSI numbers. Set aside the low numbers for fast devices such as the hard disk and network interface cards, and use higher numbers for slower devices such as DAT backup and CD-ROM devices (Table 4.3).

RAID technology

In most networks the piece of hardware most prone to failure is the file server's hard disk. This is purely because it is the most frequently used piece of mechanical hardware; it is under constant use during working hours. It is remarkable how reliable hard disks have become. I have seen a file server with a 1.2 Gbyte hard disk that has been in constant use for three years without any problems. However, when a system fails the probability is that the failure will affect anything mechanical.

When deciding on a hard disk, you need to ensure that it is very reliable and mechanically sound. However, manufacturers are constantly striving to achieve hard disks with greater and greater capacities, and these two requirements are normally contradictory.

RAID technology has attempted to bring these two goals together. RAID (redundant array of inexpensive disks) attempts to provide the file server with an array of hard disks, providing vast storage capability while allowing for intrinsic tolerance towards faults.

Table 4.3 Recommended SCSI device numbers.

SCSI ID	Device usage
0	Normally used by the adaptor card
1	Hard disk 1
2	Hard disk 2
3	Hard disk 3
4	
5	CD-ROM
6	DAT backup

How RAID works

The basic concept of RAID is beautifully simple. It utilizes an array of standard off-the-shelf hard disks connected to a single hard disk controller, which can operate all of them simultaneously (Figure 4.14).

Data is then spread across the array of hard disks so that the user thinks it is accessing one vast hard disk, even though it is actually a collection of inter-working hard disks. When the user's data is organized appropriately across the hard disks the RAID disk driver can provide a user with data at a far faster rate then a single hard disk system, because the RAID controller can use all the hard disks simultaneously to satisfy the user's request.

The clever thing about RAID drivers is the way they scatter the user's data across the hard disks so that they are fault-tolerant. This is not a new idea; mainframes and minicomputers have been using this technology for years. The thing that is relatively new is PC-based RAID controllers. And running multiple hard disks

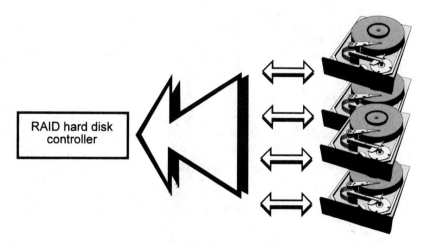

Figure 4.14 RAID basic structure.

off a single hard disk controller is not new either; PC users have been doing this for years with the humble ST-506 and IDE controller cards. You can hang two hard disks off each card, but you can only access one at a time. With SCSI you can daisychain up to seven hard disks together but, again, only one of them can be in command of the SCSI bus at any one time. The difference with a RAID hard disk controller is that it can read and write to all its hard disks simultaneously.

This technology has always been associated with the very powerful servers, such as the machines available from Compaq and Dell. Each manufacturer used to implement their version of the RAID controller card and incorporate it in their own proprietary machines. RAID technology is now becoming standardized; we should see prices beginning to drop as more third-party manufacturers produce RAID disk controller cards.

There are now six well-recognized levels in the way that RAID organizes its data across the hard disks. Generally speaking, the higher the level, the more sophisticated the system, and the greater its tolerance towards faults. Level 0 is the most basic level, and level 5 is the most sophisticated. In all the RAID levels, spindle synchronization can be used to significantly improve the performance of the hard disk. When hard disks are all in spindle synchronization, they spin in such a way that sectors appear under the heads of all the drives at the same time on each rotation.

RAID level 0

This level has no tolerance towards error development, but it uses the technique of scattering the data across the hard disks in a way that significantly improves performance.

In RAID 0, sectors from a given file are written across all the hard disks one after another, with each disk storing one sector at a time. This is sometimes called data stripping. No provision is made for any form of data redundancy; if any one of the hard disks fails the result can be disastrous. This level is excellent for applications that require speed but are not concerned with fault tolerance. It is also extremely cost-effective; it has the benefits of excellent performance without the overheads necessary to hold redundant error recovery data on the hard disk.

However, for today's file servers, I would not recommended the use of level 0; it is potentially too dangerous. I would suggest, if possible, that you look at the higher RAID levels, such as 3 or 5.

RAID level 1

This is an enhancement of level 0, which adds fault tolerance in the shape of disk mirroring. Data is duplicated on two separate disks, so that if one fails there is always another copy. It does mean, however, that you have halved your storage capacity in comparison with RAID level 0.

RAID level 2

This level introduces the concept of reserving a hard disk purely for storing error-recovery data for the remaining hard disks. Unlike levels 0 and 1, where stripping takes place at the sector level, RAID 2 uses the bit level for stripping. The data for a given file is written across all the hard disks, with each disk storing one bit at a time, and the last controller being used as a parity check. It is organized so that if any part of the hard disk goes down (so long as it is not the parity check disk itself), the information can be reconstructed dynamically. The error-correction data stored by the parity drive is calculated by doing a bit-wise calculation on the data and storing the result. If a bit goes missing on the failed disk, the bit that has failed can be recalculated by combining all the other bits and the value stored on the parity drive.

RAID level 3

In RAID level 3, data is not stripped at the sector level as with RAID 0 and 1 or at the bit level as with RAID 2, but at the byte level. Level 3 works on a similar principle to level 2: it sets aside a redundant hard disk to store error-recovery data for the other active hard disks.

RAID level 4

This is the same as level 3 except that it works by stripping data at the block level. The block size is calculated by the RAID controller card. It selects an optimum block size by matching the maximum data that the controller can transfer to the number of hard disks that it has at its disposal at each read or write operation.

RAID level 5

This is the 'de luxe' level. The error-correction information is not just kept on one disk, but is spread evenly across all the drives. Data stripping is at block level, as for level 4. Because no single parity disk has to be used during writing of data, RAID level 5 can handle multiple simultaneous writes far more efficiently. All drives are perceived as being of equal importance, with sufficient redundant information on the others to be able to afford any one of the disks failing. By using the information on the remaining disks the information on the failed hard disk can be reconstructed.

Strategy

If you are installing or are considering installing a medium-to-large network that requires a powerful file server, then RAID technology is definitely worth considering. I suggest you look at RAID level 5. If you can afford the extra expense, it is an ideal level to use on powerful file servers. Traditionally, the RAID hard disks are housed in a rack, stacked one on top of each other. Each hard disk ideally should have its own power supply, but this is rather impractical, so I suggest you always invest in a UPS (uninterrupted power supply) to back up the whole file server, with extra lines to support the RAID hard disks.

   RAID technology does not come cheap. Assuming you want a 1 Gbyte hard disk on a file server, and it is to have some fault tolerance for its ten users, do you use RAID technology? In situations such as this you need to cost the benefit against the outlay on purchasing redundant hardware. If you use a RAID controller card you need to acquire at least two other hard disks as spares in the event of any drive failure. This mean you need to cost for three 1 Gbyte hard disks, pushing up the purchases bill significantly, especially if you are working to a tight budget. My advice in situations such as this would be to use the mirroring or duplexing functions of the Novell operating system and to forget about RAID technology – for the time being, anyway.

To summarize the main points:

✓ increased data security

✓ extend hard disk capacity by using an array of hard disks

✓ use off-the-shelf hard disks

✓ transparent to the users

✓ increased performance

✗ RAID cards are more expensive than SCSI or IDE

✗ RAID hard disks need an external storage rack

✗ extra expense on buying redundant hard disk storage

✗ potential compatibility problems with Novell's own hard disk storage

Preparing the server hardware for action

Here is an action plan of the steps that you should carry out before installing the Network operating system on the file server:

- Assemble all the hardware (memory, printer/serial ports, NIC, and the hard disk controller) for the server
- Boot up using DOS
- Use programs such as CheckIt or MSD to check hardware
- Test to check that memory is OK
- Test to check that interrupt lines are not clashing
- Check that printer and serial ports are all working OK
- Record the CMOS configuration and keep it in a safe place
- Now you are ready to start with the Novell installation

How much hard disk storage?

Overview

One of the most important aspects of recommending a file server configuration is deciding on how much hard disk storage you really need. This is not as simple as it might seem; there are a lot of factors to take into account before you can come up with an overall size recommendation.

The general principle is: if in doubt, overestimate. As the price of hard disk storage comes down, the demands on the storage capacity of file servers are going up. The average serious Windows application nowadays can easily take up 40 Mbytes. Microsoft recommend that the average stand-alone Windows user should have a 150 Mbyte hard disk.

In this section I shall identify the four important elements that you need to consider when you are evaluating storage capacity for your new file server. I am only concerned with user-accessible disk storage area, and not with any duplication. If, for example, you decide to mirror your hard disks for fault tolerance, you obviously need to double your disk costs. If you decide to use RAID technology, which if you decide on large capacities such as 3 Gbytes or above is most likely, then you will also need to cost in for a number of redundant hard disks, depending on which level of RAID you decide to use.

Estimating file server disk size

You need to work out a figure for each of the following, and then add them up to get your overall hard disk storage requirements:

- network operating system
- application and data storage requirements
- total users' home storage requirements
- hot fix area

A typical calculation might look like that shown in Table 4.4.

We shall now look at each of the four components in greater detail. Once the figure for each category has been estimated you can use Table 4.4 to consolidate them into a grand total.

Estimating network operating system size

This is very easy to estimate. If you use the following formula, you get a good overall approximation of the requirements of the operating system.

- For NetWare 2.x, allow 20 Mbytes

Table 4.4 Estimating file server disk size (Mbytes of storage).

Item		Individual totals	Total
Network operating system		20	
Application and data storage requirements		600	
Total users' home storage requirements		300	
Subtotal			920
Hot fix area (based as % of the subtotal)	5%	46	
Total disk storage requirement			966

- For NetWare 3.x, allow 30 Mbytes
- For NetWare 4.x, allow 60 Mbytes
- For every 20 potential user accounts, add another 5 Mbytes to the total
- For every potential printer server, add another 30 Mbytes to the total

These rules have been used to fill out Table 4.5.

This total is very easy to estimate. It deliberately makes an allowance for the number of users recorded on the system: the more users registered on the system, the greater the number of script files and MAIL home directories that the system has to create. You also need to estimate the potential number of print servers being serviced by this file server. This rule allows for the extra storage requirements of the print queues. Print queues are considered as part of the operating system, and are kept in the file server volume SYS: under the SYSTEM subdirectory (Figure 4.15).

Every time a new print server is created, a new subdirectory will be created with a unique number under the SYS:\SYSTEM subdirectory. When a queue is created another subdirectory is created, which is automatically given a unique number followed by the type .qdr, such as 08000002.qdr or 09000001.qdr. This is where the jobs to be printed get spooled. Deciding how much room to set aside for the print queues is the most unpredictable part of this calculation, since they have the habit of temporarily expanding to very large size and then shrinking again as the jobs get printed. I have known a print job to be as large as 90 Mbytes for the duration of the printout, and then shrink to 0 Mbyte after printing.

The figure of 30 Mbytes allowed for each print server's exclusive use is an average derived from a lot of installations. It is based on the assumption that the system has an average selection of Windows users, and around five different queues on each print server. The users are using typical packages such as Microsoft's Word for Windows, Excel, or the average off-the-shelf dBase IV type of application. If you are doing a lot of text-based printing you would probably not need to set aside that much storage. Conversely, if you are handling a lot of highly graphical printout, then you would probably need to set aside more.

The total figures derived represent a good generalization of the amount of storage required to store the following:

- network operating system programs

Table 4.5 Estimating network operating size.

	Comment	Space required in Mbytes
Network operating system size	NW386	30
Number of potential users	40 users	10
Number of potential print servers	2	60
Total network operating system size		966

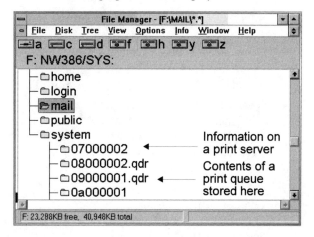

Figure 4.15 System print-related subdirectory.

- network operating system public files
- login directory
- NetWare system MAIL subdirectories for users
- printer queues storage

Estimating application and data storage size
This is very hard to estimate. Applications are getting bigger all the time. The sort of programs that only a few years ago would fit on a 360 kbyte floppy disk now come in a set of ten high-density 1.2 Mbyte diskettes. I know of a game called Wing Commander II that requires at least 20 Mbytes of storage. The Borland C++ application, when fully installed, requires at least 50 Mbytes of storage. In this section I shall try to suggest a way of categorizing applications so that you can realistically estimate their storage requirements.

I classify applications into the following five categories in terms of their disk storage requirements. Once you have categorized applications in these terms you can carry out an audit of software application size.

- **DOS-based applications (minor).** These are normally stand-alone applications that came on one or two disks at most when they were first installed. These types of program are not graphical. Examples are Norton Commander and virus check programs. Allow 1 Mbyte for each.

- **DOS-based applications (major).** These are normally DOS-based applications that come on from three to eight disks, but they run under DOS and are not graphical. Examples of such programs are PC Tools, Norton Utilities and Clipper. Allow 10 Mbytes for each.

- **Windows-based applications (minor).** These Windows-based programs are normally add-on utilities that come on one to two disks. Examples of such programs are Microsoft Write and Sound Blaster media support. Allow 2 Mbytes for each.

- **Windows-based applications (major)**. These are major Windows programs. They come on three to fifteen disks. Example of such programs are Word for Windows, Excel and Corel Draw. Allow 40 Mbytes for each.

- **Special applications**. These are special applications that have to be audited individually, since they potentially can consume a large amount of storage. Examples of such programs are an internally developed database program, the organization's accountancy package, and a storage-hungry desktop publication package. You need to audit each such application individually.

Doing an application size audit

This is not an easy job. To do it properly you need to set aside a day or two, depending on the size of your system. The ideal solution would be audit every single current application and then do a survey of the future software that you are going to buy. This is a bit unrealistic. I have tried to simplify the operation by categorizing applications together.

Each category except the last one has a suggested storage figure for that type of application. Remember, this is an average; there will be some applications that need more and others that need less. The figures are on the generous side, to take into account any data that might be temporarily required, but they are only meant as a starting point. You should review them and adjust them where you see fit. The aim of this section is to present a method of doing a software size audit; you can then customize the figures to meet your requirements.

In your estimate, you need to take account not only of the current applications being used but also of any new applications that might be bought in the near future. This requires some creative accounting and some imagination. If yours is the average sort of installation, with users constantly updating their application to the next release, then you can use a trick to approximate future software requirements. All you do is calculate last year's disk storage space for new software, and then double this to give a rough approximation of this year's requirements. Hopefully, you already have an idea of which applications are being used. You then need to sit down and estimate how many fall into each category.

As the potential storage requirement of an application increases you need to be more precise in your approximations. For the hundreds of small applications it is not worth being very precise; just estimate their numbers and multiply by their average size. You do need to identify which are going to be the biggest packages in terms of storage requirements and audit them individually under the special application category.

You can get a good idea of your future storage requirements by looking at past requirements and then doubling them.

I suggest you use the forms shown in Tables 4.6–4.8 to fill in when you are doing a software size audit. Tables 4.9–4.11 show their use in a typical audit.

Table 4.6 Software size audit forms for categories 1–4.

Application categories	Estimated number	Estimated average size	Estimated total storage in bytes
(1) DOS (minor)			
(2) DOS (major)			
(3) Windows (minor)			
(4) Windows (major)			
Total of application categories 1–4			

Table 4.7 Software size of special applications.

Special application name	Estimated size requirements
Total of all special applications	

Table 4.8 Summary of the software size audit.

Application categories	Estimated size requirements
(1) DOS (minor)	
(2) DOS (major)	
(3) Windows (minor)	
(4) Windows (major)	
(5) Special applications	
Total	

Estimating users' home storage requirements

This section is not as hard to estimate as applications. Thanks to the Novell operating system, it is very easy to limit users' disk storage on the file server. It is important that, where possible, you do use this facility. If users are given access to what seems like an endless storage capacity they will soon fill it up, without ever bothering to delete files or keep their home data files in good tidy order.

Table 4.9 Typical completed software size audit form for categories 1–4.

Application categories	Estimated number	Estimated average size	Estimated total storage in bytes
(1) DOS (minor)	50	1 Mbyte	50 Mbytes
(2) DOS (major)	10	10 Mbytes	100 Mbytes
(3) Windows (minor)	5	2 Mbytes	10 Mbytes
(4) Windows (major)	10	40 Mbytes	400 Mbytes
Total of application categories 1–4			660 Mbytes

Table 4.10 Typical software sizes for special applications.

Special application name	Estimated size requirements
dBase accounts package	100 Mbytes
PageMaker	50 Mbytes
Mailshot program	150 Mbytes
Total of all special applications	300 Mbytes

Table 4.11 Summary of typical software size audit.

Application categories	Estimated size requirements
(1) DOS (minor)	50 Mbytes
(2) DOS (major)	100 Mbytes
(3) Windows (minor)	10 Mbytes
(4) Windows (major)	400 Mbytes
(5) Special applications	300 Mbytes
Total	**860 Mbytes**

One of the most effective ways of ensuring that users keep their files in order is to limit their disk size. This forces them to think about the file server as being a limited resource that they must use effectively. This is specially true of users who see themselves as networking experts; these are exactly the type of people who could waste storage space, since they cannot be bothered to remove unnecessary data. We shall see later that there are a number of good third-party tools, such as Fry net utilities, that can produce a list of users classified by the amount of disk storage that each has consumed.

Every time a new user is created you can limit the disk storage space available to them. As they store information on the file server it comes out of their own budget. Novell provides two tools for limiting user disk space: SYSCON and

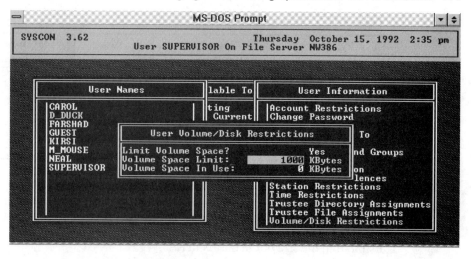

Figure 4.16 Using SYSCON to limit users' disk storage space.

DSPACE. Most people use SYSCON to limit users' disk storage space. In the example in Figure 4.16, the SYSCON utility has been used to limit the user D_DUCK to only 1 Mbyte of storage of the volume SYS: on file server NW386.

Always try to limit users' disk space, even if they are 'super users'.

In estimating how much disk storage space to give to users, I first classify them under three different categories, and then allocate home storage size depending on their classification. The categories are as follows:

- **Type A**. These users make very little demand on the system. They are not power users, and store very little on their own home directory. They can be typically part-time or external users with a minimum amount of rights on the system. Limit storage to 2 Mbytes.

- **Type B.** These are normal users, making average demands on the system. They are probably Windows users as well. They have average rights over the resources of the file server. Limit storage to 40 Mbytes.

- **Type C.** These are the power-hungry users. They have above-average rights on the network. They probably act as supervisors or workgroup managers. It is especially important to limit this kind of user; in my experience they tend to be the greatest offenders in wasting disk space. Limit storage to 100 Mbytes.

Once you have classified your users in these categories, you can start to estimate how much globally to allow for their storage requirements (Table 4.12). Note: only count people once. If they sometimes log in as type 1 and at other times as type 2, then only count the higher value.

Table 4.12 Estimation of user personal storage requirements.

User type	Estimated number	Estimated average size	Total storage in Mbytes
Type A: minimum		2 Mbytes	
Type B: normal		40 Mbytes	
Type C: power		100 Mbytes	
Total storage requirements			

The actual figures used are an estimate. You can change them or perhaps even increase the different types of user. The aim here is to present a technique that you can use in estimating home storage requirements.

Estimating the size of the hot fix area

The hot fix area is a very useful feature of the NetWare operating system. It is part of the Novell SFT (system fault tolerance) level 1. It helps to prevent data from being written to bad blocks on the hard disk. You need to set aside some storage as the hot fix redirection area. This will be used when a bad block is found; it can then be redirected to the area set aside for hot fix blocks. Normally, Novell set aside 2% of the total storage for hot fixing. I like to increase this to 5%. This gives you a bit more time before the hard disk completely fails, if bad blocks are beginning to appear.

The way these bad blocks get consumed is very interesting. They start extremely slowly and then, as the hard disk starts to deteriorate, the number of blocks that need to be hot fixed into the redirection area seems to increase exponentially. This means that, whatever figure you came to in adding all the previous parts, you need to increase that figure by the hot fix percentage.

The hot fix redirection area is created when a NetWare partition is created. Once a block has been recorded as being defective, the file server won't try to store data in it again. Hot fix is transparent to the user.

Allow for data fluctuations.

After you have derived a figure, add 30% to it. This allows for unforeseen growth in the future.

Good rule of thumb: every two years, hard disk storage requirements double.

Good rule of thumb: always try to keep the hard disk less then 75% full.

CPU chip selection

Any self-respecting Novell file server of today would not be seen dead running on an 80286 processor. Up to last year, the standard CPU used for a Novell 386 file server was an 80386 processor running at 33 MHz. That situation has now changed radically. The price of the more powerful 486 chip has come down dramatically, so much so that it is now the standard chip to use if you are considering installing a file server. The 486 processor outperforms the 386 processor significantly for very little price difference. In fact, some manufacturers are already stopping shipment of 386 PC machines in favour of the 486-based PCs. The question today is: Do I go with 486 33 MHz, 486 50 MHz, 486 66 MHz or should I wait for the 586 (Pentium) chip?

Not surprisingly, tests show that the higher the clock cycle, the higher the potential throughput from the file server, assuming (and this is the crunch) that you have not hit a bottleneck from some other module within your file server.

Table 4.13 Chip types.

Chip type	Description
8086/88	This processor could address up to 1 Mbyte of memory (now obsolete)
80286	A superior chip, based on the 8086, but able to address 16 Mbytes of memory. About two to three times faster then the 8086/88 (becoming obsolete)
80386DX	A super set of the 80286, it can be configured into real and protected memory mode. Ideal for multitasking operating systems, it can also support a 32 bit address I/O bus. About twice as fast as the 80286
80386SX	The same as the 80386DX except that it has only a 16 bit I/O address line, just like the 286 chip
80486SX	This is essentially the 80386DX but it can work at faster clock cycles, such as 33 MHz and 50 MHz
80486DX	This is the same as the 80486SX chip, but it contains an integrated maths co-processor and 8 kbytes of very fast memory. It can run at nominal speeds 20 MHz, 33 MHz and 50 MHz
80486DX2	This is the double clock-speed chip. This means that internally it is running at twice the speed of the motherboard. For example, the 486DX2 at 66 MHz works internally at 66 MHz, but when it comes to external devices such as RAM or the DAM controller chip, it slows down to 33 MHz
80586 or P5 Pentium	This is the chip of the near future; it should have hit the market by the time you read this book. Unlike its predecessors it is not just two or three times faster than the previous chip type: it is radically redesigned, based around the RISC (reduced instruction set computer) technology. It will operate at 100 MHz clock cycles. It is to be followed by the P5 DX2 and a 200 MHz version. As they say, watch this space!

CHIP selection strategy

Because of the dramatically falling price of CPUs, my advice is to consider using 486 at 50 MHz or better. This would give you good flexible future growth, at a negligible price difference. Avoid the 486 DX2 chip; although it appears to be cheap, it performs worse than the equivalent 486 DX. The pure 486 DX motherboards are normally far better built, have to work at higher clock cycles and conform to higher tolerances. In terms of expenditure, it is worth paying a small extra amount.

The different types of CPU

The biggest manufacturer of CPU chips in the world is the Intel Corporation. They were the first to bring the 8088 and the 8086 processors onto the market, and they have dominated the PC CPU market ever since. The monopoly that they have held for so long is beginning to erode away, thanks to chip manufacturers like Cyrix, NEC and AMI. They are all keeping up the pressure on Intel not to overcharge, by bringing out their own versions of Intel-compatible CPU chips.

It is an interesting trend that every two to three years Intel seem to bring out the next generation of processors, which on average is twice as fast as the previous fastest CPU chip. If we continue at this rate of processing power, I should not be surprised if by the end of the century we all have as much power sitting on our desktop PCs as we today associate with the Cray mainframe 'supercomputers'.

Table 4.14 Chip summary.

CPU	Landmark	Maximum address	Data bus	Clock speeds (MHz)	Year
8088	1	1 Mbyte	8 bits	4.7	1979
8086	1	1 Mbyte	16 bits	4–10	1978
80286	10–12	16 Mbytes	16 bits	6–16	1982
80386SX	20–30	16 Mbytes	16 bits	16–33	1988
80386DX	30–60	64 Gbytes	32 bits	20–40	1985
80486SX	115–180	64 Gbytes	32 bits	20–25	1991
80486DX	115–180	64 Gbytes	32 bits	20–50	1990
Pentium	*	*	64 bits	100–200	1993

* No firm data was available at the time this table was compiled, but the figures promise to be very impressive.

Performance difference between a 486 33 MHz and a 486 50 MHz

Figure 4.17 illustrates the performance differences between the two processors as the number of workstations increases. The 50 MHz chip starts to have the edge over the 33 MHz at around the 15-user mark.

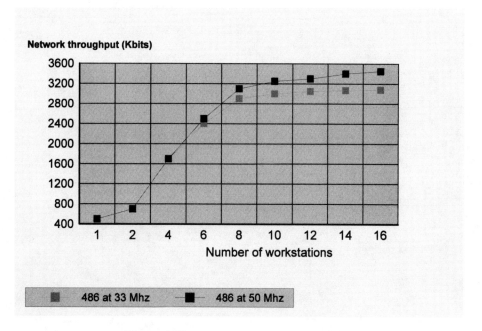

Figure 4.17 486 33 MHz versus 486 50 MHz.

5

NetWare disk, volume and file management system

NetWare filing system

Overview

When it was first introduced, NetWare 3.0 came with an impressive filing system, capable of enormous disk storage: up to 32 Tbytes per disk. Volumes can now span across multitudes of different types of disk drive, and several million file entries can appear in any directory. This has brought to the PC world the sort of specifications that we have always associated with mainframes.

The NetWare filing system also has an intrinsic series of procedures that make it tolerant towards faults developing: these are referred to as Novell SFT (system fault tolerance).

Filing system optimization

The Novell filing system uses some very clever techniques to improve the file server's ability to satisfy users' requests to read and write to the hard disk.

Directory hashing

Hashing is used to locate one item from a large list of items. This is particularly useful in a networked system. When a user makes a request to read or write a file, the NetWare filing system must, as quickly as possible, determine whether such a file exists from millions of potential entries (Figure 5.1).

The technique that Novell uses is a hashing algorithm: this is a mathematical formula imposed upon a given filename that the user provides. The result of this

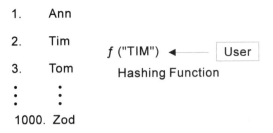

Figure 5.1 Hashing function.

calculation is a number indicating the location of the file within the list of files in the relevant directory. This technique is very fast, because you do not need to take the suspect word and then either sequentially or by using some binary chop technique go through each item in the list to check to see if it exists. It is in fact a form of direct random access. NetWare actually creates two tables for each volume directory and stores them in memory. The first is the hash table: the mathematical groups of directories and filenames. A second special hashing table is also kept; this is for the so-called wild card method, used in situations where the user provides only part of a filename, leaving the rest as wild cards.

Elevator-seeking optimization

Another technique that Novell uses to optimize the performance of the hard disk is called elevator seeking. This takes its name from the way that lifts and elevators work. Let us assume that you are on the top of a building and that the lift is on the ground floor. If you press for the lift, then it is instructed to come from the ground floor to collect you at the top floor. If somebody on an intermediate floor requests the lift to take them to the top floor while the lift is ascending, it will stop and pick them up.

The elevator-seeking function of Novell works in exactly the same way. The Novell filing system constantly monitors the demands and calculates the minimum path required to satisfy the user's request. In effect, NetWare reorders the request in order of priority, based upon the current position of the disk heads. It is ordered so as to minimize head movement and maximize response time (Figure 5.2).

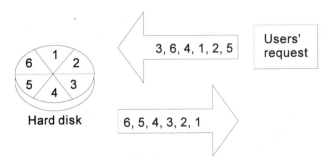

Figure 5.2 Disk elevator optimization.

What is interesting is that this has to be a continuous, dynamic process. As it meets the current demands, more and more requests pour in. It must therefore constantly take snapshots of where the head is and what the demands on it are, and then attempt to satisfy these demands with the minimum amount of movement. It must do this while responding to and reordering the new requests, and calculating the minimum paths required to satisfy the new situation.

Disk caching

Caching has been around for a long time. The Novell NetWare filing system makes full use of caching techniques to optimize the performance of the disk. In fact, instead of applications making direct requests to the hard disk, they make requests to the caching process, which has cached memory at its disposal. Normally, this is an area of main memory that has been set aside for exclusive use as caching memory (see Figure 5.3).

When the file server receives a request to read a block of data, it instructs the hard disk to collect that data and additionally collects other nearby data blocks in anticipation of future user requests. This extra data is then stored in the cache memory on the basic principle that it is quicker to read from memory than from the hard disk. In fact, the success rate of the caching algorithm as used by Novell can be as high as 98% in predicting the next user request: an astonishingly high hit rate!

The caching process also helps with improving disk writing. When a user makes a request to write a block of data, it is put into the cached memory and the user is informed that it has been written. The NetWare operating system now waits either until the caching write buffer is full or until there is a lull in disk activities, in which case it will then start to write back all the blocks to the hard disk. If necessary it will also take this opportunity to reorder the way in which it will write the hard disks back in order to minimize head movements.

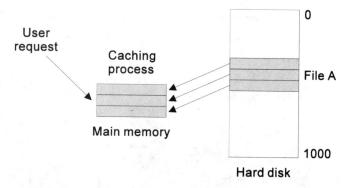

Figure 5.3 Disk caching.

System fault tolerance I, II and III

Novell defines three different levels of system fault tolerance. Levels I and II are well documented in Novell's own manuals. However, SFT III is something that is becoming a reality, after many years of being 'promiseware'.

SFT Level I: Media corruption

This is designed to prevent errors on blocks of data occurring on the hard disk. All file entries in directories and their associated FATs (file allocation tables) are duplicated by the system. The two entries are kept in two separate areas on the hard disk, thus reducing the probability of both being lost at the same time. If an error occurs in one copy, the other copy is temporally used by the system, and the error is reported on the server console. The corrupted copy is rebuilt from the working copy on a different area of the hard disk. This is all handled by the NetWare operating system. If things really get out hand, the network manager should then dismount the volume and use the VREPAIR.NLM program to attempt a complete repair.

Novell can perform automatic read-after-write verification. This is used to ensure that the data is written correctly on the hard disk. After writing a block of data it is re-read from the disk and compared with the original data, still kept in memory. If all is matched up the write is considered to have been successful. If the data does not match up the hot fix function comes into action. This sets aside a small portion of the hard disk (normally 2% of the usable disk storage area) as the hot fix redirection area.

I used to recommend increasing the hot fix area to 5%, for extra tolerance to errors developing within the hard disk. However, since hard disks are now more reliable, this is optional.

The hot fix area is used to receive all the data from the block that failed the read-after-write verification test. It also stores blocks that, in the opinion of the system, will go bad in the near future.

One of the most important and simple things that you can do to monitor the health of your hard disk is to check the hot fix area regularly.

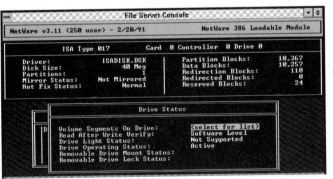

Network manager needs to keep a regular eye on the hot fix redirected blocks, using MONITOR program

Figure 5.4 Monitor hot fix area.

**Understanding the assortment of disk
block information provided by Monitor**
With regard to the hot fix function there are a number of important parameters
that you should know about. Note all blocks are measured in 4 Kbyte units.

- **Partition blocks:** This is the total number of 4 Kbyte blocks that are
  defined on the disk

- **Data blocks:** Total amount of partitions blocks available to store files and
  directories

- **Redirection blocks:** This is the total number of blocks set aside for the hot
  fix area

- **Redirected blocks:** This is the key field; it shows how many blocks have
  been hot fixed

- **Reserved blocks:** This area is set aside for the exclusive use of hot fixing
  the operating system

Note: if your **Redirected Blocks > (Redirection + Reserved Blocks)** then
your hot fix has failed.

If you see the number of redirected blocks slowly starting to creep up, you
should be considering changing the hard disk soon. You should also, as a matter of
urgency, be reviewing your backup procedures, ensuring that a backup copy of the
data is taken frequently.

**When the hot fix area starts to be used up, it does not go in a
linear fashion. It starts up very slowly but towards the end of the
hard disk life, the hot fix area is consumed on an exponential
basis (Figure 5.5).**

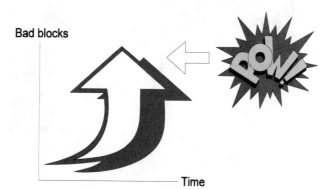

Figure 5.5 Hot fix area is usually used up on an exponential basis.

SFT level II: hard disk protection

Hard disk mirroring (Figure 5.6) will allow for simultaneous duplication of data on paired disks: one is the primary disk; the other is a standby secondary disk. Data is written to both disks. If one disk fails the other disk can continue to operate without the loss of users' data.

Disk duplexing (Figure 5.7) extends the concept of disk mirroring, not only by protecting against hard disk failure, but also by protecting against hard disk controller failure. This has the added advantage that the performance of disk reads is significantly improved. When the Novell filing system sees a duplexed disk, it will make 'split seeks': during read requests, NetWare uses the drive that will satisfy the request the faster. Also, on retrieving very large files, it is possible to send the primary disk to retrieve the first section while the secondary disk is instructed to retrieve the next section.

SFT level III: full server duplication

Novell has been promising system fault tolerance level III for as long as five years now, and we are finally beginning to see its implementation. The aim of SFT level III is to back up file servers completely, so that when one server goes down the other can immediately take over the operations. This is something that major financial institutions and mission-critical establishments are desperately awaiting.

System fault tolerance level III (Figure 5.8) represents true mirrored server technology. Two file servers are connected together by an umbilical cord, in effect as a standard NetWare IPX point-to-point connection link. In Novell terms this will be called the mirrored server link, abbreviated to MSL. This is a bi-directional link used to synchronize the two file servers, normally implemented on a very fast network of around 100 Mbit/s. The two file servers connected by the MSL are also in direct connection with the network providing the service to users.

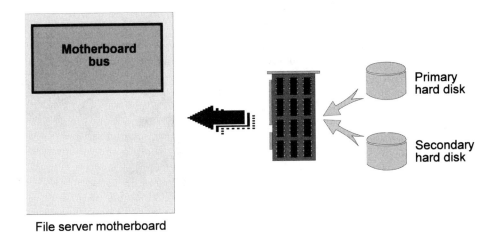

Figure 5.6 Disk mirroring.

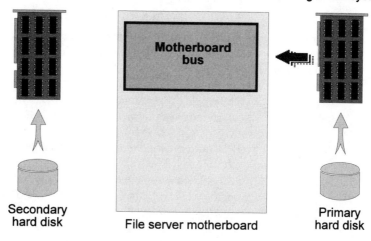

Figure 5.7 Disk duplexing.

One file server will be active, the other passive, but both monitor each other's health. If one of the file servers fails because of a hardware problem, the second server will automatically take over its operation. Novell claim that this will take place without any interruption or loss of services to the user on the network: an ambitious claim, and it will be interesting to see how it bears out under varying circumstances.

SFT level III will provide some useful opportunities for network managers. For example, when the primary file server goes down, a message will be sent to all users informing them of this and that they are now connected to the second server. The manager can now correct the hardware problems and restart file server one. When the secondary file server detects that the first server is healthy once again, it will automatically resynchronize all the changes that have taken place while it was inactive and update so that both file servers are synchronized once again. It will then pass control back to the primary file server and return to its original role.

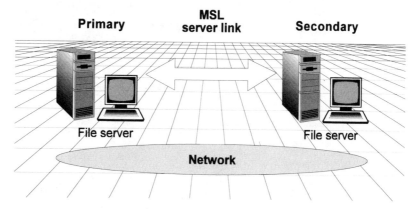

Figure 5.8 SFT III mirrored file server.

On-line maintenance also becomes very straightforward. The manager can down one file server to maintain the hardware and possibly update, upgrade, or change memory while the other file server continues, and then resynchronize the two servers when finished.

Novell first promised SFT level III in 1987, and have been widely criticized for their slowness in bringing this product to the market. One of the main reasons for the delay is that sufficiently stable hardware has not been available until now. The technology uses standard and (now) relatively inexpensive equipment: identical 386, 486 or 586 servers, working simultaneously together. Novell have implemented a special version of NetWare 3.1, which has SFT support, on a number of different sites; this will be available on a commercial basis on the NetWare 4 release.

Novell are one of the first LAN vendors to provide full fault tolerance – on a par with what we associate with mainframes – at a highly competitive price, on standard off-the-shelf hardware platforms. The alternative from Microsoft and its LAN Manager product is the domain replicator. In this, the two file servers are connected up through the network. Novell make the point that this congests the network, by transferring traffic from one file server to another across the network. In Novell's solution, the umbilical cord connecting the two file servers together is fast and independent, irrespective of the type of network used.

Novell currently claim that there are 500 different sites implementing SFT III utilizing a special version of Novell NetWare 3.1, and NetWare 4.x, a commercial version of SFT III, is now slowly becoming available. It supports TCP/IP, Macintosh, UNIX and NetWare for NFS. The NetWare 4.x code operating system contains as standard many of the commands that are required for supporting SFT III.

A number of major vendors have started to support SFT level III, including companies such as Eagle and Thomas Conrad. The dedicated umbilical cord runs at about 100 Mbit/s, using either fibre or coaxial cables to connect the two file servers. In addition to the normal network card required, this involves putting two special network cards into the file server.

NetWare disk and volume management

Overview

Novell use a number of terms in relation to defining and using hard disk storage space. It is important to be aware of what these terms mean, and how they can be exploited. These issues are discussed in this section.

NetWare device numbering

To physically address a hard disk with the NetWare operating system you need to provide three items of information: the disk, the hard disk controller and the board number.

The disk drive number identifies each hard disk running off a given hard disk controller. For ST-506 controllers this is number 0 or 1, since only two can be supported. For SCSI controllers, it can be from 0 to 7. Since NetWare can support a number of hard disk controllers simultaneously, each controller is also given a unique number, working from 0 as the first one. The NetWare server can further support multiple motherboards, on which can reside multiple disk controllers, which can in turn control multiple hard disks. These boards are typically defined by Novell as DCB (disk co-processor boards) (Figure 5.9). However, usually there is only one board (the main motherboard) referred to as board = 0.

A typical boot-up disk drive will normally be given the following physical address:

board = 0, disk controller = 0, disk number = 0

NetWare has two basic numbering schemes for identifying connected hard disks: the physical device number and the logical device number. They are defined as follows.

Physical device number

This address uniquely identifies the hard disk to the system in hardware terms. A five-digit code is used to define the physical hard disk, its hard disk controller, and the board containing the controller. The code has the format shown in Table 5.1. For example, 21101 means that the hard disk is: drive type 21, on board 1, on hard disk controller 0, and it is the second hard disk.

Logical device number

NetWare assigns a unique logical device number to each physical disk as it is recognized during the boot-up sequence. The first drive is given the device #0 code, and the numbers are assigned sequentially, working upwards. Hence any device has two type of address, one physical and one logical. NetWare keeps a table that relates physical address to their equivalent logical identifier.

Using NetWare device addresses

These address codes are used by a number of the NetWare utilities, such as INSTALL and MONITOR. For example, from the MONITOR program under disk information you might see the following:

```
Device #0 (20000) ISA Type 017
```

Device #0 means that it is the first logical hard disk, whose physical address is defined by (20000). This can be broken down as (20-0-0-0). The 20 is the disk driver ID number assigned by Novell. The next 0 means that it is located on the first board. The next 0 means that it is on the first hard disk controller on board 0. The last 0 means that it is the first hard disk on that hard disk controller. Following the device code is a string identifier that defines the brand or manufacture of the hard disk.

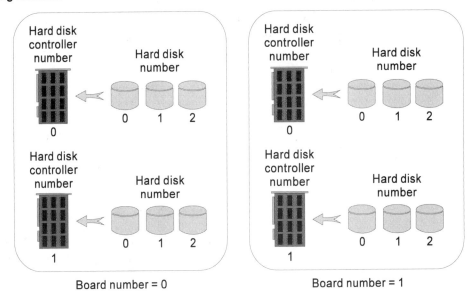

Figure 5.9 Novell disk addressing.

Table 5.1 Physical device number.

Digits	Description
1–2	Drive type number
3	Board number (normally 0)
4	Hard disk control number (0 is first controller)
5	Disk number (0 is first disk)

NetWare partitions

The partition is the most fundamental division of any hard disk area. It breaks the hard disk up so that it can potentially support different operating systems. The DOS user would usually use the FDISK program to break the hard disk up into different partitions: primary and extended. The first partition, of around 10 Mbytes, is normally made DOS bootable, because NetWare 3.x and 4.x are not self-booting operating systems. The rest of the hard disk is then left unused. During installation of NetWare 3.x or 4.x this unused partition is initialized by the NetWare operating system, which subdivides the area into volumes.

You can only define one NetWare partition per hard disk. Physical NetWare partitions are split into the hot fix redirection area, and the logical NetWare partition. (Figure 5.10). The logical partition is the area from the end of the hot fix block to the

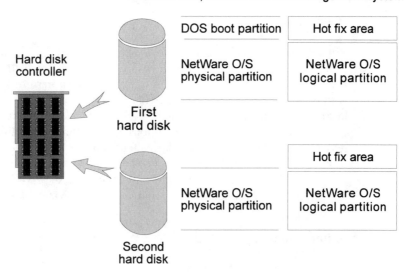

Figure 5.10 NetWare partitions.

end of the physical partition area. On start-up, Novell assigns a logical identification number to each physical partition. If disks are mirrored or duplexed, NetWare uses a common logical partition number to group the two physical partitions together (Figure 5.11).

> **If you plan to mirror or duplex physical partitions, for best results ensure that the two disks are the same size. If they are different sizes, then NetWare will ignore the extra storage on the larger disk. This is a waste of valuable storage.**

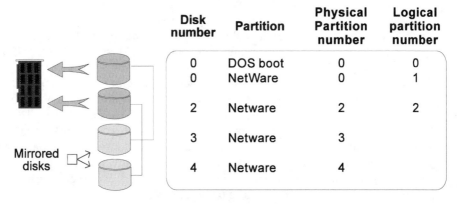

Disk number	Partition	Physical Partition number	Logical partition number
0	DOS boot	0	0
0	NetWare	0	1
2	Netware	2	2
3	Netware	3	
4	Netware	4	

Figure 5.11 Partition numbering.

NetWare volumes

Within each partition, NetWare defines volumes. These are where users' data is kept. Each NetWare server must have at least one volume, called the SYS: volume. It is possible to create multiple partitions on a given hard disk. It is also possible, with NetWare 3.x and 4.x, to span volumes across many disk drives, which means that a single volume can span a number of logical partitions. NetWare keeps track of which volume is over which partitions in a volume definition table. For safety reasons, each NetWare partition keeps four separate copies, on separate parts of the disk, of the volumes defined across itself.

In NetWare 3.x and 4.x the maximum size of a volume is limited to 32 Tbytes. This is 32 million Mbytes: well above the capacity of any hard disk as yet!

Volume management tips

How many volumes to define

When you first install NetWare 3.x or 4.x, the volume SYS: will be created automatically. The big decision now is whether to create any more volumes. There is no absolute answer to the question; it depends on how you plan to use the server.

One approach is to break up the server's hard disk into multiple volumes. You give each volume a logical name, and store the relevant data within the volumes. By splitting up the server's storage over many volumes, it is easier and quicker to get to any file, than if all files were in the same volume. However, as time goes on these volumes will start to fill up. What happens when some of them are full, while others are still half empty? You then have to go through a lot of housekeeping, moving files from one volume on to another.

Another common approach is to define just one volume, which uses all the disk storage. This is the SYS: volume. All files will be stored in this volume. Instead of creating other volumes, each volume is given a unique directory. Users' data is organized around a subdirectory tree structure. This has the advantage that users' disk storage is not limited by volume size, but by the hard disk storage capacity. If the manager wishes to limit a given user's disk storage, the SYSCON or DSPACE programs can be used.

There is no ideal solution: you have to decide which approach is best for you. Usually, the solution lies somewhere between the two options above. A common approach is to have two different volumes, SYS: and VOL1:. The SYS: volume is normally about 100 Mbytes, and contains all the system and public files. All the remaining disk space is allocated to VOL1:, which is allowed to grow to accommodate all the users' applications and data files. The advantage of this approach is that if the volume SYS: ever gets corrupted, it can be recreated from scratch without loss of data (except bindery files).

Volume space allocation

If you are defining a volume to span across a partition, don't allocate all the available space to the volume: keep about 10% unused. When your volume becomes full, you can give yourself a little extra lease of life by extending the size of the volume to use the unused space. This will give you enough time to obtain a bigger hard disk. It is very easy to extend volume size dynamically, through the INSTALL program. The existing data on the volume will not be lost. However, you cannot reduce the size of a volume without losing its data.

Spanning across many hard disks

Be very careful when you span volumes across many hard disks that are not mirrored; if one of them fails you could lose the entire volume's information. Another common problem when volumes are spanned is that the hard disks do not all work with the same performance. This will mean that some files can be accessed quicker than others. Where possible, define volumes within the confines of a single hard disk. However, if you are planning to mirror or duplex drives, then spanning volumes across two hard disks can be an excellent idea. When volumes are split across physical disks, NetWare optimizes its read and writes across both disks. This improves the performance significantly.

Naming volumes

You can give volumes names from two to fifteen characters, but long volume names are hard to work with. Try to keep them less than eight characters; three or four is ideal.

6

Managing your PC's configuration, memory and network adaptor cards

Analysing your PC hardware configuration

Using diagnostic programs

There are a number of excellent PC diagnostic programs available. These can provide an insight into what is going on inside your machine. Three of the most used programs are:

- **CheckIt Pro from TouchStone**: This is by far the most popular PC diagnostic program. It not only provides an excellent set of diagnostic data, but can also be used to extensively test your machine (Figures 6.1 and 6.2). This is one of those programs that you cannot live with out; I highly recommend it. The new version comes in two volumes, the first of which is for system information, while the second provides tests and diagnostic tools. One of the great functions that CheckIt Pro provides is its ability to investigate the PC I/O port addresses. This is shown in Figure 6.2. You can select an individual I/O port or investigate all of them. This is useful if you wish to avoid conflicts when adding new PC add-on cards. This ability is not normally found in other diagnostic tools.
- **SI.EXE from Norton Advanced Tools** (Figure 6.3).
- **MSD.EXE from Microsoft:** This comes free with Microsoft Windows. It was put together with the Windows set of programs so that when the Windows user reports an error to Microsoft, they can be asked to run a standard diagnostic program. This information is then used to analyse what could have caused the error. The opening screen provides a summary of the version

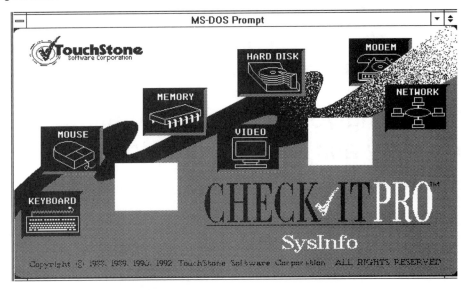

Figure 6.1 CheckIt Pro front screen.

numbers of all the major components being used inside the machine. Memory maps can be drawn, showing the position of each TSR. Device drivers used, conventional, extended and expanded memory are all shown. The WIN.INI and SYSTEM.INI can also be browsed through. On the whole, it is an excellent free program to use to see what is going on inside your PC.

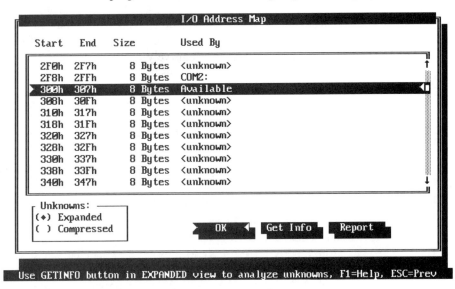

Figure 6.2 I/O address map.

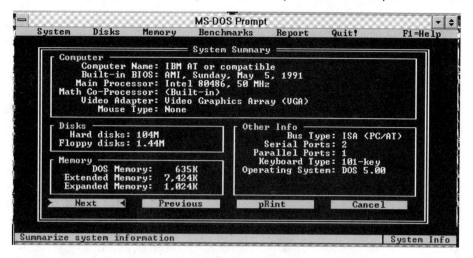

Figure 6.3 System Information from Norton Advance Tools.

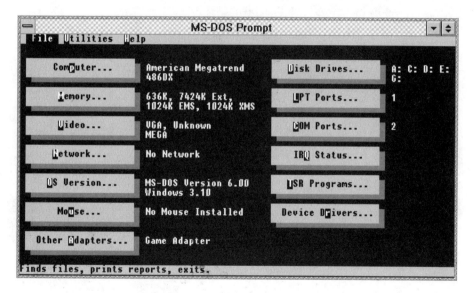

Figure 6.4 Microsoft diagnostic program.

The PC boot-up sequence explained

To understand what goes on inside your PC-based workstation it is important to know what steps are carried out during the boot-up of the machine. This information should help in troubleshooting a PC that fails to start up properly.

Power supply test

When the PC workstation is first switched on, the power supply carries out a self-test: if all is well a 'power good' signal is sent to the PC motherboard.

CPU activated

When the 'power good' signal is received, the CPU is activated and automatically initializes itself by starting to execute instructions found in the address location FFFF:0000. This is where the BIOS ROM has been placed.

ROM BIOS

The code in the ROM BIOS is now activated, and checks to see whether it is a cold or warm boot-up. If it is a warm boot-up then the next step (a POST) is omitted.

POST

The POST (Power On Self Test) consists of a number of tests that check the PC hardware. This sequence tends to differ from one ROM BIOS manufacturer to another: for example the POST test from AWARD BIOS is different from the IBM BIOS test. However, there are some common denominators, although some tend to be more thorough than others:

- motherboard integrity
- CPU
- interrupt controller chip
- DMA controller chip
- chip
- display adaptor
- system main memory
- any extended memory
- keyboard
- floppy disk
- hard disks

If any error occurs, you sometimes hear a beep-like noise. This differs from one BIOS to another, but the standard IBM POST audio message is outlined in Table 6.1.

Run any additional ROM on add-on cards

BIOS now searches through the user memory between 640 Kbytes and 1 Mbyte and searches for an add-on card with on-board ROM. When it discovers one with the appropriate signature, it passes over control and its program starts to run. This could be your hard disk controller, VGA and any network interface cards. Each card would then initialize itself, and if necessary attach itself to the resources of the PC. As each card completes its initialization code, control is passed back to the PC BIOS.

Table 6.1 IBM POST audio messages.

Message	Meaning
None	Power supply could be faulty
Continuous beep	Power supply could be faulty
Repeating short beeps	Power supply could be faulty
Dash–beep	Motherboard faulty
Dash–beep–beep	Video card is faulty
Beep	Normal start-up

Try to boot up drive A:

The BIOS now attempts to load an operating system from floppy disk drive A. If it finds one, it sends the drive head to the boot track, which is always track 0, sector 1. If it fails to load a floppy disk, the BIOS jumps to the next step.

If you have a diskless workstation – one without a floppy disk – but a network interface card (NIC) with a remote BOOT option, the NIC will make a request across the network to find a file server that has an image of a boot-up floppy disk drive. The NIC will pull the data across the network and feed the BIOS as if it were booting up a floppy disk drive locally.

Try to boot up drive C:

The BIOS now attempts to load an operating system from the hard disk drive C:. If it finds one, it sends the drive head to the boot track, which is always track 0, sector 1.

If it fails to load the operating system from the hard disk, the BIOS jumps to try to load the IBM ROM-based BASIC. It is at this point that you might see 'ROM BASIC not found'.

Boot up DOS

The boot track stores the load program that contains the type of network operating system that has to be loaded. In this case we shall assume that we are loading IBM DOS v5.0.

- **Load IBMIO.SYS**: This contains a patch to the internal PC BIOS. It introduces DOS device drivers such as KBD, COM1, NUL and LPT1. It starts to initialize the DOS environment using the SYSINT code, and then attempts to load the IBMDOS.SYS.
- **Load IBMDOS.SYS**: This program when running will start to initialize all the system interrupt lines.
- **Start to read the CONFIG.SYS file**: The CONFIG.SYS file is then located in the \ root directory. It is opened and the text processed. Each of the drivers is located, loaded in the appropriate place and initialized. A typical CONFIG.SYS could look like this:

```
Buffers=20
Files=20
```

```
DEVICE=HIMEM.SYS
```

In this case the IBMDOS program would set the internal DOS buffers to 20 and set parameters to hold up to 20 files open. It would then look for the HIMEM.SYS driver, load this into the DOS memory and pass control to it, enabling it to initialize itself.

- **Run COMMAND.COM**: This is the DOS shell. Interestingly, COMMAND.COM is loaded just as if it was any old DOS program by making the DOS EXEC call to interrupt 21 hex function 4B hex. This program is the front-end shell for DOS: it provides the user with the DOS prompt line.

DOS, when loaded in memory, is split into two sections (see Figure 6.5): the static part (IBMIO.SYS and IBMDOS.SYS), and the transient part (COMMAND.COM).

Managing network interface cards

Overview

In the rapidly growing world of PC networking, NICs are becoming very big business. Market research statistics indicate that in 1993 75% of all PCs will have a NIC installed.

Back in 1998, these cards were large and relatively expensive. A typical Ethernet card would cost $400, while Token Ring (4 Mbit/s) would set you back $600. Prices have fallen dramatically within the last few years, and today a typical NIC card costs around $150.

NIC technology has come a long way; already we have the $10 chip set containing Ethernet or Token Ring, and a number of Taiwanese manufacturers are currently gearing up to produce motherboards that have on-board network interface capabilities as standard.

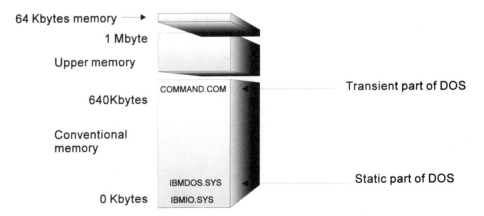

Figure 6.5 DOS static and transient sections.

Gone are the days of having to gain access to the jumper on the NIC every time you added a card to the PC that conflicted with the old NIC. You had to establish what was clashing, open the machine, change the jumpers of the NIC and then change the Novell network IPX drive to reflect the new NIC setting. Not much fun, especially with a large number of users using an assortment of different cards! Modern NIC cards are mostly (with a few exceptions) software-switchable.

This enables you to plug your NIC into all your PCs and run one common software package. The card would be set up appropriately for each PC. The Novell network driver (IPX or the ODI – see later) will also be common to all as they will ask each NIC for its current setting. Each card has its own non-volatile memory that records its own interface parameters, such as what interrupt it is using. This is automatically used by the universal Novell driver. However, this does mean that a different driver is needed for each different type of NIC. You can therefore simplify things immensely by using the same NIC card throughout. Since each card is self-configured, all the network software drivers will be the same on the PCs.

Network adaptor resources

A normal network adaptor requires the use of three resources to communicate with the computer system:

- IRQ (interrupt request channel)
- I/O base address
- RAM buffer area.

The LAN adaptor does not have the capability to share these resources.

The one common resource that most NICs seem to insist upon is access to a unique interrupt line. Normally the choice is between one of the following:

IRQ	DOS device
3	COM2
4	COM1
5	LPT2
7	LPT1

Typically, IRQ 3 is used as a safe default interrupt, unless COM2 is being used, in which case the next most popular interrupt is IRQ5.

> If you are planning to use IRQ 5 for your adaptor card, be careful: it is very common for SCSI controller cards to use the same interrupt.

Managing the interrupts on the PC

Use Table 6.2 to determine which interrupt is most suitable for the LAN adaptor. Most NICs on the PC use interrupt 2, 3, 4, 5, 6 or 7. Typically, IRQ 3 is used as a safe default interrupt, unless COM2 is already being used, in which case the next most popular interrupt is IRQ5.

Table 6.2 outlines the functions for each of the relevant interrupt lines. This is not the full hardware interrupt list; it is the most common interrupts on the PC, and their meanings. Against each interrupt is a warning on what it is normally responsible for and when it should not be used for setting up NICs.

If you are using an 80286 chip or above, such as a 386, 486 or the Pentium (586) CPU, you have extra interrupt lines to choose from (Table 6.3).

Software interrupts

Software interrupts are generated by programs issuing the INT instruction. This is a low-level command that instructs the process to jump to the interrupt service routine that is pointed to by the software interrupt number.

Most DOS commands are sent to the DOS control program thorough a software interrupt. In this case the DOS interrupt number is 21 hex. When the user wishes to request a DOS function, the registers are preconfigured for the requested function, and then the INT 21 hex is issued. DOS will then service that request and return control back to the calling programs.

Table 6.4 lists some of the most used software interrupt numbers.

I/O base address

This is a special area in memory that the computer system uses to communicate with external devices. It is sometimes referred to as dual port memory, because as one computer writes to this location, the computer on the other side of this memory can read off this location.

Table 6.2 Standard hardware interrupt settings for NICs.

Number	Potential conflict with device	Avoid using this interrupt when
IRQ 02	Usually available	EGA or VGA installed
IRQ 03	COM2:, SDLC, BSC	Second serial port installed
IRQ 04	COM1:, SDLC, BSC	First serial port installed
IRQ 05	Hard disk (in XTs) LPT2: (in ATs)	Some SCSI cards
IRQ 06	Floppy disk	System uses a floppy drive
IRQ 07	LPT1:	First parallel port installed

Table 6.3 Extra hardware interrupt settings for NICs.

Number	Potential conflict with device	Avoid using this interrupt when
IRQ 08	Real-time clock IRQ	Used by computer system. Don't use it!
IRQ 09	Software INT 0Ah (IRQ 2)	Software redirected to IRQ 2. Don't use it!
IRQ 10	Usually available	Could be used
IRQ 11	Usually available	Could be used
IRQ 12	Usually available	System uses a floppy drive. Don't use it!
IRQ 13	Used by system	Is the co-processor IRQ
IRQ 14	Used by system	Fixed disk controller. Don't use it!
IRQ 15	Usually available	Could be used

Table 6.4 Software interrupt numbers.

Number	Software interrupt name	Address	Owner
05	Print screen	F000:FF54	BIOS
08	System timer	137D:0000	WIN386.EXE
09	Keyboard	1052:0045	DOS system area
10	Video	1388:000F	WIN386.EXE
13	Fixed disk/diskette	0070:0774	DOS system area
14	Asynchronous comms	F000:E739	BIOS
15	System services	133F:0000	WIN386.EXE
16	Keyboard	F000:E82E	BIOS
17	Printer	F000:EFD2	BIOS
20	Program terminate	011C:1094	DOS system area
21	General DOS functions	04C7:2819	DOS system area
22	Terminate address	140E:01DC	COMMAND.COM, Copy2
7A	Novell NetWare (API)	0000:0000	Unused

How to find an I/O base address to use

Table 6.5 illustrates the most common devices and their I/O ports. Use this table to ascertain what kinds of device normally use these addresses. If you think you have such a device in your machine, avoid using that particular address and seek an alternative.

RAM base address memory

This is an area between 640 Kbytes and 1 Mbyte called the upper memory. Normally, NICs request a contiguous block of 8, 16 or 32 Kbytes, depending on the manufacturer. You need to find a UMB (upper memory block) that is not being used by any other device.

Occasionally, when the NIC has a remote boot option, it needs another block in the upper memory: this can be anything from 16 to 32 Kbytes long.

Table 6.5 I/O base addresses.

Base address	Potential conflict with device
[200]	Game controller/joystick (200–20F)
	Expansion unit (210–217)
[220]	Novell NetWare keycard
[240]	Normally available
[260]	LPT2: (278–27F)
[280]	LCD display on Wyse 2108 PC
[2A0]	Normally available
[2C0]	Normally available
[2E0]	COM2: (2F8–2FF)
	COM4: (2E8–2EF)
	Data acquisition (2E2–2E3)
[300]	3 Com EtherLink factory setting is 300–31F
[320]	XT hard disk interface (320–32F)
[340]	Normally available
[360]	LPT1: (378–37F)
[380]	SLDC/secondary bi-sync interface (380–38C)
[3A0]	Primary bi-sync interface (3A0–3A9)
	Monochrome display (3B0–3BB)
[3C0]	EGA display control (3C0–3CF)
	Colour graphics display: CGA (3D0–3DF)
[3E0]	COM1: (3F8–3FF)
	COM3: (3E8–3EF)
	Floppy disk controller (3F0–3F7)

Important notice to Windows users
Portions of upper memory are sometimes used by memory management utilities like QEMM 386 and Microsoft Windows. It is a good idea to inform them that a range of upper memory is not to be re-mapped or tampered with. Microsoft Windows has a means of excluding these portions of memory.

For example, if you are using Windows and have installed a LAN adaptor at D8000–D9FFF (assuming 8 Kbyte LAN adaptor RAM), you would add the following line to SYSTEM.INI:

```
EMMExclude=D800-D9FF
```

If your machines hang when running Windows and the network adaptor, try using the Windows EMMExclude=????-????? command to exclude the portion of memory block from the Windows environment. Also, check in your CONFIG.SYS for the exclude command on the EMM386.SYS parameter line.

NIC management strategy

Restrict the number of NIC vendors

Wherever possible, standardize on one or at most two vendors for all your NIC purchases. This form of restraint has the following advantages:

- Only one type of NIC device driver need be issued to workstations
- The same type of NIC driver can be used for all workstations
- You can use a common NIC diagnostic tool on all nodes
- You can react to NIC problems quickly, since the NIC is well known
- It is easier to train users on one type of NIC than a variety of different types

However, there is the danger that if the selected vendor falls behind technologically you will be left with a selection of obsolete equipment.

Most organizations I have come across have a policy of buying only one type of NIC such as 3-COM or SMC. However, do not forget that each manufacturer will provide different models of NIC: these could be the 8, 16 or the 32 bit versions.

Who to buy NICs from

My recommendation is to strictly stick to the big names, such as 3-COM, IBM, SMC or Intel. Do not be seduced by this week's latest offering of very cheap NICs. Unlike the big players, who have been around a while, all sorts of NIC vendors come and go every week. They all claim that their NIC is cheaper, faster and fully compatible. Each NIC needs a special NIC driver, and these companies rarely put into their drivers the same amount of research and conformance testing as the bigger companies. You also have no guarantee that they will still be around to release the next version of the NIC device drivers.

Standardize NIC settings and documents

Try to standardize a set of NIC interface settings across your organization and then record it formally. You do not want the situation where every workstation is using a different set of NIC interface parameters, which could lead to an assortment of specific problems on specific machines. The aim of the network manager should be to standardize the set-ups across the whole organization.

I suggest that you adopt the same strategy as some of the major organizations, and restrict the NIC hardware set-ups to two: type A and type B. Type A is the company default set-up; type B is used only in machines that cannot work with type A. It is up to you, as network manager, to decide what these settings should be.

The exact parameters selected will depend on:

- the type of NIC being used
- the NIC vendor's default recommendations
- any extra hardware that has to sit alongside the NIC on most machines

Type B should use parameters that are completely independent of type A, so that this approach can also be used in machines that require two NICs to be installed at the same time.

In machines that require two NICs, use one NIC as Type A and the other as Type B.

Figure 6.6 provides a form for you to use to record your standard settings for NIC types A and B, to keep for future reference.

Managing the DOS workstation memory

This section first defines the underlying concepts of the PC memory structure, introducing the important memory terms, and how they function. It then makes some suggestions on how you can use these memory structures effectively. In particular, it discusses the MEMMAKER program from DOS 6.x.

Network Adaptor Set-up Form

Network adaptor type A (default)

Board Type	IRQ	I/O base address	RAM base address	DMA channel	ROM base address

Network adaptor type B (Alt)

Board Type	IRQ	I/O base address	RAM base address	DMA channel	ROM base address

---

Figure 6.6 Form for recording your standard NIC parameters.

Understanding PC memory structure

DOS is the most popular operating system on the PC. However, there has always been the great problem of the 640 Kbyte barrier in DOS, even with the advent of programs like Windows and DESQview. The problem really started back in 1980, when the most popular PC was the Apple II EuroPlus, which came with 16 Kbytes of memory as standard. If you were a serious user, you would upgrade your machine to 32 Kbytes; however, for the real power-hungry Apple user there was the possibility (for $500) of supercharging your Apple to the maximum of 64 Kbytes – a considerable luxury at the time. In those days you could run programs like WordStar or dBase II within 32 Kbytes using the CP/M operating system.

It was against this background that Intel developed the 8088 processor, which can address up to 1 Mbyte of memory. Bill Gates of Microsoft won from IBM one of the most lucrative contracts ever, to write an operating system to use the new chip. IBM had made the major decision to enter the PC market by bringing out their own PC based on the Intel chip and using the Bill Gates operating system, called DOS.

DOS was designed to address 1 Mbyte of memory, but the region from 640 Kbytes to 1 Mbyte was left for the system to map special drivers and adaptor cards. A decade later we still have the 640 Kbyte barrier: although processing chip technology has moved on, so much software has been written for DOS that we continue to inherit the classic 640 Kbyte 'RAM cram'.

One of the most challenging issues for today's network manager is how best to manage the DOS workstation memory to load all the drivers. The Novell shell TSRs (terminate and stay resident) can utilize the PC memory very effectively, leaving plenty of conventional memory to run applications.

Basic 8086 memory structure

DOS was designed to work with the Intel 8086 chip. This can only address 1 Mbyte of memory, or 1024 Kbytes to be precise. This is because it has only 20 address lines, giving it 2^{20}=1024 Kbytes. The memory is split into two sections (Figure 6.7). The first is called conventional memory; this is where all the normal user programs are executed. The DOS operating system is used in this area. The second area, from 640 Kbytes to 1 Mbyte (384 Kbytes) is set aside to be used by video display adaptors, I/O device drivers, NICs and other add-on peripherals. Microsoft breaks this area up into UMBs (upper memory blocks), which are contiguous ranges of upper memory.

You need to be careful here; there are many different terms with the same meaning. For example, I have heard people refer to the first 1 Mbyte as conventional memory, and then divide it into low DOS and high DOS: all very confusing!

A typical snapshot of the workings of a PC memory is shown in Figure 6.8. Using CheckIt, or the MEM command from DOS 5, you can gain information on how the two different blocks of memory are used.

Conventional memory

This is the area that DOS uses by default to run programs, in addition to storing the applications' data while executing in memory (Figure 6.9).

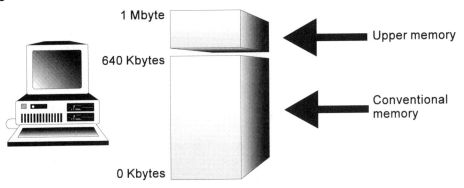

Figure 6.7 Basic 8086 PC memory structure.

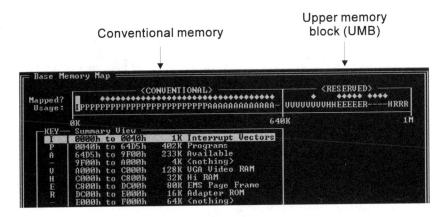

Figure 6.8 Conventional and UMB memory.

In addition to loading DOS applications, TSR programs are traditionally loaded into conventional memory. Examples of such programs are IPX.COM and NETx.COM. Each one of these TSR programs must be loaded and active while the DOS user runs other programs to access the Novell network. Some of the valuable conventional memory is used each time you load these Novell TSRs. This could result in normal DOS programs that were previously running showing the 'not enough memory available' error when the Novell TSRs are loaded. However, you can manage your workstation memory to minimize this potential problem by placing the bulk of the NetWare shell outside the conventional memory area, thus releasing more memory for conventional DOS programs to run.

You can get a detailed map of the conventional memory status by using the DOS 5 or DOS 6, command MEM /C. It should provide the following type of information. Note that the information is provided in logical address order.

Using MEM /D gives even more detail...

```
Modules using memory below 1 MB:
```

Name	Total	=	Conventional +	Upper Memory
SYSTEM	20157	(20K)	17085	(17K)	3072	(3K)
HIMEM	1168	(1K)	1168	(1K)	0	(0K)
EMM386	3120	(3K)	3120	(3K)	0	(0K)
DBLSPACE	44352	(43K)	44352	(43K)	0	(0K)
COMMAND	2992	(3K)	2992	(3K)	0	(0K)
win386	47456	(46K)	16432	(16K)	31024	(30K)
WIN	2304	(2K)	2304	(2K)	0	(0K)
LSL	5008	(5K)	5008	(5K)	0	(0K)
SMC8000	8928	(9K)	8928	(9K)	0	(0K)
IPXODI	18656	(18K)	18656	(18K)	0	(0K)
VLM	39776	(39K)	39776	(39K)	0	(0K)
COMMAND	3200	(3K)	3200	(3K)	0	(0K)
ASPIDISK	2640	(3K)	0	(0K)	2640	(3K)
ASP	2496	(2K)	0	(0K)	2496	(2K)
SETVER	624	(1K)	0	(0K)	624	(1K)
ASPI2DOS	11360	(11K)	0	(0K)	11360	(11K)
DOSKEY	4144	(4K)	0	(0K)	4144	(4K)
Free	488000	(477K)	488000	(477K)	0	(0K)

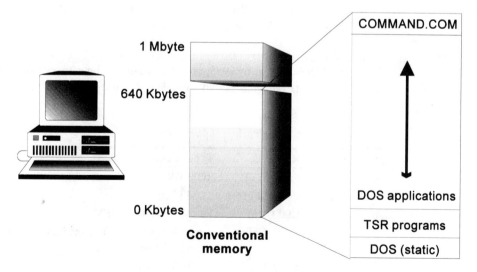

Figure 6.9 Conventional memory structure.

```
Memory Summary:

Type of Memory        Total       =       Used        +   Free
---------------       --------------      ----------------    ---------
Conventional          651264  (636K)     163264  (159K)      488000
Upper                  55360   (54K)      55360   (54K)           0
Adaptor RAM/ROM       135168  (132K)     135168  (132K)           0
Extended (XMS)       7546816 (7370K)    6498240 (6346K)     1048576
---------------       ------------------  ------------------    ---------
Total memory         8388608 (8192K)    6852032 (6691K)     1536576

Total under 1 MB      706624  (690K)     218624  (214K)      488000

Total Expanded (EMS)                    1048576 (1024K)
Free Expanded (EMS)                     1048576 (1024K)
 Largest executable program size         487984  (477K)
 Largest free upper memory block              0    (0K)
MS-DOS is resident in the high memory area.
```

Upper memory: detailed structure

As stated earlier, the upper memory is the area from 640 Kbytes to 1 Mbyte (384 Kbytes). It is set aside to store the BIOS (Basic Input Output System), video display adaptors, I/O device driver, network interface cards, hard disk controllers and other add-on peripherals. Microsoft breaks this area up into UMBs (upper memory blocks): contiguous ranges of upper memory.

The upper memory is divided into six blocks of 64 Kbyte segments. Memory within these segments is allocated to resources in units of 4 Kbytes. Table 6.6 shows how each of the six blocks is generally used.

Basic 80286 memory structure

When the 80286 arrived in 1985, it was designed to be a successor to the old 8086 chip, emulating its functions but able to address a maximum of 16 Mbytes of memory

Table 6.6 Typical usage of the upper memory.

Block size	Range	Typical applications
64 Kbytes	F000–FFFF	ROM BIOS (bootstrap)
64 Kbytes	E000–EFFF	ROM BIOS
64 Kbytes	D000–DFFF	Network adaptors or EMS page frames
64 Kbytes	C000–CFFF	Network adaptors, EMS page frames or video display adaptors
64 Kbytes	B000–BFFF	Video display adaptors
64 Kbytes	A000–AFFF	Video display adaptors

(Figure 6.10). It was also roughly three times faster. All the programs that could run on the old system, including DOS, could run on the new chip.

The 80286 chip defined two different types of operation: real mode and protected mode.

> Note: Not all 286 systems can support UMB blocks.

In real mode, the 286 chip forgets about its extra memory, and concentrates on being a powerful 8088/86 processor. This means that it ignores memory above the 1 Mbyte line (Figure 6.11).

Because of a small error in the Intel design of the 286 chip (which for reasons of compatibility has been copied onto the 386 and 486 chips), it is possible to access

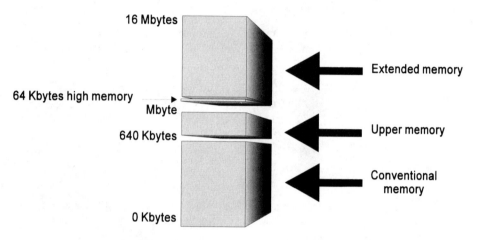

Figure 6.10 Basic 80286 memory structure.

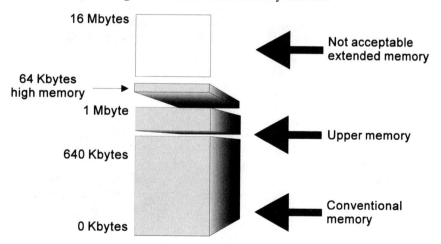

Figure 6.11 286 chip real mode.

the first 64 Kbyte block above the 1 Mbyte line. This is now referred to as the high memory area (HMA). This is nicely exploited by DOS 5 (or above), which loads part of itself in this area, thereby releasing room in the conventional memory.

The HMA is 65 520 bytes, which is 64 kbytes minus 16 bytes. DOS can now address this extra piece of space in the real mode of the 80286, 386 or 486 chips. To do this you do need to load up the HIMEM.SYS driver as part of CONFIG.SYS. HIMEM.SYS, when loaded, activates address line 20 (A20) on all AT machines, which enables the chip to address the HMA.

A typical CONFIG.SYS might look like this:

```
FILE=30
BUFFERS=30
DEVICE=HIMEM.SYS
```

There are a number of important parameters that can be used to select different options when the HIMEM.SYS driver is loaded into memory:

```
DEVICE= [drive:][path] HIMEM.SYS
       [/A20CONTROL:ON|OFF] [/CPUCLOCK:ON|OFF]
       [/EISA] [/HMAMIN=m]
       [/INT15=xxxx]
       [/NUMHANDLES=n]
       [/MACHINE:xxxx]
       [/SHADOWRAM:ON|OFF]
       [/VERBOSE]
```

However, in most cases you do not need to specify any options. The standard defaults will work for most circumstances. This, when the machine is started up, should show:

```
HIMEM: DOS XMS Driver, Version 3.07-02/14/92
Extended Memory Specification (XMS) Version 3.0
Copyright 1988-1992 Microsoft Corp.

Installed A20 handler number 1.
64K High Memory Area is available.
```

This means that the A20 line has been enabled, and that DOS and other drivers can be loaded into the HMA.

> Warning: On some machines you might get an error 'Failed to connect to A20'. This is usually because some motherboards (often from the Taiwanese manufacturer Elite) having their own HMA handler implemented in the chip controller, so that the software cannot get hold of it. The solution is to go through the CMOS setting of the machine and disable the on-board HMA handler. This should cure the problem.

If you experience problems with the A20 handler, you might have to specify a value for the type of machine being used from the following list. This is done using

```
DEVICE=HIMEM.SYS /Machine=xxx
```

where the number *xxx* is taken from Table 6.7.

There is an important point to made about this area. Normally, only one program at a time can control the A20 line, so that only one program at a time can use the HMA. This means that you should try to load as much as possible into the 64 Kbytes of HMA.

It is important that programs or drivers placed in the HMA are very well designed and behave appropriately. They must only enable the A20 line while they are running. When not in use, they must disable it so that, when other programs are running, they see only the normal 1 Mbyte.

In protected mode the chip can address the full 16 Mbytes of physical memory. It still maintains the division into conventional memory and upper memory for introducing external devices, but now extra memory above the first 1 Mbyte, called extended memory, is directly addressable.

Extended memory

The old 8086/88 chip cannot address any extended memory. In the 80286 processor the extended memory is up to a maximum of 16 Mbytes; in the 386 chip this is further extended to a theoretical physical memory of 4 Gbytes, which is the same as the addressable limit of the NetWare 386 network operating system.

Table 6.7 Devices and A20 handlers.

Code	Number	A20 handler
Pt	1	IBM PC/AT
Ps2	2	IBM PS/2
Pt1 cascade	3	Phoenix Cascade BIOS
Hpvectra	4	HP Vectra (A and A+)
Att6300plus	5	AT&T 6300 Plus
Acer 1100	6	Acer 1100
Toshiba	7	Toshiba 1600 and 1200XE
Wyse	8	Wyse 12.5 MHz 286
Tulip	9	Tulip SX
Zenith	10	Zenith ZBIOS
At1	11	IBM PC/AT
At2	12	IBM PC/AT (alternative delay)
Css	12	CSS Labs
At3	13	IBM PC/AT (alternative delay)
Philips	13	Philips
Fasthp	14	HP Vectra

While DOS applications can only address the conventional 640 Kbytes, memory management programs such as Windows, when run on a 286 chip or better, can extend DOS to take advantage of the workstation's extended memory. These programs use the XMM extended memory manager that conforms to XMS specification v2.0 or above. When you load the HIMEM.SYS driver, you see on your screen that the XMS driver has been loaded: you must do this if you want to run WINDOWS under the standard or enhanced mode.

Expanded memory

This was designed to increase the memory of systems not originally intended for extra memory support. It was supported on a separate memory expansion card. Essentially, expanded memory is an illusion; it fools the system into seeing more memory than it can actually address directly (Figure 6.12).

To use this kind of memory, the computer needs to load the EMS (expanded memory standard) as a driver. It will then physically map pages of memory into the upper memory block. This means that applications have to be aware of the EMS driver and make the appropriate request to it before benefiting from this service.

LIM/EMS standards

The three companies Lotus, Intel and Microsoft (LIM) got together in 1985 to bring out the official release of the EMS standard, to be called LIM version 3.2. This defined the device driver, and how application developers were to utilize the standard. It created a 64 Kbyte page frame in the upper memory that the expanded memory driver was to use exclusively to map pages of memory in and out as requested. The 64 Kbyte pages were themselves divided into four 16 Kbyte units. This division was used internally by the driver to optimize the memory management. The LIM 3.2 standard allowed for up to 8 Mbyte of expanded memory to be used.

LIM/EMS v4.0

In 1987 the EMS standard became 'extended' thanks to the new version, LIM v4.0, which dramatically improved performance and flexibility. With this standard, you are not restricted to a page memory size of 64 Kbytes; page memory of up to 1 Mbyte is possible. The new standard also allows for up to 32 Mbytes of expanded memory to be addressed. The most important aspect of the standard is its multitasking ability: it can simultaneously support the memory requirements of several programs from a common memory pool. One very important program that utilizes such a function is Microsoft Windows 3.1.

Practical Point

Extended and expanded memory sound very similar, and it is easy to get them confused. A useful mnemonic to distinguish between the two is to remember that if the word has a 'p' in it (ex*p*anded) then think of *p*age memory; otherwise think of good news, and the flat memory model of extended memory.

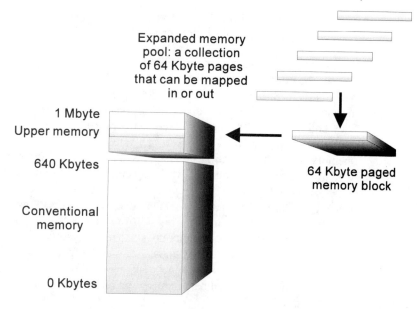

Figure 6.12 Expanded memory model.

Objectives of PC memory management

It is essential to maximize the amount of conventional memory made available to users after all the drivers have been loaded. The aim should be to provide 600 Kbytes or more of free conventional memory at the DOS prompt line; thus giving users the opportunity to run a wide range of programs.

Another important objective is to give the user a solid and reliable memory architecture. There are a large number of drivers that, when put into high, extended or expanded memory, cause a deterioration in the machine's reliability.

Whatever method you decide upon, the machine should not hang or reboot unconditionally. Unfortunately, these two objectives are sometimes contradictory: as you increase the number of drivers located outside the conventional memory area, there is increasing potential for the PC memory architecture to become unstable.

Management strategy for expanded memory

The LIM (EMS) standard is not ideal; it was a bit of an afterthought, and its popularity is now beginning to diminish. Nevertheless, there are still a lot of applications that use it, but if you can avoid using it, do!

I have often encountered machines that seem to 'blow up' for no apparent reason; on further analysis I discover that they are using an expanded memory driver that is incompatible with the applications they are running. If you do need to use this standard, be aware of the different versions, and always ensure that the applications being used are compatible with the driver!

Mapping network adaptors into upper memory

One of the most important memory areas in a PC from a network manager's point of view is the area between C000 and E000. Traditionally, this is where the NICs are normally mapped. This rule applies to workstations as much as to file servers, since they both share the PC memory architecture, even though one runs under DOS and the other under the NetWare operating system: they both map NICs into the upper memory. Note that sometimes this area is shared with the EMS page system. Figure 6.13 gives a typical example of what is occurring in the upper memory.

To establish what your current NIC is using you can use a program like CheckIt or Norton Utilities SI. An alternative way for checking your memory setting is to use the IPX-I command. This will only be useful if you are not using ODI drivers, and the IPX you generate does not refer to software-configurable adaptors, which nowadays are quite rare; most NICs are software-configurable. In this case you need either to check the original disk provided by the manufacturers of the NIC, which will show the actual hardware setting on board the NIC, or use programs such as CheckIt.

When you come to install multiple NICs, you must change the NIC defaults so that they do not clash. This is when you need to be fully aware of where each NIC is mapped into your system. They must each be given a unique location that is not being used by any other device.

DOS 6 and MEMMAKER

A powerful memory management tool

MEMMAKER is a superb program. It is worth upgrading to DOS 6 just for this function alone. It provides much-needed automation for getting the best out of your

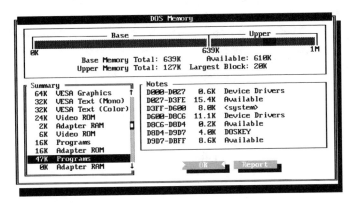

Figure 6.13 DOS memory map.

DOS workstation's memory. It is ideal for those manager who cannot remember all the different options with HIMEM.SYS, EMM386.EXE, LOADHIGH and DEVICEHIGH. When MEMMAKER is run it starts to investigate every device driver named in the CONFIG.SYS and TSR programs loaded from AUTOEXEC.BAT.

Then, by using artificial intelligence techniques, it will attempt to optimize your computer's memory by moving device drivers and memory-resident programs to upper memory if possible. It will exploit the ability of the new LOADHIGH and DEVICEHIGH facilities to specify particular regions within upper memory. This program can only be run on the 80386 and 80486 chips.

MEMMAKER is a superb program, It can save a lot of time – and memory. I have used it with great success on client sites.

MEMMAKER in action

Here is a typical example of the usage of MEMMAKER.EXE. Before it was run, the CONFIG.SYS file looked like this:

```
DEVICE=C:\DOS\HIMEM.SYS
DEVICE=C:\DOS\EMM386.EXE
BUFFERS=15,0
FILES=20
DOS=UMB
LASTDRIVE=Z
FCBS=4,0
device=C:\DOS\SETVER.EXE
DEVICE=C:\ADAPTEC\ASPI2DOS.SYS /D
DOS=HIGH
STACKS=9,256
DEVICE=C:\ADAPTEC\ASPIDISK.SYS /D
DEVICE=E:\SB16\DRV\ASP.SYS /P:220
SHELL=C:\DOS\COMMAND.COM
DEVICE=C:\DOS\DBLSPACE.SYS
```

This configuration gave the workstation 521 Kbytes of conventional memory:

Memory Type	Total	= Used	+ Free
Conventional	636K	115K	521K
Upper	0K	0K	0K
Adaptor RAM/ROM	132K	132K	0K
Extended (XMS)	7424K	6400K	1024K
Total memory	8192K	6647K	1545K

The MEMMAKER program was then run on the workstation; it automatically analysed the system and modified CONFIG.SYS to the following:

```
DEVICE=C:\DOS\HIMEM.SYS
DEVICE=C:\DOS\EMM386.EXE NOEMS HIGHSCAN
BUFFERS=15,0
FILES=20
DOS=UMB
LASTDRIVE=Z
FCBS=4,0
DEVICEHIGH /L:2,12048 =C:\DOS\SETVER.EXE
DEVICEHIGH /L:2,18048 =C:\ADAPTEC\ASPI2DOS.SYS /D
DOS=HIGH
STACKS=9,256
DEVICEHIGH /L:1,7616 =C:\ADAPTEC\ASPIDISK.SYS /D
DEVICEHIGH /L:1,5008 =E:\SB16\DRV\ASP.SYS /P:220
SHELL=C:\DOS\COMMAND.COM
DEVICEHIGH /L:3,44400 =C:\DOS\DBLSPACE.SYS
```

This new configuration gives the same workstation 605 Kbytes of conventional memory: a saving of 605 − 521 = 84 Kbytes. Most of this extra memory has been derived from using the DEVICEHIGH command to load the DOS drivers into the HIGH memory.

```
Memory Type          Total = Used   +   Free
----------------     ------   ------    ------
Conventional          636K     31K      605K
Upper                 126K    126K       0K
Adaptor RAM/ROM       132K    132K       0K
Extended (XMS)       7298K   6274K     1024K
----------------     ------   ------    ------
Total memory         8192K   6563K     1629K
```

7

Managing the NetWare workstation environment

Overview

There are many different types of user. The new breed of user, the heavily input-intensive Windows user, is slowly replacing the DOS text-based user. However, regardless of type, all users have a lot in common, and in this chapter we look at how to improve the workstation environment for them. The emphasis is on how to get the best out of DOS and the Novell shell for maximum flexibility and efficiency. We also look at the ODI (open data link) interface. This is Novell's way of enabling multiple protocol stacks to be supported simultaneously.

You will learn:

- how the Novell shell integrates with DOS
- where to put IPX and NETX for maximum main memory
- how to use the new burst mode NETX
- how to manage NetWare shell updates
- how to support multiple protocols by using ODI
- how to support multiple protocols by using NDIS
- how VLM programs, introduced with NetWare 4.x, can be used.

The Novell shell

What is the Novell shell?

'The shell enhances the local workstation operating system to enable programs to use the shared resources of the Novell network (Novell corporation).

Novell has defined a series of universal function calls that any Novell user can make from the file server (Figure 7.1). These high-level function calls are all made in the same way, regardless of the user's operating system or the type of machine being used. These high-level functions are defined as part of the NCP (NetWare core protocol).

The kinds of high-level request made by NCP calls are such things as requesting to log in, reading directory access rights, asking who is logged in, and reading a file. Thanks to the NCP standard these commands are universal, regardless of the user operating environment.

The Novell shell acts as a form of translator between the user's own operating system and the universal high-level language that the Novell file server understands. The program that converts the user command, where relevant, to the universal NCP command is NETX.EXE. This has to be specific to the user's operating system, which is why historically we used to have different versions of NETX.EXE according to the type of DOS being used (Table 7.1).

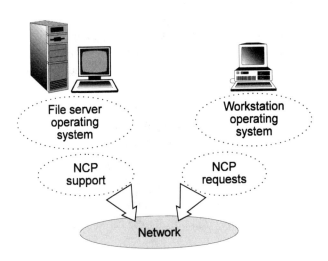

Figure 7.1 NCP calls across the network.

Table 7.1 Novell shells.

Workstation operating system	Shell to use
DOS 3.x	NET3.COM
DOS 4.x	NET4.COM
DOS 5.x	NET5.COM
All DOS versions	NETX.EXE (latest version)
All DOS versions	BNETX.EXE (burst mode)
All DOS versions	NETX.VLM (VLM version)
All DOS versions	BNETX.VLM (burst mode VLM version)

The same principle applies if you are using OS/2 or Apple Mac: there would also be an equivalent of the NETX program that would act as an interface between local operation and triggering of NCP universal calls from the file server.

Novell also define another standard, called the IPX (Internet Packet Exchange) protocol as their universal postal system. This standard defines NetWare's lowest and fastest means of communication from point to point, regardless of the underlying type of network being used (Figure 7.2). IPX works equally well across Ethernet, Token Ring or FDDI; it can be configured to work across practically every conceivable type of network. Once activated, the Novell system can use the universal function as defined in IPX to transfer data from point to point (sometimes called a datagram service).

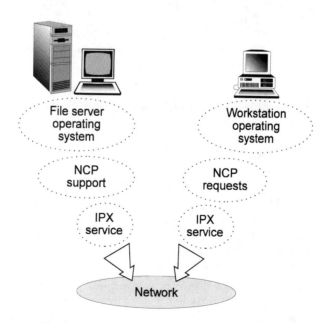

Figure 7.2 NCP and IPX calls across the network.

Traditionally, the Novell shell uses the IPX function to communicate across the network; this is an implementation of the IDP (internetwork datagram packet) originally designed by Rank Xerox.

Novell always uses IPX by default, although as we shall see later you don't need to use IPX; in theory you could use alternative protocols such as TCP/IP to communicate across the Novell network.

The IPX program is implemented by running a program called IPX.COM. In what is called the native IPX implementation, you need to tell the IPX program the type of network card being used. Thanks to the ODI (open data link) standard, there is now an alternative; in addition to its other benefits, it abolishes having to customize the IPX to the network adaptor.

When IPX is run it checks for the network adaptor and initializes it. It then loads as a TSR (terminate and stay resident) program and starts to provide a universal point-to-point communication service. When NETX is loaded it first checks to see that IPX is activated, and that its communication service is available. It is on top of this service that the NCP command is carried to the Novell file servers.

When IPX.COM is loaded, two types of communication are implemented. Novell defines a second, more reliable, service called the SPX (sequenced packet exchange) protocol that can be used as a more reliable means of communication (Figure 7.3). SPX is a connection-oriented protocol. Unlike IPX, which cannot guarantee that the other side has actually received the data, SPX can guarantee point-to-point communication. It is the 'value added' version of IPX. When used, SPX uses the services of the underlying IPX to provide its service. As always, there is a price to pay; according to Novell, calls to SPX are 5% slower than calls to IPX. Where IPX is fast, SPX is robust!

SPX and IPX fit well into the framework of the seven-layer OSI model (Figure 7.4). IPX works at layer 3 (the network layer), whereas SPX works at layer 4 (the transport layer).

How the Novell shell integrates with DOS

The Novell shell integrates well with DOS, and enhances its functionality. Once loaded into the DOS workstation it will include the resources of the remote file server as if they are an extension to the DOS environment. The DOS user can address the resources of the file server just as if it was an extension of the local hard disk. The shell intercepts all the data coming from the user. If the data refers to local workstation resources the shell passes it on to DOS; if it refers to a resource on the network, the shell intercepts the command and issues the appropriate Novell command across the network. In effect, the shell acts as an interpreter between the Novell operating system and the DOS environment. Novell also provide shells for OS/2, Apple Mac and UNIX workstations; the basic idea is the same.

If you are going to use NetWare 4.x then you will need to familiarize yourself with the new NetWare redirector concept; it is radically different from the NetWare shell concept.

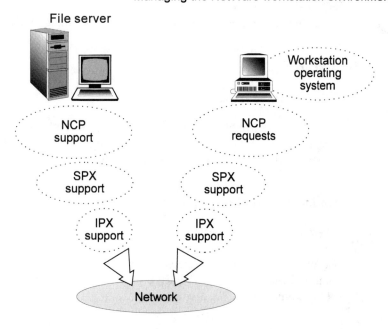

Figure 7.3 NCP, SPX and IPX calls across the network.

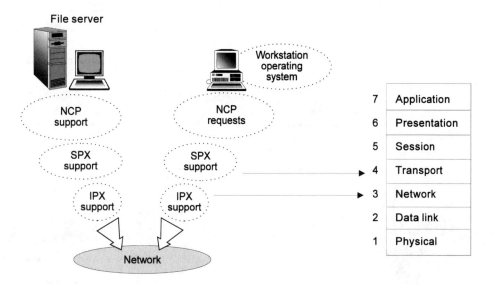

Figure 7.4 NetWare protocols in relation to the seven-layer OSI model.

See the section on the NetWare 4.x VLM redirector at the end of this chapter.

Novell shell start-up

What actually happens?

When you are troubleshooting, it is important to understand what actually happens when the PC first boots up. If you can recognize each step then it becomes much easier to decide which element of the workstation is faulty.

Understanding IPX/SPX and NETX

There now follows a basic overview of the steps required to establish a connection with a file server. It is assumed that you are connecting to a NetWare 2.x or NetWare 3.x server. The steps required to connect to a NetWare 4.x server are slightly different, since you must use the VLMs (virtual loadable modules) instead of the equivalent NETX program.

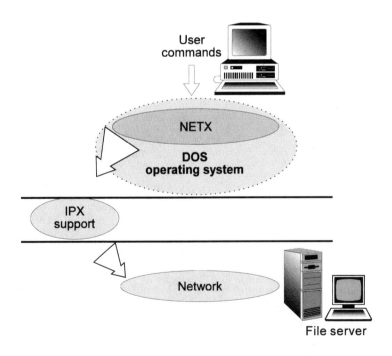

Figure 7.5 Basic NETX and IPX functions.

First, the workstation operating system is loaded. Then the Novell IPX (interpacket exchange) program is loaded to provide a standard protocol for the Novell operating system to talk across the LAN cards. This is a TSR program Finally, the Novell NETX program is loaded This works on top of IPX to provide for:

- locating and connecting to a file server
- enhancing the operating system
- enabling the Novell file server to be accessed through standard workstation operating system commands

Multiplatform shell

The shell works across a range of Novell file servers (Figure 7.6), and can be used for connecting up to different types of NetWare operating systems simultaneously. This make it far easier for the network manager to administrate different kinds of Novell file server.

There are four basic different types of NetWare operating system:

- NetWare 4.x (you need to use VLMs instead of NETX)
- NetWare 3.x
- NetWare 2.x (advanced)
- hosted NetWare running on mini or mainframe computers

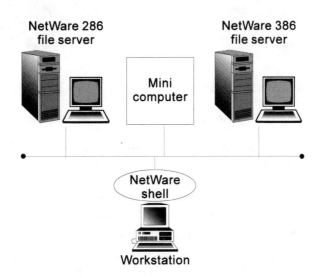

Figure 7.6 The NetWare shell can support different types of server.

The ODI IPX versus dedicated IPX

There are two different approaches to producing the Novell shell: the dedicated IPX.COM method, and the ODI path.

Dedicated IPX.COM method

This is the old way of generating a shell for the workstation. Dedicated IPX drivers are being phased out. Novell discontinued the certification of dedicated DOS IPX drivers in June 1992.

The WSGEN program is used to generate a dedicated IPX. These dedicated IPX drivers have been used for most NetWare installations since NetWare version 2.0A. This technology was created to act as a bridge between adaptor boards and the network communication protocol, connecting hardware with the network operating system. However, many companies have now moved to larger and more complex systems where dedicated IPX drivers have limitations. The growing need for added flexibility in network communications spawned the development of the open data link interface (ODI).

ODI based IPX and other protocols

The ODI path is now becoming the standard approach to activating the Novell shell. In addition to its many advantages, it does not require the use of WSGEN.COM to generate a customized IPX.COM. In some ways the installation is far easier to set up and manage, but yet potentially far more powerful.

Nowadays, network managers should be thinking of moving towards ODI drivers and away from the old dedicated IPX method.

Novell IPX.COM native drivers

Generating the IPX shell using WSGEN.COM

Assuming that you are producing a Novell shell for a DOS/Windows-based workstation (Figure 7.7), the basic steps required are described below. Before generating WSGEN, it is worth gathering some basic information. Record the following for the workstation you are about to generate for:
- the workstation owner or location
- the workstation operating system
- the type of network adaptor in the workstation
- your name as the workstation installer
- the configuration of the network adaptor

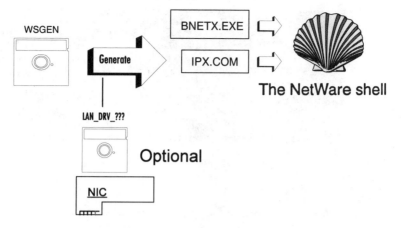

Figure 7.7 Generating NetWare IPX.

How to produce the IPX program

- Insert the WSGEN (formerly SHGEN) disk. Type WSGEN. Press <ENTER> for a list of all the drivers that can be used to link with the IPX.OBJ to produce a customized IPX.COM program.

- Select from the list of network card names (drivers) the one that matches your card in the workstation (Figure 7.8). If the network driver is not shown in the list, press the <INSERT> key. You will be prompted to put in the third-party network disk driver. The program will now read the drive and add it to its list.

- Select the relevant configuration option for the NIC (Figure 7.9). A number of options are displayed, showing the different parameters for which the network adaptor can be configured. These settings are dictated by the make of card that you use. Each card has a default setting. Most cards are software-selectable. You do not need to state which hardware parameters are to be used at this stage; you simply instruct the driver to ask the card itself. These cards store a series of hardware settings in non-volatile memory. If two or more of the same type of card are being used in the same workstation, each can be instructed to

```
Select the driver that matches the network board in your workstation.

 ▲ IBM LAN Support Program Driver  v2.60 (901031)
   IBM PCN II & Baseband  v1.15 (900905)
   IBM Token-Ring  v2.60 (901022)
   NetWare Async Remote Router COM1/COM2 V1.2
   NetWare NE/2  v2.02EC (900718)
   NetWare NE1000  v3.02EC (900831)
   NetWare NE2000  v1.05EC (900718)
   NetWare Turbo RX-Net  v2.11 (901217)
   SMC EtherCard PLUS V4.00EC (910924)
   Western Digital EtherCard PLUS v3.12EC (910808)
```

Figure 7.8 Selecting a network card driver.

```
Select the configuration option that matches the setting on your network
board.

            ┌─────────────────────────────────────────┐
            │ Network Board Driver:                   │
            │   SMC EtherCard PLUS V4.00EC (910924)   │
            └─────────────────────────────────────────┘

  ┌────────────────────────────────────────────────────────────┐
  │ 0: First Software Configured Adapter                        │
  │ 1: Second Software Configured Adapter                       │
  │ 2: Third Software Configured Adapter                        │
  │ 3: Fourth Software Configured Adapter                       │
  │▼4: IRQ=3, I/O Base=280h, RAM at D000:0 for 16k              │
  └────────────────────────────────────────────────────────────┘
```

Figure 7.9 Selecting interface parameters.

use a different set of parameters: this is why you will see options such as first, second, third and fourth software-configured adaptor.

If you are not sure which setting to use, and cannot easily find this out, select option 0. This is the most frequently used option, and nine times out of ten will be sufficient.

- Generate workstation software. NetWare incorporates the information about your network board into the IPX.COM file.
- Issue IPX.COM and NETX.EXE. These files, which are now on the WSGEN disk, can be copied to the user's workstation

Running WSGEN

The WSGEN utility is normally supplied on one disk that comes with the Novell 386 and Novell 286 (ADV) set of master disks. The disk is the same for both Novell file server operating systems.

Always use the latest WSGEN disk from either set (NW386 or NW286) as your standard WSGEN disk, since it is universal.

This disk contains all the programs required to generate the IPX and ODI drivers. We shall ignore ODI drivers for the time being, and concentrate on generating native IPX. The ODI driver, which is now preferred over this method, is discussed in the next section.

WSGEN is a user-friendly program; it acts as a menu-driven front end for the Novell linker; NLINK.EXE. This program links IPX.OBJ and the network driver *.OBJ together, producing IPX.COM.

WSGEN can be run from floppy disk or hard disk. The latter need not be local; it might be found on a network drive.

WSGEN default drivers support

Novell supports a limited number of network adaptors. Figure 7.10 shows a list of the network cards that Novell supports by default. The drivers are automatically found on the WSGEN disk.

```
3Com 3c503 EtherLink II   v3.01EC (901101)
3Com 3c505 EtherLink Plus (Assy 2012)  v4.12EC (910117)
3Com EtherLink/MC 3C523   v2.36EC (901207)
IBM LAN Support Program Driver   v2.60 (901031)
IBM PCN II & Baseband  v1.15 (900905)
IBM Token-Ring  v2.60 (901022)
NetWare NE/2   v2.02EC (900718)
NetWare NE1000   v3.02EC (900831)
NetWare NE2000   v1.05EC (900718)
NetWare Turbo RX-Net   v2.11 (901217)
```

Figure 7.10 WSGEN default drivers support.

If you are using one of the cards listed in Figure 7.10, you do not necessarily need any other disks in order to produce an IPX.COM. However, you might find that the drivers provided by Novell are now out of date, and that you have a far more efficient driver contained in the original network card package. If you do not see your network adaptor card listed, or if you wish to overwrite the driver with a more up-to-date version, then you must add another driver to the list.

Adding network drivers to WSGEN

Manufacturers of network adaptor cards generally provide Novell network support by issuing the Novell drivers on one disk. WSGEN can then be instructed to read any third-party drivers by pressing the <INS> key when the driver list is presented. These third-party disks are recognized by WSGEN because they have the following type of disk label:

LAN_DRV_xxx

The xxx is designated by the network adaptor manufacturer.

At the top level on each one of these disks you should find two different types of file (Figure 7.11).

- The first type are the *.LAN files. These store information regarding the type of driver available and what the parameter options are.

- The *.OBJ files are the object files used in the linking process to be combined with IPX.OBJ to produce the IPX.COM program.

When WSGEN starts to run, it automatically searches through all the floppy disk drivers, looking for disks with the LAN_DRV_xxx label. If successful, it automatically starts to read the description inside each *.LAN file. It then presents them to the user as part of its normal list of drivers, which can be selected by the user to generate an IPX.COM file.

Warning: WSGEN is notorious for dying on you. It is constantly looking for add-on disks, and if it finds a disk which even half conforms to its expectations then it seems to hang without generating any error message. In such situations you should reboot, but before you run WSGEN again, check the floppy disk labels, and also check for the existence of the *.LAN and *.OBJ files at the disk's top level.

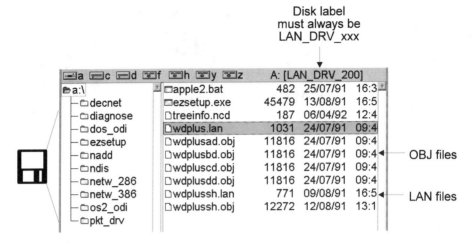

Figure 7.11 Format of LAN driver disks for IPX generation.

Running WSGEN from floppies

Wherever possible you should run WSGEN from the hard disk. However, if you are going to visit workstations or clients on site, it is very useful to be able to generate IPX from one of two floppies. This method is ideal for the *ad hoc* approach. It is an important addition to your first-aid kit of troubleshooting disks that you need to carry when you visit clients or users (Figure 7.12).

To run WSGEN from floppy disk you need to copy the WSGEN master disk to another disk. This has to be done, because owing to copy protection the WSGEN program will attempt to write back on the disk the newly linked IPX.COM file. Make

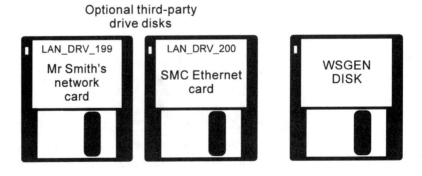

Figure 7.12 WSGEN and adaptor card driver disks.

sure you use DISKCOPY to copy the disks and not just COPY or XCOPY, since it is important to copy the disk labels. You also need a driver disk from the manufacturer of the network adaptor, if it is not one of the cards that Novell supports by default.

Next put in the WSGEN disk and type WSGEN to start the program. Press the <INS> key to introduce the third-party Novell disk driver to the available list of network adaptors supported. Most LAN cards require the use of three resources to communicate with the computer system. These are:

- IRQ (interrupt request channel)
- I/O base address
- RAM buffer area

The LAN adaptor does not have the capability to share these resources.

Running WSGEN from a hard disk

This method is not discussed in the Novell manuals, but I have been using it for many years. It is a far more convenient approach for system administrators when using floppy disks to generate the IPX. It is fast and easy to use, and all the drivers that might be required for the different types of network adaptor are on the hard disk.

The technique consists of setting up a set of appropriate directories and subdirectories, from which you can generate IPX.COM without the use of any floppies. The suggested structure is as follows (Figure 7.13).

First, create a directory called NWSHELLS: this is your main directory from which you run the WSGEN.EXE program. Under this directory you create a subdirectory called WSGEN, into which you copy all the contents of the Novell-issued WSGEN disk. It is best to use XCOPY A:*.* /s/e for this instead of just the COPY program in case there are any subdirectories on the disk.

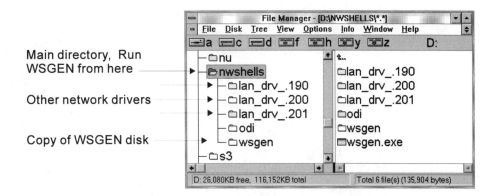

Figure 7.13 A suggested directory structure for setting up WSGEN on a hard disk.

Next, copy all the optional LAN drivers potentially required in the future for your system into subdirectories under the NWSHELL directory. Give each subdirectory the same name as the electronic disk label. This should always take the form LAN_DRV_.???.

Note: since you can only have eight characters in DOS for a directory name, with three letters for the extension, you need to split a given disk label such as LAN_DRV_190 into LAN_DRV_.190.

Now copy WSGEN.EXE from the WSGEN subdirectory to directory NWSHELL.

You are now ready to run the WSGEN program by going to the NWSHELL directory and running WSGEN.EXE. It should automatically detect all the extra network adaptors that could be defined within your system.

Managing multiple different network adaptor drivers

Using the above structure you can put all the different types of network adaptor in one place. You must document what you have done, so that other network managers understand and adhere to the system.

When any new network adaptor becomes available in your system, all you have to do is create yet another subdirectory to accommodate it, and give this the appropriate name. Every so often you need to review your directory structure to remove obsolete drivers from the system; always make sure that you have a backup copy first, in case of error.

The manufacturers of network adaptors are not renowned for being very imaginative. You might come across two disk labels that are the same; for example SMC Ether cards use disk labels LAN_DRV_200, while the old Western Digital Ethernet card also use LAN_DRV_200. In situations like this you must decide which takes priority and disable the other by changing the directory name to a non-standard name structure until needed.

Novell ODI drivers

Overview

The ODI is a data link specification jointly developed by Apple Computer and Novell and published to the networking industry in 1989. The strategic goal of ODI is to provide seamless network integration at the transport, network and data link levels. ODI simplifies the development of network drivers for a wide variety of network adaptors and network transport protocol stacks. The result is easier access to a wide variety of networked resources without requiring multiple network connections or additional investments in hardware and software.

Understanding ODI drivers

ODI provides an alternative to the use of WSGEN to configure IPX.COM to support a specific network adaptor card. As the IPX program talked directly to the adaptor card, it was not possible to allow other protocols to use its services (Figure 7.14).

This led to Novell developing the ODI standard: their answer to users who require to run more than one protocol simultaneously, such as Novell's IPX and the UNIX TCP/IP protocols (Figure 7.15).

Novell decided to solve the problem by using yet another level of redirection. They devised a universal set of functions with the ability to describe any network card, and then bind this to standard protocols such as IPX.

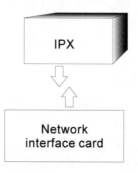

Figure 7.14 Dedicated IPX takes control of NIC.

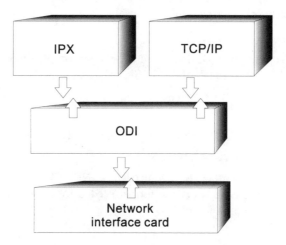

Figure 7.15 An example of a typical ODI set-up.

Strategy in using ODI drivers

ODI drivers provide the network manager with a far more flexible method of defining protocols over networks. One set of protocols can be issued to all users with different network adaptor types, whereas previously each IPX.COM had to be customized. It also provides a very user-friendly method of supporting different protocols on the same network. However, if you have no intention of using TCP/IP, if you never require UNIX NFS support, or if you are a pure IPX user, then you do not need to bother with ODI drivers. Nevertheless, it is still worth considering using ODI drivers, for the following reasons:

✓ Extra memory-saving benefits

✓ No need to generate IPX.COM for each type of NIC

✓ ODI multi-protocol support

✓ Novell commitment to ODI as its future development platform

✓ Novell only supports TCP/IP on ODI drivers

✓ Easier to manage

✓ Easier to configure thanks to the NET.CFG file

The disadvantages are:

✗ More files required to be run at the workstation

✗ IPXODI is slightly less efficient then the native IPX (assuming same packet size)

✗ Slightly higher memory requirements (by 2 kbytes)

The good points, I believe, outweigh the bad points; I suggest that Novell network managers should consider ODI drivers as standard on all workstations.

How to use ODI drivers

To load the ODI drivers on a Windows or DOS workstation, you need to load four different files, all of them TSR programs:

• MLID.COM (customized for your network adaptor card)

• LSL.COM

• IPXODI.COM (to be bound to the LSL protocol)

• NETX.EXE (or BNETX.EXE for the burst mode version)

A further file is needed – NET.CFG – which stores all the hardware parameters in a text file format needed for the drivers. It is read by NETX.EXE at the time they are loaded.

ODI architectural structure

The ODI standard is not just one standard, but is made up of a collection of interconnecting standards. Novell, when designing ODI, had the OSI seven-layer model very much in mind. It fits in very well with that model.

The ODI standard is broken up into two main sublayers (Figure 7.16). The upper layer is the LSL (link support layer), which manages communication with the protocols. The lower layer is the MLID (Multiple Link Interface Driver), pronounced 'EMLID'. In terms of the OSI model, LSL is equivalent to the services provided at the logical data link layer, which is part of layer 3

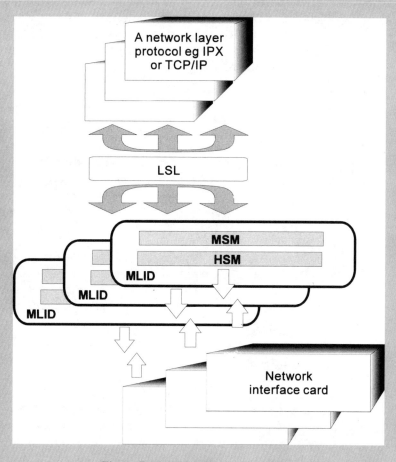

Figure 7.16 ODI architecture structure.

(network layer). It defines a set of universal functions that can be used for point-to-point communications, regardless of the type of underlying network, such as Ethernet or Token Ring.

The services of the LSL driver are used by protocol developers to bind their protocols to the services of the network, without having to worry about the type of network actually being used. The LSL provides its service thanks to the MLID layer, which is actually responsible for managing the network adaptor hardware.

The LSL also operates as an automatic switchboard, allowing for multiple protocols to access the resources of the adaptor card simultaneously.

The future, according to Novell, is to use ODI drivers, rather than native IPX drivers. I suggest that, where possible, you try to implement ODI drivers on workstations, to benefit from ODI's better memory management, and its potential for supporting multiple protocols.

The MLID layer

The MLID is a network interface card driver developed to the ODI specifications. The MLID controls communication between the LAN board and the link support layer. It is divided into two sublayers: the media support module (MSM) and the lowest-layer hardware support module (HSM). The MSM is source code provided by Novell that implements the standard functions of LAN drivers into ODI for each of the standard media types. The HSM is the code written by the developer to handle the LAN board details.

When the MLID receives a packet of data, it removes the media access information (MAC header) and passes the packet up to the LSL. Since the media details are invisible to the LSL, this modular design provides true media independence.

Link support layer (LSL)

The LSL is the clever part of ODI. It allows a single driver to support multiple protocols, and a single protocol to use multiple drivers. When the LSL receives a packet of data from the MLID, it acts as a switchboard by determining which protocol stack should receive the packet. This eliminates the need to write separate drivers for each frame/protocol combination, thereby dramatically reducing the number of drivers that a developer has to write and a customer has to install.

Protocol stacks

The ODI structure allows multiple protocol stacks to receive packets of information from the LSL (Figure 7.17), whatever medium or LAN board type is used for communication. The LSL removes the protocol-specific header information and passes the packets on to other higher-layer protocols or applications. The most popular types of protocol stack are NCP/SPX/IPX, NFS/TCP/IP and OSI. The modular design of ODI is the key to its flexibility. This modularity is created by making sure that the protocol stacks are unaware of media knowledge and that the MLIDs are unaware of protocol knowledge. The drivers and the protocol stacks operate independently of each other, making it easy to add new media or new protocols to the file system.

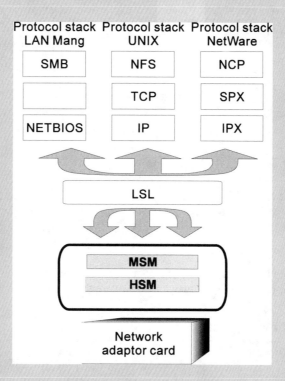

Figure 7.17 An example of ODI multiprotocol support.

Comparing IPX ODI and dedicated IPX

Comparing functions

Frame types supported

Dedicated IPX	ODI
Ethernet frame types supported: 802.3, Ethernet II	Ethernet frame types supported: 802.2, 802.3, Ethernet II, SNAP
Token Ring frames supported: 802.5	Token Ring frames supported: 802.5, 802.2, SNAP

When using ODI, a driver allows the user to support multiple frame types easily on the same network. This opens the network up to more products and platforms.

Protocol types supported

Dedicated IPX	ODI
Supports a single protocol stack	Supports multiple protocol stacks simultaneously
IPX, AppleTalk (on the server)	IPX, TCP/IP, AppleTalk, OSI, etc.

The ODI drivers benefit from their ability to support multiple protocols under a single card and driver. This provides easier maintenance for hooking up multiple clients to a single server and accessing resources from host servers.

Physical board support

Dedicated IPX	ODI
Supports up to four physical boards in server	Supports up to 255 logical boards in server or as many physical boards as will fit in the machine

The ODI standard provides support for a larger number of LAN boards. This allows for balancing of network load over multiple cards.

Throughput capacity

Dedicated IPX	ODI
Maximum packet size: Up to 4 only in powers of 2 (512 bits, 1 Kbyte, 2 Kbytes, 4 Kbytes)	Maximum packet size: Up to 24 Kbytes depending on media and board limitations

The ODI drivers can substantially increase total network throughput.

Ease of maintenance

Dedicated IPX	ODI
Drivers may not be unloaded	Drivers can be loaded on the fly

Additional features

Dedicated IPX	ODI
	Lanalyzer for NetWare
	Packet burst
	Locally administered node addresses

The ODI driver provides a number of functions that are not available when using the dedicated IPX drivers.

Performance test: dedicated IPX versus ODI IPX

Figure 7.18 shows the results of a comparison test between IPX.COM and IPXODI.COM, performed using the PERFORM3 program. All the parameters on the network were kept identical during the two tests; the only difference was the version of the IPX program. Therefore any differences highlighted in the test results were due to the different IPX implementations.

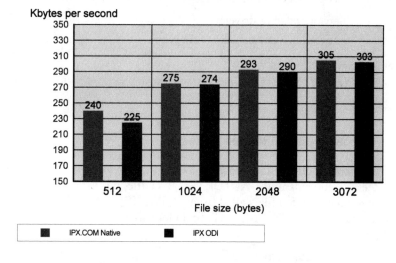

Figure 7.18 Testing workstation network performance:
IPX ODI versus native IPX.COM
(test performed on a NetWare 3.11 server with one user).

From the figures in Figure 7.18 it can be seen that there is a slight difference between native IPX and ODI IPX; the IPX ODI version just has the edge over the native IPX.COM, even though it has to use an extra software layer for data transmission. However, it is internally optimized to a greater extent than the native IPX.COM.

Installing ODI drivers

To activate connections using ODI drivers to a Novell file server, there are a minimum of four distinct files that have to be loaded as TSR programs. It is essential that they are loaded in the correct order. They are:

(1) link support layer (LSL.COM)

(2) network adaptor ODI driver

(3) protocol support (IPXODI.COM)

(4) NETX.EXE or BNETX.EXE (the burst mode version)

Each one of these modules can be loaded in a number of different ways. The most basic is under conventional memory. However, most of these drivers can be loaded high using the DOS 5.0 (or above) command LOADHIGH.

Workstations that support source routing on Token Rings will also need another program called ROUTE.COM

When loaded, the ODI software looks for a text file called NET.CFG. This contains defaults covering three important areas stored under different headings:

• network adaptor driver

• network driver hardware settings

• protocol bindings

The NET.CFG file is normally stored in the same directory as all the other ODI programs.

Typical batch file to load drivers

Normally, you would load the network drivers via a batch file. Some people put these commands in the AUTOEXEC.BAT file, but I think it is better to place them in a separate batch file, called from AUTOEXEC.BAT. This file, which we can give a name such as NOVELL.BAT, could look like this:

```
C:
CD \NOVELL\ODI
LSL
REM Load the specific LAN Adaptor driver
WDPLUS
```

```
IPXODI
BNETX
F:
LOGIN
```

We shall now examine each component in greater detail.

The LSL.COM program

The link support layer has to be the first program loaded, because it establishes the groundwork for the ODI drivers. Basically, the LSL acts as the intermediary between the network adaptor and the protocols that will be bound on the network adaptor card.

The LSL program is very flexible; it can provide for one network card to service different types of protocol, or it can provide for several different network adaptor cards to service the same protocol. It can also perform any combination of mixing and matching different protocols to different network adaptor cards.

When run, the program looks something like this:

```
C:\NOVELL\ODI>lsl
NetWare Link Support Layer  v2.00 (920904)
(C) Copyright 1990, 1992 Novell, Inc.  All Righ's Reserved.


Max Boards 4, Max Stacks 4


C:\NOVELL\ODI>
```

The program has reported that it is set up to define up to four different network cards. This number can be increased. Each network adaptor can potentially have a different associated protocol stack.

LSL.COM is a very small program; it normally takes up about 5 Kbytes of memory. To check this, type the DOS MEM/C command:

```
C:\NOVELL\ODI>LSL
C:\NOVELL\ODI>MEM /C
```

```
Conventional Memory :
```

Name	Size in Decimal		Size in Hex
MSDOS	15440	(15.1K)	3C50
HIMEM	1072	(1.0K)	430
EMM386	3232	(3.2K)	CA0
SSTORDRV	44496	(43.5')	ADD0
COMMAND	2624	(2.6K)	A40
DOSKEY	4128	(4.0K)	1020

```
   Name              Size in Decimal        Size in Hex
   ------------      --------------------   ------------

   LSL               4912     (  4.8K)      1330
   FREE                64     (  0.1K)        40
   FREE               160     (  0.2K)        A0
   FREE            579056     (565.5K)      8D5F0


Total  FREE :      579280     (565.7K)


Total bytes available to programs
(Conventional+Upper) :         649216     (634.0K)
Largest executable program size :
                               579056     (565.5K)
Largest available upper memory block :
                                37232     ( 36.4K)


   4587520 bytes total EMS memory
   4194304 bytes free EMS memory

   7602176 bytes total contiguous extended memory
         0 bytes available contiguous extended memory
   3129344 bytes available XMS memory
           resident in High Memory Area
```

In this case you can see that LSL.COM has only taken up 4.8 Kbytes of memory.

Reducing LSL.COM memory overhead

If even this is too much, LSL.COM can be loaded into high memory using the LOADHIGH LSL command, or just LH LSL as part of the normal batch file sequence. If you load LSL.COM using the LOADHIGH command, assuming you have set up all your HIMEM.SYS drivers correctly and have enough room in your high memory for LSL.COM, you will see the following improvement. In this case LSL.COM is unloaded from the conventional memory by typing LSL U, and then reloaded into high memory:

```
C:\NOVELL\ODI>LSL U
C:\NOVELL\ODI>LH LSL
C:\NOVELL\ODI>MEM /C

Conventional Memory :

   Name              Size in Decimal        Size in Hex
   ------------      --------------------   ------------

   MSDOS             15440    ( 15.1K)      3C50
   HIMEM              1072    (  1.0K)       430
   EMM386             3232    (  3.2K)       CA0
```

```
     Name                   Size in Decimal        Size in Hex
 -------------          ----------------------    -------------

    SSTORDRV               44496    ( 43.5K)         ADD0
    COMMAND                 2624    (  2.6K)         A40
    DOSKEY                  4128    (  4.0K)         1020
    FREE                      64    (  0.1K)         40
    FREE                     160    (  0.2K)         A0
    FREE                  582864    (569.2K)         8E4D0


Total  FREE :            583088    (569.4K)


Upper Memory :

     Name                   Size in Decimal        Size in Hex
 -------------          ----------------------    -------------

    SYSTEM                176720    (172.6K)         2B250
    LSL                     4912    (  4.8K)         1330
    FREE                     160    (  0.2K)         A0
    FREE                   41472    ( 40.5K)         A200
    FREE                   24544    ( 24.0K)         5FE0


Total  FREE :             66176    ( 64.6K)


Total bytes available to programs
Conventional+Upper) :        649264    (634.0K)
Largest executable program size :
                             582864    (569.2K)
Largest available upper memory block :
                              41472    ( 40.5K)


   4587520 bytes total EMS memory
   4194304 bytes free EMS memory

   7602176 bytes total contiguous extended memory
         0 bytes available contiguous extended memory
   3129344 bytes available XMS memory
           MS-DOS resident in High Memory Area
```

Table 7.2 Loading LSL.COM: summary of conventional memory requirements.

Using conventional memory	Using upper memory (via LOADHIGH)
4.7 Kbytes	0.1 Kbytes

The network adaptor driver

This is the program that actually makes the connection between the physical network adaptor and the logical requests that are made upon it. This program is normally provided by the manufacturer of the network adaptor card. If it is an ODI-compliant driver, it will conform to the MLID standard. The program name will differ from one manufacture to another. Examples of typical names are listed in Table 7.3. All these drivers have a number of things in common, as detailed below.

Loading and unloading drivers dynamically
Each one of these drivers can be loaded and unloaded dynamically. In the following example I have loaded up and then unloaded the WDPLUS driver:

```
C:\NOVELL\ODI>wdplus
Western Digital LAN Adaptor MLID v1.02 (910621)
Copyright Western Digital Corporation 1991,
All rights Reserved.

EtherCard PLUS (WD8003EB)
Int 5, Port 2A0, Mem D4000, Node Address C0952D1C
Max Frame 1514 bytes, Line Speed 10 Mbps
Board 1, Frame ETHERNET_802.3

C:\NOVELL\ODI>wdplus u

WDPLUS MLID successfully removed.
C:\NOVELL\ODI>
```

Loading into upper memory
Like the LSL.COM program, the ODI network driver can be loaded into upper memory, thus freeing conventional memory. This is done using the LOADHIGH command:

```
C:\NOVELL\ODI>lOADHIGH WDPLUS
Western Digital LAN Adaptor MLID v1.02 (910621)
Copyright Western Digital Corporation 1991,
All rights Reserved.

EtherCard PLUS (WD8003EB)
Int 5, Port 2A0, Mem D4000, Node Address C0952D1C
Max Frame 1514 bytes, Line Speed 10 Mbps
Board 1, Frame ETHERNET_802.3

C:\NOVELL\ODI>
```

Table 7.3 Typical network adaptor ODI drivers.

Network adaptor	ODI driver name
SMC EtherCard PLUS	SMC8000.COM
WD EtherCard PLUS	WDPLUS.COM
Novell 16 bit Ethernet	NE2000.COM
Novell 8 bit Ethernet	NE1000.COM
3COM 3c503 cards	3C503.COM

Table 7.4 Loading a typical network adaptor driver: summary of conventional memory requirements.

Using conventional memory	Using upper memory (via LOADHIGH)
4 Kbytes	0.1 Kbytes

Use NET.CFG configurations

They all refer to the NET.CFG text file for information on the hardware setting of the adaptor card installed. These are categorized as shown in Table 7.5.

Each network adaptor, depending on how it is configured, may require a different set of the options in Table 7.5 to be specified within the NET.CFG file. There is so much variety that it is difficult to generalize. The best advice here is to read the manuals that come with the actual network adaptor card, under the section ODI drivers. In that section you will find a copy of a typical NET.CFG file for the particular card. This file could now be used to build around all the other options that are required to go into NET.CFG. However, if you already have a NET.CFG, you would now append the two files together by using the normal DOS APPEND command:

```
append [existing NET.CFG]to[new NET.CFG]
```

where both the existing and the new configuration files must include the current path designations.

NET.CFG stores a lot of different information: not only the hardware setting, but also the different options associated with the protocols. When a new network adaptor is installed it is very important that only the section within NET.CFG dealing

Table 7.5 Network adaptor hardware setting in NET.CFG.

DMA [#1 | #2] channel_number

INT [#1 | #2] interrupt_request_number

MEM [#1 | #2] hex_starting_address [hex_length]

PORT [#1 | #2] hex_starting_address [hex_number_of_ports]

NODE ADDRESS hex_address

SLOT number

with hardware setting and driver name is changed; everything else must be left unaltered.

Some network cards need special DMA channels, and others need special memory ports. However, one common parameter that most cards seem to insist upon is exclusive access to an interrupt line. This is discussed in Chapter 6.

Normally, if you are using the network adaptor card in its default setting you do not need to put any hardware-related command into the NET.CFG file

A typical NET.CFG that contains relevant information for the LAN driver might look like Figure 7.19. In this case network adaptor number 1 is defined as follows:

- I/O port   =   2A0   for 20 hex bytes
- Mem   =   D4000 for 2000 hex bytes
- Interrupt   =   5

The driver is called WDPLUS. This driver is extremely important in the ODI standard. By using this name we shall later bind different protocols to the network card.

There are two other very interesting software-related settings that the network adaptor drivers can use:

- FRAME frame_type
- PROTOCOL name hex_protocol_ID_frame_type

The FRAME type option
This is designed for network adaptors that can internally support different types of protocol packet, such as the Ethernet 802.3 and Ethernet II standards. Using this

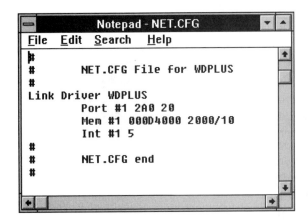

Figure 7.19 Typical NET.CFG.

option you can tell the network card what type of packet it is to use at the data link layer. Note that you are only working at OSI layer number 2 (the data link layer), and not at any higher layer, such as the packet size of IPX.

The most common types of packet are:

- ETHERNET_802.3
- ETHERNET_802.2
- ETHERNET_II
- ETHERNET_SNAP
- TOKEN-RING
- TOKEN-RING_SNAP
- IBM_PCN2_802.2

You do not normally need to specify this option at all, because the default is acceptable. In this case, for example, if you type this line in NET.CFG:

```
Frame ETHERNET_802.2
```

the frame type is reassigned as Ethernet 802.2. The default frame type is ETHERNET_802.3.

The PROTOCOL option

This field is not often used. It allows a new protocol to be handled by the existing network card. This is done by giving the protocol a unique identifier. To change the protocol name, add the following line to NET.CFG:

```
Protocol <name> ID <frame type>
```

where <name> is the protocol name, ID is the protocol ID number, and <frame type> is the frame type being used. The frame type is defined by the FRAME option used for the protocol. For example:

```
Protocol IPX 8137 Ethernet_II
```

This indicates that the protocol name is being changed to IPX-designated protocol ID 8137 within the Ethernet II frame type.

I have known this technique to be used by a company which wanted its network packets to be secure, so they gave all nodes on the network the same unique protocol number.

Some typical protocol identifiers are listed in Table 7.6.

The IPXODI program

This program will bind itself to the appropriate network adaptor and provide the IPX protocol service to other programs. It actually loads not one but three different

Table 7.6 Typical protocol identifiers.

Protocol frame types	Identifier code
ETHERNET_802.3	0
ETHERNET_802.2	E0
ETHERNET_II	8137
ETHERNET_SNAP	8137
TOKEN-RING	E0
TOKEN-RING_SNAP	8137
IBM_PCN2_802.2	E0
IBM_PCN2_SNAP	8137
NOVELL_RX-NET	FA
IP	800
ARP	806

protocols, the most important of which is IPX, which is normally loaded by IPXODI.COM:

- IPX (interpacket exchange) at layer 3
- SPX (sequenced packet exchange) at layer 4
- diagnostic responder protocols at layer 7

IPXODI has the following options:

```
C:\NOVELL\ODI>ipxodi -?

NetWare IPX/SPX Protocol  v2.00 (920904)
(C) Copyright 1990-1992 Novell, Inc.  All Rights Reserved.

Available command line options:
/?      Display this help screen.
/D      Eliminate Diagnostic Responder - Reduces size by 3K.
/A      Eliminate Diagnostic Responder and SPX - Reduces size by 9K.

/C=[path\]filename.ext
        Specify a configuration file to use (Default is NET.CFG).

/U      Unload resident IPXODI from memory.
/F      Forcibly unload resident IPXODI from memory, regardless of
        programs loaded above it.  Using this option can cause a
        machine to crash if applications are still using IPX/SPX.


C:\NOVELL\ODI>
```

As can be seen, you do not need to load all three layers of protocol. Most Novell-aware programs only use IPX and not SPX calls, so if memory is tight you can try to do away with the SPX calls support, saving about 5 Kbytes. You can also do away with the diagnostic responder, saving another 3 Kbytes. However, I think it is well worth loading the full IPX ODI option, especially for its diagnostic responder option. This is particularly true in large network installations. It can then be used by special Novell management programs to integrate the performance remotely and troubleshoot the workstation.

Just like the other programs, IPXODI can be loaded into HIGH memory:

```
C:\NOVELL\ODI>lh IPXODI


NetWare IPX/SPX Protocol  v2.00 (920904)
(C) Copyright 1990-1992 Novell, Inc.  All Rights Reserved.


Bound to logical board 1 (WDPLUS) : Protocol ID 0


C:\NOVELL\ODI>
```

This can provide the memory savings listed in Table 7.7.

Loading ODI drivers

As previously discussed, the ODI drivers eliminate the requirement to generate IPX. There is a set sequence of operations that must be executed in order to load the ODI drivers; however these operations are very flexible. Each section can be modified or controlled by the NET.CFG file: this is a simple text file, containing all sorts of parameters that will be referred to in the loading of the ODI drivers.

To connect to a NetWare server using ODI drivers, you need these four basic programs:

- LSL.COM: this is the link support layer program, which is TSR program
- the actual ODI LAN driver that comes with the NIC: this is normally provided by the manufacturer of the card:
- the protocol that gets bound to the NIC. In Novell terms this would be the IPXODI.COM program; you could just as easily also have had the TCP\IP protocol drivers

Table 7.7 Loading the full IPXODI.COM: summary of conventional memory requirements.

Using conventional memory	Using upper memory (via LOADHIGH)
15 Kbytes (full)	0.1 Kbyte
12 Kbytes (IPX and SPX)	0.1 Kbyte
7 Kbytes (IPX only)	0.1 Kbyte

- the NETX program: this provides the NetWare core protocol support, and also acts as a translator between the workstation operating system and the Novell NetWare core protocols

  To summarize, the sequence of operations is:

- LSL.COM
- ODI NIC drivers
- bind protocol
- load BNETX (or NETX non burst mode version)

Converting IPX to ODI IPX

Because of the advantages of ODI drivers compared with dedicated IPX, Novell are to assist in upgrading DOS workstations from dedicated IPX drivers to ODI. This will be achieved by the utility WSUPGRD, which is intended to be used by system administrators on large sites to upgrade a number of workstations that are all similarly configured. It is executed from the system log-in script. It then scans for the dedicated IPX.COM file on the workstations, and determines which driver was linked in with the SHGEN utility and what hardware options were selected.

It will then reference an installation file created by the system administrator to select the appropriate ODI driver, and will install it along with the ODI LSL module and an appropriate NET.CFG file (which may be configured by the system administrator).

NDIS drivers

Understanding NDIS drivers

Simply put, NDIS is to Microsoft what ODI is to Novell. Each standard has been developed to allow multiple protocol stacks to be supported simultaneously on the same NIC. It also allows for supporting the same protocol on multiple network cards, or on any combination. The network device interface standard (NDIS) was jointly developed by 3Com and Microsoft. It is now widely used. Microsoft are pushing this standard very hard. It is used extensively in Windows NT. Other major networking companies have decided to adopt the NDIS standard by default rather than ODI from Novell, including Banyan-Vines and DEC Pathworks.

Internal NDIS structure

Figure 7.20 shows the basic structure of the NDIS standard.

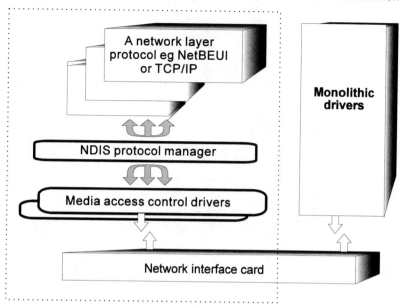

Figure 7.20 NDIS basic structure.

The NDIS standard defines the following:

- how network/transport protocols should be written by third-party developers so that they can make service calls to the protocol manager
- Microsoft/3Com NDIS protocol manager code
- how media access control drivers should be written by third-party NIC hardware manufacturers so that they can be used by the NDIS protocol manager

Network/transport protocol drivers

Network protocol drivers manage the transfer events between the higher protocols and the media access control drivers. They are hardware-independent.

Protocol manager

The protocol manager is the heart of the NDIS standard. It is a special driver (PORTMAN.OS2 for OS/2 or PORTMAN.DOS for DOS) that is loaded as part of the CONFIG.SYS file. It can support multiple protocols, acting as a switching system to pass the appropriate data between the network protocols and the adaptor cards. When a system uses multiple protocol stacks, the protocol manager daisychains the packets from stack to stack until the packet is recognized and received. When it is loaded it looks for the PROTOCOL.INI file, which contains configuration information about all the protocol and adaptor drivers that it has to manage.

Media access control drivers

Media access control drivers ensure that all NICs from different manufacturers can be used in the same way. Once the appropriate media access control driver has been configured, all NICs look the same to the NDIS protocol manager. They work directly with the NIC, acting as an intermediary between the protocol manager and the hardware.

Monolithic drivers

These are special drivers that combine the network layer protocol and media access control function into a single driver. This means that they directly talk to the NIC. Although in theory they can be slightly faster, they are very inflexible. They are also unable to cope with multiple protocol support on the same NIC. This means that they are not NDIS-compliant. An example of a monolithic driver is the old Novell IPX.COM, which had to be generated for each type of NIC.

ODI versus NDIS

Overview

The NDIS and ODI protocols are very similar; they were both designed to solve the same problem, and both specifications promote schemes to support multiple protocols on a network. There are various technical differences, which are outlined below.

Protocol media awareness

NDIS protocol stacks have some media awareness. Some NDIS compliant-protocol stacks recognize and support different media frame formats, such as Ethernet 802.3 or Token Ring 802.5, or both. ODI was designed to support any network transport transparently, regardless of the underlying medium. For example, it will integrate FDDI, wireless technology or other media types into your present network without the need to rewrite or change the protocol stacks.

Multiprotocol switching

The NDIS protocol manager daisychains the packets from stack to stack, until the packet is recognized and received. This means that the order in which protocols are loaded is important. It works well as long as the data packet always needs to go to the first protocol stack in the chain, but if the traffic is evenly spread across several stacks, or a new stack is added later, then the protocol manager will spend a lot of time toggling between stacks looking for the right route for data transmission. Microsoft have suggested that NDIS protocols should be loaded in order of network traffic use to speed up the throughput.

Under ODI, the LSL determines which protocol stack should receive each packet of information, and the loading order is irrelevant. A stack can be added to the system and ODI automatically supports it.

Loading drivers

This is one of the nicest things about ODI compared with NDIS. You can load and unload ODI drivers from the DOS prompt line; the NDIS protocol manager (v2.01) has to be loaded in the CONFIG.SYS file, while ODI is a TSR.

Version compatibility

Another important distinction between the two specifications relates to backward compatibility. NDIS tends to demand greater compliance with use of the latest drivers then ODI. For example, if you are using NDIS v2.0 drivers and want to upgrade to Windows NT, you need to update your NDIS drivers, since the NT protocol manager requires all NDIS drivers to be v3.0 drivers. This is also sometimes true with ODI drivers, but each ODI layer seems to operate far more independently. In the above example, if you do not have the latest NDIS drivers, but have access to the card's ODI drivers then it can be used to connect into Windows NT through Novell's ODI-to-NDIS conversion program, called ODINSUP. This module allows the customer to talk to the NDIS protocol stacks unmodified over the ODI driver.

Summary of differences

ODI

- ✓ Backed by Novell as default
- ✓ Drivers loaded from DOS prompt line
- ✓ Direct switching between Protocol and adaptor drivers
- ✓ Used by default in NetWare 4.x and above.
- ✗ Not supported by Microsoft
- ✗ Cannot dynamically change node address

NDIS

- ✓ Backed by Microsoft
- ✓ Widely supported
- ✓ Supported as default by Banyan-Vines and DEC Pathworks
- ✓ Supported as default in Windows NT
- ✗ Daisychain switching between protocol and adaptor drivers
- ✗ Driver has to be loaded in CONFIG.SYS
- ✗ Some NDIS protocols are media aware

ODINSUP.COM: the ODI to NDIS converter

Overview

The support program ODINSUP.COM implements the NDIS standard on top of the ODI standard. This means that ODI adaptor drivers can now talk to NDIS protocol stacks, allowing users to standardize on ODI device drivers regardless of whether they are using NDIS- or ODI-compliant protocols (Figure 7.21).

The ODINSUP program acts as a translator between the NDIS and ODI standards. It creates a special ODI protocol stack that is then used to support NDIS drivers. This allows NDIS protocol stacks to run unmodified over the ODI LSL and talk to an ODI LAN driver. NDIS protocols such as IBM's NetBEUI or DEC's LAT can now run over ODI drivers unmodified.

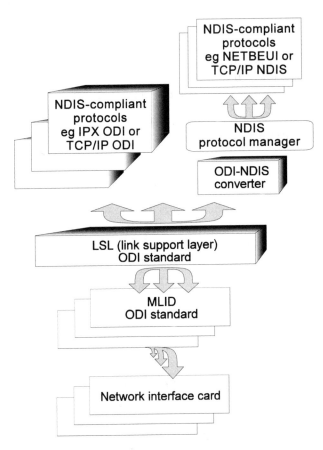

Figure 7.21 ODI to NDIS architecture.

Advantages of ODINSUP.COM

✓ Users can standardize on ODI NIC

✓ Novell ODI users can now use NDIS-compliant protocols

✓ ODI protocol stacks can now coexist with NDIS protocol stacks

✗ Extra memory overhead

✗ Two configuration files needed: NET.CFG for ODI and PROTOCOL.INI for NDIS

✗ Can get very confusing

✗ Difficult to troubleshoot

Using ODINSUP.COM

To get ODINSUP working in your machine, you need to do the following:

(1) Ensure that you have all the up-to-date ODI MLID network adaptor drivers; the old NDIS drivers will no longer be needed

(2) Ensure that the NDIS PROTMAN device driver is loaded in CONFIG.SYS. It must be loaded before the ODINSUP module is loaded

(3) From the DOS command line, load the ODINSUP.COM module after loading the ODI LSL program. It is a simple, small TSR program that can easily be loaded as part of the AUTOEXEC.BAT sequence or as a special log-on batch file. An example of a typical log-on batch file is given in the next section.

Detailed installation considerations

NET.CFG modification

To get ODINSUP working correctly, you need to modify the NET.CFG file, to introduce to LSL a special protocol stack called the NDIS translator. This takes the following form:

```
Protocol ODINSUP
    Bind SMC8000
    BUFFERED
```

This assumes that you are using the SMC Ethernet card.

The BUFFERED command is very important. It must be placed after the Bind command.fIt allows double buffering of received packets for presentation to the NDIS protocol stacks. Some NDIS protocols rely heavily on the MAC interrupt request function, which may not perform very well with ODINSUP if it is not BUFFERED. When activated, it provides the ability to generate asynchronous interrupts on demand by the protocol. Since ODINSUP does not have direct access to a hardware device, this function must be emulated in software.

One of the peculiar aspects of ODINSUP is that it requires that the underlying Ethernet or Token Ring ODI LAN drivers have a number of different frame types enabled at the same time. These are:

Ethernet	Token Ring
ETHERNET 802.2	TOKEN-RING 802.5
ETHERNET SNAP	TOKEN-RING SNAP
ETHERNET_II	

This is very simply done through the NET.CFG file. The different frame types support is requested by specifying the frame keyword under the appropriate ODI LAN drivers section header.

Typical additions to the NET.CFG file might be as follows:

```
Link driver ne1000
        frame ethernet_802.3
        frame ethernet_802.2
        frame ethernet_snap
        frame ethernet_ii
```

A typical NET.CFG could look like the following:

```
#
#       NET.CFG File for SMC PLUS
#

Protocol ODINSUP
 Bind  SMC8000
 BUFFERED

Link Driver SMC8000
 Port20
 Mem #1 000D4000 2000/10
 Int #1 5
 slot 1
 Frame ETHERNET_802.2
 Frame ETHERNET_II
 Frame ETHERNET_SNAP
 Protocol IPX 0 ETHERNET_802.3
#
#       NET.CFG end
#.
```

On running the appropriate MLID driver, in this case the SMC Ethernet driver, you might get something like the following:

```
C:\NOVELL\ODI>smc8000
SMC EtherCard PLUS Family DOS ODI Driver v3.04 (921104)
(C) Copyright 1992 Standard Microsystems Corp.   All Rights
Reserved.

    Adapter 8003EB, Int 5, Port 2A0, Mem D4000, Node Address
C0952D1C L
    Max Frame 1514 bytes, Line Speed 10 Mbps
    Board 1, Frame ETHERNET_802.2, LSB Mode
    Board 2, Frame ETHERNET_II, LSB Mode
    Board 3, Frame ETHERNET_SNAP, LSB Mode

C:\NOVELL\ODI>
```

NDIS PROTOCOL.INI modification

Unfortunately, the NDIS PROTOCOL.INI file has to be manually modified to tell the NDIS protocol manager which protocols it should bind to and use. However, you can get rid of the hardware interface parameters information for NDIS drivers; the system will not use them, since everything is routed to the ODI device drivers.

For each NDIS protocol used there must be a section in PROTOCOL.INI. The most important command is the Bindings statement, which specifies which NDIS MAC(s) driver the protocol is going to bind with. The NDIS driver must be the same name as specified under NET.CFG.

If the ODI LAN driver's name starts with a number (e.g. 3C503) the NDIS MAC name to use for the Bindings statement must be preceded with the letter 'X' (e.g. X3C503).

A typical PROTOCOL.INI file might look like the following:

```
[PROTOCOL_MANAGER]
      DriverName = PROTMAN$

[ETHERAND]
      DriverName = DXME0$
      Bindings   = SMC8000
```

Running ODINSUP.COM

This program must be loaded after the ODI MLID drivers. If it is loaded correctly, it will look something like this:

```
C:\NOVELL\ODI>odinsup
```

```
ODI Support Interface for NDIS Protocols  v1.21 (921113)
(C) Copyright 1992 Novell, Inc.  All Rights Reserved

MAC Name = [SMC8000] : Using first SMC8000 MLID.
Execute NETBIND to activate.
```

```
C:\NOVELL\ODI>
```

Next the Microsoft NETBIND must be run.

Typical startup AUTOEXEC.BAT file

```
lsl
SMC8000
ODINSUP

REM ...Load NDIS Protocols if not loaded in CONFIG.SYS

netbind

REM ...Load ODI Protocols
IPXODI
BNETX
```

NDIS does not provide a dynamic interface for its protocols and MACs; the ODINSUP.COM module is *not* unloadable.

Installation: general points

ODINSUP is loaded after the LSL.COM and ODI LAN drivers. The ODI protocols should be loaded after NETBIND.EXE and the NDIS protocols have been loaded. This will allow the ODI protocol modules to be unloaded.

After installation, ODINSUP.COM consumes approximately 5 Kbytes of DOS memory. On top of that, each additional adaptor that ODINSUP is bound to will increase memory usage by approximately 3 Kbytes.

The normal optional NDIS MAC capability that allows users to modify the node address dynamically is not supported by ODINSUP, as ODI MLIDs do not support this. You need to modify NET.CFG to support node address overrides for the ODI MLID driver.

Strategy

If possible, do not use ODINSUP.COM; it can make things far more complicated. Standardize on either NDIS or ODI; do not mix the two. If you use NDIS you can still connect up to Novell networks, because Microsoft provides an NDIS-compliant IPX protocol. However, if you mainly use Novell, then the ODI drivers would be the best bet.

Novell Shell for DOS workstations

SHELL.CFG and NET.CFG files

These are ASCII text files containing parameters to customize NETX.EXE, IPX.COM and the NETBIOS.COM programs. Novell are slowly attempting to move users away from SHELL.CFG to the alternative NET.CFG text file. The difference between the two text files is that SHELL.CFG is used by their dedicated native IPX.COM environment, whereas NET.CFG is the equivalent in the ODI standard. In this section we shall concentrate on SHELL.CFG, but most of its functions can also be defined in NET.CFG. However, it can store many more options, such as support for multiple protocols. See the section on Novell ODI drivers in this Chapter for more information on NET.CFG files.

When NETX.EXE or IPX.COM are run, they automatically look for SHELL.CFG. If it exists they read it and adjust themselves appropriately. A good analogy is to say that SHELL.CFG is to the Novell shell what CONFIG.SYS is to DOS. The parameters in SHELL.CFG can be used to set a wide range of parameters, including:

- preferred file server for connections
- optimizing workstation performance
- minimizing the NetWare shell memory requirements
- the number of concurrent sessions supported
- management of local printers and the shell
- set-up information on workstations

Because SHELL.CFG is one file utilized by a number of different programs, the commands within it are split into a number of different groups in order to initialize themselves into the workstation memory:

- IPX protocol driver
- SPX protocol driver
- NETX program
- EMSNETX program
- XMSNETX program
- NETBIOS program

A typical SHELL.CFG or NET.CFG file might look like this:

```
PREFERRED SERVER   =NW386
SPX CONNECTIONS    =60
LONG MACHINE TYPE =TOSHIBA
```

This file should be found in the same directory as IPX.COM and NETX.EXE (Figure 7.22).

Adjust the SHELL.CFG options to eliminate the majority of problems associated with printing, or the inability to open a large number of files.

Optimizing Novell workstations (useful SHELL.CFG or NET.CFG settings)

Some of the following settings are used to improve the performance of the workstation; others enable the shell to do things normally not possible if you stick to the default figures. Attempting to fine tune the workstation is no easy task; there are so many different types of workstation configuration. Fortunately, Novell has provided an abundant set of options that can be configured when the Novell shell is activated. I shall concentrate on some of the most useful parameters and tricks most commonly used by Novell experts. Most of these options can be set-up permanently on the appropriate workstation.

I have broken this section up into problem areas. Instead of simply showing all the SHELL.CFG or NET.CFG options, I have grouped statements together under relevant headings.

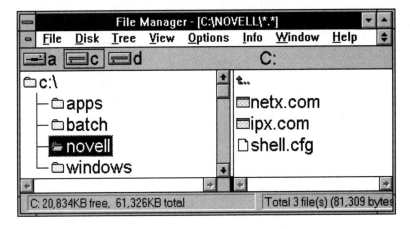

Figure 7.22 SHELL.CFG file locations.

Improving workstation performance

```
IPX PACKET SIZE LIMIT= number
```

This is a neat trick used to improve the performance of the workstation, especially when using Ethernet. When Novell sends out IPX packets the default maximum packet size is 4160 bytes. If you are using Ethernet, it can only cope with a packet size of 1500 bytes; with Token Ring it is around 5 Kbytes (Table 7.8).

Figure 7.23 illustrates the potential misfit of IPX packets on Ethernet. This means that the default IPX packets have to split up over several Ethernet packet sizes, whereas Token Ring can cope with delivering an IPX packet in one go. So if you are using Ethernet it is well worth limiting the IPX packet size to be equal to the maximum Ethernet size: this actually increases performance by splitting IPX packets over multiple Ethernet packets.

This is done by adding the following line to SHELL.CFG or NET.CFG:

```
IPX PACKET SIZE LIMIT = 1500
```

The range of allowable IPX size is from 576 up to 6500 bytes.

If you are getting 'out of memory' problems on your workstations, try reducing the size of the IPX packets. This will reduce the memory requirements of the shell, but at the expense of performance.

Table 7.8 NetWare packet types and maximum default sizes.

Packet type	Maximum default size
IPX	4160 bytes
Ethernet	1536 bytes
Token Ring	4160 bytes

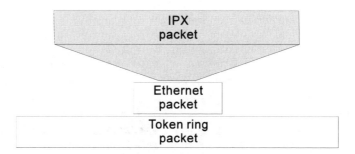

Figure 7.23 An IPX packet can misfit into an Ethernet or Token Ring frame.

```
CACHE BUFFERS =n
```

This is a straightforward option. It attempts to improve the performance of the workstation, at the expense of utilizing extra memory. It allocates RAM to be used as local caching for sequential reads from the file server.

The default set-aside block is five buffers. Each buffer takes up to 512 bytes. This option has no limit to how many buffers could be used. You obviously have to weigh up the advantages of having faster read access time over loss of memory.

Generally, if you are running applications that do not use all the available conventional memory, it is well worth experimenting by increasing the number of cache buffers. However, if you are using Windows v3.1 and have activated the SMARTDRV option, it is not worth having two duplicating caching programs.

```
CACHE BUFFERS = 10
```

If you are getting 'out of memory' problems on your workstations, try reducing the number of CACHE BUFFERS. This will reduce the memory requirements of the shell, but at the expense of performance.

Managing multiserver environments

```
PREFERRED SERVER= name
```

This is a very useful option when you have a multiple file server network. Normally, when NETX.EXE is activated, it sends out a packet requesting a connection from the nearest Novell file server. In a multiple file server environment, if no preferred file server is defined, the user takes a gamble as to which file server they connect up to. This can cause considerable confusion, as user rights may vary on the different file servers daily. If you do not want the default file server, you can use the preferred server option to specify a particular file server. On logging in, you instruct the connection to be moved over to an alternative file server.

For example, instead of just saying

```
LOGIN a-user
```

you can qualify your name with

```
LOGIN NW386/a-user
```

To direct NETX.EXE to search for a specific file server name you add the following line to the SHELL.CFG or NET.CFG file:

```
PREFERRED SERVER = name
```

When the preferred server option is used, NetWare will poll up to five different file servers to locate the file server specified.

Managing printers

```
LOCAL PRINTERS = n
```

This option can used to identify the number of local printers installed in the workstation. The trick here is to set it to

```
LOCAL PRINTERS = 0
```

This means that there are no printers installed in the PC. This option will take priority over any contradictory information that might have been set in CMOS on the motherboard. The advantage of this is that if the user presses <SHIFT> <Prt Scrn>, the machine will not hang. However, if LPT1: is captured to a queue then the <Prt Scrn> key will work.

```
SPX CONNECTIONS = n
```

The SPX connection specifies the maximum number of sessions that the SPX protocol can support. This has to be increased if you want to use the workstation as a dedicated print server. You need to increase the default of 15 up to a recommended 60:

```
SPX CONNECTIONS=60
```

Managing workstation identifications

```
SHORT MACHINE NAME = name
```

You can automatically give a machine a name during the log-in process. This can be very useful, since it can then be passed as a variable into the script files, which in turn can be used to make a number of different decisions based on the machine's name.

The default name is IBM but the other name often set-up is CMPQ, meaning that it is a Compaq type machine. Although in theory the name can be anything, it should in fact be four characters or less. This is because Novell uses this name to load the name $RUN.OVL file.

The SHORT MACHINE NAME is used to load an appropriate screen driver for the Novell menu system.

$RUN.OVL is used to store the screen driver for the Novell menu system. When you buy the standard Novell system, you get two different files: IBM$RUN.OVL and COMQ$RUN.OVL. This is why the short name is normally set to IBM or COMQ.

Sometimes it is better to set SHORT NAME = COMQ, rather than IBM, since COMQ$RUN.OVL is far easier to read than IBM$RUN.OVL on some screens, such as laptops.

```
LONG MACHINE NAME = name
```

You can automatically give a machine a meaningful name during the log-in process. This is very useful, as this name can then be passed into the script files as variable %MACHINE. The name can be up to six characters. For example:

```
LONG MACHINE NAME = IBMPC
```

The default is IBMPC. The difference between this and the SHORT name is that this name can be slightly more meaningful. It is not used by the Novell system to load up an appropriate screen driver for the menu system. However, the name is often used to select an appropriate DOS version to put into the user path.

Changing workstation NIC settings

```
CONFIG OPTIONS = 1...10
```

This option can be used to modify the hardware configuration that IPX.COM will try to use to initialize the NIC inside the workstations. In theory, this means that when you change the setting in your NIC you do not need to regenerate the IPX again using the WSGEN program. You simply select a different set of parameters from the set of ten that IPX stores internally. The default set is the options that were selected when you generated IPX with WSGEN. By typing IPX -D you can establish at any time what options are available for dynamic selection:

```
C:\NOVELL>ipx -d
Novell IPX/SPX  v3.10 (911121)
(C) Copyright 1985, 1991 Novell Inc.  All Rights Reserved.

LAN Option: Western Digital EtherCard PLUS v3.12EC (910812)
Hardware options available:
      0. IRQ=3, I/O Base=280h, RAM at D000:0 for 16k
      1. IRQ=5, I/O Base=300h, RAM at CA00:0 for 8k
      2. IRQ=10, I/O Base=2A0h, RAM at CC00:0 for 16k,
         16 Bit Only
      3. IRQ=2, I/O Base=240h, RAM at D800:0 for 32k
    * 4. First Software Configured Adapter
      5. Second Software Configured Adapter
      6. Third Software Configured Adapter
      7. Fourth Software Configured Adapter
      8. Driver Configurable by Jumpers Utility
C:\NOVELL>
```

The * against the option indicates the current default setting. You can easily change this – for example, from the 'First Software' setting to the 'Second Software' setting by using the /D option after IPX. In this case it would be

```
IPX /D5
```

This is suitable for quick changes; you can perform this change permanently by adding the following line to SHELL.CFG or NET.CFG:

```
CONFIG OPTION = 5
```

Managing files and directories

```
SHOW DOTS on/off
```

In Novell, the default is that when directories are shown, the 'parent' and 'current directory' dots are not shown.

This is a normal directory listing showing the dot directories:

```
C:\NOVELL>dir

 Volume in drive C has no label
 Volume Serial Number is 2D62-11CD
 Directory of C:\NOVELL

.               <DIR>       10-02-92  11:06a
..              <DIR>       10-02-92  11:06a
IPX      COM     28794 09-14-92   5:01p
NETX     COM     52443 03-10-92   3:10a
SHELL    CFG        72 10-22-92   7:38p
         5 file(s)       81309 bytes
                      21385216 bytes free


C:\NOVELL>
```

You would not see these directories if this was a Novell directory. Instead, you would see the following:

```
Q:\NOVELL>dir

 Volume in drive Q is SYS
 Volume Serial Number is 9190-7CD9
 Directory of Q:\NOVELL

IPX      COM     28794 09-14-92   5:01p
NETX     COM     52443 03-10-92   3:10a
         2 file(s)       81237 bytes
                      23494656 bytes free


Q:\NOVELL>
```

unless you give the following command:

```
SHOW DOTS = ON
```

> You used to put 'SHOW DOTS = ON' in your NET.CFG file when using Microsoft Windows v3.0. This is no longer needed for Windows v3.1.

This is very important for some programs. They require that the current directory and the parent directories are shown as dots in the directory listing.

Windows is such a frequently used application that this entry is now considered standard in the SHELL.CFG or NET.CFG.

```
MAX CUR DIR LENGTH size
```

When the DOS request 'Get Current Directory' call is made, the name of the directory is returned. In the Novell shell, version 3.01 and above, the name is limited to a maximum length of 64 characters. You can increase this length to a maximum of 255 characters. This is very useful if you have users who get carried away with the creation of sub-, sub-sub- and sub-sub-sub directories! However, if you find that you need to change this parameter, then there is a possibility that something is going wrong. Instead of attempting to allow for ever-larger path lengths, ask yourself whether you could reorganize the directory structure more efficiently.

```
MAX PATH LENGTH size
```

When you read files across a Novell network, it can be qualified by a directory path. The Novell shell has limited this maximum length to 255 characters.

DOS has a default limit of a maximum 128 characters for the path length.

```
SEARCH MODE = number
```

This is used to define what happens if a file is not found in the local directory, and what the system should do in terms of searching in other places for the specified file. The request could either come from the DOS prompt line, or from DOS programs. The default is:

```
SEARCH MODE =1
```

There are eight different search mode numbers; each one defines a different type of procedure in searching for a file. Table 7.9 lists their meanings.

Loading Novell drivers automatically

A typical sequence for log-in commands is:

```
IPX
NETx
F:
LOGIN
```

One of the ways to help the user to log in automatically is to write a batch file. I have outlined here a very useful batch file that will load IPX.COM and NETX.EXE and, if not told otherwise, will also automatically log in the user name.

This batch file can be placed in the directory with all your batch files, or alternatively can be stored under the \NOVELL subdirectory with all the other Novell drivers. I call it NOVELL.BAT, but you can give it any name.

Table 7.9 Search mode numbers.

Search mode	Meaning
0	No search is attempted
1	This is DOS default. If the file is not found in the current directory, the DOS path is then sequentially searched
2	Only search through the current directory
3	If a directory path is specified in the executable file, the file searches that path. If not, the file searches the default directory; then, if the open request is read-only, the file searches the search drives
4	Reserved
5	Search the current directory and the DOS path, whether or not the path has been specified in the executable file
6	Reserved
7	Search the current directory and the DOS path, whether or not the path has been specified in the executable file, if the program opens a read-only data file

The contents of NOVELL.BAT are:

```
REM This batthe name Farshad with your own user login name
REM Replace the Preferred file server NW386 with your own name
C:
CD \NOVELL
REM **** Load up the IPX/SPX protocol
IPX
REM **** Load up NETx with preferred file server name NW386
NETX PS=NW386
F:ch file start up a Novell Work Station.
REM Replace
IF X%1==X GOTO FARSHAD
G:LOGIN %1 %2 %3
GOTO END
:FARSHAD
LOGIN FARSHAD
:END
```

To log in automatically, the user would just type

```
NOVELL
```

However, if another user wants to log in on your PC, all you do is to qualify the NOVELL batch file with their own user name:

```
NOVELL AN-OTHER
```

What happens when NETX is run

When the NETX program runs, various things happen, culminating hopefully in the message on the screen saying, 'Connected to a file server'. It is always good to see this message; there could be many different problems causing the alternative message, 'File server not found'.

To understand what could have gone wrong it is useful to understand the sequence of operations that NETX performs on execution. These are described below.

Check for IPX

First, NETX looks for the IPX driver in the workstation's memory. It uses the IPX driver to carry information across the network. If it finds that it has not been loaded as a TSR, then NETX will abort, with an appropriate message.

Send out Get Nearest File server request

Assuming IPX is found, NETX then attempts to deliver a special packet requesting to connect to the nearest file server. This is part of Novell's SAP (service access protocol). The packet is actually called a GetNearestServer request.

File server responds

As the packet flows through the network, active file servers on the network search for such packets coming from workstations. The first file server to grab the packet starts to satisfy the request. It then sends out a response SAP packet to the workstation request. This packet contains the name of the file server plus other information, such as a connection number allocated to this session, and how many routers the packet had to go through before it reached the file server. This is Novell's equivalent of establishing the distance of the file server from the workstations.

Response packet picked up by NETX

This packet is then picked up by the NETX program, and the name of the attached file server is then printed on the screen.

Time/date requested from file server

By default, NETX reads the time and date from the file server. It then updates the local workstation time and date to be the same as the file server.

Map to a log-in drive

NETX's next big task is to provide a platform for the user to log into the network. It does this by mapping the F: drive to the file server directory SYS:\LOGIN. If the F: drive actually exists, Novell will allocate the next available drive working from F: upwards, unless there was a statement about the LASTDRIVE in the CONFIG.SYS file, such as:

```
FILES=20
BUFFERS=20
```

```
LASTDRIVE=G:
```

In this case NETX allocates the next letter following the one specified by the LASTDRIVE parameter.

> Beware of setting LASTDRIVE=Z. This causes lots of problem with the old NetWare shell. It stops it from being able to assign a log-in drive. However, if you use the new NetWare VLM redirector, you *must* set LASTDRIVE=Z!

This can be very useful in standardizing the log-in drive across a network that comprises a collection of different workstations, some with no hard disks, some with a C: drive, some with C: and D: drives, and others with C:, D:, E: and F:. In such cases, if you insert in the CONFIG.SYS file in all the workstations:

```
LASTDRIVE=F
```

then you would always log in from the G: drive, regardless of the type of machine used to log into the network. This is very good news in terms of managing the system, because it means that you can develop batch files that can be used across all the workstations.

NetWare protocol packets and NETX

There follows a breakdown of the actual NCP (NetWare core protocol) packets that are sent between the file server and a workstation when NETX.EXE is run. This assumes that everything is up and running as it should be. To keep the example simple, we are assuming that there is no preferred file server.

Basic operation

When NETX is run, it must establish a connection with a file server; the file server will respond with its name. Then IPX routing packets are sent to find the most suitable path between the workstation and the file server. Once this has been established the workstation requests an exclusive connection number from the file server. The user will later log in on this number.

The workstation now negotiates with the file server the maximum packet size acceptable to both sides. It also requests the file server type and version. Once this is done, a LOGOUT request is automatically made to the file server. This ensures that the connection number is available to the user to log in; anybody else currently logged in on this connection number is automatically logged out.

The workstation requests the time and date from the file server; this is used to initialize the local workstation time and date.

Summary of basic operations

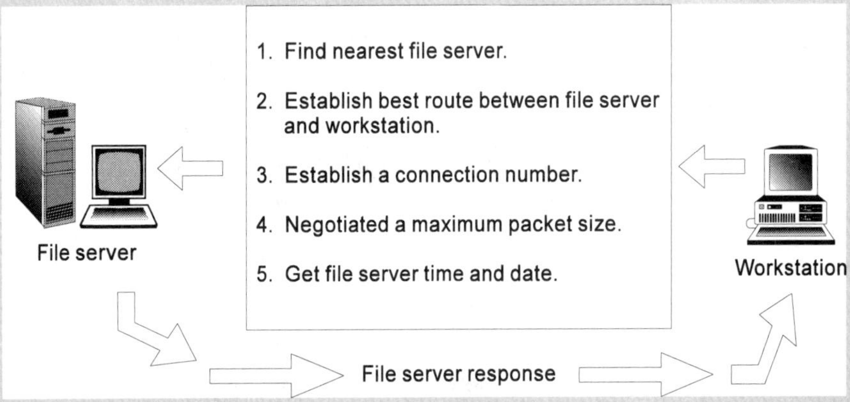

1. Find nearest file server.

2. Establish best route between file server and workstation.

3. Establish a connection number.

4. Negotiated a maximum packet size.

5. Get file server time and date.

File server

Workstation

File server response

Figure 7.24 Summary of packets sent during NETX activation.

Table 7.10 Packers sent between workstation and file server during NETX activation.

Frame	Destination	Source	Summary-(NCP)
1	BroadcastAll	WorkStation	NCP Cmd Find Server (File Server)
2	WorkStation	FileServ_NIC	NCP Rep Service Response (F/S Name=NW386)
3	BroadcastAll	WorkStation	IPX (Routing Information) Request (RIP)
4	WorkStation	FileServ_NIC	IPX (NetWare) Response (RIP)
5	FileServ_NIC	WorkStation	NCP Cmd Create Service Connection
6	WorkStation	FileServ_NIC	NCP Rep Create Service Connection (OK)
7	FileServ_NIC	WorkStation	NCP Cmd Get Server Version
8	WorkStation	FileServ_NIC	NCP Rep Get Server Version NW386
9	FileServ_NIC	WorkStation	NCP Cmd Negotiate Buffer Size 1024
10	WorkStation	FileServ_NIC	NCP Rep Negotiate Buffer Size 1024 (OK)
11	FileServ_NIC	WorkStation	NCP Cmd Logout
12	WorkStation	FileServ_NIC	NCP Rep Logout (OK)
13	FileServ_NIC	WorkStation	NCP Cmd Get Server Date/Time
14	WorkStation	FileServ_NIC	NCP Rep Get Server Date/Time
15	FileServ_NIC	WorkStation	NCP Cmd End-of-Job
16	WorkStation	FileServ_NIC	NCP Rep End-of-Job (OK)

Detailed analysis of the protocol packets

In order to examine the sequence of operation in greater detail, I have used a protocol analyser called LANdecoder/e from Triticom to capture the packets and decode them.

Figure 7.25 shows the captured packets going between the workstation and the file server.

Finding the nearest file server

The first packet sent out makes a request for the services of a file server. This is done using the NetWare SAP (service advertising protocol). SAP is used by NetWare for all servers to advertise their services to the network users. This includes all types of server, including file servers, print servers, routers and communication gateways. Novell has given each server a unique advertising code. This number is then used to request access to particular types of server.

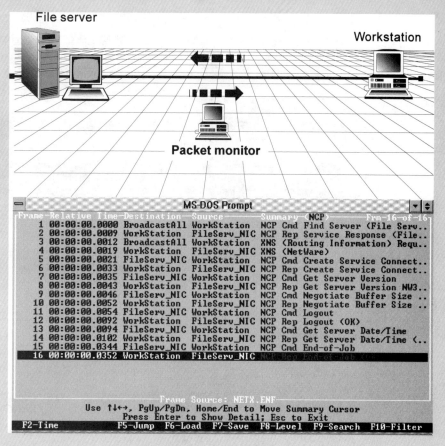

Figure 7.25 Packet transfer between file server and workstation.

In Figure 7.26 you can see that an NCP packet is making the request to find a server type 4 (Novell's advertising number for a file server). Other important server numbers are listed in Table 7.11.

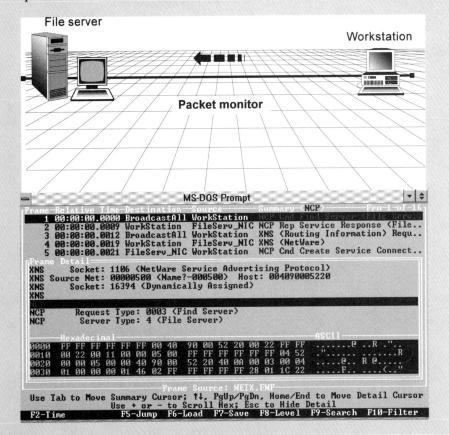

Figure 7.26 Workstation requests the services of a file server.

Table 7.11 NetWare service advertising codes.

NetWare server type	Advertising number
File server	4
Print server	7
Archive server	9
Remote router server	24
Router server	26
Portable NetWare server	9E
NNS domain server	133

NetWare has dedicated a special socket from the XNS protocol to be used exclusively for packets that carry SAP information across the networks. The socket number is 452h. The appropriate NCP packets ride on this type of packet, which makes the appropriate service advertising requests.

The file server is constantly looking out for SAP request packets requesting the services of server type = 4. It then picks up these packets and responds to the workstations, as shown in Figure 7.27.

The file server is now responding with a complementary SAP packet, informing the workstation of its details. This includes such information as the server name, the network number and its unique internal network number.

Get routing information

Now the workstation investigates the best route between itself and the file server. This is done by using the RIP (routing information protocol) packets. These are actually a special type of IPX packet, with socket number = 0453h.

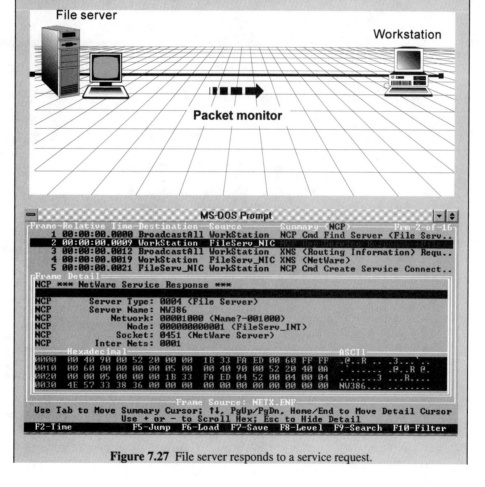

Figure 7.27 File server responds to a service request.

Whenever Novell sees this type of packet, it assumes that it is investigating the best route between two points. In this case it is very simple because we only have one network connecting the two devices together.

A general request is made by the workstation to the file server to identify which network number it is sitting on (Figure 7.28). All this is done using IPX socket = 1107 (0453 hex).

The file server then responds with the packet shown in Figure 7.29. This shows that the file server and the workstation are sitting on the same network. If

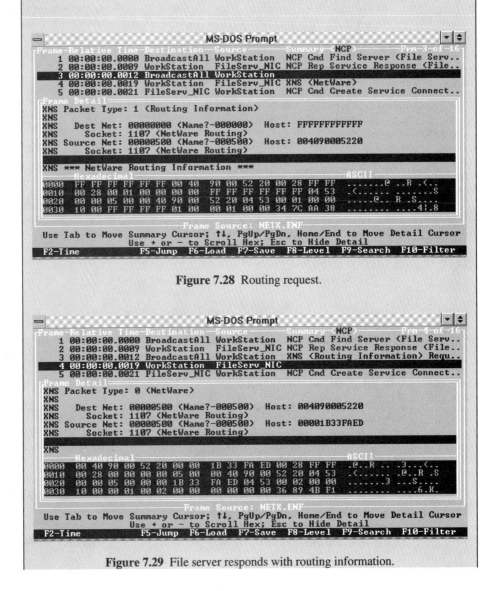

Figure 7.28 Routing request.

Figure 7.29 File server responds with routing information.

this was not the case, then an extra series of packets would be generated by the workstation. This entails broadcasting to all routers on the network the request to return the faster route to the file server. These requests are all part of the Novell RIP protocol. When the response packets return, the workstation will select the fastest path if there happens to be a multiple path, by selecting the path with the minimum number of hops. (One hop is defined as a packet's having to go through one router. Therefore a three-hop route means that the packet has to get through three routers before it reaches its destination.)

Connection number request

The next important step is for the workstation to obtain a connection number, which is used later to attach and log into the file server. When the workstation closes a connection, it is then returned to the file server pool, ready for allocation to some other user.

Connection numbers are normally assigned from 1 upwards, unless they are requested by an NLM running on the file server, in which case they seem to be assigned from 255 downwards. When you type USERLIST, you will see the actual connection number assigned to your workstation and the file server, as below:

```
C:\WINDOWS>userlist

User Information for Server NW386
Connection   User Name        Login Time
----------   --------------   --------------------
      1    * FARSHAD         11-01-1992  9:02 pm

C:\WINDOWS>
```

The connection number remains unchanged for the duration of the user's session. Even if the user logs out and logs in again, the same connection number will be active.

A request is sent out to the file server for the connection number to be filled in with an appropriate number. A suggested number of 255 is sent out (Figure 7.30).

The file server now responds with the next available connection number to be set aside for the exclusive use of communicating with this workstation (Figure 7.31). In this case the allocated connection number is 2.

Get server information

The workstation now makes an information request regarding the file server: the file server responds with the information shown in Figure 7.32. It reports the name and version number, and provides additional information: for example, how many user licences the file server is valid for, and how many current connections are in use.

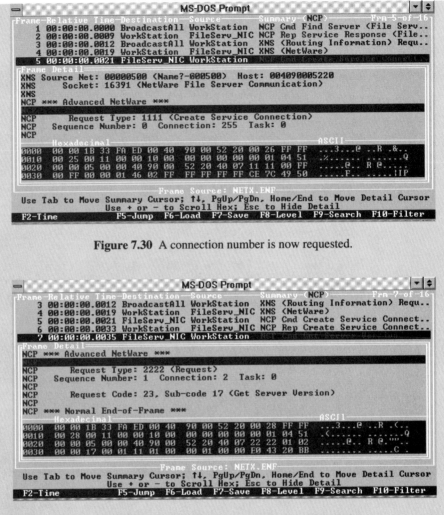

Figure 7.30 A connection number is now requested.

Figure 7.31 The connection number is assigned.

Negotiating buffer size

Both sides now have to negotiate the maximum acceptable packet size that they can accommodate. Normally, this is about 1024 bytes, but it depends on the underlying network being used. In Figure 7.33 the workstation requests a packet size of 1024 bytes and then awaits a response from the file server. The file server responds by confirming that it can cope with the packet size request size of 1024 bytes.

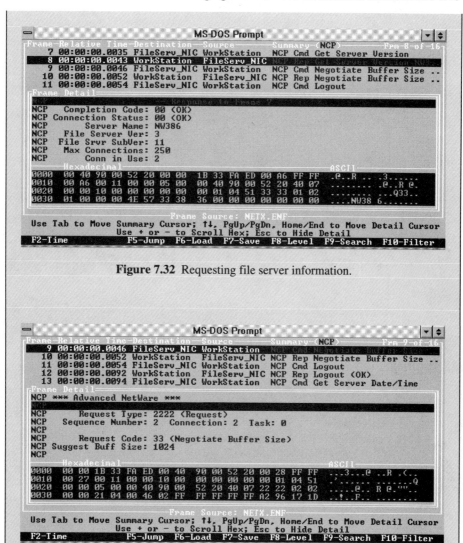

Figure 7.32 Requesting file server information.

Figure 7.33 Negotiating buffer size.

End of job status

The end of job request unlocks and clears any open files or active records that are active on this connection (Figure 7.34). This request is normally called to reset the error mode, and to release any resources that might have been used by applications (it is normally called when the applications have been terminated).

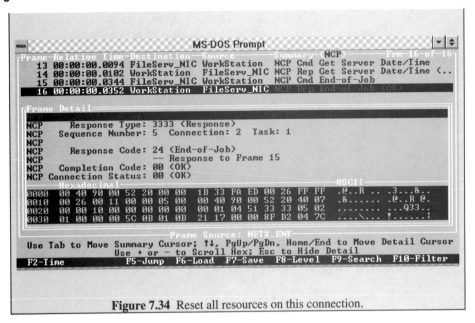

Figure 7.34 Reset all resources on this connection.

Managing shell updates

Overview

WSUPDATE.EXE is a very useful command that, if necessary, allows for the NetWare shell to be automatically updated across the network. This program will check for the time and date stamp on the workstation files and, if necessary, will update copies of the NetWare shell from the file server copy. It is a simple program; all it does is compare the two files and, if the time and date differ, copy one on top of the other, making a backup copy first.

This is very useful for updating the next release of NETX.EXE to be placed on all workstations, or to update all the workstation shells to support burst mode. You would run this command in the standard system script file instead of updating each workstation with the new shell commands. Each time a user logs into a workstation, its shell is compared with the standard shell layout on the file server, and WSUPDATE will update the workstation if it is out of date.

Basic WSUPDATE syntax
The syntax of WSUPDATE is:

```
WSUPDATE [source path] [destination drive(s):destination
filename] /option
```

There are a number of options, which are explained well in the Novell manuals. The one that we are going to use is the /F command:

```
/F= <path> <filename>
```

This option is used when we want to issue commands from a text file. The commands are entered into this file as if they were being typed from the command line. Each line will be interpreted separately.

For this program to work well you need to standardize, on as many workstations as possible, where the local Novell program is loaded during the boot-up sequence into the Novell file server. Most users seem to boot up via the C: drive, and on that drive under a directory, say for example C:\NOVELL, they store all the boot-up NetWare files. Of course, if you have a diskless workstation this approach will not work, as you need to update the boot-up image files: this is beyond the scope of the WSUPDATE program.

However, if your network comprises mostly workstations that boot up via the C: drive or even the floppy drive A:, this method of automatically updating the NetWare shell is extremely efficient.

I once worked for a company that had 247 workstations, all booting up from the C: drive and storing NetWare shell files on the C:\NOVELL directory as standard. Using 15 people and WSUPDATE we managed to update all the workstations within 20 minutes. In fact, all they had to do was log in as a special updating user in all the machines; the rest was automatic.

A framework for managing shell updates

First, create a directory on the file server where you will store all the latest NetWare shell files. You will if necessary update workstation shell files from this master directory on the file server (Figure 7.35).

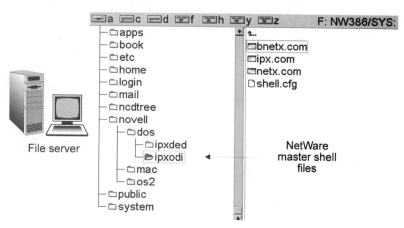

Figure 7.35 A proposed framework for keeping copies of the NetWare shell files.

You will notice that the shells are categorized according to the type of workstation operating system. This is because NetWare shells are specific to the workstation operating system. The directory is further subdivided into the old dedicated IPX technology and the new ODI-based IPX technology. It is not advisable to combine them; keep them in separate directories for future administration.

We now create a text file that contains the names of the files we want to check, and automatically update it if these files are found to be different from the master set. In the example in Figure 7.36, WSUPDATE receives its commands from the file WS_DOSUP.CFG.

How to check for updates when necessary

The final step is to put a statement into the system script file that will automatically load up the WSUPDATE program, and check for any required updates. The problem with this method is that if you put an unconditional command to run WSUPDATE, you will be constantly rechecking every time a user logs into the system, and hence slowing down the logging-in procedure. The other problem with different types of workstation operating system is knowing which set of programs to check for.

Here I suggest you use the trick of creating a special updating user on the system. These users are employed to activate the workstation update programs. They can also be specified according to the type of workstation operating system that you wish to check.

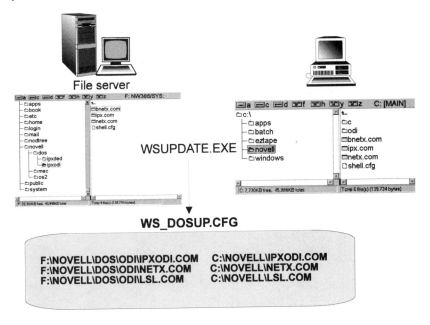

Figure 7.36 Automatic update of NetWare shell.

Some typical user names could be:

- User – UPDOS
- User – UPOS2
- User– UPUNIX

This means that the system will not check for updates on any other user, so that time is not wasted when a normal user wants to log in. It also has the advantage that each special updating user can be specific to the type of workstation operating system that you wish to check for or update.

If you call all your special updating users UP something, such as UPDOS or UPUNIX, then it easy to manage them, as they will appear one after another in the user list. Also, you can make them members of a special group with rights only to the relevant updating directories

For each updating user you might have a different configuration file. So a typical system script file could look something like Figure 7.37. Note that instead of checking for each different type of updating user, we just put them all in a group called 'updaters', and check for that first, before wasting time checking for each different type.

Burst mode and IPX technology

Overview

Novell have introduced burst mode technology. This is in effect an enhanced version of NCP (NetWare core protocol). It uses the IPX (internetwork packet exchange) protocol in a slightly more efficient manner that will significantly improve the transfer of large files across the network. Novell claim that by using burst mode technology you can improve performance by anything from 10% to 300% depending on the size of file being transferred. This technology is particularly useful in a Microsoft Windows environment, because Windows-based applications tend to read and write large data files across the network. Burst mode is normally used with ODI drivers, but it can also work across the old dedicated IPX implementation. It is in effect a replacement for NETX.EXE.

Old technology: request followed by response packets

The normal sequence of operation for reading a large file is to break it up into multiple packet size requests. Each packet is then requested in sequence from the file server. This means that to read a file of 100 Kbytes, such as the LOGIN.EXE file, would require on average 100 IPX requests of 1 Kbyte size to be made to the file server. Each time, the file server will respond by sending back the next 1 Kbyte of the file. This is then reconstructed in the workstation into a 100 Kbyte file (Figure 7.38).

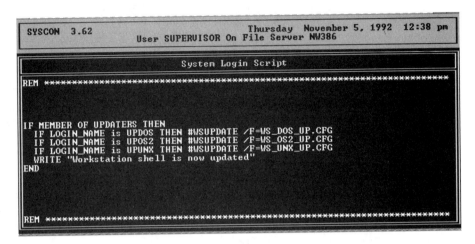

Figure 7.37 Typical script to automatically update workstation files.

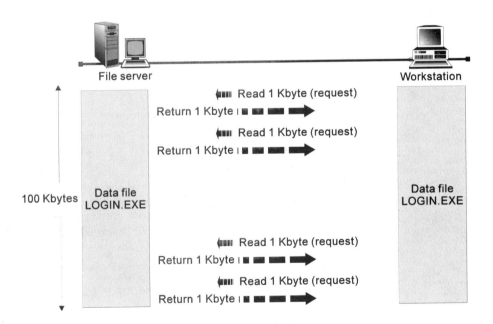

Figure 7.38 Normal IPX packet request–response sequence.

New technology: overview of burst mode functionality

Taking the previous example, and assuming that we are now implementing the new burst mode technology, the number of IPX requests sent across the network will now be radically reduced. However, the amount of information that each IPX packet can carry has been radically increased (Figure 7.39).

In burst mode, a client can make a single read or write request for a data size of up to 64 Kbytes. The new flexible IPX packet sizes are used by an enhanced NCP that is burst mode-compliant. Normal read and file requests across the network are now intercepted by the NCP protocol, which in turn makes requests for very large IPX packet sizes.

Before this technology can be used, burst mode has to be implemented on both sides of the communication – workstation and file server – via a burst mode-compliant NCP. This is done on the workstation by loading BNETX.EXE on top of NETX.EXE, and on the file server by loading a special NLM called PBURST.NLM. In theory, burst mode technology should be completely transparent to the user.

Burst mode in mixed platform

Burst mode is totally compatible with any node on the network that might not support burst mode technology. In these cases it would default back to the normal NCP calls. If, for example a workstation is running burst mode and it is then connected up to a different file server that does not, it can communicate with both using the appropriate NCP calls (Figure 7.40).

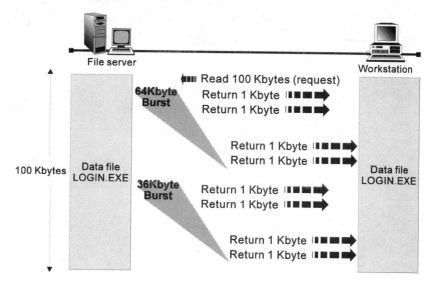

Figure 7.39 Burst mode protocol.

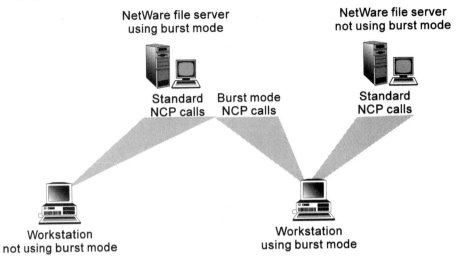

Figure 7.40 Burst mode protocol.

Implementing burst mode

To implement burst mode on a Novell network you need to do the following (Figure 7.41):

- Execute PBURST.NLM on the file server
- Execute BNETX.EXE on the workstation, replacing the old NETX
- Set up the appropriate buffers at the workstation

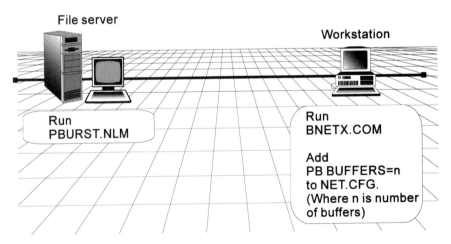

Figure 7.41 How to implement burst mode across NetWare.

PBURST.NLM includes support for NCP Packet Signature, an enhanced security feature. To utilize this feature, you must obtain a number of new NetWare files, including server NLMs and supervisor, print and other utilities.

If you wish to use PBURST.NLM and BNETX.EXE without implementing the security feature, enter the following line at your file server console (you may add this line to the AUTOEXEC.NCF file):

```
SET NCP Packet Signature Option = 1
```

To implement burst mode at a workstation, add the following line to your NET.CFG (or SHELL.CFG) file:

```
PB BUFFERS = 3
```

This technology is designed around NetWare 3.x and 4.x and is not supported as yet on NetWare 2.x file servers.

Installing burst mode on the file server

To install burst mode on a file server, you need to load a special NLM program that activates a special burst mode-compliant NCP. This means that the File server can now satisfy the special burst mode request that might be made by workstations.

The installation steps required are:

- Copy the file PBURST.NLM from the DOS_CLIENT master disk into SYS:\SYSTEM

- Now run PBURST.NLM on the file server (Figure 7.42).

This command should be placed in AUTOEXEC.NCF after the BIND IPX to the network card command (Figure 7.43).

> Make sure you use PBURST.NLM version 2.0 or above, since the early version did not work very well.

I have found that you must update your CLIB.NLM to ensure that the packet burst option works correctly.

Installing on a workstation

This is a very simple operation. Instead of the NETX.EXE program, Novell have introduce the burst mode version, BNETX.EXE. In theory, this program behaves exactly the same as the old NETX.EXE. The burst mode part of BNETX.EXE is only activated if an appropriate entry has been made in NET.CFG or SHELL.CFG.

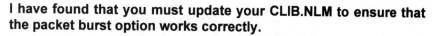

```
File Server Console
:load pburst
Loading module PBURST.NLM
   NCP Packet Burst Support, Large Internet Packets And Packet Signatures
   Version 2.00    November 12, 1992
   (C) Copyright 1983-1992 Novell Inc.
       Patent Pending - Novell Inc.
:
```

Figure 7.42 Loading PBURST from the console command line.

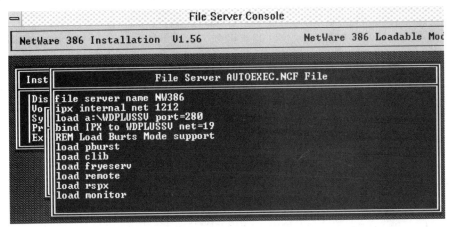

Figure 7.43 Modifying the NetWare 3.11 server.

You will find this program on the DOS_CLIENT master disk, which comes with the standard NetWare DOS workstation support disk pack.

If you are already running NETX.EXE, you must remove it before starting the BNETX.EXE program. To remove it, and install the new NETX, you would type the following from the DOS prompt line:

```
NETX /U
BNETX
```

New NET.CFG and SHELL.CFG option

Burst mode is activated when the following line is entered in NET.CFG or the equivalent SHELL.CFG file:

```
PB buffers = <number>
```

where <number> is a value from 2 to 10. This parameter specifies how much of the workstation memory is to be set aside for burst mode operations. To implement burst mode at a workstation, add the following line to your NET.CFG:

```
PB BUFFERS = 4
```

To disable burst mode operation, set the buffer size to zero:

```
PB buffers = 0
```

Try setting the buffer size to 4. I have found that, for the average Windows based workstation, this figure is a good compromise between performance and minimizing memory usage.

Burst mode and workstation memory

One of the problems with burst mode is that, at present, it can only use conventional memory. The burst mode program requires a minimum of 4–5 Kbytes, plus the memory allocated to buffers. The total amount of workstation memory allocated to burst mode buffers will be dependent on:

- the number of burst mode buffers set up in the NET.CFG file
- nine of the negotiated buffers

Although this is a small amount, in a workstation that has a very tight conventional memory usage, burst mode technology can cause all sorts of memory problems; programs that used to run before burst mode was introduced may cease to work correctly.

The actual size of a buffer is defined by the following standard formula:

One buffer size = negotiated packed size + 102

The negotiated packed size is defined when the connection is established between a workstation and the file server. In Ethernet it is normally set to 1024 bytes. For more information about packet size negotiation, see the section on negotiating buffer size in this Chapter. The protocol information overhead is normally 102 bytes. This contains information such as the NCP controlling information for the start and end of the burst.

The total amount of required for burst mode is:

Buffer memory size × Number of buffers

The number of buffers is defined in the NET.CFG file as

```
PB BUFFERS = <N>
```

where <N> is the number of buffers.

Thus the total memory requires to implement burst mode on a workstation is given by

Total memory = 5 Kbytes + Total buffer memory

Selecting the right burst mode buffer setting

Generally speaking, the higher you make the number of buffers, the greater the performance. However this is only true up to a point. Sometimes increasing the number of buffers is actually detrimental to performance. Just increasing the number of buffers up to the maximum 10 will not necessarily mean maximum performance. There are a number of factors to consider before coming up with the optimum figure for the workstation, as listed below.

On-board NIC buffers

Does the workstation have a network with on-board buffers? If so, large burst mode buffers are not necessary, and may in fact reduce operating performance. There is no point in having two buffers doing the same thing.

Workstation CPU speed

The faster the machine, the quicker it can use the buffers to its full advantage. In a slow workstation, however many buffers you allocate to it, unless it can move the data into the buffers fast enough, they are wasted.

Amount of conventional memory available

Since, on average, each buffer might take up as much as 1 Kbyte of conventional memory, you need to carry out tests to check whether there is enough conventional memory to be exclusively allocated to burst mode operations without interfering with other programs.

Management strategy

In general, start by setting buffer size as low as possible. This means starting at two buffers, and then carrying out a simple test, such as a large file transfer across the network, timing it and then repeating the test with an increased buffer size. Generally speaking, four buffers gives a good overall figure for the average 386 workstation running standard 16 bit Ethernet cards such as SMC's EtherCard PLUS Elite16 Series.

Performance of burst mode versus standard NCP calls

The test in Figure 7.44 was carried out to compare NETX.EXE with BNETX.EXE on a workstation. All parameters were kept the same, except for the different workstation shell. The system was evaluated using Novell's PERFORM3 test with a burst mode buffer size of four.

On file sizes less than 1 Kbyte, the old NCP calls work faster than burst mode, because there is a slightly greater protocol overhead. However, as the file sizes reach 4 Kbytes or more, burst mode performance outstrips the old method.

VLM redirector (introduced with NetWare 4.0)

With the release of NetWare 4.0, radical changes have occurred to the old NetWare shell concepts. NETX and BNETX have been replaced by the more flexible concept of the VLM (virtual loadable module), because of the increased functionality required by NetWare 4.x. The old NetWare shell NETX concept was limited to 64 Kbytes, and could not cope with the new demands. The new NetWare redirector breaks this barrier, and can be highly tuned to meet the demands of users.

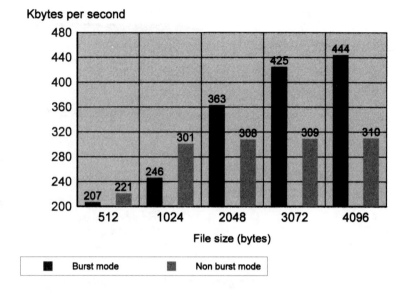

Kbytes per second

File size (bytes)

■ Burst mode   ▨ Non burst mode

Figure 7.44 Testing network workstation performance: NETX.COM versus burst mode BNETX.COM.

The new NetWare client redirector is functionally the same as Microsoft's own network redirector: hence integrating between Windows NT, LAN Manager and NetWare 4.x will be far easier.

Note: the NetWare DOS redirector is *not* compatible with NETX.COM, BNETX.COM or NETX.EXE; it is a total replacement. If you need to use NETX, then use NETX.VLM for compatibility with shell calls.

NetWare DOS redirector architecture

The new architecture (Figure 7.45) utilizes the DOS redirection facility. Whereas before, the old NetWare shell used to keep its own redirection table separate from DOS, the new system integrates it into the DOS redirection table.

There are three basic layers. At the top is the DOS redirection layer, which will make a network server look like a standard DOS drive. The special VLM to do this is called REDIR.VLM.

In the middle is the service protocol layer. It is here that other VLM programs can be loaded to enhance the client's workstation environment, such as:

- NetWare protocol support (NWP.VLM)

NetWare DOS redirector

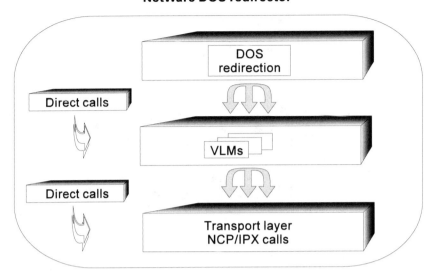

Figure 7.45 NetWare DOS redirector.

- NetWare file input/output support (FIO.VLM)
- NetWare print support (PRINT.VLM)

At the bottom is the transport protocol layer. This is concerned with maintaining connection to network resources, and providing a reliable data transportation service. It will typically use the services of the IPX protocol, which in turn will most probably be using the ODI drivers.

All three layers are supervised and managed by the VLM.EXE programs. These programs define the VLM system bus, which then can be used to load VLM programs.

Installing DOS requester

To install the new NetWare DOS requester on a workstation, there are a number of changes that have to made to the NET.CFG, CONFIG.SYS and SHELL.CFG files. You can do these manually, but Novell have provided a special menu-driven program to simplify things, by doing the following things:

- It will check your NET.CFG files and optimize your ODI drivers. It will make any changes that might be needed in the NET.CFG file. It creates a new header under NET.CFG called the NetWare DOS REQUESTER. All the new redirection parameters are placed under this section.
- Add the following line to your CONFIG.SYS file:

```
LASTDRIVE=Z
```

The NetWare DOS requester uses the drive *before* the LASTDRIVE. You can define the letter of the first log-in drive by placing the following line in the NET.CFG file:

```
Network DOS requester
    FIRST NETWORK DRIVE = F
```

- It will ask if you wish your Windows drivers updated. These are: NETWARE.DRV, VIPX.386, and VNETWARE.386

Loading sequence of VLMs

To start off, you must load the ODI driver, and then bind to it the normal IPX ODI protocol. Now instead of loading up the old BNETX or just NETX programs you load VLM.EXE. This loads the VLM system bus. It will automatically select the best memory position available, trying to load itself in the following order: extended memory; then expanded memory; finally, if all else fails, conventional memory.

```
C:\NOVELL\NW4>vlm
VLM.EXE - NetWare virtual loadable module manager BETA 1.1
v1.0 (921228)
(C) Copyright 1992 Novell, Inc.  All Rights Reserved.

The VLM.EXE file is pre-initializing the VLMs.............
The VLM.EXE file is using extended memory (XMS).
You are attached to server NW40

C:\NOVELL\NW4>
F:\>LOGIN
```

Within NET.CFG, on top of the normal default VLM you can specify which other VLMs are to be loaded. In the example in Figure 7.46, NETX.VLM is loaded so that bindery servers can also be supported. Alternatively, if you do not state which VLM is to be loaded, a default selection will be automatically loaded.

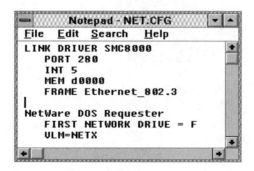

Figure 7.46 Typical NET.CFG configuration as used by the NetWare VLM programs.

> Warning: the log-in drive prompt appears to be a root-mapped drive. This is because the NetWare DOS requester uses DOS's own redirector facility. It defines that no directory path can be in the drive structure maintained by DOS when the parent of the directory is inaccessible. This is the case with an unauthenticated connection and the drive mapped to the SYS:LOGIN directory. Users might see 'F:\>' instead of the old 'F:\LOGIN>' when first trying to log into the system.

VLM memory utilization

The VLM.EXE program uses a special transient swap block of around 8.5 Kbytes to swap modules of data between conventional memory and the extended or expanded memory that it is using. This swap memory block is located in the PC's upper memory block (UMB) (Figure 7.47). In this area, there is also a global memory block of about 22 Kbytes. However, if the VLM is not using any upper, extended or expanded memory, the transit and global data blocks would both have to be accommodated within conventional memory.

VLM loading order

Table 7.12 lists the various VLM programs that can be loaded. You do not need to load every one. A few are essential; the others can be loaded on demand.

If you plan to use just bindery services, then you do not need NDS.VLM; conversely, if you plan to use NDS exclusively, you do not need BIND.VLM. However, if you wish to use both, then both BIND.VLM and NDS.VLM must be loaded.

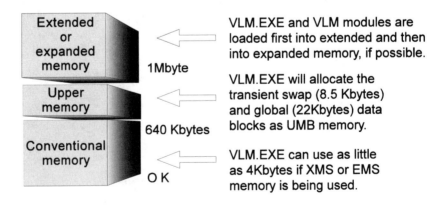

Figure 7.47 VLM memory utilization.

Table 7.12 VLM programs.

VLM name	Function	Load order	Required
CONN	Connection table manager	1	Yes
IPXNCP	IPX/NCP support	2	Yes
TRAN	Transport protocol manager	3	Yes
SECURITY	Enhanced security support	4	No
NDS	Directory services	5	Yes
BIND	Bindery services	6	Yes
NWP	Protocol multiplexer	7	Yes
FIO	File input/output support	8	Yes
GENERAL	Miscellaneous functions	9	Yes
REDIR	DOS redirector	10	Yes
PRINT	Print redirector	11	No
NETX	NetWare shell compatibility	12	No
RSA	RSA encryption for NDS	13	No
AUTO	Auto re-connection module	14	No
NMR	NetWare management responder	15	No

The normal set of VLM files required to support NetWare directory services is shown in Figure 7.48. These modules are loaded from the NET.CFG configuration file.

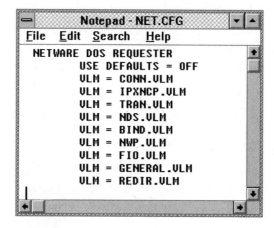

Figure 7.48 VLM load-up sequence.

Loading VLM and Microsoft Windows

There are a number of minor considerations that you need to take into account when running the Windows environment over the NetWare DOS redirector.

- Novell recommend that you should not use the expanded memory option. You can run Windows with the NetWare DOS requester only if you use the extended memory option. If that is not possible you might need to use the conventional memory option.

- Novell also recommend that the Windows SYSTEM.INI configuration file needs to be edited. The following parameter must be added and/or set to a non-zero value under the [386Enh] section of the SYSTEM.INI file:

```
TimerCriticalSection = <milliseconds>
```

For example:

```
TimerCriticalSection = 10000
```

Enhancing VLM performance

There are a number of VLM parameters that can be set up to optimize the performance of the redirector. Some of these parameters need to go in the NetWare DOS requester section of NET.CFG. The improvements are normally at the expense of extra memory utilization. The most important performance related parameters are listed below. For other general parameter settings for improving performance see section on optimizing Novell workstations in this Chapter.

```
LOAD LOW CONN = ON
```

This option relates to the connection manager, which keeps an active table of all connections. It takes up around 3 Kbytes; if you can keep this in the conventional memory, it will improve you redirector performance.

```
LOAD LOW IPXNCP = ON
```

This relates to the IPX transport layer service. If this can be kept in conventional memory, at the expense of 4 Kbytes, it will also lead to improved performance.

```
CHECKSUM = 1
```

This refers to the NCP checksum. This means using a checksum with all protocols except the Novell default Ethernet 802.3 frames: the more checksum calculations that have to be executed, the slower the processing speed of the redirector.

```
LARGE INTERNET PACKET = ON
```

This allows for supporting large internetwork packets greater than the default 512 bytes. This is a very useful option, especially if you are connecting to servers across routes. It can improve performance significantly.

```
SIGNATURE LEVEL = 1
```

This relates to the signature level security offered by the NCP. If this option is disabled, performance can be improved by about 10 %.

```
CACHE BUFFERS SIZE = 512
```

This is very important; it should be set to the size of the physical packet size being supported for maximum utilization. This means that in Ethernet it is normally (1500 – 64), whereas in Token Ring it is (1500 – 64).

```
CACHE WRITE = OFF
```

This option allows your program to fill the local cache buffer, before it is written to the network. It can significantly improve your network's performance.

NetWare workstation drivers management strategy

ODI drivers

Wherever possible, you should use use Novell's ODI drivers. This is Novell's preferred path for the near future. They are including only ODI drivers with the NetWare v4.0 operating system. Older dedicated IPX drivers are being phased out. Novell Labs discontinued the certification of dedicated DOS IPX drivers in June 1992.

However, there are a few considerations that might make the above suggestion unrealistic.

• If you are using a diskless workstation, then traditionally you could not use the new ODI drivers to boot remotely. However, this is already beginning to change; the latest release has addressed this problem.

• IPX.COM takes slightly less memory then the IPX ODI version, since LSL.COM is required.

NetWare shell (NETX) or NetWare redirector (VLMs)

The NetWare shell, in the form of NETX and BNETX (burst mode version), has been superseded by the new NetWare redirector in the form of VLMs. However, you do not need to get rid of your NetWare shell; it has its uses.

When to use the NetWare shell?
If you only connect up to NetWare 3.x or NetWare 2.x servers, then for the time being you can happily continue to use the NETX or BNETX programs. However, do investigate what new functions would be available to you if you did convert your workstation to VLMs: SNMP (simple network management protocol) support, for

example. Even if you do not have a NetWare 4.x server, you can replace your NetWare shell with the new NetWare redirector.

NetWare
4.x

When to use the NetWare redirector

If you need to connect to a NetWare 4.x server at any time, you will need to use the NetWare redirector, in the form of VLMs. It is also possible to connect to NetWare 3.x and NetWare 2.x servers. The NetWare redirector is becoming Novell's own preferred workstation environment over the old NetWare shell concept.

Opt for burst mode

Where possible, select the burst mode drivers. Remember Novell's claim that the use of burst mode technology can significantly improve performance depending on the size of the file. This technology is particularly useful when running a Microsoft Windows environment across a network.

When using burst mode, in the early versions you could not instruct it to use any of the high memory; it would only work under conventional memory. Memory-hungry programs that worked under non-burst mode drivers might not work under burst mode. Check this point when you decide to use burst mode on your workstations.

8

Managing network drives, directories and applications

For the user, the most crucial aspect of any network is the type of application that can be run across it. You might have the fastest, securest and most efficient network possible, but without the right applications the system is almost useless.

Selecting the right application is not as easy as it might seem. Some applications can be loaded satisfactorily on the network, so that all users can access them via a common directory. Others need to be partly across the network and partly on the local workstation's hard disk. Some applications should not be networked at all, because of performance considerations.

Sometimes it is prudent to resist the temptation to install an application across the network. Wrong or badly installed applications can cause a lot of problems. The user becomes complacent and moves on to the next problem once the application has started to work. This is particularly true of Microsoft Windows; there are a large number of parameters that can be modified to optimize performance, but most users are blissfully unaware of these parameters, and happily tolerate substandard performance.

Evaluate new applications

When you are deciding which new applications to install on your network, the most important and obvious consideration is: will a given application do the job that the users require? There are also some other, more subtle consideration, as follows:

- The application should have a good proven record. Don't be the first to try out an application. Let someone else try it first. Then, when most of the bugs have been ironed out, or have at least been adequately reported on by others, you can consider implementing the application on your system. I know of at least one company that has a corporate policy never to buy any application with version 1.0 on its label.

- **Minimize radical new applications** Try to maintain a continuity of applications from the same series of companies. Many managers forget the hidden costs incurred by changing applications. Retraining staff, for example, can increase the original price of the application by a factor of ten. Such costs can be reduced significantly if you stick to the kind of application that staff are used to.

- **Stick to major software houses** It is important to know that the application you are about to recommend to your organization will continue to be supported in years to come. Although no one can guarantee this, your chances are greatly increased by sticking to the big names such as Microsoft, Borland, IBM or Lotus.

- **Network compatibility** Look for applications that are truly network-aware. They are far easier to install across the network, and tend to be cheaper to license. They can utilize the resources of the network fully, as they see not only DOS drives, but also see the name of each file server and all volumes at each server. Network-aware applications can see network queues and automatically redirect their printouts to network printers. Ask the manufacturer of the application which version of the Novell shell it supports.

Always ask the provider of the application for a statement of network compatibility in writing. A telephone conversation may not stand up in court, if things ever come to litigation.

Although most applications for DOS are not networked, they can usually be 'massaged' to work across the network. The scale of problems encountered will depend upon the type of application and how you want to use it.

Types of network application

There are three types of application:

- network-ignorant
- network-aware
- network-dependent

Network-ignorant

Most DOS software falls into this category. Such applications know nothing about networks. They assume that they are running on a single-tasking operating system. However, they can be massaged to work across the network. thanks to the elegant way in which the Novell shell integrates into the workstation's operating system. It adds extra resources to the workstation operating which the 'dumb' application can then use, thinking it has exclusive use over it while in reality it is being shared.

The following command can fool the application into thinking that it is using a local disk drive, when it is actually using a directory found on a file server far away across a network:

```
MAP E:= NW386/SYS:\APPS\DATA
```

This adds to DOS a new drive letter E:, which is actually DIRECTORY \APPS\DATA under volume \SYS on file server NW386.

Network-ignorant applications can also be fooled into printing on shared printers, by assigning the standard DOS LPT: port to print queues:

```
CAPTURE l=1 Q=Q_LaserIV
```

This command will assign line printer LPT1: to the network print queue Q_LaserIV.

Since most DOS-based applications are network-ignorant, the workstation environment is 'supercharged' by NetWare so that these applications can use network resources.

Network-aware

These are applications that used to be network-ignorant, but can now recognize directly the type of network being used. They also are aware that files might be simultaneously accessed by other users. They therefore normally implement some form of file or record locking. They can usually be run on stand-alone workstations or over a network.

Most major software applications are now network-aware; examples include dBase IV, Windows 3.1 and AutoCAD.

Network-dependent

These are applications that from the outset were designed for a network environment. Most were originally developed to run on mainframes or minicomputers, but nowadays are commonly made available across PC networks. Examples of such application are SQL client server and E-mail applications. (There is no point in running E-mail on a stand-alone machine!)

The anatomy of an application

An application can be broken up into distinct parts (Figure 8.1). The main parts are the executable code and its associated data files. Most applications also have a special configuration set-up file. This is normally a special data file that tells the application what type of environment it is to be run over. In Microsoft Windows such files are

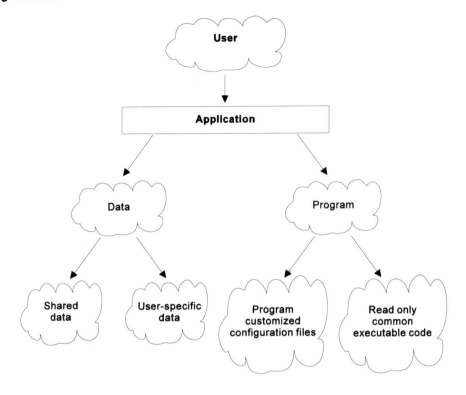

Figure 8.1 The anatomy of an application.

called INI files. They store all sorts of facts about the system, including hardware information, such as the screen drivers used, and software information, such as the user's colour screen preferences. These configuration files are normally stored in the same directory as the executable code.

The basic mode of operation

When applications are run over a network they can be configured in a variety of different ways. The three basic parts of any application are:

- the executable code
- the configuration data
- the data files

These can be spread around the network in many different permutations.
The three basic locations for storing an application are:

- a common network directory accessible to all licensed users
- a private network directory accessible only by a specified user

- a directory on the local drive accessible only by the workstation

There is no universal rule as to where you should place an application. The questions that you need to ask include the following:

- Does the data file need to be shared?
- Can users customize the application?
- Does the application require workstation hardware customization (Windows does, for example)?
- Is the application very input/output intensive?

Some of the answers to such questions can be contradictory.

Mapping Novell drives

Overview

Novell have provided a powerful tool for running applications across the network, in the form of the MAP command. This can be used to enhance the workstation DOS environment by mapping drives, and by adding to the normal DOS search path to use the directories found on file servers.

Creating network drives

The MAP command can be used to create DOS-like drives that are mapped to directories on the file server, which the user happens to have access rights to. To map a drive in DOS you would use the MAP command as follows:

```
MAP J:=NW386/SYS:\APPS
```

In this example a new network drive J: is to be mapped to the directory APPS which is under a volume called SYS: on file server NW386.

Figure 8.2 shows how it is done when you are using Microsoft Windows.

Enhancing the DOS search path statement

The MAP command integrates well with the DOS path statement; it can manipulate the path to include searches across the networked subdirectories.

Network drives

Different drive types

Novell DOS workstations can have three different types of drives. By typing MAP at the DOS prompt line you receive a description of all active drives:

```
C:\WINDOWS>map
```

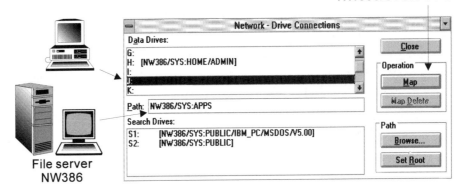

This button will now map drive J: to NW386/SYS:\APPS

Figure 8.2 Mapping to a network drive from Windows.

```
Drive  A:    maps to a local disk.
Drive  B:    maps to a local disk.
Drive  C:    maps to a local disk.
Drive  D:    maps to a local disk.
Drive  E:    maps to a local disk.
Drive  F: = NW386\SYS:  \LOGIN
Drive  H: = NW386\SYS:HOME\FARSHAD   \
       -----
SEARCH1:  = Z:. [NW386\SYS:PUBLIC\IBM_PC\MSDOS\V5.00   \]
SEARCH2:  = Y:. [NW386\SYS:PUBLIC   \]
SEARCH3:  = C:\BATCH
SEARCH4:  = C:\APPS\DOS
SEARCH5:  = C:\APPS\UTL
SEARCH6:  = D:\NU
```

The same information from the Windows File Manager program is displayed as shown in Figure 8.3. Note that the current version of File Manager does not make any graphical distinction between the search and network drives. This is to be corrected in NetWare NT.

There are two major categories of drives: physical and logical (Figure 8.4). Physical drives are referred to by Novell as local drives, while logical drives are subdivided into network and search drives.

Local drives

These drives are considered by the Novell shell as being physically connected to the local workstation. They normally include the two floppy disk drives A: and B:, and hard disk drives C: and D:.

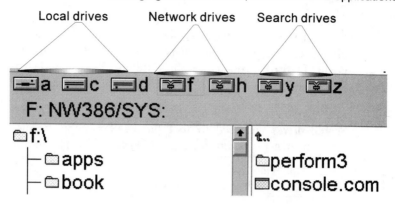

Figure 8.3 Local, network and search drives.

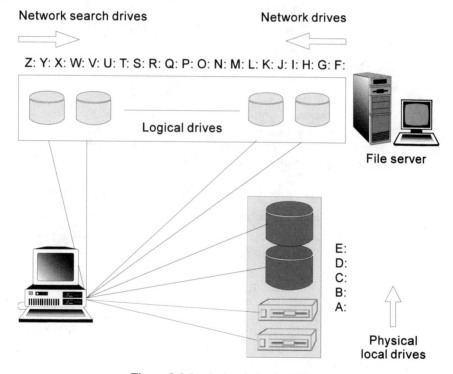

Figure 8.4 Logical and physical drives.

Network drives

Network drives are made to look like local drives to the DOS user. However, they are actually mapped to a particular directory at the file server. The user can use all the normal DOS commands, and, assuming the appropriate access rights were given to the user, the directory will behave as if it is attached locally.

The first network drive is usually the F: drive. It is sometimes called the log-in drive. NetWare, unless told otherwise, assumes that the first potential drive to log in is the F: drive. To change this, use the DOS LASTDRIVE command in the CONFIG.SYS file.

Search drives

Search drives are used to fool the DOS prompt statement into searching for programs in network directories as well as in the local directory.

> The Windows File Manager program shows search drives using the same icon as network drives, which can be confusing.

- A search path is a list of directories that is searched by DOS only if the command was not found in the current directory
- Novell search paths extend DOS and OS/2 paths
- The Novell MAP command can be used to add/delete/modify any of the DOS paths
- Search drives are priority numbered. You can have up to 16 search drives

Mapping drives

At the workstation you can create a mapped drive at any time during your session. When the user logs out of the system, all the mapped drives are automatically removed, and the DOS search path is restored to the original format that it had before log-in. Normally most of the MAP commands are executed at the NetWare system script file.

To map a drive to a network directory, you need two things:

- You *must* have access rights to the directory that you wish to map to.
- You *must* allocate a unique drive letter (from A to Z).

Overview of mapping strategy

The MAP command is one of the key tools that network managers have at their disposal. Used correctly, it can make a significant difference in ensuring that applications are run as efficiently as possible. However, it is a tool that has to be used with care.

Aim, as far as possible, to standardize the use of the MAP command across your network. You need to develop a corporate-wide standard for mapped drives for all your users. This will entail universal letters for mapped drives, which will be available to every user on logging in. Each mapped drive will store a universally understood type of information, such as public files or a user's home directory. These drives would be available regardless of the type of PC being used. This standard should be flexible enough to allow for an assortment of different uses, and to provide sub or supersets of itself if required.

This leads to the development of two different standards. The first is a universal workstation MAP set-up. This includes standard network settings and network path settings. This fact that this setting is universal has a number of advantages:

- It makes it easier to educate users in the effective use of the network, as you can advertise the name of the common drive letters and what they mean to all users.
- It is easy to write universal batch files.
- You can place some important subdirectories in all user standard network search paths. This is done through the system script file.

This approach is called the core map set-up. Using it means that you must be careful to organize the file server directory structure correctly, since your system core map setting is based around it.

The second standard works on the first to create dynamic set-ups specific to particular applications. When the application is terminated these temporary set-ups are removed and the core map set-up is restored.

Core search path set-up

To make network administration easier, it is well worth having a number of search paths that appear in all users' PATH statements. These search paths are universal to all users, and can be set up in the system script file.

Dynamic search paths

Dynamic search paths are set up specially, before a particular application is run, and are then removed after its termination. This approach allows you to reorder the search path to optimize the application's performance. It also allows you to keep the number of core mapped drives to a minimum.

Using the MAP command makes it easy to add, delete or reassign search paths dynamically. This is done using the following format:

To insert a search path at position x, use:

```
MAP INS Sx:= < Volume > / <Directory>
```

To delete search path x, use:

```
MAP DEL Sx:=  < Volume > / <Directory>
```

To redefine search path x, use:

```
MAP Sx:= < Volume > / <Directory>
```

A typical sequence of commands before running an application is as follows:

```
REM Insert new search paths
MAP INS S1:=< Application directory >
```

```
<Run application>
MAP DEL S1:
```

The advantage of using search path 1 is that the directory that the application is going to use is placed at the top of the search list. The application can therefore find its files far more effectively, as it does not have to go through all previously assigned search paths.

On completion, the original search paths are restored by removing all such dynamically assigned search paths. I have known network managers go the other way and install all the dynamic searches from S16. They argue that this search path will least affect the existing search set-up. This might have been sensible in the days when it was not possible to insert paths into the search path. However, now that you can insert and delete search paths dynamically, it is better to work from S1 downwards.

Summary of suggestions

- Use MAP from Shell v 3.01 or above
- Try to give each mapped drive letter a universal meaning
- Root mapping logical disk drive
- Define network drives as either fixed or dynamic drives
- Try not to have more than ten mapped drives at any given time
- Search priority order is very important
- DOS search paths are restored on log-out
- Use the INSERT for search drives where possible
- Root mapping search disk drive

Organizing file server directory structure

The recommended framework shown in Figure 8.5 can be used to organize the applications stored on the file server. It is flexible enough to cope with most configurations. If implemented, it can make it far easier to manage the network, not only because the directory structure is laid out logically, but also because it simplifies the process of giving rights to appropriate groups of users.

Novell standard directories

When Novell NetWare is installed on a hard disk, it creates a basic directory structure, which is normally kept in the standard volume SYS: The directories that it contains are:

- SYS:\SYSTEM

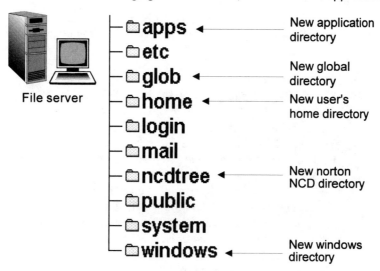

Figure 8.5 A suggested framework for organizing the file server directory structure.

- SYS:\PUBLIC
- SYS:\LOGIN
- SYS:\MAIL

SYS:\SYSTEM

This is the most important directory in the whole system. All the important network operating system files are stored in it. This directory should only be accessible to supervisors.

The kind of information stored in the SYS:\SYSTEM directory includes:

- bindery files
- NLM files
- print servers and queue directories
- special system administration programs

The bindery files store all the important information about the network: user accounts, account restrictions, passwords, group accounts and printer definitions. For NetWare 3.x, these files are:

- NET$OBJ.SYS (identification for each bindery object)
- NET$PROP.SYS (the bindery objects' properties)
- NET$VAL.SYS (the values of each bindery object)

For more information, see the section on Novell bindery files in Chapter 16.

All the NLMs that need to be run from the file server console are normally placed in the SYS:\SYSTEM directory. For example, when a console operator types

    :LOAD INSTALL

at the file server, the system automatically looks for such a file under the SYS:\SYSTEM subdirectory for the INSTALL.NLM program. This is useful to know, especially if you want to run a new NLM program on the file server. You first log in as supervisor and copy the new NLM program to the SYSTEM directory. Then you log out, go to the file server console, and type LOAD followed by the name of the newly installed program. The system will now load the program from the SYS:\SYSTEM directory.

Every time a new print queue or print server is created, a new subdirectory will be created under the SYS:\SYSTEM directories. Each of these subdirectories is automatically assigned a bindery number by the network operating system. You can tell the two different directories apart by looking at the extension. If it is QDR, all spooled data for a given queue will be stored under this directory (Figure 8.6). If the directory only has a hex number and no extension, it is probably storing information about a print server.

Do not limit these directories. If you have a large print job it all has to be sent here before printing. Running out of directory space will result in a printing failure.

There are a number of special files reserved solely for the supervisor's use in system administration. These are usually very sensitive programs that need to handled with extreme caution. Users should not be allowed to run any program located on this directory, unless they have supervisor-equivalent privilege rights. Some of the important programs found in SYS:\SYSTEM are listed in Table 8.1.

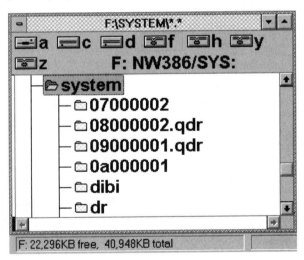

Figure 8.6 Typical print queue and print server subdirectory.

Table 8.1 Some important programs located in SYS:\SYSTEM.

File name	Description
BINDFIX.EXE	Checks bindery files for inconsistency and attempts to fix any errors. Keeps a copy of all the old bindery object files, by calling them NET$OBJ.OLD, NET$VAL.OLD and NET$PROP.OLD
BINDREST.EXE	Restores the previous versions of bindery files before being BINDFIXed. Reactivates the information found in the .OLD files produced by the BINDFIX program
DOSGEN.EXE	Used to create an image for a diskless workstation (see Chapter 20)
PAUDIT.EXE	Allows viewing of the system accounting log record
ATOTAL.EXE	Allows viewing of individual items being accounted for on the network, such as read, write block and connection times
SECURITY.EXE	Checks for potential security holes across the whole system
WSUPDATE.EXE	Used to update workstation shells automatically against a common standard
RSETUP.EXE	Makes a customized boot disk to support remote file server boot-up. Not used very often
RCONSOLE.EXE	Enables complete control of the file server screen and keyboard from any workstation on the network. You can now load and unload any NLM program
ACONSOLE.EXE	Like RCONSOLE but designed to work across a modem

SYS:\PUBLIC

Under this directory, all the normal public standard utilities, command line drivers and menu-driven programs are available to all networks.

SYS:\LOGIN

Users who have not logged into the network are connected to this directory when they first establish a connection with the file server. Normally, the most important program stored here is LOGIN.EXE. Other important files stored here are bootable image files, which are used by diskless workstations.

SYS:\MAIL

Every time a user account is created, NetWare automatically gives them a unique bindery number. This number is then used to create a subdirectory exclusively assigned to the user. The supervisor is always given number 1 as bindery ID. Other users are given a seven hex digit, such as F000001 (Figure 8.7).

Novell no longer provide a free electronic mail package, but there are a number of third-party E-mail packages that utilize this disk structure. NetWare automatically maintains the directory structure. It is also used to store users' log-in script and print job configurations.

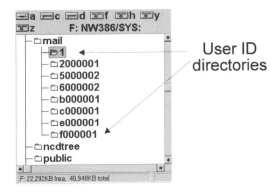

Figure 8.7 User ID directory structure.

When you remove users from the system, their subdirectories are not automatically removed from the SYS:\MAIL directory. You need to run BINDFIX, found in the SYS:\SYSTEM subdirectory, to force NetWare to remove all redundant users' mail subdirectories.

Do not try to remove or rename any of the subdirectories under SYS:\MAIL; you can easily confuse the system bindery files.

New directory structures

Managing different workstation operating systems

It is an excellent idea to store on the file server all the normal utilities provided with the operating system, so that the user need only have the minimum boot-up file stored on their machine. Logging into the network would automatically provide access to the set of standard tolls provided with their own operating system.

I am going to use DOS as an example, but in theory the system can work for other operating systems. At first sight it would seem easy to create a subdirectory, copy all the standard DOS files into it, and ensure that all users automatically have a search path statement to this directory.

The problem with this method is that there is more than one type of DOS. Even versions of DOS with the same version number may have been produced to work with different hardware. We need a flexible framework that can cope with different workstation hardware, different types of operating system, and all their different versions. Such a structure is easy to create in Novell, and if correctly maintained can make the life of the network manager far easier.

In Figure 8.8, workstations running different type of operating system can automatically insert a search path statement to pick up the relevant operating system from the file server. This is done by using a command such as:

```
MAP INS s3:=SYS:\PUBLIC\%MACHINE\%OS\%OS_VERSION
```

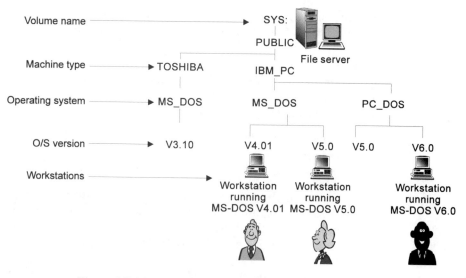

Figure 8.8 Managing different workstation operating systems.

Whenever you declare search drive it is always a good idea to root them. This makes them easy to refer to, and gives you root level security.

This is how you insert into the user path a reference to a specific directory that contains all the relevant utilities for the workstation operating system. This command line is best placed in the system script file. It uses normal script variables such as %MACHINE to select automatically the relevant directory to connect to. As supervisor, you would copy all the appropriate DOS files to each of the relevant directories.

Make sure you mark them 'sharable and read only', by changing to each directory in turn and issuing the following command:

```
FLAG *.* SRO
```

I suggest that, at the same time, you re-map the COMSPEC command. Some programs, when executed, destroy the transit part of DOS, which means that a copy of COMMAND.COM has to be reloaded when the program terminates. DOS uses COMSPEC to find a copy of COMMAND.COM to be reloaded. In this case, the relevant commands would look like this:

```
MAP INS ROOT s3:= SYS:\PUBLIC\%MACHINE\%OS\%OS_VERSION

COMSPEC= s3:\COMMAND.COM
```

If you point your DOS COMSPEC SET command to a directory on the file server, when you log out from the network it is not reset to what it originally was before logging in. This could cause the 'COMMAND.COM not found' error when you run programs after logging out. If you need to do this then be careful to reset COMSPEC to the local copy of COMMAND.COM.

Structuring network applications

The normal method of organizing applications on the file server is to install them all under a single subdirectory called APPS. This can be improved upon by subdividing them into three categories (Figure 8.9):

- general applications
- secure applications
- system batch files

General applications are DOS-based programs that will be made available to all licensed users on a read-only basis. They might include standard tools, utilities and standard applications, such as Norton tools or anti-virus software.

Security-sensitive applications might include payroll programs and internally developed database packages: basically, any application that requires special rights to be given to groups of users before it can be used. Unlike general applications, programs stored under this section might have common read and write privileges given to the appropriate group of users. Most applications fall under this category, but splitting them from the general applications makes it much easier to manage them when allocating the appropriate rights to groups of users.

The batch file directory can be used to store all the batch files that users can call up to start applications. A reference to this directory is automatically inserted into the user search path. This is part of the core mapping set-up common to all users. It is very convenient to have one directory that all users are mapped to in their search paths; whenever you place a new batch file in the directory, it will automatically become available to all users Of course, although the batch file is available to be run by all users, if they are not authorized to execute the application concerned, they will merely get an error message.

In order for these batch files to work, they must make some common assumptions as to the drive letters under which they will find the appropriate application before trying to run it. This builds upon the core mapping set-up for all

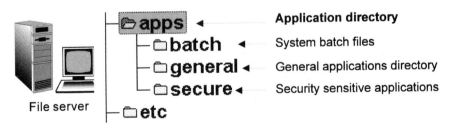

Figure 8.9 Suggested framework for organizing the application directory.

users. These are assigned when the user first logs in. As part of the core mapping set-up, all users are automatically given a special drive through the system script file, which they can use to access each of the different application directories. In the example in Figure 8.10 these are given arbitrary letters of K: (for applications) and I: (for internal, security-sensitive applications). The choice of letters is arbitrary: the important point is that there should be a common standard drive letter.

Whenever you create a new mapped network drive, try not to use letters Z to U, as these are normally used for search paths.

The network drives are all map rooted, giving good security. You do not want users to move up one level from the assigned directories. The user can at any time go to the I: or the K: drive to see a list of all the applications available to them. Potentially, every user could see a different set of available directories, depending on the access rights granted to them over the subdirectory applications.

A search path to the SYS:\APPS\BATCH directory is also automatically inserted into the user path statement.

It is common practice to give users a special directory (their home directory), normally given the same name as their log-in name, for their exclusive use. Each user is then given exclusive rights (except supervisory) to their own directory.

Remember to limit the users' disk utilization when you create home directories; otherwise they will quickly fill up their hard disks with massive amounts of data, at the expense of all other users.

The home directory is normally seen by the user as the H: drive. When each user goes to the H: drive, they will see a different directory on the file server (Figure 8.11). The setting to accomplish this is normally done in the system script file, using the user log-in name as a variable to select the appropriate directory:

```
MAP H:=SYS:\HOME\%LOGIN_NAME
```

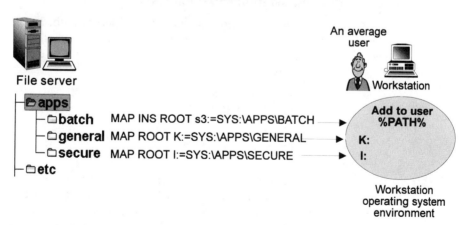

Figure 8.10 User perspective of the application directories.

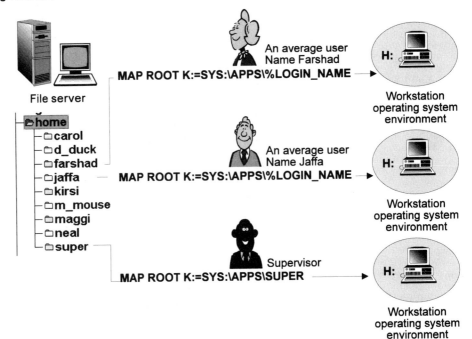

Figure 8.11 User perspective of home directories.

Where the %LOGIN_NAME is variable, it will return the actual user's log-in name. This is why it is important to keep user log-in names to less than nine characters.

Always keep users' log-in names to less than nine characters. When it comes to creating a home directory with the same user ID name, DOS imposes an eight-character limit for directory names, ignoring the three-letter extensions.

This system works very well, but what happen when the supervisor tries to log in? Because the word 'supervisor' has ten letters, it is not possible to give it a unique eight-letter directory name. The usual trick is to create a directory called SUPER and to do the following:

```
IF %LOGIN_NAME is "SUPERVISOR" THEN
  MAP H:=SYS:\HOME\SUPER
ELSE
  MAP H:=SYS:\HOME\%LOGIN_NAME
END
```

It is very useful to have one common directory accessed by all users (the global directory). This is similar to the company scratchpad available to all users. This means that it is an insecure directory, and all users must understand that any files copied or subdirectories created under this directory will be seen by all users.

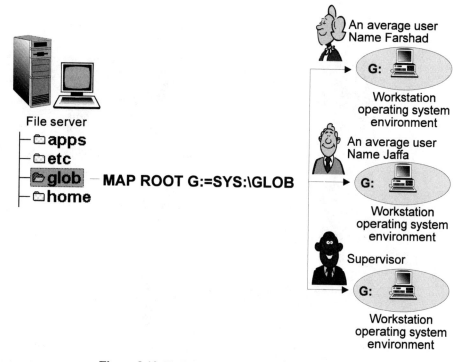

Figure 8.12 User perspective of the global directory.

I suggest you give everyone all access rights, except supervisory, to this directory. Set the purge flag on this directory, using the Novell FILER.EXE program. This is for security reasons; when a user deletes a directory or file, it cannot be salvaged by another user (Figure 8.13).

It is very easy for the user to store large files under the global directory and then forget to delete them afterwards. Limiting this directory using the DSPACE.EXE utility is a good way to prevent this situation from getting out of hand. The size will depend on the actual volume size, but I normally find 10% of the total volume size is an appropriate figure (Figure 8.14).

In theory, the global directory is a temporary storage area. Every so often it is worth looking at it and questioning why files and directories have been left there. I have known companies that extend this idea by having an program that automatically removes all files found under SYS:\GLOB. In my view, this is potentially dangerous.

It is important to limit the GLOBAL directory using the DSPACE.EXE Novell utilities.

Dear Editor: Here are the screen shots re-done.

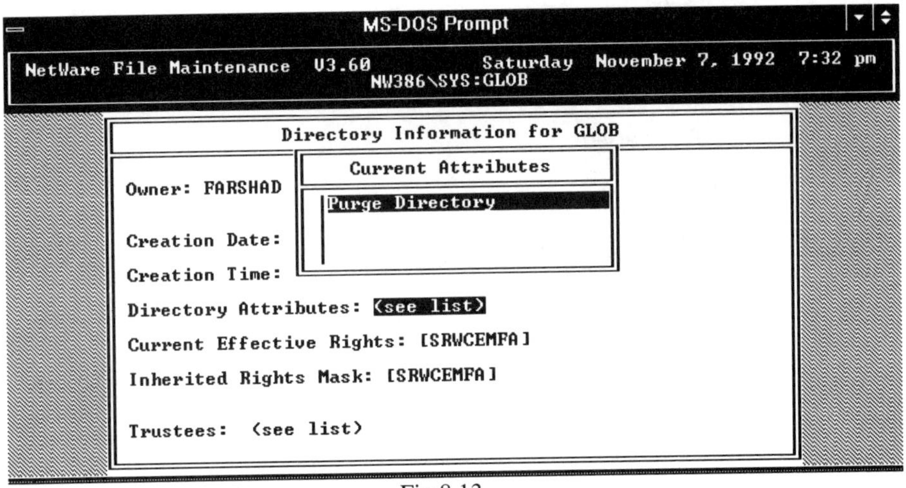

```
┌─────────────────────────── MS-DOS Prompt ──────────────────── ▼ ┃ ♦ ┐
│ NetWare File Maintenance  V3.60        Saturday  November 7, 1992  7:32 pm │
│                              NW386\SYS:GLOB                                │
│  ┌──────────────── Directory Information for GLOB ────────────────┐      │
│  │                  ┌──────── Current Attributes ────────┐        │      │
│  │   Owner: FARSHAD │ Purge Directory                    │        │      │
│  │                  │                                    │        │      │
│  │   Creation Date: │                                    │        │      │
│  │   Creation Time: └────────────────────────────────────┘        │      │
│  │   Directory Attributes: (see list)                             │      │
│  │   Current Effective Rights: [SRWCEMFA]                          │      │
│  │   Inherited Rights Mask: [SRWCEMFA]                             │      │
│  │                                                                │      │
│  │   Trustees:  (see list)                                        │      │
│  └────────────────────────────────────────────────────────────────┘      │
└───────────────────────────────────────────────────────────────────────────┘
```

Fig 8.13

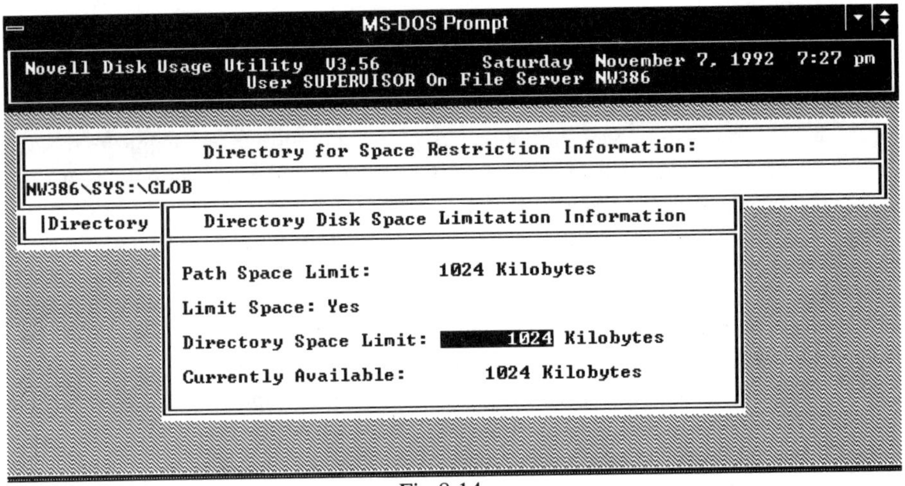

```
┌─────────────────────────── MS-DOS Prompt ──────────────────── ▼ ┃ ♦ ┐
│ Novell Disk Usage Utility  V3.56       Saturday  November 7, 1992  7:27 pm │
│                       User SUPERVISOR On File Server NW386                 │
│  ┌──────────── Directory for Space Restriction Information: ──────────┐   │
│  │ NW386\SYS:\GLOB                                                     │   │
│  │ │Directory  ┌──── Directory Disk Space Limitation Information ────┐ │   │
│  │            │                                                     │ │   │
│  │            │  Path Space Limit:      1024 Kilobytes              │ │   │
│  │            │  Limit Space: Yes                                   │ │   │
│  │            │  Directory Space Limit:        1024 Kilobytes       │ │   │
│  │            │  Currently Available:   1024 Kilobytes              │ │   │
│  │            └─────────────────────────────────────────────────────┘ │   │
│  └────────────────────────────────────────────────────────────────────┘   │
└───────────────────────────────────────────────────────────────────────────┘
```

Fig 8.14

Windows applications

Microsoft Windows is becoming such an important environment that it is worth giving it its own subdirectory at the highest level. The installation of Windows and its related applications is an enormous topic, which is covered in subsequent chapters. In this section, I am merely laying down a suggested directory structure on which we shall build later. What I have tried to do is to come up with a flexible structure that is easily managed later on. It can cope with different version of Windows, and with upgrading from one version to another.

This structure is not appropriate in all cases. This method might not be appropriate in cases where copies of Windows are installed on the local hard disk. In this section I am looking strictly at the issues involved if you wish to store Windows across the network. There is no perfect set-up, and neither Microsoft nor Novell imposes any rigid structure for implementing Windows. It is up to you!

I have introduced a special group of users called WINDOWS_USERS, to which all Windows users will belong: this is used to make the appropriate mapping assignments. I have broken the Windows structure into two parts:

- master copy of Windows
- Windows applications

Master copy of Windows

Master copies of all versions of Windows that may be required are stored on the network. A full set of the programs and drivers supplied with each version of Windows is stored under these directories. For Windows 3.1, this means copying the seven high-density disks into the relevant directory: this will become the master copy of Windows for users to refer to. As part of the core set-up, the user gets a drive, which I call the W: drive. This is automatically mapped to the master copy of Windows for all Windows users.

There are two important points about this assignment. First, since there are different versions of Windows – 3.0, 3.1 and NT – I prefer to install a subdirectory with the appropriate version of Windows (Figure 8.15). This approach makes it much easier to update from one version of Windows to another. It also allows for different versions of Windows to be supported across your network, just like different versions of DOS.

Second, I use a network drive assignment:

```
MAP ROOT  W:=SYS:\WINDOWS\V3.1
```

as opposed to putting the following in the user's search path:

```
MAP ROOT S7:=SYS:\WINDOWS\3.1
```

This is because I wish to know which drive letter will be used in batch files. One of

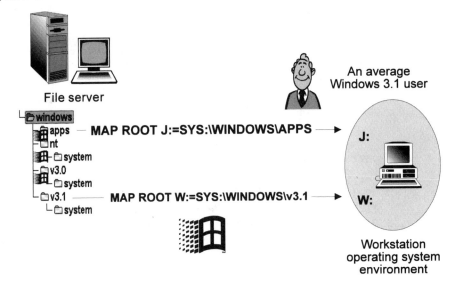

File server

Figure 8.15 User perspective of the master set of Microsoft's Windows directories

the problems with assigning search paths is that you cannot be sure of the drive letter that will be allocated. We need to know this letter, as we shall be using it to run a series of batch files and to configure Windows: INI files to refer to it.

The disadvantage of using a network drive assignment is that a user must actually be taken to the W: Windows directory before they can run Windows. This is not a major problem, since we can use a batch file called WIN.BAT, which is kept in the \APPS\BATCH directory, to call up the Windows program automatically from W:.

Master copies of Windows applications

It is very useful to keep master copies of Windows applications in a separate directory from the Windows master directory. This is because most Windows applications work across a number of different versions of Windows. It is far easier to manage each version separately, rather than have the two systems mixed together.

The Windows user is given direct access to all Windows applications through a special drive, which I call the J: drive,. to fit in with the other drive letters (Table 8.2).

Table 8.2 Application-oriented drive letters.

Assigned drive letter	Meaning
I:	DOS-based secure applications
J:	Windows-based applications
K:	DOS-based public applications

File server directory framework

Figure 8.16 summarizes the structure that could be used to organize the file server. The drive letters used are largely arbitrary, and can be changed to suit your own environment. This structure is then used to create a static set of drives that are always available to the user as part of the core mapped drives automatically set up by the system script files. Once such a framework is developed it is well worth documenting for users what each network drive is called and what sort of information they might find under each drive letter.

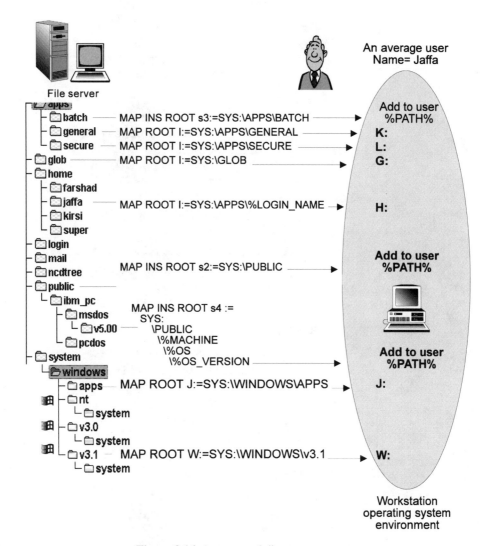

Figure 8.16 A suggested directory structure.

These assignments are performed through the system script file. There now follows an extract from a typical script file that might be used to make the appropriate assignments:

```
REM ***********************************************************
REM Do the Core set-up Mapping

MAP DISPLAY OFF
MAP ROOT I:= NW386\SYS:\APPS\secure
MAP ROOT K:= NW386\SYS:\APPS\general
MAP ROOT G:= NW386\SYS:\GLOB

IF MEMBER OF "WINDOW_USERS_3.1" THEN BEGIN
   MAP ROOT W:= NW386\SYS:\WINDOWS\V3.1
   MAP ROOT J:= NW386\SYS:\WINDOWS\APPS
END

REM ***********************************************************
REM Assign a home directory to the H: drive:
REM If the user is the SUPERVISOR use the
REM  special directory HOME\SUPER as the SUPERVISOR home dir
IF "%LOGIN_NAME"= "SUPERVISOR" THEN
 MAP ROOT H:=NW386\SYS:HOME\SUPER
ELSE
 MAP ROOT H:= NW386\SYS:HOME\%LOGIN_NAME
END

REM ***********************************************************
MAP INSERT ROOT S1:= SYS:PUBLIC/%MACHINE/%OS/%OS_VERSION
MAP INSERT ROOT S2:= SYS:PUBLIC
REM ***********************************************************

MAP DISPLAY ON

REM ***********************************************************
REM ****** Set COMPSPEC for the correct version of DOS on each
REM *******   Workstation as they come on the network.
COMSPEC=S1:\COMMAND.COM
REM NOTE IT could cause problems not resetting after logout.
REM ***********************************************************
```

If the user has been defined as a member of the WINDOWS_USERS_3.1 group, they might see the following drive setting if the MAP command is issued:

```
C:\>map

Drive  A:   maps to a local disk.
Drive  B:   maps to a local disk.
```

```
Drive  C:    maps to a local disk.
Drive  D:    maps to a local disk.
Drive  E:    maps to a local disk.
Drive  F: = NW386\SYS:  \LOGIN
Drive  G: = NW386\SYS:GLOB  \
Drive  H: = NW386\SYS:HOME\FARSHAD  \
Drive  I: = NW386\SYS:APPS\SECURE  \
Drive  J: = NW386\SYS:WINDOWS\APPS  \
Drive  K: = NW386\SYS:APPS\GENERAL  \
Drive  W: = NW386\SYS:WINDOWS\V3.1  \
       -----
SEARCH1: = Z:. [NW386\SYS:PUBLIC\IBM_PC\MSDOS\V5.00 \]
SEARCH2: = Y:. [NW386\SYS:PUBLIC  \]
SEARCH3: = X:. [NW386\SYS:APPS\BATCH  \]
SEARCH4: = C:\BATCH
SEARCH5: = C:\APPS\DOS
SEARCH6: = C:\APPS\UTL
SEARCH7: = D:\NU


C:\>
```

This structure, or a modified version of it, should be publicized to the users, so that they become aware of the meaning of each drive and what sort of information is available under each drive letter. I have designed a simple form that can be filled out explaining what each drive means (Figure 8.17).

	User view of network drive	
Drive letter	**Description**	**Who has access**
G:	Global directory	Read/write to all
H:	Home directory	Exclusive use to user
I:	DOS-based secure applications	Applications only available to authorized groups
K:	DOS-based public applications	Application available to licensed users
J:	Windows-based applications	Application available to licensed users
W:	Windows master copy	Available on a read-only basis to licensed Windows users

Figure 8.17 Summary of typical network drive letter assignments.

A blank form is provided for you to record you own drive settings if they are different; you can then give this to users (Figure 8.18).

Managing memory with MS-DOS 5.0, Windows 3.1 and Novell NetWare

One of the notable things about MS:DOS version 5 compared with earlier versions is its ability to load itself into the high memory area. To do this you have to load

	User view of network drive	
Drive letter	**Description**	**Who has access**

Figure 8.18 Network drive asignment form.

HIMEM.SYS, which is an extended memory manager for programs, such as Windows, that need to use extended memory. It also provides access to the 64 Kbytes of high memory that lie above the 1024 Kbyte boundary.

With these two drivers loaded into high memory, you can load other devices and drivers into high memory using the LOADHIGH and DEVICEHIGH commands. You can also say that DOS is equal to HIGH UMB; this places DOS into the high memory area and establishes a link between DOS and the upper memory block areas.

DOS 5.0 also provides a program that has been available as shareware for some time, called MEM. You can use this to keep track of where your programs have loaded into conventional, upper and high memory.

The DOS 5.0 and Windows 3.1 system disks both provide HIMEM.SYS and another memory manager called EMM386.EXE. Always use the latest one: in this case, the one supplied with Windows 3.1. When the next release of either DOS or Windows comes out then use the drivers that come with it as they will be the latest versions.

DOS 5.0 enables us to load TSR programs, such as the Novell drivers IPX and NETX, into high memory, thereby releasing conventional memory. Novell also provide two special versions of the NETX.COM program: EMSNETX.COM for loading into extended memory and XMSNETX.COM for expanded memory.

Understanding HIMEM.SYS

The HIMEM.SYS program must be loaded as part of the CONFIG.SYS. It is essential to the running of Windows and DOS 5. It makes extended memory and the high memory area available for use by applications. It normally does this by tapping onto the notorious A20 address line.

For more information on HIMEN.SYS, see Chapter 6.

A simple framework for installing applications

This section outlines an approach that can be used to install most applications across the network; it needs to be extended and modified to meet the requirements of the specific applications. It is based on batch files that call up the applications. All users are automatically mapped to the batch file subdirectory, which contains batch files for all possible potential network applications. This is placed into their path statement when they first log into the system, as part of the system script file. I have called the directory that they all map on to \APS\BATCH: this is where supervisors will write an appropriate batch file that a user can call up to run an individual program.

Let us follow the sequence of installing an imaginary application called WhizzBang, which we want to enable all users to run. It is a DOS-based application that requires one driver to be loaded up before, and removed after, its execution. It is supplied on four disks. (We shall assume that all software licence details are in order.)

Installing the application

Armed with the WhizzBang master set, as supervisor you log in to the network. Go to the K: drive, where public applications are to be stored, create a subdirectory called WHIZZ, and perform the normal installation sequence specified for the WhizzBang software, ensuring that you specify K:\WHIZZ when prompted to choose a drive to install it to (Figure 8.19). Try to complete a full installation at this stage if the application provides such an option, rather than a customized installation. Now you are ready to write a batch file.

Creating a batch file

You now go to the batch file directory. All users should have an entry in their path statement pointing to this directory, so anything placed in here will be available to all users. You create an appropriate batch file (in this case we shall call it WHIZZ.BAT), which specifies the sequence of operations required to load WhizzBang and start execution (Figure 8.20).

You can do a number of things inside this batch file. First, you can create dynamic search paths or reorder the existing paths to enable WhizzBang to run slightly faster. If the software requires access to yet another directory in its search path you can add this path to the existing list and then remove it on termination. You can also take this opportunity to end this batch file and move the user either to their

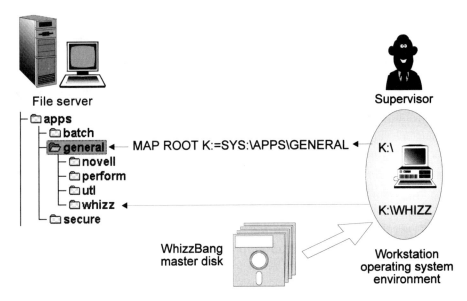

Figure 8.19 Installing applications on the file server: stage 1.

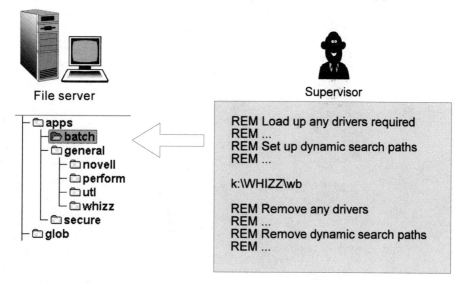

Figure 8.20 Installing applications on the file server: stage 2.

home directory or to a common directory. Bear in mind that this batch file is executed from the workstation. Because of your core map set-up, all users should have access to the K: drive.

By simply pointing to the directory K:\WHIZZ\ followed by the program name (let us call it WB.EXE), you can then run the WhizzBang program. On completion within your batch file you can remove any specially loaded dynamic search paths, programs and drivers. This is particularly useful for programs such as AutoCAD which require special TSR programs to be loaded. In particular, screen drivers need to be removed on termination so that you can release memory for other programs. You can also use the batch file to provide standard messages that inform the user of their next actions.

User viewpoint

A user can now execute WhizzBang from anywhere (Figure 8.21). Once they have logged into the system an automatic entry is made in their path statement referring to the common batch file directory that contains the batch file that loads WhizzBang. So in any drive the user can type WHIZZ, which loads WhizzBang.

Advantages of this approach

Most problems in computing can be solved by adding another level of indirection. In other words, do not point to objects directly: refer to an object which in turn points

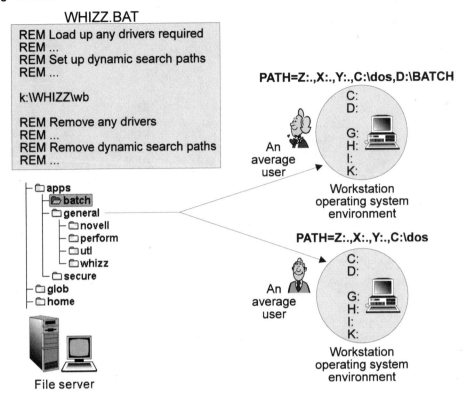

WHIZZ.BAT

```
REM Load up any drivers required
REM ...
REM Set up dynamic search paths
REM ...

k:\WHIZZ\wb

REM Remove any drivers
REM ...
REM Remove dynamic search paths
REM ...
```

PATH=Z:.,X:.,Y:.,C:\dos,D:\BATCH

An average user

C:
D:
G:
H:
I:
K:

Workstation operating system environment

PATH=Z:.,X:.,Y:.,C:\dos

An average user

C:
D:
G:
H:
I:
K:

Workstation operating system environment

```
├─ apps
│   ├─ batch
│   ├─ general
│   │   ├─ novell
│   │   ├─ perform
│   │   ├─ utl
│   │   └─ whizz
│   └─ secure
├─ glob
├─ home
```

File server

Figure 8.21 Installing applications on the file server: stage 3.

to your required object. This is definitely true when loading applications. Instead of allowing the user to load the application directly across the network, by using a batch file you can control the sequence of operations that the user has to go through before the application is run, and also the sequence of operations required to terminate the program gracefully.

There are many different types of applications. Some will require data to be stored exclusively by user; others will require access to shared data storage. There are also some applications that have to store special configuration files, depending on the type of hardware that the user is running the software on.

The framework described here is a starting point; it needs to be modified appropriately depending on the requirements of the application. For example, how can we cope with applications that require a customized configuration for each user? This is not too difficult. The common batch file that loads up the application can initially point the user to a specific home directory, where a customized copy of their preferences and configuration files is stored, before loading the application (stored in the APS subdirectory) across the network. We shall look at this in greater detail when we consider Windows, which deserves its own substantial section. Another very important consideration is the software licence, which we shall also examine later. However, the simple technique outlined in this section can be used to ensure that only one copy of a given application is run at any given time; basically, the application is locked.

Archiving using PKZIP

Minimizing file clutter around the file server is one of the vital jobs of the network manager. One of the most popular programs for this purpose is PKZIP, which is an extremely useful file-compression utility.

Look for the latest version of PKZIP. It should be v2.0g (or above); it has been significantly improved.

This program is one of the most widely used shareware programs on the market. For the network manager, it is a useful tool for:

- moving the contents of a directory and its subdirectories into a single file
- long-term storage
- copying files to diskette
- sending data across telephone lines

Using it, you can normally expect to save at least 50% of storage space.

PKZIP version 2

The latest version of PKZIP has the following features, most of which are very good news for the network manager:

- Novell NetWare aware: it uses NCP directly, rather than the standard DOS file transfer calls
- improved compression: PKZIP 2 implements deflating
- multi-volume archive support: it can create .ZIP files larger than a single floppy disk. This means that a large file can span many floppy disks. You will automatically be asked to enter each disk
- automatic detection and utilization of 80386 and 80486 CPUs
- full use of EMS and XMS memory
- easily configured to suit your needs, through the use of the PKCFG program
- password encryption: sensitive data files can be scrambled with password protection. The security of this feature has been improved in PKZIP 2
- authenticity verification: users requiring authentication of archive files may request an authenticity verification code. This allows users to create .ZIP files that reveal tampering

- data encryption: it offers the ability to protect stored data through encryption. You should use PKZIP's encryption facility in the place of any other encryption on files that you intend to compress

> Be careful: PKZIP v2.04c had a number of problems, especially when used over multi-floppy disks. Check your version, and upgrade as soon as possible if it is 2.04c.

Where to get the latest copy of PKZIP

The PKWARE BBS bulletin board offers the latest in PKWARE shareware as well as many other files for downloading. PKWARE BBS has multiple phone lines for your convenience.

```
PKWARE BBS, (414)354-8670
CompuServe. PKWARE Support Technicians maintain a discussion
forum on CompuServe. To get to the forum, simply type "GO
PKWARE" from any CompuServe prompt. PKWARE CompuServe ID#
75300,730

For more information:
PKWARE Inc., 9025 N. Deerwood Dr., Brown Deer, 53223
(414)354-8699, (414)354-8559 FAX, (414)354-8670 BBS
```

9

Windows and NetWare: a happy marriage?

If everybody on the network had the same machine and preferences, then installing and using Microsoft Windows across the network would be simple. However, in reality the network manager will probably have to deal with different machines, with different types of screen, and with varying user preferences. The installed copy of Windows must cope with this variety, and the result is a veritable minefield of potential problems.

Microsoft and Novell are both working hard to ensure that the two products integrate effectively. At the same time Microsoft are working independently to develop their NT technology, which they see as a replacement for Novell NetWare. However, until this comes to fruition, Novell NetWare remains the leading network in the world, and Windows has become the most important user interface.

This chapter is concerned with getting the best from both Windows and Novell taking all the potential variations into consideration. Microsoft provide remarkably little information on the integration of their products with Novell NetWare, and Novell's contributions are very technically oriented and generally not particularly user-friendly. In order to keep you sane, and to help you find your way through this jungle of variations and permutations, I shall outline a framework that you can use to install Windows on the Novell file server. It is sufficiently flexible to cope with the variety of different configurations. I shall also examine available third-party products that help to achieve the smooth integration of Windows and Novell.

The Microsoft Windows product range

Microsoft have a range of Windows-based products, each with its own networking capabilities. The current range is:

- the very popular Windows 3.1
- Windows for Workgroups

- Windows NT
- LAN Manager

The network device interface standard (NDIS) is very important to the Windows for Workgroups, NT and LAN Manager products. For more information about NDIS, see the section on NDIS drivers in Chapter 7.

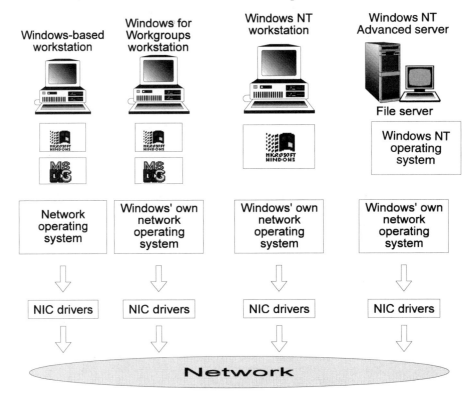

Figure 9.1 Microsoft Windows product range.

Microsoft Windows 3.1

This is one of the most popular programs in the world. It is made network-aware during the set-up procedure. It can work with a multitude of different underlying network operating systems, the most important of which is NetWare. It has no intrinsic networking capabilities; it only sees the network through the add-on network drivers. This means that it can work equally well with dedicated IPX, NDIS or ODI drivers.

Regardless of the underlying network operating system, be it Novell or LAN Manager, Windows sees the underlying network in the same graphical manner. The main difference is that more options are available under some network operating systems than under others. It seems likely that, in the future, this product will be merged with Windows for Workgroups.

Windows for Workgroups

While we wait for Microsoft's Windows NT technology to arrive, Windows for Workgroups is already here. This special version of Windows 3.1 is a peer-to-peer DOS-based network operating system. Microsoft would be the first to admit that it is not intended for large networks; they provide the OS/2-based LAN Manager for such applications. Windows for Workgroups is an entry-level product, aimed at networks of between two and five users, although in theory it can go up to 20 users. Microsoft's aim is to get Windows users used to networking. It is also an attempt to hold back Novell, with its bundled software package of DR-DOS (Digital Research DOS) and NetWare Lite, Novell's equivalent for peer-to-peer networking. Microsoft have claimed that, by 1995, as much as 20% of all PCs within networks will be using this product.

Windows For Workgroups version 3.11

Microsoft is currently working on a new version of Windows for Workgroups 3.11 (is this Microsoft's answer to NetWare v 3.11?). It will turn the product into a more attractive proposition for the large corporate users. The new system will include a 32-bit filing system to significantly improve the disk performance. The most significant changes in this product from the Novel point of view is that it will support ODI drivers as well as NDIS. It looks very likely that this product will be incorporated into the next major release of Windows operating system.

Underlying technology

Windows for Workgroups supports most of the standard network interface cards from companies such as 3-Com, Intel and SMC(WD). It also supports IBM Token Ring cards. The key thing about this product is that it uses the NDIS standard. This means that any card that has an NDIS specification can be used by Windows for Workgroups. As for LAN Manager, the underlying protocol is NETBEUI (NETBIOS extended user interface), but because Workgroups uses NDIS it can also use other protocols, such as TCP/IP.

Set-up security

On installation, each Windows workstation is given a physical name. This is not the user name, but a name that will be physically associated with the particular PC on which you install Windows for Workgroups. When you install the system, you are prompted for a password. This is used to control who can start the network service in the future. From then on, every time Windows for Workgroups is started it prompts the user for the password before activating the network function.

Sharing resources

To share the contents of your directory with another Windows user, you use the specially extended version of the File Manager program. Instead of giving remote access rights to your actual subdirectories, you give any directory to be shared a logical name, referred to as the shared name such as DataBase=C:\C. This name can then be used by other Windows users to tap on to your resource.

In Figure 9.2, the shared directory is shown by the special hand icon. When a directory is shared, any of its subdirectories are also made available to the remote user, but higher-level directories are not accessible. So if you make your top-level directory shareable, such as C:\, then other users can access the whole of your C: drive.

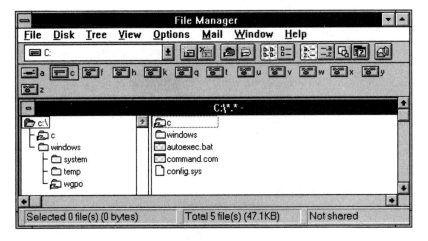

Figure 9.2 Windows for Workgroups enhanced File Manager.

Controlling the network

There is a special network icon in the control panel that opens the Workgroups network control panel. From here you can adjust all sort of things about the network. This includes changing the network card type, defining the opening password, and specifying how much processing time priority users should be given at the expense of applications that might be running on your machine.

DDE across networks

Dynamic data exchange is a technique that enables applications to link data together via DDE channels. So if you change the data in one application, then the same data will be automatically updated by Windows in the other application. DDE has now been extended to work not only across applications on the same machine, but across several machines simultaneously. This should allow applications to link together across the network. Windows NT and Windows for Workgroups support DDE across the network.

E-mail

Windows for Workgroups is supplied with a free E-mail package: in effect, a cut-down version of Microsoft's Mail package (Figure 9.3). It is not as comprehensive as Lotus's cc-Mail, but it is an excellent E-mail package for beginners.

Schedule

Windows for Workgroups also includes a workgrouping package called Schedule. This can be used to organize users around a schedule, which can be interrogated by a number of users on the network. You can use this program to bring people together: for example, if you need to arrange a meeting, you can look through everyone's schedule from you own workstation to set the next suitable date and enter the time and location of the meeting into their schedules. Each user will be informed of the upcoming meeting when they next use the Schedule program.

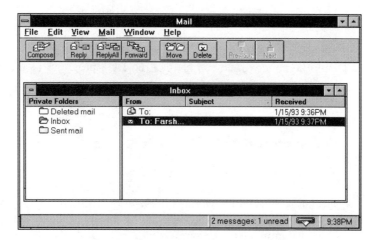

Figure 9.3 Windows for Workgroups: E-mail package.

Novell and Workgroups

Using the NDIS standard and the special version of IPX that is NDIS-compliant, it is possible to connect up to a Novell file server whilst using resources from other Windows for Workgroups users. The only problem is that you must use the special IPX (NDIS) provided by Microsoft and not the one provided by IPX (dedicated or ODI versions) from Novell.

Network-monitoring programs

Two programs are provided for monitoring the network. The first is called WinMeter. This program monitors network traffic, and shows how much of the processor was taken up at any time to service user requests rather than running your own applications. The second is called Net Watcher: this is a very simple program that shows you who is currently using the resources of your machine.

Strategy

Although Windows for Workgroups software is a very interesting product, it should be thought of as an entry-level product that paves the way for Windows NT. Use it for testing and experimentation. It is ideal for a small number of Windows-based users (from two to five), but above this you should be looking at alternative network operating systems, such as Novell 3.x, 4.x or the Windows NT advanced server.

Windows NT (new technology)

This is the product that should see Windows into the 21st Century. In this product DOS is done away with, and a complete 32-bit flat memory architecture is implemented. This leads to a far more efficient and reliable operating system: a true multitasking environment that can run DOS programs as part of its sessions. It has intrinsic networking capabilities, and requires a strict adherence to the Microsoft NDIS standard.

New security features

Unlike Windows 3.1, Windows NT is a secure system; users must log in before using their files. Like LAN Manager, Windows NT introduces a supervisor: a special user called the administrator. In order to create users you first log in as the administrator and create accounts for users. It is these accounts that users must use to log in before using the system.

Files are protected under the Windows NT system by using NTFS (new technology filing system). This is similar to the HPFS (higher performance filing system) that is provided under OS/2. With DOS, anyone can boot up DOS and read files. Under NTFS, you can only read files after you have logged into the system, and even then only the files that the administrator has given you jurisdiction over.

Windows NT system files

Windows NT stores all the system information, such as user passwords and directory rights, within files called registries. These are analogous to Novell's bindery files, and are the most important files for the operating system. They store all the important objects used within the operating system. The registry files are never accessed directly; they are manipulated through standard tools provided within the Windows NT operating system, including the control panel and a special user manager program. However, there is a special registry program made available to all administrators that allows manipulation of the registry files.

New Windows NT filing system (NTFS)

Windows NT does away with the old DOS FAT format but, most importantly, it is a secure system; you must authenticate yourself to the system by typing your user ID password before the filing system will allow you to assess the required files. Other major differences are as follows:

- NTFS allows for long names; the eight characters and three extension characters associated with DOS filenames are eliminated.
- File size is limited by hard disk storage only.
- Transaction tracking facilities are now provided.
- Massive large volumes can now be defined (NTFS volumes are similar to those in the Novell filing system)
- Performance is significantly improved over DOS.
- NTFS will also support FAT and HPFS filing systems.

Networking and Windows NT

Windows NT has intrinsic networking capabilities that allow for peer-to-peer file- and print-sharing facilities. A collection of control programs are automatically provided through the File and Print Manager. You can easily share directories or print over the network. Windows NT uses the preferred Microsoft NDIS standard as a means of defining network interface cards. It is supplied with a comprehensive list of supported network cards from the major manufacturers.

Enhanced MS-DOS 5 commands

Windows NT enhances most of the commands that we associate with MS-DOS 5 to take into account the new facilities offered by the NT environment. For example, the DOS COPY command can now be used to address file server names directly.

Windows NT and the future

Microsoft are working hard to implement a coherent distributed computing environment (DCE), which will allow users of the future to run applications being processed on other Windows NT machines, leading to the world of distributed processing. A Windows NT machine will then become a processing server: something that Sun UNIX people have been doing for years.

Microsoft are also working on a project called 'Cairo'. This is their distributed object-oriented technology that should emerge in mid-1994. From the limited details currently available, it seems that Cairo will define object linking and embedding (OLE) across networks. It will provide object-oriented file systems that can be distributed around the network. It will also let users locate documents or resources on the network, regardless of their actual location. Could this be Microsoft's answer to the NetWare 4.x Directory services?

NetWare 4.x and Windows NT

Windows NT promises to have plenty of applications written for it, with most of the big names in the software business gearing up to producing Windows NT applications, although it is worth recalling that the same thing was said about OS/2 when that was introduced.

As far as running Windows NT on servers is concerned, Novell's development of UnixWare in conjunction with USL (UNIX System Labs) has put a lot of pressure on Microsoft to ensure that Windows NT is great success. It is a new operating system, and has yet to prove its reliability in the real world.

While NT is under attack as an operating system from UnixWare, its networking facilities are under attack from Novell's NetWare 4.x product, which will support a far superior worldwide directory service, making it much easier to create new users or resources. A NetWare 4.x manager can manage the resources of the enterprise-wide network from a single point, whereas the Windows NT manager can only cope with managing network domains (a domain being a collection of servers). This advantage makes NetWare 4.x far more appropriate for large corporate organizations. The equivalent of NetWare's directory services is not expected to appear in Windows NT for another year or so.

However, it is likely that Microsoft will ensure that Windows NT running on workstations will offer most Windows 3.1 users enough tempting reasons to want to upgrade. They are working hard to make the transition between 3.1 and NT as smooth as possible. The Windows 3.1 user will see the benefit of the improved performance and functionality. In my view, most of today's Windows 3.1 users will soon be using Windows NT as their standard GUI. However, when it comes to networking functionality, I believe that NetWare 4.x will dominate the world market, but your guess is as good as mine.

Comparing Microsoft Windows products

Table 9.1 outlines the main differences between Microsoft's various Windows products. At the most basic level is Windows 3.1; at the top end is LAN Manager for Windows NT, sometimes called the Windows NT advanced server. This is a special version of the old LAN Manager program, which used to run under the OS/2 environment, but has now been ported onto the Windows NT platform.

Windows basics

Why use Windows?

Why is Microsoft Windows so popular, and why do most organizations now seem to fully standardize their application around the Windows environment?

Table 9.1 A comparison of Microsoft Windows products.

Function	Windows 3.1	Windows for Workgroups	Windows NT	Windows NT advanced server
GUI	yes	yes	yes	yes
Peer to peer	no	yes	yes	yes
E-mail	no	yes	yes	yes
Scheduler	no	yes	yes	yes
File server	no	no	yes	yes
Single domain management	no	no	yes	yes
Multiple domain management	no	no	no	yes
Hot fix	no	no	yes	yes
RAID 5 support as standard	no	no	no	yes

Here are some of the important reasons for Windows great success:

- Windows defines a graphical user interface, providing a far friendlier environment for new users than the DOS text world.

- It is from Microsoft.

- Microsoft Windows standardizes the user interface across many different applications. In the old days the network user was faced with an assortment of different DOS-based applications, each requiring a different sequence of keys to perform similar tasks. The unified interface provided by Windows is of the greatest importance for today's network manager, because once the network has been installed most of the problems seem to take place at the application layer. The other advantage is that users will become more productive; it is said that the average manager is able to spend only 20 consecutive minutes on a particular application before being interrupted by the telephone etc.

- Windows not only provides a universal environment for applications to run upon; it also standardizes some of the key sequences. For example, in all Windows applications function key F1 triggers the help button. Every application runs within a window and can be resized and moved; you also can flick from one application to another. Once the user is accustomed to the concept, then regardless of the type of application they will be able to find their way around and will be familiar with the ways of selecting menu and submenu options.

- Once you have told Windows what type of printer, screen or mouse you are using, most applications will use the same standard. In the old days every application had to be configured differently, depending on the type of screen you were using.

- A correctly installed version of Windows allows the network manager to change the configuration at one administration point, and this will automatically be reported and used by all relevant Windows applications.

What happens to all those people who have old applications and would like to move on to Windows? In most systems the two approaches seem to coexist, with users slowly moving from the old DOS-based applications to a new generation of Windows-based applications. One interesting point about Windows is that you can run a DOS-based applications as yet another task within the Windows environment.

When Windows is networked it has a number of advantages for the user. It can hide the different types of operating systems that it is manipulating; the user can map and move around network drives from a Windows environment regardless of the type of network operating system that they are using. For example, if in the future they decide to move from Novell NetWare to UnixWare, then Windows simply has to be reconfigured to use the new underlying network operating system. For the front-end user, most things remain unchanged. It is also worth saying that Windows is great fun to use.

However, there are problems. Windows-based programs are usually processor-hungry compared with DOS-based applications, because information displayed in a graphical format requires far greater processing speed. As corporations standardize on Windows applications they find that users are demanding far more powerful processing capabilities, with a consequent increase in cost. A typical Windows user would require a 386 33 MHz machine with a minimum of 4 Mbytes of memory.

Another disadvantage is that you will probably need a mouse on all machines; again, this is not required in most DOS-based applications. The disadvantage here is not so much the cost, which is minimal, but more the extra hardware and cabling required on the desk top.

However, the disadvantages are completely outweighed by all the advantages. I see the future moving further and further towards Windows technology, reflected in the number of developments currently taking place. Most major manufacturers are bringing out Windows-based versions of their products. With Windows NT the future of Microsoft Windows is, I feel, assured.

Starting Windows in different modes

With Windows 3.1 and higher versions, there are two different modes in which you can start the Windows program: standard and 386 enhanced mode. There used to be a third mode, called real mode, that was available in Windows 3.0, but it is not available in Windows 3.1, and is therefore not discussed in this section. As a general rule, opt if possible for starting Windows in 386 enhanced mode.

Standard mode
In standard mode, Windows needs to be running on a 286 machine or higher. This is the normal operating mode on a 286 workstation. It makes full use of extended memory as a continuation of conventional memory. It is a simple, fast mode in which Windows applications treat conventional and extended memory as a continuous memory block.

There are a number of problems associated with the standard mode: expanded memory is not supported, and you cannot create virtual memory by the use of swap files. To run Windows under standard mode you must already be running HIMEM.SYS.

386 enhanced mode
This is the preferred mode for running Windows on a 386 or higher processor. In this mode, as with standard mode, all conventional and extended memory is treated as a continuous block of available memory that can be used by Windows applications.

Windows 386 can also emulate expanded memory. In this mode you can multitask non-Windows applications, by creating a number of virtual machines, each one having a unique pseudo-DOS environment. Enhanced mode employs the concept of virtual drivers. Each DOS session window, just like the drivers in the DOS

CONFIG.SYS file, loads a set of drivers for the DOS environment. These virtual drivers, when loaded, will be exclusively used by the program that will be run within the DOS window. In this mode you can run non-Windows DOS-based applications within a window.

Multitasking Windows applications is not particularly efficient, compared with multitasking applications under UNIX. Windows slows down considerably when it has to multitask applications.

Warning: Resource conflicts can occur when running multitasked applications within Windows. For example, it can lead to lots of problems if two applications try to use the same serial port at the same time.

Windows INI files

Windows uses text files with the INI extension to store an assortment of information that defines the Windows environment. Some of these files are intrinsic to Windows itself, such as WIN.INI and SYSTEM.INI; others, such as EXCEL.INI and LOTUS.INI, are created and maintained by specific Windows applications.

Format of INI files

All .INI files have the following features in common. They are normally stored as text files. Each file is divided into a number of logical groups called sections. Each section is further divided into a number of subsections. Each subsection is identified by a keyname. Against each keyname there can be a list of parameters that define its value.

Each section has the following format:

```
.

.

[Section Name]
Key name = parameters
Key name = parameters

.

.
```

Each section can contain a series of keynames. Each keyname can have any number of parameters, although normally there is only one value against each keyname in each section. The order in which the sections appear is not important. At any point in the INI file, comments can be added, by using a semicolon in the first column followed by any remark.

Figure 9.4 shows a typical INI file. It has three sections. The first section [datasets] shows three different keynames; the second [console] shows one key name; and the last section [refresh] shows two different keynames.

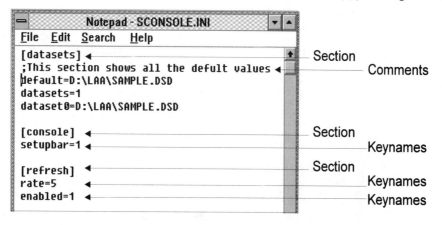

Figure 9.4 Format of INI files.

Microsoft recommend that you only use Notepad, the Windows text (ASCII) editor, to edit INI files. This is because other editors might add special characters, which could cause a problem with the application. In general, if you are not sure whether a line in the INI file is still needed, do not delete it. Put a semicolon in front of it, thereby turning it into a comment. You can always remove it later after your Windows application has run successfully.

Windows INI files

Windows has a number of important initialization files. These contain information that defines the Windows environment, and the applications and drivers that are to be supported (Table 9.2).

The two most important Windows INI files are WIN.INI and SYSTEM.INI.

Table 9.2 Windows INI files.

INI filename	How Windows uses it
WIN.INI	Stores the Windows user's preferences
SYSTEM.INI	Deals with the hardware set-up of the Windows environment.
CONTROL.INI	Stores the list of currently installed drivers, and default colour schemes
PROGMAN.INI	Defines how Program Manager displays program groups
WINFILE.INI	Used by File Manager to store the user's selected default set-ups

WIN.INI

This file primarily contains the settings that Windows uses to customize its environment according to the user's preferences. Far too many Windows applications also place all sorts of information within this file instead of creating their own INI files. Even Microsoft's products are not entirely innocent in this respect. However, although WIN.INI can get very long, all entries are placed under meaningful headings so, technically speaking, it is easy to see which application has added a given section to the file.

SYSTEM.INI

This file primarily contains the settings required to customize the user's hardware environment. However, there are also a large number of entries that are configuring the Windows software environment. An example of this is the default FONT selection.

Application INI files

Potentially, each Windows application can define its own specialized INI file. These files are normally used to store user preferences and default selections for the given application. An example of such a file is shown in Figure 9.5: this is the INI file produced by the Minesweeper program.

Figure 9.5 A typical application INI file.

Swap files under Windows

What are swap files?

When running Windows 3.1 and above under 386 enhanced mode, you can use a swap file to create virtual memory. This extra memory is then presented to your Windows application as if it were extra PC RAM memory. This can be very useful when you are running out of real memory. The main price you pay is that this type of memory is slow to utilize, and will require disk storage. Windows swap files create virtual memory support by using the hard disk.

> Warning: do not create swap files on compressed disk drives, produced by products such as SuperStor and Stacker. They tend not to use a standard configuration of 512 bytes per sector, which makes them non-standard as far as Windows swap files are concerned.

How it works

When swap files are set up, Windows can then fool applications into thinking that they have more memory than is actually physically available in RAM. In broad terms, Windows reports to the application:

$$\text{Total memory available} = \text{Actual RAM storage} + \text{Swap file size}$$

When an application requests more memory than is actually available, Windows automatically swaps some memory usage from RAM to the swap files. This normally means that it suspends part of an existing application and stores its contents in the swap file. It then releases the area to meet the memory request from the current application.

The virtual memory manager (VMM) uses the least recently used (LRU) technique to swap pages. It maintains a table of all pageable memory, in which two flags are associated with each page: the last accessed flag means that the page has been accessed, and the dirty flag means that the page has been recently modified. The VMM uses these two flags in deciding which page to swap in or out.

Setting up swap files

You activate the swap file through the Windows Control Panel 386 Enhanced icon. From there you then select the Virtual memory button (Figure 9.6).

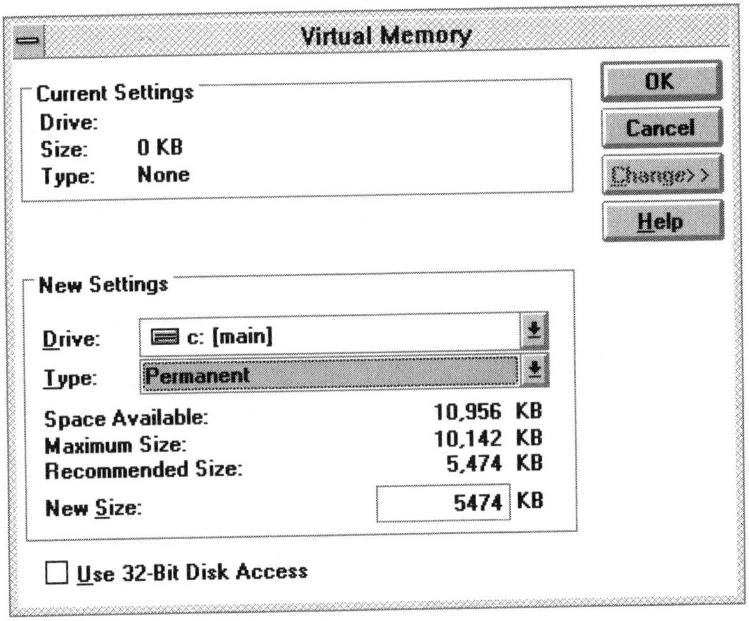

Figure 9.6 Creating virtual memory.

Swap files can be either permanent or temporary.

Permanent swap files improve the speed of the Windows virtual memory system compared with temporary files, because they occupy a contiguous block of sectors on the disk, so that accessing them requires less overhead then the normal files created by temporary swap files.

Swap files normally have the following format:

Typical file name	Description
386SPART.PAR	Permanent swap file
WIN386.SWP	Temporary swap file

If you use the permanent option, it will have to be of a fixed size and occupy a contiguous portion of the disk, whereas temporary swap files are deleted at the end of each Windows session, releasing the space back to other applications.

Before setting up swap files on local hard disks make sure you run a defragmentation program, such as SD.EXE from Norton Advanced Utilities.

Using swap files across the network

It is possible to use swap files across the network, but it is not a very good idea, because it can severely congest the network and reduce Windows performance for the user. However, sometimes you have no choice: for example, if you have a diskless workstation with little main memory.

In the network environment observe the following points:

- The user must be given read and write access to the location of the swap file
- The user must have access to the swap file before running Windows
- The networked swap file means that the user must be prepared for a slow Windows start
- You cannot create permanent swap files over networks

You can fool Windows into treating a temporary network swap file as semi-permanent by the use of the WIN.INI file under the [386Enh] heading. Typical entries would be:

```
[386Enh]

Paging=Yes
PagingDrive=H
MaxPagingFileSize=2048
```

Paging means that the virtual memory has been activated. The paging drive is where the swap file is going to be found. Be careful in selecting a value for MaxPagingFileSize. Select a value of 1024 Kbytes or above; anything below that would be almost useless. A typical value is 5 Mbytes.

Swap file management issues

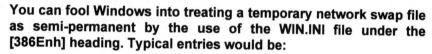

One of the easiest ways to ensure that Windows runs fast and trouble-free is to give it lots of memory. The average Windows workstation should have a minimum of 4 Mbytes and preferably 8 Mbytes or more.

Swap files are all very well for machines with low memory, but they can be very slow, especially if you create swap files across the network. However, there are times when it is useful to increase Windows memory size temporarily at the expense of performance, in which swap files are a perfect answer.

My advice is, where possible:

- Add plenty of memory to the workstation to do away with swap files
- If you need to use swap files, opt for permanent ones
- Try not to use swap files across networks

Installing Windows over the network

Anatomy of Microsoft Windows

When you look at the full Windows program set, you can identify four different types of file:

- shareable code files
- configuration files
- swap files
- data files

It is important to be able to recognize the different types of file, because you need to decide on the best location for storing them across the network.

Shareable code files

These are dynamic link library (.DLL) files, and other Windows applications such as WRITE.EXE and FILER.EXE. This type of program gets read and will not be changed by any application. This means that this type of file can be kept in a common directory that is available on a read-only basis to all users.

Configuration files

These are normally user-specific files that contain information on the user's preferences and configuration. They also contain information on the specific hardware used on the workstation.

This type of file normally has an INI (initialization) or a GRP (group) extension. WIN.COM is an interesting program that also falls into this category; this program can be modified by the user.

When a user makes a change to the configuration of Windows it is recorded in this type of file. For the changes to take place, the user must make sure that read and write access is available. The network manager therefore normally keeps these files in a different subdirectory from the shareable code files, which are always read-only, regardless of the user.

Swap files

Most users run Windows under 386 enhanced mode, thus providing the opportunity to create swap files to increase available memory size by utilizing disk storage. Swap files, as described above, can be either permanent or temporary. A permanent swap file has to be of a fixed size and occupy a contiguous portion of the disk; temporary swap files are deleted at the end of each Windows session, releasing the space for other applications.

Data files

This type of file is created by Windows applications for storage of their own data. To decide where these files should be stored, you need to take into account the type of application and whether it is going to be shared among users. Example of such files are *.DOC files from Microsoft Word, *.WRI from the Windows Write program and *.CDR from the Corel Draw package.

Network installation overview

When you purchase Microsoft Windows 3.1 you receive seven high-density disks full of compressed files. To install Windows from the master set you use the Setup program, normally found on the system 1 disk. Setup automatically stores Windows onto any hard disk that you choose. So a simplistic approach would be to run Setup and install Windows on a remote network drive. Setup will automatically read the configuration of the workstation that it is actually being run on; it will look for any network drivers and install the appropriate ones on the designated drive.

However, using this approach can cause problems when you have installed this copy of Windows on the network and users with different configurations wish to run it. It would be better, therefore, to separate the main program files from the configuration files. The core program set would be loaded from a central master directory available to all users across the network, but Windows would load the appropriate individual configuration file for each user or workstation

Now comes the big decision. Where should the individual configuration files be stored: on the user's local drive, making them specific to the workstation, or under the user's home directory on the file server (Figure 9.7)?

There are different schools of thought on this. Storing the configuration file on the local drive makes it specific to the workstation, so if a user logs on to another machine with a different type of screen or mouse driver, then the appropriate configuration file is automatically loaded from the local station. However, if it is installed in the home directory, then if the user logs on to another machine with the same type of hardware they can still use Windows under their own log-in name because their configuration file is automatically made available to them through the network. Also, of course, there are no local drives on diskless workstations, so in this case the configuration file has to be stored in the home directory.

So far, most organizations that have installed Novell and Windows seem to have adopted the policy of putting users' configuration files on the local drive, usually on the C: drive under a subdirectory called C:\WINDOWS. However, there does now seem to be a trend towards storing configurations in the home directories.

The Windows configuration problem

One problem with the current version of Windows 3.1 is that the configuration files it produces contain a mixture of information. Some is hardware-specific, relating to the types of screen and mouse drivers that are supported; some is application-oriented and relates to user preferences such as background screen colour, and the number of windows last opened.

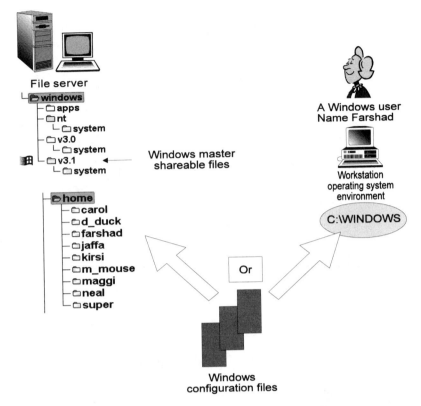

Figure 9.7 Where to put users' configuration files.

It would be nice if you could separate the two, with the hardware-specific information that is local to the workstation stored on the C: drive, and the user-specific information stored in the home directory on the file server. Unfortunately, Windows will not let you do this; the two configurations are stored in the same set of files. In general, the WIN.COM file contains user preferences and application-specific information, while SYSTEM.INI stores hardware information and the drivers required to run Windows. But the split is not clear-cut, which means that the two types of information cannot easily be separated out.

Different approaches to Windows installation

There are three different approaches to installing Windows on the network:

(1)   full local hard disk installation

(2)   shared code and configuration files on the local hard disk

(3)   shared code in a common network directory, configuration files in the users' home directory

Approach 1: full local hard disk installation

This is the simplest approach. All the Windows shared files, user configuration and any swap files are all stored locally on the hard disk. This approach is normally used where there is a large local hard disk, and the user is going to be running Windows applications that are very input/output-intensive. The advantages and disadvantages are as follows:

- ✓ You do not congest the network by having to read Windows files
- ✓ Response is fast, as Windows is stored locally (assuming you have a fast hard disk)
- ✓ You can operate Windows when the network is not active
- ✗ A lot of hard disk space is required on each workstation
- ✗ Backing up Windows configuration files is much more problematic
- ✗ The user cannot run Windows on another machine, as all the user configuration files are on the original workstation.
- ✗ The biggest problem is that you cannot administrate the Windows configuration for all users through the network

Approach 2: shared code and configuration files on local hard disk

The Windows shareable files are put into a common network subdirectory to which all Windows users are given access via their own search path statement. All the user configuration and swap files are stored on the local hard disk. The advantages and disadvantages of this approach are as follows:

- ✓ Most of the Windows common files only need to be kept once on the network for all users, thus saving local hard disk storage, for all Windows users
- ✓ Configuration files are made specific to the workstations
- ✓ Swap files are kept local and can be made permanent
- ✗ If the user runs Windows on someone else's machine they will not get their own customization.
- ✗ Local storage of user configurations means that you cannot administrate user configurations via the network
- ✗ Backing up Window configuration files is much more problematic
- ✗ You cannot operate Windows when the network is not active

Approach 3: shared code in common network directory, configuration in user's home directory

This is the most network-dependent approach. It relies on storing all the shared files and configurations on the network. The shared files are placed in a common network subdirectory to which all Windows users are given access via their own search path statement. The user's configuration files are kept in their own home directory. Swap files, if required, can be stored locally on the hard disk. The advantages and disadvantages of this approach are as follows:

✓ All the Windows shared files are kept once on the network for all users, thus saving local hard disk storage

✓ You can run Windows from any workstation (as long as the hardware is the same)

✓ You can run Windows from a diskless workstation

✓ It is very easy to back up user configuration files

✓ In theory, you can change some or all of the network Windows user configuration files from one administration point

✗ If you try running Windows on a machine with different hardware you might be in big trouble

✗ All Windows files have to be loaded across the network

Strategy consideration

I am going to concentrate on approaches 2 and 3. Approach 1 does not really use the network, since all the Windows files are stored locally on the hard disk.

Most network managers adopt approach 2 or 3, and there is a movement away from approach 2 to approach 3, because it is much easier to manage a network from a central administration point if all the relevant files are kept on the network. There are some excellent programs that will automatically manage the users' INI files across the network, including Windows Workstation from Automated Design Systems and Saber Menu System for Windows.

The installation framework described below stores users' configuration files on the network in their own home directories rather than on the local hard disk. This is essential, of course, if you have a diskless workstation.

There are five stages:

(1) the prerequisites before installing Windows on the file server

(2) installing the master copy

(3) laying the foundation for user installations

(4) installing a shared copy of Windows for users

(5) writing a batch file to load Windows

These stages are described below.

Prerequisites before installing Windows on the file server

Before installing Windows on the file server, you need a minimum of 20 Mbytes of storage on the file server to store the Windows master files. This could easily be doubled in terms of the future storage requirements of the Windows subdirectory.

In practice you need much more than 20 Mbytes, as many Windows applications will automatically store files under this directory.

Ensure that you have a licence to use Microsoft Windows on more than one machine.

Decide whether any of your workstations might be diskless in the near future. This information might affect your approach to the next few stages.

Installing the master copy

As supervisor, you log into the network and map yourself into the drive where you will install the master set of Windows. I suggest that you map to a subdirectory called \WINDOWS\V3.1 rather than just \WINDOWS. This allow the flexibility of storing other version of Windows, such as Windows NT, within the same framework, so that you can support them from the same file server.

Once the Windows drive has been mapped – in this example drive W: – you are ready for the Windows installation. This is referred to as the Windows administration set-up.

From the first set-up disk in the Microsoft Windows disk set, run

```
SETUP /A
```

The /A means that it is a special administrative option that instructs the Setup program to install the whole set of programs and associated drivers from the master disk on the network drive (W: in this example) automatically (Figure 9.8). Setup reads all the compressed files on the disk one by one and decompresses them onto the W: drive. This normally takes approximately 20 minutes, so have a cup of coffee ready!

This option is new with Windows 3.1. Under Windows 3.0 you had to run the EXPAND *.* program on each disk yourself, but it is now done automatically by SETUP /A. This stage of the installation is very simple, and the only questions that you will be asked are your user and company name. This is Microsoft's slight (but welcome) attempt at copy protection, ensuring that any future copies of Windows run from this master set will have the associated user and company name.

Before you run SETUP /A stop the reception of network messages from other users, which has been known to cause problems with the Setup program, by typing CASTOFF ALL.

Laying the foundation for user installations

Once you have copied all the disks onto the file server, you have a number of actions to perform.

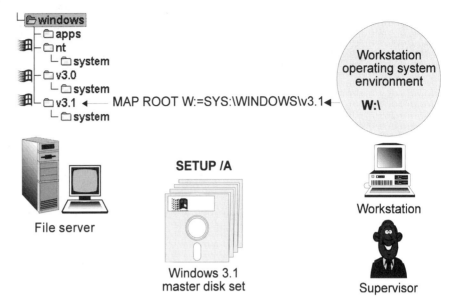

Figure 9.8 Installing a master copy of Windows 3.1 on the NetWare server.

Step 1

Go to the relevant directory and make all files read and file scan only, by using the FLAG or the ATTRIB command:

```
FLAG *.* SRO
```

This makes all the files in the Windows directory shareable and read-only, thus ensuring that they cannot be modified and changed in the future.

Step 2

Next, create a new user group called Window_Users and place all the users that will be using Windows in this group (Figure 9.9). Everyone in this group will be given read and file scan rights to the Windows master subdirectory.

I like to qualify this user group with the version of Windows that they will be using; in the example in Figure 9.9 it is Window_Users_3.1. In this way you can separate different types of Windows users.

Step 3

When the Windows users log into the network, two special network drives are created: the Windows master copy of all shareable files, and the location of all the shared Windows applications. In this example they are the W: and J: drives.

Just before the user starts to run Windows, a reference to the W: drive is placed in their search path, through the use of a batch file (Figure 9.10).

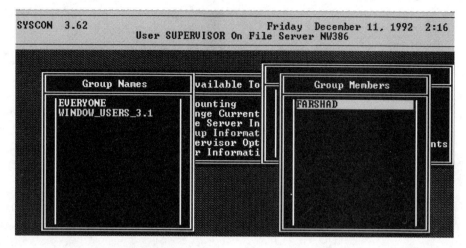

Figure 9.9 Adding Windows users to the relevant group.

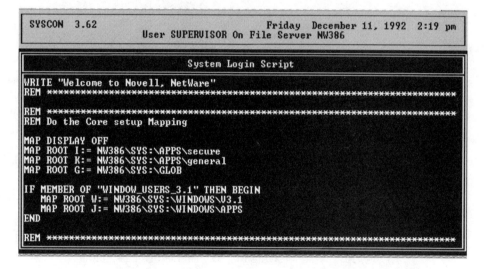

Figure 9.10 Typical script file for Window_Users.

Installing a shared copy of Windows for users

The Windows network set-up option allows you to install a shared copy of Windows for a given user. This is done by running

```
SETUP /N
```

This option generates a specific set of Windows configuration files based on the workstation hardware and on any stated user preferences. These files normally take up about 500 Kbytes. Setup will ask you whether you want to store the customized files on the C: drive or on the user's home drive.

Before you run SETUP /N it is important to load all the Novell drivers first. As seen earlier, this normally consists of loading the ODI or native IPX drivers, and then choosing between running NETX and BNETX. The latter is the burst-mode version of NETX, which is optimized and recommended for the Windows environment.

Try using the burst-mode NETX for improved performance. See the section on burst-mode NETX in Chapter 7.

The two different approaches to installing user configuration files were outlined earlier. Under installation approach 2, you would send the Windows customization file to a subdirectory located on the local hard disk, such as C:\WINDOWS. Under approach 3, you would send the file to a Windows subdirectory under the user's home directory, such as H:\WINDOWS, where this has been mapped by

```
MAP ROOT H:=\HOME\<UserLogInNameDirectory>
```

Writing a batch file to load Windows

If you have been following the suggested directory framework structure, the system script file should have automatically inserted in every user search path a reference to the network batch file directory, as part of the core mapping set-up that all users have in common. The batch files are thus available to be run by all users, but unauthorized users who do not have access rights to a particular application will get an error.

Using this structure, the network manager can create a batch file that the user can call to load up Windows. The structure of this file is as follows:

(1) Add to the user's search path a reference to the main Windows directory

(2) Load any special TSR required by Windows, such as TBMI2

(3) Change directory to the location of the user's Windows configuration files

(4) Run WIN, allowing for parameters to be passed to it

(5) Unload any special TSR such as TBM12

(6) Reset the user search path to what it was before this batch file was run

I shall call this batch file WIN31.BAT. Although it could be called anything, I prefer to incorporate the version number. In this way it is easy to cope with Windows NT, as that could be called WINNT.BAT.

The exact format of this batch file will largely depend on how you have decided to install, but Figures 9.11 and 9.12 show examples of batch files for both types of approach under discussion.

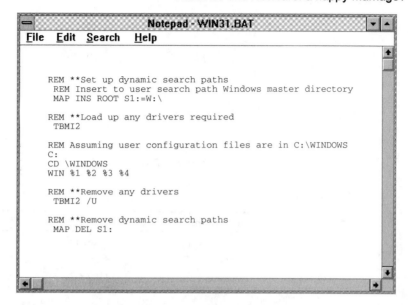

Figure 9.11 Batch file to load Windows: approach 1.

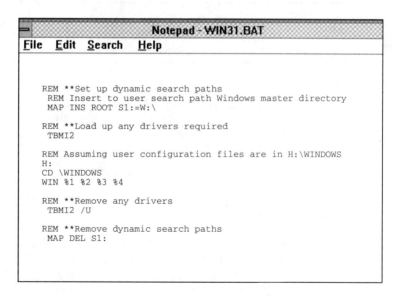

Figure 9.12 Batch file to load Windows: approach 2.

Running Windows over NetWare

If you want to utilize NetWare and Windows fully, make sure that you are using the latest Novell drivers.

Update NetWare drivers as necessary

You should be using the following drivers (or a higher version). Windows version 3.1 already includes some of these updated drivers for Novell NetWare.

IPX options

Name	Minimum version	Description
IPX.OBJ	Version 3.10	Native IPX
LSL.COM	Version 1.21	ODI driver
IPXODI.COM	Version 1.20	ODI driver

NETX options

Name	Minimum version	Description
NETX.COM	Version 3.26	Non-burst mode
BNETX.COM	Version 3.26	Burst mode

> Warning: the EMS NetWare shell (EMSNETX.EXE, etc.) is not supported when Windows is running in 386 enhanced mode.

Other support TSR programs

Name	Minimum version	Description
TBMI2.COM	Version 2.1	Tasked switched manager

To check the current NetWare driver in use, just type NVER (Figure 9.13).

Additions to NET.CFG

In addition to any previous entries, there are a number of specific entries that can be placed within the NET.CFG file to ease the Windows–Novell integration. This should normally be located in the same directory in which NETX (or BNETX) and IPX.EXE (or IPXODI.COM) are kept. These command are as follows:

```
Show Dots=On
```

```
H:\>nver

NETWARE VERSION UTILITY, VERSION 3.12

IPX Version: 3.30
SPX Version: 3.30

LAN Driver:  SMC EtherCard PLUS Family DOS ODI Driver  V1.00
             IRQ 5, Port 0280, Memory D400:0

Shell:       V3.31 Rev. A
DOS:         MSDOS V5.00 on IBM_PC

FileServer: FS311
Novell NetWare v3.11 (250 user) (2/20/91)

H:\>
```

Figure 9.13 Checking your NetWare driver versions.

This is because, by default, the Novell Windows driver does not show the double dots found in a directory listing, unless you tell it otherwise. This command used to be essential in the old Windows 3.0 system. With Windows 3.1 it it no longer needed.

```
File Handles=60
```

NetWare by default only gives access to 40 simultaneously opened files across the network. It is very easy to exceed this limit when you running a number of Windows applications across the network. Sixty is a safe figure. To activate this, you also need to add the following line to the boot up CONFIG.SYS file:

```
FILES=60
```

NetWare drivers for Windows

Windows NetWare device drivers

In addition to the normal NetWare drivers, there are a number of special NetWare device drivers that Windows needs to load before it can work properly. It is very important that you use the latest versions of these drivers. The minimum version numbers recommended by Novell are as follows:

- NETWARE.DRV (minimum version 2.0): This is the main NetWare device driver from Novell. It displays the NetWare Windows dialogue boxes and can execute a number of NetWare utilities. You can call it up by selecting the network icon from the Windows Control Panel (Figure 9.14).

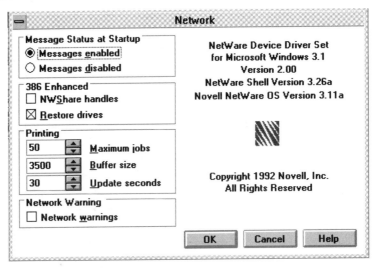

Figure 9.14 NetWare device driver V2.0.

- NETWARE.DRV (version 3.01): With the introduction of NetWare 4.0, a new version of NETWARE.DRV has been released. Its main differences from the old version are that it now supports the NetWare directory services as well as the old bindery servers, and that it integrates with the new NetWare Windows tool (Figure 9.15). You can easily check which Novell network driver version is in use by selecting the network icon from the Windows Program Manager. It will then show the current NetWare driver version (Figure 9.16).

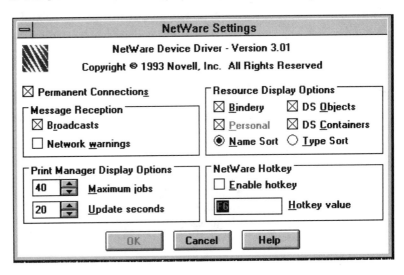

Figure 9.15 NetWare device driver V3.01.

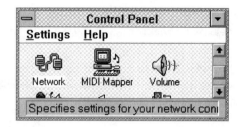

Figure 9.16 The network icon with control panel.

- NETWARE.HLP (minimum version 2.0): This is the help support program for NETWARE.DRV.

- VNETWARE.386 (minimum version 1.04): This program is used only under the Windows enhanced mode. It provides the function normally associated with NETX.COM from the Windows DOS prompt line.

- VIPX.386: This program is used only under the Windows enhanced mode. It provides the function normally associated with IPX.COM from the Windows DOS prompt line.

- NWPOPUP.EXE: This displays broadcast messages from NetWare.

Windows requires different set of NetWare drivers, depending on the mode it is running under:

Windows mode	Required NetWare files
Standard	NETWARE.DRV, NETWARE.HLP, NWPOPUP.EXE
Enhanced	NETWARE.DRV, NETWARE.HLP, NWPOPUP.EXE, VNETWARE.386, VIPX.386

Novell INI changes

There are some specific additions that you need to make to the WIN.INI and SYSTEM.INI files when you are running Windows across Novell networks.

Under the [Windows] section of WIN.INI, add the following:

```
Load= NWPOPUP.EXE
```

This will automatically load the NetWare pop-up message utility.
The following lines should exist within SYSTEM.INI:

```
[boot]
network.drv=netware.drv

[boot.description]
network.drv=NetWare Device Driver Version 2.0
```

```
[386enh]
network=*vnetbios, vnetware.386, vipx.386
```

The first part loads the very important NetWare driver NETWORK.DRV. The second part loads a description of the version. The third part is only relevant when Windows is running under the enhanced mode. For a description of these drivers, see the earlier section on NetWare drivers.

Modifying the Windows NetWare environment

The most important driver as far Novell and Windows are concerned is NETWARE.DRV. There are a number of settings that can be customized when you are running Windows over Novell networks. These are stored in WIN.INI, SYSTEM.INI or NETWARE.INI. The precise storage location depends on the type of change you want to make. Windows provides a user-friendly way of changing these settings without having to make change to these files yourself. These changes allow you to:

- stop or start receiving messages
- stop or start receiving network warnings
- set up driver management information for enhanced mode (386)
- set up parameters for network printing

These are all accessed via the network icon found in the Windows Control Panel (Figure 9.17).

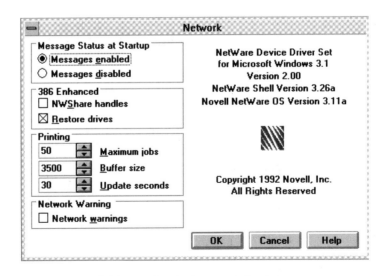

Figure 9.17 NetWare device user-defined parameters.

Messages enabled

This option will enable or block incoming messages popping up on top of your Windows application. These settings take effect immediately.

Network warning field

This option is very useful in troubleshooting situations. It is well worth switching on, as it provides information on the following situations:

- The NetWare shell is not loaded
- An earlier than recommended version of the NetWare shell is running
- Memory is insufficient to load network support

It is well worth having this field always selected, especially during the initial stages of an installation.

These settings take effect immediately.

386 enhanced fields

These are two very interesting fields, which are only available when Windows is running in enhanced mode on a 386 CPU or above.

- NWShare handles: This means that once the drive mapping setting is changed under one DOS session, it will affect all other sessions. This be can very useful. By default, NWShare is not activated.
- Restore drives: If selected, this will instruct Windows to restore the previous mapped drives when it is exited.

Printing fields

These fields are used to configure the Print Manager:

- Maximum jobs: This sets up the number of print jobs shown under the Print Manager. Maximum, 250; minimum, 1; default, 50.
- Buffer size: This sets up the maximum buffer size (in bytes) for printing. Maximum, 30 000; minimum, 3500; default, 3500.
- Update seconds: This sets the time interval given to updating the Print Manager queues. Maximum, 65; minimum, 1; default, 30.

Drive mapping under enhanced mode

When the enhanced mode is active, each DOS session is given its own set of drive mappings. These would at first be inherited from the parent Windows, but then any changes within the DOS session will be unique to itself. So, as shown in Figure 9.18, if two DOS sessions have been activated, and on one of them a new L: drive is created, it is not reflected in the other DOS session unless the NWShare was set up as active.

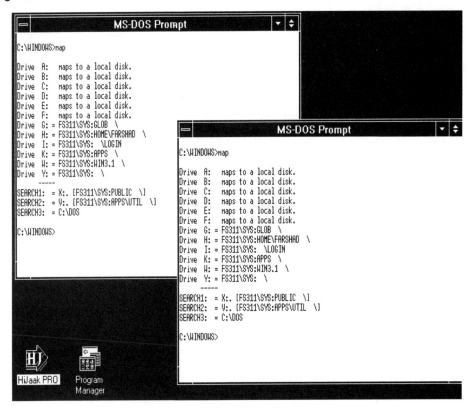

Figure 9.18 Two DOS windows with the same MAP assignments.

This default setting can be changed by making mapped drives shareable, which is done by selecting NWShare Handles from the network icon found in the Control Panel. You can test this facility in action. Open up two DOS sessions; within one, change the NetWare mapped drives, then go to the other session and type MAP and see that the changes have come through from one session to the other (Figure 9.19).

Management strategy

I strongly recommend updating your NETX to the burst-mode version. Novell claim that this will significantly improve the performance of Windows across the network. If possible, try to get hold of NETWARE.DRV version 3.0 or above and the associated NetWare Windows tool, which was issued with NetWare 4.0; it is far superior to the old NetWare tool. It should be available through your normal Novell dealer channels.

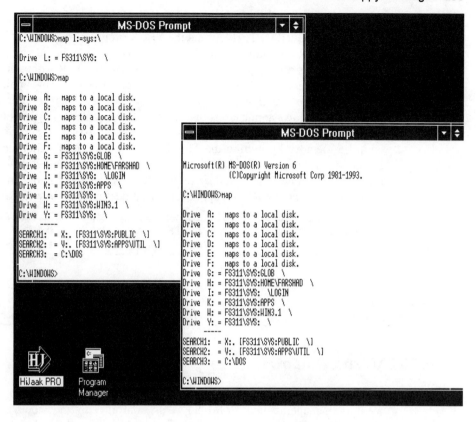

Figure 9.19 The mapped L: drive is not shown in the second DOS window.

Managing TSRs and Windows

TSR and Windows guidelines

There are three different ways of loading TSR programs:

- as part of AUTOEXEC.BAT from the DOS prompt line
- as part of the Windows WINSTART.BAT (a special batch file automatically executed whenever Windows runs in 386 enhanced mode)
- within a DOS window under 386 enhanced mode

   Each method has its advantages and disadvantages.

   Try to load the minimum number of TSR programs either from AUTOEXE.BAT or from the DOS prompt line before you start 386 enhanced mode.

The most important TSR program at this stage is probably the network drivers: for example, the Novell ODI drivers and the NETX program.

If a TSR program is required by a single DOS-based application while Windows 386 is running, the best approach is to run the TSR within the virtual DOS window, just prior to starting the application itself. As soon as the application ceases to run within the virtual machine window, the TSR is automatically removed.

For Windows applications that require access to TSR programs that are never referred to or required by non-Windows or DOS-based applications, you can optimize memory by putting the TSR in WINSTART.BAT. This means that it is available to Windows-based applications. Whenever you request a virtual machine to be created in a DOS window, more room is made available in conventional memory for the non-Windows application, as it does not require the TSR.

How the TSR is started	Is the TSR available to Windows applications?	Is the TSR available to virtual DOS machines?
At DOS prompt line	Yes	Yes, to all
Using WINSTART.BAT	Yes	No
Within a DOS virtual window	No	Yes, only to that virtual machine

EMM386.EXE and Windows

When you buy DOS.5.0/6.0 or Windows 3.1, Microsoft give you an expanded memory manager called EMM386. This conforms to the Lotus/Intel/Microsoft (LIM) 4.0 standard memory specification, which runs on 386 and higher CPUs. This program is provided either as an .EXE file, or in .SYS form, the latter meaning that it can run as a DOS device driver within the DOS CONFIG.SYS file.

When this program is used in conjunction with MS-DOS 5.0 or 6.0 you have the ability to load TSRs into the upper memory block between 640 Kbytes and 1 Mbyte.

Before you can use the EMM386 program:

- You must be using MS-DOS 3.3 or higher. The DOS 6.0 EMM386 is preferable.
- You must have a continuous block of 64 Kbytes free in your upper memory.
- You must have HIMEM.SYS already installed and active.

Potential problem areas

Not enough free space
The most common reason why EMM386 fails to work properly is that it fails to find at least 64 Kbytes of continuous free space. You can check this by running programs

such as CheckIt, or SI from Norton Utilities. These will tell you whether you have a continuous block of 64 Kbytes for the expanded memory manager to use.

Memory-mapping conflicts

EMM386 uses a very clever algorithm to find unused memory between 640 Kbytes and 1 Mbyte memory. Sometimes, devices use memory in those regions, but don't reserve and flag it for their exclusive use. This means that EMM386 grabs an area that can later on conflict with some other device, leading to all sorts of problems, most of which reveal themselves as random errors. A classic symptom of this is the machine either hanging, or else rebooting itself.

> Warning: A common conflict occurs when the network adaptor card driver is loaded into the upper memory block, clashing with Windows' special memory area for your SVGA card. Be careful; avoid conflicts! In cases like this, you will have to identify what area is being used, and then exclude that memory region from being used by Windows.

Using upper memory blocks without using EMM386

One of the nice facilities with EMM386.EXE is that it allows you to manage the upper memory block without providing the expanded memory specification. This assumes that none of the applications that you are running will require the expanded memory manager. In such cases you can save 64 Kbytes of memory in your upper memory block by instructing EMM.386 EXE on loading, via the parameter switch noems. This tells the program to provide the upper memory block manager, but not to provide the expanded memory manager facility.

> Warning: Be very careful if you encounter programs that require expanded memory management, as they can fail because of incompatibilities. They may show 'out of memory' messages, or they may just lock up without any error messages at all.

Use the EMM386 program from DOS 6.0 rather than that supplied with DOS 5.0 or Windows 3.1. It is better in performance, and integrates nicely with MEMMAKER.EXE, which is a special program issued with DOS 6.0 that will automatically attempt to work out your best memory setting.

TBMI2 program

TBMI2 is a TSR program that may be required before loading Windows. TBMI2 stands for 'task-switched buffer manager version 2'. It is supplied on the Windows Workstation support disk from Novell, called TBMI2.COM. It works with IPX and SPX, enabling them to run in a multitasking environment such as Microsoft

Windows. It is possible to open up different sessions of DOS environments within the Windows world and see different IPX protocol servers. Each window activates a different IPX.

The DOS operating system, with a few unusual exceptions, is considered to be a single-tasking program. This means that only one program can be executed at any given time (Figure 9.20). IPX and SPX were also originally designed as single-user services, with DOS very much in mind. However, in a multitasking environment, multiple programs could be running simultaneously. Each program might need the services of an exclusive IPX/SPX server.

This is where TBMI2 comes in. Multiple sessions of DOS are created in multitasking environments such as the one provided by Windows. A single-tasking DOS program can be executed inside each session. These programs are fooled into believing that they are running on a single-tasking operating system (in a DOS world), and that they have exclusive access to IPX/SPX services. However, the controlling Windows environment can swap between each session, giving the impression that they are all activated simultaneously (Figure 9.21). If there is not enough memory in the workstation to hold all the sessions simultaneously, the current DOS session is moved from conventional memory to disk, and the next session is loaded from disk and its execution is continued.

It is important to note that if a program calls NetWare through the NETX program it needs TBMI2. As the NetWare Shell already does its own multitasking, this is only necessary for programs that need direct access to IPX/SPX services.

When to use TBMI2

The times that you need to install TBMI2 are few and far between. In practice, it depends largely on the type of program that you will be running under Windows. You only need to use TBMI2 when you are going to run multiple sessions of applications that call IPX/SPX services directly.

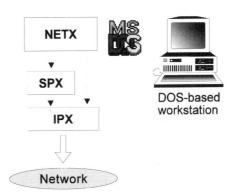

Figure 9.20 Basic NetWare workstation environment.

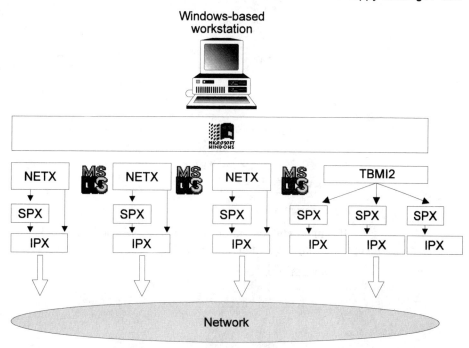

Figure 9.21 NetWare TBMI within Windows.

If you are unsure whether you need TBMI2, run it before you start your normal programs. Then, when you return to the DOS prompt line, type TBMI2 /D. This will show you how many times it has been used, if at all. Look for the field Far Call Usage; if it is zero TBMI2 has not been used, and loading it into memory was a waste of time.

Running TBMI2

If required you would normally run TBMI2 after loading the IPX drivers. With this restriction in mind, this program can be loaded from the DOS prompt line at any time. However if you are in a DOS session under Windows, you should not attempt to load and cannot unload it. This can only be done from the pure DOS prompt line.

```
C:\NOVELL\ODI>tbmi2 /?

Task Switched Buffer Manager for IPX/SPX - version 2.1
(C) Copyright 1990,1991 Novell Inc.  All rights reserved
```

```
Usage: TBMI [option]
valid options:
        /U           Unload resident TBMI
        /I           Display version and load information
        /?           Display this help screen
        /H           Display this help screen
        /D           Display diagnostics information
        /C=<file> Load with alternate configuration file
                     default configuration file = NET.CFG
Note: Only if no parameters, or the /C option is used
does TBMI attempt to load and remain resident.


C:\NOVELL\ODI>
```

It is important to load this program before you load Windows. Use the TBMI2 /D option at any given time to look at the number of calls made to it:

```
C:\NOVELL\ODI>tbmi2 -d


Task Switched Buffer Manager for IPX/SPX - version 2.1
(C) Copyright 1990,1991 Novell Inc.  All rights reserved


TBMI is currently resident
Interrupt 2Fh hooked
Interrupt 64h hooked
Interrupt 7Ah hooked


TBMI Buffers in use          : 0000
TBMI Max buffers used        : 0000
TBMI Unavail buffer count    : 0000
TBMI Old int usage count     : 0000
TBMI Far call usage count    : 0000
TBMI Task Buffering Enabled : 0000
TBMI Current Task ID number : 0000
TBMI Outstanding ID count    : 0000
TBMI Configured ECBs         : 0014
TBMI Configured Data ECBs    : 003C
TBMI Configured sockets      : 0014
TBMI Current sockets         : 0000


C:\NOVELL\ODI>
```

Keep an eye on the Far Call field to see if the program is being used.

Warning: To use this program you must be using the latest version of the IPX driver; it must be IPX v3.02 or above.

Normally, the best way to load TBMI2.COM in memory, if required, is to put it in the batch file used to load Windows, and then unload it when you quit Windows. The batch file could then look like this:

```
REM...
TBMI2
WIN
TBMI2 /U
REM..
```

Some Windows secrets

Creating your own WIN.INI and SYSTEM.INI format files

If you are installing Windows from the master network directory, you can design your own standard WIN.INI, SYSTEM.INI and CONTROL.INI files. As long as the Windows master disks were all copied to the Network directory using the SETUP /A option, a number of .SRC files will be found on that directory. These are:

- WIN.SRC
- SYSTEM.SRC
- CONTROL.SRC

They are used automatically by the SETUP /n program to create user-specific WIN.INI, SYSTEM.INI and CONTROL.INI files, respectively. The newly created files will then be placed in the relevant user home directory. By editing the contents of each .SRC file, you can customize the relevant INI file for the new Windows user.

The BOOTLOG audit

You can load Windows using a special switch that instructs Windows to record all the drivers that it loads up during the start-up process:

```
WIN /B
```

This option will create a BOOTLOG.TXT file that looks like Figure 9.22. This is very useful in troubleshooting.

Understanding Windows system resources

It is important to understand what Windows means by system resources. If they are fully utilized, they can inhibit the loading of any further applications, even though there is plenty of available memory. When you select the About box from the Program Manager, it shows the available memory to application and system resources. The figure for the system resource is shown as a percentage (Figure 9.23).

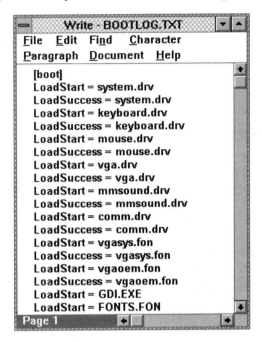

Figure 9.22 Typical BOOTLOG record.

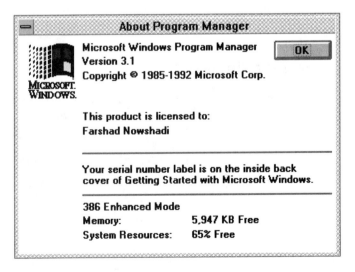

Figure 9.23 About Windows Program Manager screen.

This figure represents a combination of two different type of heap: the application and the GDI (graphical device interface) heap. Each is 64 Kbytes in size. The percentage shown represents the most used of the two heaps. So if the GDI heap has 65% free while the user heap has 80% free, the system resources figure will be shown as 65% free (Figure 9.24).

SYSEDIT

This program is a system configuration editor. It is one of those very useful undocumented programs that is automatically shipped out as part of the Windows package. You can find it under the \SYSTEM subdirectory. It allows for easy editing of the four very important text files that are used in the normal Windows boot-up sequence:

- CONFIG.SYS
- AUTOEXEC.BAT
- WIN.INI
- SYSTEM.INI

On running SYSEDIT.EXE from the Program Manager Run option, you get each of the four text files automatically shown within its own window, ready for editing (Figure 9.25). This is very useful for *ad hoc* changes to this type of file.

There are rumours that this is a program full of bugs. I have not found any, but be careful!

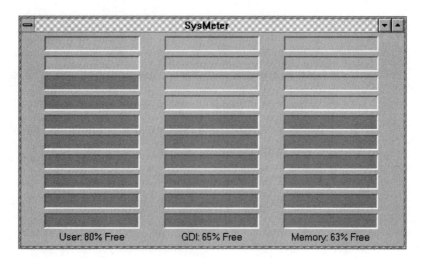

Figure 9.24 Windows resources gauge.

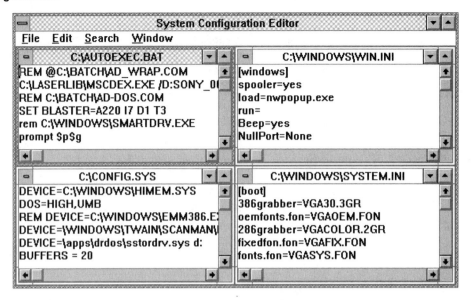

Figure 9.25 SYSEDIT system configuration editor.

Loading Windows more quickly

Here is a very easy way to get Windows loading just that bit quicker. Try typing

```
WIN :
```

This will ensure that you skip over the opening greeting screen, and hence Windows will load more quickly, especially if it is being loaded across the network.

Just for fun: the Bill Gates Windows animation screens

To see an animated Windows credit screen presented by Bill Gates do the following:

- Select About... from the standard Program Manager help menu
- While holding down the <Ctrl> and <Shift> keys, double click on the Windows icon on the top left-hand side. Click OK to close the About window. You will see nothing special yet.
- Repeat the first two steps. You should now see the Windows flag blowing in the wind:

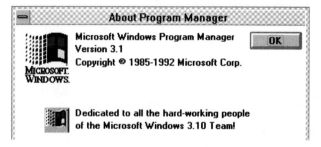

- Now close the window and repeat the first two steps again. This time you will see the real Windows credits animated screen:

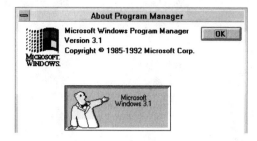

If you want to see a really nice version of the same idea, try it out on Corel Draw versions 3.x and 4.x. Click on the balloon for an uplifting experience!

10

Managing Windows applications over NetWare

Managing installation of Windows applications

Overview

Most applications that are designed to use the Windows environment install themselves automatically within the user's environment. Nine times out ten, this process consists of running the application's own SETUP.EXE, which is found on the first diskette that comes with the application. The SETUP.EXE program is normally started from the Program Manager window, using the Run command from the File menu.

Normally, the Windows application asks which drive/directory you would like the application installed on. The application will then check to see if there is sufficient storage space available, proceeding if everything is OK.

It is important to remember that installation of a Windows application is generally far easier than installing a sophisticated DOS-based program. The application need not ask the user for any information regarding the hardware, such as the screen card, printer or mouse type being used. All of this information is derived automatically from the Windows environment.

Windows applications across networks

Windows provides a wonderful facility for Windows applications: the applications don't need to find out about the user's hardware or Windows environment details. All these details are provided by the underlying system, and all of the issues are automatically handled by Windows. The network manager can install one copy of the application across the network and make it available to all licensed users. This has a superb implication: all users can use the same application even though they might each have different Windows environments (see Figure 10.1).

Managing network applications

When you install Windows applications across the network you must think about where they are going to be installed and how the licensed users are going to use them.

In this section I will outline an approach that can be used to install applications on the network.

Another important issue, which a large number of installers tend to overlook, is what happens when you wish to remove the application from your system?

Windows applications have a habit of changing a number of the standard Windows .INI files, the most important being the WIN.INI and SYSTEM.INI. Some

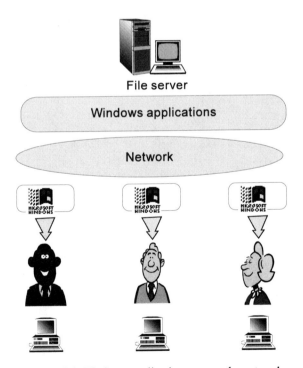

Figure 10.1 Windows applications across the network.

also have the habit of adding one or more extra lines to your AUTOEXEC.BAT file, and even sometimes to your CONFIG.SYS. There are programs that do this without even bothering to inform you! I have devised a simple batch file, outlined later, which will take a snapshot of the Windows environment: this should be used before any Windows application installation. Once this is done, you can always restore the Windows environment to its original pre-installation state.

Always take a copy of the WIN.INI, SYSTEM.INI, *.GRP and *.INI files before an installation, just in case you want to undo the installation.

Networked Windows applications

As stated earlier, it is extremely useful to keep master copies of Windows applications in a separate directory from the WINDOWS master directory. This is because most Windows applications work across a number of different versions of Windows. It is far easier to manage each separately, as opposed to having the two systems inter-mixed. The Windows user is given direct access to all windows applications through a special drive, which I call the J: drive (see Figure 10.2). This letter is arbitrary: you can select any other appropriate letter to fit in with your own system.

This means that, when you install a new Windows application over the network, it will be installed on the J: drive. The network manager will then give appropriate rights over the newly created directory to all the licensed users. These rights should be R and F (Read and File scan) unless otherwise stated.

Application installation modifies Windows configuration

During their installation processes, Windows applications have a habit of changing a number of the standard Windows .INI files, possibly creating a new .INI file,

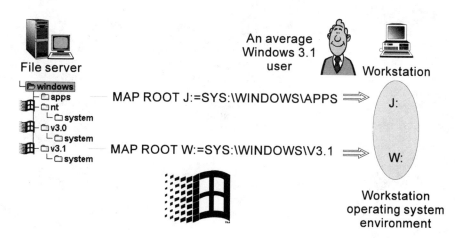

Figure 10.2 User's perspective of the master set of Windows programs.

modifying .GRP files and/or modifying the AUTOEXEC.BAT and CONFIG.SYS files.

Most good Windows applications create their own application .INI file, which is used to store all the application's own parameters, instead of adding a special section to the WIN.INI file. Unfortunately, some application developers are too busy to manage their own .INI file and simply modify the standard WIN.INI file. This is bad news because it becomes very difficult to keep applications and their configurations grouped together. There are a number of applications that do both, that is, modify the WIN.IN and then create their own application .INI file – this is very bad news!

During their installation, almost all Windows applications modify the .GRP files. These are the files that are used by the Windows Program Manager to display groups of applications which the user can run. They can either add themselves to an existing group or create a new group which is placed in the PROGMAN.INI file. Figure 10.3 shows an example: an application called WHIZZ has just been installed and has created a new group 12. Inside the file WHIZZ.GRP is a selection of ICONS that are part of the WHIZZ application.

Sometimes, applications do not create a new group but allow the installer to add the new application icons to an existing .GRP group file. In this case, the PROGMAN.INI is not changed, but a relevant .GRP is enhanced. It is important to

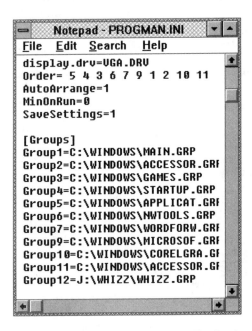

Figure 10.3 Example result of a Windows application installation on the PROGMAN.INI file.

bear in mind that since this is a networked application, all the licensed users should have at least read access to the newly modified .GRP file.

Table 10.1 lists files that might be modified during installation of a Windows application.

The problems start when you want to delete an application from the Windows environment. Unfortunately, Windows applications are not as efficient at removing their 'droppings' as they are at inserting them during the installation process.

Preparation prior to installation

Before you install a Windows application, it is wise to take a few precautions. The installer should always take a snapshot of their Windows environment prior to installation. Subsequently, if there is a problem with the installation process, you can always restore your old Windows configuration. Also, if after using the application you wish to get rid of it (which is often the case), you can remove the application code from the system completely.

Table 10.1 Files that might be modified by installing a new Windows application.

File name	Description
WIN.INI	Normally a new section is created with a title similar to the application's name.
SYSTEM.INI	Most applications do not modify this file, but some do!
PROGMAN.INI	Modified when a new Program Group is created.
application.INI	This is the application's own newly-created .INI file. Not all applications create this file: some just use the WIN.INI file.
application.GRP	Created when a new Program Group is defined.
existing.GRPs	If the application allows it, during the set-up process any existing .GRP file could be modified to include the new application icons. The actual file will depend on the Windows installer's instructions.
AUTOEXEC.BAT	Sometimes, applications modify the user's AUTOEXEC.BAT. This normally involves adding a few DOS SET commands. Be careful if you are booting up from diskless workstations: the image file has to be changed.
CONFIG.SYS	Very rarely changed, but there are some applications that will modify the CONFIG.SYS file. This is normally done to add special drives, or to modify and enhance some of the CONFIG.SYS parameters. Once again this can cause all sorts of problems for diskless workstations. The image file has to be changed.

Taking a snapshot of your Windows configuration

I have written two batch files that can be used to take a snapshot of the Windows environment:

(1) WIN_TAKE.BAT

(2) WIN_REST.BAT

The two batch files work as a pair. They work by storing a Windows configuration under a name provided by you. This name is normally connected with the name of the application that you are about to store, or possibly a date. By using a name to store a snapshot of Windows, it is possible to keep multiple different Windows configurations. Each configuration can be used to restore Windows to its configuration prior to the recent Windows application installation.

The batch files each create a special directory with the following format: <Name>.CFG, where <Name> is the name you provide to the batch file as a parameter. The batch file WIN_TAKE uses PKZIP.EXE to compress the Windows configuration and store it under your new directory <Name>.CFG, so that minimum hard disk storage is used.

These batch files can also be used to store and restore different network users' configurations on a single directory.

These batch files are shown here for you to use as they are, or as a framework for you to modify to meet the requirements of your own system. Do study them to see how they could be used in your own system.

The advantages of using this type of batch file are:

✓ It is easy to restore a previous working Windows configuration.

✓ It is easy to keep multiple versions of Windows configurations.

The disadvantages of using this type of batch file are:

✗ You need to type two BATCH files.

✗ Extra directories are created.

On the whole it is well worth having some sort of batch file as shown below.

```
@ECHO OFF
REM Farshad Nowshadi Utility
REM
REM ===========================================================
REM WIN_TAKE.BAT: Takes a snapshot of the Windows environment.
REM              It works in conjunction with WIN_REST.BAT.
REM              To run this BATCH file you must be in the
REM              user's directory where WIN.COM and WIN.INI
REM              are located.
REM -----------
```

```
REM Parameters required:
REM -------------------
REM Batch files require one parameter: the name of application
REM to be installed
REM Examples
REM  WIN_TAKE Lotus  or WIN_TAKE Excel
REM =========================================================

REM How it works:-
REM This batch file does the following
REM   1) Creates a sub directory to store configuration files.
REM   2) Takes a copy of all the .INI and .GRP files.
REM   3) Takes a copy of AUTOEXEC.BAT and CONFIG.SYS.
REM   4) Compresses all files using ZIP into one file.
REM =========================================================

REM Check to see if parameter is given
IF a%1==a GOTO ERRORNOPARAM

MD %1.CFG > NUL:
CD %1.CFG

REM Take copy of all *.INI and *.GRP files
copy ..\*.INI > NUL:
copy ..\*.GRP > NUL:

REM Take a snapshot of your DOS boot up files
@echo on
copy C:\AUTOEXEC.BAT
copy C:\CONFIG.SYS
@echo off

REM Compress the files
call PKZIP -m %1 *.*
REM Go back to the Windows main directory
CD ..

ECHO
*************************************************************
ECHO A snapshot of the Windows pre installation of %1 is now
ECHO complete.
ECHO The files are now stored in the
ECHO     directory %1.CFG as a compressed ZIP file.
ECHO To restore them type:-
ECHO     WIN_REST %1

GOTO End
```

```
:ERRORNOPARAM
ECHO Error you must specify a name for this SNAPSHOT.
ECHO  Example:  WIN_TAKE Excel
:END
```

The second file is called WIN_REST.BAT. This is used to restore Windows to its original configuration, that is, its configuration when the WIN_TAKE.BAT took a snapshot of its environment.

```
@ECHO OFF
REM Farshad Nowshadi Utility
REM ============================================================
REM WIN_REST.BAT: Takes a snapshot of the Windows environment.
REM              It works in conjunction with WIN_TAKE.BAT.
REM              To run this BATCH file you must be in the
REM              user's directory where WIN.COM and WIN.INI
REM              are located.
REM ------------
REM Parameters required:
REM ------------------
REM Batch files require one parameter: the name of snapshot
REM file.
REM Examples
REM  WIN_REST Lotus  or WIN_REST Excel
REM ============================================================

REM How it works:-
REM This batch file does the following
REM 1) Goes to the sub directory where the configuration files
REM    are stored.
REM 2) UN-compresses the files.
REM 3) Copies back up all the .INI and .GRP files.
REM 4) Replaces AUTOEXEC.BAT and CONFIG.SYS (making a backup
REM    first)
REM ============================================================

REM Checking to see if compressed file already exists in the
REM snapshot directory
IF NOT EXIST %1.CFG\%1.zip GOTO ERRORPARAM

CD %1.CFG
REM UN-compress the files
PKUNZIP %1

REM Replace copy of all *.INI and *.GRP files
copy *.INI ..      > NUL:
copy *.GRP ..      > NUL:
```

```
REM Replace DOS boot up files
REM After making a backup copy (just in case)

copy C:\AUTOEXEC.BAT C:\AUTOEXEC.BAK  > NUL:
copy C:\CONFIG.SYS   C:\CONFIG.BAK    > NUL:
copy AUTOEXEC.BAT    C:\              > NUL:
copy CONFIG.SYS      C:\              > NUL:

REM Go back to the Windows main directory
CD ..
@ECHO OFF
ECHO ************************************************************
ECHO The Windows environment is now restored to what it used
to
ECHO be pre installation of %1.
ECHO ************************************************************
ECHO  Make sure:
ECHO  1) You remove any old directories and code that the
ECHO     application has created.
ECHO  2) Check the AUTOEXEC.BAT and CONFIG.SYS to see if it is
ECHO     all correct.
GOTO End

:ERRORPARAM
ECHO Error: Two possible errors could have occurred
ECHO   1) You have not specified a parameter for the Directory
ECHO   2) The directory %1.CFG does not exist
:End
```

Top tips for networking Windows

Always, if possible, set the Windows TEMP= command to a local drive. This will considerably reduce network congestion and increase workstation performance. However, it is not much use on diskless workstations.

Remove all the files from the TEMP directory after exiting Windows. This can be done as follows. After exiting Windows but before logging out of the network, type:

DEL %TEMP% > NUL

This command will delete all the files in the TEMP directory.

Test and then re-test any new modification to the Windows environment to ensure that it is going to work correctly for the users. There is nothing more damaging to your credibility than for a user to discover that their system, which was working fine, has stopped due to your actions!

 Back up all important files before changing the Windows environment. Constantly ensure that you are using the latest NetWare Windows drivers. This is a never-ending task!

 Try, where possible, to standardize all your Windows workstation hardware. Work towards installing a similar super VGA card and an appropriate screen for all workstations. This will reduce hardware maintenance time, and means that spares can be easily managed.

 Remove all unnecessary TSR programs before running Windows.

NetWare standard tools for Windows

NetWare 2.x and 3.x tools

Novell provides a standard set of basic Windows-based tools, which come free with the latest NetWare Windows Workstation Services diskette. These tools (see Figure 10.4) are all basic in nature, but integrate nicely with the Windows 3.1 environment.

You can perform most of these commands manually if you jump to a DOS window.

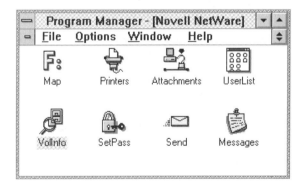

Figure 10.4 NetWare 2.x and 3.x tools.

This package updates all the Windows NetWare drivers and NetWare .DLL files, and provides NetWare application tools. These tools provide services such as:

- Attaching to file servers
- Sending grouped messages (very useful)
- Mapping network drives (not a great advantage, since you can do this already using Microsoft's File Manager program)
- Listing network users (useful)
- Changing passwords
- Viewing volume information (very useful)

NetWare 4.x standard issue Windows tools

With the introduction of NetWare 4.0, Novell has improved the old NetWare for Windows tools. It has combined all the functionality of the previous selection of programs into one program. Each function can now be started from an icon tool bar (see Figure 10.5).

This new set of tools does practically everything the old version did, but it also supports the new NetWare directory services, as well as the old bindery-based servers.

If you are using the old NetWare Windows tools, on a NetWare 3.11 server, try to get hold of the NetWare 4.x Windows Tools program. It should work on your system and prove to be far more elegant.

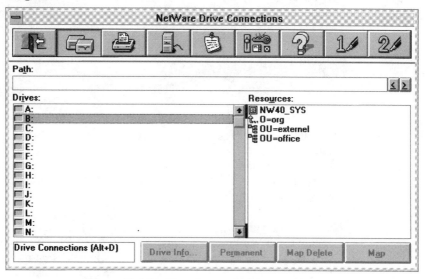

Figure 10.5 NetWare 4.x standard issue tools.

> Warning: You will need to ensure that the NETWARE.DRV you are using is Version 3.0 or above before you can use this program.

Setting up the NetWare Windows tools

The program NWSETUP.EXE uses a Windows application to install the NetWare Tools and to update the NetWare driver files. The NetWare Tools program, when installed, adds a special group called [Novell NetWare] and adds the following files to the Windows SYSTEM directory:

- NETWARE.INI: the initialization for NetWare Tools
- NWTOOLS.EXE: starts NetWare Tools
- NWTOOLS.HLP: the help file for NetWare Tools
- NWT.DLL: works with NETWARE.DRV to access NetWare Tools

The Map tool
This tool is not particularly exciting, as you can perform most of the functions using Windows' own File Manager program. However, it is slightly easier to use, and looks more like the normal MAP command used at the DOS prompt line.

The Attachments tool
This tool allows you to login to a number of different Novell file servers at the same time.

The UserList tool
This is a useful command which shows all the active users (see Figure 10.6).

The VolInfo tool
This tool is better presented than the DOS version. The pie charts show the amount of storage space left on each volume (see Figure 10.7).

The Send tool
This is a very useful tool, which allows you to send messages to a single user or a group of users (see Figure 10.8).

The SetPass tool
This is the same as the Novell DOS command SETPASS. It allows you to change your user password.

The Printers tool
This tool is the Windows equivalent of the CAPTURE.EXE command. It allows you to connect your printer port connections to available print queues. On establishing a connection, you can specify a number of print options such as number of copies and whether to use print banners or not.

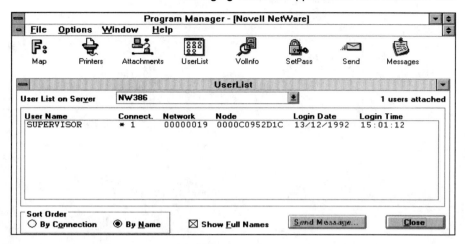

Figure 10.6 The user list tool.

Creating a corporate-wide Windows menu

You can use the Program Manager to create a corporate-wide standard group menu (see Figure 10.9). This can be very useful, as it means that all users see a standard menu on top of all their normal groups. This menu can be administered from a single point, by the network manager.

This is potentially a god-send for the network manager. No longer does the manager have to add icons to each Windows user's environment. I have found this approach to be highly satisfactory.

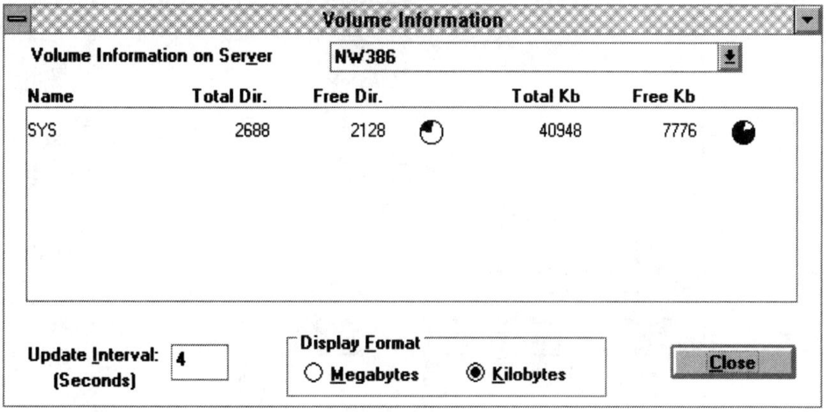

Figure 10.7 The volume information tool.

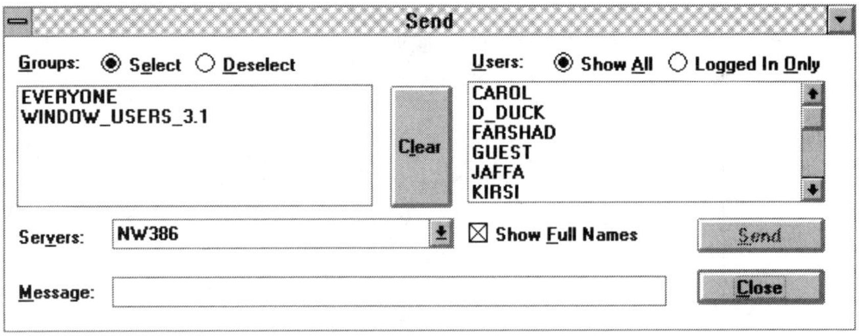

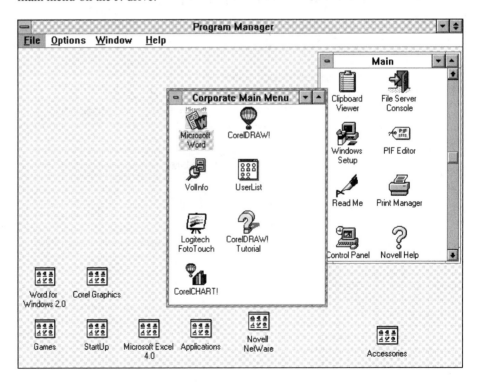

Figure 10.8 The Send tool.

How it works

To create a corporate-wide main menu, you use the PROGMAN.INI file to point to a group in a read-only network directory. In Figure 10.10, I have put the corporate main menu on the J: drive.

Figure 10.9 Example of a corporate-wide main menu.

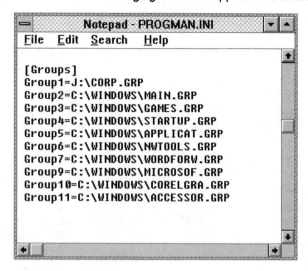

Figure 10.10 The [Groups] section of the PROGRAM.INI file.

The [Groups] section lists all the grouped Windows applications that will be shown to the user. Each group is represented by its own .GRP file. They are loaded in order. In this case, I have used the network J: drive to create a special application called CORP.GRP (which stands for corporation-wide standard main menu). This application could be called anything: you might want to give it the name of your organization.

In this example, the users are allowed to change and modify all Groups from 2 to 11. However, the line `Group1=J:\Corp.GRP` points to a group that is under the control of the network manager. As far as the users are concerned, this group is read only: they cannot change the corporate main menu. If the manager ensures that all the relevant users have a reference to this group across the network, it becomes very easy to introduce new applications to all the users.

Changing the corporate main menu

To change the menu, the network manager should login as normal and ensure that full access rights are given to the directory where the CORP.GRP is stored. It can now be changed in the normal way as if it were any normal group application window. The next time other users come to use Windows they will see the network manager's changes to this program group.

User viewpoint

The great advantage of this approach is that a user is allowed to change any of his or her own program groups but not the corporate main menu. This is illustrated in the following example. As you can see from Figure 10.11, when the user selects the corporate main menu, he or she is not allowed to Delete or Move any of the icons. The user can, however, run any of the applications. However, a user can Delete, Move or re-arrange the icons on his or her own group menus (see Figure 10.12).

Restricting the Program Manager for network users

The Program Manager stores its preferences and default settings in the PROGMAN.INI file. These settings can be very useful to the paranoid network manager. They allow the manager to restrict the way users can use and modify applications from the Program Manager. Most Windows applications are started from the Program Manager; this provides the network manager with a powerful tool for controlling the user's environment. The PROGMAN.INI has three parts: [Settings], [Groups] and [Restrictions] (see Figure 10.13).

The [Settings]

This section has a number of lines regarding the pre-selected default parameters, such as the location of the Program Manager window.

The [Groups]

This section shows all the groups of applications, represented by their own .GRP files, that are loaded by the Program Manager. Each group is loaded in order.

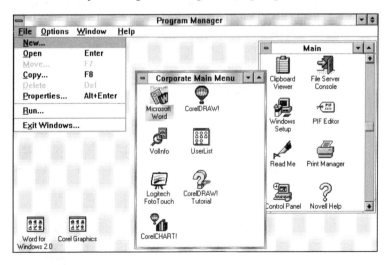

Figure 10.11 Users cannot Move or Delete icons from the corporate main menu.

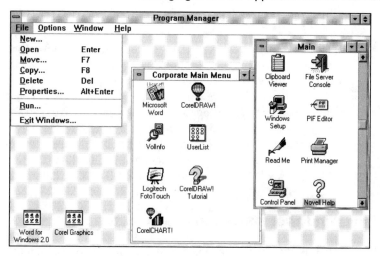

Figure 10.12 Users can Move or Delete icons from their own group menus.

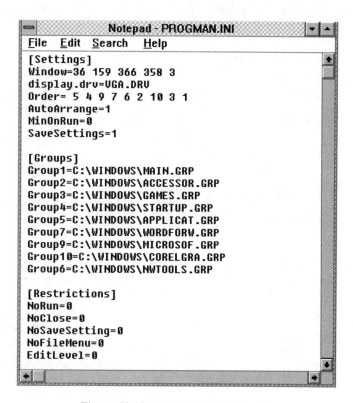

Figure 10.13 The PROGMAN.INI file.

The [Restrictions]

This is the interesting part from a management viewpoint. It allows the network manager to make the restrictions outlined in Table 10.2. (The possible values for x, in the EditLevel line, are given in Table 10.3.)

These options are very useful in situations where you do not want the network users to change any program group settings. I have also found these options to be very handy in situations where you need to provide Windows on an open environment basis. For example, this could be in the show room where any user can come along and run the Windows application. By carefully setting up the PROGMAN.INI, you can create a relatively secure environment.

Word for Windows: installation case study

In this case study, we look at installing a network version of one of the most popular word processing systems of all time: Microsoft Word for Windows v2.x. This case study acts as an excellent example of the sort of steps required to install most Windows-based applications, in particular Microsoft's own products. For example, the installation of Microsoft Excel is very similar to that of Word. By studying the installation of Microsoft Word, the installation of Excel becomes trivial due to the similarities.

Table 10.2 Restrictions imposed using the PROGMAN.INI file.

Network manager's imposed restrictions	Line in PROGMAN.INI
User not allowed to use the Run command	`NoRun=1`
Disable the File menu	`NoFileMenu=1`
User not allowed to exit Windows	`NoClose=1`
User not allowed to save settings	`NoSaveSetting=1`
Set up the user's restriction on subgroup windows	`EditLevel=x`

Table 10.3 Possible values for x in the `EditLevel` line.

Edit level	Description of restriction
0	No restriction on users
1	Prevents users deleting, creating or editing group window names
2	Same as 1, but also prevents users deleting or creating program icons with group windows
3	Same as 2, but also prevents users changing the program command lines
4	Same as 3, but also prevents users changing any program items

The following text describes the steps required for the installation of Word for Windows.

> Warning: You must obtain the appropriate Microsoft Word for Windows licence for each Word user. A licence is obtained by buying a retail package or a Microsoft Licence Pack.

Overview of the installation

There are number of different ways that Word for Windows can be installed; each is described below.

Stand-alone installation

The first approach is the simplest and is called either Complete installation or Custom installation. This will create a single-user version of Word for Windows, by copying all the appropriate master files into the user's directory. This means the user can run Word on a stand-alone basis; only a single-user Word for Windows licence is required.

Networked installation

Word for Windows calls the second method the Workstation installation method. This is the real networked version installation. Using this approach, a shared version of Word is kept on the file server and specific customized files are kept under users' own directories. This means that the vast majority of Word program files are actually located on the server. Each user's WIN.INI has an appropriate reference to the shared copy of Word across the network. The shared copy of Word keeps a special file called REG.DAT, which contains the licence agreement and each user's registration details.

Under this option, the installer first installs Word on the server. This creates a common core of Word shared program files. Then the Word set-up program is run again to carry out a workstation user-specific installation. This will copy the user-specific files into the users' directories.

Application installation considerations

The main decision to be made is where to store the Word user-specific files. Should they be on the user's hard disk or in the user's home directory on the file server?

There is no perfect answer to this question. As a general rule, you should follow the precedence that has already been set within your system. If users have their WINDOWS master directory on the local hard disk, then the Word files should be stored in this directory. On the other hand, if the users store their WINDOWS master directory on the network under their own home directories, then the Word-specified directory should go under this. This is a general rule, and there are times when it is not appropriate. The greater the standardization and uniformity the network manager can impose on the system, the easier the system will be to manage.

If I had to make a choice between the two approaches, I would install the

Word user-specific files under the users' home directories for the following reasons:

✓ Backing up is easy.

✓ You can cope with diskless workstations.

✓ You can physically modify any user configuration files from any workstation.

✓ Less local hard disk space is needed.

On the other hand:

✗ The program can be slower.

✗ The users are totally reliant on the network.

Objectives of this installation

Since Microsoft Windows can be installed in many different ways, I have limited the goals of this case study as described below.

We are going to assume we are installing the networked version of Word for Windows. This means that we are going to install a common shared version of the Word programs to which all licensed users will be able to refer. A workstation-specific installation will take place.

A master copy of the main program modules will be stored under a directory called, in this case, \WINDOWS\APPS\WORDWIN2. This directory will be referenced by all Word users when they load Word for Windows, .DLL files, standard dictionaries and thesauruses. However, each user stores their own configuration file WINWORD.INI in their own Windows home directory.

To run Word for Windows, the users will select the appropriate icon from the Windows Program Manager. It will load up the mass of common Word for Windows programs from the common directory; however, the customised configuration is kept under a special directory in the user's own home Windows directory.

Figures 10.14 and 10.15 show two different methods of installing Word for Windows across a network.

Installation steps required

The installation of Word for Windows is divided into two major parts. The first part consists of installing a 'once and for all' copy of Word on the server. The second part involves installing a customized working copy of Word for Windows for each of the licensed users.

Overview

The following is an overview of the installation process:

(1) Prepare for installation.

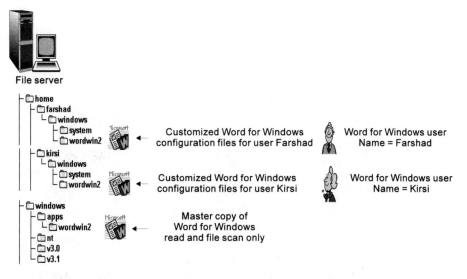

Figure 10.14 Installing Word for Windows, method 1.

(2) Install a master copy on the file server.

(3) Take a snapshot of your Windows environment, using the suggested batch files.

(4) Install an individual working copy to each licensed user.

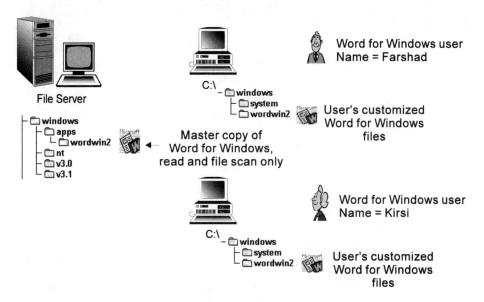

Figure 10.15 Installing Word for Windows, method 2.

(5) Give each licensed user access rights to the master copy of Word for Windows.

(6) Login as a user and ensure that Word for Windows is working correctly.

Installing Word on the network server

Login with supervisory rights

This means that the users must have read and write access rights over the network, shared master Windows directory. In this case, since Word will be installed under the WINDOWS\APPS\ directory, the installer must be able to write files in this directory (Figure 10.16).

I have found it very useful to create a special user for installing Windows applications. Create a special user called WinApps which has special supervisory rights over the shared Windows master directories. This will allow someone else other than the supervisor to install Windows applications.

Server installation

(1) Using Disk 1 of the Word for Windows diskettes, run the SETUP program.

(2) Enter the name of your organization.

(3) Type the network path that Word for Windows is to use for its server installation.

(4) The SETUP program will now present the user with a number of installation options (see Figure 10.17): select the server installation. This option will now copy all the files as defined in Table 10.4.

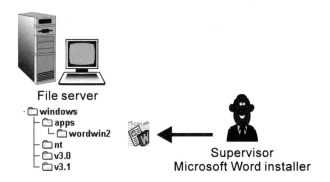

Figure 10.16 Supervisor installing Word for Windows.

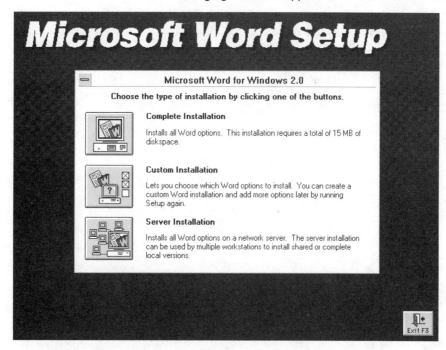

Figure 10.17 The installation options.

The SETUP program creates directories and sub-directories on a network server hard disk and copies the files listed in Table 10.4.

Installing Word on a workstation

Check that the user has access to the Word master directory
Now log in as the new Word for Windows user. Go to the user's WINDOWS directory and ensure that he or she has read and file scan access to the Word master directory.

Take a snapshot of the user's Windows environment
Take a snapshot of the user's Windows environment: this is just in case there is a problem with the installation process.

The snapshot process consists of taking a backup copy of the *.INI, *.GRP, WIN.INI and SYSTEM.INI files. Earlier in this section, a series of batch files were described that can be used for this purpose (see 'Taking a snapshot of your Windows configuration'). If you use these batch files, the first command you type might look like this:

```
WIN_TAKE word
```

Table 10.4 Shared files on a server.

Shared directory name	Contains files	File name
\WORDWIN2	Program file	WINWORD.EXE
(named by installer)	Grammar checker	GR_AM.LEX, GRAMMAR.DLL
	Spelling checker	SP_AM.LEX , SPELL.DLL
	Thesaurus	TH_AM.LEX, THES.DLL
	Hyphenation	HY_AM.LEX , HYPH.DLL
	Help	WINWORD.HLP, WPHELP.DLL
	PCL V printer driver	FINSTALL.*, HPPCL5A.*
	Screen fonts	DIALOG.FON, SMALL.FON, WINLD.FON
	Utilities	MACRODE.EXE, SETUP.EXE, WWORD20.INF
	Text conversions	*.CNV
	Associated sample files	*.TXT
	Word macro conversion	*.GLY
	Document templates	*.DOT
	Information files	*.DOC
	User licence register	REG.DAT
WORDWIN2\CLIPART	Sample ClipArt files	
WORDWIN2\DLL	DLL files	*.DLL
WORDWIN2\GRPHFLT	Files for graphics filters	
WORDWIN2\EQUATION	Microsoft Equation Editor files	
WORDWIN2\MSDRAW	Microsoft Draw files	
WORDWIN2\MSGRAPH	Microsoft Graph files	
WORDWIN2\PCLFONTS	Files for downloadable symbol fonts for HP printers	
WORDWIN2\WINWORD.CBT	Files for online lessons	
WORDWIN2\WORDART	Microsoft WordArt files	

WIN_TAKE is the name of the batch file; 'word' is a parameter name that is used to store the snapshot of the Windows configuration.

Now if there is a major disaster in the installation process, the user's Windows configuration can always be restored to its previous working configuration. This can be achieved by running:

```
WIN_REST word
```

Run Word SETUP

(1) From Windows, run the SETUP.EXE program (it is on the path where Word was installed on the network).

(2) Enter the user's name.

(3) Select the location of the user's own directory. The SETUP program will store the Word user-specific customized files. This is normally in a directory under the user's \WINDOWS directory, for example:

<User's own directory> \WINDOWS\WORDWIN2 (see Figure 10.18).

(4) The SETUP program will now present the user with a number of installation options. Select the Workstation installation option and follow the setup instructions.

Table 10.5 shows the files that will now be installed in the user's Word directory.

Using Word over Novell networks

Modifying the WIN.INI Word section

There are a number of very useful options that Microsoft Word for Windows stores under its own section of the standard WIN.INI file. These options can easily be adjusted to integrate the Word application into your own network.

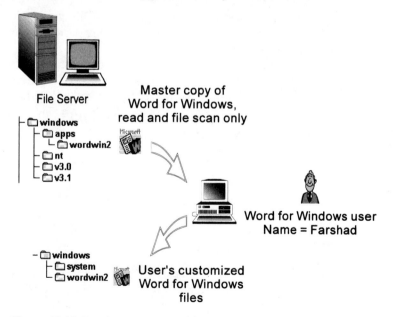

Figure 10.18 Creating user-specific Word for Windows configuration files.

Table 10.5 User-specific files.

Shared directory name	Contains these files	File name
WORDWIN2	User-specific .INI file	WINWORD.INI
	User-customizable document templates	*.DOT
	Word's information files	*.DOC
	User's own document files	*.DOC
WINDOWS\SYSTEM	Word's own .DLL files	OLE???.DLL, SHELL.DLL, VER.DLL
	Screen fonts	WINLD.FON
	VGA-specific files	SMALLE.FON, MTEXTRAE.FON, MTSYMBOLE.FON, FENCEE.FON, MTSYMITE.FON

Microsoft recommends in its Word for Windows documentation that you should put the following line into the WIN.INI file under the [Microsoft Word 2.x] section:

NovellNet=Yes

This makes the way Word checks for a valid directory name *fully* compatible with NetWare.

These parameters can be changed directly from Word for Windows, by choosing Options from the Tools menu, then choosing the WIN.INI Category (see Figure 10.19).

Table 10.6 lists some of the important parameters that can be changed to integrate the Word files into your own system. All the following key words should appear under the [Microsoft Word 2.0] section in the WIN.INI file.

Most of these changes to the WIN.INI file do not take effect until you restart Word.

Saber Windows Menu System

Overview

Saber provides one of the most useful networked Windows menu management systems on the market (the Saber standard menu screen is shown in Figure 10.20). In fact there are strong rumours that the Saber menu system is being incorporated in the next standard release of NetWare.

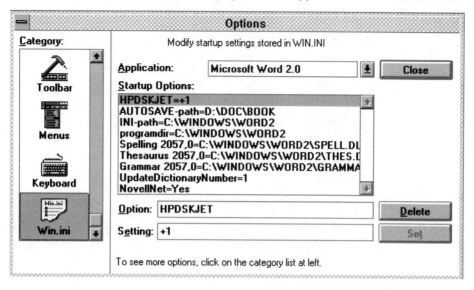

Figure 10.19 Changing parameters in WIN.INI, via Word for Windows.

The Saber Menu System allows the network manager to create a single standard intelligent menu for all users. The system will dynamically check for the user's identifiers or groups and display itself appropriately. Figure 10.21 shows a sample Saber menu. The system allows the network manager tremendous control via a range of different parameters that can be used to limit user actions. A major advantage of this approach is that the network manager need only update and modify one menu for all users.

Table 10.6 Important parameters, from a networking viewpoint.

Keyword	Word is looking for	Description
programdir=path	WINWORD.EXE	The Word for Windows master program
INI-path=path	WINWORD.INI	Location of user's Word .INI file
DOC-path=path	User documents	Default user home directory
AUTOSAVE-path=path	Automatic saving of .DOCs	programdir=C: \WINDOWS\WORD2
Spelling *lang,type* = path	Spelling checking programs	Spelling tools
Thesaurus *lang,type* = path	Thesaurus checking program	Thesaurus tools
Grammar *lang,type* = path	Grammar checking program	Grammar tools
NovellNet =Yes		NovellNet=Yes

Figure 10.20 Saber Menu System standard menu screen.

Saber has always been known for its excellent DOS-based menu systems. Its original menu system was developed to overcome the limitation of the old Novell free menu (MENU.EXE) system, which came as standard with NetWare 2.x and 3.x. The Saber Menu System seems to have become the industry standard for big Novell networks requiring a DOS-based menu system. Saber have now produced their own Windows version of this very popular system.

The Saber Menu (SMENU)

The Saber Menu (SMENU) is a tool you can use for quick access to your

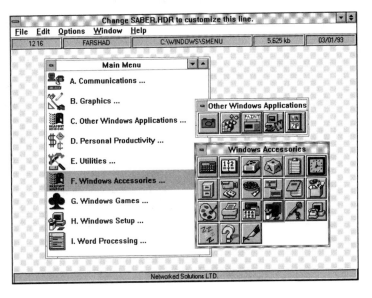

Figure 10.21 A sample Saber menu.

applications and programs. You can use SMENU to create a personalized desktop, create menus, start applications and run programs. In SMENU, your applications and programs are listed on a personal or shared menu. You can choose from four display styles for the menu window: list, icons, icon listed or icon pallets. Some of SMENU's main advantages are described below.

Displaying menus and items based on certain criteria

The LAN administrator can define menus and items to be displayed for particular networks, user names, user groups, workstations, hardware, work surfaces (for example, DOS or Windows) or passwords (see Figure 10.22). This is one of its nicest features. It is a godsend for the network manager as it works very well and is a pleasure to use.

Password-protected windows

One excellent feature of Saber is that each program group can be protected with a password which can be set by the supervisor. It is also possible to instruct the system to use the user's Novell-defined password.

In the example shown in Figure 10.23, the Windows setup option is password protected.

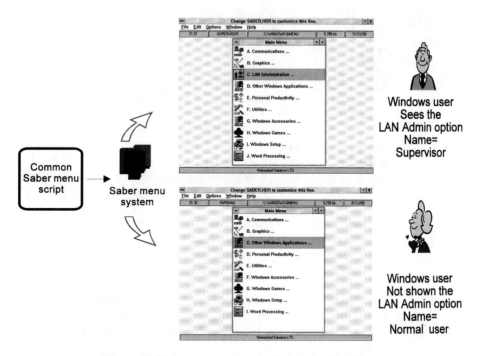

Figure 10.22 A common menu is displayed with different sets of options, depending on the user.

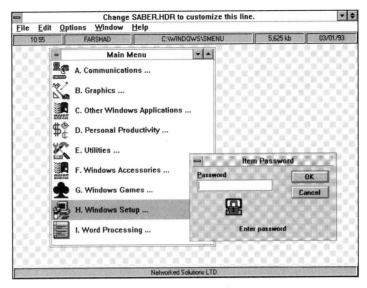

Figure 10.23 A password-protected option.

Be careful! Saber checks passwords using the unencrypted technique, so you might need to adjust the file server appropriately.

Triggering applications through script files

Users can make menu selections to execute a series of DOS and Windows applications when they select an ICON.

Usually, users can run DOS applications without creating special .PIF files. These scripts can run the appropriate .EXE file or cushion it with a series of elaborate functions: attaching network drives (via the Saber NLINK command); attaching to file servers; or prompting the users for all sorts of data before triggering the application (such as a file name or desired directory path).

Locking a menu according to the user's identifier

This option lets the administrator define shared drives and add drives and directories to the search path before a menu item is executed.

Screen blanking

Security for workstations is provided through screen blanking which also extends the life of the monitor. The difference between this and Windows' own standard screen blanking is that users are asked to re-enter their password before the screen is restored.

Workstation clock

The Saber Wait option allows users to schedule programming scripts to be executed at predefined times (see Figure 10.24). This can be very useful.

.INI control manager

The system comes with a host of different minor utilities, the best of which is the
.INI file control manager. This tool is extremely useful for controlling users' .INI
files, especially the SYSTEM.INI file. INIMAN allows the LAN administrator to
establish and maintain hardware-, network- and installation-specific settings in .INI
files, without changing set preferences such as desktop colours.

    The system works by running a special pre-Windows program which ensures
the correct .INI files are loaded for the execution of Windows from a particular
workstation. The INIMAN program automatically updates your .INI files before
starting Windows, so that you always run the most up to date version of LAN
applications. It is a bit complicated to set up, but once mastered it can make the life
of a network manager far easier. When a new Windows application is installed on
the network, it is no longer necessary to change .INI files on every workstation.

```
REM **********************************************************
REM *  This sample batch file demonstrates how to use INIMAN
REM *  prior to starting Windows.  It assumes that the files
REM *  WIN.DEF and SYSTEM.DEF have been created and, along with
REM *  INIMAN.EXE, can be located along the path.
REM *
REM *  A DOS environment variable, S_MONITOR, is used to store
REM *  the workstation's monitor setting and to make sure the
REM *  right WIN.COM file is copied to the user's current
REM *  directory for display of the Windows logo in the right
REM *  display resolution and to make sure that the user's
REM *  current directory is used by Windows to read and write
REM *  .INI file settings.
REM **********************************************************
```

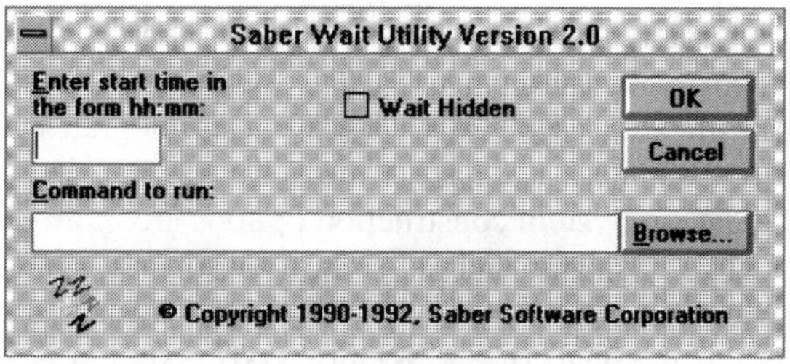

Figure 10.24 The Saber Wait utility.

```
@Echo off
CD X:\WINDOWS
COPY X:\WINDOWS\%S_MONITOR%\WIN.COM WIN.COM /b
INIMAN WIN SYSTEM -s
WIN
DEL WIN.COM
CD X:\
```

Installing the Saber Menu System for Windows

The installation is very simple; the software comes on a couple of disks. The system is installed by running the Windows application INSTALL.EXE found on the first disk (the *Install disk*). The system will now copy all the appropriate files across. During the set-up process you can scan network or local drives for applications to be included in the Saber menus. Another option is presented which will take your existing Windows Program Manager groups and convert them into a Saber menu which you can later change and enhance.

Management issues

This is an excellent package. If you are serious about providing standard Windows menus for all your network Windows users, Saber is well worth the investment. The Saber Menu System for Windows is very good and will become an industry standard. The great advantage is that menus developed under Saber can be used universally, either in the DOS text world or the graphic Windows world. In fact a Saber Menu can have both items which are displayed only if it is running under Windows and items which are displayed only if it is running under DOS.

The .INI manager is a great idea, although practically speaking I have found it problematic as it requires a lot of manual massaging to get it working properly.

Windows Workstation

An alternative to the Saber Windows Menu System is the Windows Workstation package from Automated Design System, Inc. This package is very similar in its capabilities to the Saber system. It integrates very well into the Windows environment, in some ways much better than its Saber equivalent. However, the Saber Menu System construction options are more powerful. It is amazing to look at these two packages and to see how similar they are in functionality. Who has been copying whom?

At the heart of the Windows Workstation is a replacement for the Windows Program Manager (see Figure 10.25). It contains a graphical menu system for organizing programs into single or multi-user groups for easy network access.

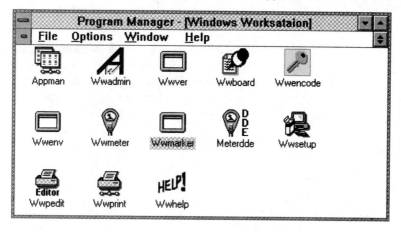

Figure 10.25 Windows Workstation – the Program Manager window.

Application management

The main features of the package are:

- Centralized control of menus
- Each menu can have common network groups and personal user groups
- Each menu or submenu can have user rights and password assignments
- Creation of application-specific help screens
- Customized groups for users' personal files
- An excellent script language to run the MultiSet application
- Multiple choices for viewing and arranging the users' workspaces
- Menus can be displayed as a list of icons

Network security

The Secure Station option provides security at the workstation level; it provides a password-protected screen blanking option.

Workstation clock

This program allows the user to set alarm messages and, more importantly, to schedule programming scripts to be executed at predefined times.

Workstation Print Manager

This program is designed to make the management of tasks related to printing across the network far more intuitive and user friendly. It is a superset of Windows' own Print Manager. One example of its flexibility is that all the connected network printers can be shown as icons. Each can be described by their location. The program can also change banners on printouts.

11

Managing IPX numbers and network interconnections

Managing NetWare IPX network numbers

The NetWare addressing system

In order to understand the workings of NetWare internetwork connections, it is necessary to understand the NetWare addressing system. The heart of the IPX is its addressing system. It uses three basic components to identify any unique process across its environment:

(1) The network address

(2) The node number on the network

(3) The actual process on the node (known as the socket)

The IPX address is formed as shown in Figure 11.1.

IPX addressing structure

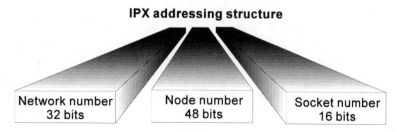

| Network number 32 bits | Node number 48 bits | Socket number 16 bits |

Figure 11.1 IPX addressing structure.

Each IPX packet carries the sender and destination address as it is sent around the Novell network. Figure 11.2 shows a typical IPX packet. It is shown carrying an NCP packet, since IPX is carrying as its data a packet type 17, which is the NCP signature. The destination of the IPX packet is the NCP socket 4003 on server with network card (0080C71E9783) on network number (10410000).

The IPX packet format

The IPX packet structure is very simple, compared with other protocols. Its header is 30 bytes in length. It does not use a checksum since the Checksum is always filled up with FFFFh. Figure 11.3 shows the details of the IPX header.

Length field

This field stores the total length of the IPX packet including the IPX header plus the size of the data it is carrying. Normally the maximum size of this is 1518 bytes.

The maximum length of the IPX packet is 1518 over Ethernet unless you are using the Large Internet Packet protocol.

HOPs

This shows the number of routers the IPX has crossed over. This field is set to zero by the sender and as it is relayed across each router it is incremented. The IPX packet is discarded if this field reaches 16 HOPs. Sometimes this field is referred to as the transport control field.

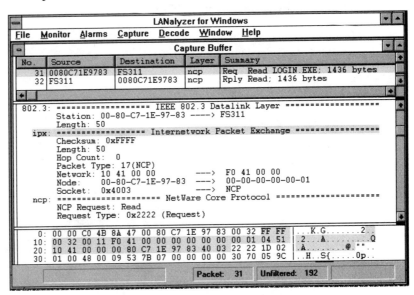

Figure 11.2 A typical IPX packet.

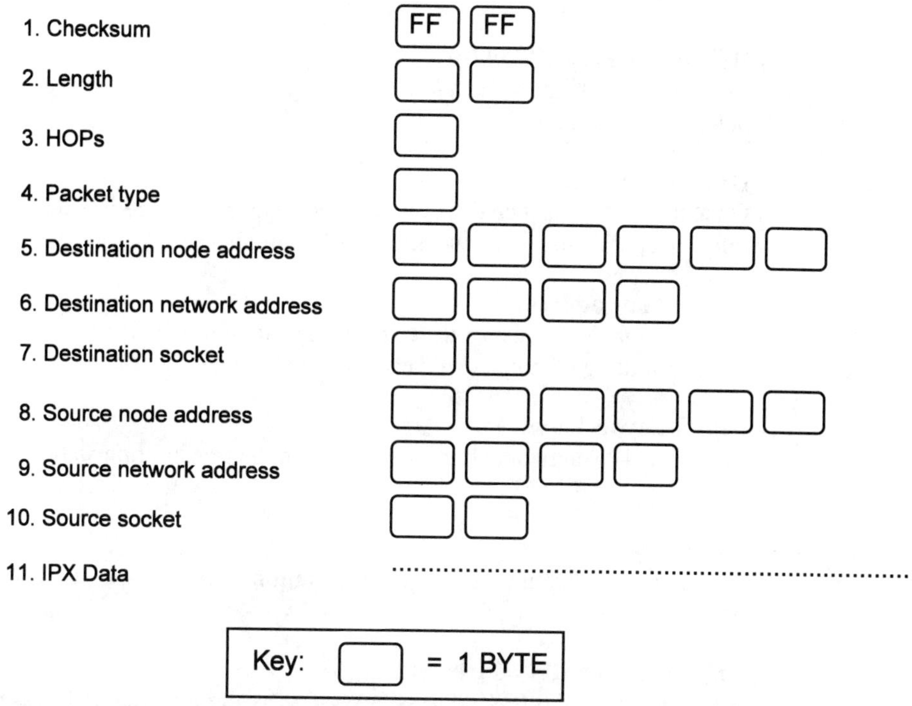

1. Checksum [FF] [FF]

2. Length

3. HOPs

4. Packet type

5. Destination node address

6. Destination network address

7. Destination socket

8. Source node address

9. Source network address

10. Source socket

11. IPX Data

Key: [ ] = 1 BYTE

Figure 11.3 The IPX header.

Packet type
This field indicates what type of NetWare protocol packets this IPX packet is carrying. Some well known packet type numbers are shown in Table 11.1.

Destination node address
This is the node address of the destination station, its value is normally the same as the destination station's network adaptor address.

Table 11.1 Common IPX packet types.

Packet type	Value (in hex)
IPX communication	0
RIP	1
SPX	5
NCP	17

Destination network address

This is the IPX network address that the packet has to get to before it can be delivered to the destination node address.

Destination socket

Once the packet has been delivered to the destination node it is then passed on to the relevant application using the given socket number.

Source node address

This is the node address of the transmitting station. Its value is normally the same as the transmitting station's own network adaptor address.

Source network address

This is the IPX network address from which the transmitting station has sent the IPX packet.

Source socket

This is the socket number that a transmitting process has used to send the IPX packet.

An analogy for IPX addressing

An analogy for the IPX addressing system is the everyday addressing system that we all use (see Figure 11.4). To identify a given person in a town you could use the following:

(1) The road name

(2) The house number on the road

(3) The name of the house occupier in that road

An internetworked environment can be seen as a town of linked roads. Each road has a unique name and is connected with other roads at traffic junctions.

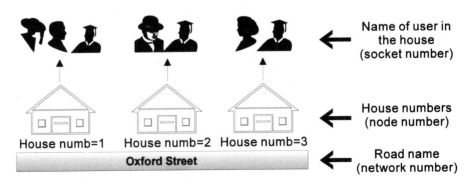

Figure 11.4 An IPX addressing analogy.

An analogy for IPX routing principles

The following analogy can help us understand the function of a router. Of course, in real life, things are more complicated, but it does highlight the basic principles. An internetworked series of Novell networks can be seen as a town of linked streets, all connecting by junctions. Each street has a unique name. Streets are only connected at traffic junctions. Each junction asks an approaching car (data packet) what its destination is. It then directs the car onto the next appropriate junction towards its destination.

Sometimes users talk to each other within a given street. In this case the traffic is isolated to the given road. On the other hand, when a user wishes to send data to a user on another street, it must go through the traffic junctions (routers) before it can reach its destination. The clever thing about these traffic junctions is that they understand the addressing system.

Let's examine the basic sequence of events involved in User A sending data to User B, as illustrated in Figure 11.5. In this analogy, we assume that the services of a chauffeur (IPX driver) are used. This chauffeur is informed of the destination address, which is the street name (network number), house number (node number) and user name (socket number). The chauffeur takes the data and drives along the street to the first junction. On approaching junction Stage 2, the chauffeur informs the junction of the final destination, in particular the name of the street the chauffeur wants to go to. If the traffic junction does not connect directly to that street it refers to a map of the town. This map is kept internally by the traffic junction and is updated regularly. It shows the name of all the streets that are accessible from this junction. It also shows the next junction the data needs to be relayed onto so that it can travel towards its final destination.

A typical map for the above junction might be similar to Table 11.2.

The junction now automatically relays the chauffeur and car onto the next traffic junction at Stage 3, which in turn inspects the destination and discovers the chauffeur wants to go to Street 4. In this case, since the junction is directly connected to Street 4, it does not need to refer to its relaying map. It now directs the car to its final destination.

It stands to reason that each road on the interconnected system must have a unique name. This is exactly the same for IPX networks. Each IPX router must connect differently numbered networks.

NetWare addressing system

NetWare identifies different applications running on different nodes by using the following addressing system. NetWare tackles the addressing issues at the IPX protocol level. It is at this level that the address is read to ensure the correct delivery of data to users (or processes).

The NetWare address system consists of two parts. The first part identifies the actual node address, the second part identifies the application running on the node. Figure 11.6 shows the IPX addressing structure.

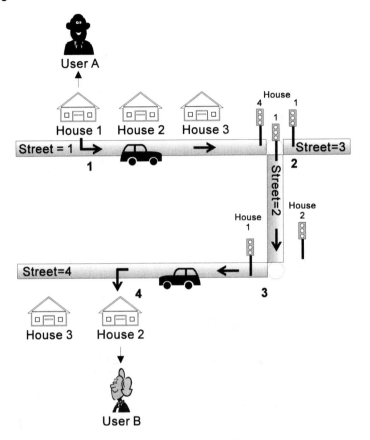

Figure 11.5 An analogy for IPX routing.

Identifying a unique node on any network

To identify a unique node on any network, we use the network number (**Internet address**), in conjunction with the node identifier across the network (**Station address**).

Table 11.12 Internal traffic junction map.

To get to	Number of junctions	Forwarding street
Street 1	1	Street 1
Street 2	1	Street 2
Street 3	1	Street 3
Street 4	2	Street 2

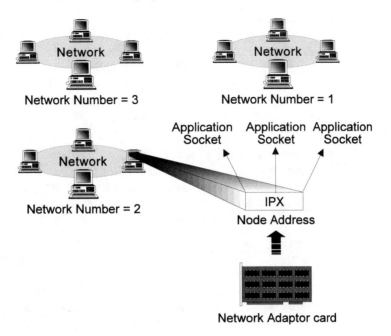

Figure 11.6 IPX addressing structure.

Most real networks are actually made up of a collection of physically distinct networks, normally interconnected by routers. NetWare gives each of these distinct physical networks a unique Internet address. This Internet address is then used to address an individual network. The address is normally a number specified in hexadecimal and can be up to eight digits (64 bits) in length.

Each workstation on a network must be identified by a unique address. This ID is normally read directly from the network adaptor card. When started, IPX automatically reads the physical network adaptor card address, and uses it as its IPX node identifier (station address). No user intervention is required, since Ethernet, Token Ring and FDDI adaptor cards are all given a universally unique adaptor address. This address then becomes the IPX node identifier. In theory, two nodes can have the same IPX node ID as long as they are on different networks or, in other words, each must be qualified by a different Internet address. The node address is normally a number specified in hexadecimal and can be up to 12 digits (96 bits) in length.

Application address

An application running on a node is identified in two parts: the **connection number** and the application **socket number**.

Each time a user runs the NETX.COM, a connection is established between the workstation and the file server. This is purely a logical connection assigned exclusively between the workstation and the file server. All further data transferred between the two nodes will take place along this connection number. NetWare assigns connection numbers to nodes on a next-available-connection-number basis, working from 1 upwards. The actual number is limited by the software licence of the NetWare package. This means that, for a 20-user NetWare licence, the file server can only establish up to 20 connections. If users fails to establish a connection they cannot login. The rather confusing error then shown says File server not found.

If you see the error File server not found, go to the file server console and check that you have not run out of connection numbers. If your software licence connections limit has been reached, remove any connections that show NOT-LOGGED-IN. This should release the connection number, enabling you to connect to the file server.

Any node on the network could potentially be running several different processes, all concurrently engaged in some sort of connection with the file server. NetWare identifies each process by its application socket number and automatically assigns sockets or logical ports to these processes. IPX sets aside a number of sockets for its own exclusive administrative usage (for example, see Figure 11.7).

As far as NetWare is concerned, the most important NetWare socket numbers are shown in Table 11.3.

These socket numbers are all well defined. There are a range of socket numbers available for third-party use (above 8000h up to FFFFh). Normally, to gain wide acceptance you need to apply to Novell for an allocation of socket numbers. If granted, this will then be listed within the public domain, enabling others to use your socket (or, more to the point, to be aware of your socket number and leave it well alone!).

Internal and external network numbers

When you install a NetWare file server or a NetWare router, you are always prompted for a network number, to be associated with each network adaptor that is

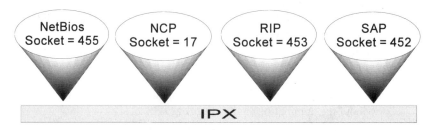

Figure 11.7 Some classic IPX socket numbers.

Table 11.3 Important NetWare socket numbers.

Socket number	Description
17	NetWare Core Protocols (NCPs)
451	NetWare File Server Packets
452	NetWare Service Advertising Protocol
453	NetWare Routing Information Protocol
455	NetWare NETBIOS Emulation Packets
456	NetWare Diagnostic Packets

to be configured inside the machine. You can have up to four different ISA network cards or six EISA NIC cards. Each has to be given a unique number. These numbers are used by the IPX RIP (Routing Information Protocol) packets to route traffic from one segment on to another.

These numbers are arbitrary numbers between 1 and FFFFFFFF. However, they have to be assigned using the following rules:

Each network number must be uniquely assigned to each network segment.

This becomes its unique address. No two segments can have the same number.

Each NetWare 3.x or 4.0 server must be treated as having an internal network segment. This is given another unique network number, called the **internal network number**. In effect, this logical network acts as a roundabout connecting a number of physical networks via the file server.

Figure 11.8 shows the difference between NetWare 386 logical and physical network numbers.

The internal network number must be unique amongst all other file servers and the numbers given to all the physical network segments.

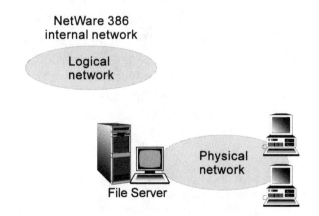

Figure 11.8 NetWare 386 logical and physical network numbers.

Unfortunately, unlike TCP/IP, which has a far cleverer network numbering system (such as 178.188.12.3 which allows you to break up the numbers into sections and subsections), in NetWare 386 you have only one number to assign. So it is very important to create a good system for managing them.

You do not need to panic too much if two networks are accidentally given the same network number: NetWare will inform you through its file servers which two networks have identical numbers. You can then simply change one of them to a new number. Of course it is far better to have devised a system beforehand so that this situation can be avoided.

Managing number assignment

It is very important to keep a record of IPX network number allocation at a centralized place. Some companies keep a special book at their head quarters called the IPX Network Number Book. All network installers have to consult this common book for a network allocation number.

If you wish to connect your interconnected IPX network to other IPX networks from other organizations, then you will need to request IPX numbers from Novell and use the IPX numbers assigned to you.

See the section on the IPX network registry service for further information.

However, if you plan to only interconnect your organization's IPX network across multiple LANs or WANs, then you can use your own IPX numbering format.

You might consider using the form shown in Table 11.4 to allocate your network number. This is my own standard that I have developed over the years: it can be adapted to your own purposes. I have defined three different types of network. Two of them are Novell's own standards and the third I have introduced (it has been very useful when interconnecting networks through WANs):

(1) Internal networks found on NetWare 3.x and 4.x file servers

(2) Physical networks (or a given LAN cabling system)

(3) External networks: these are remote or external networks

The table only includes some simple numbers, as an example, but it shows the basic idea. You could keep a different sheet for each type of network, which would make allocation far easier.

As your network begins to expand, you must know what numbers have already been assigned so that new ones can be accommodated. It would be nice if you had a numbering scheme that was also meaningful, so that, by looking at a given network number, you could have a good idea what its address is. The addressing scheme described below may give you some ideas.

Table 11.4 An example network number register.

Network number	Network type	Description
F 044 10 10	File server	In UK site 10, Number 10
F 001 69 08	File server	In USA site 69, Number 08
F 001 09 03	File server	In USA site 09, Number 03
2 001 F3 68	Thin Ethernet LAN	In USA site F3, Number 68
1 098 04 78	10BaseT LAN	In IRAN site 4, Number 78
E 358 87 08	External WAN	Starts in Finland site 87, Number 8

A proposed addressing scheme

There are many different numbering schemes and each one has its good points and bad points. The important thing is to *have* a scheme: it does not really matter what it is, as long as it is logical and ensures that all network numbers are unique. You might want to consider using the following addressing scheme. It might not be appropriate in all cases, but there should be something useful in it for everyone.

The range of numbers you can use is from 1 to FFFFFFF. I suggest you always use the full eight characters when assigning numbers, filling in with 0s if necessary.

I have used an addressing idea similar to TCP/IP's, which breaks up network addresses into sections and subsections, and have added a new idea. The value of the first character will tell you what type of physical cable is being used or if it is an internal or external network.

The network address key

Each network address has the following format:

F.FFF.FF.FF

t.aaa.ss.nn

The addressing system is defined as follows:

- **t** is one of the values listed in Table 11.5.
- **aaa** is the area code. This could be the country's telephone code if the organization is international, for example, 044 for the UK and 001 for the USA. Or, if it is a national organization, it could be the local city code. You should decide how to define an area which is suitable for your organization.
- **ss** is the sub-area code. Once again, it is up to you to define a suitable subdivision area code suitable for your organization. This should, however, bring you down to a building/site level.
- **nn** is the network number. This should define the actual network number within the site.

Table 11.6 shows some example network addresses and their meanings.

Table 11.5 Possible values for **t**.

Character	Meaning
F	File server (internal network number)
E	External network (connects to a WAN)
2	LAN using Thin Ethernet (10Base**2**)
5	LAN using Thick Ethernet (10Base**5**)
6	LAN Token Ring **16** Mbytes
4	LAN Token Ring **4** Mbytes
1	LAN 10BaseT

See Appendix A for a ready-made form which you can copy and use.

IPX network registry service

In April 1993, Novell made a public statement about their intention to set up an IPX number registration service. This will form the foundation of a worldwide network for NetWare IPX users, and will be in parallel to the TCP/IP Internet service. It began with the US Department of Defense Advance Research Project Agency (DARPA) network. It has grown with the increasing popularity of the TCP/IP protocol. The Internet service has had an IP number registration service for many years, enabling over one million nodes worldwide to interconnect to each other. The Novell press release states that the intention is *not* to compete with the Internet, but to enable IPX users to enjoy similar worldwide interconnection facilities as those enjoyed by IP users. The IPX worldwide network could end up being larger than Internet as there are about 20 million IPX users worldwide. This is a very important statement of intent from Novell; the press release of April 19th 1993 is shown below.

Table 11.6 Example network addresses and their meanings.

Network number	Meaning
F 044 10 12	File server in UK site 10, Number 10
F 001 69 08	File server in USA site 69, Number 08
F 001 09 03	File server in USA site 09, Number 03
2 001 F3.68	Thin Ethernet LAN in USA site F3, Number 68
1 098 04 78	10BaseT LAN in IRAN site 4, Number 78
E 358 87 08	External WAN connecting Finland site 87 Number 08

Novell announces the Novell network registry
San Jose, California, April 19, 1993

As a service to its customers who are building enterprise networks, Novell today announced the Novell Network Registry, a network registration service to be administered by Novell. The Registry, an optional service, facilitates network administration by eliminating name and address conflicts among geographically dispersed networks. Working with assigned network names and numbers from the registration service assures customers they will have a unique set of network identifiers, enabling reliable communications worldwide.

The Novell Network Registry is a key part of Novell's strategy to empower NetWare customers with comprehensive tools for enterprise-wide management and administration. The Novell Network Registry is a natural complement to NetWare 4.0 Directory Services, NetWare Global MHS and the NetWare MultiProtocol Router. The Novell Network Registry's name and address structures are fully compatible with the technology in Novell products and those of partners throughout the industry.

NetWare users with large corporate networks benefit from the Registry service, as do those with any size networks who use the network to communicate with other organizations. "As NetWare networks are connected into global information systems, our customers have asked us to organize a database of unique network names and addresses, allowing them to participate in worldwide IPX Internetworks without address conflicts" said Navindra Jain, vice president and general manager of Novell's Network Management and Internetworking Products Division. "The Novell Network Registry brings structure to IPX Internetworks and serves as the foundation for a new generation of global information sharing. I encourage all NetWare customers who are now internetworked, or who plan to communicate with other NetWare sites outside their immediate environment, to take advantage of this service."

Customers contact the Registry to reserve an organization name, or a range of addresses, or both. An organization name is selected by the requesting user and recorded with the Registry administrator. A unique range of IPX addresses is allocated by the Registry with a size matched to the user's needs.

"The Novell Network Registry will help us provide an easy migration path for interconnecting our international networks and easily connect our networks to external companies or providers" said Dr. Hans W. Barz, international telecommunications coordinator for Swiss-based pharmaceutical, biological and chemical company CIBA (formerly CIBA-Geigy). CIBA employs more than 91,000 personnel and maintains offices in 62 countries, including the United States.

How the Registry works

The Novell Network Registry consists of two separate but complementary services. Customers can register their organization names, or apply for a unique set of IPX addresses, or both.

- The Novell Network Registry reserves a top-level organization name for an enterprise. The customer's network administrator manages the names of departments, users and servers within the enterprise. Since the naming structure is hierarchical, it facilitates sharing the administrative workload.

- Once the Novell Network Registry assigns a range of IPX addresses, the customer's network administrator subdivides the range to meet local needs, and assigns individual network numbers to servers, routers and network segments.

The service does not require any special software. The Novell Network Registry is an optional service; NetWare, as before, operates with independently assigned names and addresses.

Pricing and availability

Registration fees start at US$100.00 and range higher depending on the number of IPX addresses requested. These fees cover the costs of processing requests and maintaining the database. The service is available now (as from April 1993).

For more information

A Novell Network Registry information package can be ordered by calling USA-408-321 1506. The fax request number is 1-408-9560463. In addition, the Novell Network Registry can be contacted by Internet e-mail at the following: `registry@novell.com`; or MHS NHUB e-mail at `registry@novell`.

Internetworking NetWare

The basics of network interconnection

Overview

A few years ago the big question was how to use a network to interconnect workstations. One of the biggest issues facing managers today is how to connect all of our fast growing networks together in a way that increases facilities at no expense to performance (generally a contradiction in terms!). When interconnecting networks you can benefit from factors other than simply extending the services available. Some of these fundamental benefits are more subtle than others.

It used to be true that managers of small unchanging networks did not need to concern themselves with network interconnection, whereas managers of large networks were forced to face the interconnection challenges. Things have changed: all network managers should now be aware of the products that interconnect networks and the issues confronting them.

Novell sees the area of network interconnection as a very important aspect of NetWare. Most of the development in NetWare 4.x has gone into providing improved NetWare interconnection facilities.

We will concentrate on routers, the area of fastest growth within network interconnection, which is also fully supported by Novell's products and protocols.

The OSI Reference Model

If you are familiar with the seven-layer OSI Reference Model, you can omit this section.

In 1979, the International Organization for Standardization (ISO) began work on defining a conceptual model for the purposes of data communications. This gave rise to the Open Systems Interconnection Reference Model. ISO define the purpose of the model as follows:

> The purpose of this International Standards Reference Model of the Open Systems Interconnection is to provide a common basis for the coordination of standards development for the purpose of system interconnection, while allowing existing standards to be placed into perspective within the overall Reference Model.

Open Systems Interconnection (OSI) refers to a conceptual environment (the OSIE) which aims to allow all the computers in a particular OSIE that adhere to the standards to exchange information easily, reliably and in a harmonious manner. Computers or terminals which adhere to the OSI standard are referred to as being 'open', since all open systems will be able to exchange information, irrespective of their manufacture.

The central purpose of OSI is to provide a comprehensive framework for the high-level interaction of users and applications in distributed processing environments, incorporating a wide variety of computer and communications equipment.

The functions that must be performed to accomplish this task are modularized amongst the seven layers of the OSI architecture (see Figure 11.9), in a hierarchical arrangement that proceeds from hardware-specific, bit-encoding functions in the Physical Layer all the way up to abstract, structured-data exchange functions in the Application Layer. The function of each layer in the Reference Model is shown in Figure 11.9.

Protocols in the lower four layers (Physical, Data Link, Network and Transport) are communications oriented. They build a uniform, reliable data transport service that does not depend on the characteristics of specific underlying communications facilities.

Protocols in the upper three layers (Session, Presentation and Application) are application oriented; they create a coordinated framework based on the exchange of data using the Transport Service.

Why interconnect?

Reasons for interconnecting networks include the following:

- To expand the services to users.
- To extend the number of stations on the network.

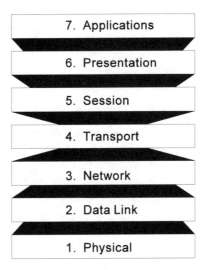

Figure 11.9 The seven-layer OSI Reference Model.

- To extend the distance of networks.
- To apply a structured numbering system to identify any user on any network.
- To connect different types of network, for example, Token Ring and Ethernet.
- To improve network performance. This is achieved by isolating the network traffic. In the example in Figure 11.10, the network is divided into two, giving each user their own network for connecting to the file server. In this case, this is done simply by splitting the network and terminating each section at the file server. Now the traffic produced by each user is isolated in their own network, thereby improving overall performance. Note that the two can still talk to each other through the file server.

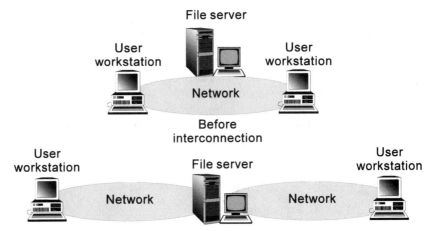

Figure 11.10 Interconnection can improve performance.

- To improve fault tolerance. By interconnecting networks, you can develop multiple paths from the source to the destination. This means that if one path fails the data can be routed through another path, thus giving the network fault tolerance. A typical example of such a set-up is shown in Figure 11.11. Two backbone networks connect all other networks in such a way that if any cable fails there is an alternative path for the data to take.

The tools of interconnection

There are four basic types of product that can be used to interconnect different types of network:

(1) Repeaters

(2) Bridges

(3) Routers

(4) Gateways

They all provide the means to extend the range of a LAN, but work at different levels of the OSI protocol (see Figure 11.12). It is important to understand what these products actually do and what their limits are. Generally speaking, the higher the protocol layer these products work on, the more expensive and complicated they become. However, what you lose on the one hand you gain on the other because they also become more intelligent and sophisticated.

Repeaters

Repeaters work at the Physical layer. They normally consist of a simple box which

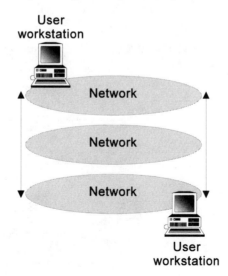

Figure 11.11 Interconnection can improve fault tolerance.

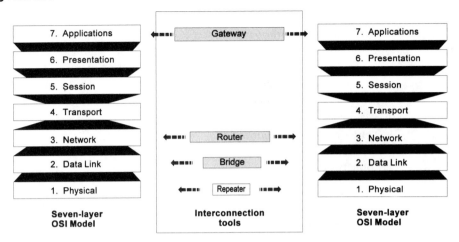

Figure 11.12 The tools of network interconnection.

boosts cable signals from one medium to another (see Figure 11.13). This enables the length of the network to be extended. The repeater does not understand the actual meaning of the signals that it is transferring, it just re-transmits the signals from one network onto the other. Repeaters are most commonly used in Ethernet networks to extend the network over two or more segments.

Repeaters can do the following:

- Boost signals across different media types
- Boost signals across an extended cable
- Send signals out to all network segments

Some repeaters can isolate a fault on one segment and not pass this on. Repeaters are used primarily in linear networks such as Ethernet.

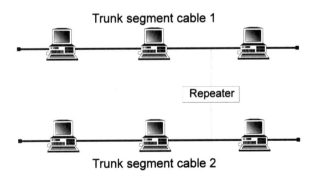

Figure 11.13 Example of a repeater.

When to use repeaters

They are typically used when cabling distance limits have been reached. Generally speaking, they are not very effective when used for network interconnection because they cannot isolate traffic. They simply broadcast all data from one segment to all others.

Most hubs and cable concentrators are forms of repeater, so without knowing it you might already be using repeaters in your network. When your network is cabled around such devices it is advisable to follow the manufacturer's suggested method for extending the local interconnection.

If you require further network interconnection, it is advisable to look at other products such as bridges and routers: they can possibly do the job of extending your network instead of a repeater.

If you plan to use a repeater, see if you can get hold of a fault-isolating version. It will isolate traffic if it detects a network segment has become saturated and, therefore, stop the congestion from being passed on to the next segment. In the long term, the extra expense is well worth it.

Bridges

A bridge connects two or more networks together at the Data Link layer (OSI layer 2). Bridges work at the Media Access Control (MAC) level. This means that two or more separate networks can be connected into one large logical network.

Typically, a bridge is used to connect an Ethernet IEEE 802.3 to another Ethernet IEEE 802.3 or a Token Ring network to another Token Ring network. Any network that conforms to the MAC standard can, in theory, be bridged with other MAC-conformant networks. Bridges can also bring together more than two different networks. In the example shown in Figure 11.14, a bridge is used to connect an Ethernet to a Token Ring network. All users on the Ethernet side see the Token Ring users as fellow Ethernet users, and vice versa. These types of bridges work by converting the protocols from Ethernet into Token Ring format and vice versa.

Basic internal structure of bridge

A bridge works by utilizing the LLC (Logical Link Controller) as defined by the IEEE 802.2 standard. The OSI Data Link layer is divided into two sub-layers which the bridge uses to interconnect networks. These sub-layers are the LLC (Logical Link Controller) layer and the MAC (Media Access Control) layer. The LLC layer defines a universal standard that all networks should conform to. The MAC layer defines an actual physical network implantation. This explains why you have many different MAC implementations such as Ethernet (IEEE 802.3), or the MAC that supports Token Ring (IEEE 802.5). They all, however, conform to the services demanded by the common LLC layer. This means that the LLC layer can act as a universal

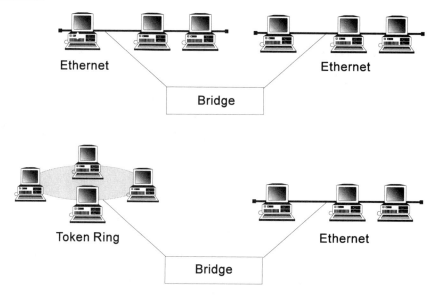

Figure 11.14 Examples of typical bridge usage.

translator between one type of MAC and another. It is an intelligent form of switchboard. Figure 11.15 shows an example of the internal structure of a bridge.

Using the example in Figure 11.15, let's assume that a data packet needs to go between the Ethernet and Token Ring networks. The basic sequence of operation is as follows:

(1) An Ethernet frame arrives at the bridge.

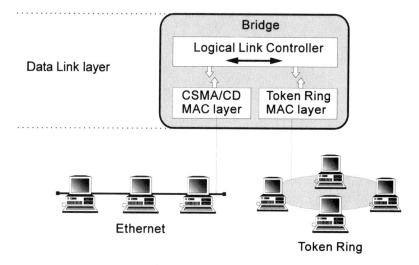

Figure 11.15 An example of a bridge's internal structure.

(2) It is processed by the bridge's Ethernet card.

(3) The bridge's Ethernet MAC layer sends data up to the LLC layer.

(4) The LLC formats the data ready for sending over to the Token Ring MAC.

(5) The Token Ring MAC is activated.

(6) It uses the bridge Token Ring card to send the data onto the ring.

This is a very simple overview of the operation. In practice, it is much more complicated than the above suggests, especially when managing the addresses of users on either side. A bridge will somehow have to decide which users are on which side and forward relevant data. This gets even more complicated when there are many bridges interconnecting many sub-networks. How do these bridges decide which path the data should take? These problems have been solved by today's intelligent bridges, which have an awareness of each other. They are normally categorized under the 'learning' or 'spanning tree' categories.

Bridge classification

There are three basic types of intelligent bridge; each is described below.

Static bridges were the first-generation bridges. Using a keyboard (or, even worse, dip switches), the network manager had to physically tell the bridge the address identity of all the nodes that the bridge was to connect. These bridges are now becoming very rare. They do however still have a use in networks where security is essential and the network manager wants to physically define who can talk to who. They are, by their very nature, inflexible and hard to manage in a fast-changing network environment. This is why most people choose more intelligent bridges.

Learning (or adaptive or spanning tree) bridges are popular in the Ethernet world. They are primarily used to connect many Ethernet networks together. Called many different names, from 'learning' to 'spanning tree' bridges, they are all the same. They work by building a dynamic table of who is on which network, and maintain an internal table of each sub-network that they bridge. These type of bridges are transparent to data.

The tables are built up dynamically. When the bridge is first switched on it enters into the promiscuous mode: this means it allows all data traffic to go through it. It observes the traffic as it passes. The observed addresses are used to dynamically update the tables. The bridge knows the origin of each packet and can build up a picture of the network. These tables only store the current live session, not all the possible connections that can be made. After a fixed time of inactivity, the table entries are reset and new ones established.

Source routing bridges are primarily used to connect multiple Token Ring networks. Here the bridges are told what to do by the packets, unlike the transparent bridges. The source node must include routing information in the data packet that it wishes to send and the bridges are designed to act upon this information.

A connection is established as follows:

(1) The source node sends out a number of discovery frames.

(2) Each frame then takes a different path through the bridges in attempting to reach the destination.

(3) The first packet to reach the destination returns to the source taking the same path home.

(4) The source then records the path of the fastest packet.

(5) Meanwhile, all the lost frames are destroyed by bridges since they were all given a limited life span.

(6) This path is now used in data transmission to the destination.

Source routing transparent bridges are capable of handling both transparent and source routing data. They can act as a translator between the two systems. They are *very* clever!

Bridge management issues

Bridges are far less sophisticated at distributing network traffic than routers. There are times, however, when you need to use bridges, especially if multiple different network layer protocols are being used. In these situations, opt for intelligent bridges. There is no problem using spanning tree bridges over Novell Ethernet networks, since they are transparent. Far greater problems arise when you use source routing bridges on Novell Token Ring networks. You must modify the user's workstation environment by running a special TSR program called ROUTE.COM after loading up the MLID device driver. This is yet another burden placed upon the network manager. If you have the choice, go for routers, since no special change to the workstation is required.

Spanning tree bridges under NetWare

To use spanning tree bridges under NetWare, you need to run the following programs:

- ROUTE.NLM on the file server
- ROUTE.COM on the workstations

These programs provided by Novell allow users running NetWare 3.x to communicate across IBM Token Ring network bridges. They also allow IBM applications that require source routing support to run unmodified on NetWare.

On the file server, copy the ROUTE.NLM to the SYS:\SYSTEM sub-directory. From the console, type:

```
LOAD ROUTE
```

On the ODI workstation:

(1) Load the ROUTE.COM file found on the DOS/ODI Workstation Services diskette to the user's normal network boot-up directory.

(2) Set up the appropriate parameters for ROUTE.COM. The default parameters for ROUTE.COM can be used with most network communications.

(3) Run ROUTE.COM after the Token Ring MLID driver, such as TOKEN.COM, but before loading the protocol stack, such as the IPXODI.COM driver.

Routers

Figure 11.16 shows an example of a router.

Because they work at the Network layer, routers are aware of the protocol flowing through them, such as IPX or the IP part of TCP/IP. One of the wonderful features of routers is that they are generally aware of each other and can cooperate in ensuring a good data flow through the interconnected networks. Most network protocols have a built-in facility for working out the best route through a network of routers. Examples of such protocols are Novell IPX and the UNIX TCP/IP protocols. Routers talk to each other via the RIP (Routing Information Protocol). The IPX protocol has the identification of a station node on a uniquely identified network number built into its addressing structure.

Routers have the following characteristics:

- They filter packets of data.
- They cooperate with each other in the transmission of data across interconnected networks.
- They isolate traffic.
- They connect different Data Link layer types of network together.
- They use intelligent routing algorithms.
- They see each network as having a different network number, used for routing.
- They are network-protocol-dependant, such as IPX or the IP part of TCP/IP.
- They translate between different protocols, at the Network layer.

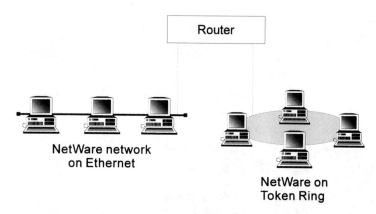

Figure 11.16 A router connecting Ethernet and Token Ring NetWare networks.

Basic router operation

A router monitors the data packets and examines routing information files contained within the protocols. It then determines the best route for each packet to take. It can forward packets to fellow routers, which in turn relay the data until it reaches its destination. Routers see the network as being made up of a collection of segments. These segments are the logical building blocks upon which routers operate. They connect them together, enabling data to be transferred from its logical source to its logical destination. By using segmentation, network traffic can be isolated, preventing unnecessary data transfer across networks. A protocol-specific router can only handle data packets of that protocol type, such as the very common NetWare-specific IPX routers. A multi-protocol router, on the other hand, can cope with different protocols and can translate between the internetwork addressing of one type of protocol and another.

Different factors affecting the routing path

Routers have clever algorithms which decide on the best path for data transmission. Most routers take a combination of the following factors into account in deciding upon the best path:

- The minimum number of **hops** (a hop is jump across a router)
- Time (**ticks**) as a deciding factor
- Speed
- The cost of each path

For example, NetWare routers take the number of hops and number of ticks into consideration.

A router is normally bought to support a fixed protocol.

Cisco: the big name in routers

Cisco is the company that dominates the internetwork market. In 1993, Cisco was estimated to have 30% of the market share (Vitalink having 20%, 3Com (Inc. BICC ISOLAN) 10%, and Proteon a 5% share). In this dominant market position, Cisco is the company that most others compare themselves against. Its popularity is due to a number of factors:

- Its routers fully support NetWare protocols, and perform substantially better than Novell's alternative (at an extra cost, however).
- Cisco routers can support multiple protocols, such as IPX to IP and vice versa.
- They have excellent LAN/WAN connectivity options.
- IBM SAN and the recent APPN support are excellent.

If you are looking for a fast router, look at what Cisco has to offer. Of course it will largely depend on what you want to route and how, but generally speaking this company is on most people's short list.

OSI routing view

The OSI seven-layer model defines two protocols for routing. They define how the two basic components within the network should talk to each other. These are the users at the End System (ES) and the router itself, called the Intermediate System (IS). The protocols have been developed using these basic components. The first part defines how the users at the ES can make use of the services of the IS (router). The second part of the protocol defines the inter-routing protocols used by the interlinked routers, so that the user data can be relayed across the network until it reaches its destination. This is called the IS-IS protocol. This IS-IS protocol is the heart of the system. The interlinked routers use this standard to talk to each other. They build a picture of the interlinked networks so that the data can be transferred across them. Figure 11.17 illustrates the OSI routing protocols.

The OSI has defined a routing algorithm called the Open Shortest Path First (OSPF). This is used by OSI-compliant routers to develop their routing tables. OSI has also introduced the concept of **areas**: these are level 1 and level 2 routers. The level 1 routers are aware of sub-networks within a defined area. This area could be a local area as defined by the organization. Packets of data that are outside the area are then forwarded to level 2 routers. This approach means that routing information needing to be stored within each router is reduced, leading in turn to simplified implementation on large networks.

Brouters

'Brouters' combine the features of bridges and routers in one product. They behave as a router if they recognize the Network layer packets and like a bridge if they don't.

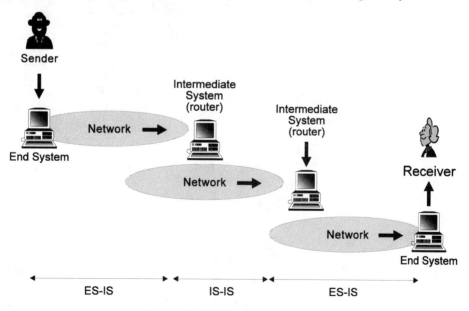

Figure 11.17 OSI routing protocols.

Be careful: some brouters use the proprietary method of routing, limiting you to a specific manufacturer's hardware. Where possible, go for routers that use standard industry protocols and that can also bridge if necessary.

Bridges versus routers

The market is moving away from bridges towards routers, because the latter have far more sophisticated multiprotocol support and can be easily managed. The projected worldwide sales of the two products, shown in Figure 11.18, speak for themselves. Novell has concentrated on providing routers for its users.

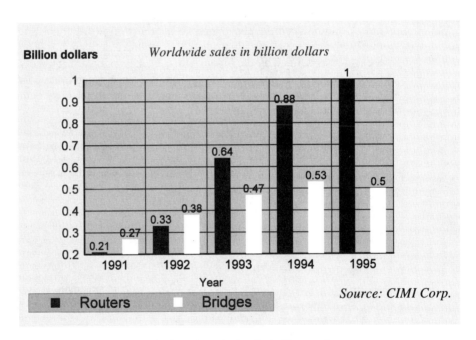

Figure 11.18 Projected sales for bridges and routers.

12

Managing Novell routers

Overview

A NetWare router (previously referred to as an 'intelligent Novell bridge') can be a NetWare file server, a dedicated or non-dedicated workstation or just a special router box bought from a third party. This area has traditionally been one of the strengths of the standard NetWare package as compared with other network operating systems. With NetWare, you get a free program called the ROUTEGEN program. Using this program you can turn any PC into an IPX router capable of routing four different networks all together. Novell call this an **external router**.

Each NetWare server can very easily be turned into a router, since they can normally accommodate up to four different network cards internally, and bind to each one's protocols. Novell call this an **internal router**. The NetWare file server provides an incredible amount of flexibility. You can either bind the same protocol to all network adaptors or bind different protocols on to the same card, or any combination of the two. The incredible thing is that all this can be done dynamically while the file server is providing a server through its other resources.

Novell routers seem to concentrate on the two most popular protocols: IPX and the IP part of TCP/IP. They come free with the NetWare file server package. I will be concentrating on these two protocols, but it is important to make the point that other protocols are supported with the appropriate purchases of the extension disks.

Another important way that routers can be used is in connecting to WANs. These routers are sometimes called **half routers** or **remote routers**. I will concentrate on the **asynchronous routers**: they connect remote networks via an asynchronous device such as a modem.

This section will look at each type of router and the last section will look at some of the management strategy considerations.

Warning: Novell bridge name confusion!

Novell used to call routers 'bridges'. They used to say 'Novell bridges *[meaning routers]* are very intelligent; they are aware of protocols'. This confusion was probably due to marketing reasons. The Novell marketing department thought that clients would be more likely to buy bridges than routers. Novell is now using the correct name and calls its routing software a ROUTER; hence you can use the Novell ROUTEGEN program to produce Novell routers.

Understanding NetWare routers

Let us examine in detail the stages a Novell router passes through as it flows through an interlinked network.

Basic components

NetWare has built-in routing protocols as an enhancement to its IPX protocol. This is divided into two parts, described by Novell as the **router requester** and the **router service provider** (routing manager).

As part of the NetWare shell, each node on the network has the router requester code implemented. This enables each node on a network to request routing information from other routers. This is done by sending out a special type of IPX packet called an RIP (Routing Information Protocol) packet.

Novell allows for two different types of router:

(1) **Internal routers**, which function within the file server and can normally bring up to four different networks together. In the case of EISA, this can be extended to six.

(2) **External routers**, which are stand-alone dedicated routers running on workstations.

In addition to the normal routing requester, each one of these items will also have the routing service provider. The internal structure of the NetWare router is illustrated in Figure 12.1.

The routing service provider manages the relaying of IPX packets from one network to another. This is why they are found within NetWare routers.

Hopping along NetWare

Figure 12.2 shows an example of the basic steps involved in transferring a packet of data from User A to User B on separate NetWare networks.

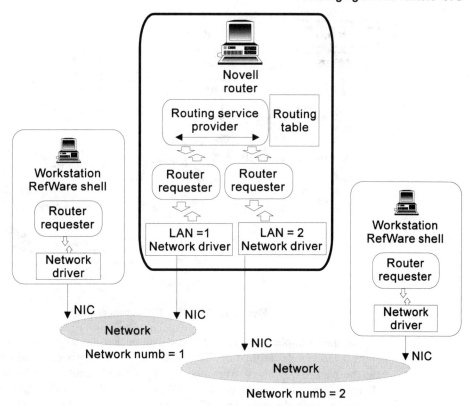

Figure 12.1 NetWare router internal structure.

It is important to note that the data packet contains two different types of addressing as it flows through the system:

(1) The IPX sender and destination address

(2) The MAC layer address for sender and destination

This can also be shown as follows:

Data	MAC address: Sender and destination of next hop	IPX address: Sender of original data; destination of user

In the case of Ethernet and Token Ring, the MAC address is normally a 48-bit address.

It is important that the IPX address part is kept constant as the packet hops along from network to network. The MAC layer address is changed automatically by the routers to transfer the packet along to the next junction. As the MAC layer address is changed, the final destination IPX address should be getting closer.

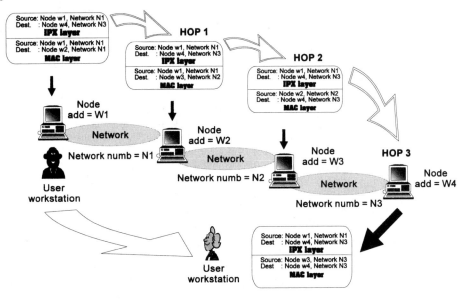

Figure 12.2 Routing IPX across networks.

In the example in Figure 12.2, the data packet has to go through two routers before it reaches its destination. The MAC layer address is changed three times to help the packet hop along from network to network until the IPX packet can be delivered. The only change within the IPX packet is the record of how many hops it has already gone through. The IPX packet calls this the **Transport Control** field (see Figure 12.3). This record is used to time out IPX packets that might have got themselves into a loop. Only the first four bits of this field are used (at the moment!). The four bits limit how many hops a frame can take (currently 15). The value 16 (or 0Fh) is used to indicate that the frame should be destroyed. NetWare defines a maximum of 15 hops. The number 16 hop is used to indicate infinity, meaning that the destination is no longer available through this route.

The routing table

The NetWare routing table has an entry for each of the networks that can be reached from the router. In the example in Figure 12.4, the router will have the table shown in Table 12.1.

The following information is found against each network entry.

(1) **Forwarding network.** This field is used to indicate which directly-connected network the router will forward the packet onto. This field in fact defines which node the packet is to go out from, on its way to its final destination.

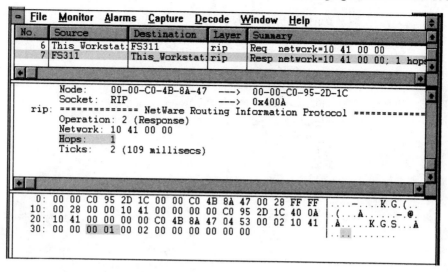

Figure 12.3 The Transport Control field.

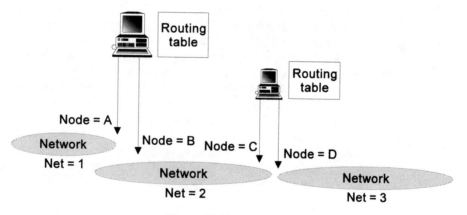

Figure 12.4 Routing tables.

Table 12.1 Router table for the example in Figure 12.4.

Network destination	Forwarding network	Forward to node	Hops to destination	Number of ticks
Net 1	Net 1	Use final node add	1	1
Net 2	Net 2	Use final node add	1	1
Net 3	Net 2	C	2	3

(2) **Forwarding node.** This is the node that the packet will be sent onto within the forwarding network. This could be either the final destination node, or the node address of the next router on the forwarding network.

(3) **Hops to destination.** This indicates how many router hops the packet is away from its final destination. This is used in working out the best path if there are a number of routes available.

(4) **Number of ticks.** The number of ticks indicates the estimated time needed to reach the destination. Each tick is roughly equivalent to 1/18 second.

RIP (Routing Information Protocol)

Novell uses RIP (Routing Information Protocol) packets to enable routers to talk to each other so that they may constantly keep their routing tables updated. Novell RIP packets are based on the Xerox Network System RIP, except that they are enhanced by the inclusion of ticks. The number of ticks indicates the estimated time needed to reach the destination. This is in addition to the information provided by the hop count. NetWare routers use this information to work out the fastest path to a given destination.

The RIP packets are recognized by NetWare because they have been allocated a special IPX socket number. This number is 453h, not to be confused with the XNS RIP packets, which use socket number 1.

The RIP format is very simple; there are only two different basic types of command, **request RIP packets** and **respond RIP packets** (see Figure 12.5).

These packets are only transmitted from one router to another. Occasionally, however, a lovely rippling of RIPs across the network occurs. As a router starts up, it requests information from surrounding routers. They in turn will need to update their tables and will make the appropriate request. This in turn activates all their neighbours and so on until the new information has flowed through the system. As

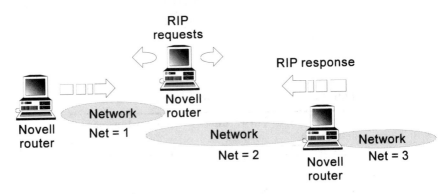

Figure 12.5 RIP request and respond commands.

the information flows, each router updates its routing table based upon the information received from its neighbours.

RIP request

This packet is used to request information from other routers regarding a given network. If it is FFFFFF, then information on all networks is requested.

RIP response

This is normally a list of all known files. Each field represents information about a given network. Each field takes the following format, which NetWare calls **tuples**:

Known network number	Number of hops	Ticks

How RIPs are sent out

RIP packets are sent out from routers to other routers on the following conditions:

- Every 60 seconds, each router transmits its routing table to all the directly-connecting networks. This allows other routers to pick up any new information and update their own tables. This can create a large overhead on slow networks such as asynchronous links or X.25 networks. In such cases, automatic updating can be suppressed.
- Every time a router is started, a request for updates is made. This alerts all the neighbouring routers to update their own tables due to the arrival of a new path. They in turn will inform all their neighbours and so on.
- Every time a router is closed down, it informs all its neighbours that the connection is no longer available. They in turn will inform their neighbours and so on.
- Issuing the **RESET ROUTER** command at the router console will initialize the routing table and issue the appropriate request along the interlinked network.

SAP (Service Advertising Protocol)

What is SAP?

SAP is another specialized use of IPX sockets. Socket number 425 is used by NetWare to advertise the services available on a network. Each server type has a unique type number. One of these services is of course the file server, but there are some other important services. Each server type is given a type number (see Table 12.2).

Table 12.2 can be very useful – keep it handy!

The SAP packets allow network servers to advertise their name and type to all others. They also allow users to search out servers of a particular type, such as a file server. The SAP packets can carry out the following operations:

- Get the name and address of the nearest server for a particular type.
- Get the name of all the servers of any type within the network.
- Get the name of all servers of a particular type.
- Respond to the `Get nearest server` command, as used by the NetWare shell NETX.EXE command.
- Respond to a general request.

See the section on network protocol packets in Chapter 7 for more details on the actual SAP packets in action.

As with the routers, each NetWare server keeps a SAP information table (see Table 12.3).

Table 12.3 shows, in a simplistic manner, the sort of information stored in a SAP table. For each entry there is: its type, how to get to it and its local bindery object identifier. This is useful for quick access.

Table 12.2 Some of the most important server types on NetWare.

NetWare server types	Advertising numbers
File servers	4h
Print servers	7h
Archive servers	9h
Remote router servers	24h
Router servers	26h
TCP/IP gateway	27h
Portable NetWare servers	9Eh
NNS domain servers	133h

Table 12.3 Example of a SAP information table.

Server name	Type	Internetwork address	Local bindery ID
s386	File server	00002:0C0123456789	F12345
DB	File server	00002:0C0654321545	F42423
R1	Router server	00002:0C0142324767	FA4132

These tables are updated in the same manner as the routing tables. Where routing tables use RIP packets, the SAP tables are updated using SAP packets. Every 60 seconds, SAP enquiry packets are sent out to find information regarding any changes in the network. This, on a large network with many different types of server, can produce a lot of unnecessary traffic.

Reduce SAP traffic by obtaining Novell's own special disk, called the *MultiProtocol router – basic support* disk, for NetWare 3.x servers, or use the standard SERVMAN.NLM program on NetWare 4.x servers.

NetWare 4.x SAP filtering

With NetWare 4.x, you get an excellent NLM program called SERVMAN.NLM. On top of its other facilities, such as providing menu-driven options to change the server's SET values, it provides a very convenient way of setting up SAP filtering.

From the IPX/SPX option of the SERVMAN menu you are presented with SAP filtering as a sub-option. When selected, as in Figure 12.6, the SERVMAN.NLM presents you with a list of known active networks so that you can start to filter out their SAP transmissions. You can now control either the transmission or the reception of SAPs, over that network, from the server. You can now create a list of server types that are either to be excluded or included in the SAP filter for the given network (see Figure 12.7).

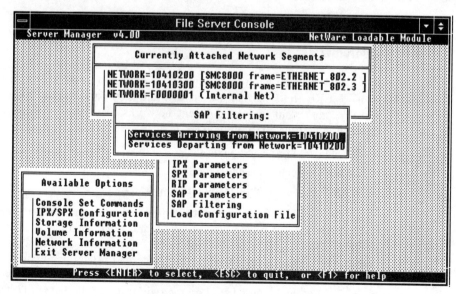

Figure 12.6 The SAP filtering option.

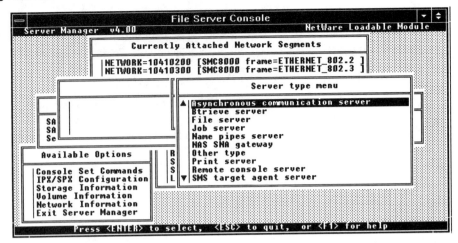

Figure 12.7 The Server type menu.

This is a very powerful and simple tool, which can increase your network security and reduce unnecessary SAP traffic.

Warning: If you are not sure what you are doing, do not set any SAP filters.

NetWare external router

Overview

The NetWare external router runs on a workstation as a DOS program called ROUTE.EXE. It is normally used to route IPX packets only between networks. Usually, this is up to four different networks. NetWare external routers can be configured in three different modes:

(1) Dedicated protected mode

(2) Non-dedicated protected mode

(3) Dedicated real mode (rarely used nowadays)

The NetWare routers can be either dedicated or non-dedicated; in a non-dedicated mode, the router can still be used as a workstation by running the NETX program. Nowadays, it is just not worth having non-dedicated routers. Stick to dedicated routers for improved performance and reliability. Figure 12.8 shows an example of an external router.

The last category is based on the old legacy of the IBM XT/PC, which could only address 640K of program memory. Novell can produce special routing software

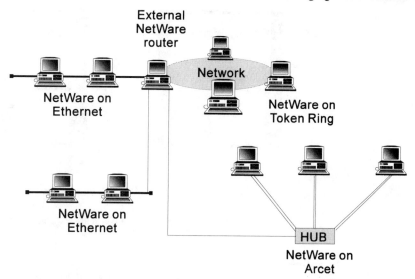

Figure 12.8 An example of an external router.

for these machines (if, that is, there are any left in use). Traditionally, under the protected mode option, the routing software (which has to run on a 286 CPU or above – not a problem nowadays) can address the first 12 Mbytes of memory. This is about to be extended, but 12 Mbytes is more than adequate for just routing packets in most cases.

See the section 'NetWare MultiProtocol Router Extension disk' in this chapter for further information.

If in doubt, always choose dedicated protected mode external routers.

I recommend that, for the average network, you use a standard 386 PC with at least 4 Mbytes of memory (8 Mbytes would be nice). Turn the PC into a dedicated router.

External router installation

The installation of a Novell external router is simplicity itself. It requires just one disk, the NetWare ROUTEGEN, and any appropriate network driver disks (see Figure 12.9).

Use the ROUTEGEN program to generate the router. This will create the ROUTE.EXE program, which can then be called automatically in the AUTOEXEC.BAT file of the dedicated workstation.

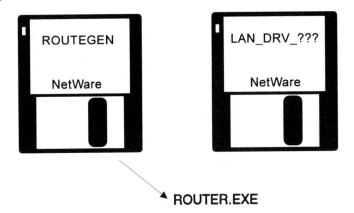

Figure 12.9 Generating a NetWare external router.

Operating mode
Dedicated protected mode routers are far more reliable, so if you want a good router select the dedicated protected mode option (see Figure 12.10). It does mean that you have to have a dedicated PC, with a 286 CPU or better, exclusively for routing.

Defining the number of communication buffers
If in doubt, choose as high values as possible. Each buffer takes up to 500 bytes of server memory. You can have a maximum of 1000 buffers, which is 500 Kbytes.

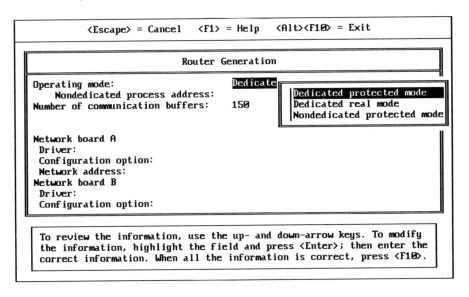

Figure 12.10 Selecting the operating mode.

Novell suggest the following formula:

- Start with 100 buffers.
- Add two buffers per workstation on the network.
- Add two buffers for each connected file server.

Nowadays, I just choose the maximum 1000 buffers. It will cost 500 Kbytes but, since the router is going to be dedicated, you might as well give it as many buffers as possible.

Define each network adaptor card

For each of the networks that the router is going to connect up, you must have a network card installed inside the machine. You must make sure the interface parameters of each NIC do not clash.

If you install different NICs with clashing parameters the software will warn you.

Warning: It is a bit difficult to ensure that the network card supports different frame types, other than the default. In the case of Ethernet, this is the IEEE 802.3 packet. If you wish to support different frame formats, it is easier to use the file server internal routing facility.

Running the external router

Boot up the device with DOS and run the generated ROUTER.EXE. The following console commands can be entered at the router console prompt line:

- CONFIG shows the current configuration of networks.
- DOWN downs the router and issues an RIP to inform all other routers that it is no longer available.
- RESET ROUTER automatically requests the latest routing tables from all other routers (good to do after any significant change on a network).
- MONITOR shows how the router is behaving (it is a good thing to have running all the time).

Management issues

Forget about using the non-dedicated mode routers: for the sake of reliability and performance, where possible go for the dedicated protected mode router.

The average machine that I recommend using is a 386 CPU with around 4 Mbytes of memory. This should give good performance for most networks. For a quick 'ready to go' router you cannot beat the ROUTE.EXE program. The good news is that it is free. The thing to bear in mind is that the ROUTE.EXE program is great if you have a simple NetWare (IPX)-only network using one common frame type such as IEEE 802.3 frames. However, if you want to support multiple frame types and multiple protocols such as IPX and TCP/IP then you have two options:

- Option 1: It will be very easy to route through the Novell file server. This does come at a price: it will place a greater burden on the file server, reducing its capacity to provide other services. However, depending on the network, this can be very insignificant.

- Option 2: Go for a third-party router. There are a number of manufacturers that will support multiple protocols, especially IPX. They tend to give excellent performance compared to the Novell equivalent, but at a price. Cisco should be on most people's short list of router manufacturers.

 See the section 'Cisco: the big name in routers', in Chapter 11 for further information.

NetWare MultiProtocol Router Extension disk

Overview

This is one of those things that should have been included free with the standard NetWare 386 system, but unfortunately you have to pay extra for it. It is important to be aware that such a product exists: most users do not know about it. The NetWare MultiProtocol Router – Basic disk is a software-only product that enables users to convert an Intel 80386- or 80486-based PC system into a multiprotocol router supporting IPX, IP and AppleTalk protocols.

There are two parts to this package: the runtime version of NetWare v3.11 which can turn a PC into a dedicated router, and a number of extra utilities to be used on any NetWare 386 file server. The package's main strength lies in the extra tools that can significantly improve the performance of your routers. These are enhanced NetWare Loadable Modules (NLMs) which have the following features:

- **Burst mode NLM support.** This is no great bargain, since you can already get it free. It improves NetWare workstation and server performance by transferring large amounts of data in response to a single request.

- **The large Internet packet exchange NLM.** This is great: it allows large packet size transmissions between servers and workstations through IPX routers.

- **The service advertising filter NLM.** This reduces SAP broadcasts over an IPX Internet. It can also be used to enhance network security.

Protocols supported

This product supports as standard the following protocols:

- IPX
- IPX RIP
- IP from TCP/IP
- IP RIP
- Novell NetBIOS
- AppleTalk
- AppleTalk RTMP

running over any of the following:

- Ethernet
- Token Ring
- LocalTalk
- ARCnet

The product is fully compatible with any Open Data Link Interface (ODI)-compatible card. This product can be used with the NetWare Link/64 or Link/T1 products to provide wide area IPX connectivity.

The required hardware

The product must run on a CPU 386 or above. Novell suggest 8 Mbytes of RAM, 20 Mbytes of hard disk space and one high-density diskette drive.

How it works

The NetWare MultiProtocol Router program is based on a runtime version of the NetWare v3.11 operating system (see Figure 12.11). It turns a PC into a dedicated NetWare v3.11 router, with the file server services stripped out. The PC should be formatted with MS-DOS or PC-DOS 3.1 or above.

Managing the SAP packets

One of the problems with SAP packets is that they can clog up a network with unnecessary packets flying all over the place. This is, in real terms, a bit of an exaggeration. In a small to medium network of 50 users, with a few servers, the SAP packet overhead is very small. However, as the network grows and the number of servers available to users increases, network performance can be affected by the SAP

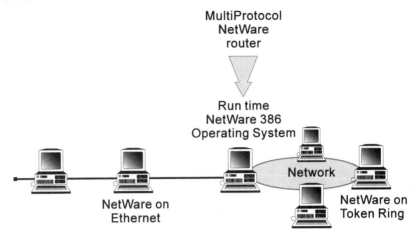

Figure 12.11 MultiProtocol NetWare Router.

packets. This is particularly of concern for networks using a relatively slow expensive medium such as asynchronous lines or X.25 connections.

Novell provide a special disk called the *MultiProtocol Router Basic Enhancement disk.* This contains some very useful programs that can be used to manage the SAP protocol flow (see Figure 12.12).

The special program SAFILTER.NLM can be used to control (in most cases this means reduce, but you could also increase) the SAP packet flow from a NetWare 386 server.

The filter might also be used as a special security measure. It can stop servers from advertising themselves to a particular section of a network. This can be very useful for defining certain sections of the network as low priority, which means they can only see a limited number of servers. On the other hand, other network segments can have high priority, with access to the full set of servers available.

The three programs are described below.

SAFILTER.NLM

This is the SAP filter administration program. It is menu-driven. The program requires you to load the SAFENG.NLM program first. The SAFILTER.NLM needs to be loaded up before binding any IPX onto the network card drivers using the BIND command. It allows you to:

- Create a SAP filter list for communicating to other servers
- Filter incoming SAPs
- Filter outgoing SAPs

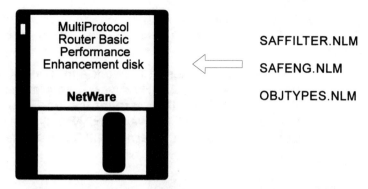

Figure 12.12 Disk containing the NetWare SAP filter program.

SAFENG.NLM
This is the SAP filter engine. It is controlled by running the SAFILTER.NLM program.

OBJTYPES.NLM
This is an object type administration program. It is an optional menu-driven program that can show the name and identifier of bindery objects on the file server or router. It basically relates the coded bindery identifier to a meaningful name.

Management issues

There are some very useful utilities on this package, on top of its routing software. If you are serious about using NetWare's own dedicated routers or using the internal facility of the NetWare 386 file server, it is well worth checking this product out. For the sake of few hundred dollars, you get a far more flexible and efficient system.

NetWare internal router

Overview

As part of the normal NetWare file server, you can normally internetwork up to four different network adaptor cards (if you are using EISA cards, this can be extended to six adaptor cards). You just define the card drive, the support frame packet types and the protocols that are to be bound onto each card: it is as simple is that. The two protocols supported as standard are Novell's own IPX and the IP part of TCP/IP from the UNIX world. This means that a NetWare file server can act as an IPX and an IP router at the same time. It is very powerful. However, it should be noted it can not translate between the two. Figure 12.13 shows an example of an internal NetWare router.

If you have an Ethernet network and use IPX, choose the default packet Ethernet 802.3. However, if you intend to use TCP/IP and IPX or just TCP/IP then standardize on Ethernet II packets. With the introduction of NetWare 4.x, Novell has changed its default Ethernet frame from Ethernet 802.3 to Ethernet 802.2.

NetWare routing terminology

Local router: Used within the cable length limitations for its LAN drivers. A remote router connects beyond its driver limitations or through a modem.

Dedicated: A computer that works only as a router. (This is the recommended mode.)

Non-dedicated: Normally an external router that works simultaneously as a router and a workstation.

Protected-mode router: Contains an 80286, 386 or 486 microprocessor. It can have up to 8 Mbytes of RAM (8 Mbytes is a NetWare router limitation).

Real mode: Contains an 8086 or 8088 microprocessor. It can access only 1 Mbyte of memory.

Routing table: Each file server and router on a NetWare network contains an internetwork router. Each router constantly broadcasts its own current status and updates other routers' distance and location in its routing tables.

Routing protocols on the file server

The following fundamental steps are required to route a protocol on the Novell file server:

(1) Define the network card by loading its driver.

(2) Select the appropriate frame packet supported by the card.

(3) Load the appropriate protocol (in the case of IPX, this is automatic).

(4) BIND the protocol to the appropriate frame on the network card (see Figure 12.14).

These commands can all be placed in the AUTOEXEC.NCF files.

Defining network cards

This is very simple if you have got the correct network card. You just load the

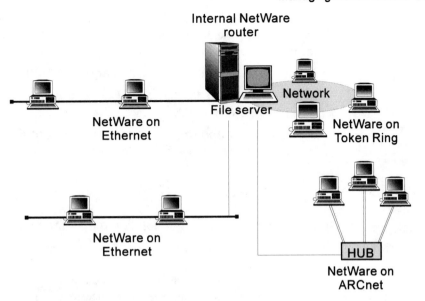

Figure 12.13 An example of a internal NetWare router.

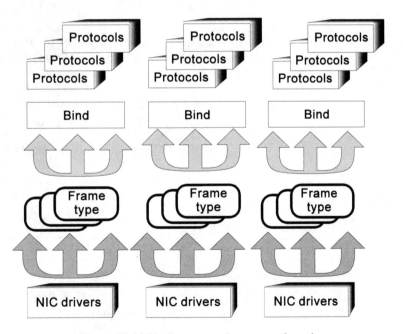

Figure 12.14 Binding protocols to network cards.

appropriate NLM. The important thing is to have the appropriate interface parameters following the driver name. This information will differ for each different type of network card and configuration. A typical command is:

```
load SMCPLUSSV port=280 frame=ETHERNET_802.3
```

This example loads the SMC Ethernet card driver on port 280, and will support frame type Ethernet 802.3

If you want to update to a new driver, do not destroy the old one. Place the new driver onto a floppy diskette and test it. For example:

```
LOAD A:SMCPLUSS port=280 frame=ETHERNET_802.3
```

If it works, you can then delete the existing drivers.

Something that I find very useful is to give the network card a name on loading up its driver. This can make life very simple, especially if you plan to install a number of different network cards in the same file server. Giving the network card your own easy-to-use name can make reference to a card very meaningful – it is much better than being forced to use the name of the LAN driver. Also, if you have several identical cards with identical drivers, naming them differently is the only way to identify which one you want to use, without having to state the port or interrupt numbers.

Give network cards a name made up of simple abbreviations of the NIC manufacturer, protocol supported and a sequential number working from 1, for example:

WD_IPX1   **The 1st Western Digital card using IPX**

SMC_IP2   **The 2nd SMC NIC using TCP/IP**

IBM_IP2   **The 2nd BM token card using TCP/IP**

> Warning: Be careful – assigning board names can get very confusing, because Novell allows for a different 'board name' for each frame format on a given network card.

Packet frame types

This is very important. The FRAME option is a parameter that is used to define the packet header format when using Ethernet or Token Ring cards, for instance:

```
LOAD SMCPLUSS port=280 NAME=SMC1 frame=ETHERNET_802.3
```

In this case, the frame ETHERNET_802.3 is now supported by the card SMC1.

Most NICs support a multitude of different frame types. Ethernet and Token Ring packets are listed in Tables 12.4 and 12.5 respectively.

When to use different packets

As a general guideline, you can use the following rules to decide which packet format you need to use:

- If you only use IPX across your Ethernet network, then use the standard ETHERNET_802.3 packets. It is far easier to configure at the workstation side and on the file server.
- If you intend to use TCP/IP and IPX across your Ethernet network, or just TCP/IP on its own, then use ETHERNET_II (default) or ETHERNET_SNAP.

The above advice is valid before Novell decided to change its default frame type to Ethernet_802.2.

See the section on different Ethernet frame formats in Chapter 3 for further information.

Supporting multiple frame packet size formats

It is very easy to allow for different frame formats on the same network card. On a NetWare 386 server, if you reload the network card driver, you will be allowed to assign a different fame format to the same card. For example:

```
:load wdplussv
Loading module WDPLUSSV.LAN
Western Digital Star/EtherCard PLUS Server Driver v2.05 (910424)
```

Table 12.4 Ethernet packets.

Ethernet packets	Description
ETHERNET_802.3	Novell standard default (pre-NetWare 4.0)
ETHERNET_II	Commonly used on TCP/IP networks
ETHERNET_802.2	Contains IEEE 802.2 (LLC) on top of IEEE 802.3 (the new NetWare default with the introduction of NetWare 4.0)
ETHERNET_SNAP	Uses the SNAP convention over Ethernet

Table 12.5 Token Ring packets.

Token Ring packets	Description
TOKEN_RING	Novell standard IEEE 802.5 packet
TOKEN_RING_SNAP	Uses the SNAP convention over Token Ring

```
Do you want to add another frame type for a previously loaded
board? y
Supported frame types for WDPLUS using I/O Port 280h to 29Fh,
Memory D0000h to D
3FFFh, Interrupt 3h are:
      1. ETHERNET_II
      2. ETHERNET_802.2
      3. ETHERNET_SNAP
Select new frame type: 1
  Previously loaded module was used re-entrantly
:
```

The above shows what happens if you reload the network driver WDPLUSSV a second time. The system automatically asks if another frame is to be supported on the same card. If you say 'yes', it shows all the other frames that can be supported. Note that it does not show ETHERNET_802.3, since it is already activated.

By typing CONFIG you get the following:

```
:config
File server name: NW386
IPX internal network number: 00001212

Western Digital Star/EtherCard PLUS Driver v2.05 (910424)
      Hardware setting: I/O Port 280h to 29Fh, Memory D0000h to
D3FFFh,                             Interrupt  3h
      Node address: 0000C0FCFB55
      Frame type: ETHERNET_802.3
      Board name: WD1
      LAN protocol: IPX network 00000019

Western Digital Star/EtherCard PLUS Driver v2.05 (910424)
      Hardware setting: I/O Port 280h to 29Fh, Memory D0000h to
D3FFFh,                             Interrupt 3h
      Node address: 0000C0FCFB55
      Frame type: ETHERNET_II
      No board name defined
      No LAN protocols are bound to this LAN board
:
```

Binding protocols

This is one of the most powerful commands within the NetWare file server. It allows protocols to be bound to networks. The BIND command in fact binds a given protocol such as IPX or TCP/IP to a given frame type, which in turn is bound to a network adaptor card. This open environment allows for tremendous flexibility. Any given protocol can be added to active network cards. Some protocols need special frame types to be declared on a card before they can be used. For example, whereas IPX is quite happy to use ETHERNET_II or ETHERNET_802.3, TCP/IP normally insists that the ETHERNET_II option is activated as opposed to the ETHERNET_802.3 frame format.

To bind a protocol to a card with an already-defined frame format, use the BIND command. For example, to bind IPX to the card, type:

```
BIND ipx TO wdplussv net=1234
```

An interesting observation is that almost all protocols that are bound to a network card must be accompanied by a network address. For example, in the case of IPX, this is a unique number whereas, in TCP/IP, this is the IP address number.

 See the section 'Managing NetWare IPX network numbers' in Chapter 11.

It is very simple to unload a protocol at any time. You just type:

```
UNBIND ipx FROM wdplussv
```

At any time, more protocols can be added to a network card, as long as the appropriate protocol support module has been loaded. In the case of IPX, this is not necessary since it is intrinsically always loaded.

The following example shows what to do if you want another protocol to be supported by the same card. The existing card has IPX bound to it on the ETHERNET_802.3 frame, but it has also been activated to support other frame formats such as ETHERNET_II and ETHERNET_SNAP. Then the TCP/IP protocol module is loaded. It is now ready to be bound to an existing network card.

```
:load tcpip
Loading module TCPIP.NLM
  TCP/IP  v1.00 (910219)
  Auto-loading module SNMP.NLM
  SNMP Agent  v1.00 (910208)
:bind ip to wdplussv
Several boards are using the WDPLUSSV LAN driver
     1. Western Digital Star/EtherCard PLUS Driver v2.05
(910424) using I/O Port 280h to 29Fh, Memory D0000h to D3FFFh,
Interrupt 3h Frame type: ETHERNET_802.3
     2. Western Digital Star/EtherCard PLUS Driver v2.05
(910424) using I/O Port 280h to 29Fh, Memory D0000h to D3FFFh,
Interrupt 3h Frame type: ETHERNET_II
     3. Western Digital Star/EtherCard PLUS Driver v2.05
(910424) using I/O Port  280h to 29Fh, Memory D0000h to D3FFFh,
Interrupt 3h Frame type: ETHERNET_SNAP
Select board to bind: 2
IP address: 147.80.20.12
```

```
IP: Bound to board 2.  IP address 147.80.20.12, net mask
FF.FF.0.0
IP LAN protocol bound to Western Digital Star/EtherCard PLUS
Driver v2.05
:
```

Seeing what is going on

At any given time, you can find out which protocols are activated on the system using the PROTOCOL command:

```
:protocol
The following protocols are registered:
   Protocol: IPX  Frame type: VIRTUAL_LAN  Protocol ID: 0
   Protocol: IPX  Frame type: ETHERNET_802.3  Protocol ID: 0
   Protocol: ARP  Frame type: ETHERNET_II  Protocol ID: 806
   Protocol: IP  Frame type: ETHERNET_II  Protocol ID: 800
   Protocol: IPX  Frame type: ETHERNET_II  Protocol ID: 8137
```

This command goes hand in hand with the CONFIG command which will show you which protocol is supported on which network card; it will also show you the network numbers associated with each network. This is a very useful command when you are troubleshooting.

```
:config
File server name: NW386
IPX internal network number: 00001212

Western Digital Star/EtherCard PLUS Driver v2.05 (910424)
     Hardware setting: I/O Port 280h to 29Fh, Memory D0000h to
D3FFFh, Interrupt
 3h
   Node address: 0000C0FCFB55
   Frame type: ETHERNET_802.3
   Board name: WD1
   LAN protocol: IPX network 00000019

Western Digital Star/EtherCard PLUS Driver v2.05 (910424)
     Hardware setting: I/O Port 280h to 29Fh, Memory D0000h to
D3FFFh, Interrupt
 3h
   Node address: 0000C0FCFB55
   Frame type: ETHERNET_II
   Board name: WDIP1
```

```
        LAN protocol: ARP
        LAN protocol: IP  address: 149.190.20.9  net mask: FF.FF.0.0
     :
```

All the network driver, frame type and protocol binding declarations are normally placed in the AUTOEXEC.NCF file.

Tracking RIP packets

Overview

NetWare automatically provides a neat utility that can be used from the file server console to monitor the Novell RIP and SAP packets as they flow in and out of your server. This is the TRACK ON/TRACK OFF function. I have found that many professional NetWare managers forget about using this tool, although it could save them a lot of time in troubleshooting. This lack of use is probably due to the unfriendly screen the utility presents: most people forget what it means and therefore don't bother using it.

To use it you just type TRACK ON from the file server or router console.

What the TRACK display shows

A TRACK screen can be rather confusing. It is important to bear in mind you are looking at two different types of information at any given time: the SAP and the RIP packets. They are displayed intermixed with each other, so it is very important to be able to tell the two apart. The formats of the two are slightly different. The main difference is that SAP record shows the name of the server, whereas the RIP record just tends to be a line of numbers. Figure 12.15 shows a typical TRACK screen.

The **hops** show the number of routers the packet has to go through. The higher this value, the slower the performance. The maximum value is 15.

If you see a hops count greater than 5, then the performance between the two devices is becoming very poor.

The **ticks** represent the time it will take to travel to the destination. This is used by the NetWare routing algorithm to work out the best path. Remember some paths might require a very small number of hops but be very slow. This is particularly true for such things as asynchronous networks. Each tick represents roughly 1/18 of a second.

If you see a number above 200, then it is most likely that the network is a WAN, such as an asynchronous line.

RIP records

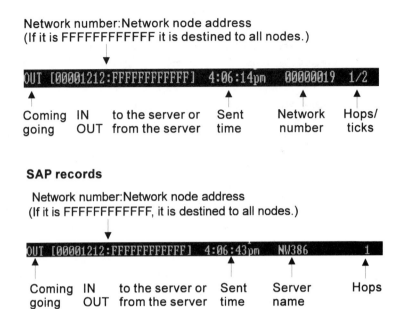

Network number:Network node address
(If it is FFFFFFFFFFFF it is destined to all nodes.)

OUT [00001212:FFFFFFFFFFFF] 4:06:14pm   00000019 1/2

| Coming going | IN OUT | to the server or from the server | Sent time | Network number | Hops/ ticks |

SAP records

Network number:Network node address
(If it is FFFFFFFFFFFF, it is destined to all nodes.)

OUT [00001212:FFFFFFFFFFFF] 4:06:43pm   NW386   1

| Coming going | IN OUT | to the server or from the server | Sent time | Server name | Hops |

Figure 12.15 The TRACK screen explained.

Quick external router installation guide

Installation assumptions

The following instructions assume that you are producing a dedicated router on a stand-alone workstation running in protected mode.

Router installation

(1) Set up the LAN driver board in the router.
(2) Check the LAN card configurations will not conflict with each other (use programs such as CHECKIT Pro from TouchStone).
(3) Boot DOS on the workstation that you will use as the router.
(4) Put the ROUTEGEN diskette into drive A: and, from drive A:, type ROUTEGEN <Enter>.
(5) Select the dedicated operating system mode.

(6) Type the number of communication buffers (select at least 300).

(7) Select a network card driver.

(8) Select the router configuration option (most boards are factory-set to Option 0).

(9) Repeat for each network board in your router: when finished, press <F10> to generate the router software. A copy of ROUTER.EXE is now on the ROUTGEN diskette.

NetWare gateways

The subject of gateways interconnection is a vast field, deserving a book to itself. It is covered briefly in this section, for the sake of completeness. Normally, when people talk about NetWare gateways, they are referring to connecting a mainframe or mini to a Novell network. This is done by having a special gateway server on the network with connection facilities onto the mainframe and then running an emulation package on each workstation which needs to connect to the mainframe. This will enable the networked workstation to be seen by the mainframe as a dumb terminal. A typical NetWare gateway is shown in Figure 12.16.

There is a very wide variety of products available, each with its own special features. To discuss each option would make this book enormous and very boring. I will just cover the most popular use of NetWare gateways.

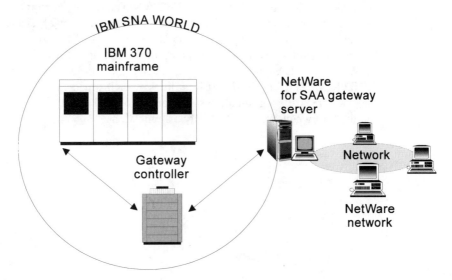

Figure 12.16 A typical NetWare gateway.

Be very careful if you are purchasing terminal software: make sure the TSR portion of the code can be loaded up outside the DOS 640K memory. This type of software is notorious at taking up a lot of conventional memory when activated.

The most popular reason for using a gateway is to connect to IBM mainframe equipment. Novell has a number of ready-made products to meet user demands.

NetWare LAN-to-IBM host and AS/400 connectivity

Novell produce a package called NetWare for SAA. It is a software-only product that provides NetWare workstations on a LAN with access to IBM mainframe and AS/400 host connectivity, while integrating with NetWare 386 file server features. It is implemented as a NetWare Loadable Module (NLM) that runs on a NetWare 386 file server. It can be run on a dedicated workstation, via a special version that uses the NetWare 386 runtime code. This is an excellent solution for a network with a heavy demand on the IBM SNA world. The runtime version is part of the SAA package.

NetWare 3270 LAN Workstation emulation package

This is an emulation package for connection to IBM mainframes. The NetWare 3270 LAN Workstation emulation package emulates an IBM terminal and printer, on a DOS, Macintosh, UNIX or OS/2 workstation. It supports up to five host sessions per workstation, which can be any combination of display, printer and Advanced Program-to-Program Communications (APPC) sessions, a DOS session, file transfer and a keyboard re-mapping utility. Designed to run on NetWare SPX, NetWare 3270 LAN allows users to transfer files to and from the host using the SEND/RECEIVE or TRANSFER utilities, which are included with the software. The TRANSFER program allows the transfer of RFT and FFT data between the PC and the host when running SAA office applications.

13

Asynchronous NetWare communication

Overview

Novell provides some very popular products to allow users to connect Novell networks using asynchronous devices such as modems. Since the price of modems is plummeting, this is going to become even more popular. The good news is that, as part of the standard NetWare package, there are already a number of free products that will allow users to use modems to extend Novell networks across telephone lines. There are a number of products that Novell provides for asynchronous communication. They all sound very similar, so it is very easy to get them mixed up. They are:

- NetWare Asynchronous Remote Router (NARR) (free). This enables two NetWare networks to connect through a WAN using a standard telephone line. They could be anywhere in the world. It supports standard Hayes-compatible modems. It comes as part of the NetWare 386 and NetWare 286 operating system.

- Stand-alone asynchronous remote IPX device driver (free). This product enables a portable workstation anywhere in the world to connect to a Novell network. It has to be equipped with a modem. It can, through an asynchronous remote router, connect to the services provided on the NetWare LAN.

- NetWare Asynchronous Communication Server (NACS) (costs extra). This product enables the sharing of a modem across the network as if it were any other resource available for sharing between authorized users. It also provides some remote management monitoring software.

- NetWare Access Server (NAS) (costs extra). This is the product to use if you wish your network to support multiple dial-in users.

NetWare Asynchronous Remote Router (external)

Overview

It is very easy to turn a dedicated workstation into an asynchronous router.

The Router provides the means by which your NetWare network can connect up to another network. It can be defined in two ways:

(1) Leased line (it connects to the host on a permanent basis).
(2) Dial-up. Using the LCONSOLE program, users can dynamically dial out to any other networks. This is the most commonly used option.

The code for the asynchronous router is produced in the same way as defining a router which is connecting two LANs, the main difference being that an asynchronous router connects up a real LAN-based network to a WAN via an asynchronous device. At the other end is another asynchronous router which will route the packets down to its local LAN. In the example in Figure 13.1, we have two LAN-based networks (numbers 1 and 3) and one WAN-based network (number 2). Sometimes, this type of router is called a 'half router', for obvious reasons. The standard software that comes with the NetWare operating system has a special diskette called the 'Asynchronous Device driver' disk. The disk is normally also labelled 'LAN_DRV_190'. On this disk are special drivers to turn a dedicated router into a remote router which uses a modem for communications.

The two basic products supported are standard Hayes-type modems and WNIM+ boards. Most people just buy cheap, off-the-shelf, Hayes fast modems. This section concentrates on the standard modem drivers, but the WNIM+ hardware adaptor, which has to be purchased separately, will provide four asynchronous ports on each card.

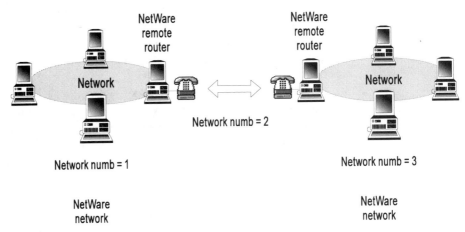

Figure 13.1 An example of a NetWare asynchronous router.

If you are installing a modem, choose one with a minimum speed of V32bis, with V42bis or MNP 5,10 error correction. Do not get a slower type. Prices are falling and soon this will be the world's standard modem configuration.

Installing the NARR

To install the NARR, you will need to:

(1) Use the ROUTEGEN program.

(2) Define two network drivers, one to connect up to your LAN and the other to drive the installed asynchronous device.

(3) Use the ACONFIG program on the ROUTE.EXE to define the asynchronous driver parameters.

(4) Run the router on the proposed workstation.

Generating the router code

To generate the code for the dedicated remote router, just follow the instructions for generating an external router. The main difference is that one of the LAN drivers will be the asynchronous device driver. If you intend to use standard Hayes-type modems or the WNIM+ device, you will need the Novell Asynchronous Device Driver disk (normally labelled LAN_DRV_190). Then run the ROUTEGEN program as normal.

See the section on NetWare external router in Chapter 12.

Make sure you are using the latest version: it should be at least Version 1.2. The old version had a lot problems. Do make sure that both sides of the communication line use the latest drivers.

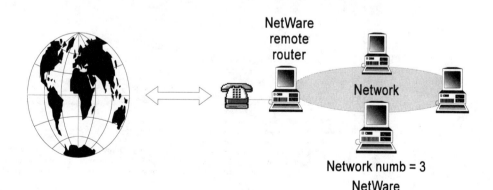

Figure 13.2 A remote asynchronous router.

Figure 13.3 shows a typical screen after the LAN_DRV_190 disk has been read. Notice that the two asynchronous drivers (asynchronous COM1/COM2 and the WNIM) have been recognized.

Once the LAN drivers have been specified, you see the screen in Figure 13.4. This screen shows a remote router being produced with the characteristics shown in Figure 13.5.

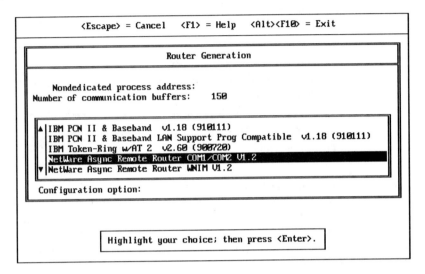

Figure 13.3 A typical screen after the LAN_DRV_190 disk has been read.

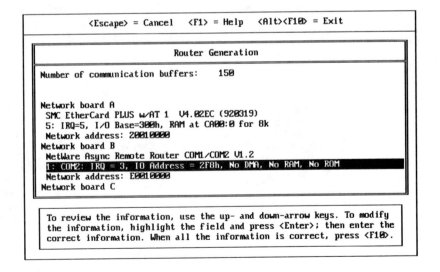

Figure 13.4 Producing a remote router.

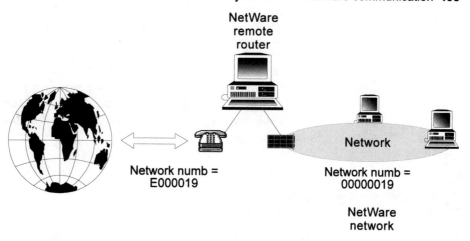

Figure 13.5 An example of a remote router.

> Warnings: Version 1.2c drivers may not work with previous versions of the NetWare asynchronous router.
>
> You must make sure that any network number that you are assigning will be unique.

See the section 'Managing NetWare IPX network numbers' in Chapter 11, for information on how this could be done.

Once all the fields have been completed, you are ready to generate the ROUTE.EXE; this is done by pressing the <F10> key. On completion you will see a screen something like this:

```
ROUTEGEN is complete.

You have created a Dedicated real mode router.

Copy ROUTER.EXE from the ROUTEGEN diskette
(or from the ROUTEGEN directory on the network)
to a DOS bootable disk.

Using the DOS bootable disk, reboot the machine
that will serve as your router then type:

     ROUTER <Enter>.

A:\>
```

However, the router is not actually ready to be used yet: you must run the ACONFIG program on it first, as described below.

> Warning: Some versions of NetWare did not have a copy of the asynchronous router. If it is not with your system disk, ask your dealer for a free update.

Using ACONFIG to set up the asynchronous router parameters

Run ACONFIG.EXE and specify the ROUTE.EXE program to be processed. You will see the screen shown in Figure 13.6. You can configure each router device and each asynchronous line.

The modem options you can choose from are:

- None
- Special configuration
- Hayes-compatible

Most modems are now Hayes-compatible, so if you are in any doubt as to the type of modem select the Hayes option (Figure 13.7). The special configuration will send an initialization string to the modem, that you can define. This is useful in cases of modems which require a special initialisation string.

One of the problems with the asynchronous driver is that, traditionally, it has been limited to 2400 bps. To improve upon that speed you need to use the WMIN+ driver, which can go up to 19.2 Kbps. I think this limit of 2400 bps on the standard COM1/COM2 drivers is there for political reasons and not for technical ones: it forces users to purchase the higher performance products.

In the Edit Router box (see Figure 13.8), set up the ID string for security reasons. It must be *exactly* the same at the other side in order for the two sites to connect up. Note that the ID string is case-sensitive.

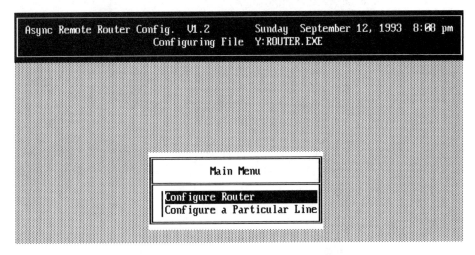

Figure 13.6 You can configure each router device and each asynchronous line.

```
┌─────────────────────────────────────────────────────────────┐
│                         Edit Line                           │
│                                                             │
│  Line Number ......................... 1                   │
│  Line Enabled ........................ No                  │
│  Flow Control Ena┌─────────────────────┐                  │
│  Data Rate ......│   Modem Type ?      │0                   │
│  Modem Type .....│                     │es Compatible       │
│    Phone Type ..│ Special Configuration│ch Tone             │
│    Modem Initial│ Hayes Compatible     │0S0=1X1             │
│    Dial String P└─────────────────────┘0DT                 │
│    Phone Number .....................                       │
│    Auto Connect .................... No                    │
│                                                             │
└─────────────────────────────────────────────────────────────┘
```

Figure 13.7 Selecting modem type for the asynchronous router.

```
┌─────────────────────────────────────────────────────────────┐
│ Async Remote Router Config.  V1.2    Sunday  September 12, 1993  8:10 pm │
│                 Configuring File  Y:ROUTER.EXE              │
├─────────────────────────────────────────────────────────────┤
│                                                             │
│          ┌─────────────────────────────────────┐           │
│          │             Edit Router             │           │
│          │                                     │           │
│          │  Number of lines ........... 1      │           │
│          │  LAN Driver ................ LAN A  │           │
│          │  Name of Router Server ..... HQ_USA │           │
│          │  ID String ................. Pass123│           │
│          │  Router Password ...........        │           │
│          └─────────────────────────────────────┘           │
│                                                             │
└─────────────────────────────────────────────────────────────┘
```

Figure 13.8 Adding the ID string: note that the ID string is case-sensitive.

The COMM1/COMM2 driver for the remote workstation shell will now support 19.2 Kbps. This enables a stand-alone workstation to connect with a router that is configured for a WNIM+ at 19.2 Kbps.

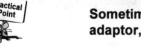

Sometimes, if the asynchronous driver is not the last LAN adaptor, all sorts of problems seem to occur.

Run the ROUTER.EXE

This program is run on the PC which is going to be the stand-alone remote router. It has to be equipped with the appropriate modem. At any given time, the following commands can be entered:

- CONFIG shows the current configuration of networks.
- DOWN downs the router and issues an RIP to inform all other routers that it is no longer available.
- RESET ROUTER automatically requests the latest routing tables from all other routers. It is a good command to use after any significant change on a network, for example, lines going down abnormally. It is like downing the server and bringing it up again.

If communications go down abnormally, instead of downing the server, you can just type RESET ROUTERS.

The occurrence of LAN F:DIED is nothing to be worried about. It just means that the connection that was established has now been terminated. As users come in and out of your router, you will see a number of LAN F: DIED messages displayed on your console screen.

Dial-up using LCONSOLE

Once the asynchronous router has been set up, it is possible to dial up other networks at will using the LCONSOLE.EXE program which is found on the LAN_DRV_190 disk.

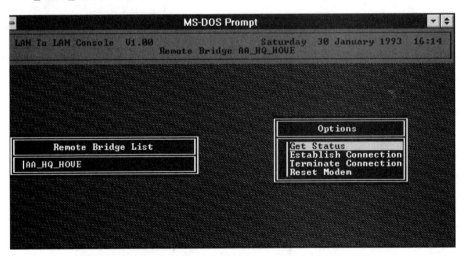

Figure 13.9 LCONSOLE locates a list of available asynchronous remote routers.

> Warning: This program calls NetWare asynchronous routers 'remote bridges', which is technically incorrect.

When started, the program makes a SAP call requesting the names of all active asynchronous routers. From there, the user can select the appropriate router and dial up at will to a number of defined telephones. These can be defined by the user. The program is very basic but it does the job. Figure 13.10 shows a typical telephone list.

Asynchronous remote workstations

Overview

It has always been very easy to set up a special version of IPX which, instead of using a network adaptor card, uses a modem to dial out to a predefined telephone number, which happens to have an asynchronous router waiting to answer the call. Once that was done, we could run our favourite version of NETX and login to any servers that might be available remotely. This is lovely clean approach, with one big drawback: slowness. In theory, anything you can do on the workstation on a LAN can be done on the remote workstation using the asynchronous driver. The difference is that all IPX packets have to flow across a slow asynchronous line, instead of a fast LAN. This means that any user from anywhere in the world can connect up a Notebook via a modem and dial into the office Novell network(s) (see Figure 13.11). This could be from a hotel bedroom in PNG (Papua New Guinea) or a public telephone in London. The problem is always the speed. It will not be fast.

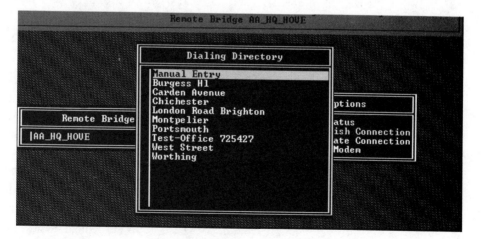

Figure 13.10 A typical telephone list.

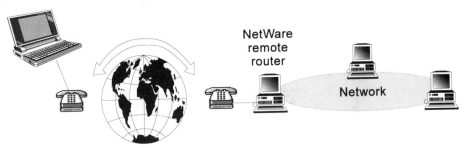

Figure 13.11 An asynchronous remote workstation.

See the section 'Asynchronous management issues' later in this chapter for a discussion of the pros and cons.

Using IPX for asynchronous modems

This can be used on a stand-alone basis on any workstation equipped with a modem wishing to connect to a remote network equipped with an asynchronous router.

There are two methods of using the IPX driver: the old method of using the IPX dedicated approach and the new ODI approach. I will concentrate on the ODI approach.

The old approach used to rely on using the WSGEN program to link a dedicated version of IPX.COM, using the asynchronous driver found on the LAN_DRV_190 disk. It then was configured with the ACONFIG program to install the telephone number. This used to be tedious and is nowadays outdated. It relied on the dedicated IPX.COM technology which Novell says is now becoming outdated. The new, open, future is the ODI method, which I strongly recommend users should move to as soon as possible.

See the section ODI drivers in Chapter 7.

ODI driver on an asynchronous router remote workstation

To produce an asynchronous driver for a remote workstation is so much easier under ODI than it used to be using the old IPX.COM approach. You no longer need to bother about the ACONFIG program. Any changes to the modem specification can be done within the NET.CFG file.

The drivers required are found on the LAN_DRV_190 disk (Asynchronous Driver disk). Look out for it – you might need to replace your old ones.

To get your workstation connected up to the remote network, you will need the special MLID driver called NARS.COM.

```
c\:> NARS
Novell Asynchronous Remote Driver v1.00 (911206)
(C) Copyright 1991 Novell, Inc.  All Rights Reserved.

c\:>
```

NARS.COM is the key file: the rest are the standard ODI files LSL, IPXODI and BNETX. The following files are needed:

- LSL.COM: the standard LSL program
- NARS.COM: the MLID asynchronous driver
- IPXODI.COM: the IPX ODI protocol driver
- BNETX.COM or NETX.COM or VLMs (from NetWare 4.x redirector)
- NET.CFG: the configuration text file

BNETX is the burst mode version of NETX. BNETX is not necessary but it is recommended, as it will improve performance. It used to be available from Novell as a extra piece of code (it should be free from bulletin boards).

ODI NET.CFG configuration for asynchronous drivers

The NET.CFG must have at least the following section headings with the following subsections:

```
1.  Link Support
        Buffers
        MemPool
2.  Link Driver NARD
        Frame Ethernet_802.3
        Protocol IPX 0 Ethernet_802.3
        int #1 [interupt level]
        port #1 [port address]
        other router id [astring]
        My Workstation Name [aname]
        baud rate [comm port speed in bits per second]
        modem type [a number from the table below]
        modem initialization string
        hardware flow control [0 or 1, see below]
        dial prefix [string to start dialing]
        dial number [the number to be dialed]
```

Most of the above parameters are obvious, but there are a number that might make you think twice.

The reason why it says `Ethernet_802.3` and `Protocol IPX 0 Ethernet_802.3` is that, at present, IPX Ethernet 802.3 is the only protocol that should be used across the asynchronous router line. This actually makes no difference to you. It just means that, as the IPX is transmitted over the asynchronous line, it is given the IEEE 802.3 frame format. A more efficient frame format will probably be available from Novell very soon but, for the time being, just use IEEE 802.3. It is important that the other router side should also support the appropriate format on its asynchronous driver, even though it might be connected to a physical Token Ring or ARCnet.

The `other router id` string is where you have to define the ID of the router on the other side of the line. Note that it is case-sensitive.

If you get this wrong you will see the message `Invalid ID String`. Delete the field and retype the correct ID.

The `baud rate` parameter is very important: it must be at least 1200 and not more than 19200. Table 13.1 shows the modems that are supported, although the most commonly used one is the Hayes-compatible, which is type 1.

As time goes on, this list will become even more comprehensive. The `modem initialization string` allows you to customize your own initialization code. The maximum length of the string is 46 characters. The classic modem initialization string for the Hayes-compatible modem is:

```
ATVOEOSO=1X1
```

Figure 13.12 shows an example of a typical NET.CFG.

To activate the connection

Activating the connection is simplicity itself. The difficult part is configuring the NET.CFG file. Once that has been done, the rest is just like loading up any normal ODI driver for a LAN.

The files are loaded in the following order:

(1) LSL

(2) NARS (the MLID driver for asynchronous communication)

Table 13.1 ODI NET.CFG configuration: modems supported.

Modem description	Type number
None (direct connect)	0
Hayes and compatibles	1
Telebit Ven\Tel PEP	2
Special configuration	3
US Robotics Courier V32	4
US Robotics Courier 24PS	5
Multimodem V32	6

```
┌─────────────────────────────────────────────────────┐
│ ─        Notepad - NET.CFG            ▼ ▲│
│ File   Edit   Search   Help                          │
│ Link Support                                       ▲│
│     Buffers 8 1586                                   │
│     MemPool 4096                                     │
│                                                      │
│ Link Driver NARD                                     │
│     Frame Ethernet_802.3                             │
│     Protocol IPX 0 Ethernet_802.3                    │
│     my workstation name FarshadsHOME                 │
│     other router id MSC                              │
│     int  #1 4                                        │
│     port #1 3f8                                      │
│     baud rate in bps 2400                            │
│     modem type 1                                     │
│     modem initialization string atv0s0=1x1           │
│     hardware flow control 1                          │
│     dial prefix atdt                                 │
│     dial number 776493                             ▼│
│ ◄                                                  ►│
└─────────────────────────────────────────────────────┘
```

Figure 13.12 A typical NET.CFG.

(3) IPXODI

(4) BNETX (or NETX)

When the NARS is run, it will try to initialize the modem and dial up into the remote Novell network.

If, after running NARS for about 10 seconds, your machine hangs on you, an error has probably occurred or your modem is not connected up properly. Check your modem and your NET.CFG setting, reset the PC and modem and start again.

Asynchronous management issues

The biggest problem with this approach is that the asynchronous router is simply a very *slow* IPX packet router that happens to operate across public telephone lines. The important thing to bear in mind is that you do not want to use this connection to run too many large programs over. It is ideally suited to the transfer of data, such as e-mail or stock updating data files. You should not run Windows applications remotely across this line (unless you can wait a very long time). The maximum realistic speed you can get out of the line is probably 19.2 Kbps, although most people only use it at 2400 bps. If you are serious about supporting remote users, you might want to consider:

- Purchasing the WMIN+ adaptor card to be placed in the router
- Using an X.25 public switching system
- Purchasing the NetWare Access Server to support several users simultaneously

The faster the performance you require, the more you need to spend. If you can keep your data flow down so that 2400 bps is sufficient, you will not have to pay for anything extra: all the required software is already bundled with the NetWare 386 3.11 and 4.x systems. Whatever you intend to do, the following ideas should be considered when setting up a system.

Minimize loading programs across the line

If you intend to connect a remote workstation to your network through an asynchronous modem link, you would be wise to load as much of the program software onto the workstation as possible and only use the link for data file transfer. So, for example, if you wish to run a Windows-based application remotely, place the Windows programs on the Notebook and establish the communication link only when you wish to exchange data files between the workstation and the remote server.

The trick is to have as much of the program to be run on the remote workstation already stored locally (see Figure 13.13). This means that even the Novell public utilities such as LOGIN.EXE should be stored on the workstation. This could save a lot of time; otherwise, you could find you are wasting a lot of time loading standard tools across your line which you could be using to transfer your real data.

Setting up special remote users and groups

I have found it very useful to set up special users exclusively for people who are going to login via a remote workstation. I have devised a convention of calling them as follows. Remote users are given the following name:

```
REM_<INITIALS>
```
I also create a special group called:
```
RemoteUsers
```

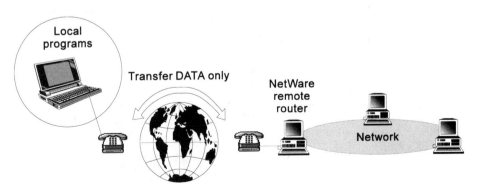

Figure 13.13 Managment considerations when using remote workstations.

For example, REM_FN is Farshad Nowshadi, member of the RemoteUsers group.

Managing remote users

The procedure for setting up remote users outlined above means that you can manage them far more effectively. For example, by typing USERLIST, you can tell which users are local and which are remote. The special RemoteUsers group can be used to adjust the execution of the system script file for any of the following reasons:

- You probably do not want the standard mapping assignments setup for the remote user.
- You probably do not want the standard CAPTURE assignment setup.
- You might want to set up new search mapping path assignments which will refer to local directories, so that the loading of standard programs across the communication can be minimized.

Modifying system script file

Most of the commands within the normal execution of the system script file will probably not be very relevant to the remote users. I suggest you identify the key elements that are common to both users and omit the rest using the IF member of the RemoteUsers group condition as your control (see Figure 13.14, for example).

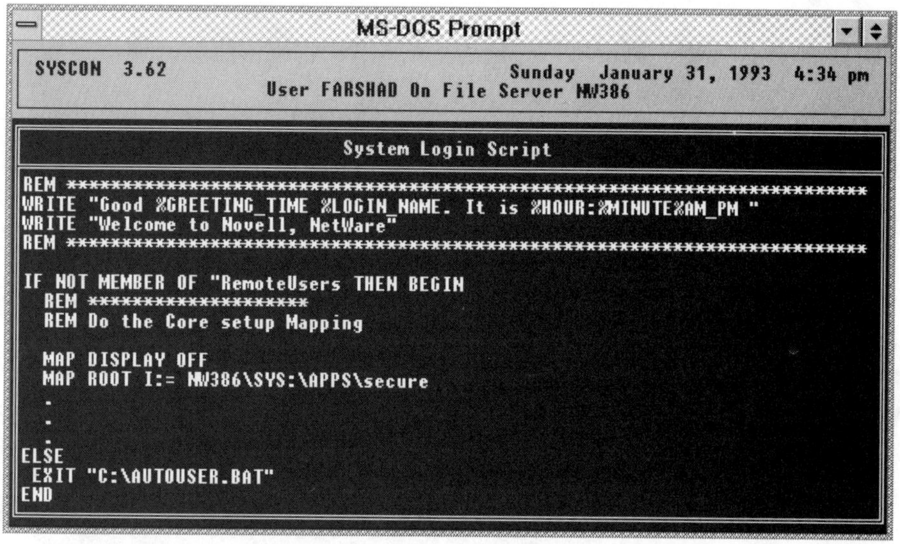

```
SYSCON 3.62                          Sunday  January 31, 1993  4:34 pm
                      User FARSHAD On File Server NW386

                            System Login Script

REM ******************************************************************
WRITE "Good %GREETING_TIME %LOGIN_NAME. It is %HOUR:%MINUTE%AM_PM "
WRITE "Welcome to Novell, NetWare"
REM ******************************************************************

IF NOT MEMBER OF "RemoteUsers THEN BEGIN
   REM *********************
   REM Do the Core setup Mapping

   MAP DISPLAY OFF
   MAP ROOT I:= NW386\SYS:\APPS\secure
   .
   .
   .
ELSE
   EXIT "C:\AUTOUSER.BAT"
END
```

Figure 13.14 Amending the system login script.

In the example in Figure 13.14, I just check to see if the user is a member of the RemoteUsers group: if so, the rest of the script is omitted and control is passed to the remote user's own C: drive, where I have a set up a batch file called the AUTOUSER.BAT.

Specification of an asynchronous external router

You do not need a very powerful PC for a remote router; a slow 386 PC with about 4 Mbytes of RAM will do just fine in most cases.

Security implications

Always remember that the remote router is open to the outside world – always set up the password option on the router. You do not want *just anybody* connecting to your system.

NetWare Access Server (NAS)

This is Novell's solution for users who wish to support multiple remote users simultaneously and efficiently. It could involve up to 16 users on any given Access Server. Figure 13.15 shows an example.

The connections do not have to be on an asynchronous line; it could be over the X.25 packet-switching system. The NAS enables DOS, Macintosh and ASCII

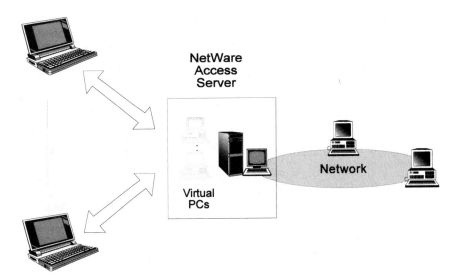

Figure 13.15 NetWare Access Server.

workstations to dial in and access all the resources available on a NetWare LAN. It has a very good dial-back facility for security. The NetWare Access Server runs programs within itself. It turns a 386 PC or higher into several virtual PCs. When the user dial ins, he or she is allocated a virtual PC machine for running DOS applications and accessing the resources of a NetWare LAN. The great thing about this approach is that programs are not loaded up across the link; they are run on the NAS, and only the screen updates and keystrokes travel over the communication line. This provides a excellent platform for accessing the LAN applications. This is the main difference between the NAS and the standard remote asynchronous link, which executes the program at the workstation site.

The NAS also allows the transfer of files from one site to another.

As well as providing a service to remote dial-in users, the NAS can also provide resources for the local LAN users. Local users can request a virtual DOS machine to run programs over. This can very useful in situations such as:

- If you want to run a process-hungry program on a 286 PC, you can use one of the 386 virtual PCs.

- When you are using an Apple Macintosh, you can run DOS applications on the virtual PCs.

- If you want to run several programs at the same time, you can use a number of virtual PCs.

Management issues

The NetWare Access Server is not just an excellent idea for remote users – it can also enhance the processing power available to your local users. It makes a virtual 386 PC DOS machine available to DOS, Macintosh or OS/2 users on demand. It has good audit trails tracking, which can significantly help in managing the system (very useful for identifying unauthorized entry, and for application and hardware troubleshooting).

I recommend, however, that you keep a sense of proportion and try not to have more than four virtual PCs running at any given time. I have found that when you go above this figure the NetWare Access Server really slows down badly.

The NetWare Asynchronous Communication Server (NACS)

This is Novell's answer to all those who keep asking why we cannot share a modem across the network. This product will do just that. It enables the sharing of a modem across the network as if it were any other available resource (see Figure 13.16). The supervisor will allow a common modem on the NACS to be used by any authorized user on any workstation. This means that your organization can invest in purchasing a few extremely powerful modems which can be used by all your network users. It also provides some remote management monitoring software.

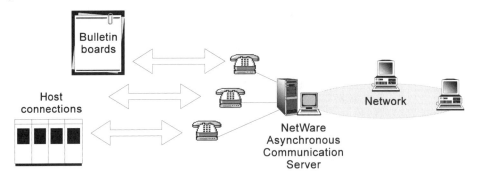

Figure 13.16 NetWare Asynchronous Communication Server (NACS).

Make sure you are using Version 3.x or above: the previous version had some problems.

The NACS can allow user NLMs to enable up to 32 users to access and share modem pools, minicomputer ports and X.25 services from anywhere on a network. Using the NACS package, a user on a workstation without a modem can use the shared modem and, using standard third-party products, connect up to bulletin boards such as CompuServe and BIX. Standard terminal emulation packages can also be run to allow users to dial out of the LAN and interconnect to host machines such as IBM mainframes. The system can also access resources on another LAN using a NetWare Access Server.

The NACS can be either run on the standard NetWare 3.x or 4.x file server as an NLM or, even more interestingly, it could be configured to run as a dedicated communication server on a 386 PC or above. This uses the runtime version of the NetWare operating system which comes with the package as standard. It can support lines up to 115.2 Kbit/s per port. Each network can support multiple NACS.

The management of the system is easy, since it is all controlled by the supervisor (in a similar way to printers). The supervisor decides which users are allowed to use the modem.

The supervisor can use the RCONSOLE program to display the communication server console.

The package makes troubleshooting easy, since it includes a diagnostic utility which allows the testing of the NACS and the modems under its control. You no longer need to go to the PC where the modem is to find out why it is not working: it can all be done remotely.

Asynchronous hardware

There are a number of manufacturers that produce special modems exclusively for use within the NACS. You can also use most of the Hayes-compatible modems.

However, the following specialized hardware has been designed and tested to be fully compatible with the NACS:

- WNIM+ (Novell)
- Hayes ESP
- Newport Systems Solutions' ACI or XCI (X.25)
- Digiboard's DigiCHANNEL PC/8e or DigiCHANNEL MC/8i

The NetWare Asynchronous Services Interface (NASI)

This is the NetWare equivalent of the Hayes modem command instruction set. It is fast becoming the industry standard when it comes to sharing modems across networks. It is now being supported by a number of major communication software packages such as ASCOM/IV, BLAST, Crosstalk for Mark 4, OnLAN/PC (Novell), Smartcom Exec (Hayes), SmartTerm 340 (Persoft) and many more.

Also, the following packages allow remote PC users who need to dial in to the LAN to use the NACS: Citrix MULTIUSER (Citrix), Co/Session (Triton Tech), pcANYWHERE IV/LAN (Symantec); there are many more.

Management issues

This is yet another great product from Novell, as long as you have the appropriate NASI-compatible software for your users to use. Remember, a potential user cannot just configure the communication software to use the Hayes-compatible command set. The software must be told to use the NASI interface. So this means you must do some research before rushing out and buying a NetWare communication server NACS, to make sure your communications are going to work!

Do not put the modem in your file server: make use of the runtime version of the NetWare operating system that comes with the package. Turn a workstation into a dedicated communication server by running the appropriate NLMs on it. This will improve the performance of your file server, and improve the overall fault tolerance of your system, since the tasks of serving communication and file services have been split up.

Before buying communication software to be run on the workstations, ask if it is going to be compatible with the NASI standard.

14

TCP/IP and NetWare

TCP/IP overview

TCP/IP is one of the world's most popular protocols, developed initially for the US Department of Defense. They had multitudes of networks worldwide and required a universal protocol to bring them together.

TCP/IP comprises a series of interrelated protocols, for example, standard applications to find out who is logged in, to send messages and transfer files across networks. The suite takes its name from two of its most commonly used components: TCP (Transmission Control Protocol) and IP (Internet Protocol). The two protocols TCP and IP are responsible for the transportation of data between nodes of networks. They are analogous to NetWare SPX and IPX respectively.

Novell has recognized the importance of TCP/IP. It is supported by Novell as its second most important protocol stack, after its own default SPX/IPX stacks. If a user wishes to use TCP/IP, they can do so by using a number of add-on programs.

It is possible to turn a NetWare 3.11 or 4.x server into a TCP/IP router. Novell also provides the LAN workplace packages. These allow Novell workstations to connect to UNIX hosts as well as Novell servers. This is done by getting the workstation to support the TCP/IP and SPX/IPX protocol stacks simultaneously, using the ODI standard. They can be bound to the same network adaptor. The number of different ways you can use TCP/IP over a NetWare network is unlimited. The question is not 'what can you do with TCP/IP?', but 'what do you really need?'

IP addressing

TCP/IP uses the underlying addressing system as defined by the IP addressing scheme. This is a 4-byte (32-bit) number which uniquely identifies a node on any network. It has certain similarities to the IPX addressing structure, in the sense they both have a network and a host number.

See the section on NetWare addressing systems in Chapter 11.

The IP address consists of two parts: the network address and the host address. The IP address is divided into three basic classes, based on the most significant bits of the first byte, as shown in Table 14.1.

The first byte of the IP address falls in the ranges shown in Table 14.2, which defines which class the IP address belongs to.

> Warning: Be aware that there are also classes D and E. Class D has a first byte of 224 and is used for multicast transmissions and class E has a first byte of 225 and is left for future use.

It important to remember that each connected IP network must be given a unique IP network address. This means that a Novell server that connects to a number of different networks must have a different IP network address associated with each LAN card.

Table 14.1 Three basic classes of IP address.

	TCP/IP class type			
	Byte 1	Byte 2	Byte 3	Byte 4
Class A	0nnn nnnn	hhhhhhhh	hhhhhhhh	hhhhhhhh
Class B	10nn nnnn	nnnnnnnn	hhhhhhhh	hhhhhhhh
Class C	110n nnnn	nnnnnnnn	nnnnnnnn	hhhhhhhh

Key:
n: the network address
h: the host address

Table 14.2 IP address ranges.

Class type	**First byte range**	**IP number range**
Class A	1 to 127	1.h.h.h up to 127.h.h.h
Class B	128 to 191	128.n.h.h up to 191.n.h.h
Class C	192 to 223	192.n.n.h up to 223.n.n.h

Subnet masking

Using subnetting, it is possible to break up a given IP network address into a series of subnets. Subnetting works by subdividing the node address into subnetworks. It is useful to consider using subnetting if your organization has been allocated a single IP network address and you wish to break up your organization into a series of subnetworks. The 4-byte IP address is then broken up as follows:

<Network address><Subnet><Host>

The network address is defined by the IP network address, while the subnet and host addresses are defined by the subnet mask. This mask can be configured by the user. The mask is a 32-bit number, just like the IP address. The mask value has all 1s (ones) for the IP network address and the subnetwork portion of the complete IP address. It then contains all 0s (zeros) for the host portion. By ANDing the IP address together with the subnet mask, the effective address is derived, in terms of the network, subnetwork and the host address:

IP address	Network address	Host address
Subnet mask	Network mask (all 1s)	Subnet mask (all 1s) : Host mask (all 0s)
Effective address	Network address	Subnet address : Host address

To make your life simple, if you decide to use subnet masking, mask off entire bytes where possible (although you can mask of individual bits).

If subnets mask are not specified, they default to the values shown in Table 14.3.

Table 14.3 Default subnet masks.

Class type	First byte range	Default subnet mask
Class A	1 to 127	255.0.0.0
Class B	128 to 191	255.255.0.0
Class C	192 to 223	255.255.255.0

TCP/IP NetWare applications

Novell provides a host of applications that can run on the server using TCP/IP (see Figure 14.1, for example). These applications are run as NLMs. They can enhance the service provided by the NetWare server. Do bear in mind that these services are in addition to the normal NetWare file server functions provided simultaneously to network users. Everything has a price: in this case, it is the expense of slowing down the performance of the Novell file server.

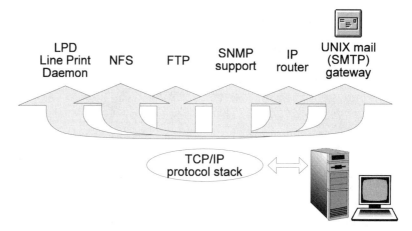

Figure 14.1 Some TCP/IP applications on a NetWare server.

Some of the most important facilities are described below:

- **NFS (Network File System)**. This Novell product allows the NetWare file server to function as a distributed file system, as originally defined by Sun Microsystems. It is normally used from UNIX workstations. A UNIX user on the network can access the NetWare filing structure as if it were a UNIX server running NFS. Since the product ultimately uses NetWare filing, it is aware of the security restrictions imposed by the supervisor. The NFS must be given the appropriate access rights before the filing system can be used.

- **LPD (Line Printer Daemon)**. This product is normally used with the NFS package. It provides TCP/IP and hence also UNIX clients with access to the NetWare printers which are serviced by the server. This integrates NetWare print servers into the UNIX print servers' environment. Since this product ultimately uses the NetWare print servers, it is aware of the security restrictions imposed by the print server supervisor. The LPD system users must be given the appropriate access rights before they can use the printers.

- **UNIX mail (SMTP)**. This is commonly known as the SMTP (Simple Mail Transfer Protocol). This standard was defined as part of the TCP/IP protocol suite. The NetWare package allows for the integration of SMTP and Novell's own MHS (Message Handling Services). It provides a gateway between the two systems, as shown in Figure 14.2. UNIX users will see the server as an SMTP.

- **FTP (File Transfer Protocol)**. This is the full implementation of FTP, as defined by the DARPA Internet protocol suite. It provides the ability to transfer files between any two nodes on the TCP/IP network. It has a set of commands for performing common directory and file operations, such as listing and file scanning a directory. It is a simple standard, mostly used to download

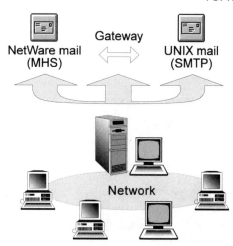

Figure 14.2 NetWare MHS and SMTP.

or upload files. The Novell implementation turns the Novell file server into an FTP server. It uses the NetWare file system. The user must, however, enter the appropriate NetWare-defined passwords before access is given.

- **IP router**. The NetWare server can be an IP router at the same time as acting as an IPX router. The two functions can operate simultaneously, without any interference from each other. This does means that, as yet, with NetWare servers you cannot get an IPX-to-IP translator or vice versa. However, there is a third-party product called Novix, from Firefox, which is an IPX-to-TCP/IP gateway.

- **SNMP support**. Novell allows SNMP agents and their associated management information database to be set up and activated on a NetWare server. This means that a rich store of management information can be requested from the NetWare server through standard SNMP calls. The functions of SNMP are normally associated with the TCP/IP protocol stack. With NetWare 4.x, however, you no longer need to run TCP/IP to use the functions of SNMP agents. You can run them over the native SPX/IPX protocols.
  See the section SNMP and NetWare in Chapter 17.

TCP/IP on NetWare servers

Both NetWare 3.x and NetWare 4.x file servers can be configured to support TCP/IP. This allows the file server to run TCP/IP applications. NetWare dedicated routers can also be configured to support TCP/IP protocols if the Novell Multi-Protocol Router package is used. The steps required to configure a dedicated router to use TCP/IP are almost identical to those required to configure the file server. This is because the code is common to both packages. Once you can configure a NetWare file server to use TCP/IP, configuring a NetWare router is a relatively simple operation.

For detailed information on TCP/IP, the following Novell manuals provide an excellent source of reference:

- *NetWare v3.11 System Administration*
- *NetWare v3.11 TCP/IP Transport Supervisor Guide*

NetWare TCP/IP files and directories

When TCP/IP is installed on a NetWare file server, the file and tree directory structure shown in Figure 14.3 is created.

The main basic file used to install TCP/IP on NetWare servers is the TCPIP.NLM. It will provide the full TCP/IP services which can be bound onto network cards installed in the server. The TCPCON.NLM provides a limited TCP/IP console menu-driven interface. The IPCONFIG.NLM program provides statistics about the performance of the TCP/IP protocol stack.

Novell provides a special file which allows for the tunnelling of IPX packets over TCP/IP packets. This is called the IPTUNNEL.LAN. Note that this is a special type of NLM: it is a LAN driver. However, as far as the user is concerned, it can be seen as yet another NLM program.

There are a number of directories created to support the TCP/IP links. These are shown in Table 14.4.

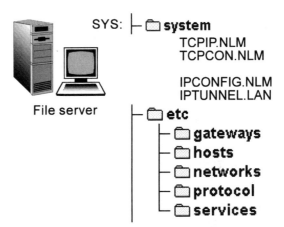

Figure 14.3 TCP/IP NetWare file structure.

Table 14.4 Directories created to support TCP/IP links.

Directory name	Contains information on
SERVICES	Services available to the IP Internet users
PROTOCOL	DARPA protocols available on system
HOSTS	Mapping host and alias names to IP addresses
NETWORKS	Known Internet networks
GATEWAY	Routing tables as entered by the IPCONFIG.NLM

Configuring TCP/IP on a NetWare server

Basic outline

Before activating the TCP/IP protocol on the NetWare file server you:

(1) Load the TCPIP.NLM program.
(2) Bind it to a network adaptor card. This is normally a card which supports the Ethernet_II packet frame format.
(3) Enter the IP address.

Once this is done, the TCP/IP protocol is activated; it is as simple as that.
We will now examine the process in greater detail.

Prerequisites for running NetWare TCP/IP

You need to have the following specification on the file server:
- Computer: 80386/80486 or P5
- RAM: at least 4 Mbytes for NetWare 3.x, 8 Mbytes for NetWare 4.x
- LAN adaptor types: Ethernet, Token Ring, ARCnet or FDDI
- LAN drivers: must be certified by Novell

Loading TCPIP.NLM

Before loading the TCPIP.NLM, you might need to need to change a few of the server SET variable parameters.

Make sure you have the following command in your STARTUP.NCF:

SET MAXIMUM PHYSICAL RECEIVE PACKET SIZE = n

where n is 1518 for Ethernet and ARCnet networks, and 4202 for Token Ring networks. This will ensure the receive packet size is large enough for IPX and TCP/IP packet sizes. The default IP route packet size is 576 bytes.

To check that your maximum physical receive buffers are sufficient for IPX and TCP/IP support, monitor the packet receive buffers as shown by the MONITOR.NLM program.

Depending on the TCP/IP application, it might be wise to increase the server's maximum packet receive buffer parameter. The default is 100 but it might be better to increase it to 200:

```
SET MAXIMUM PHYSICAL RECEIVE BUFFERS = 200
```

The TCPIP.NLM is in the SYS:SYSTEM directory. It can be loaded from the server console using the normal LOAD command:

```
:load tcpip
Loading module TCPIP.NLM
  TCP/IP for NetWare
  Version 2.02    August 7, 1992
  Copyright 1992, Novell, Inc.  All rights reserved.
  Auto-loading module SNMP.NLM
  SNMP Agent
  Version 2.01    July 24, 1992
  Copyright 1992 Novell, Inc.  All rights reserved.
  Auto-loading module AFTER311.NLM
  NetWare 3.11 Forward Compatibility Support v1.02.4
  Version 1.02d    August 31, 1992
  Copyright 1992 Novell, Inc.  All rights reserved.
  Auto-loading module TLI.NLM
  NetWare Transport Level Interface (TLI) Library
  Version 3.11d    August 24, 1992
  (C) Copyright 1989-1992 Mentat, Inc.
  Portions (C) Copyright 1989-1992 Novell, Inc.
  All Rights Reserved.
  Auto-loading module IPXS.NLM
  NetWare IPX STREAMS Driver
  Version 2.01    August 24, 1992
  (C) Copyright 1989-1992 Novell, Inc.
  All Rights Reserved.
:
```

You will notice that the module automatically loads up a number of other modules. The SNMP agent support is loaded up automatically. Table 14.5 lists a number of optional parameters that can be entered after the LOAD TCPIP command.

Table 14.5 Optional parameters that can be loaded after the LOAD TCPIP command.

Parameters	Values	Default	Explanation
FORWORD	Yes/no	No	Allows IP packets to be forwarded
RIP	Yes/no	Yes	Allows RIP (Routing Information Protocol) to be supported
TRAP	IP add	127.0.0.1	Specify the SNMP trap address

For example :

```
:load tcpip FORWARD=NO  TRAP=147.90.90.2
```

will disable the forwarding of IP packets and set the SNMP trap address to 147.90.90.2.

Loading NetWare LAN drivers with Ethernet_II packets

Before the TCPIP module can be bound to a network adaptor card, you must ensure that the card will support the Ethernet_II packet format. This is the default format that the TCPIP module requires. There is a slight problem here: Novell's own default frame format is Ethernet_802.3, whereas TCP/IP needs Ethernet_II. If you are installing the driver for the first time and do not need to support the Ethernet_802.3, you can simply do the following:

```
load WDPLUSSV port=280 name=TCPIP_WD frame=ETHERNET_II
bind IP to TCPIP_WD Addr=147.90.90.1
```

Let's assume, however, that the network driver is already loaded, with support for Ethernet_802.3, and you want to add support for Ethernet_II on the same card. In this case, you just load the network driver twice.

Loading the network driver twice

This is done by reloading the network driver. It is advisable to give it a different name on reloading it. This helps to identify it from other configurations. This will produce the following dialogue:

```
:load wdplussv name=tcpip_wd
Loading module WDPLUSSV.LAN
Western Digital Star/EtherCard PLUS Server Driver
v2.05 (910424)
Do you want to add another frame type for a previously
loaded board? y
Supported frame types for WDPLUS using I/O Port 280h to 29Fh,
Memory D0000h to D
```

```
3FFFh, Interrupt 3h are:
    1. ETHERNET_II
    2. ETHERNET_802.2
    3. ETHERNET_SNAPSelect new frame type: 1
  Previously loaded module was used re-entrantly
:
```

This allows a different frame to be simultaneously supported by the network card. You are now ready to bind the TCP/IP protocol to the network card. The above dialogue is not necessary every time: it can be entered in one go at the command line using parameters.

For an explanation of different frame types see the section on Ethernet II and IEEE 802.3 frames in Chapter 3.

Binding the TCPIP module to a network card

The BIND command will now bind the TCPIP module to the network card. It has the following basic format:

```
BIND IP TO <network Card> ADDR=<IP address>
```

A typical example is:

```
:bind ip to tcpip_wd
IP address: 147.90.90.1
IP: Bound to board 2.  IP address 147.90.90.1, net mask
FF.FF.0.0
IP LAN protocol bound to Western Digital Star/EtherCard PLUS
Driver v2.05 (91042
4)
:
```

In the above example, the adaptor card is given the name TCPIP_WD, to which the IP protocol is bound, and given the IP address 147.90.90.1.

There are a number of parameters that can be entered after the BIND command. They are listed in Table 14.6.

TCP/IP NetWare router

To set up an IP router within the NetWare file server, you simply bind the IP to each network card. The process of binding IP to a network card was outlined in the previous section. As you bind each IP to each network adaptor (assuming you have given them consistent IP addresses), they will automatically become routed to each other.

 See the section on internal routers in Chapter 12.

Table 14.6 Parameters that can be entered after the BIND command.

Parameters	Values	Default	Explanation
MASK	Net mask		Used for subnetting
BCAST	IP add	FF.FF.FF.FF	Defines the old 4.2 BSD standard (not used very much nowadays)
ARP	Yes/no	Yes	Enables ARP protocol
DEFROUTE	Yes/no	No	Used if being advertised as the default IP router
GATE	IP add	None	Used server is the default IP router
COST	Integer	1	The metric value used by RIP
POISON	Yes/no	No	Enables the RIP poison reverse function

Once you have set up a Novell router, you can check it is working correctly by using the TCP/IP *PING* program. This program is in the public domain and is available in a form that runs under DOS. Novell issue it as part of the LAN workplace series and UnixWare package. Try 'PINGing' both sides of the router to see if the packets are getting through.

TCP/IP over IPX using the Novix product

As workstations attach to NetWare LANs and wish to use TCP/IP applications, such as FTP or Telnet, twin protocol stacks will be needed: IPX and TCP/IP. The problem is that multiprotocol stacks consume valuable PC memory and they make the ODI configuration complicated. There is now a very interesting product from Firefox communication, called Novix. It takes TCP/IP host access a stage beyond Novell's own solution. NetWare users can now access UNIX-, DEC- or TCP/IP-type applications from their PCs, through the Novix NetWare file server. The wonderful aspect of this product is that the PC only needs to support the IPX NETX protocol stack. Using the Firefox product, NetWare users can now run such applications as FTP or Telnet using the standard NetWare protocol stack. On the file server, you run the Novix NLM program, which translates the IPX data into the equivalent TCP/IP packets. Once a standard TCP/IP packet has been derived it can, if necessary, be forwarded to the destination host as if it came from a normal TCP/IP user. The company providing this elegant solution, Firefox communication, signed an exclusive OEM agreement with Novell in February 1993 to supply the Novix TCP/IP package with Novell's own LAN Workplace for DOS (see Figure 14.4).

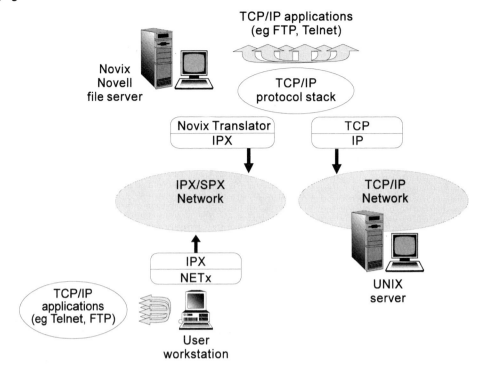

Figure 14.4 LAN Workplace for Novix.

IP tunnelling

Novell allows you to tunnel IPX packets over TCP/IP networks (see Figure 14.5). This can be very useful, especially if you want to connect two IPX networks together over a WAN. The IPTUNNEL.LAN driver allows for the encapsulation of IPX packets in the data part of the IP packets. The packet is then delivered to the other side of the tunnel as if it were a normal TCP/IP packet. When it emerges on the other side, the TCP/IP packet is then stripped away, leaving the IPX packet to carry on its journey.

Both devices at the end of the IP tunnel must support the encapsulation and decapsulation of IPX packets. The devices could be:

- NetWare 386 3.x or NetWare 4.x servers
- NetWare workstations supporting the IPTUNNEL ODI drivers
- Schneider & Koch's SK-IPX/IP Gateway/Client
- Some other third-party devices

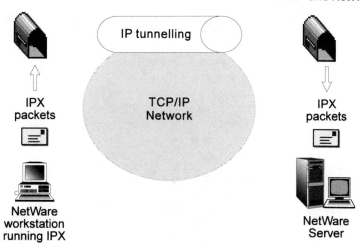

Figure 14.5 NetWare IP tunnelling.

Implementing IPTUNNEL on a NetWare server

To set up an IP tunnel on a NetWare server, you just load up the IPTUNNEL as a LAN driver. This must be done after you have set up the TCP/IP protocol on the file server.

The best way to look at implementing IPTUNNEL is through an example. Let's assume we want to connect server TOM to server ANNA. We want the IPX packets to be tunnelled across a TCP/IP network. Once the tunnel is established, the two servers will be able to receive and transmit IPX packets between themselves.

The outline of the configuration is shown in Figure 14.6.

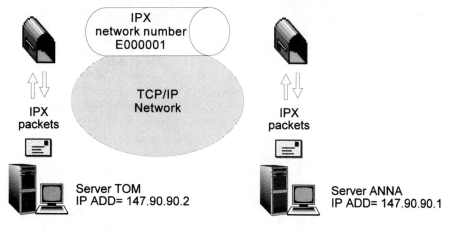

Figure 14.6 An example of a typical IP tunnelling configuration.

On server ANNA, we would issue the following command from the console:

```
:load iptunnel peer=147.90.90.2
Loading module IPTUNNEL.LAN
  IP Tunnel for IPX  v1.00 (910208)
  Version 1.00    February 8, 1991
IPTunnel: Using 147.90.90.1 as the local IP address for
tunnelling.
IPTunnel: Added 147.90.90.2 to the list of peers.
:BIND IPX to IPTUNNEL net=E000001
```

On server TOM, we would enter the following commands:

```
:load iptunnel peer=147.90.90.1
Loading module IPTUNNEL.LAN
  IP Tunnel for IPX  v1.00 (910208)
  Version 1.00    February 8, 1991
IPTunnel: Using 147.90.90.2 as the local IP address for
tunnelling.
IPTunnel: Added 147.90.90.1 to the list of peers.
:BIND IPX to IPTUNNEL net=E000001
```

This will now establish a connection between the two IPX networks. It is important to note that the IP network numbers on each side of the tunnel must be different, as must the pseudo-connecting IPX network number which in this case is E000001.

 See the section on 'Managing NetWare IPX network numbers' in Chapter 11.

Loading TCP/IP and IPX simultaneously on workstations

You can load up the Novell standard protocol SP/IPX and the TCP/IP stack simultaneously on a workstation, as long as you have the appropriate Novell ODI drivers (see Figure 14.7).

See the section on ODI drivers in Chapter 7.

The process is relatively simple. The file NET.CFG has to be modified to include information about the TCP/IP protocol. The special TCP/IP ODI driver must then be loaded onto the normal IPXODI program. Then the NETX (NetWare shell) or the new VLMs (Virtual Loadable Modules) from NetWare 4.x are loaded up as normal.

A typical NET.CFG file that can support IPX and TCP simultaneously is shown in Figure 14.8. TCP/IP must be bound to the network card adaptor driver. In this case, it is the SMCPLUS. Notice that the network card has been instructed to support the Ethernet_II and Ethernet_802.3 frame types from the NET.CFG. The Ethernet_802.3 will normally be used by the SPX/IPX protocol stack, whereas the Ethernet_II is used by the TCP/IP protocol.

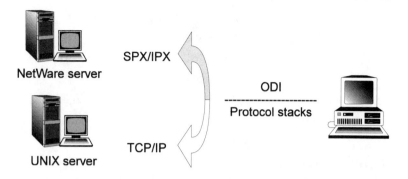

Figure 14.7 Supporting TCP/IP from a NetWare workstation.

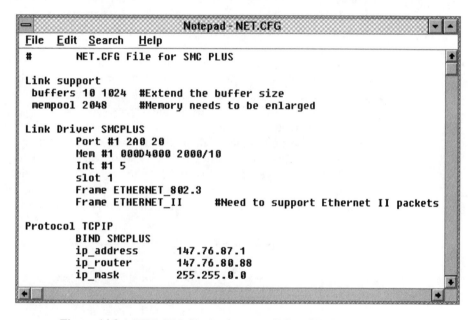

Figure 14.8 A NET.CFG file that supports IPX and TCP simultaneously.

If you want to dispense with Ethernet_802.3 completely and just use Ethernet_II frames for IPX and TCP/IP, you might need to use the Novell ECONFIG program. It is worth finding out.

To activate the protocols, you must load up a number of drivers:

(1) Load the LSL driver.

(2) Load the MLID network card driver.

(3) Load IPXODI.

(4) Load the TCPIP ODI version (new).

(5) Load up the NetWare shell or redirector. Load:

- The required VLMs, or
- BNETX (NetWare Burst Mode shell version), or
- NETX (NetWare shell).

A typical batch file to load up the drivers could look like the example shown in Figure 14.9.

Management issues

One of the major problems with Novell's TCP/IP implementation is that, to date, it is not possible to get rid of SPX/IPX completely and replace it with the TCP/IP protocol. This is a problem with the Novell NCP; although it is supposed to be an open platform, it is intrinsically linked to the SPX/IPX protocols. Future products may cure this problem.

See the next section, 'Novell announces NCP to support IP as well as IPX'.

With the development of the UnixWare product, we are beginning to see Novell move away from its insistence on SPX/IPX and towards the approach of supporting TCP/IP and SPX/IPX on an equal basis.

If you intend to use IPX and TCP/IP over your Novell networks, be very careful. Do take your time to think through the design. Where possible, try to standardize your frame type. It might be very worthwhile to run everything over the Ethernet_II frame type and to forget about Ethernet_802.3. This does mean a little more work on the workstation side. However, in the long term, you will benefit from running a standard frame type. The final choice between frame types will depend

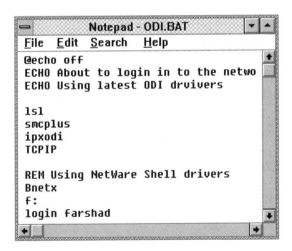

Figure 14.9 A batch file to load up the drivers.

largely on whether your organization is moving towards OSI or the more popular TCP/IP protocol suites. The IEEE 802.3 is an OSI standard, whereas Ethernet_II is a TCP/IP standard. A new alternative would be to standardize on the new Novell default frame format of IEEE 802.2 which was introduced with NetWare 4.0. It can support IPX and TCP/IP. Try not to mix the frame types together. If things start to go wrong, the less variety you have running around the network, the easier it will be to troubleshoot!

Novell announces NCP to support IP as well as IPX

In July 1993, Novell issued a press release regarding IP support over NetWare. They promised a special version of NetWare, later in 1993, that can use IP as its default Transport layer protocol rather then IPX. This is a major statement from Novell, and should bring NetWare into closer integration with UNIX, which supports IP as its standard Transport layer protocol.

15

Managing users and groups

This chapter does *not* explain how to set up a user or a group account using the SYSCON program (or NETADMIN and NWADMIN equivalents from NetWare 4.x): the Novell manuals are more than adequate in explaining this. I am assuming that the reader of this book is familiar with that type of operation, and is looking for some higher management guidelines. I wish to go beyond the Novell manuals and books by exploring strategy. Most of these publications tell you what you *can* do, but not what you *should* do. I will concentrate on strategies to use when you wish to define users or groups and allocate network resources to them.

Basic overview

SYSCON: the key to NetWare 2.x and 3.1 server administration

The SYSCON is an easy-to-use menu-driven program (see Figure 15.1). It is one of the most frequently used programs. It is ideal for creating, editing and deleting users on an *ad hoc* basis.

One of the key tools in managing networks, SYSCON can be used to:

- Manage groups and user definitions
- Create/edit user accounts one at a time
- Define users' account restrictions
- Set up the system script file
- Define groups and managers
- Set up server accounting

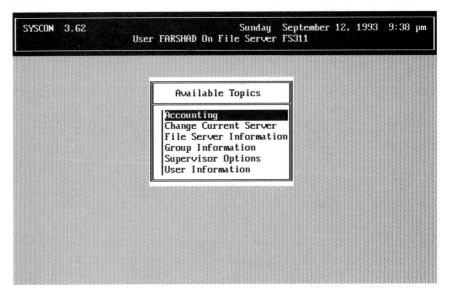

Figure 15.1 The SYSCON program.

To create multiple user accounts quickly, use the utilities MAKEUSER and USERDEF.

NWADMIN: the key to NetWare 4.0 administration

The equivalent program to SYSCON within NetWare 4.0 is the Windows-based program NWADMIN (see Figure 15.2). As well as having most of the SYSCON functions, it works within the NDS (NetWare Directory Services). There is also a DOS text version called NETADMIN, but it is not used very often.

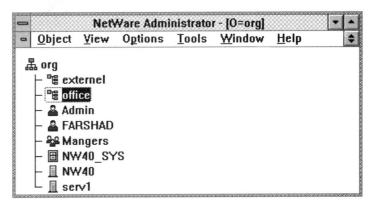

Figure 15.2 The NetWare Administrator program.

Hierarchy of NetWare users

NetWare defines a number of types of user, each with a different privilege level (see Figure 15.3). At the highest level is the *supervisor*. In other words, when the supervisor talks, all other users sit up and listen! There are five basic levels of user on the network:

- **Regular users** are only allowed to use applications according to previous authorization by a supervisor.
- **Workgroup managers** are assistant network supervisors with rights to create and delete bindery objects (such as users, groups) and to manage user accounts. These are super-users who have been given responsibility over a group of other users.
- **Account managers** are similar to workgroup managers, but cannot create users or groups.
- **Supervisors** have total control over the network and decide who are users, operators and managers.
- **Operators** are users with special rights to access and control network resources, for example, printer operators or file console operators.

At any given time, a real user might be given a number of different privileges. For example, a user can be a workgroup manager and a file server console operator.

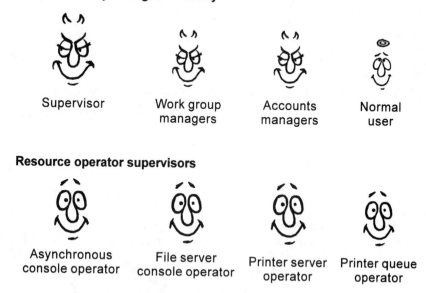

Figure 15.3 NetWare user types.

The two users automatically created by NetWare 3.11 are GUEST and SUPERVISOR. Most 'hackers' try to break into a system by using the normally unprotected GUEST user ID to identify the name of the user on the system. You should be aware of this and password protect the GUEST as well as the normal SUPERVISOR account.

Workgroup manager

Workgroup managers *can*:

- Create users and manage their accounts
- Delete users they have created
- Create groups and add users they manage

Workgroup managers *cannot*:

- Make users security-equivalent to a supervisor
- Create another workgroup manager
- Manage users or groups they have not created, unless they are designated as the user account manager
- Assign any rights that they have not been assigned by the supervisor

Group definitions

Group definitions make network management easier. They allow a supervisor to deal with users as groups. It is very important that you assign users to groups logically, not on an *ad hoc* basis. The name of the group should be meaningful.

There are many advantages of using groups, the two main ones being:

(1) It gives a group of users a common set of rights.

(2) It defines a group of users which can be managed by other users.

Managing users' accounts

When you come to define the user's login name, it is very useful to separate the users into several types. Figure 15.4 illustrates some basic user types.

A normal user will probably use his/her own first name as the login name, whereas users with supervisory-equivalent privileges are automatically recognized by the fact that their names all start with SUPER followed by their own initials, for instance SUPER_DD or SUPER_FN. This can be very useful for managing the network. By typing USERLIST, you can tell at a glance what type of users are currently logged in:

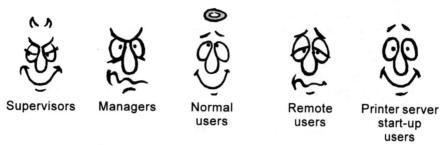

Supervisors   Managers   Normal   Remote   Printer server
                           users   users   start-up
                                                    users

Figure 15.4 Basic user types.

```
C:\WINDOWS>userlist

User Information for Server NW386
Connection   User Name          Login Time
----------   --------------     -------------------
        1      FARSHAD          2-03-1993  3:50 pm
        2    * KYLIE            2-03-1993  2:20 pm
        3      BOB              2-03-1993  1:50 pm
        4      SUPER_ID         2-03-1993  3:55 pm
        5      SUPER_MT         2-03-1993  4:00 pm
        6      REM_KOL          2-03-1993  4:00 pm

C:\WINDOWS>
```

In the example above, you can see that we have logged three normal users (FARSHAD, KYLIE and BOB), two supervisor-equivalent users (SUPER_ID and SUPER_MT) and one remote user (REM_KOL) into the system.

Whatever the logging name, it is advisable to keep it to eight characters or fewer. This is so that you can easily create a DOS-type home directory with the same name as the user's login name. Try to keep login names short: it is more user friendly.

Over the years, I have developed a special structure for allocating the user name. It works on the basis of identifying the user type and then applying a standard format in assigning their name. I identify a number of different users according to their login name format. These are shown in Table 15.1.

Naming supervisors

When you wish to login as a supervisor, it is wiser in the long term to login as a special user who happens to have supervisory privileges. This is instead of using the standard supervisor name. This is particularly true when there are a number of people who have the supervisor password. If you login as SUPER_FN or SUPER_KB it is far easier to follow which supervisor is doing what. If each supervisor is given a

Table 15.1 A system for identifying users.

Name format (less than 9 characters)	Description
<user name>	Normal LAN user
SUPER_<user initials>	Users with supervisor-equivalent privileges
MAN_<user initials>	Users with group manager or account manager privileges
REM_<user initials>	Remote users accessing the LAN
PS_<print server name>	A special login user name to start up a print server

unique name, it is easy to find out which supervisor has created certain files or directories. The suggested format is:

```
SUPER_<supervisor initials>
```

Manager names

In NetWare, you can define a workgroup manager or account manager. I like to give these types of user a special name which takes the format MAN followed by the user's initials. This makes the user's privilege level obvious to all others, and the user's ID reminds them that they are currently logged in as a manager.

A supervisor or manager should have two passwords, one which is used to carry out a manager's or supervisor's activities and a normal user ID for running normal applications.

Limit disk space

When creating a user, limit their disk space. This is essential: if you don't you will have human nature working against you! Most people will not bother deleting unnecessary files and will quickly use up disk storage. If users are given a fixed amount of storage, they are forced to keep their home directory clear of cluttering files. This rule particularly applies to supervisors: they tend to be the worst offenders! Don't forget, you can always increase the allocation at any time. Table 15.2 lists suggested allocations.

Table 15.2 Recommended allocations of disk space for different types of user.

User type	Disk space allocation
Supervisor equivalent	100 Mbytes
Normal Windows users	50 Mbytes
Normal DOS user	10 Mbytes

Managing group assignments

When assigning a group, make sure that the name you give it is meaningful. The name should indicate what sort of responsibilities the group members will be given. I recommend a maximum of 15 characters for the group name.

Where possible, each group should be related to the type of application that its users are allowed to run.

Do not assign overlapping groups

When you are assigning groups to users, make sure that groups do not overlap. The potential confusion that can be created is illustrated by the following example. Let's assume we have a user called D_DUCK who has the following group assignments:

```
F:\APPS>whoami /s
You are user D_DUCK attached to server NW386, connection 1.
Server NW386 is running NetWare v3.11 (250 user).
Login time: Thursday  February  4, 1993  5:29 pm
You are security equivalent to the following:
     EVERYONE (Group)
     GROUP1 (Group)
     GROUP2 (Group)

F:\APPS>
```

Now the groups GROUP1 and GROUP2 have the following rights assigned:

```
User Name:      D_DUCK
Full Name:      (none)
User ID:        E000001

Group Trustee Rights:
---------------------
  EVERYONE:
   [   C   ]     SYS:MAIL
   [ R   F ]     SYS:PUBLIC

  GROUP1:
   [ R   F ]     SYS:APPS

  GROUP2:
   [  W  FA]     SYS:APPS
```

The above illustration shows that GROUP1 and GROUP2 are potentially contradictory. This overlap can cause all manner of confusion. In this case, NetWare will actually add the two rights together and therefore D_DUCK will see the following trustee rights in the APPS directory: [RWFA] (read, write, filescan and access control). It is preferable to avoid this situation. The D_DUCK user should be given either GROUP1 or GROUP2, but not both. You must plan your groups carefully so that they each tackle a different application or shared item. If two groups have to give different rights to the same resources it is important that they should not be assigned simultaneously to a given user.

There are, however, times when you actually need two overlapping groups. A good example of this may occur when you are using Windows across the network. You might have two groups with the following rights:

```
Group= WINDOW_INSTALLERS
          SYS:\WINDOWS      [ RWD FA]
Group= WINDOW_USERS
          SYS:\WINDOWS      [ R   FA]
```

Any user is then given one or the other. A manager will install Windows with read and write access rights given by the WINDOW_INSTALLERS group, whereas a humble normal user will be given the WINDOW_USERS rights, that is, read file only.

Classic group names

Figure 15.5 shows some classic group names; the WINDOWS_INSTALLER and the WINDOW_USERS_3.1 groups are particularly useful. In this way, you can define groups for other types of Windows user, such as Windows NT.

It is also very useful to define a SUPERVISORS group. This will contain all the users who have supervisory-equivalent rights. This can be used in the system

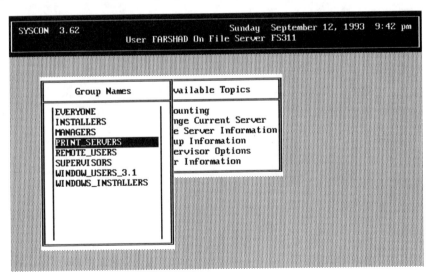

Figure 15.5 Classic group names.

script file to MAP extra facilities for this user type which would not be available to normal users.

> Warning: Do not destroy the EVERYONE group – it is very useful.

The group REMOTE_USERS is also very useful if you have a dial-in facility. Sometimes you might want to omit a number of the standard MAP assignments if the user is a remote-access user. In this case, this group is most useful.

Having said all of the above, the group names should basically describe what type of application they are covering.

Try not to assign rights to users (except in the home directory): always assign rights to a group and make users members of that group.

Managing workgroup managers

Strategy in assigning managers

It is important that you limit the jurisdiction of the workgroup manager to a specific task or department within your organization. Novell allows a workgroup manager to manage another workgroup manager, who is managing the original manager. This is a recipe for disaster and total confusion. Where possible, limit the workgroup manager to managing users as opposed to other managers.

In addition, where possible, do not split responsibilities between two managers. Keep their responsibilities separate.

Following these simple rules should make your life as a network manager far easier.

Specify passwords for all workgroup and accounts managers.

Require workgroup managers to have two user IDs: one for doing normal work and the other for doing a manager's work.

Be cautious when making anyone security-equivalent to a workgroup manager.

How to create large numbers of users quickly

There are a number of different ways to create users on Novell networks: this involves using the SYSCON, USERDEF or MAKEUSER programs.

There is a new utility that comes with NetWare 4.x called UIMPORT. This is a replacement for MAKEUSER.

See the section 'The UIMPORT tool' in this chapter for more information.

The USERDEF program

The USERDEF program is a menu-driven subset of the SYSCON program. It is useful for creating a large number of users but, although menu-driven, it can still be tedious to use. If you want to create or delete a large number of user accounts (more than 20), it is better to use the batch-file-driven MAKEUSER program. The standard SYSCON program should be used for anything below this number.

The MAKEUSER program

This is a command-line-driven program with its own control language. It is very useful for creating batches of users automatically and ideal for creating and deleting batches of users on a regular basis. A typical usage is the setting up of user accounts for students each term, and later removing their names in one go. This is the area where the MAKEUSER program is most useful.

Workgroup managers can use MAKEUSER to create users.

How it works
The MAKEUSER program is in fact a compiler; it reads a text file looking for set keywords which instruct the program on the actions to be implemented on user accounts. It then compiles the code and scans it for syntax and semantic (logical) errors. It then processes the instructions and produces a report on its actions.

Keywords
Listed alphabetically in Table 15.3 are the keywords used to create and delete users in the MAKEUSER program. As you can see, you have tremendous control in creating users.

Using the MAKEUSER program

First create a USR file
This is a text file with the USR extension. It will contain the MAKEUSER keywords to instruct the compiler to create users, assign rights, apply restrictions or just delete existing users.

Let's look at an example. Assume that we want to create the new users HARTLY, BART and FARSHAD. Each is to have a 500K space allocation and are to be members of the groups MANAGERS and DATABASE. The USR file shown in Figure 15.6 is produced.

Table 15.3 Keywords used to create and delete users (MAKEUSER program).

Keywords	Description
#ACCOUNT EXPIRATION month, day, year	Account date expiration
#ACCOUNTING balance, low limit	Accounting starting balance
#CLEAR or #RESET	Reset keyword values
#CONNECTIONS number	Maximum concurrent connections
#CREATE user name [options]	Create user's name
#DELETE user name	Delete user's name
#GROUPS group	Define group membership
#HOME_DIRECTORY path	User's home directory
#LOGIN_SCRIPT path	The LOGIN script file to be used
#MAX_DISK_SPACE vol, num	Maximum disk space on a given volume
#PASSWORD_LENGTH len	Minimum password length
#PASSWORD_PERIOD days	Number of days between password expiration
#PASSWORD_REQUIRED	Password must be used
#PURGE_USER_DIRECTORY	Used in conjunction with #DELETE
#REM or REM	A remark
#RESTRICTED_TIME day, start, end	Usage time restrictions
#STATIONS network, station	Station restriction
#UNIQUE_PASSWORD	Users cannot use previous passwords

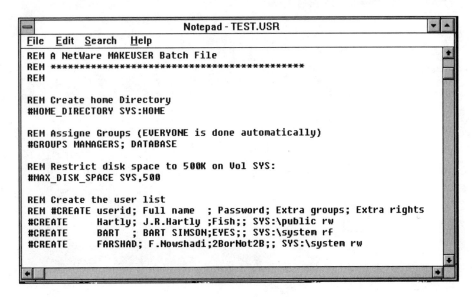

Figure 15.6 A typical USR file.

Next, compile the USR file

Once the text file is written (using your favourite text editor), it is ready for execution:

```
C:\WINDOWS>makeuser test

Error  : Line 007, Undefined keyword "#HOME"
Please fix the error(s) in the file test.USR and try it again.

C:\WINDOWS>
```

If at any time an error is detected, it is shown as above. Once the program is corrected the following is shown:

```
C:\WINDOWS>makeuser test

Processing file test.USR . . .
Check the results in test.RPT

C:\WINDOWS>
```

Finally, inspect the RPT file

On completion, a summary report is generated in the RPT file. It should be something like Figure 15.7.

The UIMPORT tool

This is available as part of the NetWare 4.x system. It is a replacement for MAKEUSER, with many more facilities. It allows the manager to import data from other databases, such as dBase IV, to create users automatically. The program uses a control file that allows the user to define the data format required to read the fields from databases.

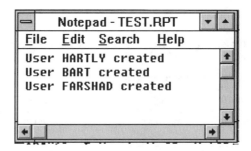

Figure 15.7 The three users created using MAKEUSER.

```
+-------------------------------------------------------------- -+
¦ UIMPORT                    General Help Screen         v4.00   ¦
+------------------------------------------------------------- ---¦
¦ Purpose: Import user objects from an ASCII file.              ¦
¦ Syntax: UIMPORT [/? [ALL | ATTR]] | [controlFileName dataFileName]¦
+--------------------------------------------------------------¦
¦ For help on:                               Type:             ¦
¦   This help screen                         UIMPORT /?        ¦
¦   Control file format and attribute names  UIMPORT /? Attr   ¦
+----------------------------------------------- ------------¦
¦   controlFileName is the name of the control file.          ¦
¦                                                              ¦
¦   dataFileName is the name of the ASCII import data file.    ¦
+--------------------------------------------------------------¦
¦ For Example, to:                    Type:                    ¦
¦  Control file name 'import.ctl'                              ¦
¦   Data file name 'import.dat'       UIMPORT import.ctl import.dat ¦
¦                                                              ¦
¦   To show all attribute names and                           ¦
¦   format of the control file.       UIMPORT /? Attr          ¦
+--------------------------------------------------------------+
F:\PUBLIC>
```

Management issues

The MAKEUSER and UIMPORT programs from NetWare 4.x are most useful commands for managing a large of number of user accounts. These programs are ideal for batching as much of your accounts creation and deletion together as possible, to be implemented in one go as opposed to on an *ad hoc* basis using SYSCON (or the NWADMIN program in the case of NetWare 4.0). A number of major companies run the create and delete user accounts batch file on a weekly basis. The advantage of this process is that you get an audit trail of what you did from the RPT files.

MAKEUSER becomes extremely useful if you can feed the user name directly from a database such as dBase IV or Paradox. It does mean you will have to write an interface to produce a text USR file. If you write such an interface, the possibilities are endless. I have successfully used Borland Object Vision to read a database and produce the equivalent MAKUSER USR file; this took an hour.

Management administration tools

It is always a good idea to have some form of hard copy of all the user accounts and their privileges, especially after an installation or major change to your system. Novell has a very limited reporting facility. There are number of third-party tools which can be used to report upon all your user accounts and group assignments.

A typical third-party product which can be very useful to the network manager is described below. This is only one of a number of products on the market, but it does show the power that these products can bring to the network manager.

The Frye Utilities NetWare management tool

This product is excellent for examining what is happening at the file server level. It provides a very elegant method of investigating user accounts, security rights and group assignments. Each of these parameters can be reported upon either to the screen, file or printer. You can even customize your own reports. Figure 15.8 shows the main screen of the Frye Utilities program.

User information
At the touch of a key, you can gain information about any users, for example: the groups they belong to, who their managers are, login script files, any restrictions and, most importantly of all, the trustee rights they have been assigned (see Figure 15.9).

Group information
Under the group subsection, you are given easy access to all the information kept against each declared group. This includes who belongs to a group, who its managers are and all the trustee rights assigned (see Figure 15.10). Once again, all this information can be reported upon.

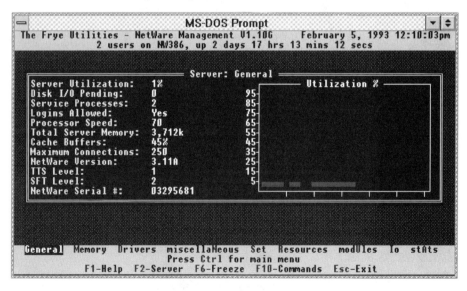

Figure 15.8 Frye Utilities monitoring network utilisation.

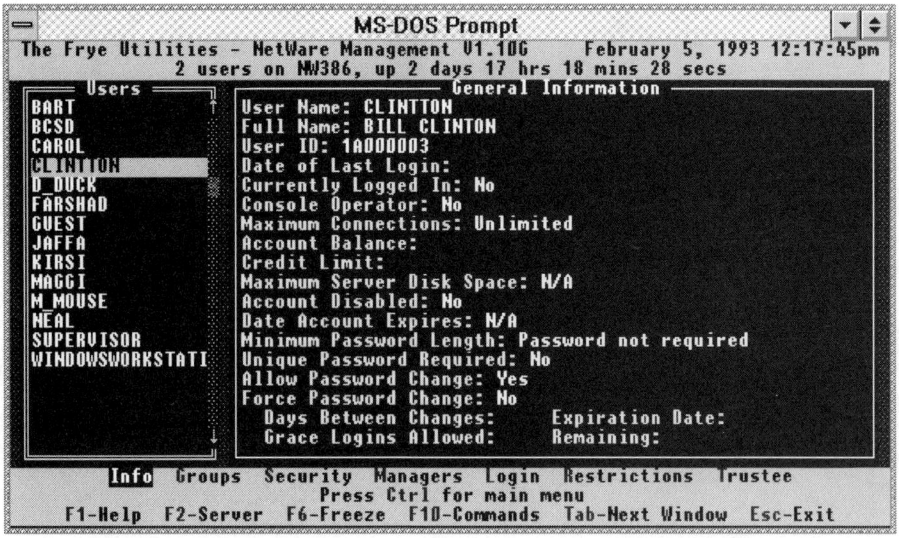

```
─                          MS-DOS Prompt                        ▼ ◆
The Frye Utilities - NetWare Management V1.10G    February 5, 1993 12:17:45pm
            2 users on NW386, up 2 days 17 hrs 18 mins 28 secs
┌─ Users ─┐  ┌──────────── General Information ────────────┐
│BART      │ │User Name: CLINTTON                          │
│BCSD      │ │Full Name: BILL CLINTON                      │
│CAROL     │ │User ID: 1A000003                            │
│CLINTTON  │ │Date of Last Login:                          │
│D_DUCK    │ │Currently Logged In: No                      │
│FARSHAD   │ │Console Operator: No                         │
│GUEST     │ │Maximum Connections: Unlimited               │
│JAFFA     │ │Account Balance:                             │
│KIRSI     │ │Credit Limit:                                │
│MAGGI     │ │Maximum Server Disk Space: N/A               │
│M_MOUSE   │ │Account Disabled: No                         │
│NEAL      │ │Date Account Expires: N/A                    │
│SUPERVISOR│ │Minimum Password Length: Password not required│
│WINDOWSWORKSTATI│ │Unique Password Required: No           │
│          │ │Allow Password Change: Yes                   │
│          │ │Force Password Change: No                    │
│          │ │    Days Between Changes:    Expiration Date: │
│          │ │    Grace Logins Allowed:    Remaining:      │
└──────────┘ └─────────────────────────────────────────────┘
      Info  Groups  Security  Managers  Login  Restrictions  Trustee
                          Press Ctrl for main menu
        F1-Help  F2-Server  F6-Freeze  F10-Commands  Tab-Next Window  Esc-Exit
```

Figure 15.9 The Frye Utilities user information screen.

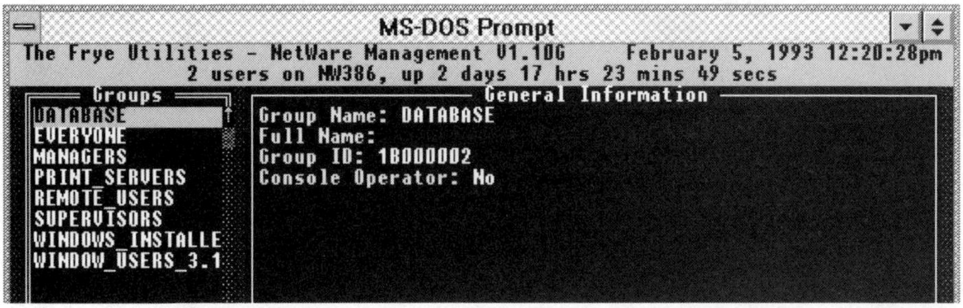

```
─                          MS-DOS Prompt                        ▼ ◆
The Frye Utilities - NetWare Management V1.10G    February 5, 1993 12:20:28pm
            2 users on NW386, up 2 days 17 hrs 23 mins 49 secs
┌─ Groups ─┐  ┌──────────── General Information ────────────┐
│DATABASE   │ │Group Name: DATABASE                         │
│EVERYONE   │ │Full Name:                                   │
│MANAGERS   │ │Group ID: 1B000002                           │
│PRINT_SERVERS│ │Console Operator: No                       │
│REMOTE_USERS │ │                                           │
│SUPERVISORS  │ │                                           │
│WINDOWS_INSTALLE│ │                                        │
│WINDOW_USERS_3.1│ │                                        │
└────────────┘ └─────────────────────────────────────────────┘
```

Figure 15.10 The Frye Utilities group information screen.

The power lies in its reports

Report generation is the strength of this type of product. As can be seen from the above, you have a nice selection of report types for the manager to choose from. As well as showing user and group configurations, these reports can also show the configuration of your file server, such as which NLMs are loaded, the contents of the AUTOEXEC.NCF and the configuration of your volume setups. The reports can also provide infromation about the configuration of the active network nodes. Figure 15.11 shows the configuration reports you can choose from.

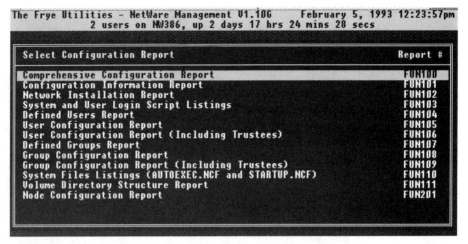

Figure 15.11 Selecting a configuration report.

A typical user's configuration report might look like this:

```
02/05/93 USER CONFIGURATION REPORT (INCLUDING TRUSTEES)  Page 1
12:27:52pm              File Server NW386              FUN106

User Name:      BART
Full Name:      BART SIMSON
User ID:        1C000001
Groups Belonged To:
-------------------
DATABASE
EVERYONE
MANAGERS
Security Equivalents:
---------------------
DATABASE                        (Group)
EVERYONE                        (Group)
MANAGERS                        (Group)
User Trustee Rights:
--------------------
     [ RWCEMFA]    SYS:HOME/BART
     [ RWCEMF ]    SYS:MAIL/1C000001
     [ R    F ]    SYS:SYSTEM
Group Trustee Rights:
---------------------
  DATABASE:
    (none)
  EVERYONE:
     [   C    ]    SYS:MAIL
```

```
    [ R    F ]     SYS:PUBLIC
  MANAGERS:
    (none)
Login Script:
-------------
WRITE "Hello"
MAP
```

User Name: **CLINTON**
Full Name: **JAMES CLINTON**
User ID: **1A000003**

```
... and so on ......
***  END OF REPORT  ***
```

16

Cracking the NetWare 3.x supervisor password, NetWare security and the virus threat

This chapter explores three major topics. In the first section I will show you how easy it is to get NetWare 3.x supervisor privileges, without those rights being issued to you by the network supervisor. There are a number of techniques, which you – as a network manager – should be aware of. By understanding these techniques you will be able to guard your network against attack. The second section explores a strategy that can be used for assigning network access rights. This is an important topic. Most NetWare users know how to assign rights, but some get very confused when it comes to dealing with IRMs (Inherited Rights Masks) and the resulting effective rights. This is not surprising, as it can become highly complicated. I will suggest a number of techniques that can be used to make the life of the network manager easier, whilst allowing him or her to retain complete control over access rights. The final section concentrates on the network virus threat.

Cracking the NetWare 3.x Supervisor password

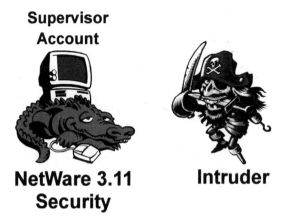

Supervisor Account

NetWare 3.11 Security

Intruder

Figure 16.1 NetWare supervisor account under attack.

> Warning: If you are new to NetWare I suggest you do not try out any of these methods, until you fully understand what is going on.

This is a topic you will not find in the Novell manuals. In this section I will show you different ways to crack the supervisor 3.x password. It is very important that you should be aware of these techniques for the following reasons:

- You can protect your network against attack from intruders
- You never know when you might need to use these techniques to recover your own supervisor account
- They shed an interesting insight on how the NetWare 3.x bindery files work

It is surprisingly easy to crack the supervisor password on a NetWare 3.x system. The key to making a mockery of the NetWare 3.11 security is to gain access to the file server console. Once you have access, with the techniques that I am about to outline you should be able to crack the supervisor account within 10 minutes.

I am about to outline three different methods which can be used to gain supervisor access rights. In the first two methods you need to modify the bindery file name, which requires no special program other the standard set of program and tools available in most organizations. The last method is an example of a specially written program such as BURGLAR, which is available on the standard bulletin boards from CompuServe.

Since the first two methods use the NetWare 3.x bindery file name structure to crack the supervisor account, to understand these methods you must be clear about the importance of the bindery files on the NetWare 3.x operating system.

What are the Novell bindery files?

The bindery files are used by NetWare 2.x and 3.x servers. They contain information such as:

- Network resources
- User accounts
- User rights
- Group assignments

Bindery files consist principally of objects and their associated properties. An object may be a user, group, file or print server, for example. In NetWare 2.x and 3.x, the bindery database is kept by the file server, under the SYS:\SYSTEM directory. In NetWare 3.x, there are three files, as shown in Table 16.1. They store the complete bindery files.

> Warning: Before you try out any of the following techniques on your own system make sure you have a backup of your system first, especially the bindery files. There is no guarantee that these methods will always work, on all systems. BE WARNED: TAKE A BACKUP COPY FIRST, JUST IN CASE.

Method 1: Initialize the bindery files to crack the NetWare 3.x security

This is a very nice method; you can use it to gain supervisory privilege over the file sever within around 10 minutes. This can be done without the use of any special software or hardware. The key to this technique is that you must be able to down the file server, and bring it back up again. It is important to make the point that you do not need to be logged in as any given user to use this method. As long as you can down the server from the console and bring it back up again, then you can use this method to gain access to the supervisor's account and any data file on the server.

Overview of Method 1

This method works by renaming the bindery files names within the SERVER.EXE program. This is very easy to do since it is a DOS program. When the file server is

Table 16.1 NetWare 3.x bindery files

Bindery file name	Function
NET$OBJ.SYS	Stores the identifier of each object
NET$PROP.SYS	Stores the property for each object as defined by the NET$OBJ.SYS file
NET$VAL.SYS	Stores the parameter values for each property defined in NET$PROP.SYS

restarted with the modified SERVER.EXE it is fooled into thinking that it is the first time it is starting up. The system will then create a new set of bindery files, with the name specified in the modified SERVER.EXE and then create a SUPERVISOR account without a password. You then login into the new system as the SUPERVISOR and re-install the original bindery files, which are still kept on the system under their original names. You can now take this opportunity to re-initialize the original supervisor password, or just use your supervisory equivalent privilege to access any data or program on the file server.

Background information

When the NetWare operating system program SERVER.EXE is started it looks for the bindery files under the SYS:\SYSTEM directory. They are NET$OBJ.SYS, NET$PROP.SYS and NET$VAL.SYS. If it does not find these files it will create a new set, with two users, SUPERVISOR and GUEST, both without an initial password. This method exploits this important detail, to crack the SUPERVISOR account.

Detailed step by step approach

The trick works by editing the SERVER.EXE program to look for another set of bindery files, instead of the normal set. When it does not find them, it will then create them and allow users to login as supervisors.

Step 1

We first make a special copy of the SERVER.EXE program, which is going to be modified. The user licence on this program does not have to be the same as the original one on the file server you are about to work on. The important thing is that the two should be the same version of NetWare. This means you can have a version of SERVER.EXE from a NetWare 3.11 disk, prepare it off-site, and take it with you on a floppy to any other NetWare 3.11 file server site.

Copy SERVER.EXE to TRICK.EXE

Step 2

Now edit TRICK.EXE using a disk editor, such as Norton DE.EXE. Change the text reference:

From:	NET$OBJ.SYS	to:	NET$OBJ.TRK
From:	NET$PROP.SYS	to:	NET$PROP.TRK
From:	NET$VAL.SYS	to:	NET$VAL.TRK

To do this look for the Text string 'NET$OBJ.SYS' within the file. This is shown in figure 16.2.

Step 3

Bring up the server using TRICK.EXE instead of the normal SERVER.EXE. Make sure you start to run TRICK.EXE from the directory where the original SERVER.EXE used to load up from. This has the advantage of loading up all the old

```
 Object    Edit    Link    View    Info    Tools    Quit              F1=Help
000CD600: 00 00 03 53 59 53 00 00 - 00 00 06 53 59 53 54 45  ..♥SYS....SYSTE ↑
000CD610: 4D 0B 4E 45 54 24 4F 42 - 4A 2E 54 52 4B 00 06 53  M.NET$OBJ.TRK..S
000CD620: 59 53 54 45 4D 0C 4E 45 - 54 24 50 52 4F 50 2E 54  YSTEM.NET$PROP.T
000CD630: 52 4B 00 00 00 00 06 53 - 59 53 54 45 4D 0B 4E 45  RK.....SYSTEM.NE
000CD640: 54 24 56 41 4C 2E 54 52 - 4B 00 00 00 00 00 00 00  T$VAL.TRK.......
000CD650: 00 00 00 00 00 00 00 00 - 00 00 05 47 55 45 53 54  ...........GUEST
000CD660: 00 00 4E 6F 20 73 70 61 - 63 65 20 66 6F 72 20 42  ..No space for B
000CD670: 69 6E 64 65 72 79 20 48 - 61 73 68 20 54 61 62 6C  indery Hash Tabl
000CD680: 65 00 2A AA 3F BF AE 22 - 2F 5C 5B 5D 3A 7C 3C 3E  e.*ª?¿«"/\[]:¦<>
000CD690: 2B 3D 3B 2C 00 00 18 A2 - 02 00 28 A2 02 00 90 4B  +=;,..↑ó¢..(ó¢.ÉK
000CD6A0: 03 00 A0 4B 03 00 AC 4B - 03 00 BC 4B 03 00 CC 4B  ♥.áK♥.¼K♥.⌐K♥..K
000CD6B0: 03 00 DC 4B 03 00 48 84 - 03 00 58 84 03 00 B4 32  ♥.▄K♥.Hä♥.Xä♥..2
000CD6C0: 04 00 C0 32 04 00 D0 32 - 04 00 80 A2 02 00 68 84  L2...2..Çó¢.hä
000CD6D0: 03 00 E0 32 04 00 38 A2 - 02 00 78 84 03 00 F4 32  ♥.α2..8ó¢..xä♥.ⁿ2
000CD6E0: 04 00 48 37 04 00 58 37 - 04 00 68 37 04 00 74 37  ..H7..X7..h7..t7
000CD6F0: 04 00 EC 4B 03 00 00 33 - 04 00 33 44 32 31 31 31  ..∞K♥..3..3D2111
000CD700: 31 32 22 32 32 31 31 40 - 32 32 34 31 44 33 31 31  12"2211@2241D311
000CD710: 31 31 32 00 00 00 00 00 - 00 00 00 00 00 00 00 00  112.............
000CD720: 00 00 00 00 00 00 00 00 - 00 00 00 00 00 00 00 00  ................
000CD730: 00 00 00 00 00 00 00 00 - 00 00 00 00 00 00 00 00  ................
000CD740: 00 00 00 00 00 00 00 00 - 00 00 00 00 00 00 00 00  ................ ↓
■
                                                 841,292      CD647
 Press ALT or F10 to select menus                          | Disk Editor
```

Figure 16.2 Using a disk editor to change bindery file extension
names from .SYS to .TRK.

boot up configuration files as before, so you do not need to re-enter any hard disk
drive or LAN card driver related information; it will be done automatically.

Step 4

Login to the file server as user SUPERVISOR. No password should be required.
Change to the SYS:\SYSTEM directory:

```
CD \SYSTEM
```

Flag the original bindery files as normal. This allows them to be renamed:

```
FLAG NET$*.SYS N
```

Rename original bindery files as *.OLD:

```
REN NET$*.SYS NET$*.OLD
```

I suggest you make another copy of these just in case the first copy gets
overwritten:

```
COPY NET$*.OLD NET$*.BAK
```

DOWN the file server again.

Step 5

Bring up the file server using its normal SERVER.EXE program. It will not
find any bindery files, since in step 4 you renamed them from their normal extension
.SYS to .OLD. It will now create a new set with extension .SYS.

Step 6

Login in again to the server as supervisor; no password should be required.

> Warning: Be very careful here, do not use BINDFIX.EXE at this stage. If you do you will lose your original bindery file information. However, you should have a backup copy of them under the name *.BAK just in case.

Restore bindery files from the SYS:\SYSTEM:

```
BINDREST
```

The supervisor password has now been cracked !

You now have full SUPERVISORY privilege over the file server, with all the original bindery objects restored to their original values. You can now change the original SUPERVISOR password if you like, using SYSCON, or access any file on the server with supervisor privileges.

Preventing an intruder using Method 1 on your system

To prevent this form of attack, it is important to keep your file server in a secure room, or in a secure box under lock and key. Outside users should not be allowed to down the server and bring up the server with their own copy of SERVER.EXE. This could mean disabling the floppy disk drive, but the problem there is that you might need to use it yourself, one day. You must also be very careful about whom you give file server console operator rights to, since they can down the file server remotely, and start it up with a special version of the SERVER.EXE that they have cleverly placed on the C:\ drive. You have been warned!

I suggest you should also use the SECURE CONSOLE command. To see how it might be useful, see the section on 'Using the SECURE CONSOLE command' in this Chapter.

Method 2: Rename volume SYS:

This second method uses the same idea as the first, but relies on renaming the SYS: volume SYS:. Not many NetWare users know that this can be done. This method is ideal if you want to have supervisory access over the file server files. It is, however, not a very good method if you want to change the supervisor's password. To do that, use method 1: it is easier. For this method to work, you must be able to create a new volume on the file server. This can only be done if you have some unallocated space on a hard disk. If the system does not have any unused disk space, you could in theory install a new hard disk, and create the new volume on top of it. Once again, for this method to work you must have access to the file server console prompt line. If you only want supervisory access rights over all the file server files this method is much easier than the first method and slightly safer.

Detailed step by step approach

Step 1

Take copies of LOGIN.EXE and MAP.EXE from the NetWare public directory and store them on a local disk. These will be needed later on.

Step 2

You now need access to the file server console. Load up the INSTALL.NLM program from the file server console. Dismount volume SYS:. You can now rename it. Let's call it SYSORG:. This is shown in Figure 16.3.

You can now create a new volume called SYS:. Mount both volumes, SYS: and SYSORG:.

Step 3

Now, using the LOGIN.EXE program from the local disk, login into the file server from a workstation. No password should be required.

To access all the NetWare public files you need to add a search path statement to the directory SYSORG:\PUBLIC. This is why you took a copy of the MAP command earlier. You could type a command similar to:

```
MAP INS S1:=SYSORG\PUBLIC
```

The Supervisor password has now been cracked

You now have full SUPERVISORY privilege over the file server, with all the original bindery objects stored in the volume SYSORG:. You have access rights over any file on any of the mounted volumes as long as you MAP to them.

> Warning: When you have finished, do remember to restore the original volume SYS: and remove the new SYS:. The following steps show you how to do this.

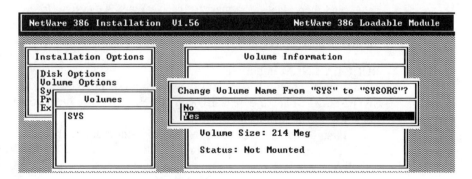

Figure 16.3 Renaming volume SYS: from the INSTALL program.

Step 5: Resetting the volume SYS:

(1) Logout from the server.

(2) Go to the server file console command line and run INSTALL.NLM.

(3) Dismount both volumes, the new volume SYS: and the original volume SYSORG:

(4) Delete the new volume SYS:. (Make sure you delete only the new volume, and not the original volume SYSORG:)

(5) Rename the original volume SYSORG: back to its proper name volume SYS:

(6) Mount Volume SYS:

You have now restored your file server back to its original state.

Preventing an intruder using Method 2 on your system

To prevent this form of attack, it is important once again to keep your file server in a secure room, or in a secure box under lock and key. Outside users should not be allowed to create a new volume on your file server. Remember, a file server console operator cannot create a new volume if all the disk space has been previously allocated, although they could just delete an existing volume and reallocate its space to the new volume SYS:. The moral of the story is to safeguard your file server console against intruder attack.

Method 3: Use third-party programs such as BURGLAR

There are a number of NLM programs produced by third parties that claim to create a supervisor account. It is not difficult to write such programs; as long as you have an NLM development tool kit, you can write one in a couple of hours. In NetWare 3.x when NLM programs run, they do so with supervisory access rights, so it is very easy to write an NLM program that stops to ask the program operator for a user name, and then places a request to the NetWare 3.x system to create a user object with full supervisory privileges. A user can now login from a workstation and use this account name and find that he has equivalent rights to the network supervisor.

BURGLAR.NLM in action

This simple program consist of two very small NLM program, one called SETPASS.NLM and the other BURGLAR.NLM. To use them you must gain access to the file server console prompt line.

First load up the SETPASS.NLM program. It does not require any parameters. It will reset the supervisor password from what it was to 'SUPERVISOR'. This is actually a very bad practice, since user names must not be the same as the user passwords, but I suppose you are going to change it again very soon. Then run the Burglar program and supply as a command line parameter the name of the new supervisor user you wish to create. In Figure 16.4 this is shown as user name FRED.

```
:load setpass
Loading module SETPASS.NLM
  Setpass
  Version 1.00     February 28, 1992

  Debug symbol information for SETPASS.NLM loaded
Supervisor Password has been set to 'SUPERVISOR'
:load burglar fred
Loading module BURGLAR.NLM
  BURGLAR - Create supervisor user. (c) 1990 Cyco Automation (bm)
BURGLAR - Create supervisor equivalent user account
          (c) Cyco Automation (bm) 1990
New user fred created
User made supervisor equivalent
```

Figure 16.4 Loading BURGLAR program.

This is the clever bit: as the new user FRED you can now login from a workstation. You will find you have full supervisory rights over all users, including the supervisor account. I have found that this program does not create a mail directory for the new user, but this is no problem: you just need to run BINDFIX and it will create it for you.

This program was written by Bart Mellirk from Cyco Automation. Apparently it was his first attempt at writing a NLM program, and he has done a very good job. Well done!

Preventing unauthorized NLM
Novell has recognized that running unauthorized NLM programs leaves the NetWare 3.x file server very vulnerable to an intruder bypassing the NetWare security system. This is why they have a special console command to stop unauthorized NLMs from running.

Using the SECURE CONSOLE command
There is a special console command called: **SECURE CONSOLE.** When this command is activated it does the following:

(1) It stops NLM programs being loaded up, from any directory other than SYS:SYSTEM. This will mean that an intruder can no longer go to console command and simply load up a copy of BURGLAR.NLM from the local drives. Of course you must make sure you have not left a copy of BURGLAR or SETPASS or any other suspicious program on the SYS:\SYSTEM directory.

(2) It prevents users changing the system date and time from the console prompt line.

(3) It removes DOS from the file server so when a user issues the EXIT command the system does not go back to DOS, but does a cold boot up. This can be very useful, since some file servers are equipped with special BIOS (Basic Input Output System) ROM that will only start to boot up if the user issues a correct password.

Summary: Protecting against an intruder attack

My advice is the three golden rules:

(1) Use the SECURE CONSOLE command

(2) Secure your file server console from unauthorized access

(3) Be on the lookout for intruders

NetWare security

Basic overview

Most of the material in this section is covered in greater detail in the Novell manuals. If you are familiar with the concepts, move on to the section on management strategy.

Novell provides four fundamental levels of security to prevent an intruder from accessing networked data. This means that a legitimate user must get through each layer of the security ring before gaining access to the desired information. The major levels of NetWare security are shown in Figure 16.5.

The **login security** layer is predominantly controlled by the login identifier and the secret accompanying password. It is at this point that the potential user is introduced to the network and his access rights are checked. If the correct password is entered, and no other account restrictions are applicable, the user is allowed to move on to the next inner layer.

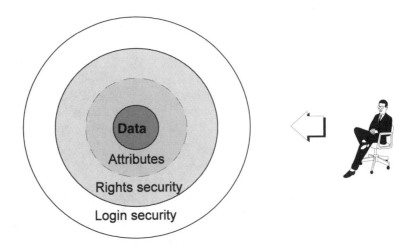

Figure 16.5 NetWare security layers.

At the login security layer, Novell allows for a host of possible restrictions that can be imposed on the user account such as:

- Requiring a minimum password size
- Insisting on a regular change of passwords
- Restricting the login time period
- Restricting the number of concurrent connections
- Restricting which workstation a user may login from

The **trustee rights security** layer provides the next important layer of security protection. Access rights are given to users for most of the resources that can be shared. This can either be done directly or via groups. There are two elements to this type of security: the user rights and the IRMs. These provide what Novell calls the *effective user rights*.

See the section 'NetWare effective rights' in this Chapter.

Unfortunately, there is a slight difference between the abbreviations used for rights in pre-NetWare 2.2 systems and those used in NetWare 2.2, 3.x and 4.x, as shown in Table 16.2.

It is important to bear this in mind when you are upgrading from NetWare 2.15 to NetWare 3.11 or 4.0. You should first upgrade to NetWare 2.2, then upgrade that system to NetWare 3.x or 4.x.

The **directory and file attributes** layer, marked 'Attributes' in Figure 16.5, is the most fundamental layer; it places access rights not against users or groups, but against shared objects such as files or directories, irrespective of who the users are. The general exception is the supervisor, who has full rights to all files (with the exception of the bindery system files).

Table 16.2 Differences between rights abbreviations used in NetWare 2.15 and 2.2/3.x/4.x.

NetWare 2.15 rights	NetWare 2.2/3.x/4.x rights
ALL = All	ALL = All
P = Parental	S = Supervisor
R = Read	R = Read
W = Write	W = Write
C = Create	C = Create
D = Delete	E = Erase
M = Modify	M = Modify
S = Search	F = File scan
O = Open	A = Access control

NetWare effective rights

The effective rights are controlled by both trustee assignments and the IRM (see Figure 16.6). The two are not simply added or ANDed – there is a complicated formula used to calculate the effective right.

A user can investigate their current effective rights using the Novell RIGHTS command:

```
F:\LOGIN>rights
NW386\SYS:LOGIN
Your Effective Rights for this directory are [SRWCEMFA]
    You have Supervisor Rights to Directory.      (S)
  * May Read from File.                           (R)
  * May Write to File.                            (W)
    May Create Subdirectories and Files.          (C)
    May Erase Directory.                          (E)
    May Modify Directory.                         (M)
    May Scan for Files.                           (F)
    May Change Access Control.                    (A)


* Has no effect on directory.


    Entries in Directory May Inherit [SRWCEMFA] rights.
    You have ALL RIGHTS to Directory Entry.


F:\LOGIN>
```

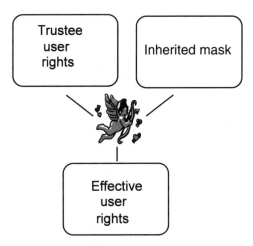

Figure 16.6 Effective user rights.

How effective rights are calculated

Figure 16.7 shows the formula used by NetWare to work out the user's effective rights.

To summarize:

- If supervisory rights are given to current or any parent directories, then all rights are given.
- If you have granted a trustee assignment to a directory, it takes precedence over any directory masks.
- If neither of the above applies, the effective rights consist of the IRM (logical) AND user rights from the parent directory.

Technical differences between NetWare 2.x and 3.x/4.x masks

In NetWare 2.x, *maximum* rights masks are used. They are static and are not inherited by the sub-directories. Any sub-directory will have the full maximum rights set unless otherwise specified.

In NetWare 3.x/4.x, *inherited maximum* rights masks are used. A fundamental difference between this and NetWare 2.x is that NetWare 3.x/4.x masks are inherited by all sub-directories.

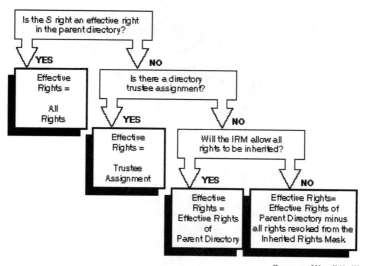

Courtesy of Novell NetWare 3.x manuals

Figure 16.7 NetWare effective rights calculations.

Managing NetWare users

The secret of effective NetWare management is KISS (Keep It Simple, Stupid). It is extremely easy to get completely confused. If you use trustee assignments and IRMs on an *ad hoc* basis, it is a recipe for disaster and an early visit to the psychiatrist! Do not get seduced by the power given to you by all the different methods of setting up rights for users and resources. It is important to have an overall policy for allocating access rights to your users.

To help you develop an easy-to-manage strategy, I recommend the policy described below.

Management strategy 1:
Work at directory level

As a matter of policy, always assign rights at the directory level; where possible, do not give rights at the file level (see Figure 16.8). If you stick to working at directory level, you make user rights management far easier. All the rights given at the directory level are adopted by default by the files inside it. There are rare occasions when going down to the file security level is unavoidable. A classic case is the FORMAT command from the DOS directory. A common practice is to give read-only access rights to all users for the shared DOS directory, with the exception of the FORMAT command. Don't forget that files which need to be treated in a slightly different manner from others can always be moved to their own unique directory.

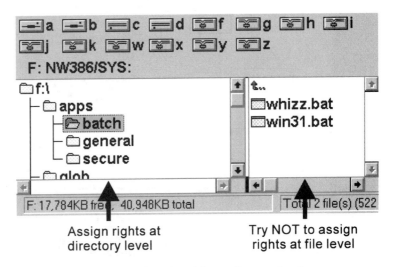

Figure 16.8 Assign rights at directory level.

Management strategy 2:
Avoid Inherited Rights Masks (IRMs)

Some of the most useful advice I can give is: *where possible, avoid using the inherited rights masks*. This will make your life much easier. It means that a user's effective rights at any directory will be user trustee rights that have been given to them by you, as opposed to the situation being complicated further by the addition of the IRM. I have come across a number of situations where a user complains that they do not have read access to a given directory. The supervisor is then puzzled because he or she is sure the user has read access. The supervisor checks, using the SYSCON program, and finds that the user has already been given read access. The problem is that another supervisor has set up an IRM higher up in a parent directory. This has been inherited and has modified the user's rights. This is a recipe for frustration on both sides. This scenario is typical of the problems you get when using the IRM.

Once again, there are times when it is useful to use an IRM but, for the majority of cases, there is a way around it using the user trustee rights. For example, one argument in favour of using IRM is when you want a directory to have certain rights irrespective of the user. It is very tempting to use the IRM at these moments; however, there is a way around this using the trustee rights. In this case, you could add the required access rights for the directory to the EVERYONE group. Since everyone belongs to this group, all users will be given the same minimum access rights to the directory, excluding the supervisor of course.

If you have to use the IRM, use it with great care – you have been warned!

Management strategy 3:
Give the minimum rights possible

Be thrifty when you are assigning rights – think of them as your hard-earned money, which you do not want to just give away. Your guiding principle is that the default user should have no access rights to any of the shared directories unless otherwise stated. The rights should be at the lowest directory level possible. By default, the parent directory should revert back to the default, that is, no access rights.

Some network installers who simply cannot be bothered to manage the rights on the system just give all users full access rights to the root volume directory. This is a cardinal sin! Figure 16.9 shows a manager giving user FARSHAD full access rights to all sub-directories. This is a very bad idea, unless of course the user is to become a manager or supervisor.

If you start off by giving the minimum rights to users, you can always increase them later on demand. It is important that you, as the manager, can monitor the validity of a user's requests for increased access rights. A user will not point out that they have been given too many rights. They probably will not even realize that they have more rights than necessary. However, they might exploit this situation if they do know!

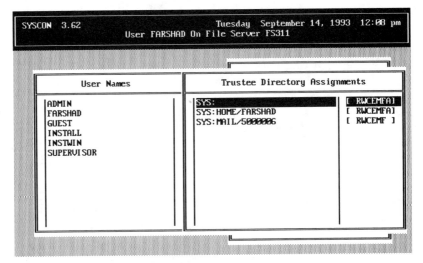

Figure 16.9 Giving a user full access rights to all sub-directories.

Normally, only give read and file scan rights to applications.

Management strategy 4:
Give trustee rights to users through groups

Where possible, do not give rights directly to the user. As a matter of policy, try to give rights to a group, and then make the users members of that group. This provides a very flexible platform for future management purposes. The only common exceptions to this rule are the user's home and mail directories.

Even though you might want to give rights exclusively for the use of a specific user, it is still preferable in the long term to produce a new group and make that user a member. This is because:

- The group name can assist in understanding the nature of the users' applications.

- If the user is run over by a big red bus, it may be tragic for him or her but, from the network management viewpoint, you just delete the user from the group and add a replacement user to the group. You do not need to redefine the user's rights.

- Any new users can just join in the group.

If, when trying to save a file, you get a DIRECTORY WRITE PROTECTED error, the chances are that you do not have (W) write and (C) create rights to the directory. Check by using the RIGHTS command from the DOS prompt line.

Management strategy 5:
Use the SECURITY program

With NetWare 2.x, 3.x and 4.x you get a free program called SECURITY.EXE. It is ideal for checking what potential security risks your file server is open to. I strongly recommend the regular use of the Novell SECURITY program. Normally it is found in the SYS:\SYSTEM directory. This program when run will monitor any loop holes in your network security. Its artificial intelligence will check the file server security risks. It checks for the following risks:

- No password assigned
- Insecure passwords
- Supervisor equivalence
- Root directory privileges: reports all users who have access privileges to the root directory of a volume
- Login scripts: ensures each user has a login script
- Excessive rights over directories
- Checks for passwords that are the same as the user name
- Excessive rights to standard NetWare directories: ensures users have no more rights than:

```
SYS:SYSTEM    [       ]
SYS:PUBLIC    [ R    F ]
SYS:LOGIN     [ R    F ]
SYS:MAIL      [ W C   ]
```

Use this program regularly, especially after making any major changes to user trustee rights.

Management strategy 6:
Force users into the habit of using passwords

With NetWare, you can specify that users must use passwords, how often they should be renewed and whether or not they should be unique each time they are renewed. You can also define the minimum length of password the user can use. Figure 16.10 shows the settings you can specify. There is a very fine line between necessary password restrictions and annoying the users with unnecessary restrictions. My advice is to adopt the following general approach:

- Users must use passwords
- Minimum password length is six characters
- Users should change their passwords every 120 days

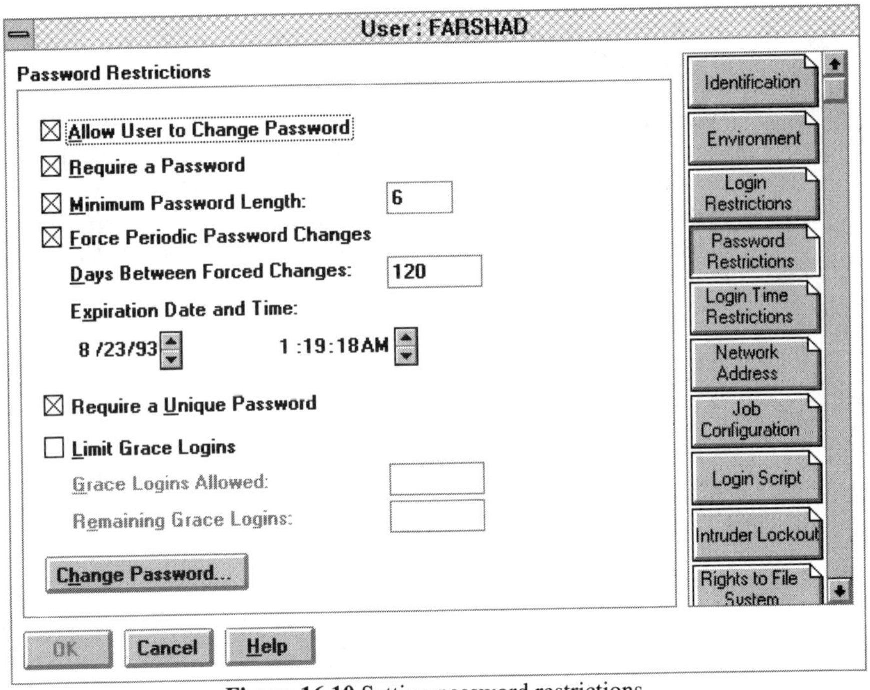

User : FARSHAD

Password Restrictions

☒ Allow User to Change Password
☒ Require a Password
☒ Minimum Password Length: 6
☒ Force Periodic Password Changes
   Days Between Forced Changes: 120
   Expiration Date and Time:
      8 /23/93   1 :19:18AM

☒ Require a Unique Password
☐ Limit Grace Logins
   Grace Logins Allowed:
   Remaining Grace Logins:

Change Password...

| Identification |
| Environment |
| Login Restrictions |
| Password Restrictions |
| Login Time Restrictions |
| Network Address |
| Job Configuration |
| Login Script |
| Intruder Lockout |
| Rights to File System |

OK   Cancel   Help

Figure 16.10 Setting password restrictions.

The above is just a general set of restrictions for most cases. However, each case has to be treated on its own merit, adding further restrictions or reducing any restrictions as you see fit.

Secure your workstation from unauthorized access

One of the commonest causes of network security breakdown occurs when users leave their workstations without logging out. Any unauthorized user can then take over the unattended workstation and change their security rights. Since most users use Windows, it is very easy to protect the workstation when they are away from their desks. Microsoft provides a primitive screen saver function, which is activated using the Setup button from the Desktop icon in the Control panel window. Using this option, you can enable the screen saver's password protection. Then, if you do not move your mouse or press any key for a fixed period of time, the screen saver will be activated. The period of time is normally set to ten minutes. The only way you can resume is to enter the previously-defined password. I prefer to use the third-party add-on program After Dark (Star Trek Edition). It has the same function as the Microsoft standard screen saver, but has a far larger range of screens to choose from and is more fun to use (see Figure 16.11).

Figure 16.11 After Dark (Star Trek Edition), password protected.

Renaming directories which have trustee rights assignment

A little known fact is that you can rename a referenced directory without having to make any manual changes to the trustee rights list. Due to the way bindery information is stored, all the rights and references of the old-named directory will be given to the renamed directory. You can try this out for yourself. Do the following:

(1) Use SYSCON to confirm that you have at least RWAF rights to your own home directory.

(2) From the DOS prompt line, using Norton NCD or another disk management tool, change your home directory name.

(3) Revisit SYSCON to see what changes have occurred to your home directory access rights.

Virus overview

How much of the talk about viruses is fact and how much is fiction? Undoubtedly, a danger is posed by the modern-day virus. It has been known for a 1500-user site to be wiped out in a few hours due to a virus. On the other hand, anti-virus software manufacturers have a vested interest in exaggerating the dangers. It is important to separate the fact from the fiction so that you can allocate appropriate resources to meet the real threats to your network.

What is a virus? It is very difficult to define, but the best definition is probably as follows:

A virus is an unauthorized program, which can normally reproduce itself.

Some people suggest that viruses are the next stage in the evolutionary process. The argument goes something like this. Viruses are reproducing themselves all the time; however, they are under constant attack from anti-virus programs. Only the very strong, resilient viruses will survive in the long term and become the so-called super-viruses of the future. If these viruses can mutate as they embark on the process of reproduction, new unimaginable forms of viruses will inhabit our networks. This is a bit far fetched, but you never know!

Returning to reality, the network manager should be aware of the ever-present threat posed by the modern-day virus. The good news is that the vast majority of virus scares tend to be false alarms; those that do turn out to be true tend to be relatively harmless.

Network and virus fundamentals

The National Computer Security Association (NCSA) in the USA have identified literally hundreds of viruses. The most common way that viruses spread themselves from one network to another is via the pirated software package. A typical scenario involves a user, with supervisory rights, who is logged into a network running a game which their friend has just bought in Hong Kong for three dollars. Surveys indicate that pirated software accounts for 80% of incidents of virus transmission. The next largest category involves bulletin boards, which account for 15%. You have been warned!

Viruses: how they work

Most viruses work by attaching themselves to programs such as .COM and .EXE files. They do this because these programs are run by the user which subsequently gives the virus an opportunity to be activated and to do its 'dirty deed'. Attaching itself to data files would be pointless as they are never run, only inspected and modified. The only reason why they might infect data files is to be awkward and cause damage to them.

There is another type of virus called the 'boot virus'. These attach themselves to the boot sector of disks and are executed as part of the boot-up sequence of your machine. They then tend to go into memory and engage in the process of replication and deception. They normally pass control back to the normal boot up sequence so that the user is not aware that the virus is sitting happily in the memory.

Viruses and NetWare

Most viruses sit in the memory and attach themselves to the interrupt lines. Every time the trapped interrupt lines are called as part of the normal operation of the PC, the virus has a good look around to see if it can do any damage. If not, control is passed to the real interrupt service routine, as though nothing unusual had happened. The situation becomes interesting when this type of virus is mixed with the NetWare shell or redirector. The IPX and NETX also attempt to take control of some of the same PC interrupt lines, the big difference being that they are useful, constructive programs (hopefully), unlike the virus programs. The NetWare shell is a TSR program and acts as an inspector. Every time a request is made to the hooked interrupts, it inspects it and, if it is network-related, takes over; otherwise, control is passed over to the original service routine that can deal with it. Some very interesting problems can arise when the two TSR programs, the virus and the NetWare shell, compete for the common interrupt lines. This opens up the possibilities described below.

Virus activated before NetWare shell

The virus is usually disabled if it is activated before the NetWare shell is started. This is because, being highly intelligent, the NetWare shell will hook itself onto the interrupts normally used by the virus and pass control back to the normal interrupt service routing, not the virus. This is not, however, true for all types of virus. It is worth noting that the IPX or NETX could be infected without passing the virus onto the network.

NetWare shell activated before Virus

This is far more problematic. If the virus hooks onto the interrupts after the NetWare shell is loaded, it is far more likely to infect the system. Results of tests performed on the most common virus in this situation reveal that the most likely outcome is that the machine will hang or that the NetWare shell will fail to operate correctly.

Network-specific viruses

To my knowledge, there are very few network-specific viruses around. However, the ones that do exist are almost always specific to NetWare. The most common NetWare virus is the *GP-virus* (Get Password). This virus is designed to sit in the user's memory as a TSR program and pass the name of all users' identifiers and accompanying passwords to a companion program using the IPX calls. God forbid the day when we see NLM-type viruses. These could be terrifying!

> Warning: Be very careful how you boot up the file server. Always use a virus-free DOS boot-up file.

Even though the virus is active, the DOS memory is cleared when the SERVER.EXE program is run. The NetWare operating system takes over, disabling any viruses.

You might get a low-level virus which is activated before the SERVER.EXE program is run. It can then do a low-level disk write access and destroy the NetWare operating system. This is why it is very important that the server DOS boot-up disk is disinfected of all known viruses, just in case.

File server-based virus protection (SiteLock)

A very useful tool in the never-ending war against viruses is SiteLock from Bright Works. It is a simple program which runs predominantly on the file server as an NLM. It has the ability to create and store checksum-like signatures for all the .EXE and .COM programs that might be run over the network. The SiteLock program compares the runtime signature against the 'registration' signature before any of the protected programs are allowed to be run over the network. If the two signatures do not match up, the program is not allowed to be executed and a system error message is generated, warning the manager of a possible virus attack. The program has the following advantages and disadvantages:

✓ The checksum verification does not rely on recognizing any particular bit patterns for virus detection and will work for any version of a virus. This means an enormous saving on your time. You do not need to update the virus software every few months, as with virus correction packages such as Dr Solomon's Anti-Virus Toolkit.

✓ Unauthorized file and local drive lockout: the program can prevent users from running unprotected files on the file server. It also has the ability to disable program execution from the local floppy or the hard disk. This can be very useful in preventing the use of pirated software.

✓ You can also use the package to meter other software. This allows only a pre-declared number of programs to be run across the network. Any user wanting to run more copies of a program than is allowed will be queued up for that application. It becomes available as soon as one of the other users releases it.

✗ It could slow down the execution of programs across the network. However, because the program is flexible, you can instruct it to check programs every other time (or more), rather than every time they are run. You also need to run an extra NLM on the file server.

✗ You must run the SWATCHER program on each workstation. This is an essential program for the correct working of the SiteLock program. This can be a bit of a problem. However, the SiteLock NLM program can be instructed not to allow any user to run a program across the network if SWATCHER is not running. It can be easily loaded up as part of the normal login procedure.

SiteLock: a demonstration

The SiteLock program is easy to use. You just run SITELOCK.NLM on the file server. Then you run the SiteLock program from a workstation (see Figure 16.12).

You now register all the programs that are to be monitored across the network. This is normally all the .COM and .EXE programs; however, it can be restricted to a given directory. This now registers each one of these files for further reference. It is at this point that you must be sure that the registered files are free of any viruses. Once this is done the system is ready. Figure 16.13 shows the list of virus-protected files.

Let's take a look at the ATTACH.EXE program. We will assume that the system is going to be infected by a virus and see how it copes.

The users *must* activate the SWATCHER program *before* logging into the system. This can be done automatically from the AUTOEXEC.BAT, or by following the execution of the script file with the EXIT 'SWATCHER' command.

To demonstrate the virus attacking the monitored program, ATTCH.EXE, I made a copy of it and changed one part of the program to simulate a virus corruption:

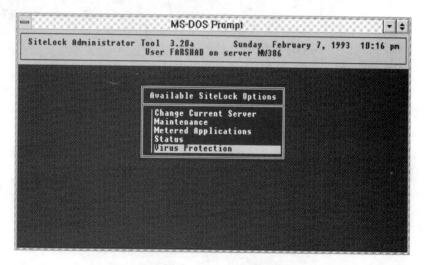

Figure 16.12 Running the SiteLock program.

Figure 16.13 Virus-protected file names.

```
ncopy SYS:\PUBLIC\ATTACH.EXE F:\LOGIN
```

A random byte is then changed to FF, using a disk editor such as Norton DE.EXE (see Figure 16.14).

The program is now executed. The message shown in Figure 16.15 is automatically generated. SiteLock detected that the program had been changed and prevented it from being executed.

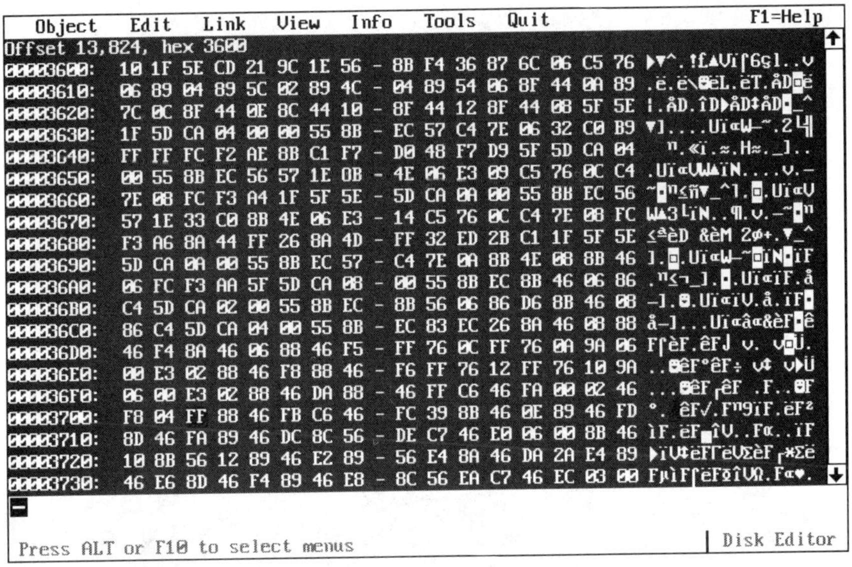

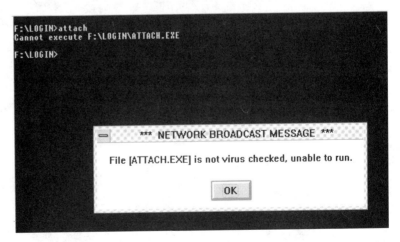

Figure 16.14 Simulated virus corruption.

Figure 16.15 SiteLock prevents the corrupted program from being executed.

Management virus summary

The impact of a virus on your network can be disastrous. You must always bear in mind that *prevention is better than cure*:

- You must develop a policy of virus avoidance. This is normally done by restricting the running of new software on your system until it has gone though your quarantine procedure.
- Develop a very strict policy about downloading software from public bulletin boards.
- Do not allow the running of illegal software on any of your workstations. There are a number of UK companies who consider this a sackable offence!
- Have two types of anti-virus software package on the network.

Virus detection software (file server based)

These are normally file server based, monitoring programs. They inspect each program for changes in program contents and warn the supervisor of potential infections. Examples of such programs are the SiteLock NLM from Brightwork and Anti-Virus for Networks v2.0 from Central Point Software.

Virus eradication software

These are normal DOS-based programs that will detect and attempt to eradicate the virus from the system. Examples of such programs are Dr Solomon's Anti-Virus toolkit for NetWare and the Norton Virus Check program.

Virus summary

Most viruses:

- Are non-destructive to data
- Are stopped by the NetWare shell: the IPX and NETX program seem to do a good job of stopping the most common viruses from infecting the network
- Are spread via pirated software (80%): as a matter of policy, stop pirated software from ever being brought anywhere near your network system
- If started on workstations, cannot normally attack the file server boot sector (as yet!)

You should:

- Use network security rights to stop infection. Give users the minimum rights necessary: viruses cannot increase user privilege rights (yet). Giving the users minimum privilege rights will stop an infection from spreading over the network.

- Use the read-only attribute to provide protection against virus infection.
- Use the execute-only file attribute on programs, which has so far been known to stop all recognized viruses affecting programs.

Educate your users

This is the best method of preventing your network from being infected by a virus. Explain what a computer virus is to your users, and what they must do to ensure a healthy network. At this point, it may be useful to put the fear-of-God into the user by over-dramatizing the danger of viruses! However, you should always keep a sense of proportion in your own mind.

Limiting viruses

- Check for viruses before loading applications on the network.
- Consider using diskless workstations.
- Write protect all original diskettes before installing software.
- Educate users about the dangers of viruses.
- Flag executable files as read only.
- Be careful of dial-in hackers.
- Get users to notify you of viruses as soon as possible.

17

Network management tools

Overview

There are some excellent management tools available for administering and trouble-shooting Novell networks. These highly sophisticated products generally fall into three basic categories: protocol analysers, and the far more sophisticated network management and LAN administration products. The distinction between these categories is becoming increasingly blurred: each product type is developing to carry out part of the functionality of the others.

Protocol analysers

These products analyse the packets as they flow around the network. They allow the manager to monitor events on the network. Although a number of these products are user friendly, they do tend to be technical in nature. They decode the packets as they flow around the network; by using artificial intelligence some will interpret the data for you and make a number of recommendations as to what you should do. This type of product is excellent for analysing errors in your communication protocols, but they are not much use for identifying network application errors. They are relatively low-level products.

Having said that, LANalyzer for Windows (from Novell) is an excellent product, which will be examined in greater detail. Other packages well worth a mention are LANdecoder from Triticom and the excellent LANWatch from FTP Software.

The advantages of these products are that they:

✓ Measure the network load

✓ Indicate if network cards are producing good data packets

✓ Check and show the network data packet error rate

✓ Display the daily network usage profile

✓ Indicate who is producing the most network traffic
   The disavantages are that:

✗ They are not normally much help with application-level problems

✗ You need to have some idea about protocols in order to use them effectively

✗ They can occasionally miss out data packets

✗ They can bring the network down if instructed to generate traffic

✗ Users normally need to go on special training courses before they can effectively use this type of product

Worldwide network management software

The art of good network management lies in having the right network management tools. There are a growing number of software packages which will provide excellent management information about the nature and configuration of your network(s). These products normally take a worldwide perspective of your network. Traditionally, they use SNMP (Simple Network Management Protocol) to gather software- and hardware-related information. They are intended to assist in the day-to-day management of networks.

 See the section 'SNMP network management' in this chapter for further details.

This information can range from file server configuration to the performance of hub cabling. Where possible, internetwork information is also gathered from such devices as bridges, routers and asynchronous links. All this information is then presented to the network manager in a graphical format. These products tend to be user friendly and based on Microsoft Windows.

Some products have physical mapping facilities. This enables the global network manager to superimpose all network logical information over a backdrop of the organization's geographic layout. This is something NetWare Service Manager does very nicely, but at a price!

The advantages of these products are:

✓ They normally use SNMP.

✓ They tend to be far more user friendly than pure protocol analysers.

✓ They can help you troubleshoot network applications.

✓ They can analyse network traffic.

✓ They can warn you of a pre-defined threshold being reached.

✓ They are normally a joy to use.

The disadvantages of these products are:

✗ They tend to be expensive.

✗ They can be time-consuming to set up globally.

LAN administration tools

There are a number of NetWare administration tools on the market which can make network administration a lot easier. Programs such as Saber's LAN Workstations combine many network administration tools in one program. They normally provide excellent reporting facilities that go well beyond the normal information provided by the standard NetWare programs. Table 17.1 shows some of the most significant products in this field.

It is very important to pick the right network administration tool for your requirements. These tools are too often bought, used for a few weeks and then neglected. Do take your time and analyse what it is you really want from these tools that you cannot get from the NetWare standard tools. These tools cover a very wide area of tasks, not all of which will be relevant to your needs.

Table 17.1 LAN administration tools.

Product	Software and hardware inventory	Print queue control	Automated user creation and definition	Software usage metering
LAN Tachometer Brightwork Developments, Inc.	Yes	Yes	N/A	Yes
Utilities for NetWare Frye Computer Systems, Inc.	Yes	N/A	N/A	Yes
Tools for Networks XTree, Inc.	Yes	N/A	Yes	N/A
LANDesk Intel Corporation	Yes	Yes	N/A	Yes

SNMP network management

In this section we look at the basic function of SNMP, what it is and how it works. If you are familiar with SNMP, you can omit this section.

SNMP: network management the simple way

SNMP is now the most popular network management protocol in use today. Regardless of their background, most vendors of network hardware and software adopt SNMP as their standard network management protocol. SNMP is simple and provides a practical working solution for the network manager. The SNMP management system is usually associated with TCP/IP networks. It only requires a basic transport service, to make it protocol-independent. The SNMP protocol can (in theory) be run over the Novell SPX/IPX protocol instead of TCP/IP.

SNMP's success lies in its simplicity: it has a command set with only three basic commands. SNMP can be used to gather information from different components of the network. It can also be used to gather up data from networks other than Novell; for example, LAN Manager, Windows NT and Banyan Vines all support SNMP commands. The SNMP serves as a common denominator for management products. Figure 17.1 illustrates the basic structure of SNMP.

The basic structure of the SNMP is divided into three separate components:

(1) Agent (or proxy agent). An agent is an SNMP program that sits on each relevant network device. It is capable of collecting information about local conditions. It is strictly under the control of the SNMP Network Manager Station. Agents can be set up on an assortment of hardware such as hubs, bridges, routers and NICs (Network Interface Cards). They can also report on software performance and configuration. For example, SNMP agents can be set up on a Novell file server. They will then report the current configuration and performance of the file server to the management monitor station. The

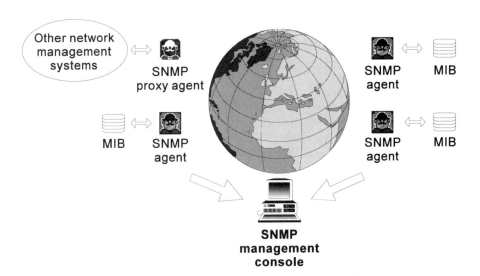

Figure 17.1 SNMP (Simple Network Management Protocol) basic structure.

agents, once told what to do, will start to collect data and store it in their MIBs (Management Information Bases).

A proxy agent is a special type of agent which sits on devices not supported by SNMP. They perform the same functions as an agent, but also serve as a protocol converter. For example, you might get a proxy agent for IBM NetView: it will convert the SNMP command into the IBM NetView command then carry out the operation and report back in SNMP terms.

(2) Manager ▣. A manager is an SNMP-based application. It can request information from its agents. It then collects and logs the information about the network activity. The manager program is referred to as a Network Management Station (NMS). The manager program is normally a Windows-based graphical environment and represents the data in a very user-friendly way. An excellent example of such a program is Novell's NetWare Service Manager.
See the section 'NetWare Service Manager' for further details.

In theory, this type of program enables the network manager to manage the worldwide network from a single point. They are also tremendous fun to use!

(3) Management Information Base (MIB) ▤. This is a local database used to store all the information that the local agents have been requested to gather.

These three basic components work together to provide a universal means of gathering information on any network system. Figure 17.2 shows a typical SNMP community.

SNMP history

SNMP was developed from the original Simple Gateway Management Protocol (SGMP). This was the first attempt at addressing the challenges facing the network managers of that time. The creators of SGMP used UNIX and hence TCP/IP as their common protocol carrier. SGMP and SNMP are still closely related to the TCP/IP protocol stack, and SNMP is very similar to SGMP in architecture and design. There are a few syntax differences which make the two incompatible. However, this is not a major issue today because usage of SGMP is minimal in comparison with SNMP.

In August 1988, the creator of SGMP formalized the SNMP structure. It was then submitted as an Internet Draft Standard. In April 1989, SNMP received its international credentials by becoming an Internet Recommended Standard (RFC 1098).

The next step in the development of SNMP, the transition from SNMP to the OSI Common Management Information Services and Protocol over TCP/IP, is being examined by the Internet Activities Board.

SNMP is considered an excellent solution to network management today by most network managers. Within the next few years, however, its popularity will be overshadowed by the more comprehensive OSI solution of CMIP (Common Management Information Protocol).

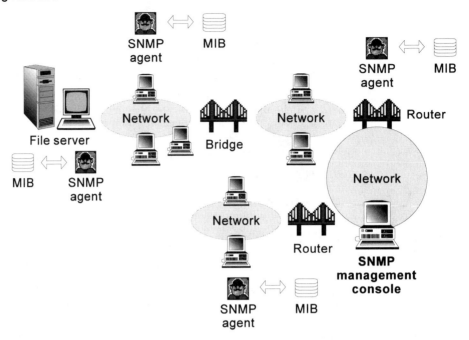

Figure 17.2 SNMP structure.

For more information on CMIP, see the section 'The OSI view of network management' in this chapter.

How SNMP works

SNMP works by sending out a number of basic commands (see Figure 17.3). There are five different types of command, called PDUs (Protocol Data Units):

- GetRequest
- GetNextRequest
- SetRequest
- GetResponse
- Trap

GetRequest, GetNextRequest and GetResponse
These are the commands that the agent will react to. It will inspect its local MIB and send back the requested data to the monitoring station. The manager can either request data on a specific item via the GetRequest command or just request the next item in the list using the GetNextRequest command. The agent then sends the data back using the GetResponse command.

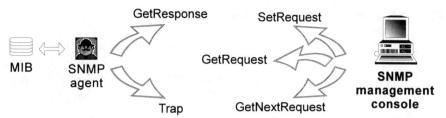

Figure 17.3 SNMP command set.

SetRequest

This is used to warn the agent to start collecting data on a specific item about the local environment. It will keep the data on its MIB ready for future inspection. SetRequest is a very powerful command and, if misused, can disrupt the system. There is also a big security implication. It must not be possible for competitors to start instructing your SNMP agents to collect data for their own use. SNMP provides a very limited security feature. It is in fact password protected, but many vendors have enhanced the basic SNMP security.

Traps

These are a number of automatic commands that agents send out to inform the manager that special events have occurred. These are such things as Initialization, WarmStart, Linkdown, LinkUp, Authentication Failure. The traps are sometimes used to control the frequency of polling, which the SNMP manager uses to monitor the agent.

SNMP Version 2 (new)

SNMP Version 2 has been significantly enhanced by the IETF (Internet Engineering Task Force). It maintains interoperability with the old SNMP Version 1 standard. Normal users would probably not recognize the differences between the two; however, SNMP Version 2 has improved network efficiency and enhanced security measures. The most important of these, from a Novell point of view, is that the standard now defines how it is run over SPX/IPX as opposed to solely being based on TCP/IP. Here are some of its notable enhancements:

- The introduction of the GetBulk command. This provides an efficient method of retrieving data on a bulk basis from SNMP agents.
- The number of SNMP detectable errors has been extended to 17.
- The MIB structure has been rationalized, so that standard and private parameters can be identified within the MIB structure.
- The SNMP manager can be given different access rights to different parts of the MIB tree.
- SNMP Version 2 will work over NetWare IPX as well as over TCP/IP.

The OSI view of network management

There is a need to standardize how networks are managed. The International Organization for Standardization (ISO) has taken up this challenge by categorizing the functions of network management, as shown in Table 17.2.

CMIP OSI management protocol

The OSI has produced a special protocol called the CMIP (Common Management Information Protocol). It is far more sophisticated than SNMP. However, they both have the same goal, which is to provide the means by which a diverse collection of network hardware and software can be managed from a single point. Both use MIBs, which are kept by agents around the network. The big difference between the two lies in the complexity of protocols. SNMP is a far simpler approach. There are some fundamental philosophical differences: CMIP uses a reporting technique whereas SNMP uses polling techniques for data acquisition.

Most people recognize SNMP as the practical management protocol of today. CMIP is a protocol waiting in the wings ready to take over in the near future.

Most products are SNMP-compliant and few can use CMIP. For the time being, Novell is backing SNMP. The majority of its network management products use the SNMP protocol, for example LANalyzer and the NetWare Management System. However, Novell has set its sights on the future and indicates that full support for CMIP (OSI N/M) will be available when the end user needs it.

Table 17.2 Functions of network management.

Category	Function	Operation
Fault management	Detect, isolate and correct problems	Ensures network availability by, for example, sounding an alarm in the event of a network fault or device failure.
Performance management	Monitor performance data, such as response times and throughput	Enables LAN Administrator to identify problems (for instance, bottlenecks and areas of degradation) and spot trends, then optimize performance by making necessary adjustments before productivity is affected.
Configuration management	Display the network map	Enables LAN Administrator to check on the state of each device.
Accounting management	Monitor the usage of network resources	Enables LAN Administrator to track costs associated with the use of network devices.
Security management	Control access to network resources	Inhibits access to data that is sensitive and/or critical to the operation of the business.

NetWare management tools

The COMCHECK tool

COMCHECK is a simple program which allows the network manager to test communication between network stations. It is free with the NetWare operating system, so use it! It is on the DOS/ODI workstation service disk. You just need to run IPX or IPXODI followed by the COMCHECK program on each of the workstations being tested. The program asks the user for a unique name, used to advertise the station name to all the other stations. COMCHECK then shows a list of all the users it has located on the network (see Figure 17.4). It is as simple as that! The program shows the network and the node number of all the devices found.

Warning: Although Figure 17.4 shows a file server, COMCHECK cannot check communication on active servers. It can only check for communication between workstations. The server in this figure was powered down and turned into a normal workstation. The COMCHECK program was then run on it and it was given the manual name 'File Server'.

The network number is shown as 00000000 if no active file servers can be found. This number will have been assigned to your network segment through the NetWare file server(s) or NetWare router(s). If they are not up and running, then the workstation cannot know the correct figure and hence the zero is shown. Don't worry about this too much – the important thing is that the node address has come through.

Warning: The COMCHECK program does not check to see if the NETX or VLMs (Virtual Loadable Modules) are working correctly. They will not load up correctly unless the file server can be located; if they can, then you do not need to use COMCHECK anyway.

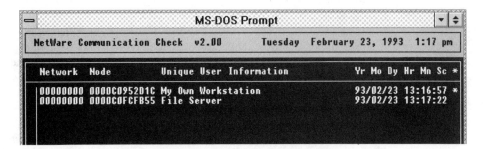

Figure 17.4 The COMCHECK program.

Management issues

This is one of those potentially invaluable tools for the network manager. When users report that the network is not working, it is usually very difficult to identify the specific point where the problem has occurred. Using this tool, you can check to see if the fundamental network communication lines between workstations and file server are working. This should help to isolate the problem(s), so that you can start to investigate the higher layers.

> Warning: It is important to point out that just because there is communication between two stations on the network does not mean that they are not suffering from massive error rates, or that the network is not massively congested. The COMCHECK program cannot inform you about these problems. To see what is really going on, use a product such as LANalyzer.

The great feature of COMCHECK is that it checks that different network adaptors from different manufacturers are talking to each other correctly. Most manufacturers of network adaptors provide their own diagnostic tools. However, they do not allow for interconnection to other types of adaptor. The COMCHECK program, since it uses IPX or IPXODI, can cope with a wide variety of different cards. It is ideal for testing individual network segments. It can also check if routers and bridges are working correctly.

Use the COMCHECK program to ensure newly-installed bridges and routers are working correctly: run COMCHECK on workstations on each side of the newly-installed device.

NetWare LANalyzer provides a more sophisticated approach to diagnosing the working of your LAN.

NetWare LANalyzer for Windows

This protocol-analysing product from Novell uses the concept of the network 'dashboard', which is just like a car dashboard (see Figure 17.5). It presents information about the network packet transfer (car speedometer), network utilization (car tachometer) and the network error rate (car engine temperature gauge). If the error rate is too high, as with the car's temperature, the network is in danger of 'blowing up'. The dashboard also shows what each workstation is doing. It shows each station's transmission, reception and any recorder errors.

One of the useful features of this product is that it automatically detects the names of all NetWare users and associates them with each physical workstation. In some products this has to be done manually.

Decoding packets

LANalyzer has an excellent packet decoding function, which can show a summary of packets. It can also do a detailed analysis of protocol packets and display themos raw hex data as they flow through the network (Figure 17.6).

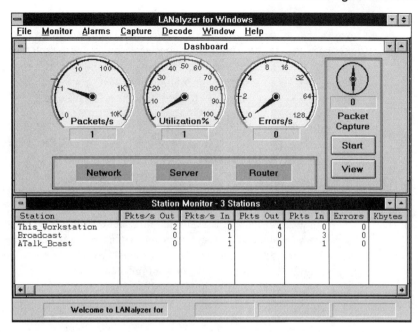

Figure 17.5 NetWare LANalyzer.

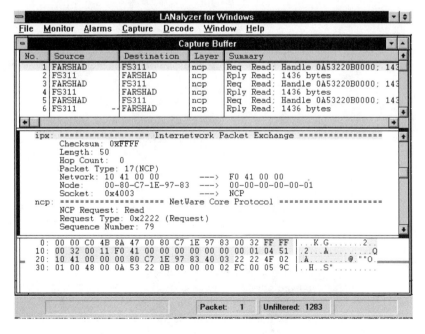

Figure 17.6 LANalyzer decoding packets.

Alerts and alarms

Alerts can be set up very easily. There are red lines around the gauges which report the alarm threshold. These can be redefined, but the defaults are sufficient for most cases. If the limits are reached, the network warning light turns red and the machine beeps. An alarm clock in the bottom left-hand corner of the window rings and a ticker tape next to it displays the type of alarm (see Figure 17.7).

Mapping the trends

At any time, LANalyzer can show its gathered statistics as a spreadsheet which can automatically be turned into a chart. This provides an easy way to review historical events and performance. You can instruct it to gather information for any period of time; every 15 minutes, it stores all its gathered data onto the disk for future reference.

In Figure 17.8, for example, the packet error rate hits very high rates on occasions. In this case, these errors all originated from the same workstation. Each time it attempted communication over the network, the network error rate increased. By changing the user network card, all problems were solved.

The advantages of using LANalyzer are:

✓ It is easy to use.
✓ It is excellent for troubleshooting Novell networks.
✓ It is excellent for identifying faulty network cards.
✓ It copes very well with Novell's own protocol.
✓ It is inexpensive.

The disadvantages are:

✗ It is limited at analysing protocols other then Novell, although TCP/IP is well supported.
✗ It is not good at analysing WANs.
✗ It cannot provide detailed data on NetWare server configurations.
✗ It does not carry out cable checking.

LANalyzer for Windows Version 2.x

LANalyzer Version 2.x is Novell's latest network analyser product. It includes a new product called the NetWare Expert, which is an intelligent trouble-shooting system which uses AI to analyse the network and make recommendations to the network manager about what could be going wrong. Version 2 also now supports Token Ring and decodes TCP/IP and AppleTalk traffic.

The NetWare Expert is unique to LANalyzer for Windows. It helps users to understand the complex information the product generates. It automatically discovers and diagnoses more than 20 common network problems and offers users suggestions on how to fix these problems. It includes an eight-hour animated computer-based

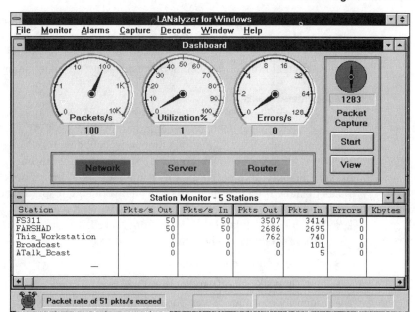

Figure 17.7 Alarm and ticker tape features.

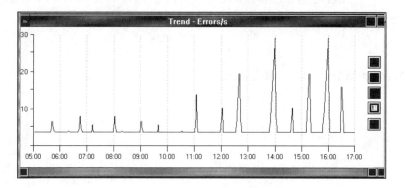

Figure 17.8 Trend-mapping chart.

training course on network analysis. Used as an adaptive learning tool, NetWare Expert quizzes users on their knowledge of Token Ring and Ethernet, identifies their strengths and trains them on their weaknesses. NetWare Expert is also a reference tool: users can select a topic, such as 'CRC errors', and NetWare Expert explains the event, lists its symptoms and causes, and suggests solutions.

The NetWare Expert also lets users obtain information about any specific network alarm by double-clicking on the appropriate entry in the event log. It lists symptoms associated with a particular alarm and offers suggestions on how to correct the problem.

With LANalyzer for Windows, you can execute a user-defined application when an alarm is generated. For example, in the event of a critical network error condition, such as an overloaded server, LANalyzer for Windows can trigger an application that notifies the technician responsible for maintaining that server.

Management issues

This is a very good product and not overly expensive. It is well worth having a protocol analyser available for troubleshooting purposes. It can pinpoint problems which might otherwise take a long time to isolate. Combined hardware and software packages are more expensive but are capable of receiving far greater rates of data packets. Frankly, in most cases, this is not an issue. The network manager normally wants to know if there is an error on the network and, if so, the cause. This is usually adequately achieved using the inexpensive software-only packages, such as LANWatch from FTP or LANalyzer from Novell.

These products can help the network manager to:

- Isolate a faulty network card
- Isolate peak network usage times
- Identify how much spare capacity there is in the network

If you are running TCP/IP and NetWare protocols on your network, I would recommend that you do not use LANalyzer. The FTP product LANWatch is more technical and does a better job of analysing TCP/IP packets. However, if you are a NetWare-only organization, you cannot beat Novell's own LANalyzer for price and performance value.

NetWare Management System

Overview

The NetWare Management System is Novell's Rolls-Royce solution to worldwide network management. It is a versatile and powerful set of products which provides a worldwide perspective of NetWare and SNMP-compliant devices. The programs can superimpose logical network data onto a geographic map of your worldwide networks. All these products are based on the NetWare Management Map (NMM). The NMM defines a set of fundamental management tools to which the user can add extension modules. The NetWare Management System is an open system environment. It allows third parties to develop extra tools which can also be managed from a centralized point using the same management tools, thanks to the NMM (NetWare Management Map) standard.

NetWare Management Map bus

Overview

The NetWare Management System is a relatively new platform defined by Novell, which allows users to physically monitor and manage multi-vendor networks. It is based on the NNM software platform, which can in effect be used to plug in a number of different management applications. These applications provide different management information about your network, but use the same facilities and services of the NMM to represent their data. The applications are currently: the NetWare services, LANtern service and hub services managers (see Figure 17.9).

- **NetWare services manager**. This first, and most sophisticated, module uses the Management Map platform to discover information about servers.

- **LANtern**. LANtern can be used to monitor network traffic. The next release of LANtern will use the NMM bus.

- **NetWare hub services**. This is another management product which uses the NMM. It is Novell's answer to intelligent hub management. It is ideal for organizations that use structured wiring and hubs that conform to Novell's HMI (Hub Management Interface) standard.

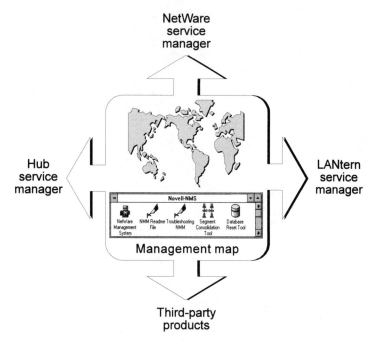

Figure 17.9 The NetWare Management System.

NetWare Management Map functions

The NMM comes as a universal software bus platform for all the other add-on, specialized Novell management tools. It provides the following fundamental tools and services for the other add-on modules to use:

- A standardized graphical user interface (Windows based)
- The ability to discover nodes on all networks
- The ability to display all the interlinked networks
- The ability to locate IPX and IP routers
- An alarm manager
- The ability to maintain and manage all objects discovered within the Btrieve database
- Support for SNMP over IPX and IP
- The ability to manage an SNMP MIB browser

How it works

To function correctly, the NMM needs to send out agents throughout its networks. These will gather up data which is then sent to the NMM monitoring station. Figure 17.10 shows the NetWare Management System monitor console.

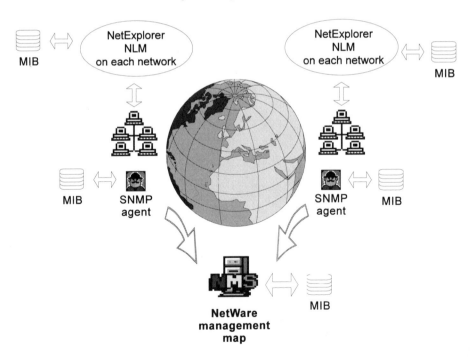

Figure 17.10 The NetWare Management System monitoring the network.

On each IPX or IP network, a special NLM program, NetExplorer, needs to be running. This will automatically discover other network devices on its network and store this information locally, ready to be sent on to the NetWare Management Map control station.

Another NLM option can be run on each file server on any given network. It is called the NetExplorer Plus NLM. This program gathers data about users' logging in names and types of network used, such as Ethernet or Token Ring.

When the NetWare management system is started it locates all its agents around the internetwork and instructs them to report on all the IPX and IP devices that they can see. They in turn pass the message on to any other agents that they can reach and the message ripples through the internetwork. All the reports are then redirected to the main management monitor. All this is largely executed by the NetExplorer NLM which resides on each network. On receiving the appropriate command from the monitoring console, NetExplorer investigates all the servers on its section and obtains their:

- Server information tables
- RIP tables
- Current connections ID

It also investigates all the routers to obtain a list of all nodes on the network, their interface cards and IPX addresses. It requests additional information concerning the network from any NetExplorer Plus NLM files. The program reports all this information back to the management monitoring station. The management station can use this information to draw a logical Internet map.

Management monitored information

The gathered data is shown in a very user-friendly manner. At the highest level is an Internet map showing all the networks worldwide. Figure 17.11 shows a discovered network with the number # 00000019.

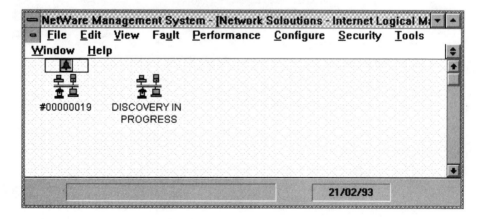

Figure 17.11 Internet map of the NMS.

Networks are shown logically linked up to each other. At each point you can gain detailed information about a given network by double clicking with the mouse. Figure 17.12 shows the sort of information given.

Finding items around the world

One of the product's most powerful features is its worldwide object Find facility (see Figure 17.13). It can help to locate a particular device in a large network anywhere on the Internet. You can look for a host of different devices, such as file and print servers, IPX routers, users' IDs, node addresses and IPX and IP addresses. The program will locate the item you specify and then display it as a flashing object on the graphical map of the network.

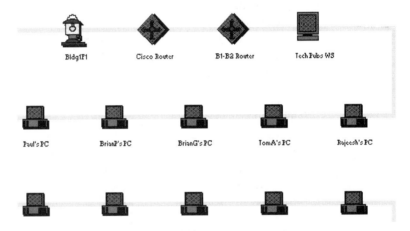

Figure 17.12 Sample network information.

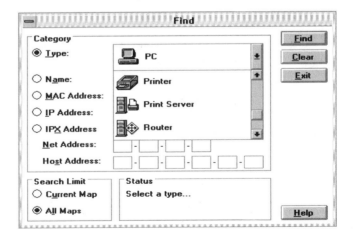

Figure 17.13 The Find facility.

Physical maps

Physical hierarchical maps can be constructed to which the network manager can associate each of the devices or network location (see Figure 17.14). This means you can really 'see' your interlinked network in action.

With each map you can do the following:

- **Create new maps**. Each map can have geographical images as a background, on which you can place objects such as countries, regions, cities, buildings, floors and physical location within offices.

- **Interlink location maps**. Through a location icon, each map can trigger another location map which might show the relevant region in greater detail (see Figure 17.15, for example).

- **Link location maps to logical network devices**. This is where the package's greatest strength lies. Each logical network device, as defined by the network segment diagram, can be linked into a location map. This could then place the object in a particular office, floor, building or a special region on the map. The organization of these is left up to user. It is very important that you organize your maps in a logical manner.

See the section 'Map design' under 'Management issues' later in this chapter for further discussion.

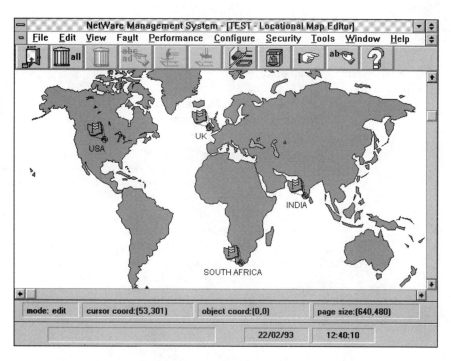

Figure 17.14 Locational map editor.

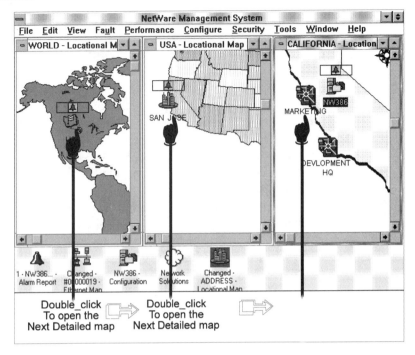

Figure 17.15 Increasing levels of map detail.

Alarm management

The NetWare Management Map system has a series of alarm-handling facilities (see Figure 17.16). Each agent in the network has a list of conditions that will cause them to send information about the potential problem up to the monitoring management station. The user is then presented with a graphical indication as to which device caused the alarm, its nature and the degree of severity. This is all kept in an alarm database which can be analysed at a later date. The alarm can be from NetExplorer or SNMP agents. This information is extremely useful to the network manager.

The alarm management facility alone justifies purchasing this product. It is excellent for troubleshooting. An audit trail of all reported alarms is kept (see Figure 17.17). Each one can be checked off once sorted out or simply ignored. The report shows what type of alarm was triggered, the severity of the error, its location and whether any other manager has made a previous note about the error.

Alarms fall into one of the following categories:

(1) Generic SNMP alarms (MIB I & II)

(2) LANtern alarms

(3) NetExplorer alarms

(4) NetWare server alarms

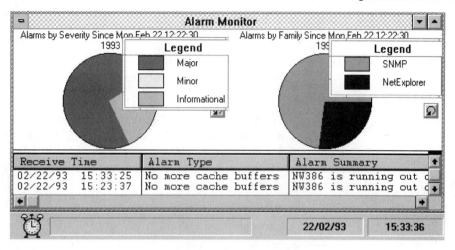

Figure 17.16 The alarm monitor.

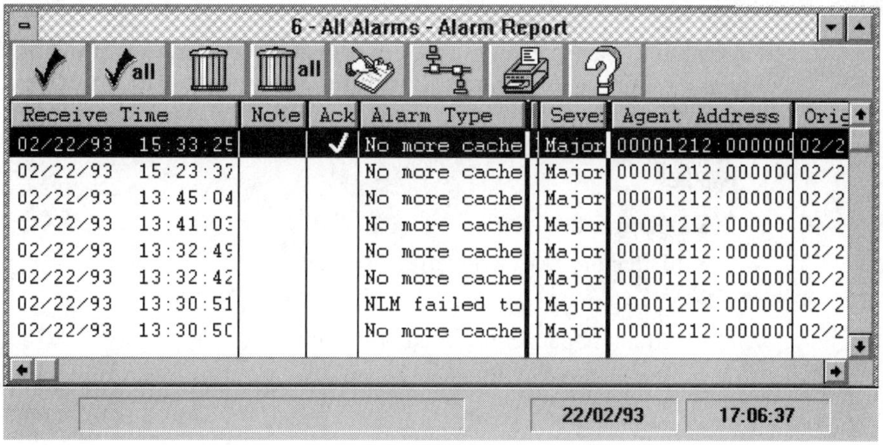

Figure 17.17 Alarm report.

Generic SNMP alarms (MIB I & II) consist of the following SNMP-defined errors:

- Cold and warm starts
- Neighbour lost
- Link down and link up (again)

LANtern alarms cover errors are normally connected with the performance of a given network segment. You need to have installed the LANtern module in the appropriate segment. The following conditions trigger off the alarms in the management monitoring stations:

- Broadcast errors
- Cable test failures
- Packet collisions threshold crossed
- Network adaptor address card duplicated
- Station active or lost connections

NetExplorer Alarms are fundamental alarms intrinsic to the NetWare Management Map system. They are sent out by the NetExplorer; they cover a large list of conditions mostly in connection with establishing links and identifying components that are then reported back to the master monitoring station. Examples of such conditions are:

- NetExplorer connection or disconnect
- Network address changed, deleted or added
- Found new world, routes, network segments, servers or workstations
- Modify information on routers, segments, servers or workstations

You need to install the NetWare Service Manager on the given server to fully activate the **NetWare server alarms** option. A very comprehensive list of conditions can then automatically trigger a NetWare server alarm. The majority of these conditions are critical. It is therefore essential that corrective action is taken as quickly as possible. Alarms provide the network manager with an excellent set of data from which he or she can troubleshoot any reported errors. These conditions can be:

- Copyright violation
- Directory read/write errors
- Disk out of space
- Memory cache threshold problems
- LAN card and driver-related errors
- Low memory errors
- NLM loading problems
- Server going down or coming up
- Volume dismounting, almost full and totally full errors

SNMP MIB browser

The NMS product comes with a tool for monitoring the MIBs of SNMP devices (see Figure 17.18). It can be very useful for manually requesting management information from SNMP agents sitting on devices. The SNMP Browser tool allows the network manager to implement any *ad hoc* investigation of SNMP devices. However, to use this tool, you must be familiar with the underlying concept of SNMP. It is not a tool for the uninitiated.

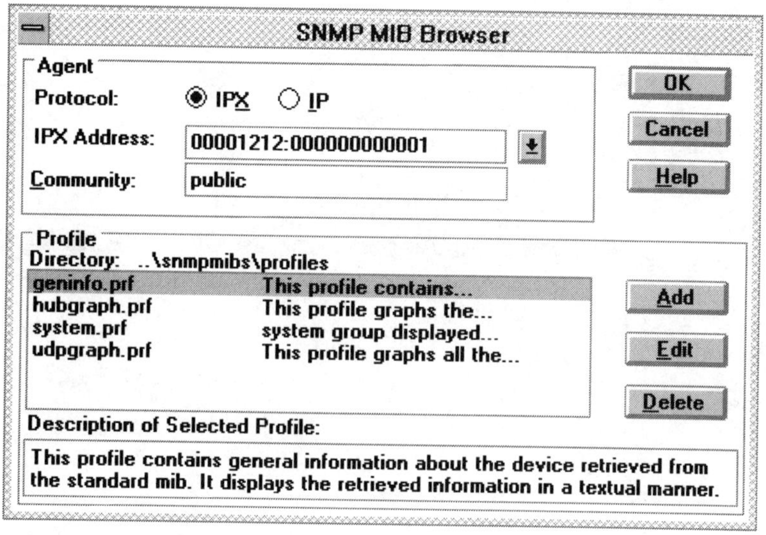

Figure 17.18 The SNMP MIB Browser.

See the section 'SNMP network management' in this chapter for further details.

You can issue the SNMP GET command with the SNMP Browser and specify which SNMP device you wish to get information from. It is also possible to issue an SNMP SET command to change the information gathered from the device. Of course you must have the correct security password before you can access the SNMP device. The tool can then be configured, through a profile, to send out requests for updates at specified intervals.

Once a connection is accepted by a host SNMP device, you can issue the SNMP GET command. It is very easy and fun to use! You simply select the information to be updated, then point to the green traffic light on the left-hand side, which then turns red. This means the SNMP command has been sent out and the Browser is waiting for a response. Once the response arrives, the information is updated and the traffic lights turn back to green. At any given time, it is possible to change the SNMP community name by selecting the lock and key icon. Once a new community identifier has been entered it is possible to access a new set of data. Figure 17.9 shows SNMP objects and their associated parameters, which were sent by SNMP agents.

This is very good tool if you want to get some hands-on training in understanding SNMP. It is well worth sitting down and playing around with this tool if you are learning SNMP. You should try to send out the SNMP GET command, and see what happens if you put the wrong community names in the SNMP commands.

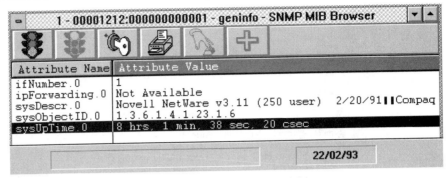

Figure 17.19 Monitoring SNMP agents.

NetWare Service Manager

Overview

The NetWare Service Manager uses the Management Map platform to discover information about servers around the worldwide network. It can dynamically report what is happening inside the NetWare servers and provides comprehensive and dynamic updating information on such things as: CPU utilization, NLMs, RAM utilization, disk performance and print queues.

Due to the NMM bus, it can report worldwide on any configured server. The product comes in two parts: the NMM (Network Management Map) and the actual NSM (NetWare Service Manager) package. As described earlier, the NMM provides the common software platform. The product integrates into the NMM system. If you double click on a NetWare server icon, a more detailed window is opened up showing the internal configuration of the server (see Figure 17.20, for example).

Features of the NSM

The NSM provides the following monitoring and management functions:

- NetWare server configuration
- Dynamic information on changes within the NetWare servers
- NetWare server alarms
- Access to RCONSOLE
- Password protection for server information

The wonderful aspect of this product is its ability to monitor the configuration of the server as it dynamically configures. There is normally a few seconds' delay before the information is updated. This is the time taken for the configuration information to get from the source to the management monitoring station. Figure 17.21 shows the type of window that can be opened to monitor server performance.

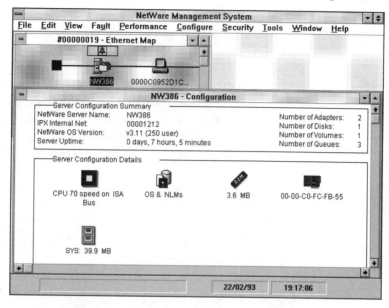

Figure 17.20 The NetWare Management System configuration window.

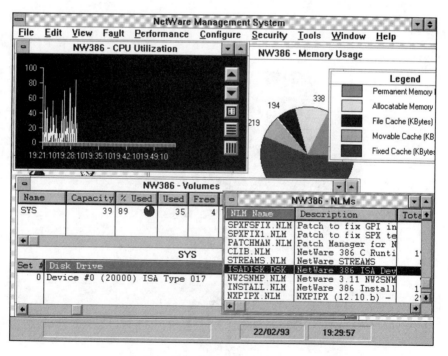

Figure 17.21 Monitoring server performance.

It is important to make the point that, while you watch, the data is being updated. This means that while you have these screens open there are a large number of investigative data packets travelling across the network. This can cause a lot of traffic, especially if the server you are investigating is many routers away.

As a general rule, the further away the server under investigation is from you, the greater the cost in terms of its communication price and the potential increase in overall network traffic. On an average network under investigation, up to 20–30% of its bandwidth can be used up by the management tools.

Gauges in action

The are a number of different gauges which allow the manager to see the information coming back from the server (see Figure 17.22). They provide information on a variety of different aspects of the server configuration, such as:

- The performance of file reading and writing
- Memory utilization
- Files currently opened
- File caching performance
- Packet buffering efficiency

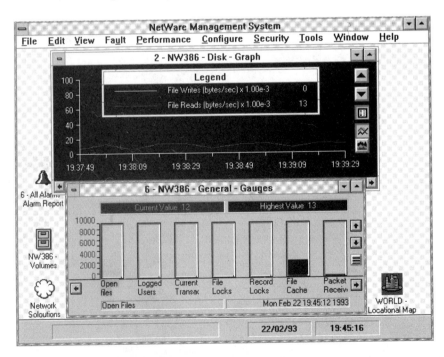

Figure 17.22 NetWare Management System gauges.

Some of these gauges can be used to set up alarms. You define the point at which an alarm should be triggered and logged into the database. This can be very useful. There are default levels, but they can be fine tuned to meet your own specific requirements.

Management issues

The NMS (NetWare Management System) is one of the cornerstones of the enhanced NetWare 4 design. To a large extent, the functions of the NMS are incorporated in the philosophy of NetWare 4. The NMS components are sold as extra modules, which enhance NetWare 4.x. I foresee the function of the NetWare Management Map system being incorporated into the next release of NetWare 4.x as standard. The user will then only need to buy the extra modules as required.

It is well worth upgrading to NetWare 4.x if you are serious about using and installing the NMS to manage your organization. It is a far superior platform for this kind of product than NetWare 3.11, especially if you want to manage a network that supports multiple file servers.

NetWare 4.x and NMM integration

It is very important to design your maps logically. This problem is very similar to designing the directory object structure within NetWare 4.x. I strongly recommend that the two structures should reflect each other as closely as possible: one should reflect the logical structure of your organization, the other the geographic layout. It is natural that the NetWare 4.x directory structure will be broken down into different sub-departments as defined by their function, whereas the NMM will be geographically based. The NMS will then be able to link the objects from the NetWare 4 directory directly onto the geographical maps of the NMM system.

See the section 'NDS tree management issues' in Chapter 18.

Map design

The outline structure of your map is going to be critical. Take your time and draw out the basic structure on paper. Think about the scope of your structure – will it allow for future expansion? The secret of designing an efficient interlinked map structure lies in ensuring that it reflects your organization's scope and breadth. At the highest point, you should have a map showing the name of your organization and its interests worldwide. Each country or organization sub-division should be shown on this map; this is the top-level map. It is essential that you get this right. Each division or country should lead to a sub-map illustrating its details. It can then be sub-divided, which in turn opens a more detailed map and a further series of sub-units, and so on.

When running on the file server, NetExplorer has a habit of constantly accessing the hard disk. I have found that you can temporarily stop this service and the disk access by unloading SIDEWIND.NLM. To activate the service, reload it.

Figure 17.23 shows a typical corporation's hierarchical tree structure. The KGB map is at the highest level showing the organization's interests in each country. Each is sub-divided in greater detail to create a 'tree' map structure of all the devices (or agents in this case) that belong to this organization. Each location is then linked to a more detailed map. At the bottom of the tree are the agents or, in NetWare 4 terminology, leaf objects. These can be such things as users, workstations, servers or routers.

A typical address within the interlinked series of maps could be constructed as follows: BUCKINGHAM PALACE.ST JAMES.LONDON.BRITAIN and so on. At the end will be a logical device. In the example in Figure 17.24, it is a file server. In NetWare 4.x, this is called the leaf object.

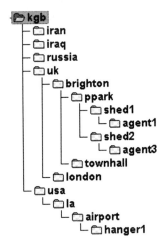

Figure 17.23 A hierarchical tree structure.

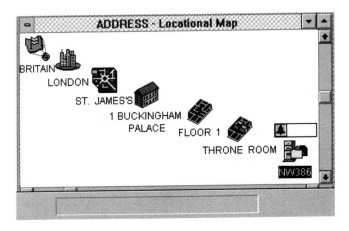

Figure 17.24 A typical address.

SNMP and NetWare

Overview

Novell has recognized the importance of SNMP in management network devices. They have chosen to support the SNMP standard in their servers. The Novell Network Management System is compatible with the SNMP system.

SNMP on the NetWare server

Novell issues a number of NLM programs as standard with the NetWare 386 and NetWare 4.x systems. They allow the server to act as an SNMP agent. The modules are:

- **SNMP.NLM**: this is the main module that turns the server into an SNMP agent (see Figure 17.25).
- **SNMPLOG.NLM**: this program works in conjunction with the SNMP.NLM and works on top of the TCP/IP protocol stacks. You must have the TCPIP.NLM program loaded. SNMPLOG will log the trapped information into the local MIB. This information can then be sent to the authorized management monitoring station.

In the old NetWare 386 3.11 system, it was common to run the SNMP.NLM on the TCP/IP stack. This meant that the TCPIP.NLM module was needed and loaded automatically, whether you wanted it or not! The current development (thanks to NetWare 4.x) allows SNMP to run over the IPX packet, without the need for TCP/IP packets. The user is then given the choice of sending SNMP packets over TCP/IP or IPX networks.

SNMP on workstations

In another new development from Novell, the workstation shells can also now become SNMP agents (see Figure 17.26). It is possible to load up an SNMP VLM with the new workstation shells that come with NetWare 4.x. Novell has replaced the concept of NETX and BNETX with VLMs. One of these modules is the SNMP agent support. It is loaded as TSR, as part of the normal network booting up sequence.

Loading SNMP.NLM
The basic structure of the SNMP.NLM is:

```
LOAD SNMP <SNMP options>
```

Figure 17.25 SNMP on a NetWare file server.

Figure 17.26 SNMP on a NetWare workstation.

Where the <SNMP options> are:

- MONITORCOMMUNITY [=< secret name>]
- CONTROLCOMMUNITY [=< secret name>]
- TRAPCOMMUNITY [=< secret name>]

Be very careful when you change these names from the default ('public'). You must make sure that they match up exactly on both sides. In other words, the agent and the monitor station must use exactly the same name.

On loading up the SNMP command, you can define a specific name for each community. This is predominately used for security reasons. The system uses this name to authenticate any incoming request from SNMP managers. They all default to the name 'public'.

These names are just a simple ASCII string of up to 32 characters. The name must be matched by the other side before any data is released by the local SNMP agent. Otherwise, the request is ignored and a record of a potential intruder is made.

There are three basic kinds of community:

(1) **Monitor community**. This group controls the requests that have read-only access to the MIB. This option is normally open to public investigation. However, to close this potential security loop-hole, both sides must agree on a new name. The default name is 'public'.

(2) **Control community**. This controls high-level access rights. It allows the user of this name to either read or alter the MIB variables. The default name is 'public'.

(3) **Trap community**. This name is sent out by the SNMP agent to the manager station as it sends out its trapped information. If this option is disabled, no

trapped SNMP information is sent out. This can be useful if you are getting bombarded with repetitive SNMP trapped information. The default name is 'public'.

The SNMP.NLM program is normally loaded from the server console prompt line or as part of the AUTOEXEC.NCF file. Here are a few examples:

- `LOAD SNMP`. This will activate all three communities and assign the name 'public' to each (not very secure).
- `LOAD SNMP ControlCommunity= CIA_BOYS`. This will only activate the Control community if the name CIA_BOYS is used.
- `LOAD SNMP TrapCommunity`. If written on its own, a name of a community is disabled. In this case, no SNMP traps will be sent out.

If your network is open to access from the outside you must ensure that you have a unique community name that will keep outsiders from accessing you SNMP MIBs. Do not leave it on the default 'public' name.

Loading SNMPLOG.NLM

This program traps the SNMP.NLM messages and stores them on the local disk. To use this module under the old NetWare 3.11 system, you must load the TCPIP.NLM first. It will only work on IP networks. The information is written to a binary file called SYS:ETC\SNMP$LOG.BIN.

Warning: Do not remove this file. Be very careful when you restore this file from a backup. It might destroy any up-to-date SNMP messages that may have been created since the last backup.

18

NetWare 4.0

Overview

NetWare 4.0 is based on NetWare 3.11 code, with some major enhancements. It was largely designed to meet the demands of the modern-day network manager, that is, to integrate networks but still be able to manage them from a single point. This has led to the most significant new development in NetWare 4.0 – the 'Directory Services' – which is set to completely change NetWare network management at the organizational level. When it comes to the fine detail of giving rights to users or groups, the concepts are significantly enhanced in comparison to NetWare 3.11.

Novell states that NetWare 4.0 is ideal for large to very large networks. It claims that the market for NetWare 3.11 will be unaffected by NetWare 4.0 developments. This could certainly be true in the short term if NetWare 4.0 only had the Directory Services to offer. However, NetWare 4.0 has many other enhancements such as disk compression, CD-ROM support, enhanced console commands, improved print servers and better Windows utilities. It seems that NetWare 4.0 is destined to become the main 'flag ship' product which will take Novell into the mid-1990s and beyond!

NetWare 4.0 is being made available at different levels, from the five-user version upwards. This means that, although Novell sees this product as being aimed at the large corporate market, it also targets the small and medium user networks.

What is new in NetWare 4.01

Most NetWare 4.0 bugs fixed
The most notable enhancement of NetWare 4.01 is that it corrects the multitude of

reported bugs that appeared in the original version of NetWare 4.0. Several hundred bugs of varying severity were reported. For example, in NetWare 4.0 when you tried to scan the NDS to find out an object's rights to other objects the system failed to work correctly. Novell now markets NetWare 4.01 as a solid, reliable platform, which makes you wonder what sort of platform previous versions of NetWare 4 were based on.

> Warning: Some of the improvements made to the NDS tree in NetWare 4.01 make it incompatible with the old NDS tree of NetWare 4.0. Novell is now recommending that all NetWare 4.0 users should upgrade their NDS tree to the NetWare 4.01 structure. They should not use the old NDS tree on top of the new NetWare 4.01 operating system.

Multi-language support

NetWare 4.01 CD now supports five different languages as standard: English, German, French, Italian and Spanish. In the old version of NetWare 4.0 only English was available as standard.

Improved VLM DOS/workstation environment

With release NetWare 4.01 Novell has updated the DO/Windows NetWare drivers. Improved version of Virtual Loadable Modules (VLMs) are now available.

Macintosh support

With NetWare 4.01, Macintosh users can now login to the NetWare server and use it as if it were a Macintosh file server.

Improved OS/2 support

In NetWare 4.01 you now get as standard a new powerful graphical utility for the OS/2 presentation manager. This is comparable to the NWADMIN program in Microsoft Windows.

NetWare 4.0 objectives

NetWare 4.0 was designed to achieve a number of objectives. The most important was to provide a set of solutions which would tempt the very large user base of existing NetWare 3.11 and NetWare 2.2 users to upgrade. Novell had to ensure that their massive user base was not alienated by this new product. The major NetWare 4.0 objectives were to:

- Provide a solution to multi-network management using Directory Services
- Consolidate the large number of NetWare programs into a few user-friendly tools (mostly Windows based)
- Provide an easy upgrade path for NetWare 3.x and NetWare 2.x servers

- Provide a network management platform
- Enhance network security services, such as auditing of files and directories
- Provide imaging services
- Provide data compression services
- Provide a new media manager
- Internationalize NetWare
- Provide NetWare 4.0 services at a competitive price (in relation to Banyan Vines and LAN Manager)

NetWare 3.11 versus NetWare 4.0 performance

A simple test was carried out on NetWare 3.11 and NetWare 4.0 file servers. The same file server hardware was used for both servers. Using a 10BaseT Ethernet network, tests were carried out with one, four and eight users. All the server's normal default SET parameters were selected. Each user requested a 100Kbyte data file from the server. The time taken to retrieve the file was recorded in seconds. The longer the time, they slower the performance of the server.

It can be seen from the results shown in Figure 18.1 that, for a small number of workstations, NetWare 3.11 seems to be more efficient. However, as the workload on the server increases, the NetWare 4.0 server begins to significantly outperform NetWare 3.11.

Note that each user in this test represents at least five normal users.

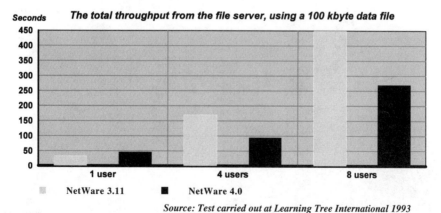

Source: Test carried out at Learning Tree International 1993

Figure 18.1 NetWare 3.11 versus NetWare 4.0 performance.

NetWare 4.0 Directory Services

Overview

NetWare Directory Services is one of the most significant new developments within the NetWare 4.0 system. The NetWare 4.0 directory system is based on the CCITT X.500 directory naming convention, with a few minor alterations.

See the section 'X.500 Directory Services' in this chapter for further information.

Basically, Novell implemented the X.500 standard in a way that made it more appropriate for NetWare networks. The old concept of bindery objects being specific to a NetWare file server is a thing of the past. Bindery objects are now logical and are stored on a distributed basis across file servers (see Figure 18.2). Objects are seen as belonging to a worldwide network, rather than to a file server. Banyan Vine's network has had this concept for years, due to its StreetTalk convention. Novell can now offer a similar facility. Its implementation is truly distributed and, best of all, is not based on any proprietary naming standard.

The NDS (NetWare Directory Services) tree provides a single logical database which users on any network can login to. It is no longer necessary to login to your nearest file server and then ATTACH yourself to other file servers. It is also no

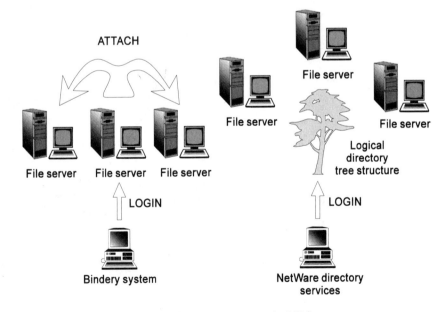

Figure 18.2 The old bindery system versus the NDS tree system.

longer necessary for the network manager to go through the tedious exercise of creating a user account on each of the file servers to be used. The network manager can now create a single account in the NDS tree, which is seen throughout the whole global network – this is regardless of which workstation the user decides to login from.

Objects: logical name and physical locations

Since all resources are contained within the single logical database, everything is given a logical name based on X.500. This is one of the great advantages of the NDS tree. This level of indirection gives the system tremendous flexibility and means that users can login to the NetWare Directory Service and use its resources without worrying about the resource location. Resources are given a logical name which the users map onto. The network manager then maps the object onto a physical location (see Figure 18.3).

Let's assume that a user is given access rights to a directory logically referred to as HQ_DATA. This data object happens to be on file server A in the SYS:\DATA directory. The user does not need to know which actual file server stores the HQ_DATA directory. The user simply uses the resources of the HQ_DATA object as if it were a normal directory. The network manager will need to have decided where to physically locate the HQ_DATA (which, in this case, happens to be on file server A). On the following day, the network manager decides to move the directory SYS:\DATA to the new file server B. A new directory called SYS:\DATA needs to be created on the new file server. Then all the data is copied from file server A SYS:\DATA to file server B, and HQ_DATA is redefined as being on file server B.

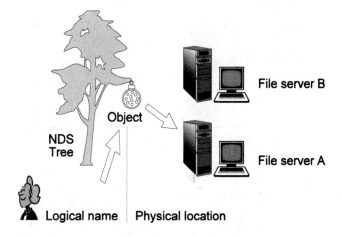

Figure 18.3 Mapping logical names to physical locations.

The great advantage of this approach is that, because the user only refers to the logical name HQ_DATA, the change is completely transparent to him or her. No changes to the user's script files or MAP commands are necessary. This is different to the old NetWare 3.11 and 2.2 systems, where any references by users to directories or files had to be made in relation to an actual file server.

Bindery structure versus new NDS tree structure

The NDS defines objects just like the old bindery system. Each object has a collection of information associated with it, referred to as its 'properties'. Each property of a given object may have a set of values. It is a very similar concept to the one used in the old bindery systems.

In NetWare 3.11, the file server keeps the bindery database to store all information regarding network objects and resources available to the server, such as users, groups of users and print servers. Under the SYS:\SYSTEM directory, three files are used to store the system bindery files (see Table 18.1).

The main difference between the old NetWare 3.11 bindery and the NDS system is that objects are now stored on a global network basis, organized on a hierarchical basis. This is in contrast to the old system which stores its objects on an individual file server basis, using a flat logical tree structure. Generally speaking, the new objects of NetWare 4.0 have a far richer set of properties and values associated with them. This is mainly due to the way that they are stored in the hierarchical NDS tree structure.

Table 18.2 gives a summary of the differences between the two systems.

Table 18.1 NetWare 3.11 bindery system files.

Bindery file name	Function
NET$OBJ.SYS	Store the identifier of each object
NET$PROP.SYS	Store the property for each object as defined by the NET$OBJ.SYS file
NET$VAL.SYS	Store the parameter values for each property defined in NET$PROP.SYS

Table 18.2 Differences between the NetWare 3.11 bindery and the NDS system.

Object/resource	NDS tree structure	Old bindery system
Structure	Hierarchical	Flat
Define users and groups	Global to the NDS tree	On a file server basis
Bindery replicator service	Yes	N/A
Volumes/directories/files	Global to the NDS tree	On a file server basis
Login	System-wide login using a single password	On a file server basis
Physical location	Distributed across the network	On a single file server

Hierarchical directory structure

The Novell directory structure introduces some new terms and concepts in its organizational style (see Figure 18.4). It is a derivation of the X.500 standard and uses a number of borrowed terms.

The terms used in the NetWare Directory Services are described below.

> Warning: Make sure you memorize these terms and that you are very clear of their meanings. They are essential to the understanding of NetWare 4.0.

Root
At the lowest level is the root. There is only one root name and that is at the most fundamental base of the NDS tree. All objects are ultimately referenced to this root name, which is normally the global name of your organization.

O (Organization) name
In NetWare 4.0, the root is normally defined using the organization's name. This is referred to as the O code. Each organization can be further sub-divided into a number of organization units. Examples of O code names might be O=IBM or O=Novell. These are good examples of O code names, as they were chosen to be the global names of those respective companies. If, for example, IBM and Novell ever decide to join forces they might also join their respective NDS trees at the organization level, creating a new NDS tree. Its new root might then be called IBM_And_Friends or even Novell_And_Friends (who knows!).

The organization name is defined by the network manager when the system is installed. Unlike the X.500 standard in NetWare 4.0, the country code is normally missed out and the root is defined at organization level.

See the section 'X.500 directory standard' for a comparison.

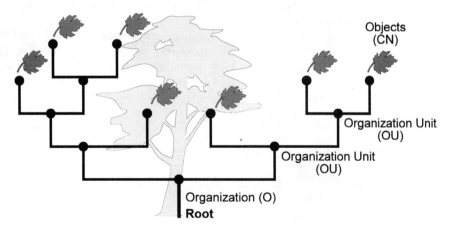

Figure 18.4 NDS terminology.

> Warning: Be careful: within the X.500 tree structure, between the root and the organization items, is the country name. This means that each organization must be qualified by stating which country it belongs to. Novell recommend that you do not use it because it makes the object naming convention unnecessarily complicated. However, it can still be used, but you should use the typeless naming capabilities, as described under 'Typeless and typefull naming conventions', later in this chapter.

OU (Organization Unit)

Each organization is normally divided into a number of distinct activities. These are then defined by the OU (Organizational Unit) names, for example, OU=Marketing, OU=Developments or OU=Staff. Within NetWare 4.0, this is a very important sub-division. Each OU can be further sub-divided into sub-organizational units, and so on. The name given to each OU is defined by the network manager. The structure of the tree should reflect your organization's activities.

Leaf objects

At the end of each branch there is normally a leaf object. There are many different types of leaf object, for example, volumes, print servers, groups of users or print queues. The leaf object is to NetWare 4.0 what bindery objects were to the old NetWare 3.11 system. Ultimately, users can only manipulate and use the resources provided by the leaf objects. The NDS tree contains the leaf objects in a hierarchical manner. Each leaf object will have a name, type and a series of values associated with it. In NetWare 4.0, leaf objects have a CN (Common Name) code. Examples of names for leaf objects are shown in Table 18.3.

Container and leaf objects

The NDS tree structure has two different types of object: container objects and leaf objects. A container object is either a parent of a leaf object or a container for other container objects held as its siblings (see Figure 18.5).

This means that any objects defined at the organization and the organization unit level are all described as container objects. This is because they are used to contain other objects, which are ultimately used to store the leaf objects. As described earlier, the leaf object normally represents some form of network resource.

Figure 18.6 shows the variety of objects that can be created under the NetWare 4.0 NDS tree.

Table 18.3 Example leaf object names.

Leaf object type	CN (Common Name)
User	Boris
User	Harry
Volume	DATA
Print server	Lasers

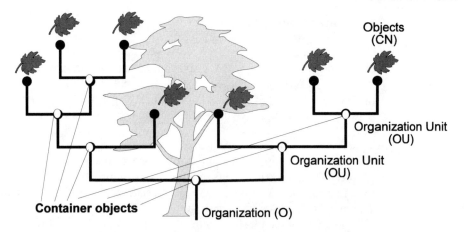

Figure 18.5 Container objects.

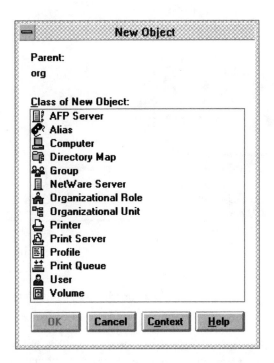

Figure 18.6 Objects that can be created under the NetWare 4.0 NDS tree.

The NDS naming convention

The naming convention in NetWare is very simple: you always start from the leaf object and work your way to the root. In the example in Figure 18.7, Agent Boris is defined as: CN=Boris.OU=Agents.OU=External.O=KGB. The last name is always the root which, in this case, is the root name. The first name is the leaf object. In between the two, you have the names of all the connecting organization units.

Typeless and typefull naming conventions

Novell NetWare 4.0 has a number of concepts making referral to leaf objects far simpler. The first is the typeless naming convention; this means that you do not need to define the O or OU codes; the appropriate code will be automatically assumed. This means that Boris can now be referred to in two ways, using either the full typefull name or the typeless method. Table 18.4 shows the difference.

The typeless naming convention is the most commonly used in NetWare 4.0, but it is worth noting that you can also use the typefull naming convention, if you so wish. In fact it is possible to mix the two conventions.

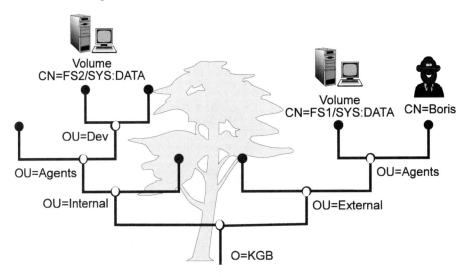

Figure 18.7 The NDS naming convention.

Table 18.4 The difference between typeless and typefull naming conventions.

Naming method	Name used
Typefull naming	CN=Boris.OU=Agents.OU=External.O=KGB
Typeless naming	Boris.Agents.External.KGB

Name contexts

Another extremely powerful function which makes referring to objects far easier is the name context parameter. Users at the workstation can set up their own naming context. This is then used by taking any object name the user provides and placing it at the end of the context name, to give the full address of the object. This means that the naming context can save the user a lot of unnecessary typing. For example, if you set up your:

```
Name Context = "External.KGB"
```

then the user can refer to Boris the KGB agent as simply:

```
Boris.Agents
```

The operating system will automatically look up the user naming context and append that to the name supplied by the user:

```
Boris.Agents.External.KGB
```

This gives the full correct name of the user within the NDS tree structure. The setting up of the name context parameter is especially useful if you only intend to work in one subsection of the NDS tree. You no longer need to constantly refer to the full name.

You set up your name context within the NET.CFG file. The format is shown in Figure 18.8.

Alias name entries

To make life simple, it is possible to create a leaf object which actually refers to an object somewhere else. In the example in Figure 18.9 (assuming you have your name context set to Agents.Internal.KGB), to send a message to Boris you just send it to the local leaf object Boris. This will then forward the information to the real Boris at Boris.Agents.External.KGB. The use of alias names can be very powerful. You can place all the objects that you commonly use from other branches of the NDS tree structure within your own scope.

> Warning: Be careful if you create a server alias object. On the original Beta version of NetWare 4.0, if you deleted this object, it would delete the server from the NDS. This bug has been fixed in NetWare 4.01.

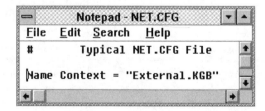

Figure 18.8 Setting up a name context within the NET.CFG file.

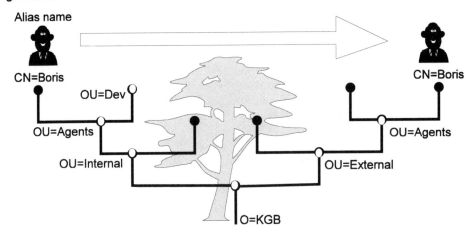

Figure 18.9 Alias name.

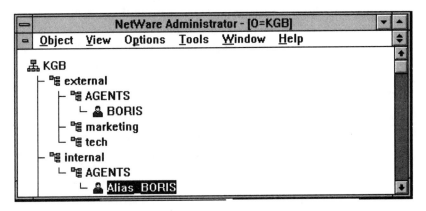

Figure 18.10 Using the alias object within NDS.

Moving leaf objects

Leaf objects can be moved from one section of the tree to another. This gives tremendous flexibility. Resources can be moved around the tree structure to reflect any network changes. When a leaf object is moved to a new place, any rights given to it over its previous local resources are lost. It will have new rights inherited from its new parents, depending upon where it is moved to.

Warning: Within NetWare 4.0, you cannot prune and graft whole branches of the NDS tree. You can only work at the object leaf level. However, it is assumed that this restriction will be removed in the next release of NetWare.

Searching through the NDS tree

The NDS tree structure can become very complicated, so NetWare 4.0 provides some excellent searching facilities. You can instruct the system to search for a given resource, such as users or printers. You can even state that you are looking for a specific type of resource. It will then start from the root of the NDS tree and travel through all its branches until it finds your specified objects. It will list their locations within the tree. In the example in Figure 18.11, a search is being requested for all user names, starting from the root of the organization and searching through the NDS tree.

Physical and security aspects of NDS

There are a number of new aspects to the NDS, as shown in Figure 18.12.

The NetWare 4.0 directory is defined as a logical tree structure, which contains all the resources of the network. The main aspects of the tree structure are concerned with how the NDS references, creates and manages each of its objects within this all-powerful logical tree. There are, however, a number of other issues.

Physical location of the NDS tree

A number of new concepts have been introduced regarding how NDS is physically organized and distributed around the network. The three most important concepts are:

(1) Partitioning. An NDS tree can be split up into sub-branches and stored on different file servers.

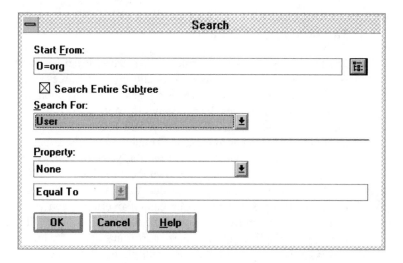

Figure 18.11 The Search facility.

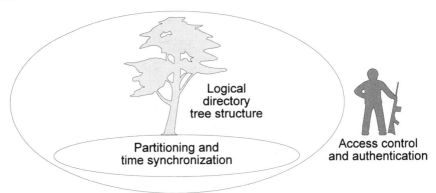

Logical
directory
tree structure

Access control
and authentication

Partitioning and
time synchronization

Figure 18.12 Aspects of NDS (NetWare Directory Services).

(2) Replications. Any NDS sub-branch can be replicated onto another device, which can be another file server, as a form of backup.

(3) Time synchronization. It is essential that the whole network has a universal master clock which can be used to synchronize the NDS activities.

Security aspects of the NDS tree

A new set of security access rights has been introduced which controls who can manage the NDS tree. This is in addition to the normal rights found in NetWare 3.x. Yet another new security concept is the new authentication process. This will ensure that each user is authenticated to the server and that their dialogue cannot be interfered with by an intruder without detection.

Partitioning the NDS tree

The NDS tree is a logical single tree structure. It defines within its branches all the resources available from its servers and other resources. However, where the NDS tree is actually going to be stored is a practical consideration. In reality, the NDS tree is stored on the file server. It is possible to split the NDS tree into partitions and keep each partition on a different file server (see Figure 18.13). In this case, the file servers must talk to each other to present a single logical tree structure to the user. There is a special directory service protocol within NetWare 4.0 which enables file severs to talk to each other and keep their own local section of the NDS tree updated.

The network manager can decide how the NDS tree is to be divided. It is important to note that partitions cannot overlap. Each partition stores a different section of the NDS tree. It is possible to store the whole NDS in one partition on a file server or split it up into many partitions, each of which can be stored on other servers. It is also possible to store multiple partitions on a single server. The way the NDS tree is partitioned and stored across the network is completely transparent to

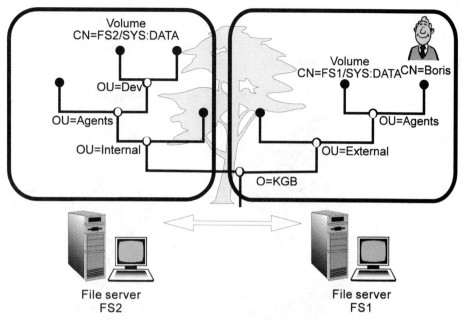

Figure 18.13 Partitioning the NDS tree.

users. It is possible to increase the performance of the network by breaking a tree into partitions and storing the appropriate sections on local file servers.

Figure 18.14 shows an example of a partition being declared on the organizational unit branch called 'external'.

Replicating partitions

NetWare 4.0 introduced the concept of replicating an NDS partition on another server as a background process. This is similar to the Microsoft LAN Manager file server replicator service. By replicating a partition, the system's fault tolerance is greatly increased and the necessity for inter-partition look-up is reduced. Local copies of replicated remote partitions can be used to look up what is stored on other servers. Of course, for this to work correctly, the two copies of the partition must be the same.

> Warning: The replication service does not provide fault tolerance for your data files. Only the NDS objects are replicated.

It is possible to create an unlimited number of replicas for each partition. They can then be scattered across many servers over the network. There are three different types of replicas:

- Master replica. Each partition has one master replica. Partition information from this type of replica can be read and changed. However, it is only from the master replica that you can change the directory structure, such as creating a new partition, for example.
- Read/write replica. You can read and modify objects within this type of replica.

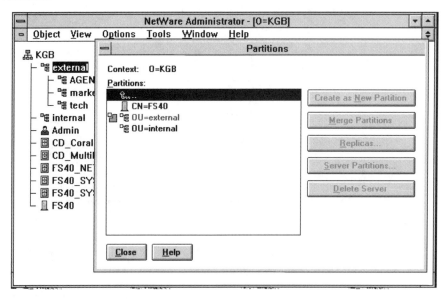

Figure 18.14 Declaring a partition.

- Read only replica. You can only read partition information from this type of replica. This means that users cannot login through this type of replica, because the login procedure needs to make changes in the NDS tree.

The replicator server is a background process automatically activated by the NetWare 4.0 services. In future releases of NetWare 4.0 the network manager will be able to define the degree of consistency. By default, the two partitions are automatically updated. When a change is made to the master partition, it is reflected in the mirrored partition across the network on the other server. However, the time taken to transfer the updating information between the two servers renders them mismatched for a short period. The faster the two servers can communicate, the higher the degree of synchronization. This should be one of the factors influencing your decision as to where you wish partitions to be replicated.

NetWare 4.0 provides a number of utilities for the administration of partitions across your network. From Microsoft Windows you can use the NetWare Administrator program or from DOS you can use PARTMGR to manage partitions and replicas. They can be used to create, delete, split and join partitions across the network.

Management considerations

Partitioning your NDS tree

How you partition your NDS tree is of utmost importance. You will need to sit down and think carefully about the design. There are two major considerations:

(1) Reducing network traffic. Where possible, try to keep partitions close to the network resources they refer to. This is sometimes impossible, since you might have a partition which has resources defined within it from a multitude of different networks and servers. In this case, you either have to split the partition into further sub-partitions or store them on the best compromise server. Don't forget you have the partition replicating service tool to improve look-ups for groups that are geographically separated.

(2) Fault tolerance. By partitioning the NDS, it is possible to mirror each partition, thanks to the NetWare replicator service. Think about developing a strategy whereby, as far as possible, most of your tree structure is replicated on another server. Try to keep the two replicating servers as close to each other as possible to minimize the amount of internetwork traffic. However, they need to be far enough apart so that, if one is hit by a disaster, the other one is a safe distance away.

> Warning: Do take into account that the file server you decide to store the partitions on will have reduced capacity for servicing its other functions.

Time synchronization services

In NetWare 4.0, information about the NDS tree is distributed around the network. In order to keep this information constantly updated it is very important that file servers keep in touch with each other. It is therefore essential that they all synchronize themselves to a common clock, which is used to time stamp all network information. The common time stamp ensures that information is updated in the correct order as it occurs. The NetWare time synchronization server defines three different servers: reference, primary and secondary.

Reference time servers are the highest-level time arbitrators. The reference time server is usually connected to an atomic clock. There is normally only one reference time server in the whole NDS tree structure.

Primary time servers are the next level down. The primary time servers get their time from the reference time server. If the primary servers do not find a reference time server, they will negotiate amongst themselves and settle on an agreed time acceptable to all. They then use this time to synchronize all the other secondary time servers.

Secondary time servers are informed of the correct time by the primary time servers.

In a small network, you would normally have one primary time server, with the others set as secondary servers. The need for multiple primary time servers arises as the network grows.

Define the time zone of each server when it is set up. This is used to ensure that users are presented with the correct local time,

even though the network functions on a universal time.

Time synchronization management considerations

Try not to make life too complicated for yourself. Novell makes the following recommendations depending on the size of your network.

For a small network (about 1 to 5 servers)
Just use one file server as the main reference point, all other servers being reset by this. Make sure that the reference time server is a very reliable machine! Check its clock to ensure that it keeps time correctly. This is an easy-to-manage simple solution, which has the benefit of minimum network traffic. However, if your system size increases and you are connecting to networks over WANs, the issue of time synchronization becomes far more critical and complicated.

For medium to large diverse networks
Use one or two primary time servers at each site, the rest being secondary time servers. If it can be justified financially, a single reference file server which can be connected to an atomic-type clock is ideal. This can then be used to set all the primary time servers on each site. They in turn will set the times for all the local secondary servers.

Directory Services access rights

A whole new dimension of security has been introduced with NetWare 4.0. It imposes a new layer of access rights on top of the old user trustee rights and IRMs (Inherited Rights Masks) used in NetWare 3.11. This new security layer controls access rights to the objects (see Figure 18.15). You must have the appropriate rights to an object before it can be used. Each object could potentially contain further sub-objects or a network resource, such as volumes or users. Each object on the NDS tree has a set of access rights associated with it. This comprises a list of users with access rights and how they can use and manage the object. The power of this approach lies in the fact that you can define trustee rights for control objects as well as for leaf objects.

Each object on the network is protected by two layers of security rights. The first layer is concerned with object protection. It defines who can manage and access objects as a whole. The next layer, property protection, is used to define who can read, modify or manage its contents. The different types of access right that can be set to protect objects and their properties are shown in Figure 18.16, Table 18.5 and Table 18.6.

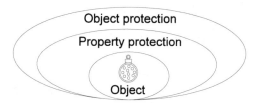

Figure 18.15 NDS object access rights.

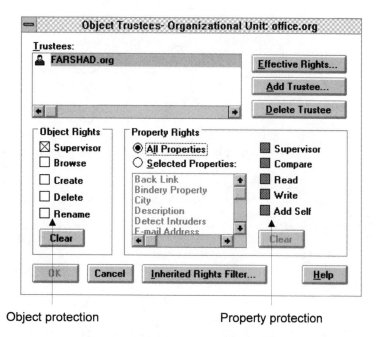

Figure 18.16 Different types of access right.

Table 18.5 Object protection.

Access rights	Definition
Browse	Can see objects in the NDS tree (by default most users are automatically given browse rights to objects)
Create	Can create sub-objects (only for container objects)
Delete	Can delete the object
Rename	Can change the object's name
Supervisor	All rights

Table 18.6 Property protection.

Access rights	Definition
Compare	The right to compare any value with the object property parameters
Read	Object properties can be read
Write	Object properties can be modified
Add (or delete) self	The right to add or remove oneself from the membership list of this object
Supervisor	All rights

Normally, to access the resources of an object, read-only property protection is sufficient.

Once set, these access rights are passed down to any sub-objects that exist under their control, unless any of the sub-objects has already had a set of specifically assigned rights (these rights will then take precedence for that object). This is exactly the same concept as file trustee rights in NetWare 3.x and 2.x.

It is also possible to use the concept of security equivalence within the NDS tree. Just as they can be made security equivalent to each other, users can also be made security equivalent to objects. This allows for tremendous flexibility and provides much room for confusion! It is possible to get yourself into loops. A user can be made security equivalent to another who is already security equivalent to the first user. Be careful!

> Warning: Use the security-equivalent function with caution, and be careful of loops!

Inherited rights filter

In addition to the normal trustee rights set for objects, you can also use the concept of the object's own inherited rights filter. This is specific to an object regardless of the user. This means that a user's effective rights are derived from a combination of their trustee rights and an object's inherited rights filter.

There is a very important difference between this system and the inherited rights filter. The supervisor attribute can now be blocked by the object-inherited rights filter.

> Warning: The administrator can be set up to have limited access rights over a given branch of the NDS tree. Make sure that before doing this there is at least one user with full supervisory rights over that tree section; otherwise, control over that section will be lost for ever!

It can be very useful to block the monolithic control that a supervisor has over the network. By using the object's inherited rights filter, it is now possible to restrict the power of the supervisor to certain parts of the NDS tree. However, you need to have supervisor access rights in the first place to set this restriction up.

The two programs that can be used to set and manage the object access rights are NETADMIN, which is a DOS text-based program, and the Windows version, NWADMIN.

NDS tree management issues

Designing the NDS tree

A well designed NDS tree can make your life as a network manager far easier, so take your time designing its construction. Novell NetWare 4.0 allows tremendous flexibility in the way the NDS tree can be constructed – it is up to you to impose limits on it. You need to create an NDS tree structure that matches the breadth and interest of your organization.

A well structured NDS tree, with a well defined standardized naming convention of objects, will have the following advantages:

- It is far easier to move around the NDS tree logically.
- Supporting supervisors can be easily trained to manage different segments of the NDS tree, providing the basic structure has been universally agreed.
- It is far easier to add new objects.
- It is far easier to train new users and administrators.
- It allows for its distribution across your worldwide networks (if you have any).
- Mistakes are less likely.
- You can achieve consistency of administration across your global network operations.

Once you have designed the basic structure of the NDS tree, it is well worth documenting and making several copies of your proposal. These copies can be distributed around your organization as a double-check to ensure that you have not forgotten some major sub-division of your organization! Although it is not difficult to change the structure of the NDS tree, it is worth trying to get it as right as possible from conception.

The way to construct a good NDS tree is to make it reflect the organizational structure of your establishment.

There are two classic approaches to constructing the tree.

You could structure the tree to reflect the geographical layout of your organization. Although this might initially seem a good idea, generally speaking, it is not. The problem is that most organizations have a hierarchy based on job activity, not location. Often, the same activities are carried out at many different locations.

Figure 18.17 shows a typical geographically-based tree.

The other, frequently used, approach is to design an NDS tree structure that reflects the company's own organizational chart. The tree will grow and change with the organization's own structure. This means dividing the company's activities into a number of major headings. These are then sub-divided into sub-activities. At the end of each branch are the organization objects. These are normally users, resources or user groups that have some form of interest within that branch of your organizational tree.

A typical company organization tree is shown in Figure 18.18.

Do not be carried away by the power of the NDS tree if you have a small network located on one or two sites. Keep life simple; as far as possible, have a relatively flat NDS tree structure and try to keep the depth of the tree to two layers.

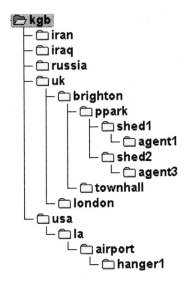

Figure 18.17 Example of a geographically-based tree.

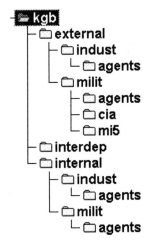

Figure 18.18 Example of a company organization tree.

> Warning: Having too many layers on your tree can make locating objects a long and tedious process and can lead to confusion. It is relatively easy to lose objects in a complicated, deep NDS tree structure. Where possible, try to structure your tree to go down no more then five levels.

Try to standardize on using one NDS tree for the whole organization. NetWare 4.0 allows for the creation of multiple NDS trees and you will need to login to each in turn. In the long term, it is generally better to implement the whole of your organization within a single, logical hierarchical tree, than to use multiple independent trees. This is because objects within the NDS tree can refer to each other and be logically grouped, which reduces the amount of repetitive management tasks. A single tree will bring your whole company together. If you are using multiple tree structures, it is not possible to group objects from different NDS trees together. NetWare 4.0 provides special merging facilities that enable two independent trees to be merged into one. This could be very useful if, for example, two companies decide to merge.

X.500 Directory Services

Overview

The X.500 standard is defined as part of the OSI seven-layer model. It is referred to as the Directory Services. The correct name is CCITT X.500, which the International Organization for Standardization calls its ISO 9594 standard. It was designed to provide a universal naming address which can be used by the X.400 E-Mail standard (see Figure 18.19). Just like the telephone directory services, the X.500 has a recognized format and aims to define a universal address for each user on the worldwide network. Any user anywhere in the world can request your X.500 number, which is then used to send you E-MAIL.

Figure 18.19 X.500 Directory Services.

The X.500 Directory Services define a hierarchical naming convention which can be used to address users worldwide. It is an international standard designed to be stored on a distributed basis. Each organization can store the names that it is responsible for and access relevant names from other organizations. Since it is a consistent standard, every X.500 will have a unique address. The X.500 standard allows each country in the world to determine how they will name their own users. This is publicized to users from other countries, providing worldwide X.500 Directory Services.

The X.500 definition defines:

- The structure of the naming conventions
- A set of directory services
- The protocols required to request information from the directory services

X.500 directory structure

The X.500 directory structure is shown in Figure 18.20. The structure of the naming convention used in the X.500 is as follows:

(1) At the highest level is the root. This is normally null.
(2) The next level is the C code for the country. Each country in the X.500 has been allocated a code called the C= (Country) code. For example, the USA has C=USA whereas Britain has C=GB.

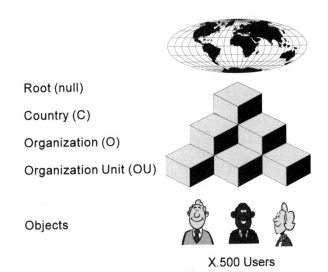

Figure 18.20 X.500 directory structure.

(3) The next layer is the O code: this is the organizational name within the country. This must be registered by the National Registration Authority.

(4) Each organization can then sub-divide itself into organizational units using OU codes. These can then be sub-divided into sub-OUs and so on.

(5) At the bottom of each address is the X.500 object or user. This is known as the CN (Common Name) code.

If you plan to use X.500, register your organizational name as soon as possible.

The X.500 directory is a collection of open systems which cooperate to hold a single logical database about a set of objects in the real world. These objects are normally users, but they can be resources or a group of users.

Installing and upgrading to NetWare 4.0

Overview

The installation of NetWare is relatively straightforward. Novell has invested a great deal of time in ensuring that the installation process goes as smoothly as possible.

The server installation is actually simpler than the old NetWare 3.x process. The new improved server installation tool (INSTALL.NLM) takes you through the installation steps logically. The major difference from NetWare 3.11 is that the new system is available on CD-ROM by default. Using CD-ROM, the whole installation process is far simpler than the old disk method, although there are more files to copy. Following the initial set of questions, instead of inserting and removing multiple floppy disks, you can sit back and make a cup of coffee. Novell issues a copy of DR-DOS with NetWare 4.0. This means that you no longer need to use a copy of your own to boot the system up before starting NetWare 4.0.

Key points regarding NetWare 4.0 installation

- A new, improved installation program (INSTALL.NLM) leads you logically through the installation process. This is shown in Figure 18.21.
- In the old NetWare 3.x system, every copy of SERVER.EXE had a unique serial number. With NetWare 4.0, there is a common SERVER.EXE for all. The installation program still checks for a serial number and user licence agreement by asking users to go through a special licensing process as part of the installation.

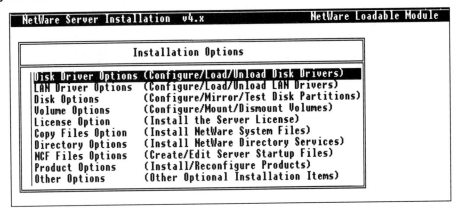

Figure 18.21 NetWare 4.0 INSTALL.NLM main menu.

- It is possible to register your newly-installed copy of NetWare 4.0 with Novell automatically. This is done on a floppy disk which is mailed to Novell. At the end of the installation process, you are prompted to enter your registration information onto the floppy.
- As part of the installation process, NetWare automatically checks what IPX network numbers, if any, are defined. It allows only the installer to define appropriate network numbers. This reduces the possibility of network numbers clashing when the server is activated.

See the section 'Network addressing system' in Chapter 11.

Server memory requirements

You can use the following simple formula to calculate the memory requirements for the NetWare 4.0 server. This is very similar to estimating the NetWare 3.11 server requirements.

See the section 'Estimating file server memory size' in Chapter 4 for information about NetWare 3.x.

Use 4 Mbyte SIMMs instead of the 1 Mbyte SIMMs where possible.

General rule of thumb for calculating memory requirements

- Start with a minimum of 8 Mbytes for the NetWare 4.0 operating system.
- If you use the CLIB, STREAMS, BTRIEVE or PSERVER NLMs, add 2 Mbytes.
- Add 1 Mbyte for each 100 Mbytes of shared hard disk, up to the maximum allowed by the file server.

- Add extra memory as required by any third-party NLM programs.
- Add a few extra Mbytes for extra caching, rounding up to the next figure divisible by eight.

This rule gives a good simple (on the generous side) approximation to memory size requirements.

Novell's method for memory calculation

Novell uses a much more complicated formula to estimate the memory requirements. It is shown in Table 18.7.

Table 18.7 Novell's method for memory requirement calculation.

Memory components	Total
System	
Add 5 Mbytes for the operating system	
Add 2 Kbytes per connection	
Add for cache memory 1 Mbyte + (Mbyte of disk storage * 5 Kbytes)	
Add 150 Kbytes for the media manager + (0.2 Kbytes * Mbytes disk storage)	
System buffers	
Add 2.3 Kbytes for each receive buffer (use MONITOR.NLM to see this figure)	
Add 4.3 Kbytes for each cache buffer (use MONITOR.NLM to see this figure)	
Add 9 Kbytes for each server process (use MONITOR.NLM to see this figure)	
NLMs	
Add 700 Kbytes if BTRIEVE is going to be used	
Add 500 Kbytes if CLIB is going to be used	
Add 600 Kbytes if INSTALL is going to be used	
Add 200 Kbytes if PSERVER is going to be used	
Add memory as required by any third-party NLM programs	
Volumes	
Add 8.2 bytes * (FAT tables volume blocks)	
Add ((BLOCKSIZE * 2)-1*4096) + (5* number of files) bytes for sub-allocation facility	
Add 250 Kbytes for file compression service	
Grand total	

As you can see, it is not the simplest formula to use. I recommend that you forget about the above, take a broad general view and use the rule of thumb explained earlier.

NetWare 4.0 installation methods

There are three different methods that can be used to install NetWare 4.0 on your new file server, as listed in Figure 18.22.

- CD-ROM method. This is the NetWare 4.0 default installation method. Using a single CD-ROM, the installation of NetWare 4.0 is very simple.
- Floppy disk method. If you do not have a CD-ROM it is possible to install NetWare 4.0 from the Novell set of master diskettes provided. You must, however, be prepared for the 'floppy disk shuffle'. It is a far slower process than the CD-ROM method, but it can be done on a server provided it has a single floppy disk drive.
- Network or local directory method. This is very useful if you wish to install NetWare 4.0 on a number of file servers. It is possible to copy all the NetWare 4.0 files to a single directory. This directory can be created on a network or local drive. From this single directory, it is possible to implement the installation process on the new NetWare 4.0 file server.

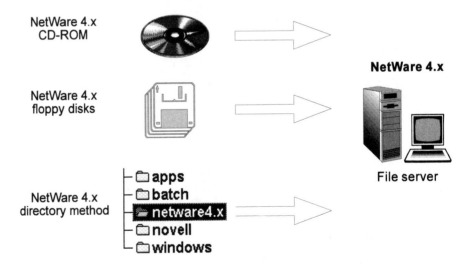

Figure 18.22 NetWare 4.0 installation methods.

> Warning: Expect problems if you try to install NetWare 4.01 with a CD-ROM on the same host adaptor as your hard disk, especially if you intend to use ASPI drivers. The reason is that the DOS ASPI drivers conflict with Novell's own CD-ROM drivers. You should contact your Novell dealer or look through Novell's bulletin board for solutions for your type of configuration.

Upgrading to NetWare 4.0

There are two approaches to updating to NetWare 4.0. If you are upgrading NetWare 3.x to NetWare 4.0, the upgrade can be implemented automatically in one step as part of the NetWare 4.0 installation. However, if you are starting from NetWare 2.x, two steps are required.

Novell also provide special interfaces to upgrade other operating systems, such as LAN Manager or Banyan Vines, to NetWare 4.0. Upgrading this type of system requires the two-step procedure.

The procedures are outlined below:

(1) Upgrading from NetWare 3.x to 4.x. This is a very simple one-step operation. You install NetWare 4.0 on top of the NetWare 3.x server; the process automatically upgrades the system.

(2) Migrating from NetWare 2.x or 3.x up to 4.x. This is a two-step process. You must first use the migration tool. It will take a snapshot of the old server's bindery information, which will be used to initialize the new NetWare 4.0 system. A copy of NetWare 4.0 is then installed on a new server. The old migration files are used to set up the new NetWare 4.0 server.

(3) Migrating from LAN Manager, LAN Server, and so on, to NetWare 4.0. This is a two-step process, as in the previous option. The only difference is that there are special drivers for each of the operating systems, such as LAN Manager or Banyan Vines, which allow the installation program to read the relevant bindery-equivalent information files.

Installing NetWare 4.0 on top of NetWare 3.11

This is very simple; however, mistakes can be fatal. If you choose this approach you must for the sake of your sanity ensure that you have a working backup of your complete system, just in case!

Always take two backup copies of a system onto two different types of medium, just in case one of them fails. Do ensure that your backups are all uncorrupted. Test them by doing a sample restore.

Migration across the network

This is a very common approach. You can use this upgrading method to update any NetWare 3.x or NetWare 2.x servers. It is also possible to upgrade other network operating systems, such as LAN Manager, using this method.

The upgrade process consists of four basic steps, as shown in Figure 18.23 and listed below.

Before you do anything, take a complete backup of your system. Once you are confident you have a full working backup of your system, including its bindery files, you are ready for the upgrade. Follow the instructions below:

(1) Using the NetWare 4.0 migration tool, take a snapshot of the old server's bindery files onto your workstation. These will be stored as a series of files in any directory you want to use.

(2) If you are ready to install NetWare 4.0 onto the target server, just use the standard installation method. This will probably be the CD-ROM method.

(3) Copy the data files and directory structures onto the new file server.

(4) Use the NetWare 4.0 migration tool again, this time to use the old migrated bindery files to initialize the NetWare 4.0 server.

You can also use the original server to act as the new NetWare 4.0 server. This makes life far more problematic in the event of mistakes, but means you do not need to have two servers. To do the above but using the same server, you do the following:

(1) Using the NetWare 4.0 migration tool, take a snapshot of the old server's bindery files onto your workstation. These will be stored as a series of files in any directory you want to use. (This is the same as Step (1), above.)

(2) Install the new NetWare 4.0 operating system on top of the original server.

(3) Restore all your original data files and directories from your backup onto NetWare 4.0.

(4) Use the NetWare 4.0 migration tool again, this time to use the old migrated bindery files to initialize the NetWare 4.0 server. (This is the same as Step (4), above.)

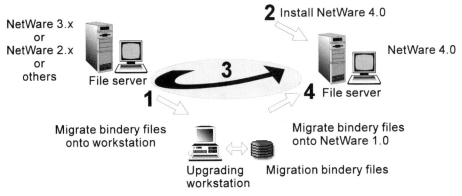

Figure 18.23 Upgrading to NetWare 4.0.

Upgrading from NetWare 3.11

When you are upgrading NetWare 3.11, you have two basic options. You can either upgrade the server directly, leaving the data files as they were, or you can go for an across-the-wire, complete re-installation onto another server. This has the very important advantage of ensuring that, whatever happens, your original data is still in working order. If you are paranoid about unforeseen disasters, then upgrading onto another machine is safer. The price you pay for this strategy is the cost of another set of server hardware. This can be very expensive and may make this option impractical. You could take the opportunity to update the client's server hardware (in particular, I normally increase the size and performance of the server's hard disks). You can then keep the old file server in a safe place for a few weeks, just in case. Then, as time goes on, the hardware can be recycled around your organization.

Should you upgrade?

This is a question that many people are now asking themselves. The answer depends upon whether you need NetWare 4.0's new facilities. If you don't find any of the features of NetWare 4.0 tempting enough, and NetWare 3.x is working just fine, then avoid NetWare 4.0 for the time being. You can afford to wait for it to settle down before you convert to it in the future. On the other hand, if you are tempted by its new features, then it is well worth considering upgrading. The decision is up to you. Bear in mind that NetWare 4.0 introduces a lot of new concepts. To use them effectively, you need to train both yourself and your support staff. The whole NDS tree directory introduces a large number of concepts which will be completely new to the seasoned NetWare 3.x manager. Putting aside the NDS, a large number of users are upgrading to NetWare 4.0 just for its file data compression facilities. Novell has produced NetWare 4.0 as its top-of-the-range network operating system. It is hoped it will put NetWare ahead of LAN Manager, Windows NT and Banyan Vines. Whether you plan to upgrade to NetWare 4.0 now or later, it is a product that puts networking into a new dimension and significantly improves network administration.

NetWare 3.11 emulation

To help users with the transition from NetWare 3.11 to the new world of the NDS tree provided by NetWare 4.0, Novell have made it possible to define an object in the NDS tree which emulates an old NetWare 3.11 bindery (see Figure 18.24). This object would in effect act as a gateway between the NDS tree and the old NetWare 3.11 system. Once access to the emulation object is given, you then need to login to the old NetWare 3.11 system to open its bindery files. Once you have been authenticated, all the resources of the file server are available to you as though you had connected to the server directly.

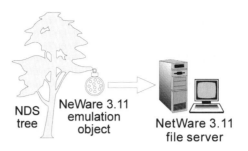

Figure 18.24 An object emulating the NetWare 3.11 server.

Installation management considerations

Before you consider installing NetWare 4.0, it is important to take into consideration which NetWare 4.0 installation method you are going to use. This could be CD-ROM, floppy disk (best avoided) or the directory method.

Tips for updating NetWare 3.x

It is possible to upgrade a NetWare 3.x server to a NetWare 4.0 server at any time. This will convert all old bindery objects to new objects within the NDS tree. This updating process will automatically update all users' script files, and show users as objects within the NDS tree.

There follows an important list of procedures you should perform before you update NetWare 3.x to NetWare 4.0:

- Back up the file server, including bindery files.
- Delete any unwanted directories.
- PURGE the system.
- Delete any unwanted user groups.
- Delete any unwanted users.
- Remove any deleted users' home directories.
- Run BINDFIX.
- Run the upgrade program provided by the NetWare 4.0 system.

Improved file server memory management

In NetWare 4.0, the internal memory structure of the servers has been completely rewritten. A number of major improvements have been incorporated. You can now run NLMs in protected memory mode. The old system was very complicated, having five different memory pools. These have now been rationalized into a single memory pool. The new memory structure has a significant performance improvement over the old NetWare 3.x servers.

Single memory pool

The NetWare 3.x system made the development of new NLMs difficult. NLM developers had to choose from five different memory pools, which were often misused. It was common to run NLM programs which would not necessarily return all their memory back to the system on unloading. This meant that, as time passed, NetWare 3.x servers slowly ran out of memory. This problem should no longer occur with NetWare 4.0. The operating system now has a single global memory pool and all NLMs are given memory from this common pool. On termination, this memory is returned to the global pool. This will make future development of NLM programs far easier.

> Warning: Not all NetWare 3.x NLMs will run on the NetWare 4.0 system. You will need to update them. Novell claims that 90% of all NLMs will run without requiring any changes.

Memory protection system

It is now possible to run new NLM programs under a memory managed environment. In NetWare 3.x, NLM programs run on the file server were not subjected to any form of memory protection. This meant that they were able to access any portion of the NetWare 3.x memory. This was very dangerous. It was possible for a misbehaving NLM program to crash the system. It is now possible to run NLM in a protected mode. This means that, whatever they do, NLMs cannot crash the system (in theory anyway).

See the section 'NetWare 4.0 file server memory structure' in Chapter 4.

The new memory protection is optional. The network manager can decide which NLM programs are to run in pure unprotected mode and which will run under memory protection.

Memory domains
The NetWare 4.0 server defines two different domains: the normal unprotected domain and the protected memory domain. When an NLM is run, it has to start up in one of these two domains.

Activating the protected memory domain

To activate the NetWare 4.0 protected memory domain manager, you will need to load the special NLM program called DOMAIN.NLM. It is used in the following manner:

- Place the following line in your STARTUP.NCF:

  `LOAD DOMAIN`

- From the server console, to select the protected domain type:

  `DOMAIN= OS_PROTECTED`

  This domain is Novell's default name; it runs at ring 3. The unprotected domain, OS, runs at ring 0.

- Load the NLM. Any programs now loaded will be activated in the last DOMAIN selected. (Note: some programs, such as MONITOR.NLM, do not run in protected mode.)

- To check the domain status type the following at the file server console prompt line:

  `DOMAIN`

  This will show which NLM programs are running under which domain.

Type DOMAIN HELP to get help on the available DOMAIN-related commands.

Management issues

For extra performance, run well known and tested NLM programs in unprotected mode. Any new, suspicious NLM programs should be run in the memory protected domain. Most manufacturers of NetWare 4.0 NLMs will recommend whether they should be run in the protected or unprotected memory domain. Programs running in the protected domain cannot access the unprotected NLM programs. This means that they cannot crash the system. They will be suspended by the NetWare 4.0 memory manager if they attempt to carry out an illegal act. All other NLMs running on the unprotected memory domain will continue as normal.

There is a price to be paid for running programs in the memory protected domain. Novell has carried out tests and claims that, on average, NLMs will run approximately 10% slower. This figure is largely dependent on the nature of the NLM and how well it has been written.

Internationalizing NetWare 4.01

Novell have decided to remove (almost) all of the text within the core code and place it in special text files. The code will then refer to the text within these files. This means that is now possible to support different languages by having a different text file for each language. This is something that non-English speaking users have wanted for a long time. Each language module is sold separately by Novell. The

English module comes as standard. The great advantage of this approach is that it is now possible to support many languages on the same network. Each user will state their preferred language and NetWare 4.0 will display its text in the user-specified language.

How it works

Users can select which language they wish to use by using the DOS SET command to set up the variable NWLANGUAGE parameters (see Figure 18.25).

The main file that stores the text is called MAP.MSG. For example, to select English MAP.MSG, you would type the following:

```
SET NWLANGUAGE=ENGLISH
```

This instructs NetWare to look up the English MAP.MSG text module in the standard directory structure. The standard client message files are stored under PUBLIC\NLM followed by the language name. Figure 18.26 shows the outline of the standard directory structure.

If, for example, NWLANGUAGE has been set to FRENCH, then NetWare will automatically look in PUBLIC\NLS\FRENCH for the language support text module.

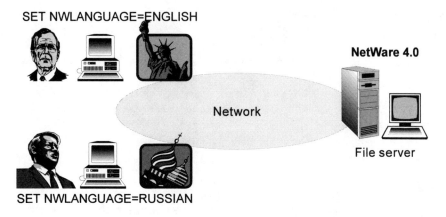

Figure 18.25 Internationalizing NetWare workstations.

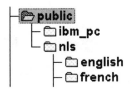

Figure 18.26 Location of standard client message files.

It is also possible to customize the file server console message. This is achieved by setting up the server console command called LANGUAGE. It is used to register new languages on the console. This means that is possible to get information on such programs as MONITOR.NLM in, for example, French or Spanish.

The language files are placed in a directory structure under SYSTEM\NLS, followed by the Novell-designated language number (see Figure 18.27).

Figure 18.27 Location of language files.

Numbers were used in preference to language names because some countries use a number of languages. For example, Luxembourg can use French or German. The text modules stored under these directories are called MONITOR.MSG. To get a list of all available LANGUAGE-related console commands, type HELP LANGUAGE. This is what you see:

```
NW40:help language
LANGUAGE                      Display current NLM language.
LANGUAGE list                 Display list of available
                              languages.
LANGUAGE name|number          Set preferred NLM language by name
                              or number.
LANGUAGE add number name      Add a new language name and number.
LANGUAGE ren number new_name  Rename the language specified by
                              number.
Example:  language spanish
NW40:
```

Novell has stated that, when menus are displayed in a different language, they will still be shown in the same order as the original English. This is very useful to know if you plan to support foreign users across the telephone.

Demonstrating multi-language support of NetWare 4.01

This is a simple demonstration of the multi-language support of NetWare 4.01 from the file server console. Figure 18.28 shows the standard front menu of the MONITOR.NLM program.

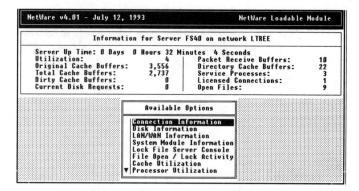

Figure 18.28 MONITOR.NLM in English.

When the following line is entered on the console prompt line:

```
FS40:language 7
   Current NLM language changed to (7) GERMAN.
```

```
FS40:load monitor
```

the same program MONITOR.NLM when reloaded shows its front menu in German (Figure 18.29).

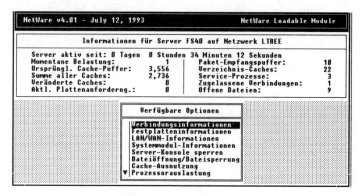

Figure 18.29 MONITOR.NLM in German.

Improved disk storage arrangement

NetWare 4.0 provides a number of improvements in the storage of files and directories, as follows:

- Volumes can now be mounted far more quickly.
- The new installation programs will automatically select the best block size.

- It is now possible to save server disk space, by sub-allocating 512 bytes of data within NetWare disk blocks to very small files. This replaces previous methods where files even 1 byte long had to take up a whole NetWare disk block of storage. Since this is normally a minimum of 4 Kbytes, it was very wasteful.

File compression system

Overview

NetWare 4.0 includes a very clever data compression facility. It differs from the normal data compression tools found in MS-DOS 6.x, Stacker or SuperStor. These are designed to work in real-time, compressing files as they are written and decompressing files as they are read from the disk. This is very different from the NetWare 4.0 solution. This works as a background process which examines each file and compresses it if it has not been recently used. The compression process is a low priority and a relatively slow process. It has been designed for very fast decompression, not fast compression. This means it will be almost as fast to read a compressed file as a decompressed file. This product is wonderful for saving space. If used properly, it can double your hard disk storage area. NetWare 4.0 file compression is transparent to users and its parameters can be customized by the network manager.

If you compress your deleted files, it is possible to un-purge many more deleted files than before.

New file attributes

A number of new file attributes have been introduced exclusively for the file compression service. They can be used to override the file compression rules used by the compression process. They are associated with each file, irrespective of the user. They can be set or reset by the normal FLAG command.

These new attributes are:

- Immediate compressed bit. This forces the compression process to compress the file on its next pass, irrespective of whether it has been used or not.
- Inhibit compression bit. This stops the compression process compressing the file.
- File compressed bit. This bit shows if the file has been compressed or not; otherwise, it is transparent to the users.

Using the file compression service

To use the file server compression service, you need to decide on the following factors:

- How many days should files be untouched before being compressed? This is a very important parameter to set. Try experimenting with this; for example, you could start off with seven days and adjust the figure as you see fit.

- What time should the data compression process start and stop? This is normally set at 2.00 a.m. and 5.00 a.m. respectively.

- What should the minimum compression gain be? If the file does not reach the set level of compression gain, it will not be compressed. I recommend setting this figure to 30%. However, it is well worth experimenting.

- Do you want deleted files to be compressed? This is a very good idea and this option is normally used.

Setting up file compression services

Using the SERVEMAN.NLM, you can change the SET variables associated with the file compression facilities.

- Select Console Set Commands, then the File System category (see Figure 18.30).

- Set the appropriate compression options (see Figure 18.31).

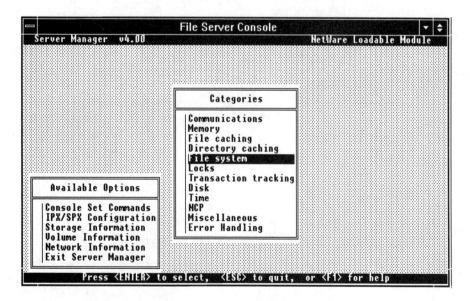

Figure 18.30 Selecting the File System category.

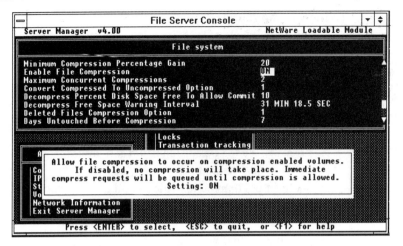

Figure 18.31 Setting compression options.

Management issues

The network hard disk is one of the most valuable resources on the network, so it is important to try to get as much use out of it as possible. It may be useful to think of network files as starting off their lives in the uncompressed mode and, as they become less used, being slowly moved over to the compressed format.

Uncompressed files
It is ideal to consider using this type of storage for files that your users frequently use, that is, files which are used at least once a week.

Compressed files
Compressed files are stored on the server's hard disk. They are available to users just as if they were stored as uncompressed. This normally means that you have a saving of at least 50% on disk space over the primary storage method. This does come at a price of deterioration of data access times. The disk decompression is very fast, but to compress the files in the first place can be time consuming. It is a good idea to instruct NetWare to compress the files that are infrequently used, for example, files that have not been accessed within the last week.

Once you have chosen to enable compression on a volume it cannot be removed without deleting the whole volume. It is, however, possible to disable it using the console SET parameter.

If you plan to decompress files, make sure you have enough room on the disk. A good tip is try to keep at least 10% of your hard disk free at any time. This is like a buffer for file expansion.

Media manager

With NetWare 4.0, Novell has introduced a Media Manager, which is a set of routines that provide a universal view on a variety of backing up devices. These routines allows third-party hardware manufacturers to produce server-based backing up devices which can seamlessly integrate into the NetWare 4.0 system (see Figure 18.32).

Data migration

The concept of data migration has been introduced with NetWare 4.0, using a special Media Manager to automatically migrate files from volumes onto a secondary medium (see Figure 18.33). This can be a CD-ROM, tape drivers or even another disk drive. The Media manager will manage the secondary storage device automatically. Files can be removed from a volume and placed on the storage device. However, user perception of the files is the same as before. It the user requests access to a file, the Media manager will automatically load the file from storage and place it back on the original volume.

Warning: You can only restore files from the secondary device if it is activated and the RTDM.NLM is running on the server.

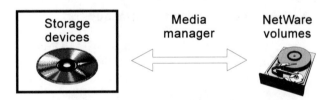

Figure 18.32 Media manager interface.

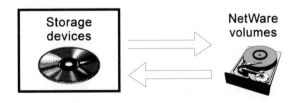

Figure 18.33 Data migration services.

Setting up migration support

This facility is implemented by setting up the appropriate parameters in the volumes and then running the special program RTDM.NLM (Real-Time Data Module). This program will use the function provided by the Media Manager to implement the data migration service.

To set up data migration

- Set up volume parameters. Using the INSTALL.NLM program, set up the data volume migration flag (see Figure 18.32).
- Run RTDM.NLM:

```
NW40:load rtdm
Loading module RTDM.NLM
  NetWare Real Time Data Migration NLM
  Version 1.16    January 6, 1993
  Copyright 1993 Novell, Inc.  All rights reserved.
  Debug symbol information for RTDM.NLM loaded
NW40:
```

CD-ROM support

NetWare 4.0 standard CD-ROM support

There is now a standard way to support CD-ROMs on a NetWare server. The special program CDROM.NLM will enable the mounting of CD-ROMs just as though they were volumes. These are then made available to users as normal directories.

```
NW40:load cdrom
Loading module CDROM.NLM
  Netware 4.xx ISO-9660 and High Sierra CD-Rom Support Module
  Version 3.00    January 8, 1993
  Copyright 1993 Novell, Inc.  All rights reserved.

For CD-ROM Support HELP enter 'cd help' on the command line.
NW40:
```

Once the CDROM.NLM has been loaded, a host of new commands are made available for managing the CD-ROM. Typing CD HELP at the server command line displays a list of these commands:

```
CD-ROM NLM Command Line Options:

  CD DEVICE LIST
```

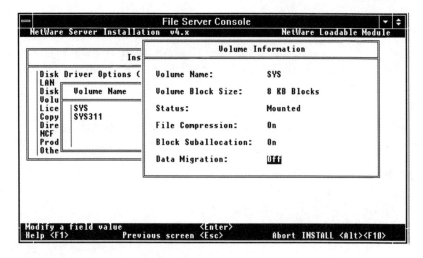

Figure 18.34 Enabling the volume migration flag.

```
CD VOLUME LIST
CD MOUNT [No.] [volume name] ('/mac', '/G=x' or '/R')
CD DISMOUNT [No.] [volume name]
CD CHANGE [No.] [volume name] ('/mac', '/G=x' or '/R')
CD DIR [No.] [volume name]
CD GROUP ([group name] and [group num])
CD HELP
```

```
The [volume name] can be obtained from the first 2 options.
The [No.] can be obtained from the first 2 options.
The '/mac' is used to add Macintosh Name Space Support.
The '/G=x' is used to set the default volume group access
rights.
The 'x' is the number listed from the GROUP Command.
The [group name] adds a group name ('del' as name removes
group name).
The [group num] adds a new group name to the group access list
(1-9).
The '/R' is used to reuse the created data file on the 'SYS'
Volume.
The '/Z' is used to remove any file with a file length of zero.
```

```
When mounting or changing a CD-ROM disc a deactivation of the
selected device will occur.   Do not be alarmed.
NW40:
```

The CD-ROM devices have to be mounted just like normal volumes, the big difference being that it is not normally possible to write back onto the CD-ROMs.

The good news is that Novell has decided to support ISO 9660, High Sierra and the HFS CD-ROM file systems. This basically means that most of the CD-ROMs available on the market can be supported as standard. The Novell CD-ROM fully supports the SCSI Adaptec ASPI drivers. So if you can connect your CD-ROM to an Adaptec card, it is very likely that it can be used on the NetWare 4.0 file server.

Kodak CD-ROM support

Novell has collaborated with Kodak to produce a writeable and readable CD-ROM.

Security auditing NetWare

Overview

NetWare 4.0 has introduced the idea of a security auditor. It can audit the NetWare network, including the supervisor's own activities. It is now possible to audit files and directories, which was something that was missing from NetWare 3.11 but commonly available on mainframe computer systems. NetWare 4.0 produces an audit trail of who did what, and to which network resource.

The auditor is totally independent of the supervisor. The auditor does not have a user account: it is password controlled and is held at the volume level. It is activated as part of the volume management. This means it is totally independent of the bindery, directory servers or user's accounts. The auditor's password is normally different from the supervisor's password. This means that the system auditor can be kept secret from the supervisor!

Audited information

All the audit information is stored on a volume as a special system file. The auditor can be set up to monitor the following activities:

- User's login and logout times can be recorded.
- Any file can be audited to show who accessed it and what they did.
- Directory creation, modification or deletion can be recorded.
- Any user trustee modifications can be recorded by the auditor.
- Any accessed NDS tree objects can be audited.
- Changes to the NDS tree objects can be recorded. This could mean mounting or dismounting volumes, creation or deletion of print queues and users.
- Any changes to a user's restrictions can be recorded. The network auditor can be set to record the changes in users' accounts or space restrictions.

For each of these activities, a record is produced showing the following information:

Date	Time	User ID	Machine ID	Operation performed	Completion status

From the collected data records, the auditor can produce a variety of reports.

Management issues

There is a small price to pay in performance loss when auditing network resources. This is because the system must create and write a special auditing record into the audit file every time an audited resource is accessed. If you decide to audit directories or files which are frequently accessed, then the most common problem you might encounter is that the audit file becomes very large. This could then fill up your whole volume.

It is possible to audit all activities on a volume; however, where possible, this should be avoided. It can produce very large audit files and significantly reduce performance. Where possible, you should start auditing as close as possible to where the sensitive data resides. In other words, just audit the files and directories that *need* auditing.

> Be careful if you try to mount an audited volume with no free space. NetWare will only mount the volume when the auditor's password has been entered. This will disable any further audits and mount the volume as normal.

If the auditor forgets the password, the only way to reset it is to backup the volume, then delete it. The volume will have to be recreated, with a new auditor defined. The original data can now be restored.

Improved on-line help documentation

With the new NetWare 4.0, you get a significantly enhanced on-line help tool. It comes as a number of different electronic documents (see Figure 18.35). Each document reflects a given supplied manual. It is a significant improvement on the old file system.

It has the following features:

- It is used from within the Windows environment.

- You can search across multiple documents. In Figure 18.36, a search is being made across all manuals for the word UNIX. Every time the word is found, a book mark is placed on the relevant manual for future easy access.

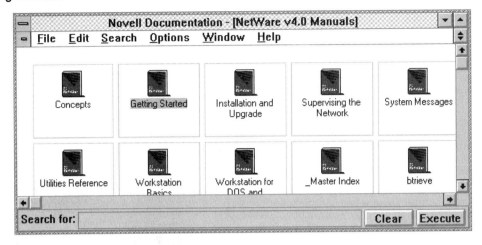

Figure 18.35 NetWare 4.0 on-line manuals.

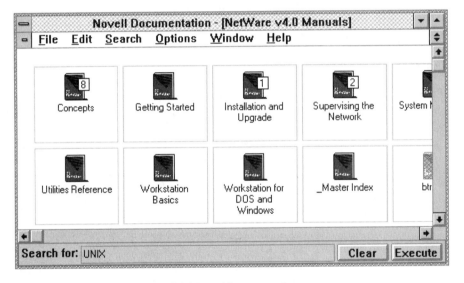

Figure 18.36 Searching across documents.

- It supports text, tables and graphics.
- It comes as a complete electronic replacement for the supplied manuals.

New console commands

With NetWare 4.0 you get limited on-line help. If you type HELP, you see the following message:

```
ABORT REMIRROR          ADD NAME SPACE          BIND
BROADCAST               CLEAR STATION           CLS
CONFIG                  DISABLE LOGIN           DISABLE TTS
DISMOUNT                DISPLAY NETWORKS        DISPLAY SERVERS
DOWN                    ECHO OFF                ECHO ON
ENABLE LOGIN            ENABLE TTS              EXIT
FILE SERVER NAME        IPX INTERNAL NET        LANGUAGE
LIST DEVICES            LOAD                    MAGAZINE INSERTED
MAGAZINE NOT INSERTED MAGAZINE NOT REMOVED MAGAZINE REMOVED
MEDIA INSERTED          MEDIA NOT INSERTED      MEDIA NOT REMOVED
MEDIA REMOVED           MEMORY MAP              MEMORY
MIRROR STATUS           MODULES                 MOUNT
NAME                    OFF                     PAUSE
#                       PROTOCOL                REGISTER MEMORY
REMOVE DOS              REMIRROR PARTITION      REM
RESET ROUTER            RESTART SERVER          SCAN FOR NEW
DEVICES
SEARCH                  SECURE CONSOLE          ;
SEND                    SET TIME ZONE           SET TIME
SET                     SPEED                   SPOOL
TIME                    TRACK OFF               TRACK ON
UNBIND                  UNLOAD                  VERSION
VOLUME                  HELP

Type HELP [command] to display specific command help
NW40:
```

Table 18.8 lists the most important new console commands.

Table 18.8 New console commands.

Command	Description
ABORT REMIRROR	Part of the SFT III support commands
LANGUAGE	Register a new language on the console
MEMORY MAP	Displays map of the server memory
REGISTER MEMORY	Register memory above 16 Mbytes on ISA machines
RESTART SERVER	You can now restart the server without having to exit to DOS first
LIST DEVICE	List the known devices on the system
SCAN FOR NEW DEVICES	OS device drivers start to look for and, if necessary, add new devices to the system

NetWare 4.0 utilities

Overview

NetWare 4.0 supplies a new set of tools in addition to some of the old favourite tools supplied with NetWare 3.x and NetWare 2.x. A number of the old tools have been combined into single more powerful programs. These new tools fully exploit the new NetWare 4.0 Directory Services. They are also capable of supporting the old bindery request. This means that the same tools can be used to manage NetWare 4.0 as well as NetWare 3.x or NetWare 2.x servers.

Novell has ensured that the majority of its powerful utilities are available in DOS, Windows or OS/2 PM. The main concentration seems to be on the Windows environment. These new tools are very user friendly.

Merged tools

Table 18.9 shows a list of NetWare 3.x tools that have been merged in NetWare 4.0.

New NetWare 4.0 tools

Table 18.10 lists new NetWare 4.0 tools.

SYSCON is dead, long live NWADMIN!
NWADMIN replaces the old SYSCON programs used in NetWare 3.x and NetWare 2.x. It is a Windows-based product and one of the most important tools available. It shows the NDS tree structure as a hierarchy of objects (see Figure 18.37).

Table 18.9 New NetWare 4.0 tools and the 3.x tools they replace.

New NetWare 4.0 tool	Old NetWare 3.x tools
FLAG	FLAG, FLAGDIR, SMODE
RIGHTS	RIGHTS, ALLOW, GRANT, REMOVE, REVOKE, TLIST
SEND	SEND, CASTON, CASTOFF
MAP	MAP, ATTACH
NDIR	NDIR, LISTDIR, CHKDIR, CHKVOL
CAPTURE	CAPTURE, ENDCAP
RCONSOLE	RCONSOLE, ACONSOLE
MONITOR	FCONSOLE

Table 18.10 New NetWare 4.0 tools.

Description	DOS text version	Windows version	NetWare 3.x equivalent
System object administration	NETADMIN	NWadmin	SYSCON
NDS partition manager	PartMgr	PAR	N/A
NetWare tools	NetUser	NWTOOLS	SESSION
Saber-like menu system	MENU (new)	N/A	MENU (Old)
Print management	PCONSOLE	NWADMIN	PCONSOLE

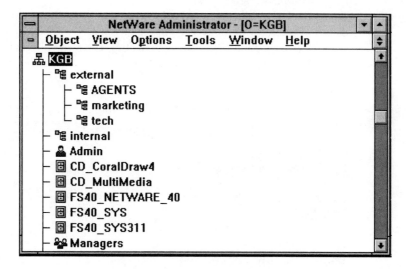

Figure 18.37 NWADMIN program.

The network manager can now create, delete or manage objects. There is also a DOS text version of the program called NETADMIN.

Partition manager
Since the NDS tree structure can be partitioned, there is a special tool that will set up partitions across the network.

User support tool
Novell provides a special menu-driven tool to allow users to change their environments. This is very similar to the old SESSION program in NetWare 3.x. There are two versions of this program, a DOS-based version called NETUSER and a much more friendly Windows version called NWTOOLS. This is a far more powerful product than the one shipped out with the NetWare client DOS/Windows disk. It includes facilities for network messaging, resource mapping of drives and managing local printer assignments.

The menu system

Novell have adopted the Saber Menu System as their replacement for the old MENU program that came with NetWare 3.x. The advantage of this product is that it will take far less memory. Each menu option can be displayed differently, depending on who is running the menu system. It is unfortunate that the Saber for Windows Menu System was not also included in this package. The DOS version is very similar to the Windows version. In fact, the code for the two systems is interchangeable.

See the section 'Saber Windows Menu System' in Chapter 10 for a description of the Saber Menu System.

Printer administration

There are few changes here. The DOS text version of the print services manager is called PCONSOLE. For the Windows equivalent, use the NWADMIN program.

See the section 'NetWare 4.0 printing enhancements' in Chapter 19 for new NetWare 4.0 printing features.

NetWare 4.x VLM workstsation support

For information on new workstation NetWare drivers, see the section 'NetWare 4.x VLM redirector' in Chapter 7.

Command line utilities

There are a number of new command line utilities; the most important of all are CX and NLIST.

The CX command

This command will probably be used frequently. The CX command is to NDS what the CD command is to DOS. It is used to change the user's name context along the NDS tree structure. It can also be used to view the NDS tree structure.

The NLIST command

This command can be used to view object properties and to search the NDS tree structure for specified objects. It can also be used to list all types of object, using the * character.

```
C:\WINDOWS>nlist *
Current context: O=org
Partial Name                                    Object Class
-----------------------------------------------------------------
serv1                                           Alias
Managers                                        Group
NW40                                            NetWare Server
Admin                                           User
FARSHAD                                         User
NW40_SYS                                        Volume
```

A total of 6 objects were found in this context.

A total of 6 objects were found.

C:\WINDOWS>

Make sure that these two commands, CX and NLIST, are available to the user from the \LOGIN directory. It is a great help to users who wish to login.

19

Managing NetWare printing

NetWare printing basics

If you are familiar with NetWare printing concepts you can omit this basic section and move onto the more advanced topics in the following sections.

What are NetWare printer servers?

A print server is a special program that controls print queues and shared printers (see Figure 19.1). Under NetWare, print servers can be run on file servers or workstations. There are three types of print server under NetWare:

(1) PSERVER.VAP on a NetWare 286 file server

(2) PSERVER.NLM on a NetWare 386 file server

(3) PSERVER.EXE on a dedicated workstation

They all look the same to users when active; the only difference is the environment under which they run. Each print server can control up to 16 printers.

Printing over the network (user viewpoint)

Accessing the network printer from workstations

Using the Novell CAPTURE program, you can redirect print output to a print queue. The program captures all the output directed to the printer ports and then redirects it to the appropriate network queue. Usually, print output goes to LPT1:, LPT2: or

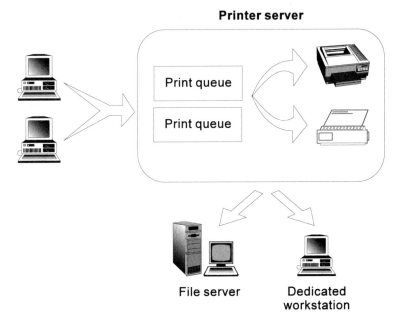

Figure 19.1 NetWare print servers.

LPT3:. Once the printer ports have been captured, any DOS program running will think it is talking to a locally-connected printer.

Connecting local print ports to print queues

The CAPTURE command has many uses, the most important of which is that it allows applications that are unaware of the NetWare print queues to use the network printers. It does this by fooling them into using the captured DOS printer ports. Capturing can be terminated at any time using the ENDCAP command. The CAPTURE command is mostly used in the login script. Examples of its use include:

- Printing from the screen, if you have captured LPT1:
- Printing to a network printer
- Printing data without exiting an application
- Printing data to different LPT ports

Four basic steps

This is how it works:

(1) You redirect the printer output to a predefined queue. Use the format CAPTURE l=<Print port number> q=<Name of a print queue>, for example:

```
CAPTURE l=1 q=Q_Epson
```

(2) You send the print output to the captured line printer port.

(3) The captured job now waits for its turn in the print queue. A print queue is a holding area on a file server. The PCONSOLE program can be used to see print queue activity.

(4) When the printer is ready for your job, the print server program opens up the print queue file and then starts to print the job line by line.

Setting up printing using PSERVER

The following are the basic steps required to set up print servers:

(1) Define a print server.
(2) Define all the printers attached to the print server.
(3) Define the queues under the control of the print server.
(4) Attach the user's printer ports to the network print queues.

Running PSERVER.EXE on a dedicated PC

The following program is used to turn a workstation into a dedicated print server. It is important that, before running this program, you create an account for the print server using the PCONSOLE.EXE program, as follows:

```
PSERVER <Print server name>
```

Since the remote printing facility uses the SPX protocol, you must add the following to the SHELL.CFG file:

```
SPX CONNECTIONS= 60
```

Once the program is run, no other program can be run on the workstation. It turns the workstation into a dedicated print server. The only way to stop it (other than pulling the plug out) is to go to another workstation and, using a program such as PCONSOLE.EXE, instruct the print server to down itself.

The user login name changes to the PSERVER name.

Remote printing

The Novell remote printing concept means that any local printer connected to a workstation can be shared across the network (see Figure 19.2).

Novell provides a special program for this purpose called RPRINTER.EXE (a TSR program). Before you can use a remote printer, you must assign control of it to a designated printer server somewhere on the network.

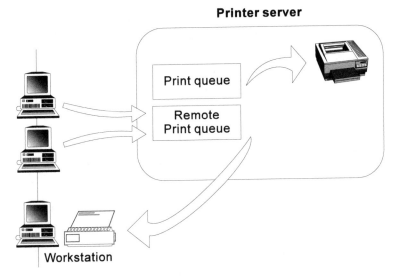

Figure 19.2 NetWare remote printing.

Printing and changing forms

With NetWare you can impose form formats on print jobs as they are processed by the print server (see Figure 19.3).

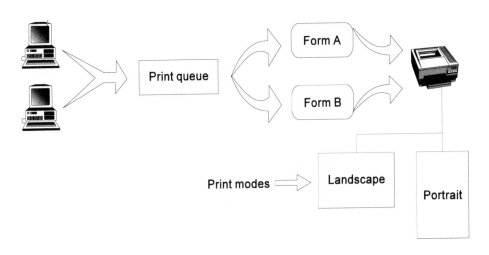

Figure 19.3 Print forms.

To impose forms on print jobs you need to do the following:

(1) Define the printer being used by Novell, using the standard Print device Definition File (.PDF) provided. Alternatively, you can define your own, using the PRINTDEF program.

(2) Define a series of print modes, such as 80 characters wide, landscape, or 16-pitch, portrait.

(3) Define a print form which uses the print mode, such as LETTERHEAD or INVOICES.

(4) When printing to a queue, users can specify the form type to be used.

Print servers are very clever and can minimize form changes.

PRINTDEF

PRINTDEF defines Novell printers. It sets up printer definitions and can be used to view the device functions, modes and forms being used. The information is then used by PRINTCON; NPRINT, CAPTURE and PCONSOLE can use the device driver via PRINTCON.

PRINTCON

PRINTCON serves as a kind of macro for printing with CAPTURE, NPRINT and PCONSOLE. If you do not use CAPTURE, NPRINT or PCONSOLE, then you don't need PRINTCON.

PSC

This program can be described as the command-line version of PCONSOLE. It is a tool for viewing or controlling print servers and network printers via DOS, rather than using the menu-driven PCONSOLE program. Use the following format:

```
PSC [PS=printserver] [P=printernumber] options
```

It is very useful for automating operations via batch files.

With PSC you can perform the following:

- See the status of one or all of the printers
- Pause the printer temporarily
- Stop printing the current job
- Start the printer
- Mark a form on the printer
- Rewind a print job

NetWare 2.15 versus NetWare print server-based printing

Old NetWare ADV 2.15 was very inflexible
Core print servers, once defined, were difficult to change. They had to be hard-coded into the operating system during installation. Printers also had to be defined during installation.

New print servers for NetWare (2.2, 3.x and 4.x)
are dynamically configured
With the new print servers, print queues and printer definitions are dynamic, print servers can be loaded and unloaded, and remote printing is now available. Multiple print servers can now be defined.

Print servers and queue directories

Every time a new print queue or print server is created, a new sub-directory will be created under the SYS:\SYSTEM directory (see Figure 19.4). These sub-directories will be given a number: this is a bindery number automatically assigned by the network operating system. You can tell the two different types of directories apart by looking at the extension. If the directory has a .QDR extension, this means that all spooled data for a given queue will be stored under this directory. If the directory only has a hex number and no extension, it stores information about a print server.

Do not limit the print related directories under SYS:\SYSTEM: if you have a lot of printing, the print spool has to be sent to these types of directory before printing. Running out of directory space will result in a printing failure.

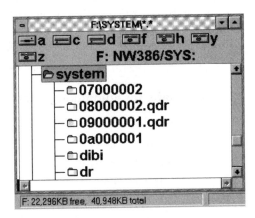

Figure 19.4 Print queue sub-directories.

NetWare Queue Management Services

Overview

As part of its NCP command set, NetWare provides a series of commands called the QMS (Queue Management Services). The QMS calls provide NetWare-aware programs with the ability to use the NetWare printing services directly. In the case of a DOS-based workstation, this means it will no longer be necessary to CAPTURE printer ports to send output to NetWare print queues. The QMS-aware application will intelligently manipulate the NetWare print queue, bypassing the workstation's own local printing facilities. For improved performance, use applications that can use NetWare QMS. The QMS system will accept print jobs on a data block basis, as opposed to using the byte-oriented method of the CAPTURE command.

QMS functions

The QMS system has facilities to:

- Manage print jobs
- Create and modify NetWare print queues
- Manage print queues
- Define and manage a number of different types of queue, such as archiving or job queues

Create print queues

The QMS provides the CreatQueue API call, which creates bindery objects with a user-specified queue name and queue type.

NetWare defines a number of different queues. As well as the obvious print queues, there are other types. The first is the archiving queue: these are special queues that can be used to archive jobs for future reference. The other type of queue is a job queue. These are queues of jobs which are awaiting execution. Table 19.1 lists some typical QMS queue candidates.

Table 19.1 Typical QMS queue candidates.

Queue type	Who services it	QMS queue ID
OT_PRINT_QUEUE	Print server	0x0003
OT_ARCHIVE_QUEUE	Archive server	0x0008
OT_JOB_QUEUE	Compiling server	0x000A

Create queue services

QMS has an API call to create queue servers. This can be anything from print servers to archiving servers. Of course, the appropriate type of queue must go the appropriate type of server.

Submitting queue jobs

The CreatQueueJobandOpenFile API command is used to add jobs to queues. When called from the user application, assuming it was successful, a DOS file handle to a queue file will have been created. This then allows the application to control the sending of data to the NetWare queue as if it were a normal write file. The job in the queue is completed by the appropriate CloseFile command being issued from the application.

Servicing queue jobs

There is a set of QMS commands which will monitor and modify queues. These commands include functions such as: putting jobs on hold, changing the order of jobs in the queues and reading the current status of all jobs in queues.

Where to get more information on QMS

For more information, I recommend the book *NetWare System Interface Technical Overview* by Novell, published by Addison-Wesley.

Print server management strategy

Defining print servers

There are a number of points to consider before implementing print servers across your network. The main point to be made is: never underestimate the time required to set up network printers. It can be very complicated. This is because Novell allows you tremendous flexibility in organizing your network printing.

Here are a number of important points to consider before installing print servers:

- **Where do you want to run the PSERVER** – dedicated on a workstation or on a file server?
- **Can you connect all the required printers up to the print server?** Will you have enough parallel and serial ports to accommodate your printer connections? If given the choice, you should try to use your parallel LPT ports first before using the serial COM ports.

- **Where are you going to put all the printers?** Check the physical position of printers. Where would you put the paper? Are there enough power points? Can you easily maintain the consumable items in the printers?
- **What are you going to call the print server?**
- **Have you made sure you can print to all printers using DOS**? Before starting up the NetWare print server, ensure that the printers are physically connected.

The naming of the print server, print queues and printers is very important. Be very careful what names you give them. The print server name should give its users an idea as to its location and maybe also its function.

Call printer servers:PS_<Location>_<Function type>

Examples: PS_LAB1 or PS_STORES_Fast

Managing printers

Before setting up, consider:

- What name to give the printer
- Which ports the printer is going to use
- Where it is going to be located

Give printers names which indicate what type of printer they are and, if appropriate, which port they use.

Call printers: P_<Type of printer>_<Port>

Examples: P_EpsonFx80_SER, P_LaserII_PAR

Managing print queues

Before you start to define queues think about:

- Which users you want to use the new print queue
- Who the queue managers are going to be
- Which shared printer(s) will be servicing the queue
- The name of the queue

Give queues names which indicate what type of printer will be servicing them.

Call printers: Q_<Printer type>_<Function type>

Examples: Q_Epson or Q_LaserII_Reports

Password protecting your dedicated print server

The following describes how you can password protect dedicated print servers, without users needing to enter a password every time the print server machine is switched on. I use a special batch file which is called from the AUTOEXEC.BAT file. It will automatically connect to the server, login as a special print server user and enter the predefined print server password. This is all done without any human intervention. Here is how it works:

(1) A special user is created exclusively to run the print server program. I normally give this type of user the following name format:

```
PS_<name>
```

where <name> is the name of the print server, for example, PS_HQ.

(2) You give this user a password, for example, PASS$123.

(3) You record this password in a text file, which will be stored in a sub-directory within the print server's hard disk. The text file can be called anything. The more obscure it is, the better. For example, a text file called XYZ.TXT is stored under the C:\NET directory:

```
PASS$123
```

(4) You connect to the network as normal, and then execute the following commands:

```
F:
LOGIN PS_HQ < C:\NET\XYZ.TXT
PSERVER PS_HQ
```

When the print server is switched on, it will automatically attach to the server and enter its user name and password. The PSERVER.EXE program is then automatically started up. The great thing about this approach is that other users cannot start the print server on their machine unless they know the password.

NetWare 4.0 printing enhancements

Overview

NetWare 4.0 has a few differences from the old NetWare 3.11 services. The main changes allow the printing services to utilize the NetWare Directory Services. According to Novell, the new printing programs are significantly more reliable. The old NetWare print services were notorious for their printing problems.

The key changes are as follows:

✓ Print servers support up to 255 printers as opposed to the previous 16.

✓ There is a new Windows version of PCONSOLE called NWADMIN.

✓ There is a new remote printer called NPRINTER.

✓ Print queues no longer need to be on the volume SYS. A print queue can be stored on any volume.

✓ Print definitions and forms can now be used and addressed globally.

✓ Print servers can also be serviced by AppleTalk printers.

✗ Novell has decided to drop the dedicated print server concept. It looks like the days of the PSERVER.EXE are numbered: workstations can no longer be used as print servers.

It is now possible to send print jobs directly to a printer name. You do not need to know the name of its assigned print queue.

Figure 19.5 illustrates the NetWare 4.0 printing environment.

Remote printing

With NetWare 4.0, the old remote printing tool RPRINTER.EXE has been renamed to NPRINTER. It has the following advantages:

• It is claimed to be more reliable than RPRINTER.EXE.

• It can be run under the Windows 3.1 and OS/2 environments.

• It can also be run on NetWare file servers as an NLM (NPRINTER.NLM).

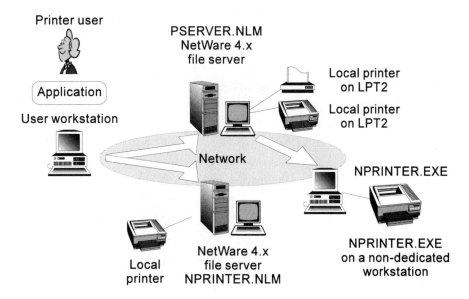

Figure 19.5 NetWare 4.0 printing environment.

Optimizing network printing

In this section, I will explore the important elements that combine to define the performance of your printing across the network. At each stage, I will also suggest techniques that can improve printing performance.

The printing process goes through a series of stages, from your application to its final destination (an actual printout from the appropriate printer). Printing bottlenecks can occur throughout the system. One of the responsibilities of the network manager is to identify where the bottlenecks are and then improve these areas. It is pointless having an extremely fast printer that can only be fed via a very slow serial cable: it is rather like feeding a waterfall from a tap. In this situation, the bottleneck is obviously the serial cable, which can be converted to parallel.

I like to look at printing performance from its starting point, which is the application, to the end point, the actual printout. Imagine water flowing through many different size pipes. The total water flow rate, from the start to the end point, is really dependent upon the thinnest pipe. The trick here is to identify all the stages involved in the flow and then work out where the 'thinnest pipe' is. This is, in fact, the same process as optimizing network performance. In a network, when data flows from the file server to the workstation and vice versa, it goes through many different stages, each of which is a potential bottleneck. Printing is very similar; therefore, to ensure optimum efficiency we need to examine all the stages involved in the transmission of the print across the network and calculate how to optimize each individual stage. It is important to remember that the total printout throughput will be determined by the weakest link in the chain.

The efficiency of the following needs to be assessed:

(1) The application, which formats its data in preparation for printing
(2) The Windows environment, which captures the application printout and feeds this through the network operating system (assuming the use of Windows)
(3) The print server, which captures the network print jobs from the workstation and starts to spool the print ready for printing onto the printer
(4) The network, which transfers the print across the network
(5) The print server, which transfers the data to the printer itself

Novell makes things a little more interesting because printers can be remote as well as local to print servers.

Each step in the process is examined below, and suggestions for improvements are made.

Applications

The print's journey commences at the application stage. It is important to have an application that can generate the appropriate print data as quickly as possible with a minimum amount of interruption to normal activities. Generally speaking, the higher the print quality required, the greater the amount of data produced to achieve the printed page. Windows applications are particularly guilty of this, especially the graphic-intensive applications. They tend to produce an extremely large amount of data for a single printed page. Typically, the average graphic page, at 300 dpi (dots per inch), will take approximately 500 Kbytes. On the other hand, a simple text-based file may require approximately 1.5 Kbytes per page.

Soft fonts versus hard fonts

Nowadays, most printers can cope with printing text out using a multitude of different fonts. The specification of the fonts can be loaded into the printer in two ways:

(1) Using software, meaning that the application producing the printout will place the appropriate instructions for the fonts to be printed in front of the data, and send this across the network to the printer.

(2) Using hard fonts, where the font description is already in the printer: this normally involves purchasing the appropriate hardware font cartridge that plugs into the printer. In these cases, the most commonly-used printers are from the Hewlett-Packard LaserJet series, for which there are very many different fonts available.

In order to minimize the amount of data being transferred across the network, it is advisable to identify the most popular fonts used in your organization. Once you have ascertained this you can purchase and physically install the appropriate hardware font. It is amazing how this can reduce the amount of print data that is spooled across the network; this is particularly true for word processing.

Typically, there may be a 100-Kbyte overhead simply to describe the font. As a comparison, printing one page in Microsoft Word for Windows with soft fonts might take 170 Kbytes, whereas hard fonts may only require 70 Kbytes. One advantage of soft fonts is that they can be varied and font format and size can be swapped and changed at will, whereas using hard fonts is a far more limited operation.

My advice here is to identify the two or three most popular fonts being used and standardize all your applications around them, implementing them by placing hard fonts in the printer. You can still have the benefits of the soft fonts to create the variety, at the expense of the extra amount of data required.

Block-oriented printing versus byte-oriented printing

Most applications rely on DOS to print through the serial or parallel ports. They direct their output to one of the byte-oriented devices such as the LPT1 or LPT2 port. Data moves through these devices on a byte-by-byte basis via DOS, which in turn uses the byte-oriented functions of the BIOS; this can be an enormous bottleneck. Imagine printing a ten-page graphical document which might require the transfer of 15 Mbytes of data: if this had to be transferred byte-by-byte, it would be a little like attempting to fill up a swimming pool with drops of water. Each time a character is requested for printing, a whole series of software and hardware interrupts is triggered off through DOS then through BIOS and then buffered appropriately. There are, however, applications that support block-oriented printing. These types of application allow the transfer of large amounts of data, such as 16 Kbytes, directly into the network's queuing system, thus bypassing all the bottlenecks imposed by the byte-oriented DOS printing facility.

NetWare provides this facility through its NCP calls under its Queue Management Services (QMS). A beautiful example of a program that uses block-oriented printing is NPRINT. To print, NPRINT opens up a spool file that is directly sent to the network file server using the QMS functions. If comparing NPRINT with DOS print, a significant performance improvement in printing is achieved.

There are products available that use the QMS facility to significantly improve the performance of network printing. It is well worth finding out if your application can send its data directly to the network print queues as opposed to relying on it being captured by the DOS print command.

Select the appropriate print server

One of the advantages of NetWare is that your print server can run on a multitude of different environments; this is one of the things that Microsoft LAN Manager has been lacking for a long time. With NetWare, you can run your print server as an NLM on the NetWare file server, or you can run it as a dedicated workstation as the PSERVER.EXE. Novell also provides facilities for direct printing via RPRINTER. As well as being locally connected to a print server, printers can be dispersed across the network on other users' workstations.

It is very interesting to examine the differences between PSERVER.NLM and PSERVER.EXE. Assuming that all else is equal, and that you have an Ethernet network, running PSERVER on a dedicated workstation will increase your overall throughput on average by 20–30%. Generally speaking, the dedicated PSERVER can handle far greater throughput of printable data than the version that runs on the file server itself. Where possible, it is advisable to use a dedicated workstation as a print server rather than using the file server. This approach also removes most of the burden from the file server, which means that most of the file server NLMs can concentrate on file server facilities.

I have found that, if the PSERVER is running as an NLM on the file server, the performance of the file server deteriorates by approximately 10–20%, depending on the printer being used.

Parallel or serial connection

Printers normally come with two options: serial and parallel connections. Both of these devices are byte-oriented, that is, they take data byte-by-byte, potentially leading to massive bottlenecks.

Parallel cabling is far more efficient and easy to configure than serial cabling. Generally speaking, the performance difference is a factor of 10 in favour of parallel cable (see Table 19.2). It does, of course, have a number of limitations; most devices allow only three parallel ports.

Always try to use up all your parallel ports first, treating serial ports as a last option.

Comparing different types of print server

Figure 19.6 shows that PSERVER.EXE on an average network has the best performance. The relative difference between PSERVER.EXE and PSERVER.NLM is largely dependent on what other activities are being carried out by the file server.

Table 19.2 Typical printer transfer rates.

Medium used	Data flow
Serial cable (14 kbps)	1.750 kbps
Parallel cable	10 kbps

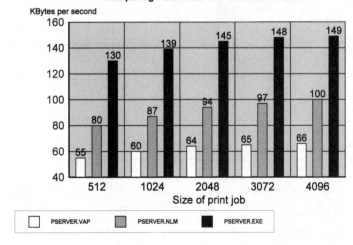

Figure 19.6 Different PSERVER performances.
Note: Different size print jobs were sent to all three.

Connecting printers directly to the network

The current trend for printer manufactures is to bring out devices that allow for direct connection to the network cable, as well as connection to PCs via serial or parallel ports. This normally involves placing the appropriate network adaptor card inside the printer. The network can feed the printer at a far greater rate than can be achieved using the old conventional parallel method. Table 19.3 shows a massive improvement in performance if printers can connect directly to the network as opposed to being fed via parallel or serial cables.

The market leader, Hewlett-Packard, produces a number of LaserJet printers specifically designed to be connected directly to the network, as in Figure 19.7. It calls the cards HP JetDirect cards. They come in Token Ring and Ethernet versions, with support for the most popular types of cabling, such as 10BaseT (UTP) and Thin Ethernet. Most of these printers come with an emulation ROM which turns the printer into a remote printer from a NetWare viewpoint. It does this by running a special version of RPRINTER.EXE actually on the printer itself. This means that the directly networked printer can now be connected to any print server as a remote printer.

This is very nice. It has a number of advantages.

✓ It does not need to use a workstation.

✓ The printer can be fed at very high rates.

✓ It can be placed anywhere on the network.

However, there are disadvantages:

✗ It can be expensive.

✗ You have to worry about whether the printer is running the latest version of RPRINTER.EXE.

An increasingly popular alternative to using a dedicated workstation as a print server is the use of intelligent print server boxes. They are normally no bigger than a book, but they can support a number of parallel and serial printers. They are directly connected to the network and are seen by NetWare as a dedicated workstation which is running PSERVER.EXE (see Figure 19.8). The Intel Corporation is one of the big names producing this sort of product.

Table 19.3 Typical printer transfer rates.

Medium used	Data flow
Serial cable (14 kbps)	1.750 kbps
Parallel cable	10 kbps
Direct Ethernet connection	1000 kbps
Direct Token Ring connection	1700 kbps

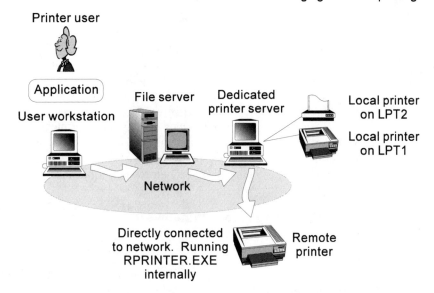

Figure 19.7 Connecting printers directly to the network.

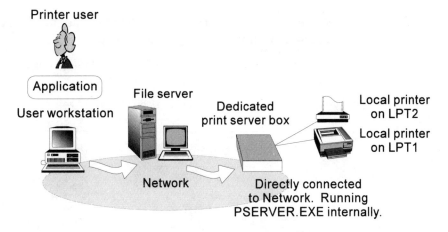

Figure 19.8 Dedicated print server boxes.

The advantages of using these are:

✓ They have a very small profile.

✓ They can be placed anywhere on the network.

✓ No screens or keyboards are required.

However, you will have the following disadvantages:

✗ You have to worry about using the latest version of PSERVER.EXE.

✗ You will have yet another type of hardware to manage.

Advice on managing print servers

Where possible, use the dedicated print server PSERVER.EXE as opposed to the file server-based PSERVER.NLM. A typical low-specification 386 PC with 2 Mbytes of memory would normally be adequate as a dedicated print server.

Minimize the number of different types of printer within the organization. This should reduce management overheads.

At large sites with multitudes of networked printers, keep users as close as possible to the printers that they intend to use. This will help users to keep in touch and troubleshoot their own printers. You need to divide users into manageable printing groups, each in control of their own printing.

Network printing across Windows

Overview

Using the network printers under Windows is very simple. The assignment can all be done within the Windows environment, in two stages:

(1) Select the correct printer driver for the remote network printer (see Figure 19.9).

For networked printers, disable the Use print manager option. There is no point in double buffering.

(2) Route the logical DOS port to the appropriate print queue. This is done using the Connect button (see Figure 19.10).

> Warning: If you mismatch the connection it will often result in the most peculiar problems.

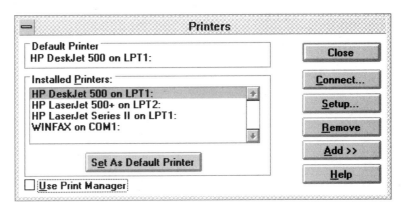

Figure 19.9 Selecting the printer driver.

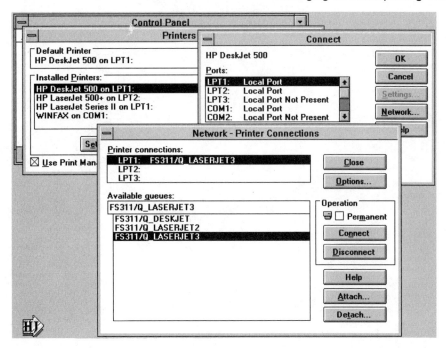

Figure 19.10 Routing the logical DOS port to the appropriate print queue.

Advice on managing printers

Try to standardize so that your Windows users use one, or at the most two, good quality printers that are to be shared. Where possible stick to industry standards such as the Hewlett-Packard LaserJet III. The fewer different types of printer being used, the fewer the problems of the network manager.

Disable the Windows Print Manager buffering. There is no point double-buffering: the Novell print server already buffers its data onto disk. This is one of the quickest ways to improve network printing with the minimum amount of effort.

20

Managing diskless workstations

Overview

Novell provides some very useful techniques for booting a workstation from remote boot image files kept on a file server. This basically means that you can do away with any floppy disk or hard disk drives on the workstation (see Figure 20.1).

This is done by simply placing an image of a network boot disk onto the file server. When the diskless workstation is booted, the remote reset ROM, which is placed on the workstation's NIC (Network Interface Card), automatically connects up to the nearest file server and starts to read the remote boot image file. It executes as if it were reading off the local floppy A: drive.

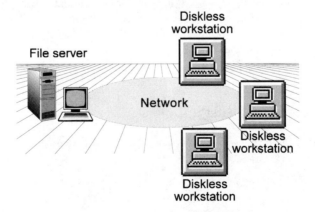

Figure 20.1 Diskless workstations.

How it works

Let's follow what really happens when a diskless PC is 'cold' booted.

The NIC, due to its programming on board the boot ROM, takes over the normal booting up sequence. This is done when the PC BIOS, as part of its normal boot-up procedure, passes control to each adaptor card in turn so that they may initialize themselves. However, unlike other normal, polite adaptor cards, the NIC does not return control to the BIOS, but instead takes on the responsibility of modifying the boot-up sequence.

First, it checks to see if a real boot disk exists on a real A: drive; if so, it will pass control back to BIOS and continue as normal. However, if no boot files are found on the A: drive, the system checks if it is possible to boot up via the C: drive. If it is possible, the system will ask if the user would like to boot from the C: drive or the network image files.

If no C: drive was found, or if the user chooses to boot from the network, the NIC starts to boot the image files from the nearest file server.

The NIC program then sends an NCP packet requesting 'Get nearest file server'.

This means that, if several file servers are on the network, the first one to respond will establish the connection. The implication is that, in order to be sure of the correct boot up, you need to place a copy of the image files in each accessible file server's SYS:\LOGIN directory.

See 'Management issues' at the end of this chapter for further discussion.

The file server then provides read access to its SYS:\LOGIN directory. The NIC proceeds to look for the file BOOTCONF.SYS. If it exists, it is investigated to see if there is a specific image file that the supervisor has set up to be run whenever that particular workstation is started; if the BOOTCONF.SYS does not exist, the default image file (always called NET$DOS.SYS) is used.

Once the appropriate disk image file has been located under the SYS:\LOGIN directory, the workstation's DOS environment is tricked into thinking it has just read a regular floppy disk from its local A: drive.

This continues until NETX (or equivalent) is executed. At this point, the execution of the remote image file is closed down. Control is now given back to the workstation and execution continues as normal.

How to create boot image files

It is very easy to create an image of a disk which can be used to boot the diskless workstation.

Warning: You cannot create a new remote boot image file on SYS:LOGIN if an existing one is already in use. You have to either create an image file under a different name or just wait for the other user to terminate connection.

Creating the boot disk

You should put all the drivers and programs required to boot up the diskless workstation onto one bootable diskette. Before you start, you must create a DOS bootable disk which should contain the following:

- The DOS operating system
- An appropriate CONFIG.SYS
- AUTOEXEC.BAT set-up

CONFIG.SYS

This file should contain all the drivers necessary for booting up. One of the most important drivers is the HIMEM.SYS. An important point to bear in mind is that, during the booting up process, all drivers have to be located on the A: drive, for example:

```
FILES=30
BUFFERS=30
DEVICE=A:HIMEM.SYS
```

AUTOEXEC.BAT

The AUTOEXEC.BAT should typically do the following:

```
PROMPT $p$g
LSL
NE2000
IPXODI
NETX
F:
LOGIN
```

Taking an image of the boot disk

To place an image of the boot disk onto the file server, use the DOSGEN.EXE (DOS Remote Image File Generation) program. This program is in the SYS:\SYSTEM directory.

Before taking the image of the diskette, I recommend that you use a disk compression utility. This will get rid of all the empty spaces and reduce the size of the image file. I use the Norton Utility SD.EXE, but the DOS 6 utility, DEFRAG, will do the same job.

The image produced must be placed in the SYS:\LOGIN directory. From the SYS:\LOGIN directory, the following command is then executed:

DOSGEN A: NET$DOS.SYS
```
Floppy Type f0 = 3 1/2 inch, 1.4 MB
```

```
Total Floppy Space 2880 Sectors
Setting Up System Block.
Setting Up FAT Tables.
Setting Up Directory Structures.
Traversing Directory Structures.
Processing IO      SYS
Processing MSDOS   SYS
Processing COMMAND COM
Processing CONFIG  SYS
Processing AUTOEXECBAT
Processing HIMEM   SYS
Processing NET     CFG
Processing SHELL   CFG
Diskette Label = DATA_01M
Processing IPXODI  COM
Processing LSL     COM
Processing SMCPLUS COM
Processing BNETX   EXE
Processing NETBIOS EXE
Transferring Data to "NET$DOS.SYS"
```

This has the effect shown in Figure 20.2.

Follow up procedures are necessary:

(1) A copy of the AUTOEXEC.BAT file found on the boot disk has to be manually copied to two different directories: the SYS:\LOGIN directory and the user's default directory (this is the directory that the user is sent to by the script file).

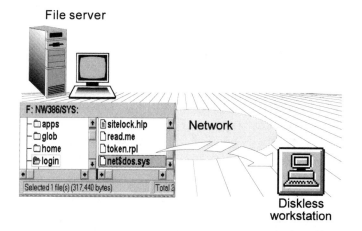

Figure 20.2 Diskless workstation's boot sequence.

(2) The NET$DOS.SYS file is now set to shareable:

```
FLAG NET$DOS.SYS S
```

(3) Finally, you need to ensure that the modify right for the SYS:\LOGIN directory is granted to all the remote boot users.

RPLFIX.COM

Due to a number of changes that Microsoft introduced with DOS 5.x, the NetWare remote load does not work unless the boot image file is modified. The program used to make this modification is provided by Novell. It is called RPLFIX.COM. When RPLFIX.COM is run, it modifies the DOS 5.x boot image file, such as NET$DOS.SYS. It does this so that it will load properly, without the characteristic problem of the workstation just hanging.

The program is simple to use; all you do is type the following:

```
RPLFIX <boot image file>
```

The program comes as standard on the latest Novell DOS workstations support disk.

Supporting multiple different remote boot disk images

Since some diskless workstations use different configurations or need to be booted up with different versions of DOS, we need to be able to support multiple boot images. Each station can have a different boot up image. This is all possible because of the text file BOOTCONF.SYS, which is kept under the SYS:\LOGIN directory. It contains a list of network node addresses and which boot image file should be loaded to each. It has the format:

```
0x <network address>,<node address> = <boot up image file name>
```

To support multiple different remote boot disk images, do the following:

(1) Boot a station from a floppy or hard disk and login as SUPERVISOR.

(2) Rename the AUTOEXEC.BAT file on the boot diskette to a name that describes the type of station (say, FRED.BAT).

(3) Copy the renamed .BAT file (FRED.BAT, in this example) from the boot diskette to SYS:LOGIN *and* to the user's default directory specified in the login script.

(4) Create a new AUTOEXEC.BAT file on the boot diskette that calls up the renamed batch file (FRED.BAT).

(5) Map to the SYS:\LOGIN directory.

(6) Run DOSGEN and indicate the new name for the image file (e.g. DOSGEN A: FRED.SYS).

(7) Create the BOOTCONF.SYS file. The file should contain a line showing the Fred workstation node and network address and the name of the image file that should be loaded up for this workstation.

(8) Flag the .SYS files in SYS:LOGIN as shareable.

(9) Grant the modify right to the remote boot users in SYS:LOGIN.

Management issues

One of the biggest problems with managing a diskless workstation on multi-file server networks is that you cannot predict which file server the diskless boot station will attempt to boot up from. In the manuals accompanying NetWare 386, Novell suggests that you place a copy of the NET$DOS.SYS program on each potential file server. This can be difficult. It would be great if you could somehow define the preferred file server at the boot-up sequence. Do not forget that the normal NETX-preferred file server option is unusable at this stage because, by the time it starts to run, it is too late – a connection has already been made.

This is a problem area that I think Novell will sort out in the near future. A possible solution is the inclusion of a special location in future copies of the boot ROM. It could contain the name of the default file server which could be blown into the ROM. However, this is currently very difficult since each manufacturer has a different ROM structure.

For the time being, I have come up with the following solution, using the file server option:

```
:SET reply to get nearest server=off
Reply To Get Nearest Server set to OFF
:
```

The above command prevents all the file servers that I do not want the remote disk to boot up from responding to the standard NCP call 'Get the nearest file server'. Each normal workstation must now use the preferred file server option, either through the SHELL.CFG or the command line NETX PS=, to login to the above file servers. This will lead to the scenario shown in Figure 20.3.

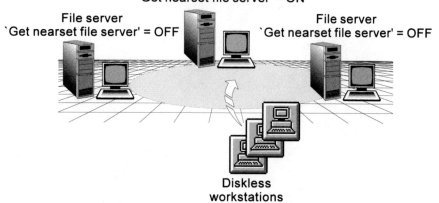

Figure 20.3 Suggested file server connection configuration.

21

Managing backups and Uninterruptible Power Supplies (UPSs)

Overview

Although backing up is usually considered boring, it can be a life saver. Taking a backup of your system on a regular basis might seem a lot of work; however, it is not so difficult once you have established a routine. Generally speaking, every moment spent in ensuring your backup system is up-to-date is worth every penny (or, in European terms, every ECU). It is also extremely satisfying and comforting to know that your system has been backed up correctly. The important point to make here is that you must develop a clear and regular backing up routine.

There are three main types of backup: full, differential and incremental (in addition, you can specify custom backups):

- Full backups include all data, regardless of when or whether it has been previously revised or backed up.
- Differential backups include all data that has been modified since the last full backup.
- Incremental backups include all data that has been modified since the last full or incremental backup (whichever was last).
- Custom backups include the data you specify.

NetWare backup programs

When you buy a copy of the NetWare operating system, you get two very good, simple backup programs:

- SBACKUP.NLM (file server-based), which is used on NetWare 386 file servers.
- NBACKUP.EXE (workstation-based), which is used to back up Novell file servers. This is not used very often these days. Most people prefer a file server-based backup system, rather than backing up a file server from a workstation.

SBACKUP.NLM

This programs needs to use a number of cooperating NLM programs in order to function correctly. The advantages of this product are that it is free and that, as well as backing up the local file server, it can back up additional file servers by running a special agent program on them (see Figure 21.1).

The following must be run on all file servers to be backed up:

- TSA.NLM: this is the Tape Service Agent (TSA), which provides the link between the data requester, SIDR.NLM, and the local filing system.
- TSA-311.NLM: this is specific to the network operation filing system. It satisfies the TSA.NLM request for local file access. In NetWare 4.x, this would be different.

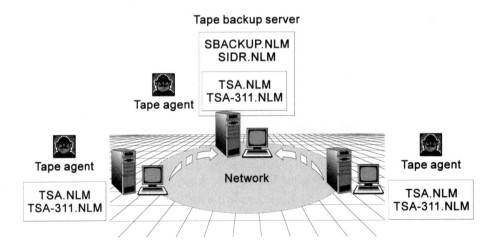

Figure 21.1 NetWare tape backup agents.

The tape backup server must also run the following programs on top of the above:

- SBACKUP.NLM: this is a menu-driven backup control program. It handles interaction between the users and the backing up process.
- SIDR.NLM: this is a data requester. It uses the SMSP (Storage Management Service Protocol) to make requests to its tape agents around the network.

NetWare 4.x

With the introduction of NetWare 4.0, it is now possible to backup and restore workstations as well as file servers. You load a special DOS TSR program called TSA_SMS.EXE; it allows the SBACKUP.NLM program to backup the workstation data.

Backup technology

The technology for backing up data has progressed significantly over the last five years. It has noticeably improved thanks to DAT (Digital Audio Tape) and the development of WORM (Write Once, Read Many). The old QIC (Quarter-Inch Tape) magnetic tapes are becoming less popular.

Quarter-Inch Tape (QIC)

This technology has been around for a long time. Up to a few years ago, it was the most popular medium for storing large amounts of data. The QIC standard supports a range of storage capacities: 40, 60, 125, 150 and 300 Mbytes. It is not the most reliable system available and is now becoming out-dated. It uses a recording technique called the *serpentine recording method.* The tape is moved back and forth across the stationary magnetic head. If the head becomes slightly out of alignment, all sorts of problems emerge.

DAT (Digital Audio Tape)

The 8 mm DAT standard
The Sony Corporation has championed this standard. It is same type of tape as used in its 8 mm camcorders. DAT uses a different recording method to the QIC tapes, called *helical scan technology.* This is the same technique used by video recorders. Both the magnetic head and tape move. The head is mounted on a drum which is spun at an angle of around five degrees to the vertical. Data is then stored in strips. As the tape is moved across the drum, the data is stored in a digital format on the

tape. This technique allows for a higher density of data compression and it is potentially more reliable than the method used by QIC tapes. A typical DAT tape can store from 1.2 Gbytes up to the very latest tape, which, it is claimed, can store up to 8 Gbytes. The other good news about DAT is that it is an order of magnitude more reliable than the old analogue storage techniques of the QIC tapes. There is now a worldwide standard that defines how the data should be laid out on the tape. This is referred to as DDS (Digital Data Storage). It defines the sequential data format. Individual files and directories can be read off the tape in any order.

The 4 mm DAT standard

Another standard pioneered by Hitachi and Sharp Electronics is 4 mm DAT. It uses the DataDAT format and allows the tape to be formatted much like a hard disk. It organizes the tape into sectors, which means it can be operated as if it were a random-access device. The advantage of this is that you can read, write and delete files, just as you can on a hard disk. However, the 8 mm tape seems to be the more popular format for backing up servers.

Advantages and disadvantages

The advantages and disadvantages of using DAT are as follows:

- ✓ A high storage rate is achieved.
- ✓ Its error rate is very low.
- ✓ The tapes are relatively cheap.
- ✓ Tape can be read and written to many times.
- ✗ It is susceptible to magnetic radiation.
- ✗ The storage medium deteriorates with time.

WORM disks

This is the same technology used by CD-ROMs, except that the WORM (Write Once, Read Many) drive can write data onto a CD. However, once it is written, it cannot be erased. This makes a permanent copy on the CD. WORM disks have the following advantages and disadvantages:

- ✓ It is not susceptible to magnetic radiation.
- ✓ Very high reliability is achieved.
- ✓ The disks do not deteriorate with time (although this has not yet been fully proved).
- ✗ The disks can only be written to once.
- ✗ They can be expensive.

Dedicated tape backup servers

This is becoming very popular. This type of product, which is a combined hardware/software package, can turn a workstation into a dedicated tape storage server. This is normally done by running a copy of the NetWare 386 run-time operating system and then loading a special backing-up NLM program. Normally, this type of workstation will have a DAT driver for backing up data. One of the most popular products is the Intel Storage Express System server.

Permanent archiving

This is a very useful concept which has been largely popularized by The Network Archivist from the Palindrome Corporation. This product sees your backup not as series of tapes, but as a collection of data that happens to be scattered over a number of different tapes. It catalogues each file as it is backed up and recognizes when file copies have become stable. When a file which has been backed up several times on different tapes remains unchanged for a long period of time it will suggest, under supervisor control, that it should be erased from your system. The space freed will then be used by more active files. This is a good idea, since the majority of the files on your system are not used very often.

This type of product allows you to control the archiving rules, which can easily be adjusted to meet your demands. These systems normally have a special NLM program which is run constantly on the file server. If a user makes a request to read a file that has been long removed and archived, the system will automatically warn the supervisor to reload the tape containing the requested data.

These products normally have both short- and long-term backup policies. The short-term goal is the normal backing up of data, whereas the long-term goal is to monitor inactive files and remove them from the system. The system normally avoids overwriting files that might be important. It uses the 'Tower of Hanoi' system, combined with regular re-checking of data, to ensure reliability and minimize tape usage.

The Network Archivist is a sophisticated backup package for a Novell system. Figure 21.2 shows a typical screen from The Network Archivist. Against each file is a rule indicating how often it should be backed up. More interestingly, it also has a column which defines the migration period, that is, how long a file may remain un-referenced before it is migrated off the system. Other excellent packages are ArcServe and TapeWare. ArcServe is compatible with the Novell tape server agent concept, which means ArcServe stations can be used by the SBACKUP.NLM program.

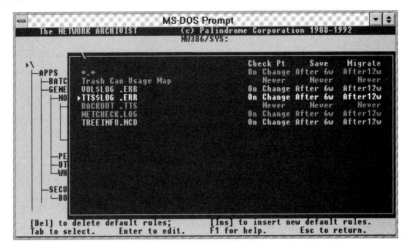

Figure 21.2 A typical screen from The Network Archivist.

Backup management strategy

Developing a backing up strategy

The key to being able to recover from a disaster is to have an up-to-date backup of your system stored in a safe place. It is generally not too difficult to get hold of replacement hardware, but to reinstate all your data from scratch could be a nightmare. Do take the following points into consideration when devising a backup plan:

- How often should a full backup be done?
- How often should incremental backups be done? Should they be done at all?
- Where should backups be stored? (are they really secure?)
- Who will be responsible for the backing up?
- How often will tapes be taken off-site?
- Who will be responsible for tapes off-site?
- How many tapes should be recycled?
- How often should tapes be set aside?

Do think about the above questions. I have suggested a number of answers in the following section, but it is ultimately up to you to devise an appropriate plan.

Management considerations

Use Novell SBACKUP.NLM or another third-party package

There is much to be said for using Novell's own SBACKUP.NLM program. It is free (but has limited third-party tape support) and, most importantly, if you use it when the next release of NetWare comes out (say NetWare 4.2), then the SBACKUP.NLM provided is guaranteed to support any bindery changes that might have occurred in the operating system. However, if you have bought a third-party backup system, you might need to go through the inconvenience of updating it before it can be used. This might take a long time, especially if the new version is not ready for shipment yet. On the other hand, the SBACKUP.NLM is very basic and there are a number of excellent third-party NetWare file server backup programs which can really make the life of the network manager easier. An example of such a program is The Network Archivist.

See the discussion on The Network Archivist in the section 'Permanent archiving' in this chapter.

Advice

If you decide to go for third-party packages, look for software that can backup local workstations as well as file servers. Unfortunately, when using SBACKUP.NLM (NetWare 3.1 version), you cannot backup workstation hard disks. However, it is possible to backup other file servers. The new SBACKUP.NLM that comes with NetWare 4.0 can also back up workstations.

Ensure that the thrid-party package complies with the Novell Storage Management System (SMS). This will ensure that it will integrate with Novell tape agent server concepts.

Whatever package you decide to use, always schedule your backup to take place when everyone is logged off and there is minimum network traffic.

The best time to backup a network is usually between 2.00 a.m. and 5.00 a.m., but each site has to be considered on its own merit. The key factor is to select a time when most networked files will be closed.

Choosing a backup medium

I recommend using DAT tapes or WORM technology for your backups. In making a choice, take into consideration price, reliability, ease of use and reusability. Either technology should be able to cope with the normal requirements of the average network manager.

Suggested routine

If you can afford it, it is well worth buying a sophisticated LAN backup package such as The Network Archivist. It will archive your files and suggest a daily routine for backing up tapes. Most users don't bother with such programs; they use Novell's free backup programs, such as SBACKUP.NLM, and develop their own backing up system. For these people, I recommend the following procedure:

- Buy 20 tapes.
- Label them as shown in Table 21.1.

From Monday to Thursday, back up every day onto the appropriate daily tape. Then use the Friday 1 tape on the first Friday of the month, Friday 2 on the second, and so on. On the last Friday of the month, instead of the normal daily or weekly tapes, use the appropriately labelled monthly tape, such as January. This system is used throughout the year, until the last Friday of the year is reached. At the end of that day, the tape labelled with the appropriate year is used to take a one-off copy of the system. This copy should be stored very carefully in a strong safe. The cycle then starts up again for the new year.

It is debatable whether the yearly tapes will be of any use in years to come, but they are worth keeping as a long-term record of your company's historical data.

The daily backup tapes will probably not last the whole year, so you should consider using a new set every three months.

With just 20 tapes used in any year, you will benefit from having full backups for the:

- Last week on a daily basis
- Weekly backups for the last month
- Monthly backups for the last year
- Yearly backups from when you started the system

Table 21.1 Tape labelling system.

Tape label	How often used
Monday	Used once a week
Tuesday	Used once a week
Wednesday	Used once a week
Thursday	Used once a week
Friday 1	Used once a month
Friday 2	Used once a month
Friday 3	Used once a month
January	Used once a year
February	Used once a year
.	.
.	.
December	Used once a year
Year 1993	Used once, set aside at end of year 1993
Year 1994	Used once, set aside at end of year 1994

Most sophisticated backup software will automatically remember the exact contents of each tape and inform you as to which tape to use next time.

Power protection overview

Most installations of Novell networks will have some sort of power supply backup. This is essential, due to the fact that the Novell file server is constantly reconfiguring its memory and hard disk status. If it is switched off suddenly without being DOWNed first, it cannot be guaranteed that you will recover from the server crash. The next time you re-boot the system, you might find that data has been lost. In real terms, nine times out ten, everything will probably be there, but it is not a risk worth taking. LAN Manager from Microsoft is much better than the Novell file server at coping with file server crashes. However, both file servers really do need to be protected against power failure. The are two different types of UPS (Uninterruptible Power Supply) on the market: the old-fashioned, unintelligent and the new, intelligent UPS devices. The difference is that the intelligent power supply is in constant communication with the file server, normally through a COM port, informing it as to the state of the power supply. If the incoming power is lost, a message is sent to the controlling program. It will then log all users out and DOWN the file server gracefully.

The other great advantage of using on-line intelligent UPSs is that they will protect your file server from very short-term power disruptions, such as voltage surges and sages.

Selecting a UPS

Power requirements
Whenever you select a UPS, you will need to know its power capacity. This can be worked out using the following formula:

$$\text{Volts Amps} = \text{Volts} \times \text{Amps}$$

Sometimes this is referred to as Watts.

The difference between VA and Watts

There is actually a difference between these two. A Watt is a measure of true power requirements, whereas the VA is a measure of power delivered. The two are not necessary the same. A correct formula is:

$$\text{Watts} = \text{Power Used Factor} \times \text{Volts Amps}$$

The Power Used Factor is normally around 60 to 70%. This is why I always increase the VA power delivery by at least 35% to get to a true Watt power requirement.

A typical file server requires 150 VA or Watts.

You need to add the power requirement of all your devices together (see Figure 21.3). It might be larger than you think.

Don't forget to take into account the power requirements of the file server monitor. If you install a black and white instead of the standard VGA colour screen, the file server's power requirement is significantly reduced.

Once the UPS power requirement has been established, you need to decide how long you need the power maintained for; for example, you can buy the Power Products UPS in the configurations shown in Table 21.2.

Connection to the file server

Most intelligent UPSs connect to the file server through the COM1: or COM2: port. Make sure that they are available on your file server and that one of the interrupts is not already used by one of your network adaptor cards.

NetWare and UPS

Novell has recognized the importance of UPS support. They issue a special UPS

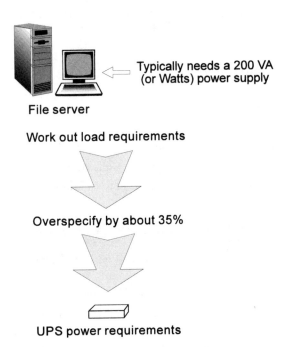

Figure 21.3 UPS power requirements.

Table 21.2 Power Products UPS configurations.

Power supply	Duration
250 Watts	15 minutes
425 Watts	30 minutes
650 Watts	10 minutes

software support program free with the NetWare operating system. This is the UPS.NLM program. The only problem with this package is that it will only work with a small selection of intelligent UPSs which conform to the Novell UPS.NLM software standard. The program is normally in the SYS:\SYSTEM directory. It has the following basic format:

```
LOAD UPS <UPS TYPE> <InterfacePort> DISCHARGE=time RECHARGE=time
```

The variables are:

- <UPS TYPE>. This is one of the Novell standard types and is defined in the manuals that accompany the UPSs. They can be DCB, EDCB, STANDALONE, KEYCARD, MOUSE and others.

- <InterfacePort>. This is the interface port number, for example, 286 or 34E Hex.

- DISCHARGE. This is the time that the file server can be kept going even though the incoming power has been lost. This is a very important figure. You must make sure you enter this figure correctly.

Always be over cautious: if the UPS guarantees ten minutes support, assume only 70%, that is, take only about seven minutes for granted. It is better to be safe than sorry!

- RECHARGE. This is the time the UPS will need to completely recharge itself once power has been restored.

Monitoring the UPS' status

Once the UPS.NLM program has been activated, it is possible to monitor the performance of the UPS using the UPS STATUS console command:

```
:
:UPS STATUS
```

This command will show a status screen similar to the one below:

```
o                     UPS Status for Server _____        o
o                                                             o
o              Power being used: Commercial                   o
o        Discharge time requested: 20 min. Remaining: 20 min. o
```

```
o                    Battery status: Recharged                o
o           Recharge time requested: 160 min. Remaining: 0 min.   o
o  Current network power status: normal                       o
o                                                             o
o  NOTICE: If your battery is over 6 months old, you may need o
o          to lower the discharge time.  (Consult the UPS     o
o             documentation for details.)                     o
```

UPS management issues

I strongly recommend that you install a UPS on your file server. The price of UPSs is falling so fast that they are becoming a very good investment. A typical starting price for an intelligent UPS can be as little as $500. The most popular type of UPS is the intelligent UPS system. The other stand-alone type is slowly becoming very unfashionable. Look for a UPS that can more than adequately keep your file server going for at least five minutes. This is the minimum needed to warn all the users to log out, and to unload all the NLM programs and dismount all the volumes. This can take a long time, especially if you have large disk sizes.

Novell's own UPS.NLM program is not very sophisticated. However, because it is from Novell, it will work, and it provides a good solution for users who do not want anything fancy. Better UPS software is available from third-party manufacturers. One package I have found very powerful is the PowerChute Smart UPS device from American Power Conversion. This product comes with an appropriate-rate UPS, PWRCHUTE.NLM and a number of workstation control programs. It is fast becoming a very popular package amongst Novell network managers.

Don't forget, when you install a UPS, to check it to see if it really does work. Log everyone out and then try to disconnect the UPS from the mains power supply and see if it lives up to expectations.

The PowerChute UPS package

This program connects the file server to the UPS via a serial port. When the PWRCHUTE.NLM is run on the file server console, it start the UPS monitoring process. Then the supervisor can run the DOS program PWRCHUTE.EXE from any workstation. It will show a screen similar Figure 21.4.

The screen shows very clearly the health of the power supply coming into your file server. Figure 21.4, for example, shows that the line voltage is normal. This means the file server is being powered from the conditioned line voltage. The program provides other valuable information, as listed in Table 21.3.

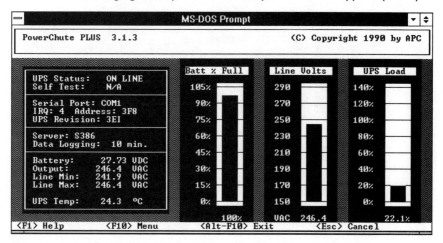

Figure 21.4 PowerChute PLUS (Example A).

If the line voltage fluctuates beyond safe boundaries, the UPS will switch to ON BATTERY to protect the equipment. The monitor screen will change to show something like Figure 21.5.

When the UPS is about to log everyone out, a Novell message is sent to all users, warning them that they are about to be logged out. This is, of course, if there are any users still active out there. While I was running Microsoft Windows, the UPS sent me the message shown in Figure 21.6.

Table 21.3 Additional information provided by PowerChute.

Item	Description
Battery Volts	Current DC battery voltage of UPS battery
Output	Voltage being supplied to the equipment
Line Min	Lowest momentary line voltage during the last 4-5 seconds
Line Max	Highest momentary line voltage during the last 4-5 seconds
Frequency	Frequency of AC being supplied to the equipment
UPS Temp	Internal UPS temperature
Batt % Full	Approximate remaining battery capacity (percentage of maximum charge)
Line Volts	The current input line voltage to the UPS
UPS Load	The current UPS output load as a percentage of full load: if this rises into the red area for more than a few seconds, the UPS will overload and shut down

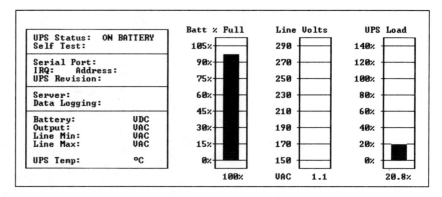

Figure 21.5 PowerChute PLUS (Example B).

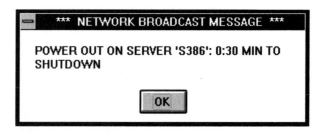

Figure 21.6 Warning message received from UPS prior to users being logged out.

22

Network performance issues

It is very difficult to get an exact benchmark of a LAN. There are so many different software and hardware parameters that it is very difficult to isolate and benchmark one single aspect of the network. Even when some of these parameters can be isolated and then benchmarked in turn, the accumulated result does not necessarily give an overall picture of network performance. Different aspects of your network, such as the hard disk and the hard disk drivers, react with each other in a non-linear fashion.

On average, 10% of the data flowing across networks is taken up by the overhead imposed by protocols.

In this chapter, I will present some of the key factors that significantly affect the overall performance of your network. I have conducted a number of tests to give the reader a flavour of the sort of performance that could be expected.

Components affecting network performance

Network type

The intrinsic type of underlying network technology limits the data transfer bandwidth (see Table 22.1).

These figures are very rarely achieved. The best I have seen was a Token Ring network with 95% saturation. Normally, the maximum you can achieve from Ethernet is around 80% of the bandwidth. You must remember that there is also a protocol overhead that starts to eat into the network bandwidth: this could be as much as 20%.

Table 22.1 Data transfer bandwidths for different network technologies.

Type of network	Maximum bits/sec	Maximum bytes/sec
Ethernet	10 Mbps	1250 KBps
Token Ring, 4 Mbytes	4 Mbps	500 KBps
Token Ring, 16 Mbytes	16 Mbps	2000 KBps
Fibre FDDI	100 Mbps	12500 KBps

The Network Interface Card (NIC)

When you buy an NIC, you have to decide how many address bits you want the card to support. The choice is normally between 8-bit, 16-bit and 32-bit cards. Obviously, the greater the number of address lines the card supports, the greater its bandwidth for shifting data between itself and your computer. Tests have shown that, for the average NIC, there is a performance difference of about 60% between the 8-bit and 32-bit NICs. My advice is to put at least 16-bit NICs in the workstations and a 32-bit NIC in the file server. The price difference between 8-bit and 16-bit cards is marginal. However, the price difference between 16-bit and 32-bit is significant, normally as much as 30–50% extra.

Use at least 16-bit NICs in the workstations; use a 32-bit NIC in the file server.

Not all NICs are the same. For example, a 16-bit Thin Ethernet card can differ by as much as 30% from manufacturer to manufacturer. This is because each manufacturer optimizes the internal performance of the NIC to a greater or lesser extent. Also, a number of NIC cards have internal buffering and caching. The general principle that you pay for what you get applies here. Do not be tempted by very cheap NIC cards selling under unknown manufacturing names for next to nothing. My advice is to stick to the well known manufacturers, such as 3-Com, IBM, SMC and Intel.

File server hard disk and hard disk controller

The performance of a network will be highly dependent on the hard disk subsystem. This is one of the areas often suspected of being a network performance bottleneck. It is important to select the right combination of hard disk controller and a fast enough hard disk to cope with the demand on the file server.

The number of routers to go through

The greater the number of routers the packets have to go through, the lower your network performance will become from the user viewpoint (see Figure 22.1). As a general rule of thumb, every time a data packet goes through a router, the maximum bandwidth is reduced by 10–20%.

Number of concurrent connections on the file server

The number of concurrent connections that the file server has to support will, not surprisingly, affect the performance of the file server; however, it is never linear. Generally speaking, user performance decreases slowly as the number of connections increases on the file server. The reason for this is that a single user does not normally fully utilize the bandwidth of the network. As users come on to the network, they start to use up the spare capacity of the file server; it is at this point that bottlenecks become obvious. The most common cause of a bottleneck is not the network, but the file server not being able to move the data fast enough from its hard disk onto the network.

How to performance test the file server

There are many tools which will provide you with an assortment of data on various aspects of file server performance. The three most commonly used indicators are described below.

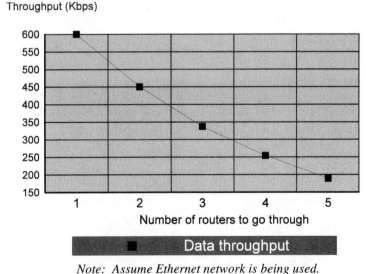

Note: Assume Ethernet network is being used.

Figure 22.1 The router performance problem.

The SPEED command

This command is available at the file server console. It provides a standard rating for the file server's CPU performance potential.

The MONITOR command

The most commonly examined field on the MONITOR.NLM screen is the file server utilization percentage figure (see Figure 22.2). This shows the current dynamic load on the file server as a percentage.

There are a number of third-party packages that will audit this figure and produce a graph of fluctuation against time. They can also be set up to trigger off warnings if utilization hits a certain high level, such as 90%.

The PERFORM3.EXE program

This program provides a standard way of finding out how a file server will cope (from the workstation viewpoint) with a series of different loads placed on it.

The PERFORM3.EXE file performance tool is provided free by Novell. This is a simple program that can provide you with a rich set of information about file server performance. You can obtain a copy of PERFORM3 from most bulletin boards, such as CIX in the UK and Compuserve in the USA.

How to synchronize the performance file server test

One of the advantages of PERFORM3 is its ability to synchronize the test across multiple workstations. All the workstations wanting to run the test at the same time must first login and go to a common directory on the file server that you want to test. The first workstation to run the test will take control, as shown in Figure 22.3.

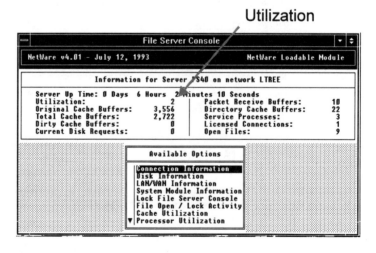

Figure 22.2 Monitoring server utilization.

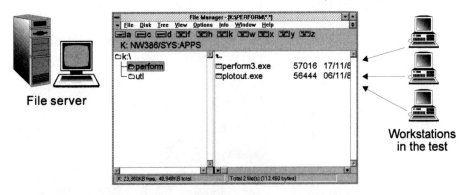

Figure 22.3 Running PERFORM3 across the network.

As other users also run the PERFORM3 program, the controlling workstation will be told that a number of other workstations have now joined in the test.

The benchmark test bed

The following are overall figures that were benchmarks on the author's company Novell file server. We used Novell's own benchmarking program, PERFORM3. The Novell file server was a 486, 33 MHz Dell PC, using a NE2000 NIC; the workstations were 486, 33 MHz PCs using 16-bit SMC Ethernet cards. The figures are very interesting: they illustrate increased memory and diminished return in performance. The graphs show that the interpretation is not straightforward: the difference in the memory configuration also seems to be related to the number of concurrent connections. The greater the number of workstations connected, the greater the difference in memory seems to be.

File server memory and performance

The following is a breakdown of how the amount of installed memory in the file server could affect network performance. The tests were carried out using PERFORM3.EXE from Novell.

When there is only a small number of workstations connected, there is hardly any difference in memory performance (see Figure 22.4).

However, as the number of workstations increases, the caching in the memory starts to play a more significant role in the overall performance of the file server (see Figure 22.5).

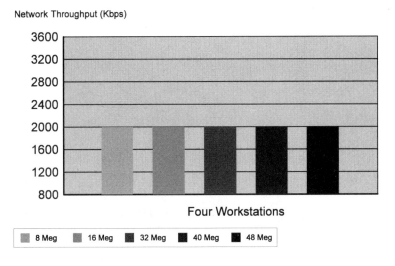

Figure 22.4 How a four-user file server's performance is affected by installed memory.

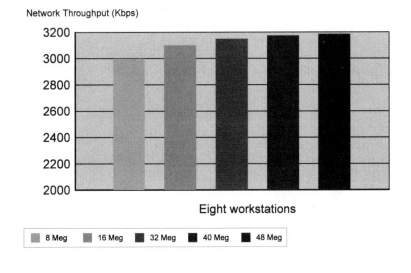

Figure 22.5 How an eight-user file server's performance is affected by installed memory.

As the demand on the file server continues to increase, the memory difference starts to play an important role in maintaining performance (see Figure 22.6). The improved performance is because the extra file server memory is being used for caching the users' I/O requests. However, after a while, as the level of installed memory continues to go up, the file server's performance levels off to a plateau. This is because other bottlenecks have started to come into action.

Strategy for improving network performance

The above factors all contribute to define maximum network performance. There now follows a number of suggestions on improving network performance.

If you find that your network is running a little slowly, and the problem is due to the underlying network, not the file server, then consider the following suggestion. One of the quickest ways of improving the file server is to split the connecting network into two or more separate networks (see Figure 22.7).

The good news is that if you are using Novell 386/486 file servers, they can support up to four different NICs inside them. This means you can connect four separate networks into the file server (see Figure 22.8). These could all be of the same type, such as Ethernet, or a mixture of networks, such as Token Ring and a combination of Ethernet and ARCnet.

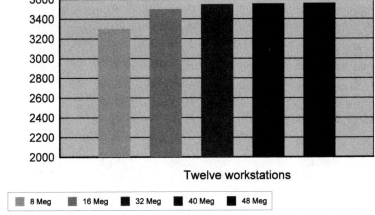

File server performance versus memory installed

Network Throughput (Kbps)

Twelve workstations

█ 8 Meg   █ 16 Meg   █ 32 Meg   █ 40 Meg   █ 48 Meg

Figure 22.6 How a 12-user file server's performance is affected by installed memory.

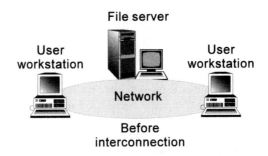

Figure 22.7 A file server on a single network.

Figure 22.8 Interconnection through the server can improve network bandwidth.

The positive aspect of this approach is that you can, in effect, multiply the bandwidth that the file server can satisfy. This technique would significantly improve those situations where the network becomes a bottleneck. However, when the next bottleneck arises will depend upon how fast the file server can satisfy the multiple networks.

The next question is how to split the users across the network. The aim of the exercise here is to put an equal load (as far as possible) on each of the connecting networks, enabling you to utilize your network effectively: this means trying to spread your power users as far as possible across the networks. This is normally hard to do, since power users tend to cluster together; it is far easier from a cabling viewpoint to put them on the same segment of the network. This is where the art of comprise has to come in, since there is a potential conflict of interests here.

In most cases, after you have split your users across a number of networks connected to a file server, you will find that, as the load increases, you experience a significant improvement over the old single-network approach. This is a very cost-effective way of improving performance. The price that you have to pay is having yet another NIC in the file server and making some minor changes to the cabling. This approach works only if the networks are going to be directly connected into the file server. If you split the network using external routers, then the bandwidth will not necessarily improve and, indeed, could deteriorate.

Figure 22.9 shows how performance was increased by splitting up the number of networks coming into a file server.

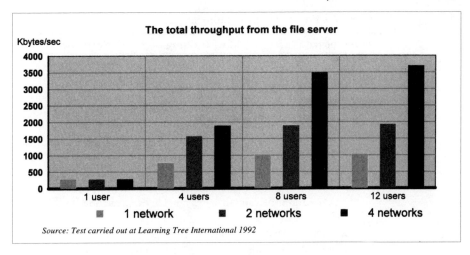

Figure 22.9 Connecting networks versus file server performance.

The NetWare 386 SPEED test

Understanding the NetWare 386 SPEED test

Novell provides its own method of speed testing the file server motherboard. This is similar to the Norton Utilities SI (System Information) test. It can be used to compare the performance of alternative motherboards for running the NetWare operating system. The higher the number returned by the SPEED program, the faster the file server can execute the NetWare 386 operating code. The test is a good overall representation of the server's internal performance. It takes into account the following aspects of the machine:

- The CPU clock speed (25MHz, 33MHz, 50 MHz, and so on)
- The CPU type used (80386SX, 80386, 80486, P5)
- The number of memory wait states (0, 1, 2, and so on)

If you become familiar with the Novell speed ratings, you can soon gain a good indication of the server's overall performance.

Generally speaking, the figures shown in Table 22.2 are those you should be achieving.

To check the performance level you are getting from your file server(s), type SPEED at the file server console. You will see something like the following:

```
:
:speed
```

Table 22.2 Processor speed ratings.

Motherboard	SPEED rating	Performance
80386SX 10MHz	70	Very poor
80386SX 16MHz	95	Poor
80386DX 16MHz	120	Average
80386DX 25MHz	242	Good
80486DX 50MHz	590	Excellent

```
Processor speed: 70

The processor speed rating is determined by

A 80386SX CPU running at 16 MHz should get a rating of about 95
A 80386 CPU running at 16 MHz should get a rating of about 120

Some machines have an AUTO or COMMON CPU speed mode that can
reduce the clock speed to as low as 6Mhz.  For NetWare 386 you
should set the CPU speed setting to the highest setting.  If
your machine has a slower rating than you expected, please
check the CPU speed setting.
:
```

You can now compare your figure against Table 22.2 in order to get an idea of the overall performance of the motherboard inside your file server.

How the Novell SPEED test works

The Novell speed test is just a simple loop that works for a set number of times. It counts how many times it manages to go around the loop within three CPU clock ticks. Novell reports this as being around 0.16 seconds. The greater the number of times the loop cycles around, the faster the SPEED rating. Before starting the test, the program shuts down the floppy disk drive (on some machines, when the floppy disk drive is active, it may cause the motherboard to go into a slow cycle).

The SPEED test does the following:

(1)   Disable floppy disk drive
(2)   Loop Counter:=0
(3)   Reset (Timer)
(4)   REPEAT
(5)   Loop Counter:= Loop Counter + 1

(6) UNTIL (Timer >= (3 CPU clock ticks have passed))
(7) SPEED:=(Loop Counter)/1000
(8) WRITE out the SPEED value

23

Documenting and auditing network hardware and procedures

Auditing the network

One of the most important aspects of effective network management is to document the network. I know it is not the most exciting task in the world, but it has to be done. (It is like your mother forcing you to take cod liver oil: it tastes horrible while you take it, but you know it is doing you good in the long term.) The documentation should cover the file server hardware and software. To be comprehensive, it would be ideal if you could also document all the workstation hardware and software. This is far more ambitious. The good news is that most of the documentation process can be automated. As the network manager, you just set up the auditing software and it will then go around the network and collect the data for you. You can then produce all sorts of reports.

Why document?

The main advantages of documenting your network are as follows:

- ✓ **Disaster planning.** The documentation will be very useful if you ever have to replace your file server in a hurry. For example, if your file server is destroyed by fire, you can easily order and set-up new hardware to replicate your original file server, using your previous documentation. This is, of course, assuming you have kept a hard copy of your documentation as opposed to keeping it on the old file server's hard disk.

  ✓ **Software rationalization**. By carrying out a software audit, you can rationalize the copies of software packages you have on the network. It is very common, for example, to find many copies of Microsoft Windows on a file server, when only one of them is being used.

  ✓ **Software licensing**. A software audit will make it very easy to know exactly what software has been installed on the file server. You can then ask yourself: 'Do I have a copy of the invoice for each of these packages?'. This might cause some sleepless nights.

  ✓ **Educating new managers**. If you go on holiday, or get run over by a big red bus, your colleagues will be left with a set of up-to-date documentation. This will be essential for any user taking over your job.

The disadvantages of documenting your network are as follows:

  ✗ **It can be tedious**. If you had to constantly go around the network and document any changes, it would make the life of the network manager very tedious. However, their are a number of automatic documentation programs, such as Brightwork's LAN Automatic Inventory and CheckIt LAN.

  ✗ **Limited shelf life**. Data can easily become out-of-date. It is a never-ending process to ensure that documentation is constantly kept up-to-date.

  ✗ **Security implication**. Be very careful who you give your documentation to. It contains the details of all your network set-ups. It might be very useful to your competitors.

LAN Automatic Inventory

Overview

This program automatically documents your network. It can collect information about most of the hardware and software on your LAN. It keeps an inventory on the file server. It can then use the inventory to check for network configuration changes. It also provides a means of entering manual information about items that could not be collected automatically.

As well as collecting information about all file servers, the product can collect information about the user workstations. It can collect information on all the programs that users have on their local hard disks. It can also take a snapshot of the installed hardware at each workstation. The system can support PC and Apple Macintosh users.

Automatically collecting information

The LAN Automatic Inventory program can collect information on the following subjects:

- Network information: user name, network address, network cards used, NetWare shell used
- Workstation hardware information: process type, bus type, BIOS version, DOS type, CMOS data, base/extended/expanded memory, floppy disk drivers, hard disk types, ports used, video adaptor type
- PC workstation software information: programs stored on the local hard disk, copies of the user's AUTOEXEC.BAT and CONFIG.SYS
- File server hardware information: LAN card used, LAN card configuration, hard disk type, CMOS data, memory size
- File server operation system information: volume name and size, copies of AUTOEXEC.NCF and STARTUP.NCF
- File server software information: software application information

Using the program

First, the program requires you to create a baseline. This is accomplished by running the LAI.EXE program. The baseline will collect as much information about the network as it can.

To take a snapshot of a user's configuration, you must run a batch file on each node. The program EQUIP takes a snapshot of a user's environment and then sends it to the common database kept on the file server.

This program can easily be placed in the system script file. If you want to be clever, you can ensure it is run not every day but once a week or month. You use the normal IF <Some Date condition> THEN run EQUIP:

```
F:\LAI>type equipmnt.bat
f:
cd \lai
btrieve /p:3072 /f:22 /t:btr.trn
equip f:
endbtrv
```

When the above batch file is run, the following information is displayed:

```
F:\LAI>f:
F:\LAI>cd \lai
F:\LAI>btrieve /p:3072 /f:22 /t:btr.trn
```

```
Btrieve/N Record Manager Version 5.10a
Copyright (c) 1982, 1990, Novell, Inc.  All Rights Reserved.


F:\LAI>equip f:
Automatic LAN Configuration Program, Version 2.0
Copyright Brightwork Development, Inc. 1991


01/12/93 19:08   00000257:0000C02E8A47
Collecting inventory for user : SUPERVISOR
        _AUTO   PCSW    NICDR   SMC LAN Adapter MLID
        _AUTO   PCSW    NICCF   IRQ 3, Port 0280, Memory D000:0
        _AUTO   PCSW    SHELL   3.31 A
        _AUTO   PCSW    IPX     IPX:3.30 - SPX:3.30
        _AUTO   PCHW    CPU     80486
        _AUTO   PCHW    BRAND   NA
```

Once the information has been collected, you can inspect it. Figure 23.1 shows a typical screen. It shows the program has located a number of active workstations on the network and a file sever called S386.

For each of the above nodes, a different set of information has been collected. It is divided into hardware and software. Figure 23.2 shows the information for a particular node being used by user FARSHAD. It lists the user's hardware equipment. This information is stored with information on all the other nodes in the common database. It is now very easy to print out a series of reports which will automatically document your network for you.

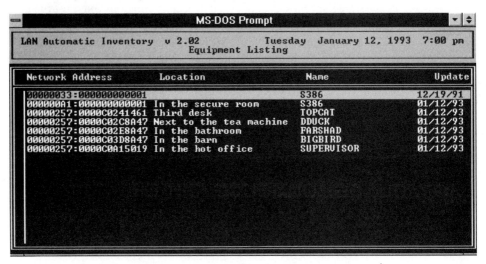

Figure 23.1 The LAN Automatic Inventory Equipment Listing screen.

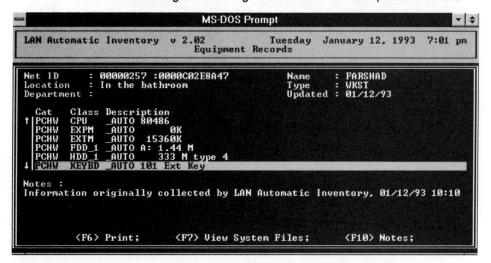

Figure 23.2 The LAN Automatic Inventory Equipment Records screen.

The power of this product lies in its report generation facilities. Figure 23.3 shows a typical report, the Equipment Summary Report. It lists all your equipment across the network and groups it by type. This will also include a list of all recognized software on your network. This will include items on the file server as well as anything found on the local workstation hard disks. This can be a very powerful tool.

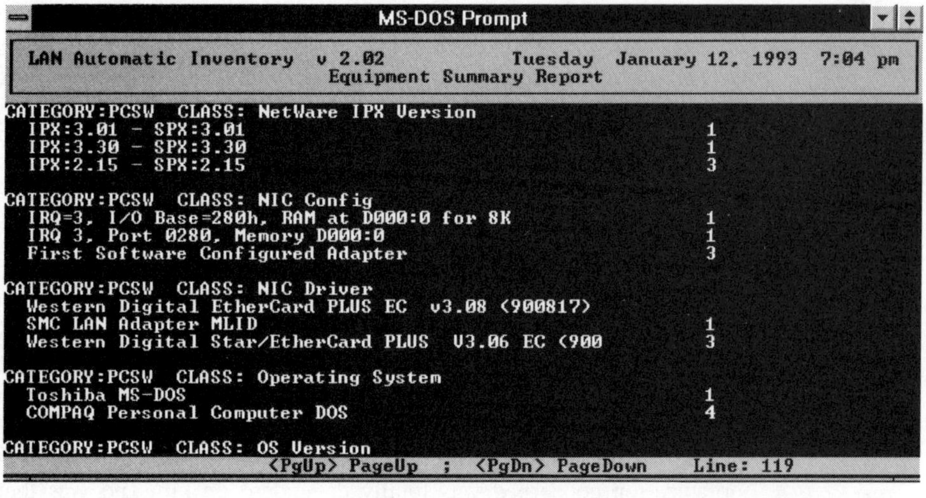

Figure 23.3 The LAN Automatic Inventory Equipment Summary Report.

The 'Don't Panic' book

Think about the unthinkable

Do not panic

Be prepared

Imagine the situation: you are the network 'whiz kid'/genius; everyone relies on you to sort their network problems out. Over the years, you have modified and optimized the network to such an extent that the others have given up trying to keep up with your changes. You can modify and change any aspects of the network without question or contradiction. Other users rely on you to sort things out. At one time, you were very keen on documentation and the people around you knew exactly what you had done to the network. Nowadays you cannot be bothered with documenting all your changes: after all, what is the point? No one else really understands it anyway! Over the years, because you are the network manager, you have slowly changed the system to keep up with the latest trends. For example, because of your expanding network, you are using some special network packets. You have developed a highly sophisticated backing up system which, of course, the other users do not understand: they just follow your instructions. You keep the system password secret for security reasons.

One day, as you are reading this book, you cross the road and get run over by a big bus. This is unfortunate for you and a disaster for your company. As the saying goes, they are 'up the creek without a paddle'!

Although this story might seem unrealistic, I was involved with a very large Novell installation (2000 users) which was supervised by a network manager. He kept his secrets. No one around him could get him to sit down and explain how the whole thing worked: he was always too busy. For security reasons he would never give away the supervisor password, although he was happy to create workgroup managers. He had placed himself in a position which made him indispensable. The organization concerned was totally dependent on him and was therefore courting potential disaster. The moral of this story is:

Think about the unthinkable and have a contingency plan.

Preparing for the unthinkable

For years, managers of mainframe installations have kept a disaster recovery, or 'Don't Panic', book which they update as the environment changes. This book is essential; it should contain the basic instructions and configurations required to recreate the current network should disaster hit the organization. The 'Don't Panic' book should be kept in safe place.

The network ('Don't Panic') book

The 'Don't Panic' book should contain the following information.

Network outline
The network outline should comprise:

- A record of the hardware specification of the network: this could be captured automatically using a program such as LAN Audit Inventory from Brightwork.
- A diagram of the network layout: this should include cable runs, positions of file and print servers and the location of workstations.

  It may be useful to list all the workstations, using the following headings:

Workstation type	Node address	User name	Screen type	NetWare DOS Shell/ Redirector version	Serial number

Network configuration
The network configuration information should include:

- Documentation of the network's directory structure, and what sort of information is stored under each directory: the main area of concentration here should be on anything unusual.
- A completed Novell standard file server worksheet.
- User configurations. You can use the following headings:

User login name	User bindery ID	Full name	Any account restrictions

Backup procedure
This should consist of:

- A detailed description of the backing up procedure in use
- Where the actual backup tapes are kept (there is no point in storing the backup tapes in an ingeniously safe place if no one knows about it)
- An explanation of any unusual modification that you have made to the network, which might be needed to recreate the network

- How to recover from a complete disaster, such as: hard disk failure, file server destroyed, binder corruption

Error logs

Error logs should include a record all the major errors that have occurred: this should help the support staff to respond to reccurring errors and improve their response time to users. It will also reduce their learning curve. You can use the following headings:

Date	Problem symptom	Solution	Who fixed it	Who reported it

Network security

This section should be kept in a secure place! The information should include:

- An explanation of how users can login to the system as the supervisor. Do not give the SUPERVISOR password, but tell the reader where it can be found. The best place is inside an envelope in a bank vault.

- An explanation of extra security features enabled in the system. For example, has the NCP security signature facility been activated?

A final word of advice

Test the 'Don't Panic' book. Can a technically competent colleague use this book to recover the system?

The most important point of all is to tell others where you are keeping this book, should the unthinkable happen. This could be the most useful book you have ever read.

Good luck! May you never have to use the 'Don't Panic' book but, unfortunately, life is just not like that!

Appendix A

Sample network number register form

The form overleaf is an example of a network number register. It has been left blank, so that you can copy and use it if you wish.

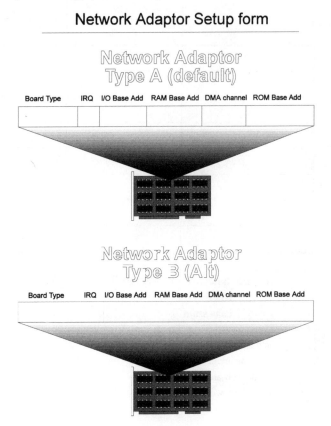

Network Adaptor Setup form

Network Adaptor Type A (default)

Board Type	IRQ	I/O Base Add	RAM Base Add	DMA channel	ROM Base Add

Network Adaptor Type B (Alt)

Board Type	IRQ	I/O Base Add	RAM Base Add	DMA channel	ROM Base Add

Network number register

Network number	Network type	Description

Key: Each network has the following format

F.FFF.FF.FF

t.aaa.ss.nn

Where:

t is for: F: File server, E: External, 2: Thin, 5: Thick, 6 :16 M Token Ring, 1: 10BaseT

aaa is the area code

ss is the sub-area code

nn is the network number

Appendix B

Quick installation guides

NetWare ADV 286 (Version 2.2)

Overview

A detailed installation guide is outside the scope of this book; this is covered perfectly well in Novell's own manuals. However, this section can be used as a very quick, basic installation guide or as a reminder of the important concepts that you need to perform for a typical installation site. You should note the following points:

- The guide is for the most common file server setup.
- It should work effectively for 90% of installations.
- It includes a number of useful recommendations.
- It aims to make your life easier.

  However, remember that each installation is different.

Installation overview

Figure B.1 provides an overview of the installation process.

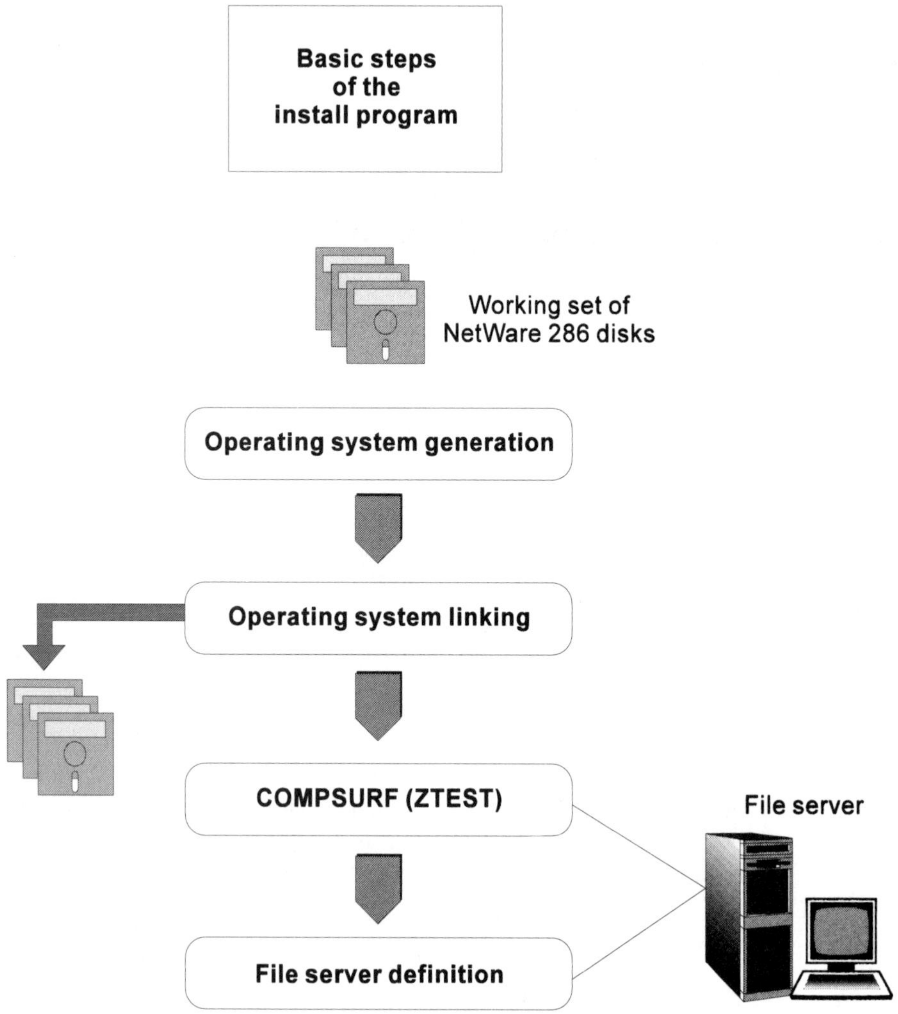

Figure B.1 Installation overview.

Before you start

Before running the INSTALL program:

- Make a working copy of the master disks:
  - SYSTEM-1*
  - SYSTEM-2*

- LAN_DRV_XXX
- OSEXE*
- OSOBJ*
- WSGEN
- ROUTEGEN
- MACINSTALL
- DOSUTL-1
- DOSUTL-2
- DOSUTL-3
- DOSUTL-4
- PRINT-1
- PRINT-2
- HELP-1
- HELP-2

Diskettes marked with an asterisk (*) are written to during INSTALL.

- Set up the file server hardware: make sure you have at least one high-density floppy disk drive on the file server.
- Boot the file server up with DOS.
- DOS 3.0 or above is required to run the NetWare version 2.2 high-capacity installation diskettes.
- Fill out the installation sheets. These are included with the standard set of Novell manuals. Whenever you have to make a selection, note it down for future reference.
- Decide on dedicated or non-dedicated server mode. The dedicated mode has full support of SFT (System Fault Tolerance) Level II functionality (disk mirroring, disk duplexing and TTS (Transaction Tracking System)). The non-dedicated mode offers SFT Level I functionality only (duplicate directories, duplicate file allocation tables, read-after-write verification and HOT FIX).
- Decide on the type of network card to be used.
- Decide on the type and size of hard disk you wish to use.
- Decide on the network address number.

Running the INSTALL programs

Run the INSTALL.EXE program found on the SYSTEM-1 disk. This will start the installation process.

Advanced INSTALL command line flags

INSTALL command line flags are advanced options for experienced installers. These flags provide access to the four INSTALL modules:

- Module 1: Operating System Generation
- Module 2: Linking and Configuring
- Module 3: Track Zero Test (ZTEST)
- Module 4: File Server Definition

  The installation-related option are as follows:

- INSTALL -E (begin module 1; end module 2 or 4)
- INSTALL -L (begin module 3; end module 4)
- INSTALL -N (begin module 1; end module 1)
- INSTALL -C (begin module 2; end module 4)

  The maintenance-related options are:

- INSTALL -M (begin module 1; end module 2 or 4)
- INSTALL -M -L (begin module 3; end module 4)
- INSTALL -F (begin module 4; end module 4)

Quick installation guide assumptions

In the following installation guide, a number of assumptions have been made:

- The INSTALL program will run from diskettes.
- The whole process will take place on the new file server.
- The file server is dedicated.
- The new print server functions will be used.
- The file server will automatically boot into the Novell operating system.
- All the hard disk partitions are given over to NetWare.

Step 1: File server network operating system generation

This step involves the following:

- Customizing the network operating system to use your network drivers.
- Customizing the network operating system to use your hard disk drivers.
- When all information is correct, INSTALL links the network operating system (NET$OS.EXE) and creates four file server-specific utilities: ZTEST, COMPSURF, INSTOVL and VREPAIR.

  If you are installing on the server, you need to use the Track Zero Test (ZTEST) module.

NetWare 286 operating system generation

Boot computer with DOS version 3.x or above.

Insert the SYSTEM-1 diskette into a high-capacity drive
and type INSTALL.

Select the Advanced installation option.

Select Operating system mode as dedicated.

Select the number of communication buffers as the
default number provided.
(Recommendation: If you have more then 30 users, use 40+n
where n is the maximum number of users.)

Type 'Y' to indicate you are running INSTALL on the server.

Type 'N' to exclude the old core printing services.

Select the network board Driver field.

Select the correct network board driver to be used
in the file server.

If you are using Novell standard drivers, insert Novell's own
LAN_DRV_XXX diskette; otherwise, use the manufacturer's
diskette which comes with the network card to read the relevant
card driver program.

Select the network board driver Configuration option (normally
option 0 for most modern cards).
(Record the driver name and option number of each network board
on the Operating System Generation worksheet.)

Specify the network address
(make sure each LAN card to be installed is
given a different number).

Repeat for each network board to be installed
in the file server.

Select the disk driver field of the first channel used
by the file server.

Select the disk driver for the file server from the list.

If you are using a non-Novell standard hard disk controller, you
need to insert the relevant diskette from the manufacturer of the
hard disk controller card (in which case, press <Insert> to add the
disk driver and insert the DSK_DRV_XXX diskette
into a floppy disk drive).

Example: SCSI card.

Select the hard disk driver for the new file
server from the expanded list.

Select the Configuration option (usually option 0).
Review the option that you have selected. Record the selected
driver name and configuration option number for each
hard disk driver on the Operating System Generation worksheet.

Repeat for any other hard disk controller card
to be used in the file server.

Press <F10> when the form is complete. This saves the
configurations as entered and continues the installation.

Step 2: Linking operating system module

Linking operating system

INSTALL program starts to link the NET$OS.EXE program.

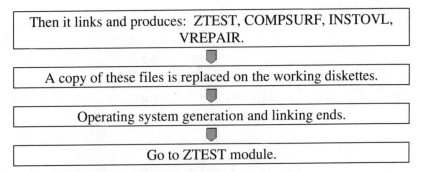

Then it links and produces: ZTEST, COMPSURF, INSTOVL, VREPAIR.

A copy of these files is replaced on the working diskettes.

Operating system generation and linking ends.

Go to ZTEST module.

Step 3: ZTEST quick installation guide

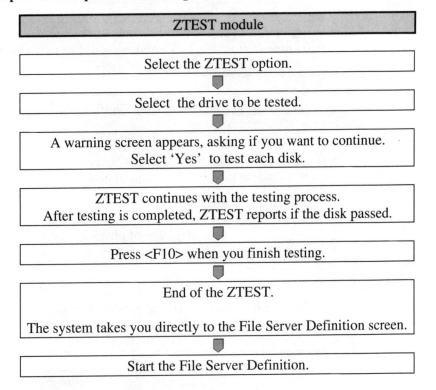

ZTEST module

Select the ZTEST option.

Select the drive to be tested.

A warning screen appears, asking if you want to continue. Select 'Yes' to test each disk.

ZTEST continues with the testing process. After testing is completed, ZTEST reports if the disk passed.

Press <F10> when you finish testing.

End of the ZTEST.

The system takes you directly to the File Server Definition screen.

Start the File Server Definition.

Step 4: The file server definition module

This must only be carried out after the operating system is generated and linked. This must be done on the file server.

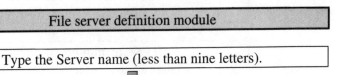

File server definition module

Type the Server name (less than nine letters).

Type the maximum number of open files.
(Recommendation: use 240 for most cases.)
Note: 100 extra bytes for each extra open file.

Type the maximum number of open indexed files.
(Recommendation use 0.)
Note: 1024 extra bytes per file.

Type the TTS backup volume name.
(Recommendation: use volume SYS:.)

Type the TTS maximum transactions.
(Recommendation: the TTS number should be twice the maximum number of users.)

Type 'Y' to limit disk space for each user.

Type 'N' to indicate no Macintosh support needed.
(If you need to support Macintoshes immediately, select the correct AppleTalk and the appropriate network driver.)

Select the logical size to define the HOT FIX area. Logical size is normally 98% of physical size.
(Recommendation: make it 95% of physical size.)

Type volume size. Maximum is 255 Mbytes.
(Recommendation: define at lease one volume SYS: with a minimum of 30 Mbytes. You can give all space to volume SYS: up to 250 Mbytes.)

Type the name of each volume:
the first volume must be SYS.

Select 'Y' to cache all the volumes.
(Volume SYS must always be cached.)

Type the number of directory entries.
(Recommendation: accept the default number of directory entries.)

Record all information on the Volume Configuration Worksheet. Press <F10> when the form is complete.

INSTALL now starts to load the operating system program (NET$OS.EXE) onto the file server.

The public and system files are now copied onto the server hard disk. (This may take a few minutes.)

The NetWare operating system is now installed.

Advanced installation techniques

Loading disks onto a hard disk

The INSTALL program modifies and creates various files. This can involve a large number of floppy disk changes. It is possible to load all the NetWare floppy disks once onto hard disk and, from then on, produce working versions of the operating system for release from the hard disk back onto floppy disk.

You may sometimes need to do this if the server you are installing is not attached to the network that you are running INSTALL on. In this case, you download these files to the working copies of your NetWare diskettes. Two programs are used for this purpose: the UPLOAD and DOWNLOAD programs.

- The UPLOAD program moves all floppy disks onto hard disk.
- From then on, the INSTALL program can work from the hard disk.
- The DOWNLOAD program copies files back to floppy disks.

Uploading software to the network or to a hard disk

Create a directory called NW22 on the hard disk. Give it the following rights: Read, File scan, Write, Create and Erase.

Create a sub-directory called NetWare. Change to the new NetWare directory. Insert the SYSTEM-1 diskette into a floppy diskette drive and type A:UPLOAD <Enter>. UPLOAD will now copy all diskettes one by one onto the hard disk. It will create a sub-directory for each diskette. To run INSTALL, go to the NetWare directory and type INSTALL <Enter>.

Downloading software to working copies of NetWare diskettes

Change to the NetWare directory on the hard disk, type DOWNLOAD [drive letter] and press <Enter>. The [drive letter] refers to the floppy diskette drive you want to download to.

You will be asked to insert working copies of the SYSTEM-1, SYSTEM-2 and OSEXE diskettes. DOWNLOAD now will copy the .CFG (configuration) and .LNK (linking) files and any server-specific utilities to the NetWare diskettes. The diskettes can now be loaded on the actual file server.

Generating multiple file servers from one NetWare directory

To generate multiple file servers from one NetWare directory, follow the instructions below:

- Delete the contents of the OSOBJ directory using DEL *.* <Enter>.
- From the new diskette set, copy all the files on the diskette OSOBJ to this directory.
- Start as normal.

Using NetWare 286 on a non-dedicated file server

The following procedure is required for a non-dedicated file server:

- Prepare a boot diskette using DOS FORMAT /S.
- Copy NET$OS.EXE and NETx.COM to the boot disk from the OSEXE and WSGEN diskettes respectively (the x corresponds to the DOS version number).
- Create an AUTOEXEC.BAT file on the boot diskette which contains four lines:

```
NET$OS
NETx
F:
Login
```

- Type CONSOLE to get the file server console prompt.
- Type DOS to change back to DOS.

NetWare 386 (Version 3.11)

Overview

A detailed installation guide to NetWare 386 (Version 3.11) is not included in this book, since it is covered well in Novell's own standard manuals. However, this section can be used as a very quick installation guide or as a reminder of the important concepts that you need to perform for a typical NetWare 386 installation site. Please note the following points:

- The guide is for the most common file server setup.
- It should work effectively for most installations.
- It includes a number of useful recommendations.
- It aims are to make your life easier.

However, remember that each installation is different.

Installation assumptions

In the following installation guide, a number of assumptions have been made:

- You have backed up the master set of diskettes.
- The whole process will take place on the new file server.
- The file server will automatically boot into DOS from the hard disk.
- The hard disk has two partitions: a DOS boot partition and a Novell 386 partition.

Outline of NetWare 386 installation (using the hard disk boot method)

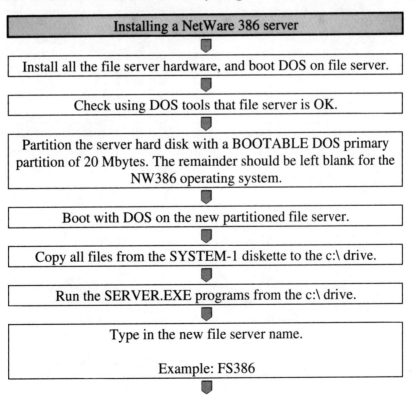

Type in the file server's internal network number.
This number must be unique to all other servers and network
addresses.

Example: F0010000

Load up the disk driver for the hard disk controller card being
used.
You might find it on the SYSTEM-2 disk.

Example: LOAD ISADISK

Now run the INSTALL program. This will set up the partitions
and volumes and load up the NetWare operating system.

Create the NetWare partition tables.

Create the NetWare volumes.
Volume SYS: is always created.
Any additional volumes should be created now.

Select the new volumes and MOUNT them.

Copy the SYSTEM and the PUBLIC files on the file server
volume SYS. Jump back to the file console command line by
pressing <ALT><Escape>.

Now load up the LAN Network Interface Card drive. First load up
the NLM manager: type LOAD NMAGENT.NLM, then load the
LAN driver(s) being used.

Example: LOAD NE2000

Now bind a protocol to the card.

Example: BIND IPX TO NE2000

Assign a Network Cable Number to the card.

Example: 20010000

Jump back to the installation program by pressing
<ALT><Escape>.

All your options are saved in two files: STARTUP.NCF and
AUTOEXEC.NCF.

Select Create from the system options of the INSTALL menu to
create a copy of both files on the file server.

File server installation is now complete.

Appendix C

Novell worldwide addresses

Novell Inc.
World Headquarters
East 1700 South
P.O.Box 5900
Provo
Utah 84606
USA

Telephone (801) 429 7000

Novell UK
Avon House
Sweetwell Road
Bracknell
Berkshire
RG12 1HH
United Kingdom

Telephone (344) 860 400

Novell Hong Kong
New Town Tower
Pak Hok Ting Street
Shatin
New Territories
Hong Kong

Telephone 852 (6) 012123

Novell Japan
Toei Mishuku Bldg. 3F
Mishuku
Setagaya-ku
Tokyo 154
Japan

Telephone 81 (3) 5481 1161

Novell International Operations
Ross Drive
Sunnyvale
CA 94089
USA

Telephone (408) 747 4000

Appendix D

Networking abbreviations

AFP	AppleTalk Filing Protocol	Gbyte	Gigabyte
ANSI	American National Standards Institute	GOSIP	Government OSI Protocol
		GUI	Graphical User Interface
API	Application Programming Interface	HDLC	High-level Data Link Control
		HFS	Hierarchical File System
APPC	Advanced Program-to-Program Communications	HLAPI	High-Level Application Program Interface
ASCII	American Standard Code for Information Interchange	ICA	Integrated Computing Architecture (Novell)
BIOS	Basic Input/Output System	I/O	Input/Output
CCITT	Consultative Committee on International Telegraph and Telephone	IPX	Internetwork Packet Exchange
		IRQ	Interrupt Request Line
CD-ROM	Compact Disc Read-Only Memory	ISO	International Organization for Standardization
CPU	Central Processing Unit	Kbyte	Kilobyte
CSMA/CA	Carrier Sense Multiple Access with Collision Avoidance	LAN	Local Area Network
		LU	Logical Unit
		Mb	Megabit
CSMA/CD	Carrier Sense Multiple Access with Collision Detection	MB	Megabyte
		MCA	Micro Channel Architecture
		MHS	Message Handling Service
DBMS	Database Management System	NACS	NetWare Asynchronous Communications Server
DMA	Direct Memory Access	NCP	NetWare Core Protocol
ELS	Entry-Level Solution	NFS	Network File System
FAT	File Allocation Table	NLM	NetWare Loadable Module
FTAM	File Telecommunications Access Method	NNS	NetWare Name Service
		OEM	Original Equipment Manufacturer

OLTP	On-Line Transaction Processor	SNADS	System Network Architecture Distribution Services
OPT	Open Protocol Technology	SNMP	Simple Network Management Protocol
OSI	Open Systems Interconnection		
PDN	Public Data Network	SPG	Service Protocol Gateway
PU	Physical Unit	SPX	Sequenced Packet exchange
QBE	Query-by-Example	SQL	Structured Query Language
RAM	Random Access Memory	TCP/IP	Transmission Control Protocol/Internet Protocol
RISC	Reduced Instruction Set Computing		
		TES	Terminal Emulation Service
ROM	Read-Only Memory	TSR	Terminate-and-Stay-Resident
RMF	Remote Management Facility	TTS	Transaction Tracking System
RPC	Remote Procedure Call	VADD	Value-Added Disk Driver
SAA	System Application Architecture	VAP	Value-Added Process
		VAR	Value-Added Reseller
SCO	Santa Cruz Operation	VGA	Video Graphics Array
SCSI	Small Computer System Interface	VMS	Virtual Memory System
		VTAM	Virtual Telecommunications Access Method
SDLC	Synchronous Data Link Control		
		WAN	Wide-Area Network
SFT	System Fault Tolerance	WNIM	Wide-Area Network Interface Module
SMB	Server Message Block		
SNA	System Network Architecture	WORM	Write Once, Read Many

Index

$RUN.OVL   199
%LOGIN_NAME   250
.DLL   282
.INI control manager   341
   management issues   342
   SYSTEM.INI   341
10Base-2   55, 57
10Base-5   55, 57
10Base-T   57
100Base-VG   58
8086/88   113
8086 memory structure 143
80286   113
80386 enhanced icon   279
80386 enhanced fields   297
80386 enhanced mode   275
80286 memory structure   146
80386 memory protection structure   81
80386DX   113
80386SX   113
80486DX   113
80486DX2   113
80486SX   113

A20 line   148
ACONFIG   404
ACONSOLE.EXE   245
Adaptec ASPI   95
addressing scheme   29
administration tools   483

After Dark   473
alarm management   500
allocation memory pool   85
Apple II EuroPlus   143
application .INI files   278
application size audit   108
application address   351
applications   233
ARCnet   72
   active hubs   74
   configuration   73
   Datapoint Corporation   72
   passive hubs   74
   SMC   73
   US   Defence Department   72
   UTP   72
ARCnet specifications   74
   cabling rules   74
   specification   74
ARCnet strategy   74
   coaxial cable specification   75
   twisted-pair specification   75
AS/400   398
ASPI   96
ASPITRAN.DSK   97
asynchronous hardware   416
asynchronous management   411
asynchronous NetWare communication   399
asynchronous remote router   400
   LAN_DRV_190   400

WNIM+   400
NARR   401
ROUTEGEN   400
ACONFIG   400
AUI   20
AutoCAD   35
AUTOEXEC.BAT   315
AWARD BIOS   134

backups   593
    management   598
    advice   599
    choosing a backup medium   599
    considerations   599
    procedure   625
    suggested routine   599
    technology   595
Bill Gates   143
bindery object   82, 243
bindery files   457
bindery system files   518
BINDFIX.EXE   245
binding protocols   392
BIOS (Basic Input Output System)   146
BNC   20, 55
BNETX   290
BNETX.EXE   219
BOOTCONF.SYS   586
BOOTLOG.TXT   305
bridges   363
    LLC (logical link controller)   363
    classification   365
    learning   365
    source routing   365
    management   366
    versus routers   370
brouters   369
buffer size   212
BURGLAR   462
BURGLAR.NLM   462
Burst mode   217, 223, 232
    buffer setting   223
    management strategy   224
    memory   223
    NCP   217
    technology   10

cable management   19
cable management software tools   34
cable scanners   26
CACHE BUFFERS   198
cache buffers   86

cache movable memory   86
cache non-movable memory   86
caching process   119
CAPTURE 1   566
CASTOFF ALL   287
CD-ROM   540, 554, 556
CheckIt Pro   131
CHIP selection strategy   114
CIA   22
Cisco   368
CLIB   13
CMIP OSI management protocol   488
coaxial cable   23
COMCHECK tool   489
COMM ports   140
COMMAND.COM   136, 247
comparing IPX ODI and dedicated IPX   174
    additional features   175
    ease of maintenance   175
    frame types support   174
    physical board   174
    protocol types   174
    throughput capacity   174
compressed files   552
COMSPEC   247
CONFIG   52
CONFIG OPTIONS   200
CONFIG.SYS   135, 148, 195, 293
CONFIG.SYS   315
connection number   211
CONTROL.SRC   305
conventional memory   413
CorelDraw   309
corporate-wide Windows menu   323
CPU activated   134
CPU chip selection 112
Crimp+   34
CSMA/CD   48
    'backing-off'   48
    collision detection   48
    CSMA/CD   48
    limitations   48
CX   562
    data blocks   121
    partition blocks   121
    redirected blocks   121
    redirection blocks   121
    reserved blocks   121

DDE   269
dedicated IPX.COM   162
DEFRAG   587

DEVICEHIGH   153
devices and A20 handlers   149
diagnostic programs   131
Digital Audio Tape (DAT)   595
directories   233
directory framework   255
directory hashing   117
Directory Services access rights   5, 530
disaster planning   619
disk and volume management   124
disk caching   119
disk duplexing   122, 123
disk information   121
disk mirroring   122
diskless workstations   585
  AUTOEXEC.BAT   587
  BOOTCONF.SYS   586
  CONFIG.SYS   587
  creating the boot disk   587
  how it works   586
  management issues   590
  RPLFIX.COM   589
  SYS:\LOGIN   586
documenting and auditing your network   619
'Don't Panic' book   624
DOS 6 and MEMMAKER   152
DOS 6x.   142
DOS   158
DOS requester   226
  CONFIG.SYS   226
  LASTDRIVE=Z   226
DOSGEN.EXE   245
DOSGEN.EXE   587
DR-DOS   4
DSPACE   111
DSPACE.EXE   251

e-mail   269
Eagle   124
effective rights   466
effective user rights   465
EIA 568   28
EISA   88
EISA buds   90
electrical interface   22
elevator-seeking optimization   118
EMM386.EXE   259, 300
EMMExclude   141
EMSNETX.COM   259
EMSNETX.EXE   292
end of job   213
ESDI   89

estimating file server disk size   105
Ethernet   47, 59
  48-bit identifier   59
  detecting a collision   61
  DIX 1.0   47
  Ethernet II   47
  frame check sequence (FCS)   60
  frame reception   63
  how Ethernet works   47
  length indicator   60
  managing an Ehternet collision   61
  start of frame delimiter (SFD)   60
  transmission   61
  truncated binary exponential back-off   62
  Xerox Corporation   47
Ethernet frame formats   53
  Ethernet 802.2   53
  Ethernet 802.3   53
  Ethernet II   53
  Ethernet SNAP   53
Ethernet IEEE 802.2 frame   50
Ethernet IEEE 802.3 packets   49
Ethernet II packets   49, 50, 52, 427
  DEC Pathworks   50
  TCP/IP   50
Excel   328
EXPAND   287
expanded memory   150
extended memory   149
external network number   352
external router   371, 372, 381
  communication buffers   382
  management issues   383
  ROUTER.EXE   383
  operating mode   382

FDISK   126
fibre optic cables   25
  Security   25
file server hard disk   88
file server hardware   77
file server memory   79
  allocation memory   79
  cache buffers   79
  cache movable memory   79
  cache non-movable memory   79
  memory protection   79
  permanent memory   79
file compression system   550
FILER.EXE   251
FLAG   247
FLAG   288

format of INI files   276
Frye Utilities   450
FTP (File Transfer Protocol)   422
full server duplication 122

GCHQ   22
groups   437

hard disk controller types   91
hard disk protection   122
hashing function 118
HIMEM.SYS   136, 148, 259
HMA   148
HMI: the Novell hub management standard   34
home storage requirements   109
HOPs   346
hot fix   120
hot fix area   105, 121
hub management   32
Hub management interface (HMI)   33

I/O address map   132
I/O base address   137, 138, 139, 140
IBM data cable types   70
   Type 1   70
   Type 2   70
   Type 3   70
   Type 6   70
IBM POST   134
IBM POST audio messages   135
IBMDOS.SYS   135, 136
IBMIO.SYS   135, 136
IDE   89
   controllers   92
   management   92
IEEE 488   94
IEEE 802   39
IEEE 802 reference model   45
   802.1   45
   802.2   45
   802.3   46
   802.4   46
   802.5   46
IEEE 802 standards   43
   IEEE 802 project   44
   IEEE 802.3   44
   IEEE 802.5   44
IEEE 802.3 packets   51
implementing burst mode   220
Inherited Rights Mask   469
INI   286
installing applications   259

installing ODI   176
INT21   138
interconnection   361
internal network number   353
internal router   371, 372, 387
   bind   388
   dedicated   388
   non-dedicated   388
   packet frame types   390
   protected-mode   388
   real mode   388
   routing table   388
internetworking NetWare   358
intruder prevention   460
IP router   423
IP tunnelling   430
IPCONFIG.NLM   424
IPX   157, 356
   destination node address   347
   for asynchronous modems   408
   length field   346
   network numbers   345
   network registry   356
   packet format   346
   packet type   347
   routing principles   349
IPX.COM   175
IPX.COM native   162
IPX.OBJ   163
IPX/SPX   160
IPXODI program   183
   potential identifiers   183
IPXODI.COM   175, 185
IRQ (interrupt request channel)   137
IRQ3   138
IRQ5   138
ISA   88
ISA system bus   90
ISO   359

labelling the cable   30
Laddr and Cam   97
LAI.EXE   621
LAN automatic inventory   620
LANalyzer for Windows   490
   alerts and alarms   492
   CRC errors   493
   decoding packets   490
   mapping the trends   492
   version 2.x   492
LANGUAGE   548
LANtern alarms   501

LANWatch   494
LASTDRIVE   205, 240
LCONSOLE   400, 406
LIM   150, 151
LIM/EMS standards   150
LIM/EMS v4.0   150
Link support layer (LSL)   172
LIPX   10
LOADHIGH   153
LOCAL PRINTERS   199
local bus   90
local drives   238
logical link controller   46
    LLC   46
    SAPs   46
LOGIN   198
LONG MACHINE NAME   199
LPD (Line Printer Daemon)   422
LSL   171
LSL.COM   177, 185
    LH LSL   178
    LOADHIGH   178
    LS U   178
    memory overhead   178

MAC (medium access control)   59
Macintosh   13
MAIL   106
MAKEUSER   445, 446
management tools   481
managing DOS workstation memory   142
managing network interface cards   136
managing shell updates   214
    a framework   215
    check for updates   216
    IPX   216
    NETX.EXE   214
    WSUPDATE syntax   214
    WS_DOSUP.CFG   216
managing the interrupts on PC   138
managing group assignments   443
    classic group names   444
    overlapping groups   443
managing number assignment   354
managing users   437, 468
    limit disk space   441
    naming supervisors   441
    manager names   441
    remote users   413
    users' accounts   440
managing workgroup managers   445
MAP   240, 298

mapping   237
mapping drives   240
MAU (multistation access unit)   68
MAX CUR DIR LENGTH   202
MaxPagingFileSize   281
MCA   88
MCA bus   90
Media Manager   553
MEM/C   144
MEMMAKER   142, 152, 153
memory protection   81
memory domains   545
memory protection system   545
MFM   89
MLID   171
MLID layer   172
    HSM   172
    MSM   172
MLID standard   180
    LOADHIGH   180
    loading and unloading drivers   180
    loading into upper memory   180
MONITOR   120
MSD.EXE   131
MSL   122
multiple different remote boot disk   589
multiple frame packet   391
multiprotocol switching   188
multiprotocol router   384
naming volumes   129

NARS.COM   408
NASI   417
NCP   156, 205
NCP   435
NCP signature facility   10
NDIS   189, 267
NDIS drivers   186
    Banyan-Vines   186
    DEC Pathworks   186
    media access control drivers   188
    Microsoft   186
    monolithic drivers   188
    NDIS structure   186
    PORTMAN.DOS   187
    PORTMAN.OS2   187
    protocol drivers   187
    protocol manager   187
    PROTOCOL.INI   187
NDS naming convention   522
NDS tree management   533
NET$OBJ.SYS   243

NET$OBJ.SYS 457
NET$PROP.SYS 243
NET$PROP.SYS 457
NET$VAL.SYS 243
NET$VAL.SYS 457
NET.CFG 181, 195, 292
    DMA 181
    FRAME type option 182
    INT 181
    MEM 181
    NODE 181
    PORT 181
    PROTOCOL option 183
    SLOT 181
NetBEUI 190
NetWare 2.2 13
NetWare 3.x supervisor 455
NetWare 3.11 emulation 543
NetWare 3.12 7
    Basic Message Handling (MHS) support 8
    Btrieve 9
    CD-ROM installation 8
    improved disk performance 9
    improved Novell menu 10
    Macintosh support 9
    manuals and on-line help 9
    new CD-ROM support 8
    patches and fixes 8
    VLM 9
NetWare 4.0 513
    alias name entries 523
    audited information 556
    CD-ROM 554
    container and leaf objects 520
    data compression 550
    disk storage 549
    inherited rights filter 532
    internationalizing NetWare 4.01 546
    leaf objects 520
    moving leaf objects 524
    name contexts 523
    NDS tree structure 518
    NET.CFG 523
    NetWare 4.01 513
    NetWare Directory Services (NDS) 516
    new file attributes 550
    objectives 514
    object protection 531
    objects 517
    on-line help documentation 557
    Organization (O) name 519
    Organization Unit (OU) 520

partition 526
partition manager 561
performance 515
replicating partitions 527
root 519
searching through NDS 525
time synchronization services 529
user support tool 561
utilities 560
what is new 513
X.500 Directory Services 516
NetWare 4.0 installation 537
    CD-ROM 540
    INSTALL.NLM 537
    installation methods 540
    server memory requirements 538
NetWare 4.0 printing 574
    NPRINTER.NLM 575
    remote printing 575
NetWare 4.X 4
    file server memory structure 6
    internationalizing NetWare 6
    multiple processor support 7
    Novell Windows-based tools 7
    server memory structure 81
NetWare 4.x 272
NetWare 4.x and NMM integration 507
NetWare 4.x Windows tools 321
NetWare 86 2
NetWare 3270 LAN 398
    APPC 398
    SEND/RECEIVE 398
    TRANSFER 398
NetWare Access Server (NAS) 399, 414
NetWare addressing system 349
NetWare and UPS 602
NetWare Asynchronous Communication Server
    (NACS) 399, 415
NetWare Asynchronous Remote Router
    (NARR) 399
NetWare device numbering 124
    logical device number 125
    NetWare device addresses 125
    physical device number 125
NetWare Directory Services 516
NetWare DOS redirector 225
NetWare external router 380
NetWare filing sytem 117
NetWare gateways 397
NetWare Kernel 11
NetWare Lite 16
NetWare loader 11

NetWare Management Map   494
NetWare Management System   494
    how it works   496
    NMM   494
    management monitored information   497
NetWare partitions   126
NetWare printing   565
NetWare router   371
NetWare security   464
NetWare server alarms   502
NetWare server memory   78
NetWare Service Manager   504
    features   504
    gauges in action   506
NetWare service advertising codes   208
NetWare service manager   17
NetWare standard tools for Windows   320
NetWare users   439
    account managers   439
    operators   439
    regular users   439
    supervisors   439
    workgroup managers   439
Netware volumes   128
NETWARE.DRV   293
NETWARE.DRV   298
NETWARE.INI   295
NETWARE.INI   322
network adaptor resources   137
network application   234
    network-ignorant   234
network drives   233, 237, 239
Network File System (NFS)   422
network adaptor setup form   627
network address   345
network management software   482
network performance   607
    file server memory   611
    hard disk controller   608
    improving network performance   613
    network interface card   608
    network type   607
    number of routers   608
NETX   161, 204, 205
    Get Nearest File server request   204
    map to a log-in drive   204
    SSAP   204
NETX.EXE   156, 195
new applications 233
NFS   16
NIC   136
NIC management   141

NLINK.EXE   164
NLIST   562
NLM programs   11
NLM support BUS   11
NNS   5
node number   345
NOVELL   1
    'Super Set'   2
    AT 7 T   4
    IBM's SNA   3
    UNIX   2, 3
    Windows NT   4
Novell DOS 7   17
Novell shell   156
NOVELL.BAT   176, 203
Novix product   429
NPRINTER   575
NTFS   270
NVER   292
NWADMIN   438
NWADMIN   560
NWLANGUAGE   547
NWP.VLM   225
NWPOPUP.EXE   295
NWSETUP.EXE   322
NWShare handles   297
NWTOOLS   561
NWTOOLS.EXE   322

ODI   189
ODI architectural structure   171
ODI driver on an asynchronous router   408
ODI drivers   168, 231
    Apple Computer   168
    Novell   168
    strategy in using ODI   170
    WSGEN   169
ODI IPX   162
ODI versus NDIS   188
ODINSUP   189
ODINSUP.COM   190, 191
    AUTOEXEC.BAT   194
    BUFFERED   191
    installation   194
    NET.CFG modification   191
    PROTOCOL.INI   193
    PROTOCOL.INI modification   193
    strategy   194
optimized network printing   576
OS/2   271
    workstation support   12
OSI reference model   359

Physical   359
Datalink   359
Network   359
Transport   359
OSI routing view   369
OSIE   359
OS_PROTECTED   82

PABX   35
partitioning the NDS tree   528
partitions   127
PARTMGR   528
PATH   241
PB BUFFERS   221
PBURST.NLM   219
PC boot-up sequence   133
PC hardware configuration   131
PC memory management   151
PC memory structure   143
PCI (peripheral component interconnect)   90
Pentium   113
PERFORM3   175
PERFORM3.EXE   610
performance testing the file server   609
permanent archiving   597
PKZIP   263
POST   134
power supply test   134
power protection overview   601
PowerChute UPS package   604
PREFERRED SERVER   198
preventing unauthorized NLM   463
primary time servers   529
print manager   582
print server management   572
print servers and queues   570
PRINTCON   569
PRINTDEF   569
printing across Windows   582
    Hewlett-Packard LaserJet III   583
    managing printers   583
    print manager buffering   583
    remote printer network   582
PROGMAN.INI   314, 324, 326
PROTOCOL   394
protocol stacks   173
protocol analysers   481
PROTOCOLS   52
PSC   569
PSERVER   567
PSERVER.EXE   578
PSERVER.NLM   578

quarter-inch tape   595
queue management services   571
    create print queues   571
    create queue services   572
    functions   571
    servicing queue jobs   572
    submitting queue jobs   572
quick installation guides   629
    NetWare ADV 286   629
    NetWare 386 (version 3.11)   638

RAID   101
    level 0   102
    level 1   102
    level 2   102
    level 3   103
    level 4   103
    level 5   103
    technology   100
RAM base address   139
RAM buffer area   137
RAM cram   143
REDIR.VLM   225
reference time servers   529
remote printing   567
repeaters   361
restricting the Program Manager   326
Ring 0   79
Ring 2   79
RIP   209
RIP tables   497
RJ-45   24
RLL 2,7   89
RLL 3,9   89
RLL   89
ROM BIOS   134
ROUTE.COM   176
ROUTE.COM   366
ROUTE.NLM   366
ROUTEGEN   371, 381
ROUTER.EXE   406
routers   371, 367
    asynchronous router   371
    half router   371
    operation   368
    remote router   371
    routing path   368
Routing Information Protocol (RIP)   376
    how RIPS are sent out   377
    request RIP packets   376
    RESET ROUTER   377
    respond RIP packets   376

RIP request   377
RIP response   377
Xerox network   376
routing table   374
    forwarding network   374
RPLFIX.COM   589
RPRINTER.EXE   580

Saber Menu (SMENU)   338
Saber Windows Menu   336
SAFILTER.NLM   386
SAP   209
SAP filtering   379
SBACKUP.NLM   594
    TSA.NLM   594
    TSA-311.NLM   594
schedule   269
SCSI 2 standard   98
SCSI   89, 96
    managing SCSI ID numbers   100
SCSI and CD-ROMs   98
SCSI hardware configuration   98
    SCSI ID numbers 98
    termination   98
SCSI history   94
SCSI LUN and IDs   99
SCSI management strategy   99
SCSI software drivers   94
SCSI technology   93
SD.EXE   587
SEARCH MODE   202
search drives   240
secondary time servers   529
SECURE CONSOLE   463
    BURGLAR.NLM   463
    EXIT   463
    SETPASS   463
SECURITY   471
security Services   10
security auditing NetWare   556
SECURITY.EXE   245
SERVEMAN.NLM   551
server memory   82
    active bindery objects   82
    caching   83
    data packet   83
    directory entries   83
    File allocation table (FATs)   83
    NetWare loadable modules   83
    Network operating system   82
server memory pools   84
Service Advertising Protocol (SAP)   377

advertising numbers   378
get nearest server   378
SERVMAN.NLM   379
SERVMAN.NLM   379
SETUP /A   287
SETUP /N   289
SFT III mirrored file server   123
SHELL.CFG   195
SHGEN   163
SHORT MACHINE NAME   199
SHOW DOTS   201
SI.EXE   131
signal transmission   21
    deterioration   21
    radiation   22
signature security enhancement   10
SIMM   86
single memory pool   545
SiteLock   476
SNMP   18
SNMP alarms (MIB I & II)   501
SNMP and NetWare   509
    control community   510
    loading SNMP.NLM   509
    loading SNMPLOG.NLM   511
    monitor community   510
    SNMP.NLM   509
    SNMPLOG.NLM   509
    SNMP on workstations   509
    trap community   510
SNMP MIB browser   502
SNMP network management   483
    agent   484
    how SNMP works   486
    manager   485
    Management Information Base (MIB)   485
    SetRequest   487
    SNMP history   485
    SNMP Version 2   487
    traps   481
SNMP support   423
socket   345
socket number   351
software interrupts   138
SPEED test   615
split seeks   122
SPX   13, 158
SPX CONNECTIONS   199
ST-506   88
ST-506 interface   91
Stacker technology   17
standard mode   275

STP   20
STREAMS   13
structured cable management   28
supervisor password   455, 456
swap file management   281
swap files   279, 280
  memory   279
  virtual memory   279
  virtual memory manager   279
SYS:\LOGIN   245
SYS:\MAIL   245
SYS:\PUBLIC   245
SYS:\SYSTEM   106, 243
SYSCON   111, 437
SYSEDIT   307
System fault tolerance   120
  SFT Level I   120
  SFT Level II   122
  SFT Level III   122
SYSTEM.INI   278, 284, 313
SYSTEM.INT   295
SYSTEM.SRC   305

TBM12 program   301
  IPX   302
  NETX   302
  running TBM12   303
  TBM12.COM   301
TCP/IP   419, 425
  Class A   420
  Class B   420
  Class C   420
  IP addressing   420
  subnet mask   421
TCP/IP and IPX simultaneously   432
TCP/IP files and directories   424
  TCP/IP.NLM   424
  IPTUNNEL.LAN   424
TCP/IP NetWare applications   421
TCP/IP NetWare router   428
TCP/IP.NLM   425
TDR   26, 27
TEMP directory   319
Thick Ethernet   20, 56
  AUI   56
Thin Ethernet   20, 55
  BNC   55
  T-BNC   55
Token Ring cables   69
  ICS (IBM cabling system)   69
  large unmovable cabling system   70
  small movable cable system   70

Type 1   70
Type 6   70
Token Ring management   71
Token ring   63
  Active monitor present (AMP)   68
  beaconing   68
  connecting   68
  electromagnetic interface   69
  IBM   63
  interface to the ring   67
  management   67
  MAU   68
  stand-by monitor   68
  token   64
  von Willemjin   63
topology   41
  evaluating different topologies   43
  logical versus physical   42
  multipoint   41
  point-to-point   41
TRACK ON   395
tracking RIP packets   395
  hops   395
  ticks   395
transceiver   58
TRICK.EXE   458
TSR   132
TSRs and Windows   299
  386 enhanced mode   299
  AUTOEXEC.BAT   299
  WINSTART.BAT   299
twisted pair cable   23

UIMPORT   445, 448
UMBs   146
uninterruptible power supply (UPS)   593, 601
  management   604
UNIX mail (SMTP)   422
UNIX Version 5.4   16
UnixWare   14, 274
  Application Server Edition   15
  NFS   14
  Personal Edition   15
  TCP/IP   14
  USL   14
unshielded twisted pair (UTP)   24
upgrading from NetWare 3.11   543
upgrading to NetWare 4.0   541
upper memory   146
  blocks   301
UPS.NLM   603
USL   272

UTP 20, 24

VESA 90
VIPX.386 295
virus management 479
viruses 455, 473
   how they work 474
   NetWare shell 475
   network-specific viruses 475
   shell activated before virus 475
viruses and NetWare 475
VLM 161
   loading 228
   memory 228
   performance 230
   programs 229
   redirector 224
VLM.EXE 227
VMM 279
VNETWARE.386 295
volume management tips 128
   SYS 128
   VOL1 128
volume space allocation 128
VREPAIR.NLM 120

WIN /B 305
WIN.BAT 254
WIN.COM 282, 284
WIN.INI 278, 281, 295
WIN.INI 313
WIN.SRC 305
Windows 3.1 266
Windows and NetWare 265
Windows applications 253, 311
   installation 313, 312
   networked 313
   SETUP.EXE 311
Windows configuration 316
   WIN_REST.BAT 316
   WIN_TAKE.BAT 316
Windows for Workgroups 267

Windows INI files 276
   SYSTEM.INI 276
   WIN.INI 276
Windows NT 270, 272
Windows v3.0 201
Windows-based applications 108
Windows-based tools 320
Word for Windows 328
   EditLevel 328
   installation 328
   PROGMAN.INI 328
   server installation 332
   SETUP program 332
   WIN.INI 335
   WIN_REST 332
   WIN_TAKE 334
   workstation 333, 342
workgroup manager 440
Workgroups version 3.11 267
WORM disks 596
WSGEN 162, 163, 164
   *.LAN 165
   *.OBJ 165
   adding network drivers 165
   default drivers support 164
   I/O 167
   IPX.COM. 164
   IPX.OBJ 164
   IRQ 167
   LAN_DRV_xxx 165
   RAM 167
   WSGEN from floppies 165
WSUPDATE.EXE 214

X Windows 16
X.500 directory services 535
   directory structure 536
X500 5
XMSNETX.COM 259
XNS 209